Endorsements

"This book accomplishes what few others in the field have. It successfully speaks to the needs of the policymaker, the student and an informed citizenry. In language that is clear and jargon-free, the authors provide remarkably lucid analysis of the dynamics and impacts of globalization. They provide well-reasoned and lucid prescriptions for both current and looming economic problems, while their crystal clear view of the global landscape provides policymakers with a guide for making their own informed economic and political decisions. Moreover, the breadth of views represented in the book makes it an invaluable resource in undergraduate and graduate courses which cover the complex issues around globalization. By also addressing the role informed citizens can play in shaping globalization trends, and making the debates about economic issues understandable to diverse audiences, the book is in a class by itself in terms of versatility. A must read for any professional or lay person interested in penetrating the complexity of the economic and political issues facing this and future generations."

Ross Harrison, faculty member at Georgetown University, School of Foreign Service and author of *Strategic Thinking in 3D: A Guide for National Security, Foreign Policy and Business Professionals*

"For many years now it has been evident that many problems faced by nation-states cannot be tackled by them acting in isolation; national answers to problems created by interdependence have failed to provide real solutions. This book explains that the need for a global perspective will deepen in the decades ahead. Behrman and Fardoust have assembled together a notable group of experts who convincingly argue that core areas of public policy like economic growth, population mobility, trade, finance, and climate change need to be addressed from a global perspective; creating in turn new challenges for the institutions and mechanisms of global governance. This excellent book makes a solid contribution to the debate as to how the world economy needs to be managed in the twenty-first century by nation-states, or by the not-necessarily-so-far-fetched concept of the citizen of the world."

Santiago Levy, Vice-president for Sectors and Knowledge, Inter-American Development Bank

"In *Towards a Better Global Economy*, a team of prominent economists reports on the longer-term implications of major global developments—particularly the fundamental economic forces that are shifting the center of gravity of the global economy toward Asia—for average citizens around the world. Their research shows that the politics, rules, and institutions of cooperation among nations have not kept up with the demands from citizens for changes in the global political order and suggests that unorthodox policies for promoting growth should play a greater role in lower-income countries."

Justin Yifu Lin, Honorary Dean, National School of Development, Peking University, and former Chief Economist and Senior Vice President, the World Bank

"This book provides a very persuasive discussion of the key global economic trends, and helps readers think through some of the main policy issues of our time: globalization, income distribution, and policymaking in an increasingly connected world where citizens are becoming-and need to become-more involved in debates about economic policies. I particularly appreciated the emphasis on the need for a debate on the aspects of economic governance that should be addressed at national versus global levels, particularly in countries undergoing fundamental changes such as those in the Middle East and North Africa. The book is important reading for those interested in where the world is going and how to think about solving some of the daunting problems the global economy will be facing."

Adnan Mazarei, Deputy Director, Middle East and Central Asia Department, International Monetary Fund

"The global economy is shaped by powerful forces including trade, entrepreneurship, technology, communications, migration, politics, conflict, environment, and climate. And the financial and economic crises of the period since 2008 have shaken confidence and led to reappraisals of what policy and institutions can deliver in influencing these forces and their outcomes for the benefit of global citizens. This book, with contributions from some of the leading thinkers of our time, provides crucial insights into actions we can take now and the way our ideas can and should be changed by experience. It is very timely and of great value."

Nicholas Stern, Lord Stern of Brentford, IG Patel Professor of Economics & Government, LSE, President of the British Academy

"In the aftermath of the global financial crisis, with future growth in advanced economies potentially slower, many developing economies are facing the risk of adverse implications for poverty reduction and development. This book pays much-needed attention to identifying the most appropriate policy responses, at both national and global level, so as to address looming risks and restore strong and sustainable growth while advancing social progress. The analyses, ideas and proposals authoritatively developed are set to inform many ongoing policy debates about how to make progress, in a post crisis environment, toward an open and welfare-enhancing global economy. Critical issues such as global governance, the relationship between finance and economic growth, income inequality, social inclusiveness and environmental sustainability are explored in depth, with a global perspective serving to detect and analyze key changes, drivers and challenges that might influence long-term growth trends and their distributional consequences."

Ignazio Visco, Governor, Bank of Italy

Towards a Better Global Economy

Towards a Better Global Economy

Policy Implications for Citizens Worldwide in the Twenty-first Century

Franklin Allen, Jere R. Behrman,
Nancy Birdsall, Shahrokh Fardoust,
Dani Rodrik, Andrew Steer,
and Arvind Subramanian

OXFORD
UNIVERSITY PRESS

OXFORD
UNIVERSITY PRESS

Great Clarendon Street, Oxford, OX2 6DP,
United Kingdom

Oxford University Press is a department of the University of Oxford.
It furthers the University's objective of excellence in research, scholarship,
and education by publishing worldwide. Oxford is a registered trade mark of
Oxford University Press in the UK and in certain other countries

First Edition published in 2014

Impression: 1

Published in the United States of America by Oxford University Press
198 Madison Avenue, New York, NY 10016, United States of America

British Library Cataloguing in Publication Data

Data available

Library of Congress Control Number: 2014942169

ISBN 978-0-19-872345-5

Printed and bound by
CPI Group (UK) Ltd, Croydon, CR0 4YY

Foreword

The global economic crisis of 2008–9 had a significant impact on most countries. As a result of the vast trade and financial channels that now link markets, production processes, and aggregate demand across countries, very few emerging economies or developing countries avoided large declines in their economies caused by the massive shocks in the United States and other advanced economies. As of early 2014, global economic growth was slowly improving. But official and private sector growth forecasts remained subdued, highlighting significant downside risks emanating from high volatility in capital flows and exchange rates and the continued fragility of financial markets.

Over the past 25 years, extreme poverty rates plummeted in the developing world, key global social indicators improved, and a large majority of people everywhere began living longer and healthier lives. Still, a significant segment of the population in many countries lives in abject poverty, and within-country income and wealth inequality are rapidly increasing in the majority of both advanced and developing countries, although global inequality and extreme poverty both have fallen considerably. The global economy as a whole has benefited enormously from the technological innovation and breakthroughs in information technology—but automation and other labor-saving technological progress has led to high unemployment rates among low-skilled workers and nearly stagnant real wages for average workers across most advanced economies. It appears that automation has enabled the owners of capital to capture a rising share of income—at the expense of workers. Continuation of this trend could lead to social and political instability in even the most stable and mature democracies.

Over the longer term, demographic changes and fundamental forces of convergence and competition are likely to bring about massive shifts in both the sectoral and geographical composition of global output and employment. The center of gravity of the global economy is likely to continue to move toward Asia and emerging economies elsewhere. Emerging resource constraints, environmental problems, and climate change are further complicating the economic outlook, introducing greater uncertainty and significant downside risks, particularly for developing countries and the poor.

A key finding of this volume is that developing countries will face stronger headwinds in the decades ahead, both because the global economy is likely to be significantly less buoyant than in recent decades and because technological changes are rendering manufacturing more capital- and skill-intensive. The challenge is therefore to design an architecture that respects the domestic priorities of individual countries while ensuring that major cross-border spillovers and global public goods are addressed in today's hyperglobalized world economy.

A key mission of the Global Citizen Foundation, a not-for-profit foundation with commitment to the welfare of average citizens around the world, is to undertake, commission, and participate in research and educational programs on global economic, social, and justice issues as well as policies that could enhance the welfare of the world's citizens and promote global economic growth. In the context of the global crisis and ongoing changes in the global economy, the Foundation has made a substantial effort to understand the impact of the crisis as well as some of the most important megatrends (including demographic and environmental changes and hyperglobalization) on average citizens around the world through various channels (such as macroeconomic stability and growth, the trade and financial sectors, poverty, and labor markets, and their implications for income and wealth distribution).

In line with its overarching goal of undertaking and commissioning research that can enhance the well-being of global citizens, the Foundation launched its first research project—"Towards a Better Global Economy"—in mid-2012. The goals of the project are to identify key global trends and their potential distributional implications, to help craft a set of policies that could lead to improvements in the economic well-being of all citizens of the world, and to disseminate the results broadly. The main purpose of the effort is to inform the debate about how the global economy best moves forward.

Toward these ends, the Foundation brought together a small core group of leading economists with varied expertise in the academic, policy, and private sector worlds to guide the project through several stages. Members of this group, along with leading experts who reviewed and commented on their research, supported the research effort in 2012–13. Their research covered six topics:

- Economic growth, led by Professor Dani Rodrik (Institute of Advanced Studies, Princeton).
- Population and human development, led by Professor Jere R. Behrman (University of Pennsylvania).

- Globalization and international trade, led by Dr. Arvind Subramanian (Peterson Institute and Center for Global Development).

- Finance and growth, led by Professor Franklin Allen (University of Pennsylvania).

- Natural resources, climate change, and growth, led by Dr. Andrew Steer (World Resources Institute).

- Global economic governance, led by Dr. Nancy Birdsall (Center for Global Development).

Professor Behrman acted as the project's overall research manager. Dr. Shahrokh Fardoust, the former Director for Strategy and Operation in Development Economics at the World Bank, coordinated and managed the entire effort.

All of the studies presented in this volume, as well as the comments on them by world-class experts, consider a horizon that extends well into the twenty-first century. All of the book's contributors address economic growth, equity, and the welfare of average citizens, as well as ethical aspects of the current mode of globalization, based primarily on market forces and determined to a large extent by national interests rather than a multilateral framework and approach.

The policy-relevant research papers were prepared through teamwork and close collaboration by the research team. A series of virtual meetings and in-person workshops was held in Geneva, Switzerland in December 2012 and at the University of Pennsylvania in March 2013. Together with their policy implications and the comments by the project's peer reviewers, the papers provided a framework for a discussion and exchange of views at the High-Level Conference on Towards a Better Global Economy, held in July 2013 in Geneva. The objective of the conference was to highlight the longer-term implications and related policy options of major recent and projected future developments in the global economy for citizens around the world. Participants in the conference also examined ways in which global citizens can deliberate on policy options and reveal their preferences for policies that would enhance their welfare.

Going forward, to improve the welfare of global citizens and ensure social justice, policymakers, development practitioners, private sector leaders, and global thinkers need to better understand and respond to global citizens' preferences and thereby try to optimally allocate resources and factors of production to facilitate achievement of those economic and social goals that reflect citizens' preferences.

The time has come to think seriously about how improvements in official global governance, coupled with and reinforced by the rising activism of global citizens, can lead to welfare-enhancing and equitable results through better national and international policies. We hope that the findings and recommendations presented in this volume of high-quality research will shed light on some of the most pressing economic and social issues of the twenty-first century and encourage debate on policies to address them.

Theophilos Priovolos
Global Citizen Foundation

Acknowledgments

This book is the result of a joint effort by a core team of researchers comprising Franklin Allen, Jere R. Behrman, Nancy Birdsall, Shahrokh Fardoust, Dani Rodrik, Andrew Steer, and Arvind Subramanian, with important support from a world-class group of experts who reviewed and commented on the research output of the "Towards a Better Global Economy" project. The project was conceived and organized by Dr. Theophilos Priovolos, whose support is very gratefully acknowledged. The team is also very grateful to the Global Citizen Foundation, which provided generous financial support to the project and organized and financed a high-level international conference on the topic "Towards a Better Global Economy" in Geneva, Switzerland in July 2013.

Coauthors, commentators, and peer reviewers greatly contributed to the quality of this book. Coauthors include Elena Carletti, Martin Kessler, Hans-Peter Kohler, Christian Meyer, Jun "QJ" Qian, Alexis Sowa, and Patricio Valenzuela. Peer reviewers include Stijn Claessens (finance), Kemal Derviş (economic growth), Bernard Hoekman (international trade), Chang-Tai Hsieh (economic growth), Ronald Lee (population and human development), Pratap Mehta (global economic governance), and Jeremy Oppenheimer (resources and climate change). In addition, Thorsten Beck, Branko Milanovic, and Zia Qureshi provided detailed and substantive written comments on the financial sector, income distribution, and economic growth, respectively. Comments by all reviewers are published in this volume.

The core research team is also very appreciative of the significant contributions made by other discussants, including chairs and panelists at the high-level international conference held in Geneva in July. This group included Karl Aberer, Amar Bhattacharya, Uri Dadush, Sebastien Fanti, James Fishkin, Robert Fishkin, Jean-Pierre Hubaux, Sebastian Jean, Homi Kharas, Arancha Gonzalez Laya, Santiago Levy, Wonkyuk Lim, Ed Luce, Wolfgang Lutz, Adnan Mazarei, Henri Monceau, Celestin Monga, Mustapha Nabli, Thorsten Temp, Hans Timmer, Ignazio Visco, Kevin Watkins, Alan Winters, and Miranda Xafa. The keynote speakers at the conference—James Fishkin, Pascal Lamy, and Hans Timmer—provided a clear and substantive context for the deliberations and discussions of the various segments of the research program covered in this book. The research team is grateful to all of them.

The research team and the Global Citizen Foundation would like to thank Gina Papalexis and Lili Zerva for their excellent administrative support; Alexander Baltaziss for his outstanding technical support to the project's website and at the Geneva conference; and Nikki Flouris and Julie Griffin for their excellent coordination of the Geneva conference.

Finally, the research team would like to thank Barbara Karni for her highly professional editorial support and hard work in preparing the manuscript of this volume. The team would also like to thank Oxford University Press for publishing this volume and providing editorial, design, and printing services, under the direction of Adam Swallow, and with helpful coordination by Aimee Wright.

Contents

Contents

List of Tables and Figures

Tables

Figures

Contributors

Franklin Allen is the Nippon Life Professor of Finance and Professor of Economics at the Wharton School of the University of Pennsylvania and codirector of the Wharton Financial Institutions Center. He is a former president of the American Finance Association. He has written three books with Douglas Gale, on financial innovation, comparative financial systems, and financial crises. He is the coauthor (with Richard Brealey and Stewart Myers) of the 8th–11th editions of the textbook *Principles of Corporate Finance*. He holds a DPhil from the University of Oxford. His email address is allenf@wharton.upenn.edu.

Thorsten Beck is a professor of banking and finance at the Cass Business School in London and a professor of economics at Tilburg University. He is also a research fellow at the Centre for Economic Policy Research (CEPR). His research and operational work focus on the relationship between finance and economic development and the policies needed to build a sound and effective financial system. He holds a PhD from the University of Virginia. His email address is T.Beck@uvt.nl.

Jere R. Behrman is the William R. Kenan, Jr. Professor of Economics and Sociology and Population Studies Center Research Associate at the University of Pennsylvania. His research is in empirical microeconomics, economic development; early childhood development; labor economics; human resources (education, training, health, nutrition); economic demography; household behaviors; life-cycle and intergenerational relations; and policy evaluation. He has published more than 370 professional articles and 33 books, been a research consultant with numerous international organizations, conducted research or lectured in more than 40 countries, and served as principal investigator on more than 75 research projects. He a Fellow of the Econometric Society, a 40th Anniversary Fulbright Fellow, the recipient of the 2008 biennial Carlos Diaz-Alejandro Prize for outstanding research contributions to Latin America, and a member of the U.S. National Institutes of Child Health and Development (NICHD) Advisory Council. He holds an honorary doctorate from the University de Chile and a PhD from MIT. His email address is jbehrman@econ.upenn.edu.

Nancy Birdsall is the founding president of the Center for Global Development. Before launching the center, she served as executive vice president of the Inter-American Development Bank; held research, policy, and management positions at the World Bank, including as director of the Policy Research Department; and served as Senior Associate and Director of the Economic Reform

Project at the Carnegie Endowment for International Peace. She is the author, coauthor, or editor of more than a dozen books and many scholarly papers. Her most recent publications include *Cash on Delivery: A New Approach to Foreign Aid* (2010) and *New Ideas on Development after the Financial Crisis* (2011), coedited with Francis Fukuyama. She holds a PhD from Yale University. Her email address is nbirdsall@cgdev.org.

Elena Carletti is a professor of finance at Bocconi University. She is also a research fellow at the Centre for Economic Policy Research (CEPR), the Tilburg Law and Economics Center (TILEC), the Center for Financial Studies at CesIfo, and the Wharton Financial Institutions Center. Her primary areas of research are financial intermediation, financial crises, financial regulation, corporate governance, industrial organization, and competition policy. She is the coeditor (with Franklin Allen, Jan Pieter Krahnen, and Marcel Tyrell) of *Liquidity and Crises* (2011) and various books on the euro zone crisis. She holds a PhD from the London School of Economics. Her email address is Elena.Carletti@EUI.eu.

Stijn Claessens is assistant director of the Research Department at the International Monetary Fund. His policy and research interests are firm finance and corporate governance, risk management, globalization, and business and financial cycles. He has edited several books, including *International Financial Contagion* (2001), *Resolution of Financial Distress* (2001), *A Reader in International Corporate Finance* (2006), and *Macro-Prudential Regulatory Policies: The New Road to Financial Stability* (2010). He holds a PhD from the Wharton School of the University of Pennsylvania. His email address is SClaessens@imf.org.

Kemal Derviş is vice president and director of global economy and development at the Brookings Institution. After leaving the World Bank, where he spent more than two decades, he served as the executive head of the United Nations Development Programme and as Turkey's Minister of Economic Affairs. At the Bank, he held a variety of senior positions, including Division Chief for Industrial and Trade Strategy, Director of Central Europe, Vice-President for the Middle East and North Africa Region, and Vice-President for Poverty Reduction and Economic Management. He holds a PhD from Princeton University. His email address is kdervis@brookings.edu.

Shahrokh Fardoust is a research professor in the Institute for the Theory and Practice of International Relations at the College of William and Mary and the president of International Economic Consultants, LLC. A former Director of Strategy and Operations in Development Economics at the World Bank, he has more than 30 years' experience in economic development. He has published in the areas of economic development, national and subnational economic policy, long-term forecasting, and international monetary system. He is the co-editor of *Post-Crisis Growth and Development: A Development Agenda for the G20* (2010) and a member of the SovereigNET Advisory Council at the Fletcher School of Law and Diplomacy at Tufts University. He holds an MA and PhD in economics from the University of Pennsylvania. His email address is sfardoust@ InternationalEconConsult.com.

Jun "QJ" Qian is professor of finance; director, Executive MBA Program Shanghai Advanced Institute of Finance, Shanghai Jiao Tong University; deputy director, China Academy of Financial Research; fellow, Wharton Financial Institutions Center, University of Pennsylvania. His research examines how financial contracts connect laws and institutions with economic and financial outcomes. He also applies financial economic theories to the design and development of financial systems in emerging markets. He holds a PhD from the University of Pennsylvania. His email address is jqian@saif.sjtu.edu.cn.

Bernard Hoekman is professor and program director of Global Economics at the Robert Schuman Centre for Advanced Studies at the European University Institute in Florence, Italy. He is also a research fellow at the Centre for Economic Policy Research (CEPR) and a senior associate of the Cairo-based Economic Research Forum for the Arab countries, Turkey, and Iran. He held various senior positions at the World Bank, including director of the International Trade Department and research manager in the Development Research Group. He is the coauthor (with M. Kostecki) of *The Political Economy of the World Trading System* (2009). He holds a PhD from the University of Michigan. His email address is Bernard.Hoekman@eui.eu.

Chang-Tai Hsieh is the Phyllis and Irwin Winkelried Professor of Economics at the University of Chicago Booth School of Business. He is a research associate of the National Bureau of Economic Research, a senior fellow at the Bureau for Research in Economic Analysis of Development, a codirector of the China Economics Summer Institute, and a member of the Steering Group of the International Growth Center in London. He holds a PhD from the University of California, Berkeley. His email address is chsieh@chicagobooth.edu.

Martin Kessler is a research analyst at the Peterson Institute for International Economics, where he works on globalization and growth. He previously worked as a research assistant at the European think tank Bruegel and as an economic attaché at the French Embassy in Berlin. He holds a master's degree from the Paris School of Economics. His email address is MKessler@PPIE.com.

Hans-Peter Kohler is the Frederick J. Warren Professor of Demography in the Department of Sociology and a research associate at the Population Studies Center at the University of Pennsylvania. His research focuses on fertility and health in developing and developed countries. He is the author of a book on fertility and social interaction and the coeditor of books on the biodemography of human reproduction and fertility and on causal inferences in population studies. He holds a PhD from the University of California, Berkeley. His email address is hpkohler@pop.upenn.edu.

Ronald Lee is a professor of demography, the Jordan Family Professor of Economics at the University of California, Berkeley, and the founding director of the Center on the Economics and Demography of Aging. He codirects (with Andrew Mason) the National Transfer Accounts project, which estimates intergenerational flows of resources through the public and private sectors. He cochairs a National Academy of Sciences committee on the long-run macroeconomic effects of the aging U.S. population. He is an elected member of the U.S. National Academy of Sciences, the American Association for the Advancement of Science, the American Academy of Arts and Sciences, and the American Philosophical Society and a Corresponding Fellow of the British Academy. He holds a PhD from Harvard University. His email address is rlee@demog.berkeley.edu.

Pratap Bhanu Mehta is president of the Centre for Policy Research, in Delhi. He is one of eight coauthors of *Non-Alignment 2.0: A Strategic Framework for India's Foreign Policy* (2012), the coeditor (with Niraja Jayal) of *The Oxford Companion to Politics in India* (2010), and the coeditor (with Devesh Kapur) of *India's Public Institutions* (2005). He holds a PhD from Princeton University. His email address is president. cpr@cprindia.org.

Christian Meyer is a research associate at the Center for Global Development (CGD), where he focuses on poverty and inequality in Latin America, private sector development in Africa, and global governance. Before joining CGD, he worked with the United Nations Conference on Trade and Development (UNCTAD), the European Commission, the German Federal Ministry of Economics, the German Federal Foreign Office, and a management consulting firm. He holds a master's degree from the Hertie School of Governance (Berlin). He has recently joined the World bank's research group and his email address is cmeyer@worldbank.org.

Branko Milanovic is a Presidential Fellow at the City University of New York. For more than 20 years, he was a lead economist in the World Bank's Research Department. His most recent book, *The Haves and the Have-Nots: A Brief and Idiosyncratic History of Global Inequality,* was translated into seven languages and selected as the 2011 Book of the Year by *The Globalist.* He holds a PhD from the University of Belgrade. His email address is branko_mi@yahoo.com.

Jeremy Oppenheim leads McKinsey's Global Sustainability and Resource Productivity Practice (SRP), which is responsible for the firm's client and knowledge agenda on green growth, including resource productivity, resilience, climate policy, environmental finance, land use and ecosystem service strategies, circular "closed-loop" business models, clean tech, and energy policy. He is the coauthor of *Resource Revolution: Meeting the World's Needs for Energy, Food, Water, and Materials* (2011). On a year's sabbatical from McKinsey at the time of writing, he is leading the New Climate Economy Project, the goal of which is to help senior economic decision-makers identify and prioritize actions that can deliver better growth and reduce climate risk. Before joining McKinsey, he was a senior economist at the World Bank. He holds a master's degree from the Kennedy School of Government at Harvard University. His email address is jeremy_m_ oppenheim@mckinsey.com.

Theophilos Priovolos is chief executive officer of Niki Shipping Company S.A. He is member of the Council of the Global Citizen Foundation. He worked at Société Nationale Elf Aquitaine, the World Bank, and the United Nations Conference on Trade and Development (UNCTAD). He holds a PhD in economics from the University of Pennsylvania. His email address is tap@gcf.ch.

Zia Qureshi is the Director of Strategy and Operations in the Office of the Senior Vice President and Chief Economist of the World Bank, where he has held a variety of leadership positions over the past 27 years. He has led several World Bank flagship publications on the global economy, including reports prepared for the G20, and is a frequent writer and speaker on global public policy. He is the author of numerous studies and papers on a wide range of topics in economic growth and development policy. His country work at the Bank spans emerging economies in most regions of the world. Before joining the Bank, Mr. Qureshi worked at the International Monetary Fund. He holds a DPhil from Oxford University, where he was a Rhodes Scholar. His email address is Mqureshi@worldbank.org.

Dani Rodrik is the Albert O. Hirschman Professor in the School of Social Science of the Institute for Advanced Study at Princeton. He was awarded the inaugural Albert O. Hirschman Prize of the Social Science Research Council and the Leontief Award for Advancing the Frontiers of Economic Thought. He is affiliated with the National Bureau of Economic Research, the Centre for Economic Policy Research (London), and the Center for Global Development, among other research organizations. The author of *The Globalization Paradox* (2011) and *One Economics, Many Recipes* (2007), Dr. Rodrik has published widely on international economics and globalization, economic growth and development, and political economy. He holds honorary doctorates from the University of Antwerp and Pontificia Universidad Católica del Peru and a PhD from Princeton University. His email address is drodrik@ias.edu.

Alexis Sowa was a senior policy analyst at the Center for Global Development between July 2012 and November 2013. She previously worked with the Africa Governance Initiative and Malaria No More UK and at Google, where she headed the quantitative insights team for Europe, the Middle East, and Africa. She holds a master's degree from the Kennedy School of Government at Harvard University. Her email address is alexis.sowa@gmail.com.

Andrew Steer is the president and CEO of the World Resources Institute (WRI). He has three decades of experience working on international development on the front line in Asia and Africa and at a senior level in international policy roles. Before joining WRI, he served as Special Envoy for Climate Change at the World Bank. He was a member of UN Secretary-General Ban Ki-Moon's High Level Panel on Sustainable Energy for All and served on the B20 Board on Green Growth. He holds a PhD from the University of Pennsylvania. His email address is Andrew.Steer@wri.org.

Arvind Subramanian is the Dennis Weatherstone Senior Fellow at the Peterson Institute for International Economics and a senior fellow at the Center for Global Development. He is the author of *Eclipse: Living in the Shadow of China's Economic Dominance* (2011) and the coauthor (with Olivier Jeanne and John Williamson) of *Who Needs to Open the Capital Account?* (2012). In 2011, *Foreign Policy* named him one of the world's top 100 global thinkers. Before joining the Peterson Institute, Dr. Subramanian was an assistant director in the Research Department of the International Monetary Fund. He holds a DPhil from the University of Oxford. His email address is asubramanian@piie.com.

Contributors

Patricio Valenzuela is an assistant professor of economics and finance in the Department of Industrial Engineering at the University of Chile, as well as a research fellow at the Wharton Financial Institutions Center and at the Center for Applied Economics and the Center of Finance at the University of Chile. He holds a PhD from the European University Institute. His email address is patriciov@dii. uchile.cl.

1

Towards a Better Global Economy Project: Overview and Policy Options

Jere R. Behrman and Shahrokh Fardoust

1.1 Introduction

The world has experienced relatively rapid economic growth over the past quarter-century. There were significant reductions in the rates of extreme poverty and major improvements in various social indicators in many developing countries. There was—and for some observers still is—much hope that the impressive progress of the past two to three decades would continue well into the twenty-first century, mainly because of the rapid pace of economic and social progress in many emerging economies, as well as in a number of low-income countries.

In the aftermath of the Great Recession of 2008–9, there are now serious concerns about the world's economic future. The main objective of the "Towards a Better Global Economy" policy research project presented in this volume is to identify the longer-term implications for average citizens around the world—and the related policy options—of major developments in the global economy. Some of these developments now appear to have

The authors are grateful to the project's core research team (Franklin Allen, Nancy Birdsall, Theophilos Priovolos, Dani Rodrik, Andrew Steer, and Arvind Subramanian) for valuable comments. They also appreciate useful comments by Deepak Bhattasali, Ross Harrison, and Ignazio Visco. Comments or questions should be directed to jbehrman@econ.upenn.edu and sfardoust1@gmail.com.

1

been ongoing for decades, but the Great Recession changed the landscape for finance, trade, and economic growth in some important respects. The legacies of the crisis—high unemployment levels, massive excess capacities, and high debt levels—and increased income inequality have reduced the standard of living of millions of people worldwide, and there are major risks that the global recovery will remain slow and sputtering for a decade or more.

Demographic changes and fundamental forces of convergence and competition are likely to bring about further massive shifts in both the sectoral and geographical composition of global output and employment, as the center of gravity of the global economy moves toward Asia and emerging economies elsewhere. New challenges, such as risks of widespread increased income and wealth inequality within countries and degradation of the environment and climate change, will require fundamental reforms at the national level as well as truly global policy responses. The responses will need to convene all legitimate institutions, old and new, to reach solutions that address these complex and difficult global challenges and protect and improve the lives of all global citizens.

The overarching goals of this research project are to identify policies that ultimately both support global economic growth and enhance the welfare of the world's citizens, regardless of their national origin, ethnicity, race, gender, or age. It seeks to do so by fostering global cooperation and, where possible and sensible, the harmonization of policies on monetary and fiscal issues; trade and the movement of labor, capital, and technology; health, education, and population; and the environment.

In contrast to many other recent prospective studies that focus exclusively on megatrends, this research program is also concerned with income distribution (both as a key determinant of the relationship between economic growth and poverty reduction and as a barometer of social stability) and the ethical aspects of globalization within a long-term horizon. It focuses on long-term policies at both the national and global levels and the key tensions among them, using a common economic framework.

A variety of major trends and shifts identified by the studies that underpin this project are relevant. First, the pace of global economic growth is likely to be slower and unemployment higher in most countries in the next decade than in the previous two (mainly as a result of demographic, structural, and technological changes that are labor-saving in nature and thus are rendering manufacturing more capital and skill-intensive), although emerging and developing economies as a group are still expected to continue to grow at a faster pace than today's advanced economies, at least for a while. Ultimately, economic growth will depend primarily on what happens domestically in countries. The challenge is therefore to design an architecture that respects the domestic priorities of individual countries and their current social and political conditions while ensuring that major cross-border spillovers and global public goods are addressed.

Second, the rapid convergence phase of productivity levels and technology in the world economy during the past two decades was associated with a surge in world trade in goods and services, ushering in an era of hyper-globalization. During this period, growth was strong, lifting out of poverty the largest number of people in history. In the aftermath of the 2008–9 global crisis, globalization-reversing forces have set in. Countering them has required actions at both national and international levels to address the relative economic decline in the West and sustain growth in the Rest. In this context, China, which has benefited enormously from globalization, along with other middle-income countries, must remain open to trade and support the greater integration of poorer countries into the global economy. Collective action needs to be taken to strengthen the institutional underpinnings of globalization. Trade is likely to be a powerful engine of growth and global poverty reduction over the long term—but only if more low-income countries become more integrated into the supply chains of international manufacturing.

Third, rapid globalization led to substantial increases in financial interdependence and the monetization of national economies over the past two decades. Financial development has had a positive impact on economic growth at adequate levels of financial depth, but this effect vanishes, or even becomes negative, when finance becomes excessive. Excessive finance incubates economic booms and asset price bubbles that end in financial crises, followed by low rates of economic growth for sustained periods. Too little finance is not desirable—but too much finance is not desirable either. The ongoing structural changes in the global economy will have important implications for global financial markets as well as the international monetary system. A likely medium- to long-term scenario is that the Chinese yuan will eventually become fully convertible, joining the U.S. dollar and the euro as the third major reserve currency, along with smaller currencies such as the Japanese yen, the British pound, and the Swiss franc. Whether the new multicurrency monetary system will be stable will depend on the macro-financial policies in each of the reserve-issuing countries or blocs of countries and the degree of policy coordination and cooperation among them.

Fourth, population growth rates have plummeted in most world regions. Regions in which this decline has been slower will increase their share of the global population. Thanks to population momentum, Asia's share of the world population will rise, and Africa's share will rise even more as a result of its late demographic transition. Overall, the world population is projected to increase by about 2.2 billion people, to about 8.3 billion, between 2000 and 2030. Continuing rapid urbanization will mean that the urban population will rise from about half of the world population to about two-thirds by 2030, with most urban growth expected in Asia and Africa (UN DESA 2012).

Fifth, current patterns of energy and resource use, agricultural practices, and urbanization will lead to risks of increased costs and decreased productivity that will reduce overall economic growth, as conventionally measured, with sharp unpredictable threshold effects possible. The impact will be felt differentially across countries. Environmental damage already imposes a dead-weight loss approaching 10 percent of GDP in many emerging economies—even before adding likely adverse impacts from climate change. Moreover, the costs of resource depletion will not be borne equally. The bottom half of the income distribution—both across and within countries—will suffer most from the direct effects, which will include higher prices of food and fuel and lower rates of economic growth and job creation. The right combination of new technology, markets, and policy may be able to accelerate the transition to a low-carbon economy with no or little impact on aggregate growth.

Other key changes at the global level include the reduction and reversal of gender differentials in human resources that traditionally favored men and boys and the rapid expansion of the middle class in most emerging economies. Recent projections of income growth imply an increase in the size of the world middle class by between 1.5 to 3 billion persons by 2030 (depending on assumptions about income and population growth and income distribution and the definition of income class) with concomitant increases in demands on natural resources, and substantial shifts in economic activities to the developing world, with probable increasing economic interactions among countries in the developing world.[1]

This volume analyzes these major trends and other important shifts, the likely effects on average citizens, and the policy significance. An important implication of this research program and its findings is that globalization is a process that can be pushed in one direction or another, as more and more citizens concern themselves with global issues and the international spillover effects of their national policies. Empowered by the Internet and other forms of social media, global citizens may join rapidly emerging, wide-ranging, and spreading global communities to enhance the ethical aspects of the current mode of globalization, checking the capture of important financial and political levers by only a few.

As many have predicted, the coming two decades could witness the continuation of the demise of the United States' dominant status in the global economy (even though substantial influence is likely to persist given its superior military power, large economy and population, and excellent

---

[1] For more detailed discussion of these estimates, see Chapter 7, this volume, and reference there to Birdsall, Lustig, and Meyer (2014).

institutions for research and higher education). The emergence of the BRICs, particularly China and India, is the flip side of the anticipated shift in the United States' position. What is not predictable is how long developing countries, including China, India, and other emerging market economies, will continue to grow rapidly on a sustained basis. Their ability to do so will depend almost entirely on whether today's emerging market and developing countries are able to implement the structural transformations needed to continue to grow faster than the advanced economies and to make their growth process more socially inclusive and environmentally sustainable. The prospects for the global economy would become much less favorable if today's emerging economies, particularly China, were to experience a significant slowdown in their pace of growth, as they currently account for 75–80 percent of the overall rate of economic growth for the world economy.

Related critical questions remain about whether the recent ascendancy of many emerging economies from low-income to middle-income status and the significant reduction in extreme poverty that has taken place over the past two decades can be replicated by currently low-income countries, and the extent to which such possibilities depend on the international system and the national policies of current middle- and high-income countries. For these reasons, the next two or three decades will be crucial to the world's success in moving toward a better global economy.

1.1.1 The "Towards a Better Global Economy" Project

It is in this context that the research reported in this volume—which identifies national and global policy measures that address the issues faced by citizens around the globe, enhance their welfare, and promote global economic growth—was undertaken. The studies presented in each chapter are intended to stimulate public interest and facilitate the exchange of ideas and policy dialogue. It is hoped that they will help lay the foundation for developments that will eventually allow citizens across the world to exchange ideas and reveal their preferences for the formulation and implementation of policies that improve their economic and social welfare.

Fluctuations in international trade, financial markets, and commodity prices, as well as the tendency of institutions at both the national and international level to favor the interests of the better-off and more powerful, pose substantial risks for citizens of all countries. The chapters in this volume examine key factors—including scarce resources, policies, and institutions—that are most likely to facilitate the process of beneficial economic growth in low-, middle-, and high-income economies.

The ultimate goal of the "Towards a Better Global Economy" research project is to identify the key global trends and their potential distributional

5

implications, help craft outlines of policies that could lead to improvements in the economic well-being of all citizens of the world, and inform the debate about how the global economy best moves forward. Toward these ends, a small core group of leading economists with varied expertise in the academic, policy, and private sector worlds was established to guide the research project through several stages. Members of this group, along with a group of leading experts who reviewed and commented on their research, prepared the following chapters:

- Chapter 1: Towards a Better Global Economy: Overview and Policy Options (Professor Jere R. Behrman and Dr. Shahrokh Fardoust)
- Chapter 2: The Past, Present, and Future of Economic Growth (Professor Dani Rodrik)
- Chapter 3: Population Quantity, Quality, and Mobility (Professors Jere R. Behrman and Hans-Peter Kohler)
- Chapter 4: The Hyperglobalization of Trade and Its Future (Dr. Arvind Subramanian and Mr. Martin Kessler)
- Chapter 5: Does Finance Accelerate or Retard Growth? Theory and Evidence (Professors Franklin Allen, Elena Carletti, Jun "QJ" Qian, and Patricio Valenzuela)
- Chapter 6: Resource Depletion, Climate Change, and Economic Growth (Dr. Andrew Steer)
- Chapter 7: Global Markets, Global Citizens, and Global Governance in the Twenty-first Century (Dr. Nancy Birdsall, with Mr. Christian Meyer and Ms. Alexis Sowa).

All of the chapters consider a horizon that extends well into the twenty-first century. All of them address economic growth, equity, and the welfare of average citizens, as well as ethical aspects of the current mode of globalization based primarily on market forces within national policy frameworks and determined to a large extent by national interests rather than a multilateral framework and approach.

Section 1.2 of this chapter motivates the analysis presented in the rest of the volume by identifying the current conditions of the global economy and proposing possible long-term growth scenarios. Section 1.3 briefly summarizes each chapter and the comments by the peer reviewers (Prof. Chang-Tai Hsieh, Dr. Stijn Claessens, Dr. Kemal Derviş, Prof. Bernard Hoekman, Prof. Ronald Lee, Dr. Pratap Mehta, and Mr. Jeremy Oppenheim), as well as other commentators (Prof. Thorsten Beck, Dr. Branko Milanovic, and Dr. Zia Qureshi). Section 1.4 considers policy options for improving the prospects for growth and welfare of average citizens.

1.2 The Global Economy in the First Half of the Twenty-first Century

A number of leading economists, including several Nobel laureates, believe that in order for the world economy to recover in a robust and stable way and to adjust to other major changes, such as the aging and shifting distribution of the world population, governments and international organizations need to devise policies that will increase and stabilize global growth. Doing so, they argue, requires a reexamination of how the global financial and trading system works.

An important part of the global economic and financial system is the current global international monetary system. Figuring out how to replace the dollar-based system with a global system is an extraordinarily important and challenging policy area. Other important policy issues relate to humanizing finance; improving the quality and content of educational and health systems; investing in physical infrastructure and increasing its efficiency and environmental sustainability; devising better structures for the development and sharing of new technologies to promote sustainable and inclusive growth; and reducing barriers to international factor movements, including the movement of people. Political economy and distributional considerations are key to the sustainability and inclusiveness of economic growth over the longer term.

Large proportions of the population in both advanced and developing countries view current policy responses as inadequate and inherently unfair, yielding outcomes that favor the wealthy and powerful. For example, a recent survey of public opinion in the United States (Pew Research Center 2013) shows that broad majorities say the government's policies following the Great Recession of 2008–9 did too little to help the poor, the middle class, and small businesses. Large majorities (60 percent plus) said that government policies did a great deal to help large financial institutions and corporations. Nearly 60 percent thought the policy response had been more helpful to wealthy individuals. In this context, new policies are urgently needed to accelerate economic growth, improve welfare, restore investor and household confidence, increase fairness in the global economy, and exploit new opportunities.

The global economy became more interconnected and complex over the past three decades. Predicting future trends has probably become increasingly difficult, as a result of the rapid pace of economic and financial globalization; technological progress; interaction between technology and globalization; and enhanced connectivity, including that through electronic social networks. Small and seemingly isolated events can have wide-ranging regional or even global consequences. Automation and globalization have adversely affected the wages of workers in manufacturing in most advanced economies and adversely affected the level of employment in many traditional industries.

But the consequences of hyperglobalization go well beyond traditional economic channels. The self-immolation of street vendor Mohamed Bouazizi in December 2010, for instance, sparked the Tunisian revolution and subsequent upheavals in other countries in that region. The bankruptcy of Lehman Brothers in September 2008 led to one of the largest single-day drops in the history of the United States stock market and helped spread the financial crisis to the rest of the world.

1.2.1 The World Economy in Early 2014

A variety of forces are likely to influence long-term growth. On the positive side, they include building on the substantial expansion and convergence that has occurred in recent decades, demographic and human resource changes that will result in larger shares of better-educated and healthier populations in the workforce in many low- and middle-income economies, and the rise of citizen activism. They also include the multispeed recovery; the slowdown in growth; the fragility of the international financial system; the slowdown in the rate of growth of world trade; the depletion of natural resources; the rise and volatility of world food prices; demographic changes toward aging populations in many economies; massive infrastructure deficits, particularly in developing countries; climate change; and the inadequacy of global governance. The background research for this volume identified the following key challenges.

THE MULTISPEED RECOVERY
Although still fragile, the global economy is gradually moving forward at multiple speeds, according to recent assessments by the International Monetary Fund (IMF) and the Organisation for Economic Co-operation and Development (OECD). In the United States, the combination of an improved financial system and improved household and investor confidence is driving renewed growth and employment generation. In Japan, a radical new expansionary macroeconomic policy stance is being implemented to spur growth. Although the economic situation in the euro area has started to improve somewhat, moving from recession to a modest recovery, the recovery appears to be weak and uneven, and unemployment remains high. High public debt, financial fragmentation, and possible deflation (which could raise real debt levels) can adversely affect recovery elsewhere. Meanwhile, many emerging and developing economies are experiencing sustained recovery and solid

growth, although some emerging economies are experiencing inflationary pressures and high and rising asset prices. Oil exporters have benefited from high oil prices: in 2012, their combined export proceeds exceeded an unprecedented $2.3 trillion.

Such a diverse, multiple-path set of economic trajectories is likely to require adjustments to both internal and external imbalances. Current account imbalances of oil exporters and major advanced economies, such as Germany, remain large and are expected to rise over the medium term. In 2012, the United States recorded a current account deficit of $440 billion (–2.7 percent of GDP). In contrast, the euro area (mainly Germany and the Nordic countries) had a combined surplus of more than $227 billion (2 percent of GDP), Japan and developing Asia had a combined surplus of $200 billion (1 percent of GDP), and oil exporters had a combined current account surplus of more than $600 billion (10 percent of GDP). Moreover, some observers expected unorthodox monetary policies, through quantitative easing by the United States and Japan, to generate shock waves through massive swings in capital flows, particularly as they begin to be withdrawn. Adjusting the composition of the major advanced economies' national fiscal and monetary policy stances in a cooperative fashion to facilitate rebalancing and avoid potentially adverse spillover effects will be challenging but probably highly desirable.

THE SLOW PACE OF GROWTH

Many developing countries experienced unprecedented economic growth and development, including substantial progress in a number of social indicators, over the past two decades; in several Asian economies, the period of sustained high growth was much longer. In the process, significant knowledge was accumulated about important dimensions of the development process, including the determinants and impacts of technological change, financial market development, human resources, and interactions between demographic change and international economic change. While attention tends to be focused on rapid Asian growth, six of the ten fastest-growing economies in 2001–10 and seven of the fastest projected for 2011–15 are in Sub-Saharan Africa (*The Economist*, January 6, 2014). This progress has been far from universal, however. To date, many fragile and postconflict states, including many other countries in Sub-Saharan Africa, have benefited in only a limited way, if at all.

Relatively slow growth in advanced economies over the medium term is likely to have significant adverse implications for growth and poverty reduction in many developing countries. Developing countries that have thrived in recent decades—in part by engaging extensively in the international economy—are at risk of finding lower demand for their trade and less supply of international finance, as a result of slow growth in the advanced economies and concomitant new barriers to international economic interactions. Poorer developing economies that wish to emulate the recent success of the developing economies that have thrived may find it more difficult than before to expand their engagement in the international economy, for similar reasons.

CHANGES IN WORLD TRADE

The post-World War II period witnessed a phenomenal rise in trade among nations, with the volume of trade increasing 27-fold between 1950 and 2008, three times more than the growth in global GDP. Rising globalization has been associated with strong economic growth that helped improve economic performance in many trading countries and lifted hundreds of millions of people out of poverty. A key feature of this era of hyperglobalization has been the rise of multinational corporations and the sharp surge in foreign direct investment, resulting in further increases in cross-border flows of goods and services and deeper integration.

After reaching the highest level ever recorded in 2008, world merchandise trade fell by more than 20 percent, its largest decline since World War II, as a result of the Great Recession. Although world exports of merchandise and commercial services trade have since recovered, regaining their precrisis level in 2010 and reaching a record level of $22.5 trillion in 2012, the pace of growth of world trade is significantly slower than it was in the previous decade. Moreover, recovery has been uneven, and short-term prospects for more rapid growth remain subdued, largely as a result of slow economic growth in advanced economies. World merchandise trade growth fell to only 2.4 percent (almost no growth in dollar terms) in 2012, down from 6.5 percent in 2011, and it is expected to have grown by only 3 percent in 2013. World trade in commercial services (transport, travel, other services) grew by about 2 percent in value terms in 2012 and 2013, compared with 11 percent in 2011.

Advanced economies' relative share in world trade fell from 60 percent in the precrisis period to 52 percent in 2012. Over the same time period, emerging and developing economies' relative share rose from 40 percent to 48 percent. China's share in world merchandise exports reached 11.2 percent—a larger share than that of any other country, including the United States (8.4 percent), Germany (7.7 percent), and Japan (4.4 percent). The United States continued to be the leading importer of goods, with 12.6 percent of world merchandise imports in 2012. It also continued to run the largest trade deficit, accumulating massive external debt (albeit in its own currency).

These major global imbalances and shifts have been reinforced by the rising importance of south–south trade, which accounted for about 57 percent of trade in emerging and developing economies in 2012, up from only

27 percent in 1995. Much of this shift reflects the rising prominence of global supply chains. As a result, although the rising trend in global integration has slowed considerably in advanced economies, it appears to be continuing in emerging and developing economies. Short-term prospects for global trade remain uncertain and are unlikely to receive a boost from the barely moving Doha negotiations. But on balance, strong forces are likely to sustain the process of international specialization and fragmentation of production that has been a driver of trade growth in recent decades.

There were no major increases in trade barriers in reaction to the sharp economic downturn after the 2008–9 global financial crisis. Trade is likely to be an engine of growth and global poverty reduction over the long term—but only if more low-income countries become part of the international supply chains that produce manufactures. Recent developments, such as negotiations between the United States and the European Union over a transatlantic trade agreement and negotiations between the United States and Japan and ten other Pacific Rim nations, which are getting close to agreement on the Trans-Pacific Partnership—which do not include a number of important emerging economies—can pose a serious challenge to the World Trade Organization (WTO), which has been pushing for more than a decade for a more global trade deal under the Doha negotiations. However, positive developments have been seen, such as the recent breakthroughs at a WTO meeting in Bali on a modest set of reforms relating to trade facilitation, which would ease the flow of goods through borders (boosting world trade by $1 trillion and creating 21 million new jobs); a few concessions to low-income countries concerning agricultural trade and food security; and a promise to expand market access for these countries in future. The open, rules-based trading system has delivered immense benefits for many, especially today's emerging market economies. Preserving it, by continuing to resist protectionism, will ensure that low-income countries can also make successful growth transitions. Cooperation to preserve globalization, even if not in its most hyper current incarnation, is therefore of critical importance.

THE FRAGILITY OF THE INTERNATIONAL FINANCIAL SYSTEM
Many experts believe the international financial system remains fragile in the aftermath of the 2008–9 crisis. They believe that the growing interconnectedness of banking and financial markets, the increased complexity of supply chains in the world trading system, and the predominance of the dollar as an international reserve currency all played important roles in the amplification of the U.S. housing crisis into a full-fledged global economic and financial crisis.

Beyond the broad risks associated with the global recovery, most current forecasts indicate that the fallout from the crisis has already changed the landscape for finance and growth over the next decade or so. Many developing countries are likely to face reduced access to global capital flows for a protracted period. In particular, syndicated cross-border bond and bank lending, as well as portfolio equity flows, to developing countries are likely to become more constrained by the new global financial environment and as a part of the process of normalization of economic conditions and policy in advanced economies. Foreign bank participation in developing countries' domestic financial systems may also be limited by the need for parent banks in advanced countries to build up their capital in more restrictive regulatory environments, as well as by financial protectionism that puts pressure on banks to concentrate more on home markets. Lower-income countries may suffer the most from this shrinkage, as their already small share of total private capital flows dwindles. Moreover, significant downside risks associated with abrupt market volatility could result from the prospective unwinding of the quantitative easing in the United States.

Financial deepening leads to diversification of risks and greater access to a larger number of countries and firms. It can be instrumental to broadening economic development. "But there is a risk that finance turns into an end in itself, with increasing damaging consequences as the system becomes more interconnected and the potential for externalities increases" (Visco 2013).

The experience of the past two decades has shown that financial development has a positive impact on economic growth at adequate levels of financial depth but that the effect vanishes, or even becomes negative, when finance becomes excessive. Excessive finance incubates economic booms and asset price bubbles that end in financial crises, with low rates of economic growth for sustained periods.

DEPLETION OF NATURAL RESOURCES

The earth's natural resources are being depleted at what appear to be increasing rates, causing sharp movements in their prices. These relative price increases are likely to benefit owners and producers and induce expanded supplies; they will also reduce demand and increase the efficiency with which these resources and commodities are utilized. But sharp increases in prices will adversely affect users of these commodities, particularly the urban poor and middle class. A resource revolution, through a completely new approach to managing the earth's resources, may be needed to keep pace with rapidly rising demand for basic materials, food, water, and energy as up to 3 billion people join the middle class in today's emerging economies over the next two decades, as a study by Mckinsey (2011) argues. The report recommends unwinding the more than $1 trillion of subsidies on resources, including energy and water, and considering carbon prices to address climate change; removing nonprice market barriers by addressing market failures associated with inadequate property rights and principal–agent issues; innovating to encourage investment, which they estimate would need to rise by 50–75 percent (to $3.1 trillion–$3.6 trillion) to boost productivity and increase supply; investing an additional $50 billion a year to achieve universal access to energy and another $50–$150 billion a year to adapt infrastructure to the potential impact of climate change; and strengthening the resilience of society and the poor to downside risks through appropriate social safety nets.

Price spikes have already increased hunger, intensified conflict and social unrest, and caused extinction of species. Soaring commodity prices have been a hallmark of the global economic boom in recent years. When the global financial crisis erupted in 2008, the resulting contraction in global output resulted in the crashing of commodity prices; the end of the commodity boom seemed imminent. Instead, commodity prices rebounded in the early stages of the recovery, leaving the prices of many commodities near or above precrisis peaks, although by late 2013 many commodity prices (energy and nonenergy) had fallen below their 2012 levels and remained well below their 2008 peak, according to the World Bank (2014).

Physical constraints are expected to dominate the future evolution of oil output and prices. World oil production from conventional sources has more or less plateaued since 2005, despite historically high prices, and excess capacity has been near historic lows. At the same time, demand from emerging economies continues to grow, in part as a result of the precautionary stocking of crude oil. However, the discovery and development of massive shale gas and oil fields in the United States has changed the outlook for oil and gas supplies. Rapidly growing domestic production of gas and crude oil has begun to reshape the energy sector in the United States. Its crude oil production is now approaching an historical high of more than 9.7 million barrels per day; the sharp increase in the production of natural gas has led to low gas prices, a boost to gas-using industries. It is now projected that natural gas will overtake coal in power generation in the next three decades. These developments will lead to sharply lower United States imports of oil and gas, perhaps by as much as 25 percent in the next two to three years, and lower greenhouse gases in the long run than would otherwise have been the case (EIA 2013).

Nevertheless, the five-year forward price of oil has remained about $90 a barrel (about the marginal cost of shale oil production in the United States), up from $20 in the early 2000s. The relatively high expected price of oil is due in part to the relatively large risk premium associated with political and social tensions across the Middle East and North Africa region, where some of the largest oil producers and exporters are located. More important is the continued strong demand for energy from the emerging economies, particularly China and India. Although the discovery of new shale oil and gas fields in the United States and the expectation of significant further increases in supplies in the coming years have reduced the prices of oil and gas, it is not yet clear that unconventional oil and gas will lead to a new era of low prices for fossil fuels. This is because absent further technological breakthroughs, development of new fields will require massive investments and oil prices of around $80 per barrel to ensure profitability of such investments. Moreover, the Organization of the Petroleum Exporting Countries (OPEC) is likely to reduce its output of conventional oil if prices decline well below its current target of $100 a barrel, given its members' budgetary and balance of payments needs, which are likely to come under pressure over the medium term with new developments in the United States.

THE RISE AND VOLATILITY OF WORLD FOOD PRICES

Over the past decade, the interaction between low initial stocks and supply disruptions—including severe droughts in several major food-producing countries, reinforced by policy-induced incentives for inefficient use of agricultural lands in many economies and policy barriers to trade in food—has been an important factor in surges in food prices. Limited expansion of agricultural land, rising production costs (through high fertilizer prices caused by high oil prices), growing resource constraints (particularly for water), increasing pressures from environmental problems and climate change, and rising demand from China and for biofuels have kept food prices well above their average since the early 1980s (although still well below the historical highs reached in the mid-1970s). According to recent reports by the OECD and the Food and Agriculture Organization (FAO), this situation is expected to continue over the medium term for both crop and livestock products (OECD and FAO 2013). With the ratio of stocks to consumption expected to remain at historical lows for many commodities, commodity prices are expected to remain high over the next decade, with significant possibilities for further price rises, which will shift real income from consumers to suppliers. Another significant increase in oil prices is likely to slow world economic growth, pushing up food prices and leading to inflationary pressures in many developing countries, potentially derailing their growth. As Ferreira et al. (2011) show, food price increases alone can contribute to increases in the incidence of extreme poverty for food demanders. However, a more complete analysis requires taking into consideration not just the effects on food demanders but also income effects, as some of the poorest people (who work in agriculture) benefit from higher food prices.

Chandy, Ledlie, and Penciakova (2013) argue that the estimated large adverse impact on the poor of the 2007–8 spike in food prices may have been somewhat exaggerated. For some countries the rise in food prices increased poverty, but the effects varied from country to country. Moreover, domestic and international policy responses have important effects on the ultimate distributional and poverty impacts of the increase in food price. Anderson, Ivanic, and Martin (2013) find that the rapid increase in prices of four major commodities (rice, wheat, maize, and edible oils) in 2006–8 led to a rise in global poverty of about 80 million people, with the adverse impact resulting from food price insulation policies (restrictions on trade) of developing countries. They estimate that reductions in protection for these commodities would have reduced poverty by about 82 million people. Their study thus suggests that the estimated increase in poverty of about 80 million people as a result of the food spike could have been avoided by collective international action that avoided additional barriers to trade in food.

Much progress has been made in the fight against extreme poverty and hunger since 1990. Under the Millennium Development Goals (MDGs), the target for extreme poverty (cutting it in half by 2015) at the global level was met five years ahead of schedule. If the average annual rate of decline of the past two decades were to continue, the target for hunger would likely be reached by 2015. Nevertheless, it is estimated that in 2011–13, 842 million people suffered from hunger. Although this figure represents a 17 percent decline since 1990–92, it still means that about one in eight of the world's population still suffers from chronic hunger (FAO 2013).

DEMOGRAPHIC CHANGES

Recent decades have seen unprecedented changes in the quantity, quality, and mobility of world population. The world population doubled from 3.5 billion in 1970 to more than 7 billion in 2010—a rate of increase never before experienced over a sustained period and not likely ever to be experienced again. Long-term projections indicate that the world population will exceed 8 billion by 2030 and 9.5 billion by 2050. Between 1970 and 2010, the quality of the population—as measured by schooling, health, nutrition, and life expectancy—improved markedly, reducing some intra- and cross-country inequalities. Nevertheless, many lower-income countries continue to suffer from poor social indicators, massive poverty, and widespread malnutrition as a result of poor-quality social services, weak delivery systems, and inadequate resources.

Long-term projections also indicate significant demographic shifts, with important implications for global savings, investment, human resource development, growth, and climate change. In the advanced economies, particularly Europe and Japan, the average age is high and rising (the United States is somewhat of an outlier in this respect, in part because of migration). China and a number of other East and Southeast Asian developing countries also have rapidly aging populations, because they are at the stage of the demographic transition in which fertility earlier rapidly declined. These trends are well known. What is less well known is that between now and 2050, the increase in the average age of the population will be larger in Latin America and the Caribbean and in South Asia (with Sub-Saharan Africa lagging to a degree) than in Europe or East Asia, according to projections by the United Nations' Population Division. Increasing old-age dependency has already intensified pressures on private and public intergenerational transfers and pension systems in the economies whose populations have aged more rapidly.

These huge demographic shifts have important implications for advanced and developing countries. Some middle-income developing countries may be able to enjoy a "demographic bonus" that will temporarily accelerate economic growth. Exploiting this dividend may be an option in the future for many currently poorer but still high-fertility developing countries.

Their ability to realize this potential probably depends on the right policy choices and a thriving international economy, however. The differential age structures across countries in the coming decades will increase the potential social gains that can be obtained from more liberalized international migration.

MASSIVE INFRASTRUCTURE DEFICITS IN DEVELOPING COUNTRIES

Infrastructure is essential to spur economic growth and reduce poverty. Slow progress in expanding infrastructure has significant adverse effects on households, particularly poor households. Fay et al. (2011) estimate that more than 25 percent of households in developing countries have no access to electricity. Connectivity is particularly weak in Africa, where nearly 70 percent of the population remains unconnected to electric grids. Although access to power has increased, nearly 900 million people are still without access to improved water sources. The sanitation situation is much worse, with 2.6 billion people still lacking access to improved sanitation. Only 70 percent of the rural population in developing countries (and just 33 percent in Africa) has access to all-weather roads. Massive infrastructure deficits also affect productivity and thus firms' ability to compete in domestic and international markets. The unreliability of existing infrastructure also reduces firms' profitability and ability to invest and expand.

Meeting developing countries' infrastructure needs would cost an estimated $1.25–$1.5 trillion (in 2008 dollars) per year. Current spending levels are about 60 percent of that level. Nearly 65 percent of this spending is financed by the domestic budget, with the rest provided by the private sector; bilateral and multilateral financial agencies, such as the World Bank and regional development banks; and, to a limited extent, sovereign wealth funds.

To meet infrastructure development needs, annual infrastructure spending would need to more than double over the medium term to about $1.8 trillion a year (Bhattacharya, Romani, and Stern 2012). Infrastructure spending in advanced economies needs to increase by at least 1 percent of GDP, to about $1.6 trillion a year, to make up for the reductions since the 1980s as a result of budgetary cutbacks and inadequate private sector financing. Emerging and developing economies will need to increase their capital expenditure by an additional $200–$300 billion a year to make their infrastructure investments environmentally sustainable and more resilient to climate change.

These figures imply that by 2030, annual global investment in infrastructure will need to add up to about $60–$70 trillion to address gaps in advanced, emerging, and developing economies. This spending will require massive mobilization of financing, including from new, innovative sources, and will also require the active participation of sovereign wealth funds.

Both the type and scale of infrastructure investment have profound implications for environmental sustainability. Impediments to private sector investment in infrastructure can impede the adoption of newer green technologies.

CLIMATE CHANGE

Responding to climate change has become one of the world's foremost economic policy challenges, because mitigation policies may affect economic growth, saving and investment levels, capital flows, and exchange rates. As Stern (2013), the author of an influential 2007 report on the economics of climate (the Stern Review), notes, "climate change is here now and it could lead to global conflict," arising from the adverse impacts of climate change through increasingly frequent extreme weather. In its 2013 report, the Intergovernmental Panel on Climate Change noted the changing pattern of extreme weather that has emerged over the past 60 years, as the earth has warmed by about 0.7°C.

A "green growth" development policy agenda would attempt to address the critical need to decouple economic progress from environmental degradation. This agenda includes investment in natural resources that are key to economic development, particularly water. It also includes investment in technological innovation and infrastructure to reduce greenhouse gases and other sources of damage to the environment while stimulating green jobs and accelerating overall economic progress. Policies to increase green infrastructure and enhance green growth focus on increasing demand for green products and production processes, promoting green public investment and procurement, and stimulating technological innovation expenditures with potential to enhance overall productivity and growth while also reducing environmental burdens. Examples of such policies include public investments in energy-efficient infrastructure (power transmission and transport systems) and more efficient water management systems;

environmental pricing, including carbon emissions trading, more efficient water tariffs, and taxes on pollution residuals; research and development (R&D) programs and incentives for technology diffusion that enhance eco-efficient development clusters and first-mover advantages in providing new green technologies, including renewable energy; and public information campaigns, promoting efforts such as eco-labeling. The appropriate mix of measures depends on the overall state of development, the economic structure and comparative advantages, the nature of governance institutions, and the status of international agreements for protecting the global environment, especially agreements that combat climate change and ameliorate its impacts.

THE INADEQUACY OF OFFICIAL GLOBAL GOVERNANCE AND THE RISE OF CITIZEN ACTIVISM

The 2008–9 global financial crisis badly shook the global market, built on the capitalist system and on democratic and accountable government as the political guardian of that system. It will probably survive the next several decades, but it is not entirely secure. As Acemoglu and Robinson (2012) argue, democracy and accountability are the hallmark of "inclusive politics." Democratic and accountable politics in turn help sustain inclusive economics and, they argue, the nation-state itself.

The official governance of the global market is inadequate in representing and protecting the bottom half of the world's population, who live on just $3 a day in the developing world. It is inadequate to manage collective action to deal with climate change or further liberalization of international trade to reduce protection against exports of poorer developing countries. There is also a global political problem: in the advanced economies, where the middle class has seen its real income eroded in many countries and is no longer benefiting from economic growth, there is growing suspicion of the costs of "globalization" and lack of confidence that the global "system" is fair.

But there is also an opportunity, as worldwide surveys show that citizens everywhere are becoming more aware and more active in seeking changes in the global norms and rules that could make the global system and the global economy fairer—in processes if not outcomes—and less environmentally harmful. Across the world an increasing number of people, especially the more educated, see themselves as "global citizens," aware that what happens inside their own country matters for others outside and that what happens outside matters for them and for their children and grandchildren. Global citizenship is seen not in opposition to but alongside national citizenship. This sense is highest among the young and better-educated, suggesting that over time it will increase.

1.2.2 Illustrative Long-term Scenarios for the World Economy

In recent years, researchers and international organizations have developed a number of long-term forecasting models that focus on productivity, convergence, technological progress and catch-up, and economic growth (see, for example, Bergheim 2008; Conference Board 2012, 2013; Dadush and Shaw 2011; Hughes et al. 2009; OECD 2012, Johansson et al. 2013; Poncet 2006; PWC 2013;World Bank 2011, 2013). These studies use different economic models to investigate a variety of long-term economic issues, including the consequences of policy scenarios relating to specific issues, such as public sector debt, the business climate, patterns of human development and poverty, trade reform and globalization, the international monetary system, and climate change. Another set of studies focuses on emerging megatrends and, to a lesser extent, productivity and growth modeling. Only a few studies have attempted to combine growth- and productivity-based forecasts with analysis of megatrends in a meaningful way to construct a vision of the future (Fardoust and Dhareshwar 2013).

There is now widespread agreement and support among economists for growth models in which each country is projected to converge to its own steady-state trend of real income per capita, as determined by the interactions between country-specific structural conditions and polices and global technological advancement. Although all countries are expected to grow at more or less the global rate of technical progress in the long run, cross-country gaps in per capita incomes are expected to persist for some time, largely as a result of differences in the level of technology (as poorer countries will be catching up with the leading economies while the technological frontier will be moving outward, as a result of technical progress and innovation); human capital and its quality; and overall capital intensity (physical capital per unit of labor).

It is also important to consider fundamental structural changes in the global economy that have taken place over the past two decades. Derviş (2012) identifies three such trends. First, since roughly 1990, the pace of per capita income growth in emerging and developing economies has accelerated in a sustainable manner and is substantially higher than that in advanced economies. Recent data suggest that although there is a linkage between growth in advanced economies and growth in developing and emerging economies, the long-term trends and cyclical movements between the growth rates of the two groups of countries need to be distinguished. Derviş calls this a major structural shift in the dynamics of the world economy.

Second, there is continued cyclical interdependence between growth in developing and emerging economies and growth in advanced economies. The decoupling of growth rates has not led to delinking of their cyclical movements.

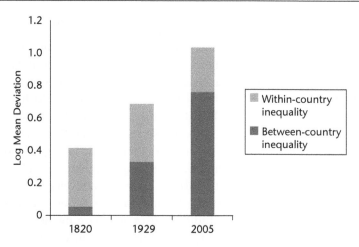

Figure 1.1 Global Income Inequality, 1820–2005
Source: Rodrik 2013 (Figure 2.2 in chapter 2 of this volume), based on Milanovic 2011.

Third, over the past two centuries, until about 1990, the global distribution of income became more unequal (Figure 1.1), driven mainly by increased inequality between countries. The situation appears to have changed radically since the late 1980s and early 1990s. The population-weighted between-country Gini coefficient declined so much that overall global income inequality fell, even though within-country income inequality increased in many advanced and developing countries during the period. Milanovic (in his comments on chapter 2) expects the between-country inequality of income to continue to shrink over the next 30 years. This new convergence has reduced the distance between advanced and developing economies (Figure 1.2), thanks mainly to the relatively rapid economic growth of emerging economies led by China and India. As noted by Derviş (2012), the delinking of the trend growth rate of emerging market countries from the 1990s onward (and that of developing countries since the early 2000s) is quite striking. On the basis of a detailed review and analysis of estimates of the historic and future scale and location of global poverty by income and expenditure, Edward and Sumner (2014, p. 75) conclude that "whatever progress is made against more extreme poverty, even under the most optimistic scenario more than half of the world's population is likely still to be not yet fully secure from poverty in 2030." Nevertheless, because between-country inequality is expected to continue to decline (because per capita GDP growth in emerging and developing economies is expected to be well above that of advanced economies), where one is born (which for 97 percent of mankind is equivalent to where one lives) largely determines one's life chances.

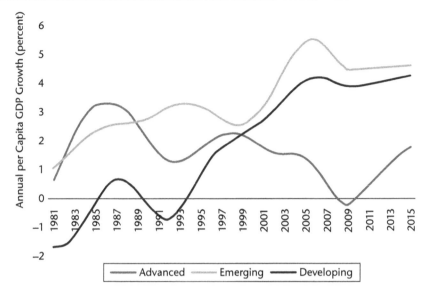

Figure 1.2 Per Capita Trend GDP Growth in Emerging, Developing, and Advanced Economies, 1981–2015

Note: Figure 1.2 shows the underlying trend growth rates calculated using a statistical technique, the Hodrick-Prescott filter, to remove cyclical movement from the longer-term trend.

Source: Reprinted from Kemal Derviş, "Convergence, Interdependence, and Divergence," *Finance & Development*, September 2012, p. 11.

In sum, the mentioned structural changes in the global economy previously described have important implications for the growth dynamics in the global economy in the next 15–20 years, and possibly beyond. Table 1.1 displays some recent long-term economic projections (GDP per capita) for illustrative purposes.

Three important characteristics of the projections in Table 1.1 are noteworthy. First, for both advanced and developing economies, growth since the middle of the twentieth century has been exceptionally rapid by historical standards. Second, since the mid-1990s, growth in developing and emerging economies, particularly China and India, has been faster than in any other major economy or group of countries since at least the 1820s (and probably ever, though data are limited for earlier periods). This rapid growth pulled hundreds of millions of people out of poverty and created large middle classes in these countries (Figure 1.3) (Ravallion 2013; Chandy et al. 2013).

Third, all of the projections reported in Table 1.1 indicate a significant slowdown in the pace of per capita income growth in advanced economies (the United States, Japan, and Western Europe) during the next 15–20 years. Although the pace of growth in developing countries and emerging economies is also projected to slow somewhat, it is nevertheless expected to remain well above that of the advanced economies.

Table 1.1 The Global Economy: Long-term Projections of Per Capita Income Growth, 1820–2030 (annual percentage change)

Country or country group	History			OECD (2012) 2011–30	Maddison (2008) 2006–30	Conference Board (2013) Base Case[a]		U.S. International Energy Outlook, (2013) Reference Case 2010–2040
	1820–1950	1950–2006	1995–2011			2014–19	2020–25[a]	
World	0.9	2.5	2.5	3.1	2.0	2.0	1.4	2.8
Advanced economies	1.2	2.5	1.5	1.7	1.8	1.6	1.2	1.7
United States	1.6	2.1	1.5	1.5	1.6	1.4	1.1	1.6
Western Europe	1.0	2.9	1.3	1.4b	1.3	1.2	1.1	1.6
Japan	0.8	4.5	0.8	1.4	1.2	1.1	0.8	1.0
Developing and emerging economies	0.5	2.7	5.6	5.2	2.5	3.0	2.0	3.8
China	-0.1	4.8	9.3	6.4	4.1	5.3	3.1	5.7
India	0.9	2.6	5.8	5.6	4.2	3.6	2.5	5.1

a. GDP growth projections by the Conference Board were adjusted by the authors for population growth to convert to per capita terms. United Nations Population Projections (medium variant) for 2010–15 and 2015–20 were used respectively for growth projections 2014–2019 and trend growth 2020–5.

b. Average of projected per capita GDP growth for France, Germany, Italy, Spain and U.K.

Source: Authors' calculations, based on Maddison 2008, "The West and the Rest in the World Economy," *World Economics* 9(4); OECD 2012, "Looking to 2060: Long-Term Global Growth Prospects," OECD Policy Paper No. 03; The Conference Board 2013; "Global Economic Outlook 2014," November, Table for Global Outlook for Growth of Gross Domestic Product, 2013–2025; U.S. Energy Information Administration 2013, *International Energy Outlook 2013*, July, Washington, DC, Table B3, p. 200.

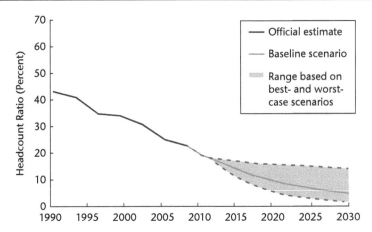

Figure 1.3 Global Poverty, 1990–2030
Source: Chandy, Ledlie, and Penciakova 2013.

At least three forces are assumed to drive growth and globalization over the next two decades: the speed of convergence between developed and developing countries, the rate of technological progress, and the pace of structural transformations and institutional reforms. A more gradual convergence—as well as headwinds that slow the pace of technological progress and structural transformation—could result in a slower pace of economic growth over the long run. A more rapid pace of convergence and structural transformation could speed the pace of growth of per capita income over the long run. There is a range of views on the probable rate of future convergence between low-income and higher-income countries and how it will compare with that during the first decade of the 2000s.

Under the optimistic scenario that poverty will continue to decline at the same pace as it did during the 1990–2010 period, Ravallion (2013) estimates that the world could see nearly one billion people lifted out of poverty by 2030 relative to the number of poor in 2010. This is consistent with the United Nations' new goal of "eradicating extreme poverty" by 2030. However, he thinks maintaining such a rapid pace of poverty reduction will be challenging. Instead, it would be likely that the pace would slow down at relatively low levels of poverty (e.g. 10 percent). It might be possible to attain a more optimistic trajectory or at least obtain a better result with a combination of economic growth and distributional changes; however, the recent rise in within-country inequality has made the task of reducing poverty substantially by 2030 even more challenging, unless countries implement policies that support faster growth and greater inclusion of lower-income groups in the growth process.

A 2012 paper presents the results from a new model projecting growth of OECD and major non–OECD economies over the long term (OECD 2012; see also Johansson et al. 2013). It assumes no major macroeconomic or financial crisis in the relevant time horizon and continued strong performance by the BRICs, particularly China, albeit at a somewhat slower pace than the past decade. It also assumes away major climate change, war, or regional conflict-induced disasters with global consequences.

These assumptions may result in optimistic projections. But the projections do not incorporate substantial changes that could occur as a result of possible policy changes such as deeper structural reforms and relaxed restrictions on international migration. If these changes were to materialize, the projections could underestimate future growth.

The main findings of this projection exercise include the following:

- Global per capita GDP could grow at about 3.0 percent a year over the next 20 years, which is about 0.5 percent higher than the growth rate projected through 2060. This growth will be enabled by continued fiscal and structural reforms and sustained by the rising share in global output of relatively rapidly growing emerging market countries.

- Growth of non–OECD countries will continue to outpace growth within the OECD, but the difference will narrow, largely as a result of the convergence effect (technology catch-up). The average annual per capita growth in non–OECD countries (emerging and developing economies) will decline from about 5.5 percent over the past decade to 5.2 percent between 2011 and 2030 and to about half that in the 2030–60 period. Annual trend GDP growth for the OECD is projected to average about 1.7 percent in per capita terms between 2030 and 2060.

- If all goes well for emerging economies and today's advanced economies continue to grow at a relatively slow pace, the next 30–50 years will see major changes in the relative size of countries' economies. Rapid growth in China and India will mean their combined GDP (measured in 2005 purchasing power parity [PPP]) will surpass that of the G7 economies and exceed that of the entire current OECD membership by 2060.

- Notwithstanding rapid growth in low-income and emerging market countries, large cross-country differences in living standards will still persist in 2060. Income per capita in the poorest economies will more than quadruple by 2060, and China and India will experience more than a sevenfold increase. But living standards in these countries and some other emerging market countries will still be only 25–60 percent as high as in the leading countries in terms of per capita income in 2060.

- In the absence of more ambitious policy changes, larger imbalances could undermine growth. As the current cycle unwinds, the scale of global current account imbalances may increase, returning to precrisis peaks by 2030. Government indebtedness by many OECD countries will exceed thresholds at which there is evidence of adverse effects on interest rates and growth. Global interest rates may therefore start to rise over the long term. Bolder structural reforms and more ambitious fiscal policy could raise long-run living standards by an average of 16 percent relative to the baseline scenario of moderate policy improvements (OECD 2012). Ambitious product market reforms that raise productivity growth could increase global GDP by an average of about 10 percent. Policies that induce convergence toward best practice labor force participation could increase GDP by almost 6 percent on average.

1.2.3 Megatrends

In order to better understand the global and regional context for the long-term macroeconomic projections just discussed, it is useful to briefly review several significant recent studies that have looked at a much broader set of megatrends. Policymakers and researchers across the world need to see the big picture if they are to deal effectively with specific challenges and opportunities over the long term. Among the many books and studies that have been published in this area in recent years, a few include lists of issues similar to the ones identified for this research program. These studies tackle the big picture from different angles, with varying success.

In *Megachange: The World in 2050*, Franklin, Andrews, and their colleagues at the *Economist* identify the trends that are transforming the world and predict how they may shape the world by 2050. Their book offers a straightforward survey of the world, together with a cautiously optimistic outlook for the global economy. According to the authors, "There is every chance that the world in 2050 will be richer, healthier, more connected, more sustainable, more productive, more innovative, better educated, with less inequality between rich and poor and between men and women, and with more opportunity for billions of people" (2012, xiv). Although the contributors are relatively optimistic about the long-term future of the world, they acknowledge that enormous challenges lie ahead, ranging from managing climate change and conflicts over scarce resources to feeding another 2 billion people and dealing with growing security threats from extremists and failed states.

At the core of *Megachange* lie two important assumptions. First, the slowing of global population growth takes the form of a baby-boomer bulge that moves from west to east (except in Eastern Asian countries that already have rapidly aging populations, such as Japan and China) and from north to south.

As a result, although growth will slow over the next 40 years in the west, it will likely accelerate in much of Asia and Africa.

Second, the pace of economic growth experienced over the past decade is likely to continue, implying greater convergence between today's advanced economies and developing countries and a more equitable distribution of income across countries. On economic matters, the authors of *Megachange* argue that the increase in inequality in today's advanced economies may turn around in coming decades and that fiscal and financial reforms will reverse the rising public debt trends, resulting in smarter and fitter states. China's spectacular growth in recent decades is projected to slow sharply, to about 2.5 percent a year by 2050. Nevertheless, a shift in economic fortunes and political and military power toward the east is likely to take place over the next three to four decades, as Asia will account for more than half the world economy.

Global Trends, by Adrian Done (2011), identifies and analyzes a dozen major long-term global trends which the author thinks will mold the twenty-first-century world. He argues that each of these trends has the potential to have major adverse effects on businesses and people's lives if not dealt with in an effective and timely manner.

According to Done, the repercussions of the economic crisis are not going to disappear in the short term. Geopolitical power will continue shifting away from Europe and the United States toward emerging economic powerhouses such as China, India, Russia, Brazil, and other developing countries. Technology will continue to develop, bringing new sources of "creative destruction." The world will continue to get warmer, and the climate will change. The worsening problem of water scarcity will continue to affect food production for the foreseeable decades, especially as nonrenewable groundwater is used up or polluted. Done's main message is that the world needs to face up to these daunting challenges as human beings have always done.

Another approach that has gained traction among policymakers around the world is the one taken by the United States National Intelligence Council (NIC). One of the NIC's key products is a global trends report produced for the incoming United States president that assesses critical drivers and scenarios for global trends over a 15-year horizon. The NIC's most recent report, *Global Trends 2030: Alternative Worlds*, was released in 2012. It provides insightful long-term predictions based on some ongoing megatrends:

- Individual empowerment will accelerate, as a result of poverty reduction, the growth of the global middle class, greater educational attainment, the widespread use of new communications and manufacturing technologies, and advances in health care.

- Power will be diffused. There will be no hegemonic power, as power shifts to networks and coalitions in a multipolar world.

- The demographic arc of instability (the large proportions of young people in some regions and high levels of unemployment) will narrow. Migration will increase.

- Demand for food, water, and energy will grow substantially, thanks to the increase in the global population. Climate change will worsen the outlook for the availability of these critical resources, such as water and access to it, which could lead to conflict.

- Asia will surpass the combined economic and military might of Europe and the United States.

Yet another approach is presented in a recent report by the Oxford Martin Commission for Future Generations (2013), a group of international leaders working to identify how progress can be delivered on critical long-term challenges such as addressing the global burden of chronic disease and the risks (and opportunities) associated with the increasingly complex and hyper-connected world. The report, entitled *Now for the Long Term*, highlights the deep global inequalities that persist in access to food, sanitation, vaccines, and health care and aims to shift government and business priorities toward longer-term challenges that will shape the world's future. The report looks at several megatrends, including large, aging populations; urbanization; the growing middle class in developing countries; inequality and unemployment; geopolitical power transitions; sustainability and resource insecurity; the shifting burden of diseases; and the information and communications revolution. It argues that in the face of complex problems, current institutions are inadequate, confidence in the ability of politicians to deal with problems is low, and short-termism is entrenched. The report suggests a range of innovative long-term ideas, including creation of a coalition of the G20, 30 companies, and 40 cities to lead the fight against climate change. It also suggests that when universal agreement on an important global issue cannot be reached, key stakeholders need to rely on a critical mass that renders opponents irrelevant.

In a recent book edited by Lomborg (2013), economists with expertise in air pollution, biodiversity, conflicts, climate change, education, gender inequality, health, malnutrition, trade barriers, and water and sanitation developed a "scorecard," using economic valuation methodology to measure actual and expected progress/change between 1900 and 2050, including actual and potential damage inflicted. They used high and low regional growth scenarios for their GDP projections (apparently with no feedback loops between the areas they investigated and the rate of economic growth). Their findings indicate that the loss of biodiversity in the twentieth century probably cost the world economy about 1 percent of GDP per year. However, for most of the topics investigated for this "scorecard" approach, improvements during the twentieth century amounted to 5–20 percent of global GDP, even though problems remain large. Lomborg and his team expect this trend to continue in most areas of investigation. Their findings also show that two key areas of biodiversity and climate change will become increasingly problematic going forward; the costs of climate change are projected to amount to 1–2 percent of GDP per year.

Studies about long-term futures serve an important purpose when they build on current megatrends and draw logical implications based on the continuation of those trends or possible reversals or significant changes in the pace of change. The policy implications and their feasibility are important and valuable public goods and necessary inputs for policy debate at both the national and international level. Each of the studies prepared for the "Towards a Better Global Economy" project provides a rich discussion of possible future trends, their implications for the welfare of average citizens, and policy options to be considered in preventing undesirable outcomes.

1.3 Towards a Better Global Economy: Summary of Research Reported in This Volume

1.3.1 The Past, Present, and Future of Economic Growth

The decade 2000–10 was an extraordinarily good one for most developing countries and their lower-income citizens. In chapter 2, Dani Rodrik asks whether this recent performance can be sustained into the future, decisively reversing the "great divergence" that has seen the world split into rich and poor countries since the nineteenth century. In answering this question, Rodrik argues that optimists would point to improvements in governance and macroeconomic policy in developing countries and to the still not fully exploited potential of economic globalization to foster new industries in the poor regions of the world through outsourcing and technology transfer. Pessimists would fret about the drag rich countries exert on the world economy, the threats to globalization, and the obstacles that late industrializers have to surmount given competition from China and other established export champions.

After reviewing recent trends, Rodrik observes that two dynamics drive growth. The first is the development of fundamental capabilities in the form of human capital and institutions. Long-term growth ultimately depends on the accumulation of these capabilities—everything from education and health to improved regulatory frameworks and better governance. But fundamental capabilities are multidimensional, have high set-up costs, and exhibit complementarities. Therefore, investments in them tend to yield paltry growth payoffs until a sufficiently broad range of capabilities has already been accumulated (that is, until relatively late in the development process).

The second dynamic is structural transformation—the birth and expansion of new (higher-productivity) industries and the transfer of labor from traditional or lower-productivity activities to modern ones. With the exception of natural resource bonanzas, extraordinarily high growth rates are almost always the result of rapid structural transformation, industrialization in particular. Growth miracles are enabled by the fact that industrialization can take place in the presence of a low level of fundamental capabilities: poor economies can experience structural transformation even when skills are low and institutions weak. Rodrik argues that this process helps explains the rapid take-off of East Asian economies in the postwar period, from Japan and Taiwan in the late 1950s to China in the late 1970s.

The policies needed to accumulate fundamental capabilities and those required to foster structural change naturally overlap, but they are distinct. The first set of policies entails a much broader range of investments in skills, education, administrative capacity, and governance; the second can take the form of narrower, targeted remedies. Without some level of macroeconomic stability and property rights protection, new industries cannot emerge. Furthermore, Rodrik explains, fostering new industries often requires second-best, unconventional policies that are in tension with fundamentals. When successful, heterodox policies work precisely because they compensate for weakness in those fundamentals.

In principle, Rodrik argues, this broad recipe can continue to serve developing countries well in the future. In particular, it can allow the world's poorest countries in Africa to embark on Asian-style structural transformation and rapid growth. But, he explains, a number of considerations suggest that developing countries will face stronger headwinds in the decades ahead.

First, the global economy is likely to be significantly less buoyant than in recent decades. The world's richest economies are hobbled by high levels of public debt, which typically results in low growth and defensive economic policies. The euro area is facing an existential crisis; even if Europe manages to stay together, its problems will continue to rein in the region's dynamism. Policymakers in these countries will remain preoccupied with domestic challenges, preventing them from exhibiting much global leadership.

Second, technological changes are rendering manufacturing more capital- and skill-intensive, reducing the employment elasticity of industrialization and the capacity of manufacturing to absorb large volumes of unskilled labor from the countryside and the informal sector. Global supply chains may facilitate entry into manufacturing for low-cost countries that are able to attract foreign investment, but they also reduce linkages with the rest of the economy and the potential for the development of local upstream suppliers. Other factors will also work against manufacturing industries. New entrants into standardized manufacturing activities face much greater global competition today than the Republic of Korea or Taiwan faced in the 1960s and 1970s or China faced in the 1990s. Most African manufacturers today face an onslaught of cheap imports from China and other Asian exporters, which make it difficult for them to survive on their home turf, let alone cross-subsidize their international activities (though there are examples of success and rapid growth, such as Ethiopia). The burdens placed on government policy to incubate and develop domestic manufacturing firms are correspondingly heavier.

Rodrik concludes that ultimately growth depends primarily on what happens at home. Even if the world economy provides more headwinds than tailwinds, desirable policies will continue to share features that have served successful countries well in the past. These features include a stable macroeconomic framework; incentives for economic restructuring and diversification (both market-led and government-provided); social policies to address inequality and exclusion; continued investments in human capital and skills; and a strengthening of regulatory, legal, and political institutions over time. Countries that do their homework along these dimensions will do better than countries that do not. The upgrading of the home market will in turn necessitate greater emphasis on income distribution and the health of the middle class as part and parcel of a growth strategy. Social policy and growth strategy will become complements to a much greater extent.

According to Rodrik, international institutions will do better to accommodate the inevitable reduction of the pace of globalization. The challenge is to design an architecture that respects the domestic priorities of individual countries while ensuring that major cross-border spillovers and global public goods are addressed.

In his comments, Kemal Derviş expresses strong agreement with the way in which Rodrik's chapter presents the broad history of economic growth, as well as with its policy conclusions. There are two aspects of the chapter on which Derviş's basic message would be somewhat different, however. The first has to do with the decomposition of global inequality into between-country and within-country inequality. Rodrik writes that "it is *increasingly* (emphasis added) the country in which one is born that determines one's economic fortune," basing his statement on evidence he cites of a continuing increase in the percentage of between-country inequality between 1820 and 2005. This powerful stylized fact was correct for the long period from the beginning of the nineteenth century through the 1990s. But, as shown in Rodrik's own chapter, the share of within-country inequality increased between 1988 and 2005, from 19.4 percent to 26.5 percent for the log mean deviation and from 22.0 percent to 26.5 percent for the Theil index. Derviş argues that this is a new trend, which emerged around 1990.

What has happened since 2005? The difference in per capita economic growth rates in the aggregate group of developing and emerging economies on the one hand and the rich advanced countries on the other widened, as a result of both continuing strong growth in the former and the 2008–09 crisis-induced recession in the latter. At the same time, the trend of increasing within-country inequality is continuing in many economies, including most of the largest countries. So one can already say with some confidence that, unlike the 1820–1990 period, the 1990–2020 period will be one in which the share of within-country inequality in overall global inequality grows very substantially.

The second point Derviş raises is his more qualified view regarding the prognosis for the future. Rodrik states that "the growth rate of economies is basically uncorrelated with their initial level of productivity or distance from the technological frontier." Derviş argues that the dividing line between manufacturing and what are broadly called "services" is becoming increasingly blurred. He concludes his comments by indicating that in terms of the basic overall message about convergence or divergence, size matters. The fact that the economies that continue to "converge" are very large (China, India, Brazil, Indonesia) will lead to a different world economy from the one that would exist if the converging economies were small.

In his comments on Rodrik's chapter, Chang-Tai Hsieh indicates that he is very sympathetic to the argument about the potential of "heterodox" versus "orthodox" reforms. There is overwhelming evidence that the kind of policies that successful countries have undertaken generally do not look like the typical "Washington Consensus" policies. However, at this level of generality, it is hard to say more. Without looking at specific policies, it is difficult to know whether heterodox policies were responsible for the rapid growth or whether some of those policies made things worse and it was orthodox policies that were responsible. Hsieh agrees that the types of reforms with the largest payoffs for most developing countries are much more nuanced than indicated by the standard Washington Consensus recipe book. The difficult question is what exactly these nuanced policy reforms are.

Hsieh questions the usefulness of thinking about forces that drive structural change (in all incarnations) as divorced from the process of institutional reform. Even if the key reforms are unorthodox in nature, it is still just as difficult to figure out which reforms might work and just as difficult to implement them. Very few countries have implemented the kind of unorthodox reforms that China has implemented, and it remains to be seen whether China's experience can be replicated successfully elsewhere.

Hsieh thinks the barriers faced by formal manufacturing may have increased in many developing countries. This view is consistent with Rodrik's argument about barriers to structural transformation, although it would still leave policymakers with the difficult task of figuring out what these barriers are and how best to tackle them.

Zia Qureshi finds chapter 2 substantive and insightful. His comments focus on the way the chapter maps structural transformation and industrialization to policies and on the role of governance in ensuring policy effectiveness. On the former, he argues that the effectiveness of unorthodox policies may not be independent of orthodox reforms. The success of unorthodox policies does not necessarily mean that the successful outcome can be entirely attributed to those policies. On the latter, the role of governance, Qureshi argues that the direct measures that worked in China or other successful East Asian countries may not be as effective in developing countries with different governance and institutional contexts. He also thinks that some discussion of comparative advantage-based specialization is warranted and notes that failing to specialize based on comparative advantage can lead to a failed industrial policy. Finally, although he agrees that future growth faces some tough challenges, Qureshi thinks that Rodrik's overall prognosis for growth in emerging economies may be too pessimistic, because it focuses too much on prospects for manufacturing. The potential for unconditional convergence remains considerable in many emerging economies, according to Qureshi.

Comments by Branko Milanovic focus on the past, present, and future of income distribution. He agrees with Rodrik that between the 1800s and 2005, the level of between-country inequality of income rose by "by leaps and bounds" and is now very high, accounting for at least three-quarters of total income inequality. Where one is born thus determines a substantial part of one's income. Milanovic agrees with Derviş that this phenomenon is becoming somewhat less important thanks to the extraordinary growth rates of China and India and the reemergence of the South as a strong global economic actor. Between 1988 and 2008, the population-weighted between-country Gini coefficient decreased to an extent that drove down overall global inequality. He expects overall global inequality will continue to decrease over the next 30 years as between-country inequality continues to shrink, and economic readjustments between Europe/North America and Asia will be made. Milanovic also argues that within the next three decades about half of the world population will be considered middle-class, about a third of the population will have an income of less than four international dollars per day, and a small segment of the population will be considered elite. Although extreme global poverty may decline to as low as 5 percent of the world population, the world will be very unequal—and different from today's world.

1.3.2 Population Quantity, Quality, and Mobility

In chapter 3, Jere Behrman and Hans Kohler argue that recent decades have seen unprecedented changes in the quantity, quality, and mobility of the population. The world population doubled from 3.5 billion in about 1970 to more than 7 billion in 2010—a rate of increase never before experienced for a sustained period and not likely to be experienced ever again. Almost everywhere, life expectancy is longer and fertility lower than in the middle of the twentieth century. The extent of these trends varies significantly across countries, regions, and sometimes subpopulations. But almost universally, the past decades brought about changes that resulted in significant increases in life expectancy, reductions in variance in the age at death and thus reduced uncertainty about survival at young and adult ages, and reductions in the fraction of the life course that is closely intertwined with childbearing and childrearing.

Over the same period, population quality (as measured by schooling and other forms of education and by health, nutrition, and life expectancy) improved markedly, and cross-country inequalities in some important aspects of population quality (such as schooling attainment, preschool programs, life expectancies, and some related health measures) narrowed. Population mobility also increased, with substantial urbanization in most regions of the world as well as substantial international mobility.

Because of heterogeneity in the stages of economic development across countries and regions as well as the timing and duration of the demographic transition, these changes have had differential effects on different regions. Despite decreases in global mortality and fertility levels—and the resulting recent declines in the rate of global population growth—the demographic transition remains an unfinished success story. High fertility and rapid population growth remain important concerns in many of the least developed countries, which may be most vulnerable to the consequences of population growth. The repercussions of these and other differences will be felt throughout the twenty-first century.

Looking forward, much of the more developed world (including middle-income countries) will experience relatively stable—or, in some cases, declining—population sizes, with rapidly aging populations and increasing aging dependency ratios. Many middle-income (and later current low-income) countries will experience declining dependency ratios and the challenges of accommodating "youth bulges." These countries will have opportunities to exploit a potential "demographic dividend" of having a relatively large share of the population of working age rather than young or elderly. Countries that currently have relatively low income and high fertility rates will be the main contributors to world population growth during the twenty-first century. As a result, both the absolute and relative size of the population of Africa is projected to increase substantially throughout the rest of the century. Asia and Africa are likely to substantially increase their shares of their populations living in urban areas, their shares of the global labor market and global human capital, and their shares of the world's total urban population.

Behrman and Kohler argue that four policy areas are particularly important and promising:

1. *Enhancing the freedom to move, internally and internationally.* Increasing internal and international mobility could yield enormous potential gains, particularly for poorer citizens, with possibly few offsetting losses for more affluent citizens. Barriers to migration within countries should be reduced, but mechanisms should be introduced so that the incentives for migration more closely reflect social rates of return. Measures could include changes in transportation systems, quality of life measures, and the mandating of green spaces. These strategies have the potential to yield "win–win" outcomes, particularly given the high prevalence of poverty in rural areas in most countries. Moreover, millions of people could move from developing countries to developed ones without reducing wages in developed countries, particularly if the pace of movement is slow enough to allow investment to adjust.

2. *Strengthening the foundation for life.* The private and social gains from establishing a stronger foundation during the early years of life—through stimulation, nutrition, and health in the first five years—are substantial, particularly for children from poorer families. Programs to increase parental knowledge about the importance of and means of stimulating their children, particularly in the early years of life, are likely to yield high private and social rates of return and benefit particularly children from poorer families. Investments in preschool programs for three- to five-year-olds and nutrition are likely to have high social rates of return, with beneficiaries concentrated among poorer families.

3. *Supporting aging with dignity and equity.* As populations age, the potential private and social returns and equity gains from increasing the labor force participation and productivities of aging adults—and providing

social support based on expected remaining life years rather than accumulated life years (age)—appear significant.

4. *Improving incentives for social service delivery.* Improving both markets for and policies regulating the delivery of services that provide essential inputs for achieving socially desired levels of human reproduction and childrearing; mortality; schooling, preschooling, and other forms of education; health and nutrition; and internal and international mobility has substantial potential for enhancing productivities and well-being, with gains often largest for poorer citizens.

Improvements in these four policy areas have enormous potential to enhance future economic growth, improve the welfare of global citizens broadly, and in many cases ensure that poorer citizens share more extensively in such growth. Moreover, many of these policies have "win–win" characteristics and disproportionately benefit the poor, justifying them both economically and morally.

Other important policies suggested by Behrman and Kohler include the following:

- In high total fertility rate contexts, increased investments in programs providing family planning information, subsidies for contraceptives, and a broader range of reproductive health services are likely to yield high payoffs.

- More than 100 million girls, most of them in low- and middle-income countries, have never been enrolled in school. Increased incentives for enrollment of girls at all levels of schooling in contexts in which significant numbers of girls are not enrolled are likely to yield high social rates of return and benefit members of poorer families. Once enrolled, however, girls on average progress more rapidly and attain equal or higher schooling levels than boys, raising questions about whether changes to improve boys' schooling performance may have high payoffs.

- Public transportation systems should be subsidized to reflect large positive externalities, and tolls should be used for private vehicles to reflect the negative externalities they generate.

- Megacities should be decentralized into independent districts with their own political leadership, but infrastructure planning should be centralized in order to increase efficiency.

- Legislation on and enforcement of quality of life issues (air and water quality, noise reduction, sewage treatment, waste recycling, energy efficiency) should be strengthened.

- Prevention of common chronic diseases should be promoted through behavioral changes (for example, stopping smoking); regulatory changes (for example, requiring that nutritional information be provided and restricting the use of certain ingredients, such as salt and transfats); and structural changes (such as creating walkable neighborhoods).

Ronald Lee strongly supports the authors' framework, which describes many of the ways in which changing demography will pose challenges for policy, income distribution, and economic development. Lee finds the "demographic transition" a useful organizing framework for the chapter and thinks the authors rightly emphasize that countries are distributed across different stages of the transition and that their positions in the transition fundamentally affect their economies.

Although he agrees with much of what the authors say, he disagrees with the discussion of aging in Asia and the classification of East Asia as being "post-transition" with an "older population age structure." He also believes that average age is not the best metric for aging, because it can rise as fertility falls with no increase in the ratio of the elderly to the working-age population. Moreover, except for Japan, Lee does not think the East Asian countries are old: they have come to the end of their first demographic dividend phase and are now poised at their peak support ratios, just about to start population aging. In an important sense, Lee argues, the full force of population aging is still decades away in every country, even the richest ones, and has yet to be experienced anywhere.

Lee does not agree with the authors' policy suggestions about pensions, arguing that further delinking them from earnings history would distort both labor supply decisions, including retirement age, and saving and asset accumulation decisions. Doing so would also imperil the sustainability of public pensions as populations age. He argues that as the population ages, the proportion of asset-holding elderly people rises, leading to capital deepening. Developing countries should encourage private saving, including through mandatory saving programs for workers, starting decades before population aging is projected to begin. Prefunded public pension programs are also possible, although in practice they run a great risk of being drained by governments.

Lee shows that the decline in fertility has been accompanied by greatly increased educational investment over the past few decades. Policy can support this natural tendency by maintaining or increasing aggregate public spending on education relative to GDP even as fertility and the population shares of children fall. Human capital deepening generates positive externalities. The increase in labor productivity helps offset the decline in the number of workers relative to the elderly as populations age.

1.3.3 The Hyperglobalization of Trade and Its Future

In chapter 4, Arvind Subramanian and Martin Kessler argue that the period of hyperglobalization that began in the late 1990s has been associated with the most dramatic turnaround ever in the economic fortunes of developing countries. This period is characterized by a number of major features, including hyperglobalization, reflected in the rapid rise in trade integration, which has occurred more rapidly than the growth in world output; the dematerialization of globalization, reflected in the growing importance of services trade; democratic globalization, as openness has been embraced widely; the rise of a mega-trader (China); and the proliferation of regional trade agreements and the imminence of mega-regional ones.

Regardless of the view one takes of the relationship between hyperglobalization and growth, it is safe to say that a broadly open system has been good for the world, good for individual countries, and good for average citizens in these countries. Going forward, even if the pace of hyperglobalization slows, the aim of policy at the national and collective level must be to sustain steady and rising globalization and avoid sharp reversals.

Three issues illustrate the proximate challenges for the open trading system: "currency wars" (the tendency to use exchange rates as a mercantilist tool); the harnessing of trade policies to facilitate climate change; and trade restrictions, which can exacerbate food and natural resource scarcity, with especially adverse impacts on the poorest around the world.

These proximate challenges can be addressed cooperatively only if the trading system can contend with more fundamental issues. Subramanian and Kessler identify three such challenges. The first is for rich countries to sustain the social consensus in favor of open markets and globalization at a time of considerable economic uncertainty and weakness: weak growth, high levels of debt, looming entitlement burdens, stagnating median incomes, and rising inequality. Especially in the United States, public support for and intellectual consensus in favor of free trade are wobbly.

The second is what might be called the China challenge. As China becomes the world's largest economy and trader, its markets become more important for other countries, especially low-income ones. Its openness, and that of other middle-income countries, will therefore be critical for the development progress of poorer countries. Relatedly, as a rising power, China will be called upon to shoulder more of the responsibilities of maintaining an open system.

If China continues to be open, trade tensions will remain contained. If China's opening slows, trading partners may be increasingly tempted to play the unfairness card, based on the disparate levels of policy openness (why should our markets be more open than the markets of a rival and equal?). In this scenario, especially if economic conditions are weak in advanced economies, the scope for trade conflict and tension could increase considerably, jeopardizing the openness of the global system.

The third challenge will be to prevent the rise of mega-regionalism leading to discrimination and becoming a source of trade conflicts. How these challenges will be resolved, the authors argue, will be determined in large part at the national level. For the United States and Europe, actions are needed to revive growth and address fiscal challenges, especially the challenges stemming from growing entitlements that are related closely to aging populations. For the United States, there is the additional challenge of addressing the problems of stagnating wages, rising inequality, and declining mobility. Success on these fronts will help ensure that globalization proceeds apace.

For its part, China should have a stake in preserving the open system for the simple reason that its rapid economic transformation over the past three decades was predicated crucially on openness. That transformation is still far from complete: China's standard of living is still only 20–25 percent that of high-income countries. Completing that transformation is critical for the political legitimacy of China's government and policymakers. In these circumstances, disrupting the open system would amount to biting the hand that has fed China and its rulers. Indeed, going forward, the Chinese agenda for reforms should be basically consistent with an open system: China's domestic needs are broadly outsiders' wants.

International/collective responses are needed to address the mobility of capital and its ability to escape taxation. Two new developments have exacerbated this problem: capital has become more mobile (reflected in growing financial globalization and increased flows of foreign direct investment), and the distribution of income in most OECD countries has moved substantially in favor of capital (and in favor of high-skilled people), increasing the size of the tax base that can elude taxation.

If countries and companies exploit the mobility of capital, the global ability to provide social insurance will decline, creating problems for globalization. Hence, there needs to be much greater cooperation between rich and emerging market countries (and, of course, tax havens) on how to tax capital and share the taxes from capital. This cooperation can take the form of greater harmonization (which would be difficult and entail a degree of regulatory convergence that countries will find challenging), or it can take the form of countries doing their best to allow other countries to better enforce their own tax rules.

At the risk of overgeneralizing, Subramanian and Kessler argue that the challenge in the trade arena can be summarized as follows: China is happy with the status quo and the United States is not. China—and the other larger emerging market countries, such as Brazil, India, and Russia—is reasonably content to have Bretton Woods rules apply to it and hyperglobalization rules apply to its large partners. China will liberalize and open up its markets in line with domestic rather than external imperatives.

The larger partners of the United States and China need to deploy a strategy that takes account of the possibility that China might occasionally be tempted into less than benign economic hegemony while reinforcing its incentives to act to preserve an open economic system. The "hyper-regionalization" of trade can be read in this context: both the Trans-Pacific Partnership and the Transatlantic Trade and Investment Partnership could have exclusionary effects on nonparticipants, especially China. But regionalism may undermine the rule-based global system.

Multilateralism could work as a defense against China in several ways: in shaping rules, in promoting adherence to them, and more broadly in defining legitimate behavior. With China's growing size, the balance of negotiating power will be with China rather than its partners. Multilateralism also ensures that China's trading partners will have enough heft to negotiate in a more balanced manner. For example, China might be willing to open its markets in return for the United States, European Union, India, and Brazil opening theirs. Its willingness to open up in a similar manner in negotiations with just the United States or European Union or with some less powerful combination is far from clear.

The open, rules-based trading system has delivered immense benefits for all, according to Subramanian and Kessler, especially today's emerging market economies. Preserving this system will ensure that low-income countries can also make successful growth transitions. It is often overlooked that the international trading system has witnessed more successful cooperation, especially between the systemically important countries, than the international financial and monetary system. Cooperation to preserve globalization, even if not in its current incarnation, is therefore critical.

Bernard Hoekman argues that the basic driver of the developments described by Subramanian and Kessler has been the steep decline in trade costs, as a result of technological change and the adoption of outward- (export-) oriented policies. Technological changes have been both hard and soft. They include advances in information and communication technology (ICT), which led to a sharp drop in the costs of international telecommunications, and the adoption of containerization and other improvements in logistics, which led to the plummeting of unit transport costs. Average tariffs were in the 20–30 percent range in 1950, complemented by a plethora of nontariff barriers (including quantitative restrictions and exchange controls) that were often more binding than the tariffs themselves. This increase in internationalization as a result of the decline in trade costs reflects ever greater "vertical specialization," with firms (plants) in different countries concentrating on (specializing in) different parts of the value chain for a final product. As a result, the share of manufactures in total exports of developing countries increased from just 30 percent in 1980 to more than 70 percent today, with a substantial proportion of this increase made up of intraindustry trade—the exchange of similar, differentiated products. Since the 1990s, intraindustry trade ratios for high-growth developing countries and transition economies have risen to 50 percent or higher. Much of this trade is intraregional—for example, about half of all East Asian exports of manufactures go to other East Asian economies, often as part of a supply chain. Many countries in Africa and South Asia, much of the Middle East, and the members of Mercosur in Latin America have not seen the shift toward intraindustry trade and participation in international supply networks that has been a driver of trade growth in East Asia, Mexico, Turkey, and Central and Eastern Europe and the emergence of what economist Richard Baldwin has called Factory Europe, Factory Asia, and Factory North America. Hoekman argues that fostering greater diversification and participation by African, Latin American, and Middle Eastern economies in international supply networks is one of the great challenges confronting governments of the countries concerned, as well as the trading system.

Technological changes have supported the long boom in trade; just-in-time multicountry lean manufacturing would be impossible without the process innovations and ICT that permit supply chain management spanning hundreds of suppliers located in different countries. Technological advances are increasingly permitting greater "dematerialization" of trade. Outsourcing and offshoring are increasingly going to be features of the organization of production and trade and a determinant of the productivity of firms. The trend toward the digitization of products, to allow them to be created in one location and transmitted to another for processing or consumption, could have major effects on the pattern and composition of trade.

Although manufactures and services account for the lion's share of global trade, agriculture remains of great significance in many low-income countries. Many rich countries subsidize and otherwise support the sector, creating negative spillovers for many of the poorest economies in the world. Hoekman argues that facilitating a continued process of broad-based beneficial economic growth in the poorer countries of the world requires that the global trading system remain open, and preferably that countries further liberalize trade.

Preferential trade agreements (PTAs) are an alternative mechanism. They have been a feature of many countries' national trade strategies for decades. What is significant is not so much the increase in the number of PTAs in recent years—many of which are not "deep," in contrast to what is sometimes claimed (including by the authors), as they often do not go much beyond the WTO in key areas, including services trade policy—but more the fact that the

United States decided to join the European Union and pursue PTAs with not only developing countries but also other high-income countries.

Given the slow pace of the Doha Round, a positive implication of the many PTAs in force and under negotiation is that governments remain willing to make binding trade policy-related commitments in treaty-based instruments. However, Hoekman argues, it is not obvious that killing off the Doha Round and launching a new "China Round" will make a difference to this dynamic.

According to Hoekman, strong forces are likely to sustain the process of international specialization and fragmentation of production that has been a driver of trade growth in recent decades. One of these forces is the fact that international production networks require low trade costs in order to operate. One reason why there was no major increase in trade barriers after the 2008 global financial crisis was that firms in countries that are most involved in supply chain trade did not ask for them, as trade protection would not have helped them. Trade is likely to continue to be an engine of growth and global poverty reduction over the next decade or two if more low-income countries become part of the international supply chains that produce manufactures.

1.3.4 Does Finance Accelerate or Retard Growth? Theory and Evidence

Finance can be beneficial for growth, argue Franklin Allen, Elena Carletti, Jun Qian, and Patricio Valenzuela in chapter 5, but it can also contribute to financial crises, which are often very damaging for growth. They suggest that financial development has a positive impact on economic growth at adequate levels of financial depth but that the effect vanishes, or even becomes negative, when finance becomes excessive. Excessive finance can incubate economic booms and asset price bubbles that end in financial crises, with low rates of economic growth for sustained periods. Too little finance is not desirable—but too much is not desirable either. They summarize what is known about finance as growth as follows:

- Long-run economic growth is positively correlated with bank credit to the private sector as a percentage of GDP. In high-income economies, however, this effect is relatively small, and it vanishes in some periods, possibly because these economies may have reached the point at which financial development no longer affects the efficiency of investment.

- Economies with small and medium-size financial systems relative to their GDP tend to do better as they put more of their resources into finance, but this effect reverses once the financial sector becomes too large relative to the productive sectors of the economy.

41

- The Great Recession of 2007–9 and the current debt crisis in Europe highlight the fact that excessive finance may have undesirable effects on economic growth. A growing body of literature finds not only a vanishing effect on the positive impact of financial development on economic growth but also a negative effect of excessive finance (excessive borrowing and lending, excessive risk-taking, poor risk management) on growth.

- Although the literature traditionally focuses on financial depth, financial structure is also important. Recent contributions focus on the optimal financial structure, which depends on a country's stage of development and endowments. Early on, for example, small banks may be appropriate for providing finance to small firms.

- Although theory predicts a number of benefits from financial openness—access to cheaper capital, portfolio diversification, consumption smoothing, emulation of foreign banks and institutions, and macro policy discipline among others—empirical studies report evidence both in favor of and against capital account liberalization.

The authors argue that these conclusions are based on the experiences of a wide range of countries. From the perspective of the average global citizen, it might be better to base policy advice on success stories. In China, alternative finance and institutions rather than traditional strong institutions and rule of law have facilitated growth. One of the most important policy conclusions is that alternative finance and the enforcement mechanisms associated with it should be encouraged rather than hindered. The conventional wisdom characterizes China's economic performance as "successful despite the lack of western-style institutions." Allen and his coauthors argue that China has done well because of this lack of western-style institutions: conducting business outside the legal system in fast-growing economies can be superior to using the law as the basis for finance and commerce. Research on political economy factors suggests that rent-seeking behavior by interest groups can turn the legal system, a monopolist institution, into a barrier to change. This view argues that by not using the legal system, alternative finance can minimize the costs associated with legal institutions. In a dynamic environment, characterized by frequent fundamental changes in the economy, alternative institutions can adapt and change much more quickly than formal institutions.

There is a dark side to finance, excessive levels of which can lead to asset price bubbles and financial crises. Other systemic risks that can lead to financial crises include panics (banking crises as a result of multiple equilibria), banking crises as a result of asset price falls, contagion, and foreign exchange mismatches in the banking system. Macroprudential policies are designed to counter these systemic risks. These policies include deposit insurance and government debt guarantees, which can prevent banking panics. On some occasions, it may also be possible to use interest rates to burst real estate bubbles. In large diverse economies such as China, the euro area, or the United States, doing so will not usually be possible, however, because bubbles tend to be regional and higher interest rates may cause slowdowns in regions without bubbles. If limits to arbitrage and other market failures lead to a serious malfunctioning of markets, it may be necessary to suspend mark-to-market accounting (the accounting practice of recording the price or value of a security, portfolio, or account to reflect its current market value rather than its book value) for financial institutions.

One of the most significant systemic risks is the raising of interest rates by central banks and markets in the post-quantitative easing era. Contagion is one of the most serious and least understood forms of systemic risk. Implementing permanent swap facilities for foreign exchange between central banks is an important policy to prevent currency mismatches in the banking system and reduce the need for large foreign exchange reserves.

According to the authors, the global imbalance in foreign exchange reserves was a significant contributor to the financial crisis, because the rapid buildup of these reserves helped fuel the real estate bubbles that triggered the crisis. Going forward, it will be important to reform the governance structure of the IMF and the other international financial institutions so that emerging economies are properly represented. This reform would help ensure that they receive equal treatment when they need financial help. It would also reduce their need to accumulate reserves to self-insure, a very wasteful mechanism from an economic point of view.

A likely medium-term scenario is that the Chinese yuan will become fully convertible and join the dollar and the euro as the third major reserve currency. Having three reserve currencies would provide more scope for diversification of risks by central banks holding reserves, and China itself would have little need of reserves.

With regard to financial inclusion, there have been several promising developments in low-income countries. Innovations in Kenya, for example, have expanded access to finance to isolated areas and minority groups. Equity Bank is a pioneering commercial bank that devised a strategy targeting low-income clients and traditionally underserved territories. Its branch expansion reached clients speaking minority languages. A key part of its strategy involved the use of low-cost services that were made possible by the use of computers.

In his comments, Stijn Claessens argues that a financial sector that serves all citizens in better ways requires better governance and engagement with a broader group of stakeholders in designing financial reforms. The recent financial crisis showed that the market-driven approach, although still the starting point for designing financial reforms, needs to more explicitly acknowledge two aspects: the many market failures that can arise in the financial sector and the large (implicit) role of the state in the financial sector, which, although necessary in many ways, has not always been productive. According to Claessens, the often poor provision of financial services and the repeated occurrence of financial crises show that regulators are still not able to design frameworks or implement them consistently in a way that creates financial systems that are efficient, serve the needs of all, and are reasonably "fail and fool proof." More therefore needs to be done regarding the "optimal" design and sequencing of financial reforms. Too little attention has been given to how to coordinate and phase various types of financial reforms. Reducing systemic risks is closely related to the need for better implementation of basic regulations, such as higher capital adequacy requirements, good supervision, clear resolution frameworks for weak financial institutions, better cross-border coordination, and incentive structures that are less prone to incentivize excessive risk-taking.

Rapid financial liberalization, including capital account liberalization, can increase the risk of crises. Some types of capital flows, such as bank flows, seem to increase countries' vulnerability to a balance of payments crisis; others, such as foreign direct investment, are less closely associated with crises. These findings suggest that in addition to basic reforms, certain types of financial systems or configurations of financial exposures or flows can make countries less prone to crises. A general lesson from recent crises is that there is a strong need for policies aimed at reducing market failures and externalities.

Crises have recurred partly because knowledge of their causes remains imperfect. With crises likely to continue to occur, the question of how to best manage their aftermath remains very relevant. The latest crisis—which has been drawn out and included large cross-country spillovers within the euro zone—is a case in point. The fiscal costs incurred may fall disproportionally on lower-income households and small and medium-size enterprises (SMEs), which may have less access to finance than large firms. Small savers may be worse off; richer households may escape the high inflation or financial repression that often follows a crisis. From an inequality perspective, there is thus a critical need to manage crises better. The main lesson is the need to absorb any losses resulting from the crisis—in the financial, corporate, or household sectors or at the level of the sovereign debt restructuring—as quickly as possible.

This area is complex and raises many fundamental questions. Financial systems typically serve a relatively small set of the population and the corporate sector; low-income households and SMEs, especially in developing countries, have little access to financial services at reasonable costs. Limited access also arises because finance has become more rules-oriented, with a multitude of new rules following the global financial crisis.

Claessens points out that capture is a big problem in the financial sector, with adverse effects on access to financial services and financial stability. Capture occurs in many ways. Some are subtle: insiders—both people within the financial services industries and important users of financial services—set the rules, standards, and institutional designs, mostly to benefit themselves. As rents are created, the costs of financial services increase and access declines for some groups. Capture can also occur in very blatant ways, such as corruption, which includes not only stealing but also misallocating resources. Capture often occurs ex post—through, for example, bailouts induced by the moral hazard of too-big-to-fail financial institutions or more relaxed monetary policy and fiscal policies to help avoid the risks of a systemic financial crisis. Overall, one should be skeptical about the scope for rapid progress in international formal governance arrangements, if only because of the multitude of actors involved.

In the end, changing the financial sector paradigm and the way in which the benefits and risks are allocated has to be about changing governance. Improving governance requires greater representation of some groups. How can the power of nongovernmental organizations (NGOs), 99 percent-type movements, and other groups be harnessed? It is also important to better understand existing stakeholders' objectives and views and to come up with an improved model. Claessens concludes by indicating that through these "answers," one can try to assess what a better model might be. He thinks political economy experts may be able to help design better ways to influence financial sector reforms for the benefit of global citizens.

Thorsten Beck, in his comments on chapter 5, focuses on three topics: the nonlinearity of the finance and economic growth literature, the conceptualization of the bright and dark sides of finance under one framework, and the channels through which financial deepening can influence societal outcomes and poverty reduction. He points to evidence that the effect of financial development is strongest among middle-income countries, that there is a declining effect of finance on growth as economies grow richer, and that the finance and growth relationship turns negative for advanced economies. He then reviews a number of explanations involving measures of financial depth and intermediation, including the relationship between financial development and productivity convergence, such that financial development has limited effect for countries at or near the technological frontier, and the possibility that the financial system can grow too large as a result of safety net subsidies that result in risky behavior that overextends the financial system. Beck then turns to cross-country evidence which shows that the positive effect of financial deepening comes mostly through enterprise credit. He indicates that the authors do not show any significant relationship between growth and the importance of household credit, particularly in advanced economies. He also points to the rising share of household credit in bank lending in advanced economies, which may explain the diminishing growth benefits from financial deepening. Other evidence, Beck argues, points to the fact that over shorter time horizons, a large financial sector may stimulate economic growth, but at the cost of increased volatility in advanced economies.

Beck then discusses "the bright and dark sides of finance," using a common conceptual framework, the financial possibility frontier—"the maximum sustainable depth, outreach or breadth of a financial system that can be realistically achieved at a given point of time." According to him, the financial possibility frontier clearly illustrates that there can be too much finance and that finance beyond the sustainable frontier does not always lead to desirable outcomes. Regarding finance and poverty, Beck concludes that it is important to look beyond direct effects to indirect and secondary effects, the differential impacts of financial deepening on labor and goods markets, and the structural transformation caused by financial deepening.

1.3.5 Resource Depletion, Climate Change, and Economic Growth

In chapter 6, Andrew Steer asks whether the recent pace and pattern of economic growth will continue throughout the current century or whether environmental and resource constraints will limit growth to lower levels. Is a greener path possible at modest cost that will enable growth and poverty reduction to continue at current rates? What is the likelihood that governments, businesses, and households will adopt such a path? Will our grandchildren inherit a healthier planet than we did?

As population quadrupled over the past century, economic production rose 20-fold, placing unprecedented stress on natural ecosystems. More than a quarter of the world's land surface has been degraded. The current rate of species extinction is 100–1,000 times higher than in prehuman days (apart from the "Great Dying," which occurred about 250 million years ago, during which up to 90 percent of all species are estimated to have gone extinct). All 13 of the planet's hottest years on record have occurred since 1998. Water withdrawals have tripled in the past 50 years. Environmental damage imposes a deadweight loss to the economy of about 10 percent a year in countries like China, even before taking account of impacts from climate change or biodiversity loss.

For the first time in history, the human footprint has the capacity to influence major planetary systems. The world is on the threshold of a new era: the

"Anthropocene." In the coming years, the human ecological footprint will likely grow even more rapidly. The number of people in the "global middle class," which grew from 1 billion in 1990 to 2 billion in 2010, is expected to rise to more than double by 2030 (McKinsey & Company 2011). This transition—in which the majority of the world will be able to afford a private motor vehicle, modern appliances, and a diet that includes meat daily—represents an important threshold (a point marking a change of a process to something else). When coupled with a changing climate, the implications are likely to be large and highly uncertain.

The challenge to agriculture is just one among many. Feeding 9.3 billion citizens by 2050 will require 70 percent more food, which will require vast amounts of water at a time when existing irrigated areas in Asia will be threatened by much more variable rainfall and rising temperatures will reduce yields in tropical areas. Today, 1.5 billion people live in water-stressed areas; by 2025, the number will be 5.5 billion.

In sum, the evidence strongly suggests that current patterns of energy and resource use, agricultural practices, and urbanization will lead to increased costs and decreased productivity to the extent that growth, conventionally measured, will be undermined, with sharp unpredictable threshold effects likely and the impact felt differentially across countries. The bottom half of the income distribution—both across and within countries—will suffer most.

Climate change is one of the most important risks the world now faces, in the judgment of some of the world's most respected economists, including Stern (2007) and Nordhaus (2013), as well as international organizations (World Bank 2012) and groups of scientists (IPCC 2013). Although global negotiators have set the target of limiting rising temperatures to 2°C, warming in the 3°C–6°C range is more likely. Estimates of economic impact from climate change vary greatly, from 2 percent to 10 percent of GDP for a 3°C increase and up to 20 percent for a 5°C increase. Research suggests that about three-quarters of the impact would fall on developing countries. Discontinuities triggered by ice melt, tropical forest die-back, ocean acidification, and other factors would multiply these impacts substantially.

Additional annual investments of about 2–3 percent of GDP would be required to limit greenhouse gas concentrations in the atmosphere to 450 parts per million, the level required to give a 50 percent chance of limiting the global temperature rise to 2°C. Reductions in growth have been estimated to be in the order of 0.2 percent per year, with global GDP in 2050 projected to be 5–6 percent lower than it would be in a world without climate change.

Although the costs of action are much smaller than the costs of inaction, they must be borne now, whereas the costs of inaction are some decades away—and conventional discounting makes the decision to act a close call.

The economics profession is sharply divided over both components of the discount rate (the pure rate of time preference and the rate at which the utility of income falls as future income rises). Mainstream economists argue that empirical evidence from consumer behavior and interest rates argue for a discount rate of perhaps 6 percent. Others, led by Nicholas Stern, argue that for several reasons, including ethics and common sense, the discount rate should be closer to 1 percent. The difference is enormous: $100 a century from now is worth 25 cents today under a 6 percent discount rate and $25 under the 1.3 percent discount rate proposed by Lord Stern.

Lack of consensus on the appropriate discount rate is just one reason why conventional cost–benefit analysis is of little help in guiding decisions on climate change. In addition, many of the "existence" and "amenity" losses embodied in an extreme climate change world cannot be captured in monetary terms. Furthermore, economists are increasingly recognizing that where truly catastrophic loss is a possibility, but with unknown probability, more sophisticated models and analysis are required than can be provided by conventional tools.

Fortunately, evidence is growing that there may be more win–win opportunities than earlier thought. But these opportunities will not happen automatically. The new "green growth" theory is predicated on two insights. First, gains that would improve both efficiency and the environment are being left unexploited because of a range of barriers, rigidities, and market imperfections. Rising concerns about resource depletion can help unlock these constraints. Roughly half of the investments needed through 2030 would be economically justified even in the absence of any environmental concerns.

Second, smart market-based environmental policies can trigger innovation and investment that can create new markets, jobs, and economic growth. For this reason, more than 50 developing countries are now imposing costs on their own citizens—through mechanisms such as feed-in tariffs and renewable energy standards—that at first sight seem not to be in their narrow interest.[2] (China, for example, introduced cap-and-trade policies for carbon emissions on a pilot basis in 2013, with a nationwide program planned for 2015.) A broad research agenda lies ahead in this field, with the issue of "green jobs" acting as a strong political impetus in many countries.

Short-termism on the part of most governments and businesses, coupled with the challenge of highly complex collective action at the global level, make the task ahead very difficult. Exploring policies with near-term economic and political gains, such as the following, will be essential:

1. *Remove harmful subsidies.* Subsidies on fossil fuels cost about half a trillion dollars a year. Subsidies encouraging overuse of water, overfishing,

---

[2] A feed-in tariff or renewable energy payments is a policy mechanism designed to accelerate investment in renewable energy technologies.

and excessively intensive agriculture add another half a trillion dollars. Smart governments are showing that the poor can be compensated for losses they would suffer from the removal of these subsidies.

2. *Price environmental externalities.* A carbon price of $25 a ton would reduce fossil fuel consumption by 13 percent and encourage new technology development. Enlightened countries are moving in this direction, but serious prospects for a global price are some years away, at best.

3. *Addressing other market failures (climb the abatement curve).* The unpriced global externality caused by greenhouse gas emissions is not the only market failure. Information asymmetry, coordination failures, imperfections in capital markets and R&D, and the existence of substantial co-benefits in the form of other environmental benefits are all discouraging action on climate change. They must be addressed through a portfolio of policies, such as emissions standards, calibrating the role of government in the development of technology, emphasis on a role for the use of public funds for renewable energy, and encouraging public–private collaboration, and incentives and public spending on green technologies.

4. *Reform global governance.* Today's global governance structures are ill-equipped to deliver the urgent actions required. Solutions are much more likely with smaller numbers of powerful players, including private companies. An explosion in such arrangements should be expected— and encouraged—to address not only climate change but also the much broader issue of resource risks in the coming decades.

5. *Give citizens a voice in the marketplace.* New technologies (such as remote sensing, crowdsourcing, and GPS tracking) and protocols for measuring emissions are enabling green companies and products to distinguish themselves. Certification schemes, commodity roundtables, environmental auditing, voluntary disclosure schemes, and integrated financial–environmental accounts are springing up in support. These mechanisms are slowly transforming supply chains among leading companies.

The case for action needs to be framed in terms of opportunities, investments, and risk management rather than in terms of burdens, costs, and uncertainties. It also needs to frame the debate in terms of a broader definition of economic and social progress beyond GDP.

In his comments on the chapter, Jeremy Oppenheim believes Steer lays out the core case for a new growth model for a low-carbon economy, but expresses doubt that the right combination of technology, markets, and policy can accelerate the transition to a low-carbon economy with no or little impact on aggregate growth. According to him, doing so requires considerable institutional sophistication to work in practice, given the risk of gaming, asymmetric information, and poorly designed policies, some captured by special interests. He thinks China provides a particularly challenging case in point. Its hugely successful transition from a low-income to a middle-income country was based largely on a resource-intensive, carbon-intensive economic model, fueled substantially by cheap coal—a very different direction from that implied by the Kuznets environmental curve. Oppenheim believes that the developed economies have not shifted their economic models in any significant way, other than offshoring a large share of their emissions to developing countries, such as China. His main point is that the theory of green growth appears to be significantly ahead of the reality. To facilitate the shift to a low-carbon economy, further research is needed in a variety of areas, including the challenge presented by cheap hydrocarbons, especially natural gas; the technology/industrial policy challenge; the distributional impact of the shift to a low-carbon model; and the case for a greater focus on local environmental goods.

1.3.6 Global Markets, Global Citizens, and Global Governance in the Twenty-First Century

In chapter 7, Nancy Birdsall, with Christian Meyer and Alexis Sowa, presents a framework for analyzing market-based growth and globalization, which have yielded many benefits. Millions of people in the developing world have escaped poverty and, for the first time in 100 years, the yawning gap between the rich countries and the developing world has narrowed, as China, Brazil, India, and other developing countries have grown and continue to grow faster than the United States, Europe, and Japan.

For the average citizen in the developing world, however, life remains harsh: half the world's people still live on less than $3 a day. The global market system is associated not only with growth but with ever greater concentrations of wealth within countries, destabilizing capital flows that hurt the average working person, new risks of job loss for middle-class people in advanced economies, and food and fuel price hikes that have had devastating effects on many poor households in low-income countries (though, of course, poor rural households whose income depends on food prices tend to benefit when those prices are higher). Even future growth in India, China, and Brazil can leave behind a large and frustrated income-insecure group. And in the absence of a dramatic technological breakthrough in the production and distribution of carbon-free energy, market-led growth is also potentially destructive because of its effect on climate change.

The enormous differences in income between the richest and poorest countries and people and the risks of unabated climate change, especially to the world's most vulnerable people, represent troubling moral challenges in an increasingly interconnected and interdependent global system. Worldwide surveys show that citizens everywhere are aware of these challenges. Millions of people in more than 50 countries, particularly young and better-educated people, see themselves as "global citizens," not in opposition to but alongside national citizenship. Substantial majorities are "strongly concerned" about climate change, and large majorities of the educated in eight high-income countries are willing to help finance the costs of meeting the Millennium Development Goals as long as other countries pull their weight.

Citizen activism in support of a better world has risen dramatically in the past decade. There is nothing new about activism, but the Internet has given citizens greater opportunities to place demands on powerful authorities beyond their borders. A good example is the citizen-based movement that in 2003 embarrassed the United States and the pharmaceutical industry into accepting a less stringent WTO approach to the global intellectual property rights that had been limiting access to anti-AIDS medications and other patented drugs in low-income countries.

Citizen-based "demand" for a fairer and more farsighted system exists, but the official supply of good global governance is wanting. The supply—the G20, the IMF, the World Bank, the WTO, the United Nations, the World Health Organization and other UN agencies, the newly created Green Climate Fund, and many other formal institutions at the regional and global level—is flawed in two ways. It is weak, and because it is inherently undemocratic it lacks legitimacy, exacerbating its weakness.

It is not the global institutions but the largest economies—including the United States and China—that are the locus of most decisions and policies that have implications beyond any one country's borders and that have the tax, regulatory, and enforcement powers to back up coordinated policies in and through the international clubs and institutions. The global institutions do provide a vehicle for countries, including the most powerful, to lock themselves as well as others into sensible rules and policies that are in their own self-interest but might be difficult to sustain domestically (for example, the open trading system) or that can be implemented at lower cost or greater effectiveness collectively (for example, World Bank lending and IMF surveillance). To the extent that these institutions bind their powerful members to sensible rules and policies, the ordinary citizen is probably better off with them than without them.

Still, the resulting global polity is a faint shadow of the sovereign state in forging and managing a domestic social contract that corrects for initial inequalities at birth and deals with such market externalities as pollution. The problem of global governance is less an intrusive "world government" than a global polity that is too weak to eliminate tax havens and restrain "race-to-the-bottom" tax competition among countries desperate to attract capital, to extend and enforce agreed safety standards to protect industrial workers at the bottom of complex multinational supply chains, to rationalize rich-country immigration policies that deprive citizens in developing countries of the right to move even as they impede growth in already rich countries, or to generate agreement to price emissions of heat-trapping gases.

A second problem is built into the nature of the system itself. The official institutions are made up of sovereign member states, themselves at best imperfect democracies; in terms of political accountability, they are at least two steps removed from the people whose lives they affect. In what they do (and neglect to do), they tend to reflect the interests and ideologies of the larger and more powerful countries, the corporate and global elite, and the well-intentioned but sometimes misguided (or driven purely by their own self-interest) NGOs of the north more than the concerns of ordinary citizens everywhere. Sometimes these institutions act for the benefit of ordinary citizens, as when the World Bank finances pro-poor cash transfers in Central America or the WTO restrains excessive patent protection in southern Africa. But because these institutions' practices often reinforce rather than compensate for the asymmetries of power within and among countries and their own governance structures reflect those asymmetries, they lack democratic legitimacy, which weakens their effectiveness.

Compounding the problems of weakness and illegitimacy is the new reality of a G-Zero (emerging vacuum of power) multipolar world, in which the decline in the overwhelming dominance of the United States is undermining its willingness and ability to fulfill the global leadership role it held in the second half of the twentieth century. The authors argue that the United States was a sort of "benign bully" because, as the most competitive and productive economy, it had an interest in open and fair global rules and practices that coincided with the interests of much of the rest of the world. With the rise in the market power of China and other emerging markets, the United States is less the economic hegemon it once was.

What can be done? One step is for empowered and enlightened citizens to find ways to amplify their influence, through the media, crowdsourcing, and the equivalent of "voting" in worldwide surveys. The world's rich—including the top 10 percent of people in the advanced economies and millions of rich people in developing countries—can support civil society and independent research and policy groups that generate information, monitor the performance of governments and intergovernmental institutions, inform the media, insist on the transparency of government and intergovernmental spending and practices, and generally contribute to deliberative discourse within and across countries.

In the world's largest economies, influential people can lobby to put their own houses in order, with a focus on changing domestic policies and practices that impose negative spillovers on the world's poor and vulnerable. The same can be said for the small but powerful corporate and political elite in developing countries.

Wherever they live, the world's rich and secure middle class have a second responsibility: to support the idea of multilateral cooperation and contribute to a narrative in their own countries in support of the multilateral institutions. In the United States, influential citizens would do well to recognize the risks to them and to the world if the longstanding bipartisan support for the IMF, the World Bank, the WTO, and the United Nations wavers. In Europe, citizens should support increased votes and influence for China and other emerging markets at those institutions, without which the rising powers will disengage.

The enormous differences in income between the richest and poorest countries—and within countries between the elite and the marginalized—constitute a moral challenge in an interconnected world. That challenge commands global collaboration to help bind all countries to trade, migration, aid, tax, anticorruption, and other policies and programs to help ensure that growth benefits the bottom half of the world's population. The number of globally minded citizens aware of that challenge seems likely to rise in this century.

Will the resultant increase in demand for better global policies increase their supply in key countries, in the form of stronger and more democratic global institutions? In the G-Zero, market-led world of asymmetric power and influence, can citizen movements, which lack the tax and enforcement powers of governments, make a real difference? Can evolving norms change global politics and bend the curve of market-led growth toward greater equity and sustainability? The authors conclude that the jury is still out.

In his comments on chapter 7, Pratap Mehta notes there is widespread agreement that there is a "global governance" deficit and that the architecture of global governance does not serve the interests of the poor. This architecture is increasingly producing a series of deadlocks on the major global challenges, including climate change, trade, inequality, and cybersecurity. It does not adequately recognize the world's deep interdependence: the political processes at the global level do not adequately take into account issues that create spillovers and affect citizens in other countries.

The authors' moderately hopeful assessment of the prospects for global governance stems from their belief that there is a greater global consciousness among the newly emerging middle classes, who increasingly think of their identity in global terms, and that truly global communication is now possible. They claim that civil society movements are now organized so that their voices are heard at the global level and that the balance of power is such that no single country or small group of countries can dominate the global system without challenge. These changes may give more incentives to countries to cooperate and create a consensus on important issues, because powerful countries can no longer assume that they can simply command and others will follow. There is an implicit normative claim that the desirability of cooperation is generally agreed upon.

Mehta thinks that most of what the chapter says is correct and characteristically well argued. However, he asks: if we are already moving in the right direction, as the authors claim, why has cooperation among nations not kept up with the demands from global citizens for a fairer and more farsighted global political order? Is it because of an undersupply of global governance, or does the problem lie in the ways in which domestic politics function? Can the seemingly propitious trends the authors describe overcome those constraints? Rather than assume that better global governance is the solution to global problems, should we not focus on how domestic governance generates these problems in the first place? The global order does not represent the poor—but neither do domestic political orders.

Mehta argues that the shift in the geopolitical balance of power creates both possibilities and pitfalls. It produces pressures for new structures of global cooperation, but it also makes collective action more difficult. Although for a while it looked as if necessity would force governments to cooperate globally on energy governance, recent developments in the United States, including the discovery of shale gas, have dimmed the prospects for the global governance of energy markets. Nevertheless, there might still be a desirable outcome for global energy, not because of more global governance but because incentives for individual countries have changed.

In other areas, such as climate change, this shift in the balance of power is making a solution difficult. The same could be argued for trade, where domestic politics rule and trump global governance, causing deadlock. In other important areas, such as the Agreement on Trade Related Aspects of Intellectual Property Rights (TRIPS), a good global outcome was achieved not because of more global governance but because domestic politics moved in a certain direction.

Mehta argues that the nature of global governance will be shaped not by the middle class, NGOs, or shifts in the balance of power but by the nature of global capitalism. According to him, the real issue is not global governance but how different states conceptualize the relationship between state and market. The global economic order, crafted under American leadership, proved fairly resilient because countries like China and India decided that it was in their interests to join that order. Doing so lifted millions of people out of poverty.

Different global issues pose different types of challenges and need different types of political responses, according to Mehta. More than institutions, they require a distinct kind of politics. He is supportive of the fact that the chapter is somewhat open-ended in its conclusions, that it does not offer the false illusion of institutional design. Instead, it reminds us that political hard work is needed at every level.

1.4 Policy Options for the Twenty-first Century and Their Implications for Global Citizens

The main purpose of the research program presented in this volume is not to make macroeconomic forecasts or develop long-term scenarios. It is nevertheless necessary to understand the major forces underpinning the pace of global economic growth—demographic transitions, climate change, technological innovations, structural reforms, trade and financial developments—and how they may affect global patterns of growth, the distribution of income and wealth, and ultimately the welfare of average citizens. Long-term economic prospects prepared by various researchers and institutions were therefore summarized in the previous section in order to provide a better understanding of the global economic context, the timing and sequencing of the policies suggested further in the chapter, and possible trade-offs and tensions among them.

Will mostly positive trends prevail, or is the world entering a new, substantially less auspicious era? The consensus (summarized in section 1.3) appears to be that growth will continue in all parts of the global economy, but probably at slower rates than in the past two decades. Whatever the future holds, policymakers should hope for the best but prepare for the worst—or at least for less positive changes than those witnessed in recent decades, when hundreds of millions of people emerged from poverty despite unprecedented population growth. The research program presented in this volume has identified some long-term policy changes at the national and international levels that, if implemented, could make it more probable that the more optimistic scenarios prevail and more pessimistic ones are avoided.

Five key questions, all of them involving trade-offs, both condition and are affected by policy decisions:

1. Will globalization and productivity convergence continue or be reversed? The two outcomes produce very different growth paths of the global economy and could have significant effects on the economic prospects of today's low-income countries and the pace of poverty reduction.

2. Is ongoing population growth likely to be accompanied by continued improvements in population quality and income, or will even the much slower population growth in the twenty-first century be incompatible

with a rapidly growing middle class in today's emerging economies, because of environmental and natural resource effects that slow the pace of growth? How would lack of progress in improving the quality of the population and its skills affect employment and productivity growth?

3. To what degree and for what types of issues should the focus be on making markets work better rather than on using top-down interventions and tighter regulation to attempt to unblock critical bottlenecks to growth, poverty reduction, an improved environment, and other goals?

4. Are key policies concerning the economic well-being of average citizens likely to be made at the level of the nation-state, or is collective action led by citizens across national borders more likely to dominate in the coming decades?

5. To what extent can emerging inequalities and inequities be addressed by equalizing access, quality, and opportunities rather than through regulation and policy interventions that may be highly inefficient from an economic point of view?

To a certain degree, differences in perceptions regarding these questions shape the analysis of policy options presented in this volume (summarized in Table 1.2). Many of the suggested policy responses to the global environment are cast in general terms, as is the guidance that would take the global economy in a desired direction. National policymakers, as well as the concerned international institutions, need to develop and customize their own policies at the country level, based on general directional guidance at the global level.

Several key megatrends and shifts underpin the analyses in this volume:

- In most countries, the pace of global economic growth is likely to be slower and unemployment higher in the next decade than in the previous two, mainly as a result of labor-saving demographic, structural, and technological changes that are making manufacturing more capital and skill-intensive.

- The rapid convergence phase of productivity levels and technology in the world economy during the past two decades was associated with a surge in world trade in goods and services, ushering in an era of hyperglobalization. In the aftermath of the 2008–09 crisis, globalization-reversing forces have set in.

- Rapid globalization led to substantial increases in financial interdependence and the monetization of national economies over the last two decades. Financial development has had a positive impact on economic growth at adequate levels of financial depth, but this effect vanishes, or even becomes negative, when finance becomes excessive. The ongoing structural changes in the global economy will have important implications for global financial markets as well as the international monetary system.

- Population growth rates have plummeted in most world regions. Regions in which this decline has been slower will increase their share of the global population. Continuing rapid urbanization, particularly in Asia and Africa, will mean the urban population will rise from about half of the world population to about two-thirds by 2030, with most urban growth expected to occur in Asia and Africa.

- Current patterns of energy and resource use, agricultural practices, and urbanization will lead to risks of increased costs and decreased productivity that will reduce overall economic growth, as conventionally measured, with sharp unpredictable threshold effects possible. Only the right combination of new technology, markets, and policy may be able to accelerate the transition to a low-carbon economy with only a modest impact on aggregate growth.

- Other key changes at the global level include the reduction and reversal of gender differentials in human resources that traditionally favored men and boys; the rapid expansion of the middle class in most emerging economies, with concomitant increases in demands on natural resources; and substantial shifts in economic activities to the developing world, with probable increasing economic interactions among countries in the developing world.

These key trends and shifts imply at least two types of challenges. First, addressing them requires both national and coordinated international actions, which may be particularly difficult at a time when many countries are facing severe fiscal and financial difficulties. Second, some policies and the underlying megatrends are likely to be complementary and thus reinforce one another (examples include improvements in infrastructure and human development indicators or openness to trade and economic growth), but other megatrends (such as the increased size of the middle class in developing countries, environmental degradation and climate change, the rapid expansion of automation/robotics and job creation, the expected slowdown in the pace of economic growth, and the continuation of globalization in its current mode) are likely to create serious tensions, making policy formulation and implementation increasingly challenging. In all these dimensions, there is also tension between market forces (or a laissez-faire approach) and multilateral action at the international level, as well as tension between inward-looking national responses to the changing world and collective international responses. Although the deepening of the financial and trade linkages across countries that occurred as a result of the hyperglobalization of the last 20 years supported rapid economic growth in many advanced and developing economies before the Great Recession, it also made countries more vulnerable to internationally transmitted shocks.

Therefore, many of the global policy changes (and country-level reforms) that aim at sustaining (or even accelerating) long-term growth need to be formulated with the knowledge that they may have important implications, sometimes in the form of unintended consequences, for global citizens through channels such as trade, finance, the environment and climate change, migration, and human development. These effects and the extent to which they may ultimately render an economy more vulnerable to shocks need to be anticipated while developing polices at the global and country levels. The broad set of policies in key areas outlined in Table 1.2 suggests a strategy that aims to maintain income growth by average citizens around the world based on continued productivity growth and convergence toward the global technological frontier in a sustainable and inclusive way. Reforms need to be calibrated at the country level and made consistent with each country's state of development.

The time has come to seriously think about how improvements in official global governance, coupled with and reenforced by rising activism of global citizens, can lead to welfare-enhancing results for all citizens, particularly poorer citizens. Cooperation among nations is either necessary (because of free-riding, as with climate change) or sensible (to ensure effectiveness at the lowest possible cost). As a recent review by IMF staff indicated, examples of international macro policy coordination have been few, and the most successful cases occurred only after the global economy entered a serious crisis. Although the G20 played a critical role at the onset of the Great Recession (Fardoust, Kim, and Sepulveda 2011), it has been unable to make headway in some important policy areas, because coordination has proved difficult and national interests diverge. The rising activism of global citizens can lead to greater awareness of potential gains from policy coordination and the need to take bold actions to remove structural rigidities and resistance to fundamental reforms, particularly in international trade and finance. The G20 agenda, as well as some key elements of the "Post-2015 Development Agenda", which cover many of the areas covered in this volume, should be revitalized and made much more supportive of global citizens' preferences and concerns.

A healthy global "system" is an outcome of, not an input to, better domestic policies that take the interests of all citizens into account. In an increasingly interdependent global market economy, countries can help one another in support of healthy domestic politics and policies through more active participation of citizens in policy debates and the assessment of key trade-offs.

Table 1.2 Matrix of Policy Options for the Global Economy in the Twenty-first Century and Implications for Global Citizens

Policy area 1: Sustaining long-term economic growth

Likely prospects in the first half of the twenty-first century	Desirable policy actions and implications for global citizens
A phase of the world economy is beginning in which East Asian-style high economic growth rates will become more difficult to sustain for the East Asian countries themselves and perhaps for the next generation of potential emulators. Important internal factors may shift economic growth from East Asia to other parts of the developing world. The "demographic bonus" of low dependency ratios that East Asia experienced in recent decades has passed in that region, but it is creating new opportunities in Latin America and South Asia, with a similar pattern projected for Africa in a few decades. Nevertheless, the future of growth, at least over the next decade, may not look like the recent past. The rate of convergence between poor and rich countries may decline from the high levels seen during the last two decades. Developing countries will probably still grow significantly faster than advanced economies, which are expected to experience slower growth in the coming decade. Ultimately, growth depends primarily on what happens at home. Whether the world economy provides more headwinds or tailwinds, desirable policies will continue to share features that have served successful countries well in the past. These features include a stable macroeconomic framework; incentives for economic restructuring and diversification (both market-led and government-provided); social policies to address poverty and exclusion; continued investments in human capital and skills; and a strengthening of regulatory, legal, and political institutions over time. Countries that do their homework along these dimensions are likely to perform better than those that do not.	1. **Support growth:** Future growth strategies may need to differ from the strategies of the past in their emphasis. Reliance on domestic and regional markets and resources will probably need to receive more attention, although trade is likely to remain dynamic and a key determinant of growth, particularly for poorer countries and commodity exporters. 2. **Reform social policy:** More emphasis on income distribution and the economic health of the lower and middle classes will be an important part of growth strategies. Social policy and growth strategy will become complements to a much greater extent. 3. **Improve policy coordination:** Globally, extensive harmonization and coordination of policies in finance and trade may not be achievable, in view of the heterogeneity of needs and preferences of citizens around the world. International institutions will need to help better manage globalization to accommodate the possible slowdown in its pace and its potential adverse effect on poorer countries. 4. **Invest in human capital:** Regions of the world with an increasing "youth bulge"—Latin America, South Asia, and, with a lag, Africa—will need to ensure sufficient human capital investments and labor market flexibility if they are to employ young people in productive activities and enjoy the more robust growth that this demographic bonus makes possible rather than suffer from growing youth unemployment. 5. **Strengthen social policies:** Higher-income countries will need to carve out some policy space to rework social bargains, just as developing countries need policy space to restructure their economies. A new settlement will need to be forged between advanced countries and large emerging economies in which the latter no longer behave as free-riders on policies of the former.

(Continued)

Table 1.2 (Continued)

Policy area 1: Sustaining long-term economic growth

Likely prospects in the first half of the twenty-first century	Desirable policy actions and implications for global citizens
	6. **Reform global governance**: Some of the shortfall between the demand and supply of global governance can be addressed by reforms and new forms of representations: by individual citizens and countries acting in ways that are more conscious of the global consequences of their decisions, by activists and regulators expanding their transnational networks, and by multilateral economic institutions improving their own governance. These changes are likely to take place in an environment with strong centrifugal forces, characterized by a growing number of actors and greater diversity of interests. If policymakers fail to take them into account, they are more likely to undermine support for than to strengthen an open global economy.
	7. **Reform national economies**: Ultimately, a healthy world economy needs to rest on implementation of structural reforms for healthy national economies and societies. Global rules that restrict domestic policy space too much are counterproductive insofar as they narrow the scope for reform, growth- and poverty-reducing policies. They thus undermine the support for and legitimacy of an open global economy. The challenge is to design an architecture that respects the domestic priorities of individual countries while ensuring that major cross-border spillovers and global public goods are addressed effectively.

Policy area 2: Enhancing the quality of the population

Likely prospects in the first half of the twenty-first century	Desirable policy actions and implications for global citizens
The quality of the population—defined here as including education and health—is the essence of development, if development is defined as increasing human capabilities. This emphasis seems intrinsically related to the Global Citizen Foundation's general concern with global citizens as well as the concerns of its Towards a Better Global Economy project. Widely improving the quality of the human population—and reducing distributional inequalities in population qualities, particularly by improving population qualities at the lower ends of the distribution—is very much consonant with this project's basic aims.	1. **Enhance migration**: Enhancing the freedom to move, internally and internationally. Increasing internal and international mobility could yield enormous potential gains, particularly for poorer citizens, with possibly few offsetting losses or even gains for more affluent citizens. Increased urbanization has substantial potential for increasing productivity, but it raises questions about policies and incentives for limiting negative externalities associated with urbanization. Gains from increased international migration could significantly exceed the gains from increased international trade. But under any plausible assumptions, the magnitude of internal migration associated primarily with urbanization is likely to dwarf the magnitudes of international migration.

2. **Strengthen the foundation for life:** The private and social gains from establishing a stronger foundation during the early years of life—through stimulation, nutrition, and health in the first five years—are substantial, particularly for children from poorer families.

3. **Support aging with dignity and equity:** As populations age, the potential private and social returns and equity gains from increasing the labor force participation and productivities of aging adults—and providing social support based on expected remaining life years rather than accumulated life years (age)—appear significant.

4. **Improve incentives for social service delivery:** Improving both the markets for and the policies regulating the delivery of services that provide essential inputs for achieving socially desired levels of human reproduction and childrearing; mortality; schooling, preschooling, and other forms of education; and internal and international mobility has substantial potential for enhancing productivities and well-being, with larger gains often accruing to poorer citizens.

Improvements in these four policy areas have enormous potential to enhance future economic growth; improve the welfare of global citizens broadly; and, in many cases, ensure that poorer citizens share more extensively in such growth. The "win–win" characteristics of many of these policies—the fact that they both enhance economic growth and disproportionately benefit the poor—justify them both morally and economically.

Because of heterogeneity across countries and regions in both their stages of economic development and the timing and duration of the demographic transition, however, these transitions have had different effects in different places in the past half century, with repercussions that will be felt throughout the twenty-first century. Differences in the stages of development and the timing and duration of the transition mean that prospects and desired policies differ across regions and countries. Much of the more developed world—including, as time goes on, more middle-income countries—will experience stable or even declining populations, rapid population aging, and rising age–dependency ratios. In contrast, many middle-income and (later) low-income countries will experience declining dependency ratios and the associated challenges of accommodating and benefiting from "youth bulges." These countries will have opportunities to exploit the demographic dividend to enhance growth—a dividend that East Asia has reaped in recent decades but will not enjoy in the future. Low-income countries with relatively high fertility rates will contribute most to world population growth during the twenty-first century (Africa's population in particular is projected to grow throughout the rest of the century, in both absolute and relative terms). In these countries, creating incentives and providing information to permit more rapid declines in fertility rates are likely to be high priorities with social in addition to private gains. In Asia and Africa, the population will become more urban, and these regions' share of the global labor market, human capital, and urban population will rise.

Policy area 3: Spurring globalization, international trade, and growth

Likely prospects in the first half of the 21st century	Desirable policy actions and implications for global citizens
Although trade has been rising rapidly, considerable potential remains for further trade expansion. On a value-added basis, the world trade-to-GDP ratio is about 25 percent. It could continue to rise over time if economic growth does not falter and the major trading countries or blocs of countries do not adopt protectionist policies. At least three forces will continue to drive globalization toward and sustain it at higher levels: economic convergence; technology; and interests, ideas, and institutions.	1. **Mitigate risk to globalization:** Collective action should help strengthen the institutional underpinnings of globalization. Actions include ensuring that domestic social insurance mechanisms are not undermined by globalization and bolstering multilateral institutions to prevent or mediate conflict between the major trading partners.

(Continued)

Table 1.2 (Continued)

Policy area 3: Spurring globalization, international trade, and growth

Likely prospects in the first half of the twenty-first century	Desirable policy actions and implications for global citizens
Headwinds are likely to limit the pace of convergence and structural change, however. As more countries continue to grow and some grow more rapidly, trade will increase. The pace of globalization will be affected by the pace of convergence. If the more sober assessment of future convergence held by some members of this project prevails, the pace of globalization may slow, but it is not likely that it will be reversed. Predicting the pace of technological progress is difficult. Revolutions in transportation, and then information and communications technology, have driven trade globalization. Even if the pace of new discoveries slows, there is scope for the spread of existing technologies, both directly and as embodied in foreign direct investment. Mobile telephony, Internet usage, and connectivity are still far from universal. Both supply and demand factors could accelerate technological developments. The very fact of hyperglobalization deepens the enmeshing of interests across countries, people, and companies. Most of the actions that will allow positive influences to prevail over globalization-reversing ones will be at the national level—namely, actions to address economic decline in the West and sustain growth in the Rest.	2. **Cooperate on taxes:** Greater cooperation on taxes may become necessary to preserve funding for mechanisms for social protection and bolster globalization. 3. **Strengthen multilateralism and global trade agreement:** The world has not yet declared the Doha Round dead, but progress has been uneven and slow. In order to move to more meaningful multilateral negotiations to address emerging challenges, including any possible threats from new mega-regional agreements, the rising economic powers, especially China and other BRICs, will have to play a key role in resuscitating multilateralism. 4. **Strengthen policy cooperation:** The open, rules-based trading system has delivered immense benefits, especially in today's emerging market economies. Preserving this system will ensure that low-income countries can also make successful growth transitions. It is often overlooked that the international trading system has witnessed more successful cooperation, especially between the systemically important countries, than the international financial and monetary system. Cooperation to preserve and achieve a more ethical globalization is critical. 5. **Reduce barriers to technological transfer:** Barriers to international technological adoptions and transfers, such as barriers related to modern agricultural developments, should be reduced or eliminated. If high-income consumers have preferences for consuming organic food and food that is not genetically modified, for example, they should be able to make and pay for those choices by being provided with that information. Governments should not restrict trade in foods using such technologies, however, as doing so has negative impacts on poor citizens in rural areas of the developing world.

Policy area 4: Supporting economic growth through finance

Likely prospects in the first half of the twenty-first century	Desirable policy actions and implications for global citizens
The global financial crises of 2007–9 and the current debt crisis in Europe highlight the fact that excessive finance may have undesirable effects on economic growth. Financial development is likely to have a positive impact on economic growth to the benefit of many citizens, but excessive finance can have a negative impact on growth and on many citizens.	1. **Discourage policies that induce moral hazard:** Deposit insurance and governmental debt guarantees can prevent banking panics. However, they create moral hazard and can be extremely costly if the systemic risk comes from collapse of an asset price bubble.

The experience of Japan, Taiwan, the Republic of Korea, and China suggests that countries can grow quickly for many years. The challenge is to understand how these countries achieved these spectacular growth paths and to implement their policies in other countries.

In China, alternative finance and institutions rather than strong traditional institutions and the rule of law have allowed this growth. One of the most important policy conclusions is that alternative finance and associated enforcement mechanisms should be encouraged rather than hindered.

Macroprudential policies—that is, macroeconomic policies aimed at building resilience to external financial shocks, especially vulnerability to capital flow reversals in the banking sector and the associated disruptions to domestic financial conditions—are designed to counter these systemic risks.

2. **Discourage the creation of asset bubbles:** In some situations, it may be possible to use interest rates to burst real estate bubbles. However, in large diverse economies such as China, the euro area, and the United States, doing so will not usually be possible, because bubbles tend to be regional and higher interest rates may cause slowdowns in regions without bubbles. When interest rates cannot be used, policymakers can limit loan-to-value ratios, which could be lowered as property prices increase at a faster pace; impose property transfer taxes that rise with rate of property price increases; or restrict real estate lending regionally.

3. **Follow prudent financial accounting:** If limits to arbitrage and other market failures lead to a serious malfunctioning of markets, it may be necessary to suspend mark-to-market accounting for financial institutions.

4. **Carefully plan existing quantitative easing:** One of the most significant systemic risks is the raising of interest rates by central banks and markets as they exit quantitative easing policy. These increases will cause asset values to fall and pose a significant risk to the stability of the banking system. The return to normalcy needs to be carefully planned and carried out over time to minimize systemic risk.

5. **Implement macroprudential policies:** Contagion is one of the most serious and least understood forms of systemic risk. Several macroprudential policies and regulations may be needed to address the different channels and types of contagion. Perhaps the most important is capital regulation.

6. **Prevent currency mismatches in the banking system:** Implementing permanent swap facilities for foreign exchange between central banks can help prevent currency mismatches in the banking system and reduce the need for large foreign exchange reserves.

7. **Reform the governance structure of the international financial institutions:** The global imbalance in foreign exchange reserves was a significant contributor to the financial crisis, because these funds helped fuel the real estate bubbles that triggered the crisis. It is important to reform the governance structure of the IMF and the other IFIs so that developing countries are properly represented. Such reform would help ensure that these countries receive equal treatment and reduce their need to accumulate reserves as a self-insurance.

(Continued)

Table 1.2 (Continued)

Policy area 4: Supporting economic growth through finance

Likely prospects in the first half of the twenty-first century	Desirable policy actions and implications for global citizens
	8. **Reform the international monetary system:** Eventually, the Chinese yuan could become fully convertible and join the dollar and the euro as the third major reserve currency. Having three reserve currencies might provide more scope for diversification of risks, and stability of the system will also require greater policy coordination among the major currency blocks.
	9. **Encourage financial inclusion:** With regard to financial inclusion, financial innovations in various developing countries show promise for emulation and replication. A key part of the strategy has involved the use of low-cost services that were possible because of the use of computers. There is no need for public subsidies. However, it is necessary that regulators permit the use of such strategies.

Policy area 5: Addressing the challenges of resource depletion and climate change

Likely prospects in the first half of the twenty-first century	Desirable policy actions and implications for global citizens
In the coming years, the human ecological footprint will likely grow even more rapidly than in recent decades. Although world population growth will slow substantially, rising per capita incomes mean that demand will increase. The number of citizens in the "global middle class" is expected to rise by up to 3 billion persons by 2030. This transition could represent an important threshold in terms of resource demands. When coupled with a changing climate, the implications are likely to be large and highly uncertain.	1. **Remove fossil fuels and other harmful subsidies:** A starting point should be the elimination of harmful subsidies, particularly on fossil fuel production and consumption, which globally amount to nearly half a trillion dollars a year. Subsidies encouraging the overuse of water, overfishing, and excessively intensive agriculture amount to another half a trillion dollars. Smart governments are showing that the poor can be compensated for the elimination of these subsidies.
The challenge to agriculture is just one among many. Feeding 9.6 billion citizens by 2050 at their higher income levels will require 70 percent more food, which in turn will require vast amounts of water at a time when existing irrigated areas in Asia will be threatened by much more variable rainfall and rising temperatures will reduce yields in some temperate and tropical areas. By 2025, the number of people living in water-stressed areas is expected to reach 5.5 billion, from 1.5 billion people today.	2. **Price carbon and other environmental externalities:** Market-based mechanisms can be significantly more cost-effective than regulatory regimes, as demonstrated by permit trading for sulfur dioxide in the United States in the 1990s. A carbon price of $25 a ton would reduce fossil fuel consumption by 13 percent and encourage new technology development. Enlightened countries are moving in this direction, and the long-term prospects for carbon markets remain strong. As a result of the need to act soon to prevent a catastrophe, a number of countries and regions are introducing trading schemes in that anticipation.

The evidence strongly suggests that current patterns of energy and resource use, agricultural practices, and urbanization will lead to increased costs and decreased productivity. The bottom half of the income distribution—both across and within countries—will probably suffer most (although some rural poor may gain from increased demand for their labor if food and other agricultural product prices increase).

Decisions on climate change need to rely on more sophisticated models and analytical tools, as many of the "existence" and "amenity" losses caused by extreme climate change are difficult to capture in monetary terms using conventional analysis.

Evidence is growing that there may be more win–win opportunities than earlier thought. Gains that would improve both efficiency and the environment are being left unexploited because of a range of barriers, rigidities, and market imperfections: half of the outlays needed up to 2030 would be economically justified even without environmental concerns. Smart market-based environmental policies can trigger innovation and investment that can create new markets, jobs, and economic growth.

3. **Climb the marginal abatement curve:** Addressing other market failures. Information asymmetry, coordination failures (the need for networks), imperfections in capital markets and R&D, and the existence of substantial co-benefits in the form of other environmental benefits are all market failures that are discouraging action on climate change. They must be addressed through a portfolio of policies such as emissions standards. "Nudge" policies, such as labeling, certification schemes, and power use monitors are also proving effective.

4. **Enforce greater international cooperation on the environment:** Today's global governance structures are ill-equipped to deliver the urgent actions required. Solutions are much more likely with a smaller numbers of powerful players, including private companies. An explosion in such arrangements should be expected—and encouraged—to address not only climate change but also the much broader issue of resource risks in the coming decades. Rewards and penalties to be instituted.

5. **Facilitate citizen voice through the marketplace:** New technologies (such as remote sensing, crowdsourcing, and GPS tracking) and certification schemes, protocols for measuring emissions, commodity roundtables, environmental auditing, voluntary disclosure schemes, and integrated financial–environmental accounts are enabling green companies and products to distinguish themselves and are slowly transforming supply chains among leading companies.

Policy area 6: Creating new global governance to enhance citizens' welfare

Likely prospects in the first half of the twenty-first century	Desirable policy actions and implications for global citizens
The global market, built largely on the capitalist system and on democratic and accountable government as the political guardian of that system, is not entirely secure. Official governance of this market is inadequate in representing and protecting the bottom half of the world's population and in dealing with climate change. There is also a global political problem: in the advanced economies and some upper–middle-income countries, where the middle class is no longer benefiting from growth or is increasingly vulnerable to poor economic performance, there is growing suspicion of the costs of "globalization" and lack of confidence that the global "system" overall is fair.	1. **Encourage citizen activism in rich countries:** The highly empowered global citizens in the world's largest economies—the United States, China, Europe, Japan—have a particular responsibility. It is their governments' actions and lack of actions on financial, trade, immigration, investment, anticorruption, tax, and climate policy that matter most for people everywhere. It is these countries' domestic policies that often impose negative spillovers on others. For citizens in advanced economies, a priority should be to lobby that their own houses be put in order (by, for example, supporting a carbon tax in the United States or fiscal expansion in Germany).

(Continued)

Table 1.2 (Continued)

Policy area 6: Creating new global governance to enhance citizens' welfare

Likely prospects in the first half of the twenty-first century	Desirable policy actions and implications for global citizens
Worldwide surveys show that citizens everywhere are becoming more aware and more active in seeking changes in the global norms and rules that could make the global system and the global economy fairer—in processes if not outcomes—and less environmentally harmful. Across the world, more people, especially the more educated and the young, are seeing themselves as "global citizens," aware that what happens inside their own country matters for others outside and that what happens outside matters for them and for their children and grandchildren. Opportunities exist to close the gap between the demands of global citizens for a better world and the supply of better global governance. Mechanisms can be exploited that amplify the voices of global citizens, strengthen the ties among them, and link their good intentions to effective national and international policies, giving global society better channels by which to influence the global polity. Individual and official supporters of reducing global inequality and managing climate change can support not only polls and informal voting but civil society groups and think tanks, including in the developing world, that generate information, monitor performance of governments and intergovernmental organizations against their commitments, inform the media, and in general contribute to deliberative discourse. They can insist on transparency of their own governments and of intergovernmental institutions as a critical input to citizen monitoring and activism.	2. **Encourage citizen activisim in emerging economies**: The small but powerful corporate and political elite within developing countries should lobby to address distortions and inequities in their own societies (for example, backing forest conservation in Indonesia, protection of indigenous people in Brazil, and reform of patronage-based school systems in India). 3. **Make governments more accountable for global policies** The first-best solution for many global problems would be a more "activist" global polity—if not a world government then something more legitimate, more democratic, and more effective than the current set of intergovernmental institutions. It is within sovereign nations that citizens of the world have the possibility and the responsibility to make their governments accountable for policies and practices that have impacts beyond their borders. 4. **Increase support for multilateralism:** The world's rich and the secure middle class wherever they live have a second responsibility: to support the idea of multilateral cooperation and to contribute to a narrative in their own countries in support of multilateral institutions. The most influential citizens in all countries, particularly in large and economically powerful countries, would do well to recognize their personal interest in a more effective and legitimate set of international institutions and the risk to them and to the world if the longstanding bipartisan support for the IMF, the World Bank, and the United Nations continues to waver. 5. **Reform global economic governance:** Global citizens should endorse governance reforms at the IMF and the World Bank that would give China and the other large emerging economies larger stakes. They should recognize that without these reforms, increasingly powerful countries will disengage, further weakening the institutions and undoing the potential benefits of global cooperation.

References

Acemoglu, Daron, and James Robinson. 2012. *Why Nations Fail: The Origins of Power, Prosperity and Poverty*. New York: Crown Publishers.

Anderson, Kym, Maros Ivanic, and Will Martin. 2013. "Food Price Spikes, Price Insulation, and Poverty." Working Paper No. 2013/11, Arndt-Corden Department of Economics, Crawford School of Public Policy, Australian National University College of Asia and the Pacific.

Bergheim, Stefan. 2008. *Long-Run Growth Forecasting*. Berlin: Springer-Verlag.

Bhattacharya, Amar, Mattia Romani, and Nicholas Stern. 2012. "Infrastructure for Development: Meeting the Challenge." Policy Paper, Center for Climate Change Economics and Policy, Grantham Research Institute on Climate and the Environment, London School of Economics, and International Government Group of Twenty-Four. http://www.g24.org/Publications/ResearchPaps/ PP-infrastructure-for-development-meeting-the-challenge.pdf.

Chandy, Laurence, Natasha Ledlie, and Veronika Penciakova. 2013. *The Final Countdown: Prospects for Ending Extreme Poverty by 2030*. Policy Paper 2013-04, Brookings Institution, Washington, DC.

Conference Board. 2012a. *Global Economic Outlook*. New York: Conference Board.

Conference Board. 2012b. *Projecting Economic Growth for Medium to Long Term*. New York: Conference Board.

Conference Board. 2013. *Global Economic Outlook 2014*. New York: Conference Board.

Dadush, Uri, and William Shaw. 2011. *Juggernaut: How Emerging Markets Are Shaping Globalization*. Carnegie Endowment for International Peace, Washington, DC.

Derviş, Kemal. 2012. "Convergence, Interdependence, and Divergence." *Finance & Development* 49(3): 10–14.http://www.imf.org/external/pubs/ft/fandd/2012/09/ dervis.htm.

Done, Adrian. 2011. *Global Trends: Facing Up to a Changing World*. London: Palgrave Macmillan.

Edward, Peter, and Andy Sumner. 2014. "Estimating the Scale and Geography of Global Poverty Now and in the Future: How Much Difference Do Method and Assumptions Make?" *World Development* 58: 67–82.

EIA (Energy Information Administration). 2013. *International Energy Outlook 2013*. July, Washington, DC.

Fardoust, Shahrokh, and Ashok Dhreshwar. 2013. "Some Thoughts on Making Long-Term Forecasts for the World Economy." Policy Research Working Paper 6705, World Bank, Washington, DC.

Fardoust, Shahrokh, Yongbeom Kim, and Claudia Sepulveda. 2011. "A Development Agenda for the G20: An Overview." In *Post Crisis Growth and Development: A Development Agenda for the G20*, ed. Shahrokh Fardoust, Yongbeom Kim, and Claudia Sepulveda. Washington, DC: World Bank.

Fay, Marianne, Michael Toman, Daniel Benitez, and Stefan Csordas. 2011. "Infrastructure and Sustainable Development." In *Post Crisis Growth and*

Development: A Development Agenda for the G20, ed. Shahrokh Fardoust, Yongbeom Kim, and Claudia Sepulveda. Washington, DC: World Bank.

Ferreira, Francisco, Anna Fruttero, Phillippe Leite, and Leonardo Lucchetti. 2011. "Rising Food Prices and Household Welfare: Evidence from Brazil in 2008." World Bank Policy Research Working Paper Series 5652, Washington, Washington, DC.

FAO (Food and Agriculture Organization of the United Nations). 2013. *The State of Food Insecurity in the World*. Rome: FAO.

Franklin, Daniel, and John Andrews, eds. 2012. *Megachange: The World in 2050*. London: The Economist.

Hughes, B., Mohammod T. Irfan, Haider Khan, Krishna B. Kumar, Dale S. Rothman, and Jose R. Solorzano. 2009. *Patterns of Potential Human Progress: Reducing Global Poverty*, vol. 1. Oxford: Oxford University Press.

IPCC (Intergovernmental Panel on Climate Change). 2013. "Climate Change 2013: The Physical Science Basis." Contribution of Working Group I to the *Fifth Assessment Report of the Intergovernmental Panel on Climate Change*, ed. T. F. Stocker, D. Qin, G.-K. Plattner, M. Tignor, S. K. Allen, J. Boschung, A. Nauels, Y. Xia, V. Bex, and P. M. Midgley. Cambridge: Cambridge University Press.

Johansson, Åsa, Yvan Guillemette, Fabrice Murtin, David Turner, Giuseppe Nicoletti, Christine de la Maisonneuve, Philip Bagnoli, Guillaume Bousquet, and Francesca Spinelli. 2013. "Long-Term Growth Scenarios." OECD Economics Department Working Paper 1000, Organisation for Economic Co-operation and Development, Paris.

Lomborg. Bjorn. 2013. *How Much Have Global Problems Cost the World? A Scorecard from 1900 to 2050*. Cambridge: Cambridge University Press.

Maddison, A. 2008. "The West and the Rest in the World Economy." *World Economics* 9 (4): 75–100.

McKinsey & Company. 2011. *Resource Revolution: Meeting the World's Energy, Materials, Food, and Water Needs*. November. http://www.mckinsey.com/insights/energy_resources_materials/resource_revolution.

Milanovic, Branko. 2011. "Global Inequality: From Class to Location, from Proletarians to Migrants." World Bank Policy Research Working Paper 5820, Washington, DC.

National Intelligence Council. 2012. *Global Trends 2030: Alternative Worlds*. Washington, Washington, DC.

Nordhaus, William. 2013. *The Climate Casino: Risk, Uncertainty, and Economics for a Warming World*. New Haven, CT: Yale University Press.

OECD (Organisation for Economic Co-operation and Development). 2012. *Looking to 2060: Long-Term Global Growth Prospects*. OECD Policy Paper 03, Paris.

OECD and FAO (Food and Agriculture Organization). 2013. *OECD-FAO Agricultural Outlook 2013–2022*. Paris.

Oxford Martin School. 2013. *Now for the Long Term: The Report of the Oxford Martin Commission for Future Generations*. October, University of Oxford.

Pew Research Center. 2013. "Five Years after Market Crash, U.S. Economy Seen as 'No More Secure.'" September, Washington, DC.

Poncet, S. 2006. "The Long-Term Growth Prospects of the World Economy." CEPII Working Paper 2006-16, Centre d'Etudes Prospectives et d'Informations Internationales, Paris.

PwC. 2013. *World in 2050: The BRICs and beyond: Prospects, Challenges and Opportunities.* January, PwC, LLP.

Ravallion, Martin. 2013. "How Long Will It Take to Lift One Billion People out of Poverty?" World Bank Policy Research Working Paper 6325, Washington, DC.

Stern, Nicholas. 2007. *The Economics of Climate Change: The Stern Review.* Cambridge: Cambridge University Press.

Stern, Nicholas. 2014. "Climate Change Is Here Now and It Could Lead to Global Conflict." February 13, *The Guardian* http://www.theguardian.com/environment/2014/feb/13/storms-floods-climate-change-upon-us-lord-stern.

UN DESA (United Nations Department of Economic and Social Affairs/Population Division). 2012. *World Population Prospects: The 2012 Revision, Vol. I: Comprehensive Tables.* New York.

Visco, Ignazio. 2013. "The Financial Sector after the Crisis." March, Lecture at Imperial College, London.

World Bank. 2011. *World Development Horizons.* Washington, DC.

World Bank. 2012. *Turn Down the Heat: Why a 4C Warmer World Must Be Avoided.* Washington, DC: World Bank.

World Bank. 2013. *World Development Horizons.* Washington, DC: World Bank.

World Bank. 2014. *Commodity Markets Outlook.* January, Washington, DC: World Bank.

2

The Past, Present, and Future of Economic Growth

Dani Rodrik

2.1 Introduction

The past decade has been an extraordinarily good one for developing countries and their mostly poor citizens—so good, in fact, that it has become commonplace to look upon them as potential saviors of the world economy. Their economies have expanded at unprecedented rates, resulting in both a large reduction in extreme poverty and a significant expansion of the middle class. Recently, the differential between the growth rates of developing and advanced countries expanded to more than 5 percentage points, assisted in part by the decline in the economic performance of the rich countries (Figure 2.1). China, India, and a small number of other Asian countries were responsible for the bulk of this superlative performance. But Latin America and Africa resumed growth as well, catching up with (and often surpassing) the growth rates they experienced during the 1950s and 1960s (Figure 2.2).

Economic growth is a precondition for the improvement of living standards and lifetime possibilities for the "average" citizen of the developing world. Can this recent performance be sustained into the future, decisively

The author is grateful for comments and suggestions by the participants in the Towards a Better Global Economy project, especially Jere Behrman, Kemal Derviş, and Chang-Tai Hsieh.

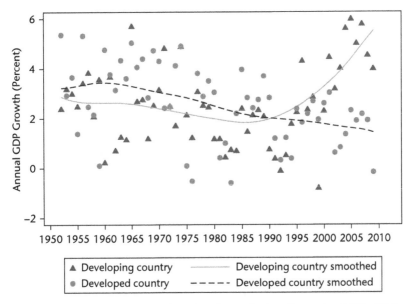

Figure 2.1 Growth Trends in Developed and Developing Countries, 1950–2011
Source: Author, based on data from Rodrik 2011b.

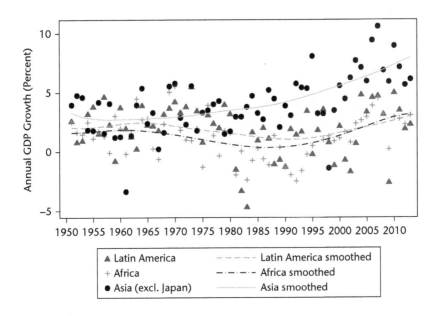

Figure 2.2 Growth Trends in Developing Countries, by Region, 1950–2011
Source: Author, based on data from Rodrik 2011b.

reversing the "great divergence" that has split the world into rich and poor countries since the nineteenth century?

In answering this question, optimists would point to improvements in governance and macroeconomic policy in developing countries and to the still not fully exploited potential of economic globalization to foster new industries in the poor regions of the world by outsourcing and technology transfer. Pessimists would fret about the drag that rich countries exert on the world economy, threats to globalization, and obstacles that late industrializers have to surmount, given competition from China and other established export champions.

The weights one places on these considerations—and many others—depend on one's views as to the ultimate drivers of economic growth in lagging countries. Extrapolation is not necessarily a good guide to where the world is headed.

We can also turn the question about the sustainability of growth around and pose it in a different form: what kind of changes in the institutional framework within countries and globally would most facilitate rapid growth and convergence? This is a normative, rather than positive, question about the policies needed. But answering it requires yet again a view on what drives growth. The more clearly articulated that view, the more transparent the policy implications.

This chapter provides a longer-term perspective on economic growth in order to deepen the understanding of the key drivers of economic growth, as well as the constraints that act on it. It presents an analytical framework that is motivated by the empirical evidence and embeds the conventional approaches to economic growth. Although orthodox in many ways, the framework highlights a somewhat different strategic emphasis that provides a better account of the heterogeneity in growth performance around the developing world.

The chapter emphasizes two key dynamics behind growth. The first is the development of fundamental capabilities in the form of human capital and institutions. Long-term growth ultimately depends on the accumulation of these capabilities—everything from education and health to improved regulatory frameworks and better governance (Acemoglu and Robinson 2012; Allen et al. 2013; Behrman and Kohler 2013). But fundamental capabilities are multidimensional, have high set-up costs, and exhibit complementarities. Therefore, investments in them tend to yield paltry growth payoffs until a sufficiently broad range of capabilities has already been accumulated—that is, until relatively late in the development process. Growth based on the accumulation of fundamental capabilities is a slow, drawn-out affair.

The second key dynamic is structural transformation—the birth and expansion of new (higher-productivity) industries and the transfer of labor from traditional or lower-productivity activities to modern ones. With the exception of natural resource bonanzas, extraordinarily high growth rates are almost always the result of rapid structural transformation, industrialization in particular. Growth miracles are enabled by the fact that industrialization can take place in the presence of a low level of fundamental capabilities: poor economies can experience structural transformation even when skills are low and institutions weak. This process helps explains the rapid take-off of East Asian countries in the postwar period, from Taiwan in the late 1950s to China in the late 1970s.

The policies needed to accumulate fundamental capabilities and those required to foster structural change naturally overlap, but they are distinct. The first types of policies entail a much broader range of investments in skills, education, administrative capacity, and governance; the second can take the form of narrower, targeted remedies. Without some semblance of macroeconomic stability and property rights protection, new industries cannot emerge. But a country does not need to attain Sweden's level of institutional quality in order to be able to compete with Swedish producers on world markets in many manufactures. Furthermore, as I discuss below, fostering new industries often requires second-best, unconventional policies that are in tension with fundamentals. When successful, heterodox policies work precisely because they compensate for weakness in those fundamentals.

As an economy develops, the dualism between modern and traditional sectors disappears and economic activities become more complex across the board. Correspondingly, these two drivers merge, along with the sets of policies that underpin them. Fundamentals become the dominant force over structural transformation. Put differently, if strong fundamentals do not eventually come into play, growth driven by structural transformation runs out of steam and falters.

This chapter is organized as follows. The next section describes the consequences of recent growth performance on the global income distribution. The salient facts that emerge from the analysis are that growth in developing countries (especially China) has been a boon to the "average citizen" of the world and created a new global middle class. Section 2.3 examines economic history. It highlights the role of differential patterns of industrialization in shaping the great divergence in the world economy between a rich core and a poor periphery. Section 2.4 summarizes the growth record to date in the form of six empirical regularities ("stylized facts"). Key among them is the presence of unconditional labor productivity convergence in manufacturing industries. Section 2.5 interprets the policy experience of successful economies in light of this empirical background. Section 2.6 presents an explicit analytical framework that distinguishes among three types of economic sectors: a traditional sector with stagnant technology; a modern service sector, where productivity depends on (slow-moving) fundamental capabilities; and an industrial sector that benefits in addition from an unconventional convergence dynamic. Section 2.7 uses the framework to present a 2 × 2 typology of growth outcomes based on the evolution of capabilities and the speed of structural transformation. The analysis yields four cases: no growth, slow growth, episodic growth, and rapid sustained growth. Section 2.8 formally defines the limits to industrialization. Section 2.9 examines the quantitative limits to industrialization. Extensions of the framework to global supply chains (section 2.9) and natural resource exporters (section 2.10) are followed by a prognosis (section 2.11) and discussion of policy implications (section 2.12).

2.2 How Is the "Average" Person Doing? Growth and the Global Income Distribution

The "average individual" can be defined as the person in the middle of the global income distribution—that is, the individual who receives the median level of income in the global economy. One way of gauging the extent of global inequality is to compare the income of the average individual to average global income (that is, global gross domestic product [GDP] per capita). Were income distributed evenly, median and average incomes would coincide. The more unequal the world economy is, the larger is the gap between the two. As the figures in Table 2.1 show, the ratio between average and median income is very large for the world as a whole—roughly twice what is observed in the world's most unequal societies (such as Brazil). Global inequality is thus much higher than within-country inequality.[1]

The good news is that this ratio has fallen significantly since the 1980s, driven by the fact that median income rose much more rapidly than average income. In 1988, the world's median income stood at $846 (in 2005 purchasing power parity–adjusted dollars). By 2005, this figure had risen to $1,209, an increase of 43 percent over the course of less than two decades. The increase in average world incomes over the same period was only 12 percent (from $3,523 to $3,946). Correspondingly, global inequality fell substantially, at least when measured by this indicator.[2] This happened even though within-country inequality rose in most large economies, such as the United States and China (but not Brazil), as Table 2.1 shows.

[1] These numbers were calculated from data put together by Branko Milanovic of the World Bank (Milanovic 2011). Because they derive from national household surveys, they do not match (and in general are lower than) income levels reflected in GDP per capita statistics.

[2] Global inequality rose by some measures, as Table 2.2 shows.

Table 2.1 Median and Average Income in World and in Selected Countries, 1988 and 2005

Economy	Median income	Average income	Ratio
World			
1988	846	3,523	4.16
2005	1,209	3,946	3.26
Percentage increase	42.9	12.0	n.a.
United States			
1988	12,327	14,819	1.20
2005	15,664	20,001	1.28
Percentage increase	27.1	35.0	n.a.
China			
1988	310	361	1.16
2005	1,013	1,303	1.29
Percentage increase	226.8	260.9	n.a.
Brazil			
1988	1,901	4,030	2.12
2005	2,107	3,890	1.85
Percentage increase	10.8	−3.5	n.a.

Note: n.a. = Not applicable.

Source: Author, based on data from Milanovic 2011.

Figure 2.3 shows the change in the global interpersonal distribution of income between 1988 and 2005.[3] It shows a rightward shift in the distribution, indicating a rise in average incomes. Much more noticeable is the change in the shape of the distribution. In 1988, the global distribution exhibited clear humps at each end, one for poor countries and another for rich countries (the latter with a much smaller mass). By 2005, the two humps had virtually disappeared, merging in the middle of the distribution. What happened in between those dates is that China, which housed a substantial proportion of the world's poor in the 1980s, filled out the middle of the distribution. Since the 1980s, China has transformed itself from a poor country, in which the bulk of its population stood below the global median, into a middle-income country, in which median income has caught up with the global median (see Table 2.1). Today, China's income distribution is centered at the middle of the global income distribution. The result is that the global economy now has a much larger middle class, with Chinese households making up a large part of it.

The impact that Chinese economic growth has had on the global distribution of income reflects an important feature of global inequality—the fact

---

[3] The distribution is generated by fitting a kernel smoothing on the ventile or decile data (depending on availability) for incomes within countries.

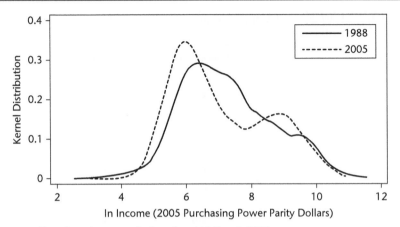

Note: Kernel = epanechnikov, bandwidth = 0.2686.

Figure 2.3 Global Income Distribution, 1988 and 2005
Source: Author, based on data from Milanovic 2011.

Table 2.2 Decomposition of Global Inequality, 1998 and 2005

Measure	Gini coefficient	Log mean deviation	Theil index
1988			
Total inequality	0.69	1.07	0.89
Percent within-country inequality	n.a.	19.4	22.0
Percent between-country inequality	n.a.	80.6	78.0
2005			
Total inequality	0.70	1.04	0.95
Percent within-country inequality	n.a.	26.5	26.5
Percent between-country inequality	n.a.	73.5	73.5

Note: n.a. = Not applicable.
Source: Author, based on data from Milanovic 2011.

that the bulk of global inequality. is accounted for by differences in average incomes across rather than within countries. The relevant numbers are shown in Table 2.2, which decomposes global inequality into within- and between-country components. It shows three measures of inequality that are based on more information than the average-median ratio: the Gini coefficient, the log mean deviation, and the Theil index. Of these, only the last two are decomposable. Depending on the measure and time period, inequality across countries—that is, differences in per capita incomes between countries—accounts for 75–80 percent of global income inequality; inequality within countries is responsible for a quarter or less of global inequality. For this reason, rapid growth in China has greatly expanded the world's middle class, despite the fact that China's income distribution has become markedly less equitable.

A longer-term perspective can be obtained by combining these data with the historical evidence on global income distribution provided by Bourguignon and Morrisson (2002), which goes back to the early part of the nineteenth century. The within-country component of global inequality remained relatively stable over the long term, but the between-country component rose sharply, from 5 log-points in 1820, to 33 log-points in 1929, to 76 log-points in 2005 (Figure 2.4). The share of global inequality that is accounted for by between-country inequality rose from 12 percent in 1820 to 73 percent in 2005. Thanks to differential patterns of economic growth in different parts of the world, the country in which one is born increasingly determines one's economic fortunes (Milanovic 2011).

To drive the point home, I often ask audiences to consider whether it is better to be rich in a poor country or poor in a rich country. To clarify the question, I spell out what I mean by "rich" and "poor." I tell them that they should think of a rich person as someone in the top 10 percent of a country's income distribution and a poor person as someone in the bottom 10 percent. Similarly, a rich country is in the top decile of all countries ranked by average income per person, and a poor country is in the bottom decile of that list. Which would they choose?

Most people have little hesitation in responding that they'd rather be rich in a poor country, which is the wrong answer. The correct answer is "poor in a rich country"—and it's not even close. The average poor person in a

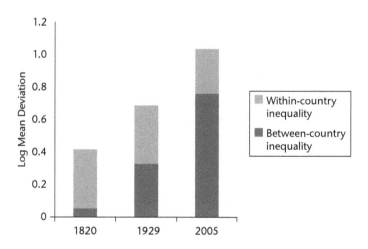

Figure 2.4 Global Income Inequality, 1820–2005
Source: Author, based on data from Milanovic 2011.

rich country, defined along the lines above, earns three times more than the average rich person in a poor country, adjusted for differences in purchasing power across countries (Rodrik 2011b). Disparities in other aspects of well-being, such as infant mortality, go the same way. The poor in a rich country have it much, much better than the rich in a poor country.

Poor countries, of course, have their own superrich. But these superrich families represent a minute share of the population in a poor country—no more than perhaps one-hundredth of 1 percent of the population. When we travel down the income distribution scale to include the top 10 percent of a typical poor country, we reach income levels that are a fraction of what most poor people in rich countries earn. Disparities in income (as well as health and other indicators of well-being) are much larger across than within countries. The country in which you are born largely determines your life possibilities.

Another way to observe the powerful impact of aggregate growth at the country level is to compare income levels over time at different points in the distribution. Figure 2.5 depicts income levels by decile or ventile (depending on data availability) in Brazil, China, India, and the United States in 1988 and 2005. The India–China comparison is especially telling. In 1988, each Indian decile was slightly richer than the corresponding decile in China. By 2005, Chinese incomes had vastly overtaken India's at all points along the income distribution. Similarly, in 1988 each Chinese ventile was poorer than the corresponding global ventile. By 2005, the poorer half of the Chinese economy had become richer than the world's bottom half.

There are three conclusions that can be drawn from recent evidence on the global distribution of income:

- The middle of the global income distribution has filled out in recent decades, thanks largely to China's rise.

- Differences across average incomes of countries remain the dominant force behind global inequality.

- Aggregate economic growth in the poorest countries is the most powerful vehicle for reducing global inequality. The more rapid growth of poor countries since the 1990s is the key behind the recent decline in global inequality.

2.3 Growth over the Long Term: Industrialization and the Great Divergence

At the dawn of the Industrial Revolution, the gap between the richest and poorest parts of the world economy stood at a ratio of roughly 2:1; the

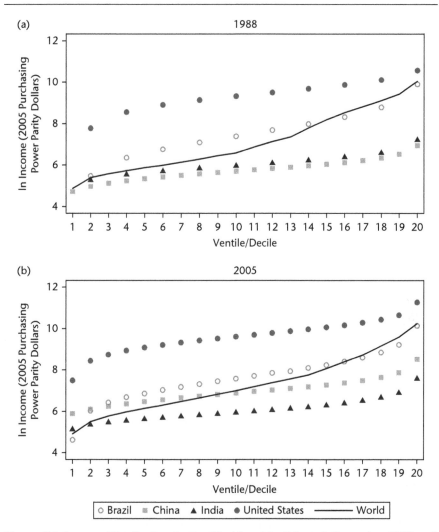

Figure 2.5 Income Distribution in the World and in Selected Countries, 1988 and 2005

Source: Author, based on data from Milanovic 2011.

between-country component of global inequality was tiny. Today, the income gap between the richest and poorest economies of the world has risen to more than 80:1. What happened in between is that parts of the world economy—Western Europe, the United States, Japan, and a few other countries—took off while the rest of the world grew very slowly when at all, often losing ground after temporary spurts (Figure 2.6). Lant Pritchett (1997) has labeled this process "divergence, big time."

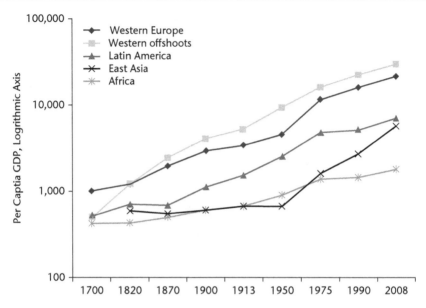

Figure 2.6 Economic Growth since 1700, by Region
Source: Author, based on data from Maddison 2010.

There is no better prism with which to view this divergence than the experience with industrialization in different parts of the world. Table 2.3 provides some interesting data from Paul Bairoch's seminal work (Bairoch 1982). The level of industrial output per capita in Britain in 1900 is fixed at 100, in order to facilitate comparisons across regions and over time. In 1750, at the onset of the Industrial Revolution, this index stood at 10 in Britain and at 8 in today's developed countries: there was virtually no difference between these countries and what later came to be called developing countries. China's level of industrialization was comparable to that of Western Europe.

From the nineteenth century on, the numbers began to diverge in a striking fashion. Industrial output per capita in Britain rose from 10 in 1750 to 64 in 1860 and 115 on the eve of World War I. Developed countries as a whole followed a similar, if less steep, trajectory. But what is really striking is not just that the gap between these countries and the countries of Latin America and Asia (except Japan) opened wide; it is also that today's developing countries typically experienced deindustrialization. Industrial output per capita in China shrank from 8 in 1750 to 3 in 1913; India's plummeted from 7 to 2 over the same period. These figures fell because industrial output failed to keep up with population growth.

The culprit was the global division of labor that the first era of globalization fostered during the nineteenth century. Cheap manufactures from

Table 2.3 Per Capita Index of Industrialization before World War I (United Kingdom = 100 in 1900)

Country	1750	1800	1830	1860	1880	1900	1913
Developed countries	8	8	11	16	24	35	55
United Kingdom	10	16	25	64	87	100	115
United States	4	9	14	21	38	69	126
Germany	8	8	9	15	25	52	85
Japan	7	7	7	7	9	12	20
Developing countries	7	6	6	4	3	2	2
China	8	6	6	4	4	3	3
India	7	6	6	3	2	1	2
Brazil	—	—	—	4	4	5	7
Mexico	—	—	—	5	4	5	7

Note:— = Not available.

Source: Author, based on data from Bairoch 1982.

Europe and later the United States, particularly cotton textiles, flooded the markets of peripheral regions, which specialized in commodities and natural resources. In the Ottoman Empire, for example, imports captured nearly 75 percent of the domestic textile market by the 1870s, up from a mere 3 percent in the 1820s (Pamuk and Williamson 2009). This global division of labor was imposed not just by markets but also by the forces of informal and formal empire: European powers, and later the United States, prevailed on India, China, Japan, and the Ottoman Empire to open their markets, and their navies ensured security for merchants and financiers.

Parts of the world that proved receptive to the forces of the Industrial Revolution shared two advantages.[4] First, they had a large enough stock of relatively educated and skilled workers to fill up and run the new factories. Second, they had sufficiently good institutions—well-functioning legal systems, stable politics, and restraints on expropriations by the state—to generate incentives for private investment and market expansion. With these preconditions, much of continental Europe was ready to absorb the new production techniques developed and applied in Britain. Elsewhere, industrialization depended on "importing" skills and institutions.

Intercontinental labor mobility was a tremendous advantage. Where Europeans settled in large numbers, they brought with them both the skills and the drive for more representative, market-friendly institutions that would promote economic activity alongside their interests. The consequences were disastrous for the native populations, who perished in large numbers courtesy of European aggression and germs. But the regions of the world that

[4] The rest of this section draws heavily on chapter 7 of Rodrik (2011b).

the economic historian Angus Maddison (2001) has called "Western off-shoots"—the United States, Canada, Australia, and New Zealand—were able to acquire the prerequisites, thanks to mass immigration. Supported by sizable capital flows from Europe, these economies would eventually become part of the industrial "core."

The impact of colonization on other parts of the world was quite different. When Europeans encountered inhospitable conditions that precluded their settlement in large numbers or began to exploit natural resources that required armies of manual workers, they set up institutions that were quite different from those in the western offshoots. These purely "extractive" institutions were designed to deliver raw materials to the core as cheaply as possible. They entailed vast inequalities in wealth and power, with a narrow elite—typically white and European—ruling over a vast number of natives or slaves. Colonies built on the extractive model did little to protect general property rights, support market development, or stimulate other kinds of economic activity. The plantation-based economies of the Caribbean and the mineral economies of Africa were typical examples. Studies by economists and economic historians have established that this early experience with institutional development—or lack thereof—produced a debilitating effect on economies in Africa and Latin America that is still felt today (Engerman and Sokoloff 1997; Acemoglu, Johnson, and Robinson 2001).

Once the lines were clearly drawn between industrializing and commodity-producing countries, strong economic dynamics reinforced the demarcation. Commodity-based economies faced little incentive or opportunity to diversify. As transport costs fell during the nineteenth century and growth in the industrial core fed demand, these economies experienced commodity booms. These booms were very good for the small number of people who reaped the windfall from the mines and plantations that produced these commodities; they were not very good for manufacturing industries, which were squeezed as a result. International trade worked just as in textbook models: profits rose in economic activities in which countries had comparative advantage and fell elsewhere.

International trade induced industrial countries to keep investing in skills, technology, and other drivers of economic growth. It also encouraged families to have fewer children and to educate them more, in light of the high returns to skills that modern manufacturing industries brought. These effects were reversed in the developing countries of the periphery. Specialization in primary commodities did not encourage skill accumulation, and it delayed the reduction in fertility and population growth: birth rates remained high in the developing world well into the twentieth century, unlike in the industrialized countries, which experienced sharp declines in fertility toward the end of the nineteenth century. In the words of economists Oded Galor and

Andrew Mountford (2008), commodity-exporting countries gave up productivity in exchange for population. Developing countries are still trying to break free of the long-term consequences of this division of labor. That escape is possible was shown by the experience of the first non-western country to industrialize before 1914: Japan.

In the middle of the nineteenth century, Japan looked no different from other economies of the periphery. It exported primarily raw materials—raw silk, yarn, tea, fish—in exchange for manufactures. This commerce boomed in the aftermath of the opening to free trade imposed by Commodore Perry in 1854; left to its own devices, the economy would likely have followed the same path as so many others in the periphery. But Japan had an indigenous group of well-educated and patriotic businessmen and merchants and—even more importantly—a government, following the Meiji Restoration of 1868, that was single-mindedly focused on economic (and political) modernization. The government was little moved by the laissez-faire ideas prevailing among western policy elites at the time. Japanese officials made clear that the state had a significant role to play in developing the economy.

The reforms introduced by the Meiji bureaucrats were aimed at creating the infrastructure of a modern national economy: a unified currency, railroads, public education, banking and other legislation. Considerable effort also went into what today would be called industrial policy—state initiatives promoting new industries. The Japanese government built and ran state-owned plants in a wide range of industries, including cotton textiles and shipbuilding. Even though many of these enterprises failed, they produced important demonstration effects and trained many skilled artisans and managers who subsequently plied their trade in private establishments. State enterprises were eventually privatized, enabling the private sector to build on the foundations established by the state. The government also paid to employ foreign technicians and technology in manufacturing industries and financed training abroad for Japanese students. In addition, as Japan regained tariff autonomy from international treaties, the government raised tariffs on many industrial products to encourage domestic production. These efforts paid off most in cotton textiles: by 1914, Japan had established a world-class industry that was able to displace British exports not just from the Japanese markets but from neighboring Asian markets as well.

Japan's militarist and expansionist policies in the run-up to World War II tarnished these accomplishments, but its achievements on the economic front demonstrated that an alternative path was available. It was possible to steer an economy away from its natural specialization in raw materials. Economic growth was achievable, even if a country started at the wrong end of the international division of labor, if it combined the efforts of a determined government with the energies of a vibrant private sector.

The Japanese experience would become a model for other countries in east and southeast Asia. Although specific policies differed, these emulators relied on the same model of export-oriented industrialization, achieved through a combination of private sector entrepreneurship and government inducements and cajoling. (The sole exception was Hong Kong, where government intervention in industry remained minimal.) I have more to say on these growth strategies further on in the chapter.

2.4 Six Stylized Facts About Economic Growth

The success of Japan and other Asian growth miracles has produced a seemingly unending debate. Are these countries examples of successful state-directed industrialization, or are they examples of what reliance on markets and globalization can produce? Framed this way, the question generates more heat than light. What works in practice is a judicious combination of markets and government encouragement, rather than a choice of one at the expense of the other.

But why is such a combination needed, what exactly does "judicious" mean, and how is the notion operationalized? To answer these questions, it is helpful to start with some basic stylized facts about economic growth. This section documents six stylized facts that are particularly relevant to the policy context. The following section provides an interpretation that is informed by these stylized facts and tries to make sense of success and failure around the world against this empirical background.

2.4.1 Stylized Fact 1: Growth Has Increased over Time

When the Industrial Revolution took hold of Britain and other early industrializers, the pickup in the growth rate of economic activity and overall productivity was so gradual as to be virtually imperceptible. To this day, it is not possible to establish the timing of the Industrial Revolution or the onset of modern economic growth with any precision: a clear break in the time series simply does not exist. Economic historians estimate that total factor productivity expanded at an annual rate of 0.5 percent in the century after 1780. This increase is clearly better than the near-zero rate of technological progress in earlier centuries, but it is a fraction of what industrial economies experienced in the second half of the twentieth century.

Figure 2.7 illustrates the increase in growth rates over time, for the world as a whole and for countries that were exceptionally successful. For each period, it shows the average growth rate of the world economy and the growth rate registered by that period's growth champion—the country or region that experienced the fastest growth. Before World War II, the most successful

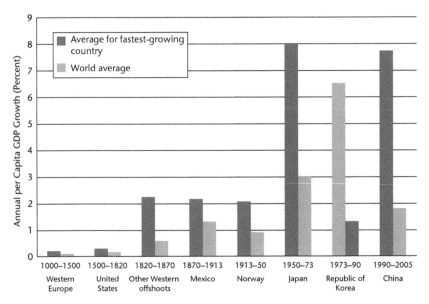

Figure 2.7 Historical Economic Growth Rates, for the World as a Whole and for Exceptionally Successful Countries
Source: Author, based on data from Maddison 2010.

period was 1870–1913, the Gold Standard period, during which the world economy expanded at an annual average rate of more than 1 percent per capita. This rate is dwarfed by the post-1950 expansion, during which annual global per capita growth reached nearly 3 percent until the mid-1970s. Although growth slowed somewhat after the oil shock of the 1970s, it was still far more rapid than anything experienced before World War II.

What stands out particularly sharply in Figure 2.7 is the stupendous and historically unprecedented growth rate experienced by the growth champions of the postwar period: Japan in 1950–73, the Republic of Korea in 1973–90, and China since 1990. These East Asian tigers, along with a few of their neighbors, grew at 7–8 percent a year in per capita terms, experiencing more rapid convergence with the living standards of the west than anything seen to date. These growth miracles were based on rapid industrialization and exports of manufactures. Clearly, the postwar global economy presented huge rewards to lagging countries that got their policies right.

2.4.2 Stylized Fact 2: Convergence Has Been the Exception Rather than the Rule

As both economic historians and contemporary growth theorists have argued, there are advantages to economic backwardness. Technologies that advanced countries have already developed can be imported and adapted; the wheel does not have to be reinvented. Global markets allow small economies to specialize in what they are good at; they are a source of capital goods and cheap intermediate inputs. Global financial markets can relax domestic saving constraints and finance investments that would otherwise not take place.

In practice, few developing countries have been able to exploit these advantages. The experience of East Asian growth champions is very much the exception to the rule. Contrary to theoretical expectations, there is no tendency for poor economies to grow more rapidly than richer economies. The experience of the past decade is not at all representative of the historical record. Over any sufficiently long time horizon, the growth rate of economies is basically uncorrelated with their initial level of productivity or distance from the technological frontier (Figure 2.8). A middle-income or rich economy is as likely to experience rapid growth as a poor economy.

In the literature on growth empirics, this result is known as the absence of "unconditional" convergence. It stands in contrast to "conditional" convergence, which is a well-established regularity in cross-country data. When growth rates are conditioned on a small set of variables, such as human capital, investment, institutional quality, exposure to trade, and macroeconomic stability, the growth residuals are systematically and negatively correlated with initial levels of GDP per capita. Empirical analysis by Barro (2012) places the conditional convergence rate at about 2 percent per year. Put differently, economic convergence is a reality only among the subset of countries that attain similar levels of conditioning variables.

The conditional convergence result would appear at first sight to be a useful one, potentially unlocking the secrets of economic growth. Unfortunately, the conditioning variables that are typically included in growth regressions are themselves outcome or endogenous variables, and they provide few operational implications about the specific policies that need to be pursued. For example, it may be helpful to know that higher levels of investment and human capital or better institutions are growth enhancing, but the result leaves unclear how these ends are to be achieved. Is human capital increased by building more schools, reducing teacher absenteeism, or providing better information to parents? Is private investment boosted by reducing red tape or providing tax incentives? Is governance enhanced by adopting legal and institutional blueprints from abroad or by engineering local solutions? From a policy standpoint, it is these questions that must ultimately be answered.

Unfortunately, econometric analyses using direct policy variables have not yielded useful results. Policy reforms are highly contextual and do not lend themselves to easy generalization (Rodrik 2007; Commission on Growth and Development 2008). I elaborate on this point further on in the chapter.

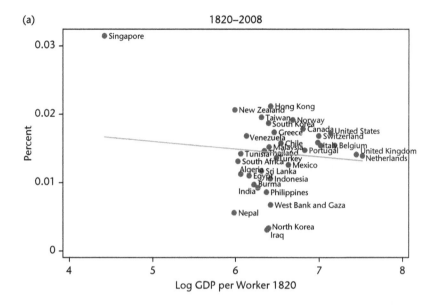

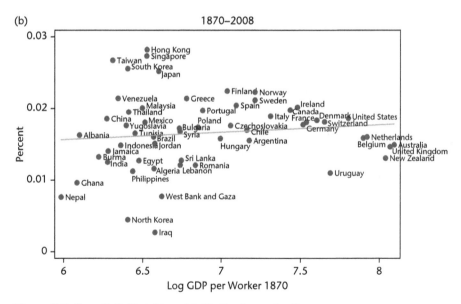

Figure 2.8 Growth Is Variable, with No Tendency for Convergence
Source: Author, based on data from Maddison 2010.

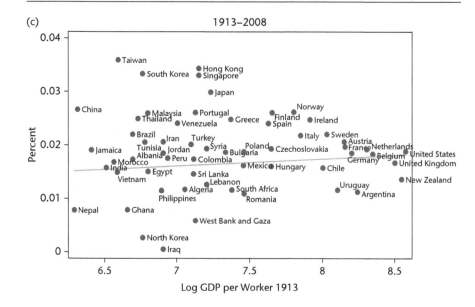

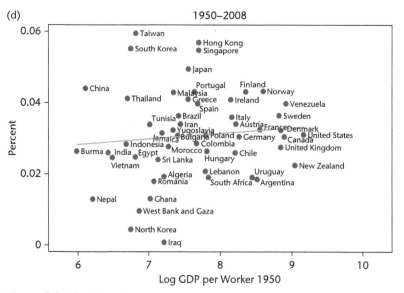

Figure 2.8 (Continued)

2.4.3 Stylized Fact 3: Economic Development Goes Hand-in-Hand with Productive Diversification

Poor economies are not shrunk versions of rich economies; they are structurally different. This key insight of old-fashioned development economics is often forgotten when modern growth theory is applied to developing economies. Developing countries are characterized by large structural gaps in productivity between traditional and new economic activities. Hence the essence of development is structural change, which entails moving workers from traditional, low-productivity activities to modern, high-productivity activities that are quite different in terms of location, organization, and technological characteristics. Rapidly growing countries are better at removing the bottlenecks that impede this transformation.

One can document this structural transformation in a number of different ways. A particularly important result was established by Imbs and Wacziarg (2003), who show that economies progressively become less specialized and more diversified as they get richer. Poor economies produce a relatively narrow range of commodities and services; as they grow, the range of economic activities expands. Past a certain point, diversification ceases, and there are hints of greater specialization at high levels of income. But the turning point comes quite late in the development process, roughly at the income level of a country such as Ireland.

From the standpoint of structuralist development thinking, the Imbs–Wacziarg result is not surprising. However, it does stand in some tension with approaches that emphasize the role of trade and comparative advantage in spurring economic development. After all, the central insight of classical trade theory is that countries gain from trade by specializing in product lines they are comparatively good at. Comparative advantage-based specialization may therefore seem to be a potent avenue for growth—and is often presented as such in policy discussions that emphasize the benefits of globalization. Whatever the benefits of trade, specialization is not the route to riches; quite the contrary.

2.4.4 Stylized Fact 4: Historically, Industrialization and Manufactured Exports Have Been the Most Reliable Levers for Rapid and Sustained Growth

The growth miracles of Japan, Korea, and China were all based on rapid industrialization. The point generalizes to other cases of catch-up as well. With the exception of a few small countries that benefited from natural resource windfalls (and managed not to squander them), virtually all countries that have sustained high growth rates for decades did so on the back of manufacturing. Industrialization is how Britain and other early emulators entered modern economic growth. It is also what has enabled successful latecomers to catch up.

Table 2.4 lists all cases of sustained, very high growth in history. I define "very high growth" as annual per capita growth of at least 4.5 percent. I define growth as "sustained" if it is maintained for at least three decades. There are not many such instances—fewer than 30, in fact. But the composition of such "growth miracles" is telling.

Table 2.4 Economies That Grew by at Least 4.5 Percent a Year per Capita over a Period of 30 Years or More

Before 1950			After 1950		
Country	Fastest annual growth rate achieved over three decades (percent)	Period	Country	Fastest annual growth rate achieved over three decades (percent)	Period
Before 1900					
Australia	5.8	1823–53	Greece	7.3	1945–75
New Zealand	7.1	1840–70	Italy	5.9	1945–75
			Spain	4.9	1949–80
			Portugal	4.6	1950–80
			Yugoslavia	4.9	1952–82
Between 1900 and 1950			Israel	4.7	1953–83
Venezuela	5.5	1907–39	Ireland	4.6	1976–2006
			Iraq	5.3	1950–80
			Libya	7.4	1950–80
			Saudi Arabia	6.1	1950–80
			Oman	7.4	1955–85
			Botswana	7.3	1960–91
			Equatorial Guinea	9.3	1974–2004
			Cape Verde	5.5	1977–2007
			Japan	7.4	1945–75
			Taiwan	7.2	1946–76
			Korea, Dem. People's Rep	4.7	1951–81
			Hong Kong	6.0	1958–88
			Singapore	6.7	1964–95
			Republic of Korea	7.3	1965–95
			Indonesia	4.7	1967–97
			Malaysia	5.1	1967–97
			China	6.7	1976–2007
			Myanmar	4.9	1977–2007

Source: Author, based on data from Maddison 2010.

Two important trends are evident from Table 2.4. First, virtually all growth miracles took place since 1950. There were only three instances before 1950: Australia and New Zealand (two western offshoots that benefited from extensive resource boom-led immigration waves during the nineteenth century) and Venezuela (which experienced an oil boom in the first half of the twentieth century). Since 1950, by contrast, there have been 24 distinct instances of growth miracles. This pattern is consistent with the increase in growth rates over time noted in stylized fact #1.

Second, most of the post-1950 growth miracles were rapid industrializers. As Table 2.4 indicates, they came in two clusters. The first cluster includes countries such as Italy, Spain, Portugal, and Greece—countries on the periphery of Western Europe that benefited first from European reconstruction in the immediate aftermath of World War II and subsequently from the European integration process. For the most part, these growth episodes had run their course by the late 1970s. The only exception is Ireland, which was a late bloomer and experienced its boom after the 1970s.

The second cluster comprises the well-known East and Southeast Asian tigers—economies such as Japan, Korea, Taiwan, Singapore, Hong Kong, Malaysia, and China. Unlike the first cluster, these countries did not share (at least initially) a geographic advantage. But the example of prewar Japanese industrialization, as well as its resumption during the 1950s, provided an important demonstration effect in the region. Korea's strategy was directly influenced by Japan's, and China's was influenced by the precedents of Hong Kong and Taiwan. Southeast Asian countries such as Malaysia and Indonesia explicitly targeted industrialization after observing the successes of the so-called Gang of Four (Korea, Taiwan, Hong Kong, and Singapore). Almost all of these economies built highly competitive manufacturing industries and experienced very rapid penetration of export markets in manufactures.

The third set of post-1950 growth miracles in Table 2.4 are countries such as Saudi Arabia, Iraq, and Botswana, which benefited from sustained booms in natural resources (oil and diamonds). These cases are reminiscent of the few pre-1950 cases. I discuss these successful instances of resource booms later in the chapter.

2.4.5 Stylized Fact 5: Manufacturing Industries Are "Special" in that They Tend to Exhibit Unconditional Convergence

I noted in stylized fact #2 that there is no tendency for developing economies to converge toward the productivity levels that prevail in rich economies. The modern, industrial parts of developing countries' economies seem to be quite different, however. Formal manufacturing industries reveal a surprisingly strong convergence relationship (Rodrik 2013). Each dot in Figure 2.9 represents the experience over a recent decade of a two-digit manufacturing industry in a particular country. As the negative slope of the scatter plot makes clear, industries that start farther away from the labor productivity frontier experienced significantly faster productivity growth—even without conditioning on the usual variables, such as human capital or institutional quality.

The convergence rate is about 2 percent a year, similar to the conditional convergence rate for aggregate GDP per worker, and it seems higher the more the data are disaggregated. This result appears to be robust to a wide variety of

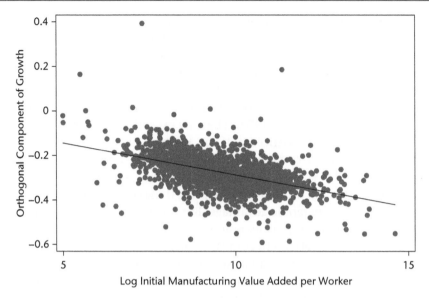

Figure 2.9 There Is Unconditional Productivity Convergence in (Formal) Manufacturing

Source: Author, based on data from Rodrik 2013.

specifications, time periods, and samples. (The benchmark sample in Rodrik 2013 covers 118 countries and more than 2,000 observations for two-digit industries.) The main shortcoming of the data (which come from the United Nations Industrial Development Organization [UNIDO]) is that they exclude the smallest or informal manufacturing enterprises in most of the poorer economies. This convergence result thus applies to only the organized, formal parts of manufacturing.

This caveat notwithstanding, this finding is remarkable. It does not denigrate the role of good policies or favorable external circumstances: as documented in Rodrik (2013), the rate of conditional convergence is even more rapid, meaning that countries with better institutions and policies experience faster rates of productivity growth in manufacturing (in particular, countries with better trade links and higher levels of financial development are likely to provide a better context for manufacturing convergence). But it does suggest that formal manufacturing industries are natural "escalator" industries that tend to propel an economy forward, even in the presence of bad governance, bad policies, and a disadvantageous context. (The countries included in Rodrik 2013 range from Ethiopia, Malawi, and Madagascar at the low end to Japan and the United States at the high end.) Productivity convergence seems to be considerably easier to achieve in this part of the economy than in other parts, such as traditional agriculture or most services. At least some of the reason presumably has to do with the tradable nature of manufacturing industries and the relative ease of technology transfer across borders. At the same time, manufacturing convergence does not seem to have picked up speed in more recent decades, under greater globalization and wider use of outsourcing. The data indicate that rates of convergence in the late 1960s and 1970s are statistically indistinguishable from rates since the 1990s. I return to these issues later in the context of the analytical framework.

This finding raises a puzzle. If manufacturing exhibits unconditional convergence, why is it not sufficient to generate aggregate convergence? The formal manufacturing sector tends to be small in low-income countries, employing less than 5 percent of the labor force in the poorest among them. Still, one would expect convergence to aggregate up to the national level, as labor and other resources move from technologically stagnant parts of the economy to the escalator industries.

The difficulty is that the requisite structural transformation is not automatic. Such transformation is a process that is fraught with both government and market failures (Rodrik 2008b). In practice, the expansion of formal manufacturing is blocked both by government policies (such as entry barriers and high taxes on formal enterprises) and by market imperfections (such as coordination problems and learning externalities), both of which push the return to investment in modern industries below the social return. The relative weights of these factors depend on the country and the context.

Manufacturing productivity thus tends to converge almost everywhere. What distinguishes successful countries from others is their ability to expand manufacturing employment and output rapidly. Successful developing economies undergo both manufacturing convergence and rapid industrialization. Underperforming economies make do with manufacturing convergence alone.

2.4.6 Stylized Fact 6: The Most Successful Economies Have Not Been the Ones with the Least State Intervention

Figure 2.10 summarizes the economic policies of four key developing countries: Brazil, China, India, and Mexico. Among these, the Asian countries have performed significantly better than the Latin American countries over the past couple of decades. As the Heritage Index ratings make clear, the Asian countries are also characterized by significantly greater government intervention—in international trade, international finance, and domestic markets.

It is difficult to find a strong correlation, in either direction, between standard measures of government activism (such as tax rates or indices of market restrictions) and rates of economic growth. It is easy to conclude that extreme controls of the central planning type, which suffocate the private

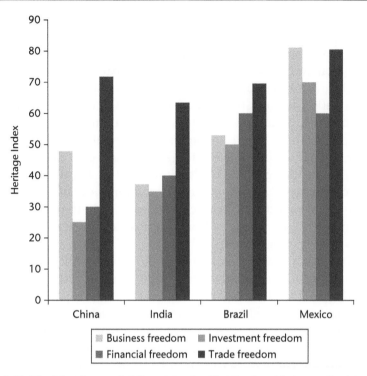

Figure 2.10 The Most Successful Countries Are Not the Least Interventionist
Source: Author, based on data from Heritage Foundation (http://www.heritage.org/index/).

sector, are bad for growth. But for countries that lie between central planning and laissez-faire—that is, almost all countries in the world—less intervention is not necessarily good for performance.

2.5 The Strategy of Reform

Obstacles to structural transformation take the form of both government and market failures. The relevant government failures are well known: excessive regulation and red tape, high taxes, corruption, restrictive labor laws, financial repression, insecure property rights, poor contract enforcement, and macroeconomic instability. All of these factors stifle entrepreneurship, especially in modern economic activities, which tend to rely heavily on the institutional environment. Efforts to fix these problems lie at the core of the "orthodox" development agenda of the Washington Consensus and its successors.

A reform agenda that focuses on eliminating these government failures would seem to be the most obvious and direct way of unleashing desirable structural change. In practice, however, it suffers from three problems.

First, it contains a blind spot with respect to market failures. New industries can fail to get off the ground not just because they face high taxes or excessive red tape but also because markets in low-income environments do not work well enough to reward entrepreneurs with the full social value of their investments. The two most important constraints are typically coordination failures and demonstration effects (Rodrik 2008a). Coordination failures occur when scale economies preclude complementary investments that would otherwise be profitable. Building, say, a successful processed food business requires significant investments both upstream (to ensure a steady, high-quality supply of raw materials that satisfy health and sanitary standards) and downstream (to ensure an efficient, timely transport and logistics network that links the operation to foreign markets). For a firm to generate profits, all parts of the chain need to be present and work well.

Demonstration effects refer to unremunerated learning spillovers. Any potential investor in an entirely new line of economic activity has to consider the risks of failure. If he goes bankrupt, he bears the full cost. But if he succeeds, he sets a model for other entrepreneurs to follow. In other words, much of the gains from new industries are socialized, whereas the losses remain private. This phenomenon acts just like a tax on new industries. Standard welfare economics justifies the use of subsidies and other government interventions in such instances.

Second, the standard approach presumes too much from reformist governments. As Washington Consensus enthusiasts discovered following the disappointing results in Latin America in the 1990s, the list of government failures that need to be fixed is neither short nor well defined. It turned out not to be enough to reduce subsidies, formal trade barriers, and state ownership. Many economists and policymakers rationalized the failures by calling for a second and eventually third generation of reforms in institutions—everything from more "flexible" labor markets to less corruption, from better courts to better governance. Apparently, standard policy reforms did not produce lasting effects if the background institutional conditions were poor. Sound policies needed to be embedded in solid institutions.

So the orthodox reform agenda became increasingly open-ended. At times it seemed as if the to-do list was designed to ensure that policy advisors would never be proved wrong: if performance lagged despite extensive reforms, the government could always be faulted for having fallen short and not having undertaken even more reforms. Paradigmatic of this approach is Anne Krueger's aptly titled 2004 speech "Meant Well, Tried Little, Failed Much." Taken to its logical conclusion, this formulation of the reform agenda was utterly unhelpful. Essentially it said: "if you want to become rich, you need to look like rich countries."

Many analysts were led down this path because of the inherently complementary nature of most of the orthodox reforms. In order to succeed in one
reform, countries need to undertake many others at the same time. For example, trade liberalization will not work if fiscal institutions are not in place
to make up for lost trade revenue, capital markets do not allocate finance to
expanding sectors, customs officials are not competent and honest enough,
labor market institutions do not work properly to reduce transitional unemployment, and so on.

To see this problem in its starkest form, consider what a conventional
reform agenda would have looked like in China in 1978—an economy that
was highly distorted as a result of central planning. An analyst would have
recognized that the right place to start reform was in the countryside, where
the vast majority of the population lived. If thoughtful enough, the analyst
would also have realized that applied in the conventional form, each reform
would require the support of others to become effective. Low agricultural
productivity would require price reform, which in turn would require property reform to become effective. Price reform in agriculture would necessitate
tax reform, as controlled prices were an important source of government
revenue. It would also require higher wages in urban areas, as food prices
rose. State enterprises would have to be allowed some autonomy to respond
to price and wage changes. But because state enterprises were monopolies,
any price autonomy would have to be matched by competition-enhancing
policies, such as trade liberalization. A rise in imports, in turn, would force
enterprise restructuring, necessitating better finance and social safety nets
for displaced workers. The causal chain of these interlinked reforms is illustrated in Figure 2.11.

Third, the standard approach overlooks the contribution of unorthodox
shortcuts. Few if any countries have grown rapidly because of across-the-board
institutional reforms of the type just discussed: successful economic transitions are marked by the sequential relaxation of one binding constraint after
another, using policy tools that are tailored to local circumstances (Rodrik
2007). Rapid growth is thus feasible in institutional environments that look
quite distorted, and policy remedies can look quite unorthodox by the standards of the conventional rulebook. China provides the most telling illustration of both of these principles, but all East Asian economies have followed
similar approaches.[5]

The list of obstacles to stimulating new industries is likely to be long,
running the gamut of government and market failures. The advantage of

---

[5] Two-track reform, the household responsibility system, and township and village enterprises were some of the innovations that the Chinese used to short-circuit institutional complementarities (Rodrik 2007).

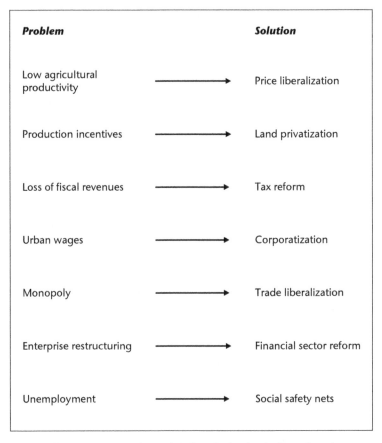

Problem		Solution
Low agricultural productivity	⟶	Price liberalization
Production incentives	⟶	Land privatization
Loss of fiscal revenues	⟶	Tax reform
Urban wages	⟶	Corporatization
Monopoly	⟶	Trade liberalization
Enterprise restructuring	⟶	Financial sector reform
Unemployment	⟶	Social safety nets

Figure 2.11 A Chinese Counterfactual: What Orthodox Reform Requires
Source: Author.

operating significantly below potential, however, is that a country does not need to get everything right in order to have a big impact. A remedy that targets a binding constraint tightly enough can produce a large investment response. A scattershot approach that tries to fix as many problems as possible may not be effective if it ends up missing the real targets. If the high cost of credit is the greatest obstacle to investment, for example, reducing the regulatory burden in product markets is unlikely to help much. Conversely, if investment is held back mainly by poor contract enforcement, reducing the cost of credit will be like pushing on a string.

Next consider how a particular constraint should be relaxed. Suppose entrepreneurship is hampered by low private returns, which may be the result of a high-risk or poor institutional environment. The most direct remedy would be to target the relevant distortions and remove them at source. But doing so may be impractical, for both economic and political reasons. Economically, it may not be possible to pinpoint the relevant distortions. Politically, policymakers may not want to step on powerful toes. An alternative strategy that is often more feasible is to raise entrepreneurs' profits in other ways—through subsidies or other instruments—in order to compensate them for the costs they incur as a result of irremovable distortions.

Most successful outward-oriented industrialization efforts have been the product of such second-best strategies. Korea and Taiwan directly subsidized exports; Singapore subsidized foreign investors; China created special economic zones and subsidized its exporters both directly and indirectly through an undervalued exchange rate; Mauritius created an export processing zone. In none of these cases did import liberalization or across-the-board institutional reform play a significant causal role in setting off the transition to high growth.

When successful, such heterodox second-best strategies can cut a path through important economic or political-economy obstacles (Rodrik 2008c). For example, China's special economic zones created new enterprises and export opportunities at the margin, without pulling the rug out from under the highly protected and less efficient state enterprises. The conventional remedy of across-the-board import liberalization would have exposed these enterprises to a severe shock, resulting in employment losses and social and political problems in urban areas. Similarly, by providing price incentives at the margin, two-track price reform in agriculture insulated government revenues from the adverse effects of incentive reform.

The bottom line is that successful growth-promoting reforms are pragmatic and opportunistic. Industrialization in particular is often stimulated by unconventional policies that compensate entrepreneurs and investors for the high taxes imposed on them by the poor market and institutional environment. In these second-best environments, more intervention can sometimes be better than less. The most effective way to counter market or government failures can be to compensate for such failures indirectly, rather than attempt to eliminate them.

2.6 An Analytical Framework

I now sketch an analytical framework that captures the salient elements of the empirical background previously discussed. The framework focuses on structural differences across economic activities as a key characteristic of developing societies and structural change as the key dynamic that drives growth. My objectives are threefold: to be explicit about the set of assumptions that lie behind the "growth model" I have in mind, to provide a consistency check for these ideas, and to provide a framework within which the future growth agenda can be discussed.

I divide the economy into three sectors, according to their dynamic characteristics. The first is a traditional sector (mainly subsistence agriculture and informal economic activities), which employs the bulk of the workforce during the early part of the development process and in which labor productivity is stagnant. For convenience, I fix labor productivity in the traditional sector at unity along with the economy's fixed labor supply: $y_T = l = 1$.

The other two sectors are modern sectors, one associated with "manufactures" and the other with "services." (This distinction does justice to neither the variety of activities under these headings nor the overlap between them in terms of the characteristics highlighted below. I use it for now to establish some ideas.) Labor productivity in services depends on the economy's broad capabilities, denoted by Θ. Specifically, Θ determines the economy's potential (or steady-state) labor productivity $y^*(\Theta)$, to which labor productivity in services, y_s, converges at the rate γ:

$$\hat{y}_s = \gamma(\ln y^*(\Theta) - \ln y) \qquad (2.1)$$

where y is the economy's aggregate labor productivity and a "^" over a variable denotes proportional changes ($\hat{x} = dx / x$). As expressed, productivity in services exhibits conditional convergence, with each economy's long-run level of productivity fixed by its capabilities.

I use the term *capabilities* to denote both human capital and institutional quality. Models of endogenous growth and financial development partially endogenize such capabilities, although policy choices ultimately remain a key determinant even in such models. I treat fundamental capabilities as one of the exogenous drivers of development. I posit that the relationship between Θ and y^* takes the logistics form depicted in Figure 2.12. Potential output initially increases slowly, as skills and institutional capabilities are accumulated, picking up speed only after Θ reaches sufficiently high levels. What I have in mind here is the multidimensional nature of the capabilities captured by Θ and the complementarity among many of those dimensions. As discussed in the previous section, effective reform in one area of the economy often requires complementary action in others. For example, a well-functioning health system relies on appropriate incentives, effective delivery mechanisms, and an adequate supply of medical professionals. (See Behrman and Kohler 2013 on the complex web of interactions involved in enhancing human capital.) Building an effective regulatory regime requires not just higher levels of human capital but also more accountable political systems and a meritocratic bureaucratic culture. An industrial supply chain

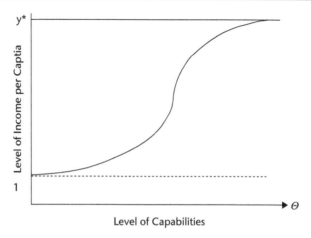

Figure 2.12 Relationship between Capabilities and Potential Output
Source: Author.

requires a substantial network of input suppliers and a wide array of specialized skills. The specific capabilities needed to increase potential output
in each of these domains are difficult to develop independently and incrementally.[6] In particular, because services are nontraded and rely on domestic
demand, their scale of operation is inherently dependent on productivity
enhancements in the rest of the economy (unlike manufactures). Successful
reform in one service sector requires successful reform in others.

This kind of context produces poverty traps and coordination failures that
prevent modern activities from taking off; it requires a "big push" to escape
(Murphy, Shleifer, and Vishny 1989; Rodrik 1996; Sachs et al. 2004). The
"big push" is often motivated by returns to scale in economic activities, but
the same idea applies equally well to circumstances in which institutional
arrangements in different areas are complementary and require set-up costs.
Unfortunately, "big bang" institutional reform is typically infeasible. It has
been accomplished in rare cases following wars (as in Japan) or through
significant surrender of sovereignty (as in former socialist countries that
joined the European Union). In other cases, institutional capabilities can be
acquired only incrementally.

Manufactures differ from modern services in that productivity also benefits from an unconditional component. The empirical justification for this

---

[6] My use of the term *capabilities* is similar to, and inspired in part by, Hidalgo and Hausmann
(2009), but I apply it not just to tradable products but also to nontraded complex services. Sutton's
interesting work on "competing in capabilities" is another important reference, although Sutton
has in mind mainly the capacity of individual firms and not economies as a whole (Sutton 2012).
The capabilities I have in mind are largely social, rather than private, and can be thought of as
public inputs from which all firms benefit (as in Ricardo Hausmann's work).

assumption is provided by the results in Rodrik (2013), which document the presence of unconditional convergence in organized manufacturing industries at a rate of about 2 percent per year. Labor productivity growth in manufacturing can thus be written as the sum of both a conditional and an unconditional term:

$$\hat{y}_M = \beta\left(\ln y_M^* - \ln y_M\right) + \gamma\left(\ln y^*\left(\Theta\right) - \ln y\right) \tag{2.2}$$

where y_M^* denotes the global productivity frontier in manufacturing. Equation (2.2) implies that low-productivity countries can experience substantial growth in manufacturing productivity even if they have low Θ — that is, even if they suffer from low skills, bad policies, weak institutions, and unfavorable geography. Increases in Θ can boost growth even farther. This specification is in line with Rodrik (2013), where the conditional convergence rate is estimated at roughly twice the unconditional rate.

As manufacturing approaches the technological frontier, the automatic convergence effect fades out. Additional increases in productivity become dependent on the presence of a complex set of capabilities, just as with modern service industries.

Let the employment shares of the three sectors be α_M, α_S, and $(1 - \alpha_M - \alpha_S)$. The economy's aggregate real GDP per worker is a weighted average of sectoral labor productivities:

$$y = \alpha_M y_M + \alpha_S y_S + (1 - \alpha_M - \alpha_S) \tag{2.3}$$

(With no loss of generality, I fix base-period relative prices at unity.) I use π_i to denote the relative productivity of each sector, such that $\pi_i = y_i / y$. Totally differentiating equation (2.3) and dividing through by y yields the following expression for growth in GDP per worker:

$$
\begin{aligned}
\hat{y} &= \left(\alpha_M \pi_M + \alpha_S \pi_S\right)\gamma\left(\ln y^*\left(\Theta\right) - \ln y\right) & \text{(A)} \\
&+ \alpha_M \pi_M \beta\left(\ln y_M^* - \ln y_M\right) & \text{(B)} \\
&+ \left(\pi_M - \pi_T\right)d\alpha_M & \text{(C)} \\
&+ \left(\pi_S - \pi_T\right)d\alpha_S & \text{(D)}
\end{aligned}
\tag{2.4}
$$

Equation (2.4) provides an organizing framework for the discussion to follow. It identifies four distinct channels for growth. The first is a process of convergence that accompanies the accumulation of fundamental capabilities such as skills and improved governance (A). It can be called the "fundamentals" channel, as it depends on broad-based investments in human capital and institutional arrangements. The second channel is the forces of unconditional convergence operating within manufactures (B). These two dynamic effects are potentially augmented by two effects of reallocating labor from traditional activities to higher-productivity manufacturing (C) and modern services (D).

The power of these channels in driving economic growth varies at different stages of development. Consider a poor economy at the very early stages of development. Such an economy faces many obstacles. Not only is Θ low, but also, increases in Θ produce only small returns in light of the logistic relationship between Θ and potential output. The growth that can be generated through channel A is therefore modest at best.

Within manufacturing, strong convergence forces are at play in light of the large difference between $\ln y_M^*$ and $\ln y_M$. But because very little of the labor force in poor countries works in organized manufacturing (that is, α_M is low), even very rapid manufacturing growth will generate only paltry GDP growth in the aggregate.

Consider, for example, a country in the bottom decile of the intercountry distribution of manufacturing labor productivity, such that $\ln y_M^* - \ln y_M \cong 2.30$ (= $\ln(10)$). Suppose α_M = 5 percent, β = 3 percent, and π_M = 400 percent—numbers that are plausible for such a country. Annual growth through channel B will amount to a mere 1.4 percent (= 0.05 x 4 x 0.03 x 2.30), even though manufacturing grows at a rate of at least 6.9 percent. The impact of manufacturing convergence is blunted by its tiny share in the economy.

Of the remaining two terms, the one relating to reallocation to manufacturing (C) is potentially by far the more important. Sticking with the parameters used previously, $(\pi_M - \pi_T)$ is about 3 (as $y_T = 1$ and the traditional sector employs the bulk of the workforce at very low levels of development). Therefore, if 1 percent of the labor force could be moved to manufacturing per year—the kind of structural transformation East Asian countries have managed—growth would increase by 3 percentage points. This is twice the bang achieved from the pure manufacturing convergence term (B).

By contrast, reallocation to services (channel D) produces little growth benefits at low levels of income, because Θ and $\ln y^*(\Theta)$ are, by definition, low in poor economies, and π_S is therefore not much higher than π_T. Indeed, service activities are likely to be dominated by petty services and informal activities. Growth does not get much of a boost when peasants migrate to urban areas only to end up in informal, low-productivity activities.

In sum, the best hope for rapid growth in a low-income setting rests on reallocation of labor to organized manufacturing (C) and, secondarily, convergence within manufacturing (B). These two channels together can generate increases in GDP per worker of 4–5 percent a year. The rest of the economy cannot contribute much, because the accumulation of the requisite capabilities is a cumulative process and takes time. Put differently, an economy with low skills and weak governance can still manage to compete with Sweden in many manufactures, but it would probably take more than a century for it to bring its institutions up to par with those of Sweden. For this reason, rapid industrialization has been the common element of all growth miracles.

However, industrialization has its limits, because manufacturing productivity growth slows as the distance from the technological frontier diminishes (per equation 2.2) and, more fundamentally, because in practice there is an upward limit to α_M. Historically, α_M has rarely exceeded about 30 percent. I consider later the determinants of this ceiling, which are related to demand, technology, and trade patterns. For now, note that the limit on α_M implies that there is only so much manufacturing can do as a locomotive for the entire economy. As the industrial share of employment reaches its limits, economy-wide growth slows unless other channels take over.

In principle, fundamental capabilities, Θ, can act as the new engine of growth. If the country in question has been investing adequately in skills and institutions, bringing the economy near the inflection point in Figure 2.12, this is exactly what will happen. New forces of convergence will be activated, identified by channels A and D in equation (2.4). The economy will now experience the "conditional" component of productivity growth in services and manufactures (channel A), and any shift of labor toward services, even if it comes at the expense of deindustrialization, will be potentially growth-increasing (channel B). In this more mature phase of growth, economic performance will increasingly rely on broad-based capabilities rather than on pushing workers into manufacturing.

Deindustrialization therefore poses little threat in economies that have built up adequate human capital and institutions. In such economies, the labor that is displaced can be absorbed into high-productivity services, at little cost to economic growth or equity.

Hong Kong provides a particularly remarkable example of this process. One of the original East Asian tigers, Hong Kong grew rapidly in the 1960s and 1970s, on the back of rapid industrialization and exports of manufactured products. Since the 1980s, it has experienced an equally striking process of deindustrialization. As Figure 2.13 shows, manufacturing's share of employment fell by more than 20 percentage points between 1990 and 2005, by which time service industries—finance, insurance, logistics, information technology—had developed so much that on average they were more productive than manufactures. Moreover, the economy's labor force had acquired the skills and human capital to be redeployed in these tradable services. The loss on account of term C in equation (2.4) was more than made up by the gain on account of D. Hong Kong's deindustrialization proved growth-promoting.

This win–win scenario often does not play out, even in more advanced economies, where capabilities have been built up but are ill-distributed. In both Britain and the United States, for example, advanced service sectors—finance, business services, information technology—have not generated enough employment to make up for the shrinkage of industrial jobs. Lower-productivity service industries have expanded alongside advanced

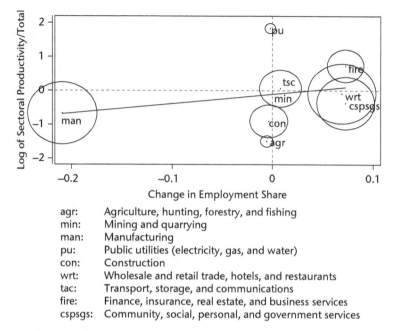

agr: Agriculture, hunting, forestry, and fishing
min: Mining and quarrying
man: Manufacturing
pu: Public utilities (electricity, gas, and water)
con: Construction
wrt: Wholesale and retail trade, hotels, and restaurants
tac: Transport, storage, and communications
fire: Finance, insurance, real estate, and business services
cspsgs: Community, social, personal, and government services

Figure 2.13 Sectoral Productivity and Change in Employment Shares in Hong Kong, 1990–2005

Note: Size of circles represents employment share in 1990. Line shows fitted values.

Source: Author, based on data from Timmer and de Vries 2009.

ones, creating a bifurcated wage structure and producing growth-reducing structural change. The situation is worse in middle-income countries, such as Argentina, Brazil, or Turkey, where much of the labor force remains excluded from the advanced sectors and has little other option than to be absorbed into informality as manufacturing jobs become scarcer (McMillan and Rodrik 2011).

2.7 A Typology of Growth Outcomes

The analytical framework presented above has two key "forcing varia-bles": the rate of industrialization ($d\alpha_M$) and the level of capabilities (Θ). The results can be summarized using the 2 × 2 matrix shown in Table 2.5, which illustrates four types of growth outcomes, depending on the evolution of these variables.

Cell 1 represents economies that fail to stimulate industrial employment or accumulate significant human capital and institutional capabilities. These economies register no or very little growth. This is the situation in which most

Table 2.5 Possible Growth Outcomes Give Rate of Industrialization and Level of Capabilities

		Rate of industrialization $(d\alpha_M)$	
		Slow	Rapid
Level of	Low	(1) No or very little growth	(2) Episodic growth
capabilities (Θ)	High	(3) Slow growth	(4) Rapid, sustained growth

Source: Author.

of the low-income countries in Sub-Saharan Africa have traditionally found themselves. They occasionally experience some growth on the basis of industrialization spurts (as in the 1960s and early 1970s) or commodity booms (during the 2000s), and many of them have enhanced their "fundamentals" through improved governance since the 1990s. But industrialization has largely petered out, and improvement in their capabilities has remained limited.

Economies in cell 2 experience significant industrialization and hence rapid growth for a while, but they eventually run out of steam—once industrialization reaches its limits—because Θ remains low. This scenario is one version of the "middle-income trap." Many countries that experienced rapid growth on the back of import-substituting industrialization eventually found themselves in this situation. Brazil and Mexico are good examples. Their growth now relies disproportionately on "fundamentals" and hence remains significantly below the rates registered during the phase of rapid industrialization (1950–80). China may eventually find itself in this situation as well, as its institutional development, particularly with regard to political institutions, lags its industrial development considerably.

Economies in cell 3 follow the conventional growth recipe: they place considerable emphasis on accumulating human capital and improving institutions. But in the absence of complementary policies that specifically promote industrialization, growth is paltry, especially at low levels of income, for the reasons discussed previously. This scenario is the typical fate of countries that adhere strictly to the Washington Consensus and its descendants. El Salvador, for example, undertook extensive institutional and political reforms following its civil war of the 1980s. It adopted a new constitution, strengthened the independence of the judiciary, consolidated its fiscal position, modernized its tax system, liberalized trade and banking, improved the regulation and supervision of its financial system, privatized most state productive assets, reformed its social security system, and expanded and granted local autonomy to the educational system. Yet after an initial period of recovery that lasted until 1997, incomes stagnated and GDP per capita relative to the United States remained just over half the level achieved in the late 1970s (Hausmann and Rodrik 2005).

Cell 4 in Table 2.5 represents the long-term successes, based on an industrialization drive accompanied by the steady accumulation of human capital and institutional capabilities to sustain services-driven growth once industrialization reaches its limits. Today's advanced industrial countries are in this category, although they too are feeling the strains of deindustrialization, as mentioned previously. Among East Asian economies, a few—including Korea, Hong Kong, and Taiwan—can be said to have joined them.

In addition to providing a useful typology, Table 2.5 helps us understand one of the more puzzling features of the cross-country data. Both institutional quality and human capital levels are highly correlated with levels of income, but improvements in institutions and human capital are not a reliable predictor of economic growth. The framework suggests that this observation is not a contradiction. Only countries that steadily enhance their fundamental capabilities eventually become rich,[7] but investments in Θ are not the easiest way of growing rich, at least during the early stages of development. Early on, it is rapid industrialization that fuels growth. Achieving it requires policies that may differ considerably from conventional fundamentals. Countries that rely exclusively on building up broad-based capabilities are rewarded with modest growth, which may easily divert them from those policies as a result.

Table 2.5 also clarifies why it is important to distinguish between "fundamentals" and "structural transformation channels" to account for existing patterns of growth. Countries that experience rapid spurts of growth over a period of a decade or two often—indeed, typically—do so without the benefit of significant advantages in human capital or institutions. There are shortcuts that can compensate for the absence of fundamentals. A fundamentals-focused perspective would have an easier time accounting for stagnation than for the spectacular take-offs in Korea in the 1960s or China in the late 1970s. At the same time, without long-term investment in fundamentals, rapid growth is unlikely to be sustained.

2.8 What Sets the Limits to Industrialization?

The peak level of industrialization, α_M, plays an important role in the analysis, as it determines the mileage that industrialization delivers. The higher

---

[7] There is a vigorous debate as to whether it is primarily the quality of institutions or the level of human capital that drives long-run levels of income (see Acemoglu, Robinson, and Johnson 2001 versus Glaeser et al. 2004). I take no position on this debate here, lumping both under the rubric of "capabilities."

α_M becomes, the longer an economy can sustain rapid growth without having to rely on adequate levels of Θ or, alternatively, the longer it can afford to wait for Θ to reach the required levels without experiencing adverse effects on growth. So a key question is what determines the ceiling on α_M.

Let the GDP deflator be the numeraire, φ (< 1) the share of manufactures in domestic expenditures, and b the trade surplus in manufactures (as a share of GDP). Earlier, base-period relative prices were fixed at 1. Because demand patterns depend on movements in relative prices, let p_M stand for the (relative) price of manufacturing. The market-clearing equation for manufactures can then be written as

$$p_M \alpha_M y_M = \varphi(1-b)y + by \qquad (2.5)$$

Note that $\alpha_M y_M$ is the aggregate quantity of manufactures produced domestically. So the left-hand side of equation (2.5) is the value of production, and the right-hand side is the value of total demand for domestic manufactures. As $y_M / y = \pi_M$, equation (2.5) can also be expressed as

$$\alpha_M = \frac{1}{p_M \pi_M} \left[\varphi(1-b) + b \right] \qquad (2.6)$$

where $p_M \pi_M$ is the relative productivity of manufacturing in value terms.

To provide some insight on this expression, I first consider a long-run equilibrium in which the trade surplus is zero ($b = 0$) and relative productivities across sectors have been equalized in value terms ($p_M \pi_M = 1$). In this equilibrium, equation (2.6) simplifies to $\alpha_M = \varphi$. Therefore, the ceiling on the employment share of manufactures is given by the share of manufactures in total domestic expenditures. This share is in all likelihood declining, as demand patterns tend to switch toward health, entertainment, and a variety of professional services as incomes rise.

In developing countries, productivity in manufacturing is typically higher than the rest of the economy (in value terms), pushing α_M farther down. Data from UNIDO in Rodrik (2013) suggest that $p_M \pi_M$ lies between 2 and 3 for a country in the middle deciles of the intercountry income distribution. If $p_M \pi_M = 2.5$, α_M can rise to only 40 percent of φ.

Note also that π_M is directly related to the skill- and capital-intensity of manufacturing activities. If global trends in technology increase skill and capital requirements in manufacturing, π_M will rise, further lowering the ceiling on α_M. To be sure, developing countries will generally rely on more labor-intensive techniques, in view of the lower cost of labor. But the extent of factor substitutability may be limited in practice.

The final determinant in equation (2.6) is the trade surplus in manufactures, b. As $\dfrac{d\alpha_M}{db} = \dfrac{1}{p_M \pi_M}(1-\varphi) > 0$, the size of the manufacturing sector can be increased at any level of income by reducing the deficit or increasing the surplus in manufactures trade. The role played by the trade balance is an important policy consideration. It makes mercantilist policies such as undervalued currencies an attractive option in low-income countries that stand to gain the most from industrialization (Rodrik 2008b).

2.9 Global Supply Chains and Changes in Manufacturing

One of the significant changes in the global economy in recent years is what Richard Baldwin (2011) calls the "second unbundling"—the development of supply chains that facilitate the distribution of production around the globe. Under the traditional model of industrialization, such as that followed by Korea in the 1960s and 1970s, countries had to build entire industries, from the input stage to the finished product. With declining costs of transportation and communication, countries can now make room for themselves along global supply chains even if they do not have a large industrial base or big domestic markets. China is often presented as the epitome of this approach, even though, of course, it has both advantages. Koopman, Wang, and Wei (2008) estimate that foreign inputs account for half of China's export value, a much larger share than in other countries, and that this ratio rises to about 80 percent for technologically sophisticated electronics products. China, where the iPhone 3G was assembled, contributed only $6.50 of the total manufacturing cost of $179 for the final product (Rassweiler 2009, cited in Xing and Detert 2010).

Baldwin (2011) argues that global production chains facilitate industrialization by reducing entry costs. Developing countries need only contribute low-cost labor; all the technologically demanding, capital-intensive inputs can be produced elsewhere. But by the same token, industrialization becomes less of a driver for the aggregate economy. Technology adoption and spillovers remain under the control of the foreign multinationals that govern the supply chains. The employment absorption of local industries (α_M) remains limited to the slices of outsourced production that managers of the global supply chain allocate to specific countries.

In such a context, the type of policies countries must follow to maximize the opportunities from industrialization do not look all that dissimilar from strategies that worked in the past. The crux of the matter remains the need to encourage investments in modern industries—or slices thereof—that the private sector would not undertake under prevailing circumstances. The focus these days may need to be more on segments of industries than on entire industries, and more on foreign investors than locals. But ultimately the principles of cooperative industrial policy based on public–private partnerships discussed in Rodrik (2007, 2008a) still apply.

Indeed, it is impossible to account for China's success in taking advantage of global supply chains without understanding the myriad state policies Chinese policymakers used to crowd in investments that would not otherwise have been made. These policies include direct subsidies, local content requirements, and an undervalued exchange rate. When Apple looked for a plant that could quickly gear up to cut a new type of glass prototype for its iPhone screens, it found a Chinese supplier that had built a new wing with help from government subsidies and was able to offer financial terms and labor flexibility few others could. "The entire supply chain is in China now," an Apple executive was quoted as saying. "You need a thousand rubber gaskets? That's the factory next door. You need a million screws? That factory is a block away. You need that screw made a little bit different? It will take three hours" (Duhigg and Bradsher 2012).

As this quotation suggests, global supply chains have not done away with the economies of agglomeration. Countries such as China that have built a large domestic manufacturing base, through a combination of low labor costs, flexible labor market practices, and government supports, find themselves much better positioned to attract new investments.

2.10 How Do Natural Resource Exporters Fit In?

The natural resource sector can be thought of as a special kind of manufacturing: a sector that converges very rapidly to the global frontier as it utilizes off-the-shelf, imported technology but has very little ability to absorb labor because it is highly capital- and skill-intensive. Furthermore, its upstream and downstream linkages are typically exceptionally weak and thus produce few spillovers to the rest of the economy. The income the sector generates comes in the form of rents and accrues to the state, a small group of (often foreign) investors, and a few privileged workers. Mining and other natural resource activities can produce very rapid growth in the boom stage, but at the cost of a highly skewed distribution of income. When the resource boom ends—because of resource depletion or a downturn in the terms of trade—there is often a collapse in economic activity. This collapse is typically magnified by macroeconomic distortions and distributional conflicts that are associated with resource booms (Rodrik 1999). The economic history of Sub-Saharan Africa and Latin America is replete with such boom-and-bust episodes.

In principle, it is possible to manage natural resource wealth to sustain continued investments in human capital and institutions and build up broad-based capabilities. Doing so would allow the transformation of resource booms into long-term economic success. This path is often blocked by unfavorable economic and political dynamics associated with natural resource-driven booms, however. Resource rents feed a small group of political elites, whose power depends on the stifling of political competition and who therefore have little interest in either broadening political participation or educating the masses (Sokoloff and Engerman 2000). A comparative advantage based on natural resources reduces returns to human capital and delays its accumulation (Galor, Moav, and Vollrath 2008). The rise in the real value of the domestic currency that accompanies the boom discourages investments in manufacturing or other nontraditional tradable activities (Rajan and Subramanian 2011). These problems are all well-known syndromes of the "natural resource curse." Their collective effect is to impede the accumulation of capabilities needed to ensure sustained growth once the initial impact of the resource boom wears off.

A few countries have managed to put their resource wealth to good long-term use. Some have benefited from special initial conditions. Australia and New Zealand are lands of recent settlement that, following the Acemoglu, Johnson, and Robinson (2001) logic, developed reasonably good public institutions early on. Norway and the Netherlands reaped windfall gains (from oil and natural gas, respectively) after they had already become rich, developed solid institutions, and accumulated high levels of human capital. Natural resource booms are less likely to turn into a curse when they happen in countries that have good institutions and high levels of human capital to begin with or are already at a relatively advanced stage of development.

The experience of Botswana is telling in this context. This landlocked southern African country grew exceptionally rapidly from the early 1960s to the second half of the 1990s, on the back of a diamond boom. Yet it started out with very little human capital and none of the institutions associated with modern, well-governed democracies. Acemoglu, Johnson, and Robinson (2003) trace the roots of Botswana's success to tribal practices that "encouraged broad-based participation"; the continued political power of rural, cattle-based interests, which reduced the urban bias typical of African polities; and the "farsighted" decision-making of post-independence political leaders. They argue that these features led to appropriate policies that maintained macroeconomic stability, kept corruption and rent-seeking in check, and fostered bureaucratic efficiency. Although public policy was not successful in all areas (Botswana was ravaged by the AIDS pandemic, for example), Acemoglu, Johnson, and Robinson's (2003) account suggests that "leadership," in combination with historical, deeper-seated circumstances, can make a difference.

Leadership also makes a difference in managing the diversification of the economy. Weaning natural resource-rich economies from their dependence requires especially proactive policies to stimulate modern industries and counter the Dutch disease. Once again, Asia has shown the way here. None of the East and Southeast Asian economies started off with a comparative advantage in manufacturing industries. Some, such as Malaysia and Thailand, were particularly well-endowed with natural resources and would have remained resource-based economies had their governments not emphasized industrialization. Thanks to their industrial policies—especially managed currencies, which prevented overvaluation—these economies industrialized to a much greater extent than Latin American countries did, even though they started out with similar specialization patterns.

The experience of many Latin American countries with the commodities boom of the last decade also leaves room for hope. Policymakers in Chile, Colombia, Peru, Mexico, and Brazil have tried to avoid the mistakes of the past and prevent unsustainable consumption and borrowing binges in response to resource windfalls. Some of these countries have passed laws that require the temporary component of export receipts to be saved. Significant investments have been made in education, health, and poverty reduction. There are encouraging indicators that such improvements in fundamentals are helping reduce the inequality and macroeconomic instability that have been the bane of Latin American countries since the nineteenth century.

Similarly, thanks in no small part to high commodity prices, Africa has experienced an economic renaissance of sorts during the past two decades, raising hopes that the continent may finally be on course for sustained development. Growth rates have been high, human and social indicators have improved, and democratic governance is becoming the norm rather than the exception. There are also some encouraging signs of positive structural change, although most of the gains are taking place in urban services rather than manufacturing (Martinez and Mlachila 2013; McMillan 2013).

What remains unclear is the extent to which these countries can continue to experience rapid growth in the absence of high commodity prices. Improvements in human capital and institutional quality promise less volatile and more sustainable growth. But manufacturing sectors have typically been battered by appreciating currencies and import competition from China. It is too early to be sanguine about the possibility that modern service industries will replace commodity exports as the growth engine in either Latin America or Sub-Saharan Africa.

2.11 Prognosis

The framework outlined above shows how fundamental improvements in capabilities (defined as both skills and institutional development) and narrower policies targeted at rapid structural change (industrialization in particular) interact to produce sustainable, longer-term growth. In the long run, convergence with wealthy economies requires the accumulation of human capital and the acquisition of high-quality institutions. But the quickest way to become rich is to deploy policies that help build modern industries that employ an increasing share of the economy's labor resources. Policies of this type overlap with policies needed to build up fundamental capabilities, but they are not one and the same, and they often diverge significantly. An excessive focus on "fundamentals" may slow growth if it distracts policymakers from resorting to the (often unconventional) policies of structural transformation required to get modern industries off the ground. Similarly, excessive focus on industrialization may set the economy up for an eventual downfall if the requisite skills and institutions are not built up over time.

In principle, this broad recipe can continue to serve developing countries well in the future. In particular, it can allow the world's poorest countries in Africa to embark on Asian-style structural transformation and rapid growth. But a number of considerations suggest that developing countries will face stronger headwinds in the decades ahead.

2.11.1 The Global Context

The global economy is likely to be significantly less buoyant than it was in recent decades. The world's richest economies are hobbled by high levels of public debt, which typically results in low growth and defensive economic policies. The euro area is facing an existential crisis. Even if Europe manages to stay together, its problems will continue to rein in the region's animal spirits. Policymakers in these rich countries will remain preoccupied with domestic challenges, preventing them from exhibiting much global leadership.

The rules of the game for developing countries have already become stricter. The World Trade Organization (WTO) prohibits a range of industrial policies (subsidies, local content requirements, copying of patented products) that Asian countries deployed to good effect in decades past to foster structural transformation.[8] Luckily, these restrictions do not apply to the poorest developing countries.

---

[8] Both China and India used local content requirements to force foreign investors to develop efficient domestic first-tier suppliers (Sutton 2004)—a strategy that would be illegal today.

Additional pressures can be expected to narrow policy space in developing countries as trade becomes more politicized in the advanced countries as a result of their economic difficulties. Subsidy schemes that have so far operated under the radar screen are more likely to be litigated in the WTO and retaliated against. With or without the acquiescence of the WTO, Europe and the United States will exhibit greater willingness to shield their industries from import surges. Developing countries that undervalue their currencies through intervention in foreign currency markets or controls on capital inflows are likely to be branded "currency manipulators." Strategies aimed at maintaining competitive currencies—another East Asian hallmark—have so far evaded global discipline. But for some years there have been efforts to render International Monetary Fund oversight over currency values more effective, and there is growing discussion about treating currency undervaluation as an export subsidy in the WTO sense. Even if these multilateral efforts do not bear fruit, domestic politics will push the U.S. government toward unilateral action against countries (such as China) that are perceived to be taking unfair advantage of global trade.

Smaller developing countries are likely to enjoy significantly greater policy space than larger ones: it is hard to imagine policymakers in Washington, DC or Brussels getting worked up over the industrial policies of Ethiopia or El Salvador. This means that the vast majority of the world's developing countries—almost all of them in Sub-Saharan Africa—will remain relatively free of external encumbrances that restrict the scope of structural transformation policies. That is the good news. The bad news is that large and systemically important economies such as India and China continue to house a substantial portion of the world's poor. In 2008, the latest year for which estimates are available, 62 percent of the world's people living on less than $2 a day lived in China and South Asia; only 23 percent lived in Sub-Saharan Africa (Chen and Ravallion 2012). The continued growth of these populous countries remains crucially important to global poverty reduction.

2.11.2 Changes Within Manufacturing

A second important source of headwinds relates to changes that are happening within manufacturing industries. Technological changes are rendering manufacturing more capital- and skill-intensive, reducing the employment elasticity of industrialization and the capacity of manufacturing to absorb large volumes of unskilled labor from the countryside and from the informal sector. Global supply chains may facilitate entry into manufacturing for low-cost countries that are able to attract foreign investment, but they also reduce linkages with the rest of the economy and the potential for the development of local upstream suppliers. The ease with which global companies sitting at the apex of the production chains can switch suppliers gives these industries a fleeting character.

In all these ways, many manufacturing industries are in effect becoming more like natural resource enclaves: skill- and capital-intensive, disengaged from the domestic economy, and transitory. A potentially compensating trend is that some service industries may be acquiring manufacturing-like properties.[9] Certain service sectors, such as food and clothing retail services, are becoming adept at absorbing technologies from abroad, employing relatively unskilled workers, and establishing significant linkages with the domestic economy (hypermarkets are one example). If such service activities are also subject to absolute productivity convergence, as seems plausible, they could act as the escalator industries of the future.

2.11.3 Increased Global Competition

Other factors will disfavor manufacturing industries. New entrants into standardized manufacturing activities face much greater global competition today than companies in Korea or Taiwan faced in the 1960s and 1970s or China faced in the 1990s. Even though its production costs have been rising, China itself poses a formidable competitive challenge to any producer attempting to make inroads on global markets. Almost all Asian manufacturing superstars started with protected home markets, which gave them a home base on which to build experience and ensured domestic profits to subsidize forays into world markets. Most African manufacturers today face an onslaught of cheap imports from China and other Asian exporters, which makes it difficult for them to survive on their home turf, let alone cross-subsidize their international activities. The burdens placed on government policy to incubate and develop domestic manufacturing firms are correspondingly heavier.

2.11.4 Environmental Concerns

Environmental concerns will play a much larger role than they did in the past, making it more costly to develop traditional "dirty industries," such as steel, paper, and chemicals. Comparative advantage and economic logic dictate that such industries will migrate to poorer countries, but producers everywhere will be under pressure to use technologies that generate less pollution and greenhouse gas emissions (Steer 2013). To the extent that environmental concerns raise the technological requirements of running these

---

[9] I am grateful to Kemal Derviş for this suggestion.

industries, they will diminish the comparative advantage of developing countries. The capital and skill requirements of green technologies are also higher. There will be the usual exhortations to the effect that these new technologies should be subsidized and made available to poor countries. Whether this will happen is an open question.

2.12 Policy Implications

These considerations suggest that a phase of the world economy is beginning in which East Asian-style growth rates will be difficult to sustain for the East Asian countries themselves and hard to attain for the next generation of emulators. The future of growth is unlikely to look like its recent past. It may well be that the six decades after the end of World War II will prove to have been a very special period, an experience not replicated before or after. The rate of convergence between poor and rich countries is likely to fall considerably from the levels seen during the past two decades. Developing countries will probably still grow faster than advanced economies, but they will do so in large part because of the slowdown in growth in the advanced economies.

Ultimately, growth depends primarily on what happens at home. Even if the world economy provides more headwinds than tailwinds, desirable policies will continue to share features that have served successful countries well in the past. These features include a stable macroeconomic framework; incentives for economic restructuring and diversification (both market-led and government-provided); social policies to address inequality and exclusion; continued investments in human capital and skills; and a strengthening of regulatory, legal, and political institutions over time. Countries that do their homework along these dimensions will do better than those that do not.

Beyond these generalities, however, the main policy implication is that future growth strategies will need to differ from the strategies of the past in their emphasis, if not their main outlines. In particular, reliance on domestic (or in certain cases regional) markets and resources will need to substitute at the margin for reliance on foreign markets, foreign finance, and foreign investment. The upgrading of the home market will in turn necessitate greater emphasis on income distribution and the health of the middle class as part of a growth strategy. In other words, social policy and growth strategy will become complements to a much greater extent.

Globally, it will not make sense to pursue the extensive harmonization and coordination of policies in finance and trade that are ultimately neither sustainable nor, in view of the heterogeneity of needs and preferences around the world, desirable. International institutions will do better to accommodate the inevitable reduction of the pace of globalization (or, perhaps, some deglobalization) than to shoehorn countries into compliance with ill-fitting rules. Industrial countries will need to carve out some policy space to rework their social bargains, just as developing countries need policy space to restructure their economies (Subramanian and Kessler 2013). A new settlement will need to be forged between advanced countries and large emerging markets in which the latter no longer see themselves as free-riders on the policies of the former.

As Birdsall underscores in chapter 7, the global economy suffers from a shortfall between the demand and supply of adequate global governance (see also Rodrik 2011b). It is possible that some of this shortfall can be addressed by reforms and new forms of representations: by individual citizens and countries acting in ways that are more conscious of the global consequences of their decisions, by activists and regulators expanding their transnational networks, and by multilateral economic institutions improving their own governance. At best, however, these changes will take place in an environment with strong centrifugal forces, characterized by a growing number of actors and greater diversity of interests. If these forces are managed well, they need not endanger economic globalization per se. But if policymakers fail to take them into account, they are more likely to undermine support for an open global economy than to strengthen it.

Ultimately, a healthy world economy needs to rest on healthy national economies and societies. Global rules that restrict domestic policy space too much are counterproductive insofar as they narrow the scope for growth- and equity-producing policies. They thus undermine the support for and legitimacy of an open global economy. The challenge is to design an architecture that respects the domestic priorities of individual countries while ensuring that major cross-border spillovers and global public goods are addressed.

References

Acemoglu, Daron, and James Robinson. 2012. *Why Nations Fail: The Origins of Power, Prosperity, and Poverty*. New York: Crown.

Acemoglu, Daron, Simon Johnson, and James Robinson. 2001. "The Colonial Origins of Comparative Development: An Empirical Investigation" *American Economic Review* 91 (5): 1369–401.

Acemoglu, Daron, Simon Johnson, and James Robinson. 2003. "An African Success: Botswana." In *In Search of Prosperity: Analytical Narratives on Economic Growth*, ed. Dani Rodrik. Princeton, NJ: Princeton University Press.

Allen, Franklin, Elena Carletti, Jun Qian, and Patricio Valenzuela. 2013. "Growth, Finance, and Crises." Paper prepared for the Global Citizen Foundation project "Towards a Better Global Economy."

Bairoch, Paul. 1982. "International Industrialization Levels from 1750 to 1980." *Journal of European Economic History* 11 (Fall): 269–310.

Baldwin, Richard. 2011. "Trade and Industrialization after Globalization's 2nd Unbundling: How Building and Joining a Supply Chain are Different and Why It Matters." NBER Working Paper 17716, National Bureau of Economic Research, Cambridge, MA.

Barro, Robert J. 2012 "Convergence and Modernization Revisited." NBER Working Paper No. 18295, National Bureau of Economic Research, Cambridge, MA.

Behrman, Jere R., and Hans-Peter Kohler. 2013. "Quantity, Quality, and Mobility of Population." Paper prepared for the Global Citizen Foundation project "Towards a Better Global Economy."

Bourguignon, François, and Christian Morrisson. 2002. "Inequality among World Citizens: 1820–1992." *American Economic Review* 92 (4): 727–44.

Chen, Shaohua, and Martin Ravallion. 2012. "An Update to the World Bank's Estimates of Consumption Poverty in the Developing World." World Bank, Washington, DC. http://siteresources.worldbank.org/INTPOVCALNET/Resources/Global_Poverty_Update_2012_02-29-12.pdf.

Commission on Growth and Development. 2008. *The Growth Report: Strategies for Sustained Growth and Inclusive Development*. Washington, DC: Commission on Growth and Development.

Duhigg, Charles, and Keith Bradsher, 2012. "How the U.S. Lost Out on iPhone Work." *New York Times*, January 21. http://www.nytimes.com/2012/01/22/business/apple-america-and-a-squeezed-middle-class.html?pagewanted=all.

Engerman, Stanley L., and Kenneth L. Sokoloff. 1997 "Factor Endowments, Institutions, and Differential Paths of Growth among New World Economies: A View from Economic Historians of the United States." In *How Latin America Fell Behind*, ed. Stephen Huber. Stanford CA: Stanford University Press.

Galor, Oded, Omer Moav, and Dietrich Vollrath. 2008. "Inequality in Land Ownership, the Emergence of Human Capital Promoting Institutions, and the Great Divergence." *Review of Economic Studies* 76 (1): 143–79.

Galor, Oded, and Andrew Mountford. 2008. "Trading Population for Productivity: Theory and Evidence." *Review of Economic Studies* 75 (4): 1143–79.

Glaeser, Edward L., Rafael La Porta, Florencio Lopez-de-Silanes, and Andrei Shleifer. 2004. "Do Institutions Cause Growth?" *Journal of Economic Growth* 9 (3): 271–303.

Hausmann, Ricardo, and Dani Rodrik. 2005. "Self-Discovery in a Development Strategy for El Salvador." *Economia: Journal of the Latin American and Caribbean Economic Association* 6 (1): 43–102.

Hidalgo, Cesar A., and Ricardo Hausmann. 2009. "The Building Blocks of Economic Complexity." CID Working Paper 186, Center for International Development, Harvard University, Cambridge, MA.

Imbs, Jean, and Romain Wacziarg. 2003. "Stages of Diversification." *American Economic Review* 93 (1): 63–86.

Koopman, Robert, Zhi Wang, and Shang-Jin Wei. 2008. "How Much of Chinese Exports Is Really Made In China? Assessing Domestic Value-Added When

Processing Trade Is Pervasive." NBER Working Paper 14109, National Bureau of Economic Research, Cambridge, MA.

Krueger, Anne O. 2004. "Meant Well, Tried Little, Failed Much: Policy Reforms in Emerging Market Economies." Roundtable Lecture, Economic Honors Society, New York University, New York, March 23. http://www.imf.org/external/np/speeches/2004/032304a.htm.

Maddison, Angus. 2001. *The World Economy: A Millennial Perspective.* OECD Development Centre, Organisation for Economic Co-operation and Development, Paris.

Maddison, Angus. 2010. "Historical Statistics of the World Economy: 1–2008 AD." http://www.ggdc.net/maddison/Historical_Statistics/horizontal-file_02-2010.xls.

Martinez, Marcelo, and Montfort Mlachila, 2013. "The Quality of the Recent High-Growth Episode in Sub-Saharan Africa." IMF Working Paper 13/53, February 26, International Monetary Fund, Washington, DC.

McMillan, Margaret S. 2013. "The Changing Structure of Africa's Economies." Background paper for *The African Economic Outlook 2013*, African Development Bank.

McMillan, Margaret S., and Dani Rodrik. 2011. "Globalization, Structural Change, and Economic Growth." In *Making Globalization Socially Sustainable*, ed. M. Bachetta and M. Jansen. Geneva: International Labor Organization and World Trade Organization.

Milanovic, Branko. 2011. "Global Inequality: From Class to Location, from Proleterians to Migrants." World Bank Policy Research Working Paper 5820, Washington, DC.

Murphy, Kevin M., Andrei Shleifer, and Robert W. Vishny. 1989. "Industrialization and the Big Push." *Journal of Political Economy* 97 (5): 1003–26.

Pamuk, Şevket, and Jeffrey G. Williamson. 2009. "Ottoman De-Industrialization 1800–1913: Assessing the Shock, its Impact, and the Response." National Bureau of Economic Research, Working Paper 14763, National Bureau of Economic Research, Cambridge, MA.

Pritchett, Lant. 1997. "Divergence, Big Time." *Journal of Economic Perspectives* 11 (3): 3–17.

Rassweiler, A. 2009. "iPhone 3G S Carries $178.96 BOM and Manufacturing Cost, iSuppli Teardown Reveals." iSuppli, June 24. http://www.isuppli.com/Teardowns-Manufacturing-and-Pricing/News/Pages/iPhone-3G-S-Carries-178-96-BOM-and-Manufacturing-Cost-iSuppli-Teardown-Reveals.aspx.

Rajan, Raghuram, and Arvind Subramanian. 2011. "Aid, Dutch Disease, and Manufacturing Growth." *Journal of Development Economics* 94 (1): 106–18.

Rodrik, Dani. 1996. "Coordination Failures and Government Policy: A Model with Applications to East Asia and Eastern Europe." *Journal of International Economics* 40 (1–2): 1–22.

Rodrik, Dani. 1999. "Where Did All the Growth Go? External Shocks, Social Conflict and Growth Collapses." *Journal of Economic Growth* 4 (4): 385–412.

Rodrik, Dani. 2007. *One Economics, Many Recipes: Globalization, Institutions and Economic Growth*, Princeton, NJ: Princeton University Press.

Rodrik, Dani. 2008a. "Normalizing Industrial Policy." Commission on Growth and Development Working Paper No. 3, Washington, Washington, DC.

Rodrik, Dani. 2008b. "The Real Exchange Rate and Economic Growth." *Brookings Papers on Economic Activity* 2008: 2.

Rodrik, Dani. 2008c. "Second-Best Institutions." *American Economic Review*, Papers and Proceedings, May.

Rodrik, Dani. 2011a. "The Future of Economic Convergence." September, Harvard University, Cambridge, MA.

Rodrik, Dani. 2011b. *The Globalization Paradox: Democracy and the Future of the World Economy*. New York: Norton.

Rodrik, Dani. 2013. "Unconditional Convergence in Manufacturing." *Quarterly Journal of Economics* 128 (1): 165–204.

Sachs, Jeffrey, John W. McArthur, Guido Schmidt-Traub, Margaret Kruk, Chandrika Bahadur, Michael Faye, and Gordon McCord. 2004. "Ending Africa's Poverty Trap." *Brookings Papers on Economic Activity* 1: 117–216.

Sokoloff, Kenneth L., and Stanley L. Engerman. 2000. "Institutions, Factor Endowments, and Paths of Development in the New World." *Journal of Economic Perspectives* 14 (3): 217–32.

Steer, Andrew. 2013. "Resource Depletion, Climate Change and Economic Growth." Paper prepared for the Global Citizen Foundation project "Towards a Better Global Economy."

Subramanian, Arvind, and Martin Kessler. 2013. "Trade Integration and Its Future." Paper prepared for the Global Citizen Foundation project "Towards a Better Global Economy."

Sutton, John. 2004. *The Auto Component Supply Chain in China and India: A Benchmark Study*. World Bank, Washington, DC.

Sutton, John. 2012. *Competing in Capabilities: The Globalization Process*. Clarendon Lectures in Economics. Oxford: Oxford University Press.

Sutton, John. n.d. "The Globalization Process: Auto-Component Supply Chains in China and India." London School of Economics.

Timmer, Marcel P., and Gaaitzen J. de Vries. 2009. "Structural Change and Growth Accelerations in Asia and Latin America: A New Sectoral Data Set." *Cliometrica* 3 (2): 165–90.

Xing, Y., and N. Detert. 2010. "How the iPhone Widens the United States Trade Deficit with the People's Republic of China." ADBI Working Paper 257, Asian Development Bank Institute, Tokyo. http://www.adbi.org/working-paper/2010/12/14/4236.iphone.widens.us.trade.deficit.prc/.

Comments on "The Past, Present, and Future of Economic Growth," by Dani Rodrik

Kemal Derviş

Dani Rodrik's chapter on "The Past, Present and Future of Economic Growth" provides a powerful synthetic overview of a huge amount of empirical and theoretical research and offers a simple but elegant and convincing analytical framework that both explains basic trends observed in the past and provides a prognosis for the future. In many ways, it is a tour de force. It distills a lot into a short space, and the analytical framework offered, while simple, draws on both the more recent "institutional–historic" literature and the "sources of growth" and "labor absorption" traditions that started with Robert Solow and Arthur Lewis. The interaction of the rate of industrialization and the development of broad institutional and human capabilities determines whether there is slow or rapid growth and whether it is episodic or sustained.

I am in strong agreement with the way in which the chapter presents the broad history of economic growth and also with its policy conclusions. The chapter emphasizes that there does not seem to be a "one-size-fits-all" recommendation that emerges from past experience and underlines how in many cases an active role of the state was beneficial to growth and development.

There are two aspects of the chapter about which my basic message would be somewhat different. The first has to do with the decomposition of global inequality into between-country and within-country inequality. Rodrik writes that "it is *increasingly* (emphasis added) the country in which one is born that determines one's economic fortune," basing that statement on Milanovic (2011) as well as the evidence presented in Tables 2.2 and 2.3 and Figure 2.4.

Figure 2.4, which presents the decomposition for 1820, 1929, and 2005, appears to show a continuing increase in the percentage of "between-country" inequality. In fact, close analysis of the data available shows that this powerful stylized fact was correct for the long period from the beginning of the nineteenth century to the 1990s. But, as shown in Table 2.2, the share of within-country inequality actually increased between 1988 and 2005, from 19.4 percent to 26.5 percent for the log mean deviation and from 22.0 percent to 26.5 percent for the Theil index.

I would argue that there are strong reasons to believe that this is a new trend, which emerged around 1990. What has happened since 2005 (the last year in the tables and figures)? Over the past eight years, the difference in the per capita economic growth rates between the aggregate group of developing and emerging economies on the one hand and the rich advanced countries on the other widened, due to both continuing strong growth in the former and the 2008–09 crisis-induced recession in the latter. At the same time, the trend of increasing within-country inequality is continuing in many economies, including most of the largest countries, such as the United States and China. Projections for the next few years move in the same direction: continued, much more rapid growth in the emerging economies and developing countries, and increasing within-country inequality almost everywhere. So we can already say with some confidence that, contrary to the 1820–1990 period, the 1990–2020 period will be one in which the share of "within-country" inequality in overall global inequality grew very substantially. What will happen after about 2020 is much more uncertain. But that there will have been this "reversal of trend" in the decomposition for close to three decades is quite clear, if current projections to 2020 are even roughly correct. In any case, the reversal has already taken place for at least 20 years.

I agree with the author's answer to his question "is it better to be rich in a poor country or poor in a rich country?" up to approximately 2010. For a long time, the broadly correct answer has been, as suggested, that it is better to be poor in a rich country. But this is changing. It still is true if by "poor countries" one takes the poorest 10 percent of countries in the world, which includes many very small or failed states. This is the definition of "poor country" the author uses. His conclusion would most likely no longer be true if he defined poor countries as the 30 percent poorest or the group of countries in which the poorest 30 percent of the world population lived. And as time has passed, over the past 25 years, stagnation of lower-income groups' incomes in the United States and now Europe, combined with accelerating income growth for the large majority of people living in emerging economies, is making it more and more likely that to be in the bottom deciles in the advanced countries may no longer be better than to be in the top percentiles in emerging economies.

I would also add that "relative" income within a society may be a better—or at least a useful additional—indicator of "happiness" or "life satisfaction" than income compared with the income of a person in a far-away country. Citizens in Spain, Greece, or the United States compare themselves with people in or close to their country, not to people in Africa or South Asia. While this point is not central to a chapter on growth per se, it does deserve mention as a qualifier to the discussion on where one would like to be born.

The second point on which I have a somewhat more qualified view has to do with the prognosis for the future. The chapter argues convincingly that unconditional or even conditional convergence in manufacturing will be insufficient to perpetuate the strong average income convergence trend observed since the late 1980s for many developing countries compared with the rich countries. Moreover, using individual countries as units of observation, Rodrik states that "the growth rate of economies is basically uncorrelated with their initial level of productivity or distance from the technological frontier." I would argue, first, that the dividing line between manufacturing and what we broadly call "services" is becoming increasingly blurred. He accepts the possibility that new forms of convergence to the technological frontier may emerge in parts, at least, of the service sector. So the strongest driving force behind convergence may affect a much larger portion of developing economies in the future. Within the chapter's analytical framework, this is more likely to happen in countries that are able to accelerate and enhance their "capabilities."

Moreover, in terms of the basic overall message about convergence or divergence, size matters. The fact that very large economies such as China, India, Brazil, and Indonesia may continue to "converge" will lead to a different world economy than if the converging countries were small economies. So both of the following statements may turn out to be true when we look back in ten years: (a) the number of developing countries reducing the relative distance between their average incomes and the average income of the richest countries may not be larger than the number of countries for which the gap widens, and (b) the relative distance between the average income of all developing countries taken as an aggregate and the average income of rich countries will decline very rapidly. Both trends have been evident in the past three decades and, in my view, are likely to continue for at least the next decade or so.

Neither of these two qualifiers detracts from the very rich analysis, the elegant simplicity of the basic framework, or the policy conclusions of the chapter. Moreover, over medium-term horizons, economic growth performance remains critically important for the well-being of most of the inhabitants of our planet. The historical, comparative, and quantitative analysis of growth found in this chapter should be invaluable for designing policies to support rapid and globally more inclusive growth.

Comments on "The Past, Present, and Future of Economic Growth," by Dani Rodrik

Chang-Tai Hsieh

I have three reactions to the chapter. First, I am very sympathetic to the argument that Dani has been pressing on the potential of "heterodox" versus "orthodox" reforms. There is overwhelming evidence that the kind of policies that successful countries have undertaken generally do not look like the typical "Washington Consensus" type of policies. However, at this level of generality it is hard to say more than this. While one can construct scenarios in which unorthodox reforms improve things, it is just as easy to construct scenarios in which they make things worse. (The same is also true of orthodox reforms.) As the chapter states, countries that experienced rapid growth implemented many unorthodox reforms, but many of the things they did were orthodox as well. Without looking at specific policies, it is difficult to know whether heterodox policies were responsible for the rapid growth, or whether some of them may have made things worse, or whether it is the orthodox policies that were responsible. That said, I completely buy the point that the type of reforms with the largest payoffs for most developing countries are much more nuanced than indicated by the standard Washington Consensus recipe book. The difficult question, which Dani has been at the forefront of trying to answer, is what exactly these nuanced policy reforms are.

I also could not agree more that structural change is an integral part of successful economies. I would add that it is even more important than one might think from looking at the manufacturing share of output. For example, even when manufacturing shares are constant, the growth of new sectors representing new technologies (for example, mobile phones) and the decline of "old" sectors (for example, textiles and apparel) is surely important to growth. And within each sector, high aggregate productivity growth is characterized by the reallocation of market shares from incumbents to new firms. The same is also true of productivity growth outside of the manufacturing sector. For example, Brazil is a country where productivity growth in agriculture in the last 20 years has been very high, and the evidence suggests that a big part of this was caused by the reallocation of land away from traditional crops toward new cash crops (primarily soybeans). The Green Revolution in India almost 40 years ago was characterized by a "structural transformation" of land away from traditional rain-fed agriculture toward irrigation and fertilizer-intensive high-yield seeds. The spread of modern retailing in many Latin American countries is also an important "structural change," albeit in the retail sector, that we know relatively little about.

What I don't buy is why it is useful to think about the forces that drive structural change (in all incarnations) as divorced from the process of institutional reform. One could argue about the precise reforms that facilitate this process and whether orthodox or unorthodox reforms are key. But even if the key reforms are unorthodox in nature, it is still just as difficult to figure out which precise (unorthodox) reforms might work, and just as difficult to implement them. Very few countries have implemented the kind of unorthodox reforms that China has implemented. Put differently, the chapter gives the reader the impression that structural change is "easy" and deep institutional reform is "hard." My reading of the evidence is that reforms that drive structural change are just as hard and just as rare. And it is not clear whether being like Sweden, where the chapter claims growth has been driven by fundamental institutional change, is different from being like China (or Korea and Taiwan). To be sure, the institutional changes behind Sweden and China are different, but they are not different in the sense that they are difficult to figure out.

Finally, the chapter points to the evidence of convergence in manufacturing productivity to argue that structural change is potentially easy—all countries need to do is to remove the barriers that prevent the productive manufacturing firms from expanding. I would be more cautious in interpreting this evidence. Our intuition of what aggregate convergence implies does not necessarily carry over to thinking about sectoral (or regional for that matter) convergence. The implicit assumption we make in interpreting aggregate convergence is that labor is not mobile across countries. This assumption allows us to interpret differences in the aggregate marginal product per worker (as measured by aggregate output per worker) as reflecting differences in aggregate productivity. At the sectoral level, convergence in sectoral output per worker also reflects convergence in sectoral marginal product per worker (in a world where the marginal product is proportional to the average product). However, convergence of the value of marginal product per worker in a sector does not necessarily imply convergence in the productivity of the sector. Sectoral marginal products reflect aggregate productivity, which is a weighted average of productivities in all sectors in the economy, and the gap between the marginal products in the sector in manufacturing versus nonmanufacturing. Convergence in marginal products in the manufacturing sector might reflect convergence in productivity in the manufacturing sector, or it might be driven by an increase in the gaps in marginal products between the manufacturing sector and nonmanufacturing sectors (or the gap between the formal manufacturing sector and the rest of the economy).

Put differently, it is not clear whether the convergence in manufacturing output per worker reflects a shift in the marginal product of labor in manufacturing or a movement along the marginal product of labor schedule. At the aggregate country level, we assume that labor supply is fixed or driven by forces exogenous to productivity, so we rule out the possibility that differences in output per worker reflect movements along the labor demand schedule. At the sectoral level, there is every reason to believe that the labor supply in a sector is a key endogenous variable, which would imply that changes in output per worker in a sector could reflect a shift in the labor supply in the sector.

I think that if Dani were to lay out an equilibrium model that generates the following three outcomes—convergence in output per worker in the manufacturing sector, a declining share of manufacturing, and nonconvergence at the aggregate level—he would find that productivity in manufacturing would not necessarily have converged. I think what he would find is that the barriers faced by formal manufacturing may have worsened in many developing countries. This result would be completely consistent with Dani's argument about barriers to structural transformation. But it would still leave us with the hard task of figuring out what these barriers are and how to best tackle them.

Comments on "The Past, Present, and Future of Economic Growth," by Dani Rodrik

Branko Milanovic

I enjoyed Dani Rodrik's chapter very much. It is a first-rate review of economic history and the factors that have led to the development of the northwestern corner of Eurasia and then spread development to the western offshoots and parts of Asia and Latin America. It weaves extremely well and persuasively the grand narrative of economic history with the author's own empirical findings on growth-promoting factors and policies. The chapter also looks at what the implications could be for the future.

My review focuses on three issues: the components of global inequality and their political significance, the shrinking space for policy autonomy, and the technological frontier and its implication for the development of poor countries.

1. Global Inequality and Global Democracy

Both Rodrik in the chapter and Kemal Derviş in his comments are right regarding the role of the between-country component of global inequality (even if they seem to disagree). Rodrik looks at the historical evolution of the between-versus-within component from the early 1800s (that is, the period for which Maddison's GDP per capita data and Bourguignon-Morrisson (2002) estimates of income distributions are available) and rightly shows that the between component has increased by leaps and bounds. Using different data from the late 1800s through 2005, I find the same result (Milanovic 2011). The level of the between component is very high. Whatever inequality measure and decomposition technique is used (Theil or Gini or Kakwani), it accounts for at least three-quarters of total inequality today. It is thus indeed the place in which one is born that determines a huge chunk of one's income. Using 2008 country percentile data (100 income percentiles per country), I find that running a regression with percentile income levels for 117 countries as a dependent variable on country dummies alone explains 65–75 percent of income variability: where you are born—which for 97 percent of mankind is equivalent to where one lives—largely determines one's life chances, as Rodrik argues.

Derviş is right that this is becoming somewhat less important thanks to the phenomenal growth rates of China and India, in particular, but also thanks to the reemergence of the global South as a strong economic actor. Between 1988 and 2008, the (population-weighted) between-country Gini coefficient decreased from 68 to 66 points, driving down overall global inequality from 72 to 70. If we use Theil (0) and Theil (1) as measures of economic inequality, which are exactly decomposable, we find that the level of between-country inequality fell by 16 Theil (0) points and 7 Theil (1) points, while the level of within-country inequality increased by 5 Theil points in both cases (Figure C3.1 shows the results for Theil (0) only).[1]

What are the prospects for the future if this trend of diminishing between-country inequality continues while inequality within counties continues to increase? If we project these trends over the next 30 years or so, we should find:

- significant decreases in the level of global inequality;
- readjustment in the component parts, with between-country inequality shrinking to perhaps 50–60 percent of the total;[2]
- economic readjustment between Europe–North America and Asia.

Now, everyone will recognize in these three points the pattern that existed before 1870. The reemergence of China and India just brings these countries back to the relative positions they enjoyed around the middle of the nineteenth century; the composition of global inequality strongly resembles the one that existed around that time too. (China, according to Maddison [2001, 2003], was the largest economy until 1870, when it was overtaken by the United States. Currently, and depending on the results of the 2011 International Comparison Project [ICP] exercise, China may already be the largest economy. If one uses Maddison's 1990 purchasing power parity [PPP] data,[3] on which the 1870 results are based, China's economy is already larger than that of the United States.)

The geographic readjustment implies a between- versus within-country inequality readjustment. The political counterpart of the decreasing importance of where one is born is the formation of a supranational economic elite, a process already evident. We can call this process *a plutocratic globalization.* As

---

[1] Theil (0) is the mean logarithmic deviation. Theil (1) is the Theil entropy index (see Theil 1967).

[2] This back-of-the-envelope calculation should (and can) be done more carefully.

[3] Data available at http://www.ggdc.net/maddison/oriindex.htm

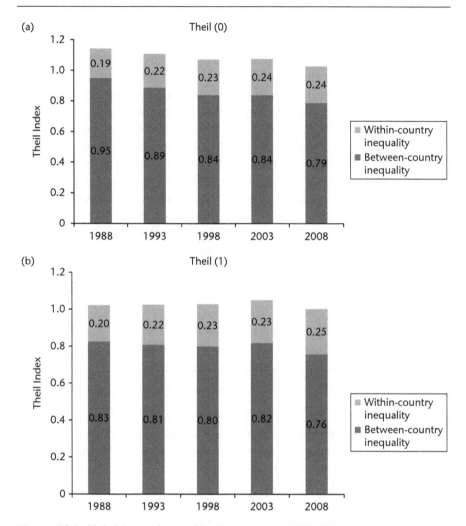

Figure C3.1 Global Inequality and Its Components, 1988–2008
Source: Author.

inequalities within nations increase and those between nations decline, members of the elite will have much more in common with one another, regardless of the country where they are from, than they will have with people with whom they share citizenship. Chrystia Freeland (2012) and David Rothkopf (2009) document this process of creation of a transnational global elite. Davoses and Bilderbergs have not arisen spontaneously and for no reason.

From the point of view of global citizenship and of people who would like to see some form of global democracy eventually emerge, this process may be welcome. If the ultimate objective of mankind is to reach some kind of global democracy, a plutocratic globalization seems to be the most realistic way to go about achieving it. The problem is that such plutocratic globalization will inevitably create tensions with the exercise of democracy at the national level. Rich minorities in their own countries will not only feel more estranged from poorer co-citizens, but the gutting of the middle class that such increased within-country inequality and polarization imply threatens the maintenance of national democracies. We are already witnessing this process. Whereas democracy, as a form of government, has in the past quarter-century become much more widespread globally, it has also become less meaningful, in both old and new democracies, as moneyed elites have bought their way to power and the choice between two or more ostensible policy options presented to the electorate has become vacuous.

The implication of the seemingly technical or arcane fact that the composition of global inequality is likely to change in the next 30–50 years has profound implications for political processes. One needs to acknowledge the potential tension between realization of the human dream of global governance and the increasing meaninglessness or subversion of national democracies that the rise of a global plutocracy may bring about.

2. Policy Autonomy

A paper, which I liked very much, that Rodrik does not mention in his review is one he wrote with Sharun Mukand in 2002 ("In Search of the Holy Grail"). This gem of a paper shows that big-time successes, like the ones featured in Figure 2.7, depend on being far enough from the ruling economic hegemon (or ruling economic policy paradigm) to be able to tinker with policies, so that countries find the best policies that suit their institutions. Quality of governance becomes key in such instances because one has to "break free" from the dominant paradigm and find the exact policy mix that suits country's institutions. But to do so, one needs "policy autonomy." China is a poster case for such an approach.

As the world becomes more globalized, the space for policy autonomy will get smaller and smaller for all countries, large and small. Tinkering with different policies will become harder. Superstar countries will be fewer in number, as policies and growth rates become more similar.

In Figure C3.2, I show the standard deviation of countries' growth rates in the past 60 years.[4] What is remarkable is that in the past 20 years, the

---

[4] Over this period, the number of countries in the sample rose from fewer than 60 to more than 160; however, from about the 1960s, the sample size is almost the same. Countries that, at a given point of time, did not exist as independent entities (for example, Bangladesh, Croatia, and Ukraine) enter the calculation with their own growth rates, as distinct from overall national growth rates.

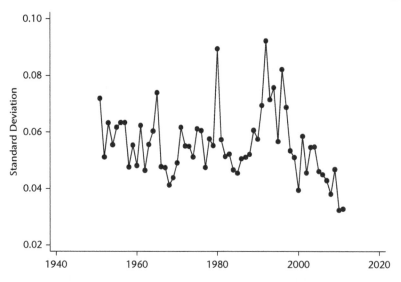

Figure C3.2 Standard Deviation of Annual National Growth Rates, 1951–2011
Source: Author.

standard deviation of countries' growth rates was more than cut in half, from about 8 percent to less than 4 percent. Growth rates are indeed converging.

If this line of reasoning is correct, we are not likely to see superstars like Japan, Korea, or China, all of which had long-term average growth rates three to four times greater than the corresponding world growth rates. This is bad news for all of Africa and other underdeveloped areas, which are unlikely to pull off the feat of almost catching up with the rich world in one or two generations.

3. The Production Possibility Frontier for Poor Countries

Robert Allen (2009, 2011) created a long-term historical series of capital per worker, matching (and using the same prices as) Maddison's (2003) series of historical GDP per capita. He estimated the relationship between capital per worker and GDP per capita at seven cross-sections (that is, across countries at different points of time) between 1820 and 1990. For each date, this relationship defines what could be considered a world production possibility frontier (PPF).

A striking finding is that for poor countries (that is, countries with a low capital-to-labor ratio and low price of labor), the PPF is at about at the same point as it was a century ago (Figure C3.3). In other words, if you are an African country today with capital/labor ratio under PPP $3,000, you have access to no more productive technologies than a country with the same

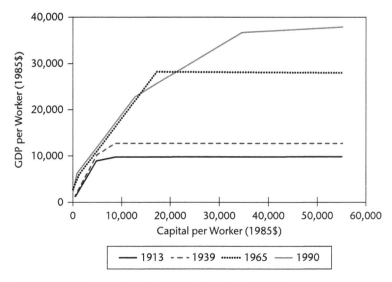

Figure C3.3 World Production Possibility Frontier, 1913–90

Source: Reprinted from *Explorations in Economic History*, Vol. 49, Robert C. Allen, "Technology and the Great Divergence: Global Economic Inequality since 1820," p. 1–16 (2012), with permission from Elsevier.

capital-to-labor ratio had in 1913. This phenomenon can be explained by the fact that technological inventions are made by countries that are rich, and inventions reflect their specific labor/capital prices. This ratio is of course high for developed countries, and the technological frontier moves outward only at ever higher labor/capital price ratios. By contrast, over the past two centuries, it has not moved up at all at low labor/capital ratios. Allen argues that the incentive to innovate exists only when the cost of labor is high (that is, when a country is relatively developed).[5] Technological innovations, which push the frontier outward, took place around the level of capital per worker of $10,000 in 1965 and $20,000 in the 1990s (both in PPP)—that is, among the richest countries at each point in time.

If this is true, then another gloomy finding for the growth prospects of the poorest countries follows: they are unlikely to benefit from technological progress as long as they remain poor. This is, in an interesting twist, the poverty trap: in order to become richer, you have to cease being poor.

---

[5] The same argument has been made to explain the startling lack of technological progress in Roman times despite a pervasive air of economic "modernity." Both Moses Finlay (1999) and Aldo Schiavone (2002) attribute the phenomenon to the abundance of cheap slave labor.

4. Conclusion

Combining the three points made above suggests a world in which readjustment between Europe–North America and Asia creates many more relatively well-off people (who may even be called a global middle class), a strong supranational plutocratic elite, and tensions between the requirements of national and global democracy—and leaves vast areas of today's poor counties still very poor. As their populations will remain smaller than the population of "the resurgent Asia" (to use Maddison's term), the between component of global inequality may still, for a while, continue its downward slide. But eventually, the population dynamics are such that the weight of the excluded regions will increase, reversing the downward-trending between-country inequality.

In the future, about half the world population will have what would be considered today a middling income level, perhaps as many as a third of the population will have an income level of less than 4 international dollars per day, and a small segment of the population will belong to the elite. Global poverty may even be driven down to 5 percent of the world population, but it would be nevertheless a very unequal world, and unequal in a different way than now and certainly than as recently as two decades ago. Would it be a better world?

References

Allen, Robert C. 2009. "Technology and the Great Divergence." Working Paper, Department of Economics, Nuffield College, Oxford University, United Kingdom. http://isites.harvard.edu/fs/docs/icb.topic725938.files/technology-6.pdf.

Allen, Robert C. 2011. *Global Economic History: A Very Short Introduction.* Oxford: Oxford University Press.

Bourguignon, François, and Christian Morrisson. 2002. "Inequality among World Citizens: 1820–1992." *American Economic Review* 92 (4): 727–44.

Finlay, Moses. 1999. *Ancient Economy,* Berkeley: University of California Press.

Freeland, Chrystia. 2012. *The Plutocrats: The Rise of the New Global Super-Rich and the Fall of Everyone Else.* New York: Penguin Press.

Madisson, Angus. 2001. *The World Economy: A Millennial Perspective.* Paris: OECD Development Centre Studies.

Madisson, Angus. 2003. *The World Economy: Historical Statistics.* Paris: OECD Development Centre Studies.

Milanovic, Branko. 2011. "Global Inequality and the Global Inequality Extraction Ratio: The Story of the Past Two Centuries." *Explorations in Economic History* 48 (November): 494–506.

Mukand, Sharun, and Dani Rodrik. 2002. "In Search of the Holy Grail: Policy Convergence, Experimentation and Economic Performance." CEPR Discussion Paper 3525, Center for Economic Policy Research, Washington, DC.

Rothkopf, David. 2009. *Superclass: The Global Power Elite and the World They Are Making.* New York: Farrar, Strauss and Giroux.

Schiavone, Aldo. 2002. *The End of the Past: Ancient Rome and the Modern West.* Cambridge, MA: Harvard University Press.

Theil, Henri. 1967. *Economics and Information Theory.* Amsterdam: North-Holland.

Comments on "The Past, Present, and Future of Economic Growth," by Dani Rodrik

Zia Qureshi

Dani Rodrik's chapter is a pleasure to read. It is substantive, insightful, and well-written. It carries his trademark out-of-the-box thinking. The chapter is impressive in the ground it covers, in terms of both the history of economic growth and growth analytics. I find myself in agreement with much of what the chapter says. There are, however, a few aspects of the chapter where I think the narrative could be somewhat different and more nuanced. I have two main sets of comments, one on the strategic and policy framework for growth and one on the prognosis for growth.

1. Growth Strategy and Policies

In this chapter, and in his other writings, Rodrik has developed well the argument for "heterodox" policies in promoting economic growth. There is now substantial supporting evidence that the successful economies employed a range of such policies. I agree with the view that "orthodox" or Washington Consensus-type policies alone may not be enough and that unorthodox policies, including a more direct and active role of government, may be necessary in specific contexts to launch and boost growth. However, I have some issues with the way in which this view is framed and presented in parts of the chapter.

The chapter identifies two "dynamics" or "forcing variables" that drive growth: it calls one "fundamental capabilities" and the other "structural transformation." One flaw that I see with this framing is that it mixes policies or inputs with outcomes. Fundamental capabilities are defined as accumulation of human capital and improvement of regulatory framework and institutions (basically the Washington Consensus-type policies); structural transformation is defined in terms of the rate of industrialization. Insofar as fundamental capabilities support industrialization and structural change, the latter is not independent of the former. It would be better to define both drivers of growth in policy terms.

When the chapter does map structural transformation or industrialization to policies, it maps it primarily to narrow, targeted, direct government policies to support the birth and expansion of new industries, in contrast to the broader reforms that enhance the fundamental capabilities. While at times the chapter recognizes the complementarity between these two sets of policies, often the narrative tends to treat them orthogonally or in a dualistic way. The effectiveness of unorthodox policies may not be independent of orthodox reforms. The mere fact that some successful economies implemented unorthodox policies does not necessarily mean that their success is wholly or mainly attributable to those policies. The prevailing context of capabilities and other reforms also matters. I am sympathetic to a similar point made by Professor Hsieh in his comments on the chapter.

The design and implementation of targeted policies require certain basic institutional capabilities. The chapter in general underplays the role of governance in ensuring policy effectiveness. The direct measures that worked in China or other East Asian countries may not be as effective in another governance and institutional context, such as in parts of Africa. The chapter appears a bit sanguine regarding the portability of the particular unorthodox interventions. I would have liked to see a clearer and more consistent message on policy interconnection and complementarity and on the dependence of the precise policy design, mix, and sequencing on the country context.

All unorthodox policies are not created equal. Justin Yifu Lin, former World Bank Chief Economist, distinguishes between what he calls "comparative advantage following" and "comparative advantage defying" industrial policies. His detailed argument is set out in two recent books (Yin 2012a, 2012b). He documents the failure of industrial policies that defy a country's comparative advantage and support predominantly import-substitution industrialization and the success of industrial policies that support outward-oriented strategies by facilitating the growth of industries in line with a country's current and potential comparative advantage. So successful unorthodox policies work with the market rather than go against its grain. I missed a reference to this work in the chapter. Comparative advantage-based specialization is not the enemy of product diversification, as seems implied in parts of the chapter, if comparative advantage is viewed dynamically.

Some of the narrative is cast in a way that brings to mind the stages-of-growth literature. There are references to poverty and middle-income traps. The point is made that narrower, targeted, unorthodox policies have a greater role to play at lower levels of income (in moving workers out of farms and into factories); at higher income levels, broader policies affecting fundamental capabilities take on a more important role (in raising productivity within factories and developing the services sector). Now it is true that the growth model and related policy challenges evolve as countries develop and move up the income scale, but this happens more as a continuum rather than in the form of sharp discontinuities or distinct stages of development. Factories do not wait until the last surplus laborer has been absorbed before they begin to improve the productivity of their workers.

On the middle-income trap, recent research at the World Bank does not find any systematic tendency for countries' growth to slow at particular middle-income levels (Bulman, Eden, and Nguyen 2012; World Bank 2012). In some cases it slows; in others it doesn't. The research does find some common attributes of countries that successfully transitioned to high-income status in the past half-century. They include faster transformation from agriculture to industry, higher total factor productivity growth, stronger outcomes on human capital and innovation, greater openness and export orientation, macroeconomic stability, and avoidance of sharp increases in inequality. This agenda spans elements of both structural transformation and fundamental capabilities in Rodrik's framework.

2. Prognosis for Growth

I agree that future growth faces some tough challenges. But in my view, the chapter's prognosis about future growth in emerging economies may be on the pessimistic side. The prognosis of a significant slowing of emerging economy growth is overly centered on prospects for manufacturing, reflecting the central role accorded to manufacturing as the driver of growth. There does not seem to be adequate recognition of new possibilities for growth in other areas, including in services, as Kemal Derviş notes in his comments, and advances in information and communication technologies, which open up new opportunities and could even allow countries to leapfrog traditional stages of development.

Using the chapter's terminology, the potential for unconditional convergence remains considerable in many emerging economies, including in some large economies that have grown rapidly in the past couple of decades. For example, despite rapid growth, China's per capita income is still only about 1/10th of that of the United States, and India's is only 3 percent. If emerging economies continue to extend and deepen progress in structural and institutional reforms, overall growth would continue to be boosted also by conditional convergence, enabling the more advanced emerging economies to avoid the so-called middle-income trap.

Part of the chapter's relative pessimism about emerging economy growth prospects stems from the less favorable external environment these economies are likely to face as growth remains subdued in advanced economies. The negative effect of weak growth in the advanced economies through the trade channel could be offset, in part at least, by the rapidly rising intra-emerging economy trade, which contributed to the relative resilience of emerging economy growth in the aftermath of the global financial crisis and continues to offer a substantial upside potential. The share of emerging economies' total exports destined for other emerging economies rose from about 20 percent in 1990 to more than 40 percent in 2012. Over the same period, the share of emerging economies as a market for the exports of advanced economies also doubled, from about 17 percent to more than 35 percent of total advanced economy exports. There is substantial scope for continued expansion of world trade—from the rise of emerging economies, the growth of global value chains, the untapped potential of trade in services, and renewed efforts toward trade liberalization. The chapter seems to underplay the potential of further advances in globalization to boost economic growth.

The chapter also mentions increased competition from China as a constraint to growth in other emerging economies. But if the increased competition reflects continued strong growth of the Chinese economy, it would be a good thing for overall emerging economy growth. And as wages rise and China moves up the value chain, its exit from labor-intensive manufacturing will create opportunities for growth in those industries for lower-income economies.

In sum, these considerations suggest that if emerging economies continue to build on structural and institutional reforms that helped improve their growth performance in the past two decades or so, they could continue to capture growth opportunities in the period ahead and sustain robust growth.

References

Bulman, David, Maya Eden, and Ha Nguyen. 2012. "Transitioning from Low-Income Growth to High-Income Growth: Is There a Middle-Income Trap?" World Bank, Washington, DC.

Lin, Justin Yifu. 2012a. *New Structural Economics: A Framework for Rethinking Development and Policy,* Washington, DC: World Bank.

Lin, Justin Yifu. 2012b. *The Quest for Prosperity: How Developing Economies Can Take Off.* Princeton, NJ: Princeton University Press.

World Bank. 2012. "Restoring and Sustaining Growth." Paper prepared by World Bank staff for the G20, June.

3

Population Quantity, Quality, and Mobility

Jere R. Behrman and Hans-Peter Kohler

3.1 Introduction

Population quality, quality, and mobility are affected by past economic development, and they help shape current and future economic development. In some basic sense, the quality of the population is the essence of development—if development focuses on increasing human capabilities as an end in itself, as Sen (1985) and others have suggested. Such a definition seems intrinsically related to the "Towards a Better Global Economy" project's concern with global citizens.

This chapter considers how population quality, quality, and mobility have evolved in recent history to their present status. It presents projections of their evolution and examines possible policy implications of their evolution that might lead to a better global economy for global citizens as the century progresses.

The next four sections set the stage by reviewing recent developments and projections over coming decades. In section 3.2, the demographic transition

*The authors are grateful to the Global Citizens Foundation and the core and project management members of the "Towards a Better Global Economy" project team, particularly Nancy Birdsall and their peer reviewer, Ronald Lee, for useful comments and suggestions on the concept notes on which this chapter is based and on the draft of this chapter that was presented at the project workshop held March 2, 2013, at the University of Pennsylvania.

framework is used to help guide understanding of the interactions between some important dimensions of population quality, quality, and mobility. Important dimensions of investment in the quality of the population are then considered as they relate to education (section 3.3) and to health and nutrition (section 3.4), and to the mobility of the population as they relate to urbanization and international migration (section 3.5). Section 3.6 discusses some major policy implications for future decades. Section 3.7 presents some concluding remarks.

3.2 Population Quality, Quality, and Mobility and the Demographic Transition

A useful framework for understanding the divergent contemporary and future trends in the quality, quality, and mobility of the human population in a global context is the *demographic transition* framework. It captures in broad descriptive terms the main trends that have, during the past one or two centuries, shaped national and global populations, and that will continue to do so throughout most of the twenty-first century.

Demographic transitions, including transitions still in process in the developing world, are frequently perceived as resulting from the economic and technological changes of the modern era that have led to economic development, mass communication, effective public health programs, contraceptive methods, and related social changes. Before the start of the demographic transition, lives were short (about 30 years on average), survival at all stages of life was relatively uncertain, fertility rates were high (with total fertility rates [TFRs] of about five to seven children per woman), population growth was slow, and populations were relatively young (Figure 3.1). During the demographic transition, first mortality and then fertility declines, resulting initially in an increase and then in a decrease in the population growth rate. The age structure of the population is also transformed. Initially, the population becomes "younger," as a result of the rapid increase of births and a decline in infant mortality; later, the population becomes "older," as a result of smaller birth cohorts, increased longevity, and the aging of the earlier large cohorts. Toward the end of the demographic transition, population growth is lower (and potentially ceases or becomes negative); fertility is lower; life expectancy is higher, with mortality risks low to very low at young and adult ages and deaths concentrated at older ages; and the population age structure is relatively old (Lee 2003, 2011). Family structures, life courses, and social and economic contexts are also fundamentally transformed (Lee and Reher 2011), with important implications for social and economic development that may further facilitate the demographic transition (Figure 3.2).

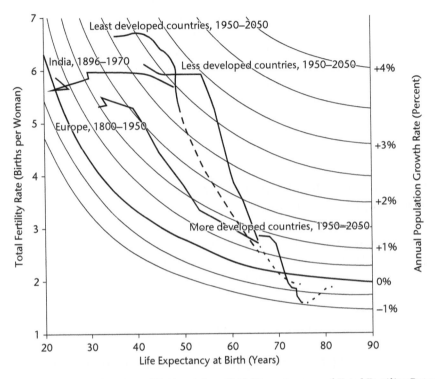

Figure 3.1 Past and Projected Trajectories of Life Expectancy and Total Fertility Rates with Population Growth Isoquants in More, Less, and Least Developed Countries

Note: The contours (iso-population growth curves) illustrate the steady-state population growth corresponding to constant fertility and mortality at the indicated levels, with zero population growth on the dark contour and positive population growth toward the upper right above this curve. The demographic transition appears first as a move to the right due to increased life expectancy with little change in fertility so higher population growth-growth contours are attained; then a diagonal downward movement toward the right occurs reflecting the simultaneous decline in fertility and mortality, recrossing contours toward lower rates of population growth.

Source: Lee (2003).

In contemporary high-income countries, the demographic transition occurred mostly in the late nineteenth and early to mid-twentieth centuries. Post–World War II population trends were often characterized by a baby boom and baby bust (including in some cases trends to very low fertility) and a continued increase in longevity. In these countries, the demographic transition often coincided with periods of rapid economic development, with the two trends inherently intertwined to facilitate broad economic growth and increases in per capita income for most citizens (Galor 2012).

In today's low- and middle-income countries, most of the demographic transition commenced after World War II. It was initially characterized by a rapid and sustained increase in life expectancy, followed more recently by an—often rapid—decline in fertility. The demographic transition in

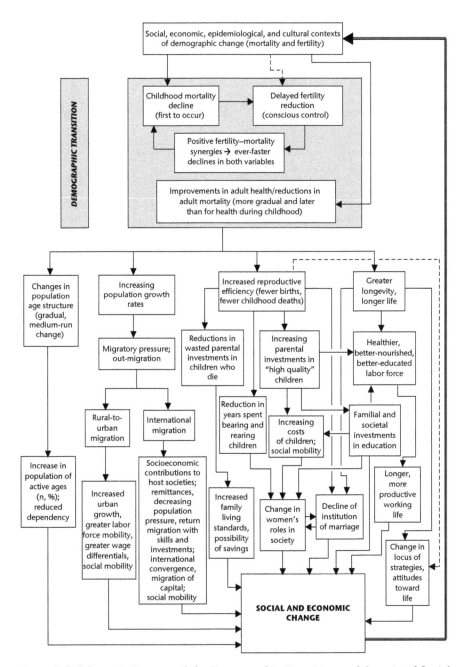

Figure 3.2 Schematic Framework for Demographic Transition and Associated Social and Economic Changes

Source: David S. Reher, "Economic and Social Implications of the Demographic Transition," *Population and Development Review*, Volume 37, Issue Supplement s1, pages 11–33, January 2011, John Wiley and Sons. © 2011 The Population Council, Inc.

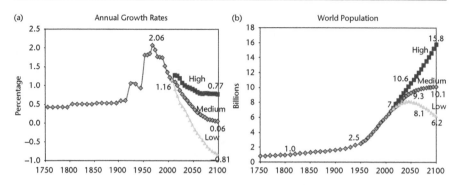

Figure 3.3 Annual Growth Rates of World Population and World Population According to Different United Nations Population Division Projection Variants

Note: The low, medium, and high scenarios assume the same mortality trends but different fertility trends with the TFR 0.5 higher (lower) in the high (low) than in the medium scenario after 2015. In the medium scenario, global TFR declines from 2.52 in 2010 to 2.03 in 2100.

Source: Global Agenda Council on Population Growth. 2012. "Seven Billion and Growing: A 21st Century Perspective on Population." World Economic Forum, Geneva.

developing countries during the second half of the twentieth century is also widely considered a "success story." Between 1950–55 and 2005–10, life expectancy in less developed countries increased from 42.3 to 66.0 years (a total gain of 23.7 years, or an average annual gain of 0.43 years); in the least developed countries, life expectancy increased from 37.2 to 56.9 (a total gain of 19.7 years, or an average annual gain of 0.37 years). These rapid rates of increase also resulted in decreasing cross-country inequalities in life expectancy. In 1950–55, for example, life expectancy in the least developed countries was 44 percent below that of more developed countries, and life expectancy in less developed countries (excluding the least developed countries) was 35 percent lower than in the more developed countries. By 2005–10, these differences were reduced to 26 percent in the least developed countries and 12 percent in other less developed countries, as a result of more rapid increases in life expectancy in those countries than in the more developed countries.[1] Fertility rates declined from a TFR in less developed countries of about 6.1 in 1950–55 to 2.7 in 2005–10 (an annual decline of about 0.062); TFR levels declined from 6.5 to 4.4 in the least developed countries during this period (an annual decline of about 0.038). Global annual population growth rates declined from a peak of 2.1 percent in 1965–70 to 1.2 percent

[1] The United Nations Population Division definitions of more, less, and least developed countries are as follows: "More developed" regions comprise Europe, Northern America (Canada and the United States), Australia and New Zealand, and Japan. "Less developed" regions comprise Africa, Asia (excluding Japan), Latin America and the Caribbean, and Melanesia, Micronesia, and Polynesia. "Least developed" countries include 48 countries—33 in Africa, 9 in Asia, 5 in Oceania, and 1 in Latin America and the Caribbean. These definitions were constant across 1950–2010.

in 2005–10 (Figure 3.3). The population growth rate in less developed countries also peaked during 1965–70, at about 2.5 percent per year; population growth rates in the least developed countries peaked during 1990–95, at 2.8 percent. By 2005–10, the population growth rates declined to 1.3 percent in less developed and 2.2 percent in least developed countries.

As a result of the global demographic transition, world population growth increased markedly in the nineteenth century and throughout much of the twentieth century, reaching a peak of 2.1 percent in 1965–70 (see Figure 3.3). The rate of global population growth declined to about 1.16 percent in 2005–10; it is expected to decline to 0.35 percent by 2050 (UN 2011).

Since the 1950s, low- and middle-income countries have been the main contributors to the significant increase in the world population, from 3 billion to 7 billion. The majority of the world population is now estimated to live in regions with TFRs below replacement (that is, less than or equal to 2.1) (Wilson 2004); the global TFR is projected to reach 2.1—the conventional, albeit globally not necessarily correct marker for replacement-level fertility (Kohler and Ortega 2002)—by 2070 (UN 2012b).

These rapid declines in mortality and fertility since the 1950s in the current low- and middle-income countries often have been associated with rapid economic development. For example, in the Republic of Korea, life expectancy increased from 47.9 in 1950 to 80.0 years in 2010, and the TFR declined from 5.1 to 1.3; annual GDP per capita growth averaged more than 5 percent between 1960 and 2010.

Although often seen as a sufficient condition for fertility decline, rapid economic development is not always a necessary condition. In Bangladesh, for example, life expectancy increased from 45.3 to 67.8 and the TFR declined from 6.4 to 2.4 between 1950 and 2010. Annual GDP per capita growth averaged just 1.5 percent between 1960 and 2010, however. Both India and China saw large fertility declines before the onset of rapid economic growth. The Islamic Republic of Iran holds the record for the most rapid decline in the TFR, from 6.5 in 1980 to 1.8 in 2010. During this time, average economic growth was relatively modest, at about 1.3 percent a year (Abbasi-Shavazi, McDonald, and Hossein-Chavoshi 2009; Abbasi-Shavazi et al. 2009).

During these diverse demographic transitions of the second half of the twentieth century, the world population grew rapidly (see Figure 3.3, panel b). It doubled from 1.5 to 3.0 billion between the late nineteenth century and 1960, doubling again from 3 to 6 billion between 1960 and 1999. In 2011, the world population reached 7 billion, adding the last billion in merely 12 years—not unlike the time periods it took to add the fifth and sixth billions to the world population.

Despite the rapid population growth during recent decades, the doomsday predictions of the 1960s and 1970s did not materialize. Not only did the world avoid the major food crises and environmental degradation predicted in books such as *The Population Bomb* (Ehrlich 1968) and *The Population Explosion* (Ehrlich and Ehrlich 1990), but various measures of average individual well-being also increased globally, in both more and less developed countries. Despite rapid population growth between 1960 and 2010, average global GDP per capita grew from $2,376 to $5,997 (in constant 2000 dollars; an increase of 152 percent); average global life expectancy rose from 51.2 to 67.9 years (an increase of 33 percent); infant and maternal death rates declined substantially; schooling levels increased, particularly among girls; global per capita food production and consumption rose; and the proportion of the global population living in poverty declined significantly (Lam 2011).[2]

This increase in well-being despite rapid population growth was far from taken for granted several decades ago. Lam (2011) attributes it to the combined effect of six factors, three economic and three demographic:

1. Market responses, which cause farmers to grow more food in response to higher food prices and people to substitute away from scarce resources whose prices increase in response to population pressures.[3]

2. Innovation, because population growth increases the incentives (and potentially also the ability) to develop new technology and knowledge, such as the technology and knowledge underlying the Green Revolution, which use available resources more productively.

3. Globalization (the increased economic integration of countries through the international flows of goods and capital), which improved the efficiency of both production and distribution.

4. Urbanization, as cities absorbed a significant proportion of the population growth in recent decades, thereby contributing to innovation, economic growth, and improvements in efficiency that helped improve living standards despite growing populations.

5. Fertility decline, which caused birth rates, with some lag, to follow declining mortality rates and lower rates of population growth.

6. Investments in child quality, which contributed to reduced fertility, improved own and child health, increased productivity, and spurred economic growth, despite rapidly growing cohort sizes.

---

[2] These dire predictions about the impacts of the population explosion were questioned at the time in the so-called "revisionist" literature. See, for example, Preston (1986); National Research Council (1986); Simon (1981).

[3] Indeed, the United States Department of Agriculture (2013) estimates that real agricultural prices from 1900 to 2010 have fallen secularly by 1 per cent per year despite the large population increases and despite short-term relatively small price increases in periods such as the 1970s and since 2000, which some interpret as reflecting basic long-run shortages.

The first three factors are the subject of other chapters in this volume. This chapter addresses the last three.

The recent decades are a unique period in global demographic history: after doubling in only 39 years from 3 billion to 6 billion, the global population is unlikely to double again. In the United Nations Population Division's medium projection, global population will level off at about 10.1 billion in 2100; even in the high-fertility scenario, global population will remain below 16 billion.[4] Estimates of the Earth's carrying capacity are of little help in assessing whether this growth is sustainable or compatible with maintaining or even improving living standards (Cohen 1995a, b). And although adding another 3 billion people to the global population without undermining past progress in global living standards or measures of well-being—or perhaps even improving upon them—will remain a challenge, the tone of the population debate and the perceived urgency of "the population problem" has dramatically changed in recent decades. The *Economist,* for example, has featured major articles with titles such as "Go forth and multiply a lot less: Lower fertility is changing the world for the better" (2009) and "The world's population will reach 7 billion at the end of October [2011]. Don't panic" (2011). Although challenges of accommodating population growth remain, most recent press coverage of the world's 7 billion population (for example, *National Geographic* 2011; Osotimehin 2011; Roberts 2011; *The Economist* 2011a, b, c) has been much less alarmist than earlier discussions, which echoed the fears expressed in books such as *The Population Bomb* (for analyses of earlier discussion of the population problem, see Wilmoth and Ball 1992). One possible reason for this shift in perceptions is that in many developing countries, as a result of substantial declines in fertility, future population growth is driven much more by population momentum— that is, expected increases in the number of people of primary reproductive age in the next decades that result from young age distributions and high previous rates of population growth—than by high current or future TFRs. The major exceptions to this trend are a set of high-fertility, low-income countries, concentrated in Sub-Saharan Africa, in which population is expected to grow significantly as a result of continued high fertility.

Because different countries have progressed (or are still progressing) through the demographic transition at different times and at different speeds, the systematic unfolding of changes in population size, structure,

---

[4] For most of the projections used in this chapter, the United Nations Population Division presents high, medium, and low variants. Figure 2.3 includes different variants. In the rest of this chapter, only the medium variant is presented in most cases, in order to keep the presentation clearer. The United Nations Population Division periodically revises its estimates. 2012 revisions were announced on 13 June 2013, after this chapter was completed (UN 2013). They imply an increase of about 3 percent for 2050 over the previous medium variant projections, a change over four decades that is within a 95 percent confidence interval for the previous estimates and that does not change anything substantive in this chapter.

and composition during the demographic transition continues to set the stage for major population trends—and major global divergences in these trends—for the twenty-first century. As a result of divergences in the global demographic transition during the twentieth century, the global population faces a set of diverse challenges in the next decades that are likely to have profound impacts on both human and economic development. The following points focus on population quantity and age structure; issues related to population quality and mobility are covered in the next three sections.

- Almost everywhere, life expectancy is now longer and fertility lower. Arguably the most profound changes during the global demographic transition have been that lives almost everywhere became longer, mortality risks at most ages declined, and fertility rates decreased. The extent of these trends varies significantly across countries, regions, and sometimes subpopulations (these differences are discussed below). However, almost universally, the past few decades brought about changes that resulted in significant increases in life expectancy (especially for children and young adults), a reduction in the variance in the age at death and thus reduced uncertainty about survival at young and adult ages, and a reduction in the fraction of the life course that is closely intertwined with childbearing and child-rearing.

- Population growth remains significant in selected low-income countries. Despite decreases in global mortality and fertility—and the resulting recent declines in the rate of global population growth—the demographic transition remains an unfinished success story. High fertility and rapid population growth remain important concerns in many of the least developed countries, which may be most vulnerable to the consequences of population growth. For example, because fertility declines in Sub-Saharan Africa in recent years were less rapid than previously expected (Ezeh et al. 2009), the United Nations unexpectedly revised its 2010 forecast for the world population to 10 billion, up from 9 billion (UN 2011). A report prepared for the 2012 World Economic Forum (Global Agenda Council on Population Growth 2012) identifies 58 high-fertility countries, defined as countries with net reproduction rates (NRR) of more than 1.5 that have intrinsic population growth rates of 1.4 percent or higher. These countries are concentrated in Africa (39 of the 55 countries on the continent have high fertility), although some are in Asia (9 countries), Oceania (6 countries), and Latin America (4 countries) (Figure 3.4). The United Nations classifies almost two-thirds of these high-fertility countries as least developed, and 38 of the 48 countries classified as least developed have high fertility. Most high-fertility countries have current population growth rates of 2.5 percent or higher, which, if maintained,

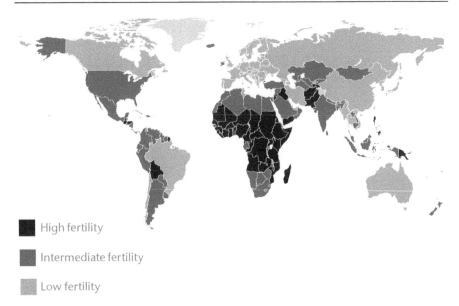

High fertility

Intermediate fertility

Low fertility

Figure 3.4 Countries According to Fertility Levels, 2005–10

Source: Global Agenda Council on Population Growth. 2012. "Seven Billion and Growing: A 21st Century Perspective on Population." World Economic Forum, Geneva.

Note: Low fertility countries have net reproduction rates (NRR, daughters born per woman) of less than one; intermediate fertility countries have NRR between 1.0 and 1.5; high fertility countries have NRR above 1.5.

would imply a doubling of the population every 27.7 years. Female education levels (as indicated by illiteracy) and contraceptive use tend to be relatively low in high-fertility countries. Despite currently having only about 18 percent of the world population, high-fertility countries account for about 38 percent of the 78 million people added annually to the world population. Based on UN median population projections, the TFR in high-fertility countries is projected to decline to 2.8 by 2050 and to 2.1 by 2100. Despite these projected declines, current high-fertility countries will make the largest contribution to the annual increment of the world population after 2018; after 2060, world population is projected to grow exclusively as a result of population growth in the current high-fertility countries. During the twenty-first century, therefore, these countries will be the major contributors to continued world population growth. Past and continued progress in reducing mortality, combined with sustained fertility levels that do not drop to 2.1 until 2100 in the United Nation's median projection, will be a primary cause of this rapid population growth (another important factor is the population momentum that results from the very young age structures in these countries). Because of these patterns, the population is projected to become increasingly concentrated in Asia and Africa (Figure 3.5). Asia is projected to

147

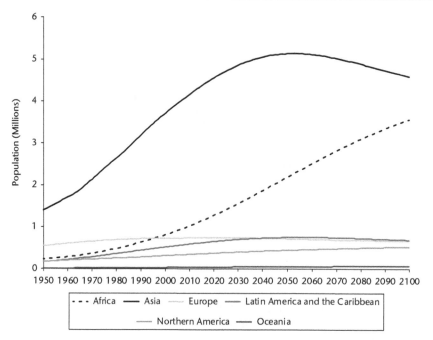

Figure 3.5 Estimated and Projected Regional Populations (Medium Variants), 1950–2100

Source: UN (2011b).

remain the most populous major region in the world throughout the twenty-first century, but Africa will gain ground as its population more than triples, from 1 billion in 2011 to 3.6 billion in 2100.

- The population is aging in high-income—and increasingly in middle-income—countries. As a result of continued progress in reducing mortality, including at old and oldest ages, and decades of low—sometimes very low—fertility, many high-income countries face rapid population aging. The most rapidly growing age segments in these countries—sometimes the only growing age segments—are old or very old, and old-age dependency ratios are likely to increase significantly in coming decades. These trends give rise to concerns about the sustainability of intergenerational transfer schemes (such as public pensions, which shift resources from the working to the elderly) and the implications of population aging on productivity; innovation; and social, economic, and psychological well-being.

- In medium- and selected low-income countries, population growth is slowing, fertility is falling, and the population is aging. Population aging in high-income countries occurs in societies with well-developed social institutions, including extensive intergenerational transfer schemes.

An accelerating trend in coming decades will be the emergence of rapid population aging in low- and middle-income countries. Slogans such as "China may get old before it gets rich" capture concerns that population changes in such countries pose unique challenges from the perspective of people and societies, including the need to provide health services to and prevent poverty among the elderly. Average ages are projected to increase most in the coming decades in Latin America and the Caribbean and in South Asia, not in high-income or East Asian countries, where the population is already relatively old. The proportion of the population that is older than 60 or 65, however, will continue to increase most rapidly in high-income countries and in East Asia in the next few decades. This is a particularly relevant group for intergenerational transfers, given age-related retirement and morbidity patterns.

- A large cohort of young people—a "youth bulge"—is transitioning into adulthood in many lower-middle income countries. In many low- and middle-income countries that have experienced significant declines in fertility in recent years, the total number of youth——often defined as 15- to 25-year-olds—is peaking, both absolutely and as a proportion of the population. This transition of large cohorts into adulthood has the potential to lower dependency ratios, yielding significant "demographic dividends" through the increased number of productive workers relative to the young and the old—but only if the large cohorts are effectively integrated into labor markets. Where such integration is not accomplished—as a result of failures of labor markets and related institutions and governmental policies—the economic benefits of low dependency ratios may not be fully realized. Moreover, a youth bulge that translates into high levels of unemployment or underemployment of young adults has the potential to cause political instability, potentially contributing to civil conflicts.

- Gender imbalances are increasing, with Asia becoming more male and the elderly population everywhere becoming more female. Sustained long-term gender imbalances are likely to characterize large parts of the global population in the next decades. In some Asian countries—including China and India—longstanding preferences for sons have caused a shift in the gender ratio at birth toward boys and a significant overrepresentation of men among young adults. In China, for example, the ratio of males to females at birth increased from 1.07 in 1950 to 1.20 in 2010, and the ratio among people under the age of 20 increased from 1.12 to about 1.19 (UN 2011). In India, these ratios increased from 1.06 to 1.08 at birth and from 1.05 to 1.09 for people under 20. Overrepresentation of men among young adult populations raises important concerns about marriage, fertility, intergenerational relations, and the support of aging populations, as well as political stability and labor markets. While men are increasingly overrepresented among young people in most of Asia (with some exceptions, such as Korea), globally the elderly population is becoming more and more dominated by women, as a result of their longer life expectancy and lower mortality.

An important aspect of this discussion is that the divergent population trends projected over the next decades are systematically related to the demographic transition—and the different timing and speed of this transition across countries and regions—during the past century or so. Countries, regions, and subregions can therefore be placed in a 3 × 3 matrix in which the three columns refer to the quantity of the population (high population growth, demographic bonus possible, and post-transition older population structure) and the three rows refer to the quality of the population (as reflected by low, medium, and high levels of human capital) (Table 3.1).

The changes in both the quantity and the quality of the population that are the driving forces behind the demographic transition are the result of billions of individual decisions made in response to the larger economic and policy environments (which themselves respond to the existing and expected quality, quality, and mobility of the population), albeit often with considerable lags. The quantity, quality, and mobility of the population are interrelated with each other and with the process of economic development, with causality arguably going in all directions.

Table 3.1 reveals strong diagonal trends, with more heterogeneity at the country level than at the regional level. Its taxonomy is useful for this chapter, because the nature of the primary issues pertaining to the quantity and the quality of populations and related policies differ depending on which cell of this table a country (or region) falls in. In contrast, population mobility relates to movements both within cells (urbanization, some international migration) and across cells (particularly international migration).

Table 3.1 Taxonomy of Population Quantity and Quality Looking Forward from 2013

		Late Stages in DT and Population Quantity		
		High Fertility, High Population Growth	Potential "Demographic Dividend"	Post-Transition Older Population Structure
Population Quality (Health, Nutrition, Education)	Low	Much of Sub-Saharan Africa	Much of South Asia	
	Medium		Most of Latin America and the Caribbean	Much of East Asia
	High			Most of Western Europe

Source: Authors.

Historically, there has been considerable controversy regarding the impacts of the quantity of the population on economic growth and the well-being of citizens, of changing age structures, and of urbanization and international migration. As a result there have been substantial debates about the rationale for various interventions. As discussed below, many policies have been and will continue to be directed toward population quantity, quality, and mobility, ranging from family planning to health and schooling subsidies to restrictions on internal and international migration.

3.3 Education

Education is the accumulation of knowledge. Standard economic models of investments in education (or other forms of human capital) imply that investments will occur at the level at which the present discounted value of private marginal benefits equals the present discounted value of private marginal costs (see, for example, Becker 1967; Behrman and Birdsall 1983). The present discounted value of the private marginal benefits of investment in education is generally assumed to be negatively related to the discount rate (which may include a risk premium, given uncertainties regarding future market developments and even the survival probabilities for the individual in whom the investment is being made) and positively related to factors such as innate ability endowments, previous human capital investments, expected returns to labor market and other activities (including market-wide effects if increasing education for many people is under consideration), and the quality of educational services. The present discounted value of the private marginal costs is generally assumed to be positively related to interest rates; private prices of other factors used in education, including the opportunity cost of time; and, if capital markets for financing investments in education are imperfect or absent, the resources or income of the investors.

This formulation points to challenges in estimating the impact of education on income because important unobserved variables (such as innate abilities and motivations) are likely to be correlated with education and directly affect the expected outcomes of interest (for example, labor market earnings) and because there may be reverse causality, with higher income causing more current education. Of course, if there are differences between the private and social expected marginal benefits or costs, the privately optimal investment is likely to differ from the socially optimal investment. Although the literature tends to emphasize that the socially optimal investment may tend to be higher because of external benefits of knowledge, the systematic empirical evidence is limited, and some factors, such as congestion costs and public schooling subsidies, may work in the opposite direction.

Family decisions to invest in education are often posited to be made simultaneously with family decisions about the number of children and therefore fertility, as in the well-known "quantity–quality" fertility model of Becker and Lewis (1973) and Willis (1973). In this model, an important component of the price of the quantity of children is the opportunity cost of the time of caregivers, generally mothers. Mothers with more schooling are posited to be able to provide quality at lower costs. Therefore, as female education increases, the prices of child quality fall relative to child quantity, inducing reduced fertility and more investment in the quality of children.

Education takes place in many venues—in households; in communities; in institutions focused primarily on education, such as schools and training programs; and in work activities. It also occurs over the life cycle. But emphasis in the literature is heavily on one form of education, formal schooling, which is generally concentrated relatively early in the life cycle.

3.3.1 Schooling Attainment

Lutz and collaborators (Lutz, Sanderson, and Serbov 2004; Lutz et al. 2007; Lutz, Cuaresma, and Sanderson 2008; KC et al. 2010; Lutz and KC 2011) have undertaken extensive work on age- and gender-specific schooling attainment in recent decades, with projections for the future in almost all countries. Their work—as well as that of others, such as Barro and Lee (1993)—suggests that despite the rapid growth of the global population in the last half of the twentieth century, schooling attainment has significantly increased—not just kept up with population pressures, but expanded despite ever-increasing cohort sizes.

Figure 3.6 summarizes their estimates for four schooling levels between 1970 and 2000. Although the number of people of 15–64 increased by about 80 percent—from a little below 2 billion to more than 3.5 billion in these three decades—the number of people with no schooling actually declined. The proportional distribution is even more striking. The percentage of the world's population with no schooling dropped substantially and the share of people with only primary schooling dropped slightly, while the shares of people with secondary or tertiary schooling increased significantly.

The figures for China and India are also striking (Figure 3.7) They reveal substantial declines in the proportion of the population with no schooling, stability or decline in the share of the population with only primary schooling, and a significant increase in the share of the population with secondary or tertiary schooling. In these two countries alone, the number of adults of 20–64 with at least primary schooling increased from about 300 million in 1970 to 1,010 million in 2000, and this is projected to reach 2,156 million by 2050 (Table 3.2). Between 1970 and 2000, the proportion of adults of 20–64

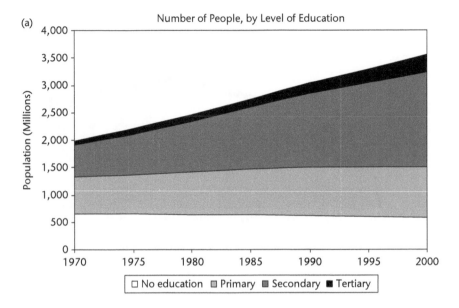

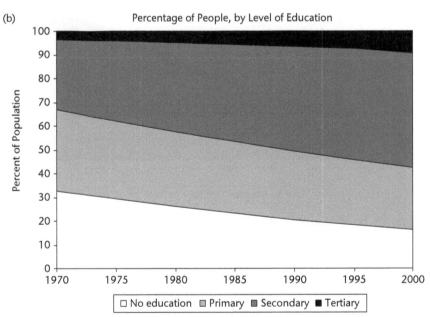

Figure 3.6 Population Distribution by Education for Population 15–64 in 1970–2000 (120 Countries/Economies)

Source: Lutz et al. (2007).

(a)

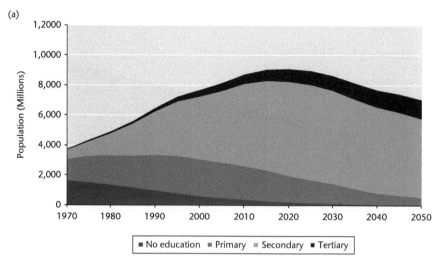

(b)

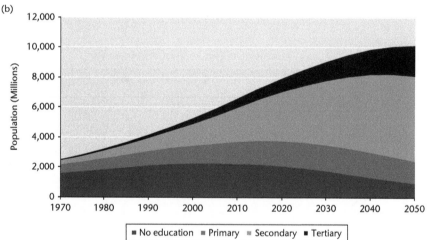

Figure 3.7 Population of China and India 20–64, by Education Level, 1970–2050

Source: Demographic Research, 22 (15), KC, Samir et al. (2010) "Projection of Populations by Level of Educational Attainment, Age and Sex for 120 Countries for 2005-2050," p. 383–472.

with secondary education rose from 17 percent to 55 percent in China and from 11.5 percent to 27.6 percent in India. The figures for tertiary education were even more dramatic, rising from 1.4 percent to 5.4 percent of the population in China and from 2.1 to 7.2 percent in India. There was thus enormous expansion in the numbers of people with at least primary schooling and a substantial shift toward higher levels of schooling in the last third of the twentieth century. Both of these trends are projected to continue until at least the middle of the twenty-first century.

Table 3.2 Estimated Past and Projected Future Schooling Attainment in China and India, 1970–2050

Country	Year	No. With at Least Primary School (Millions)	% Distribution of All Adults 20–64 with				
			No Schooling	Primary Schooling	Secondary Schooling	Tertiary Schooling	At Least Primary Schooling
China	1970	211	43.7	38	17	1.4	56.4
	2000	707	7.7	31.9	55	5.4	92.3
	2050	1070	2.3	3.5	82.9	11.2	97.6
India	1970	89	64.2	22.2	11.5	2.1	35.8
	2000	301	42.7	22.4	27.6	7.2	57.2
	2050	1086	34.2	21.4	37.5	6.9	65.8

Source: Calculations by authors from "population by education age sex 1970_2050 15 March 2010" downloaded on January 26, 2013 from International Institute for Applied System Analaysis (IIASA) World Population Program website (CEN projection for 2000–2050) http://webarchive.iiasa.ac.at/Research/POP/edu07/index.html?sb=12.

The association between schooling attainment and economic growth has been a subject of some controversy, in part because of possible reverse causality and challenges in identifying causal effects of schooling (Barro 1991, 2001; Pritchett 2001). Lutz, Cuaresma, and Sanderson (2008) use schooling attainment data by age group to estimate simple growth regressions based on five-year periods for a panel of 101 countries for which all the necessary economic and schooling data exist over 1970–2000. In their specification, schooling attainment by broad age groups enters production both as differentiated labor force inputs and through the absorption rate of new technologies, which, in turn, depend on the interaction between schooling attainment and distance to the technological frontier. They find consistently positive, statistically significant schooling effects on economic growth for some age and schooling groups, associations that may have been obscured in previous empirical investigations that used much more aggregated schooling data (for example, for all adults, as in Barro and Lee 1993, 1996) and different specifications.

They illustrate the implications of their results by simulating four scenarios based on their estimated coefficients, which they suggest roughly resemble alternative hypothetical schooling policy strategies for a poor African country (Figure 3.8). Scenario 1 is their reference case of a country with a young age structure (70 percent of the population in the 15–40 age group and 30 percent in the 40–65 age group); a low starting level of income and investment rate; and half of the population without any formal schooling, 40 percent with some primary schooling, and 10 percent who have at least completed junior secondary school (but no tertiary education). On the basis of the estimated model, such a country would have slow economic growth.

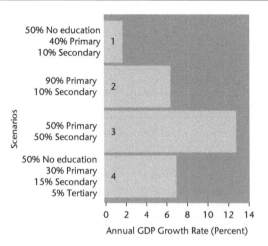

Figure 3.8 Annual GDP Growth Rates According to Four Educational Attainment Distributions

Source: From *Science*, Vol. 319 no. 5866, Wolfgang Lutz, Jesus Crespo Cuaresma, Warren Sanderson, "The Demography of Educational Attainment and Economic Growth" p. 1047–8. Reprinted with permission from AAAS.

Scenario 2 considers an otherwise identical country under the hypothetical assumptions that it has long met Millennium Development Goal (MDG) 2 (universal primary education) and that the half of the adult population that had no education now has primary education. This case would lead to somewhat higher average growth.

Scenario 3 adds widespread secondary schooling—50 percent of the population achieving at least some secondary schooling—to universal primary education. This additional investment boosts economic growth, which is more than five times as high as in the baseline scenario and much higher than in the scenario of universal primary education alone.

Scenario 4 (which somewhat resembles India, according to the authors) presents another possible direction of improvement from the baseline. In this scenario, half the population remains without education, 30 percent have primary education, 15 percent have secondary education, and 5 percent have tertiary education. This case of elitist schooling in a context in which half the population has no schooling performs better than the baseline and Scenario 1, but it falls far short of the economic growth implied by Scenario 3.

If the associations in their analysis reflect causal effects, these simulations suggest that the schooling strategy adopted by countries can have important effects on economic growth and that schooling strategies that favor "average citizens" with universal primary and broad secondary schooling should rank high among priorities even if average economic growth alone is the policy objective. Such strategies are also likely to yield more equitable growth than strategies like Scenario 4.

In addition to possible impacts on economic growth, schooling attainment may have important impacts on demographic developments, as in the quality–quantity fertility model described above. A long history of research has considered the impacts of schooling, particularly women's schooling, on demographic outcomes such as fertility and mortality (Becker 1960; Schultz 1985, 1993, 2002; Rosenzweig and Schultz 1987). Although there is some debate about the extent to which the mechanisms reflect a higher opportunity cost of time, less costly adoption of contraceptive technologies, or changes in norms and preferences, the associations between more female schooling and lower mortality and fertility appear robust.

Lutz and KC (2011) simulate the relation between schooling attainment and future population growth by comparing four school enrollment scenarios for individual countries and world regions through 2050 (all based on identical schooling-specific fertility, mortality, and migration rates):

- Fast-track scenario: All countries expand their school system at the fastest possible rate, comparable with the rates of best performers in the past, such as Singapore and Korea.

- Global education trend scenario: Countries follow the average path of school expansion that countries that are somewhat further advanced have experienced.

- Constant enrollment rate scenario: Countries keep the proportions of cohorts attending school constant at current levels.

- Constant enrollment numbers scenario: Countries keep the absolute number of students at current levels (which, under conditions of population growth, reduces enrollment rates).

Figure 3.9 and Table 3.3 give the global population projections by level of schooling for these four scenarios (Table 3.3 also includes some country examples). The differences in the scenarios by 2050 show only the beginning of the schooling effects because of lags between increased investments in schooling in girls and demographic effects when they become adults and because of population momentum. Nevertheless, by 2050 the impacts of different schooling scenarios under otherwise identical schooling-specific relations with world population size are already very strong: population in the fast-track scenario will be more than 1 billion people smaller than under the constant enrollment numbers scenario, with about half of this difference projected for Africa. (To put this figure in perspective, the difference is greater than the entire African population today, or three times the current population of the United States.) These simulations thus suggest a very

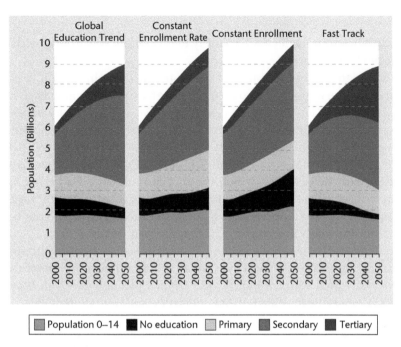

| | Population 0–14 | No education | Primary | Secondary | Tertiary |

Figure 3.9 World Population by Level of Educational Attainment Projected to 2050 on the Basis of Four Educational Scenarios

Note: Fast-track scenario (FT) = all countries expand their school system at the fastest possible rate, comparable with the rates of best performers in the past, such as Singapore and Korea; global education trend scenario (GET) = countries follow the average path of school expansion that countries that are somewhat further advanced have experienced; constant enrollment rate scenario (CER) = countries keep the proportions of cohorts attending school constant at current levels; and constant enrollment numbers scenario (CEN) = countries keep the absolute number of students at current levels, which, under conditions of population growth, reduces enrollment rates.

Source: From *Science*, Vol. 333 no. 6042, Wolfgang Lutz and Samir KC, "Global Human Capital: Integrating Education and Population" p. 587–592. Reprinted with permission from AAAS.

Table 3.3 Population of World, Regions, and Selected Countries, 2000 and 2050 (millions)

	2000	2050			
	(Base year)	FT	GET	CER	CEN
World	6115	8885	8954	9728	9977
Africa	819	1871	1998	2236	2393
Asia	3698	5102	5046	5487	5560
Latin America and Caribbean	521	718	729	809	835
Ethiopia	66	153	174	203	214
India	1043	1580	1614	1732	1789
Kenya	31	84	85	100	114
Nigeria	125	275	289	319	340
Pakistan	148	328	335	353	360
Uganda	24	89	91	105	116

Source: Lutz and KC 2011.

important interaction effect between schooling attainment and population size. But, as Lutz and KC (2011) note, there may also be important effects on other dimensions of the quality of the population, notably health and longevity (see section 3.4).

The work of Lutz and his collaborators on schooling attainment and economic growth and on schooling attainment and demographic outcomes is thus suggestive of substantial effects. As suggested at the start of this section, however, some caveats are appropriate. A large body of literature, for example, examines the possible upward "ability bias" and "family background bias" in estimates of schooling impacts at the micro level (because people with more schooling tend to have greater ability and greater motivation; receive more out-of-school investments in their human capital; live in better neighborhoods, with higher-quality schools, in their youth; and have better family connections, all of which may increase their schooling and directly affect outcomes of interest such as their adult wages and health). A number of studies suggest that controlling for such factors results in much smaller, or even negative, schooling effects.

Behrman and Rosenzweig (2002), for example, find that significantly positive associations between maternal and child schooling in the United States become significantly negative when identical twins estimates are used to control for genetic and family background endowments. They suggest that increased maternal schooling increases women's time in the labor market, reducing the time they devote to child-rearing. Other scholars, such as Black, Devereux, and Salvanes (2005), find that associations between maternal schooling and child outcomes are substantially weakened when endogenous schooling choices are controlled for using "natural policy experiments" such as changes in mandatory schooling laws. Behrman and Birdsall (1983) find that the estimated return to schooling attainment in Brazil drops about 40 percent with incorporation of school quality into the analysis. Behrman et al. (2011) find that significant associations between schooling attainment and Danish mortality and hospitalization evaporate with identical twins fixed effects estimates, suggesting that in that context schooling attainment is primarily a proxy for family background. There may also be macro effects, some of which (such as positive externalities or reduced relative cohort sizes, which increase schooling quality) may increase and some of which (such as more rapid expansion of the supply of skills than of the demand for skills) may reduce the returns to schooling attainment.

For all of these reasons, studies such as Lutz, Cuaresma, and Sanderson (2008), and Lutz and KC (2011), which are based on estimates that do not address these estimation issues, may overstate the effects of schooling attainment. Even if the true schooling effects are less than suggested by such studies, however, they are likely to be significant and important.

3.3.2 Other Forms of Education

Education takes place in many venues. It occurs over the life cycle, from conception through adulthood. Indeed, looking forward, if world markets and technology continue to change as rapidly or even more rapidly as they have in recent decades, adult education and retraining may become ever more important.

The systematic empirical evidence for most forms of such education is limited. An exception for which there has been a substantial expansion of evidence in recent years is investment in early childhood development (ECD). ECD has been widely recognized as possibly yielding high returns over the life cycle in developing as well as developed countries. The cognitive, socioemotional, and physical health developments of preschool-age children are increasingly seen as critical factors in schooling attainment, skill acquisition, and health and socioeconomic well-being later in life. In a *Lancet* symposium on ECD, Grantham-McGregor et al. (2007) estimate that more than 200 million children under the age of five in developing countries do not reach their developmental potential in part due to inadequate early life education in the form of stimulation,[5] which likely means that they are substantially less able to take advantage of educational opportunities later in life and are less healthy, less productive, and poorer as adults.

Delayed child development is a cumulative process that starts in the womb and may be difficult (or very costly) to reverse during school years and adulthood. Heckman (2006) and others argue that policies to improve human development are therefore most cost-effective if they begin as early as possible and are targeted to the most disadvantaged groups.[6] Advocacy for and resources devoted to ECD have increased rapidly, particularly in developing countries.

Figure 3.10 shows gross enrollment ratios in preschool programs in the major world regions between 1970 and 2003. It suggests that through the last decades of the twentieth century and into the early twenty-first century, preschool enrollment rates for children increased monotonically in all of the regions included, although there is a fair amount of variance across regions in

---

[5] This is the interpretation the authors give, though their empirical identification of the number of children who do not reach their developmental potential depends primarily on measures of nutritional status (i.e., stunting) and secondarily on living in poverty.

[6] This argument for investing more in early life is presumably based on perceptions that the marginal rates of returns to investing in early life are higher than the returns to investing in later life-cycle stages. It does not mean that more and more resources should be shifted unendingly from later-life to early-life investments. If enough resources were shifted from later-life to early-life investments, the marginal rates of return to early-life investments would decline and the returns to later-life investments increase until the two were equal, at which point further shifts in investments from later-life to early-life investments would not be warranted from a productivity point of view.

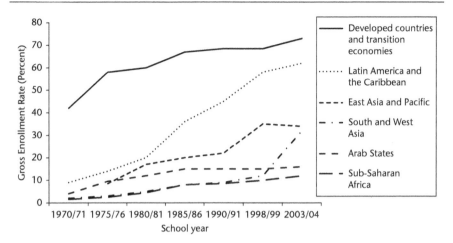

Figure 3.10 Preschool Enrollment Rates by Major World Regions, 1970/1–2003/4

Notes: Data for East Asia and Pacific are for developing countries only. Australia, Japan, and New Zealand are included with the developed economies. The broken lines reflect breaks due to a new classification.

Source: Behrman, Jere. R., Patrice Engle, and Lia Fernald, "Preschool Programs in Developing Countries," in Paul Glewwe (ed), *Education Policy in Developing Countries*, Chicago: University of Chicago Press, 2013, 65–105.

both levels and trends. Around 1970, only the developed and transition economies had enrollment rates above 10 percent (about 40 percent, increasing to more than 70 percent by 2003/04). By the end of the period covered, Latin America and the Caribbean had enrollment rates of more than 60 percent. Over the previous 30 years, enrollment increased more rapidly in this region than in any other. In contrast, none of the other developing regions included had enrollment rates of more than 40 percent, and enrollment rates for the Arab states and Sub-Saharan Africa were still less than 15 percent in 2003/04.

This monotonic trend is less clear in recent data. Figure 3.11 displays more detailed and recent preschool gross enrollment ratios for 3- to 5-year-old children for selected years for major world regions. It shows a slow increase in preschool attendance since 1990 in most regions, although in both Central and Eastern Europe and Central Asia, the ending of the Soviet Union's government-funded child care system initially resulted in rapid declines in the percentage of children enrolled. Attendance rates increased most rapidly in Latin America and the Caribbean and South and West Asia. Levels of enrollment are still low in Sub-Saharan Africa and the Arab states, although they are rising in Sub-Saharan Africa. Looking forward, there is potential for increasing preschool enrollment rates in all the major world regions, but particularly in Sub-Saharan Africa, the Arab states, and Central Asia, with intermediate possibilities in South and West Asia and East Asia and the Pacific.

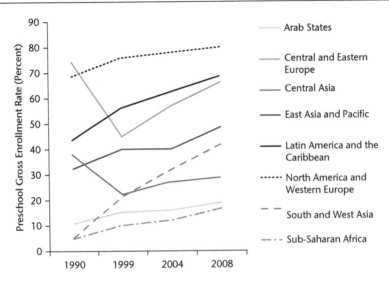

Figure 3.11 Preschool Enrollment Rates by Major World Regions, 1990–2008

Source: Behrman, Jere. R., Patrice Engle, and Lia Fernald, "Preschool Programs in Developing Countries," in Paul Glewwe (ed), *Education Policy in Developing Countries*, Chicago: University of Chicago Press, 2013, 65–105.

Most information about the impacts of ECD interventions comes from developed economies, particularly the United States. This evidence suggests that human development can be altered in early childhood by effective interventions that change the balance between risk and protection, thereby shifting the odds in favor of more adaptive outcomes. ECD programs that deliver carefully designed interventions with well-defined objectives and that include well-designed evaluations have been shown to influence developmental trajectories of children whose well-being is threatened by socio-economic disadvantages, family disruptions, and disabilities. Programs that combine child-focused educational activities with explicit attention to parent–child interactions and relationship-building appear to have the greatest impact. However, the effects of ECD programs depend on their specific designs and on characteristics of the population. Out-of-home ECD services may have positive or negative effects depending on the quality of the ECD center, parental characteristics, and the child. The effects of ECD programs are more consistently positive for cognitive outcomes than for noncognitive or social–emotional outcomes, except for high-quality child care centers.[7]

These results from developed countries cannot necessarily be safely transplanted directly to developing countries because they depend on different

---

[7] Behrman and Urzúa (2013) provide a succinct summary of these study results and references to relevant studies.

market, policy, resource, and cultural contexts. Engle et al. (2007, 2011) review the impacts of ECD programs in developing countries. The studies included in these reviews relate to programs that: promote child development through psychosocial support, such as stimulation, responsive interaction, early education, or other social investments, often in combination with health, nutritional, social safety net, or educational interventions;[8] have been in operation since 1990; include adequate comparison groups to permit causal inferences; focus on children from birth to six years old; and report cognitive, language, social–emotional, or mental health outcomes (though analyses examining related outcomes, such as parent caregiving or preschool attendance, were also included). Engle et al. (2007) identify 20 studies that meet these criteria; Engle et al. (2011) identify 42 additional studies that meet these criteria. Most of these studies are of programs that target or exclusively serve children from disadvantaged backgrounds, particularly poor children. In a gross sense, they deal with the issue of heterogeneous impacts by focusing on children from disadvantaged backgrounds.

Few studies permit even relatively crude comparisons because of the range of interventions considered and the varying approaches to estimation. Of studies that present effect sizes (calculated using standard techniques), 8 examine parenting/family-strengthening programs (often part of primary health care or other programs) and 14 examine organized early childhood learning centers (such as preschools).[9] Table 3.4 gives the medians and the ranges for the effect sizes on cognitive skills from these studies. For both parenting and center programs, the ranges of estimated effect sizes are fairly

Table 3.4 Impact of Early Childhood Development on Cognitive Skills in Developing Countries

| | Cognitive Skills Effect Sizes | | |
	Median	Range	No. Studies
Center-Based Preschool and Day Care	0.33	0.06 to 1.15	14
Parent and Parent-Child Interactions	0.28	−0.05 to 0.80	8

Sources: Compiled from Engle et al. (2007, 2011).

[8] Programs that have significant impacts on children in developing countries but do not have a psychosocial program component (such as salt iodization) are not included.

[9] For no other outcome measure are there as many as five studies with effect sizes. The estimates for comprehensive programs in Engle et al. (2007) are included with the early childhood learning centers in this summary.

large, but for both type of programs the median estimates are about 0.30, a considerable effect size.[10]

To calculate benefit–cost ratios or internal rates of return, real resource costs are as important as benefits. It would therefore make sense that there would be more or less equal efforts to assemble information on real resource costs for ECD interventions as for ECD impacts. In fact, studies of the real resource costs of individual ECD interventions are not widely available for developing countries. Engle et al. (2011) provide some suggestive estimates based on aggregate data of the potential productivity and income gains from narrowing the gap between preschool participation rates for children from families in the top quintile of the income distribution and other children in each of 73 developing countries. Subject to the caveats they discuss, their findings imply benefit-to-cost ratios in the range of 14.3–17.6 for a 3 percent discount rate and 6.4–7.8 for a 6 percent discount rate. These figures are suggestive of potentially large gains. However, they are fairly far removed from estimates for specific ECD interventions or even preschool interventions in specific contexts in developing countries, which would provide better policy guidance.

Less research has been conducted on extending education for adults. A conjunction of changes may increase the returns to such education in the future. In particular, the combination of longer expected lives, the shifts toward older age structures, the increased pressures on providing resources to aging people through traditional private or public mechanisms, and the apparently increasing rate of innovations and market integration in the globalizing economy are all likely to increase the returns to education and retraining later in the lifecycle.

3.4 Global Population Aging, Health, and the Epidemiological Transition

Investments in health and nutrition are investments in human capital, just like investments in education. The general frameworks for human capital investments and quantity–quality tradeoffs that are summarized at the start of section 3.3 thus apply equally to these investments. Although there are differences in institutions and details, the challenges in empirically identifying causal effects and differences between private and social returns carry over to health and nutrition.

[10] For the other measures used, some of the median effect sizes are of the same magnitude as for cognitive skills. One study finds a 0.28 median effect of parenting on motor skills, for example, and three studies find an effect size of 0.35 for social/emotional skills. Three other studies, however, find a median effect size of just 0.17 for the effect of parenting on the Home Observation for Measurement of the Environment (HOME) measure of the quality and quantity of stimulation and support available to a child in the home environment in which the child is reared.

Despite the rapid growth of the global population since the beginning of the twentieth century, health and nutrition have improved substantially, as reflected in part in the substantial gains in life expectancies. In some dimensions, such as life expectancy, cross-country inequalities in health have diminished, as less developed countries experienced more rapid gains than more developed countries during recent decades. Many gender differentials in health and human capital that once favored males have been reversed, with possibly important implications for productivities—at least given the concentration of women and girls in activities such as home production, which have traditionally been viewed as having large externalities. There are strong associations between increased human capital on average and economic growth, poverty alleviation, and reductions in inequality, as well as with fertility reductions, though there is some controversy about the extent of the causal impacts and reverse causality. There have been rapid changes in the provision of social sector services related to human capital investments, with increasing private provision of health- and education-related services, and significant controversy over the implications of alternative provision mechanisms. Technological innovations in these sectors also seem to be occurring at an accelerating pace, particularly regarding the use of information and mobile technologies but also, for example, in the use of genetically customized health interventions.

There has also been a shift from communicable to noncommunicable diseases as primary health concerns. The epidemiological transition that occurred in connection with the demographic transition implied a shift from communicable disease and malnutrition-based health problems to chronic health conditions related to such conditions as cardiovascular disease, cancer, chronic respiratory disease, diabetes, and mental health, with increasing relevance of certain forms of risk-taking behaviors, including diet, smoking, and inactivity. This shift toward noncommunicable diseases entails important new challenges with respect to disease prevention, the promotion of risk-reducing behavioral changes, and the provision of adequate health care with respect to ensuring (relatively) high levels of productivity and activity of people affected by chronic diseases and with respect to future improvements in health that will allow a continuation of the trend toward increased life expectancy.

The aging of the global population will imply a variety of individual-level economic and social adaptations as a result of longer lives and fewer children. With appropriate policy responses, the process of global population aging, along with its individual and population-level adaptations, has the potential to be among the most remarkable success stories of societal change during the twenty-first century, not unlike the accomplishment of much of the global demographic transition during much of the twentieth century. The share of people aged 60 and older rose from 8 percent of the world population (200 million people) in 1950 to about 11 percent (760 million) in 2010, and it is projected to increase to 22 percent (2 billion) by 2050. While the global population is projected to increase by a factor of 3.7 from 1950 to 2050, the number of people aged 60 and older is projected to increase by a factor of nearly 10, and the number of people aged 80 and older is projected to increase by a factor of 26. The share of people aged 80 and older has already edged up from 0.6 percent of the world population in 1950 (15 million) to about 1.6 percent (110 million) in 2010, with projections that it will reach 4 percent (400 million) by 2050. Globally, the 60-plus population grew about 30 percent faster than the overall population between 1950 and 2010, and the 80-plus population grew twice as fast. In more developed countries, the 60-plus population grew 2.5 times faster than the overall population, and the 80-plus population grew 4.3 times faster. Looking forward, the fraction of the population aged 60 and older will grow significantly in the next decades in developed countries, but the current developing countries will experience the most rapid rise in both the number and the proportion of older people. In addition, in 2010, women accounted for about 55 percent of people aged 60-plus, 64 percent of people aged 80-plus, and 82 percent of people aged 100-plus. In both developed and developing countries, these shares are projected to increase.

The aging of the global population is the result of remarkable and almost global increases in longevity throughout the twentieth century—with continued progress expected during the twenty-first century—and the widespread decline of fertility that has resulted in more than half the global population residing in regions with below-replacement fertility. Life expectancy increased over the past 150 years—by almost 2.5 years per decade—and it continues to rise (Oeppen and Vaupel 2002). As a result of the diffusion of health knowledge and medical technologies, less developed and least developed countries are likely to continue to narrow the gap with more developed countries in terms of life expectancy. By 2050, life expectancy in least developed countries is projected to be only 16 percent below that of more developed countries (compared with 26 percent less in 2005–10); in less developed regions (excluding least developed countries), life expectancy is projected to be just 9 percent below that of more developed countries (compared with 12 percent less in 2005–10).

The global population aging that results from these increases in life expectancy combined with declining (or already low) fertility will be far-reaching; global aging is all but certain to substantially alter the life course of people, the structure of national and global economies, and the organization of families and societies. The specifics will differ across countries, as a result of different institutional and social contexts. But several broadly similar implications of population aging will occur in both developed and developing countries.

First, global population aging arguably provides significant opportunities for improving health and well-being, including at adult, old, and oldest ages; it may set the stage for ongoing economic growth if health and productivities can be maintained across longer periods across the life course and the opportunities provided by changing population age structures—including the different timing of age structure changes across different countries and regions—can be harnessed (Bloom, Canning, and Sevilla 2002; Beard et al. 2012). However, as Beard et al. (2012, p. 2) note, if "policy-makers and leaders fail to plan adequately for the changes ahead, they will be inundated by the effects of global aging, such as a dearth of workers, strained pension systems, and overburdened health care systems."

Population aging in developed countries is a fairly well-known and widely recognized phenomenon (for recent discussions of the social and economic challenges it entails, see, for instance National Research Council 1994, 2001, 2012). In these countries, the share of people aged 60-plus rose from 12 percent in 1950 to 22 percent in 2010, and it is projected to reach 32 percent (418 million people) by 2050 (Figure 3.12). Although the social, economic, and fiscal implications of population aging often feature prominently in political debates and newspaper headlines, developed countries have the ability to mobilize significant resources to address the challenges of population aging. Moreover, improvements in the health—and arguably productivity—of the "young olds" (people aged 55–75) (Christensen et al. 2009) have created opportunities to ameliorate the fiscal consequences of population aging through adjustments in social security, related transfer systems, and labor

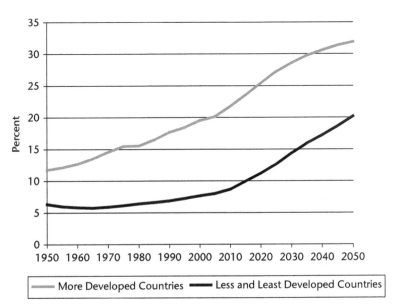

Figure 3.12 Percentage of People 60 and Over in Developed and Developing Countries
Source: Beard et al. (2012), based on data from UN (2011b).

market reforms that facilitate a relatively high participation of "young olds" in the labor market (National Research Council 2012).

Population aging in developing countries has only recently been recognized as an important challenge and opportunity. In these countries, the share of the population aged 60-plus rose from 6 percent in 1950 to 9 percent in 2010; it is projected to reach 20 percent (1.6 billion people) by 2050. Although by 2050 the proportion of the 60-plus population in developing countries will still be smaller than it is in more developed countries today, the pace of this increase means that developing countries will have a much shorter period to adjust and establish the infrastructure and policies necessary to meet the needs of their rapidly shifting demographics.

Adjustments and policy responses will be challenging given the resource constraints in less developed countries. Unlike developed countries, many developing countries will thus need to cope with getting old before getting rich. From a fiscal perspective, this phenomenon may be an advantage, as many developing countries have not adapted the extensive transfer and pension systems that characterize more developed countries—systems that may be difficult to sustain in their current form as life expectancy increases and populations continue to age.[11] But the challenges resulting from aging in developing countries will be massive. In the absence of resource transfer schemes that provide support in old age, older people in many developing countries rely on familial support, which may be increasingly challenging as migration disperses generations. Healthcare systems may be inadequate to provide prevention and treatment for the shifting disease burdens associated with population aging. Rapid urbanization may exacerbate aging in rural areas, which may be least equipped to deal with the health and social consequences of population aging.

From an aggregate economic and demographic perspective, global aging is leading societies into somewhat uncharted territory. The broad demographic changes are relatively predictable: there will more elderly people, a larger share of elderly in the overall population, longer healthy life expectancies, and smaller proportions of the primary working-age people. But the economic consequences of these changes in age structure may be complex, and they are likely to differ substantially across countries at different developmental stages and with different institutional settings and social policies.

In developed countries, alarmist views about the consequences of population aging are abundant, with worries ranging from concerns over declining rates of economic growth, overburdened family support systems, and

---

[11] A number of countries in Latin American, such as Brazil, Chile, and Mexico, as well as developing countries elsewhere, such as South Africa, have extensive pension and social security systems. Generally, however, such systems cover only workers with many years' experience in the formal sector, which excludes many adults, usually more women than men.

unsustainable pension systems (where applicable) to concerns about "too many" old and possibly disabled people draining societal resources. There are, however, some reasons to believe that such fears are exaggerated, that with appropriate policy responses and changes in the economic life course of people, the economic challenges associated with population aging are more "manageable" than is often believed to be the case. For instance, a recent report on the United States by the National Academy of Science (National Research Council 2012, p. S-3) concludes that although

> population aging is likely to result in a larger fraction of national output being spent on consumption by older persons, this does not pose an insurmountable challenge provided that sensible policies are implemented with enough lead time to allow companies and households to respond. The ultimate national response will likely involve some combination of major structural changes to Social Security, Medicare, and Medicaid, higher savings rates during working years, and longer working lives.

In the global context, Beard et al. (2012) observe that, despite declines in the global labor force participation rate (the ratio of the global labor force to the population aged 15 and over) since 1960 and the projected future decline of another 4.4 percentage points by 2050 (Table 3.5), the labor force as a share of the total population has been increasing and is projected to rise by about 1.9 percentage points between 2005 and 2050 as a result of falling fertility rates. Moreover, the actual increase might be even greater, as this projection does not account for the likely boost to female labor force participation as a result of lower fertility that has been observed in other contexts during earlier fertility declines. In the next decades, therefore, the increase in elderly dependents that many developing countries will experience will be more than offset by a decline in young dependents, especially in contexts where older people are relatively productive (for example, as a result of the absence of a pension system, which encourages relatively early retirement) and where the consumption of older people does not exceed that of prime-age adults as much as it does in developed countries, where the health care costs associated with old age are high (Figure 3.13) (Lee and Mason 2011). As a result, the total dependency ratio will increase less than the old-age dependency ratio, and the offsetting trends in the young-age and old-age dependency ratios may not necessarily pose an imminent economic crisis for the world. Quite to the contrary, research suggests that in countries that still have a relatively young age structure as a result of relatively high fertility and mortality levels (such as many Sub-Saharan African and South Asian countries), there is potential for demographic dividends (Bloom, Canning, and Sevilla 2002). These dividends result from the fact that countries face a "window of opportunity" in the demographic transition when both young-age and

Table 3.5 Actual and Projected Size of Global Labor Force, 1960–2050

	1960 actual	2005 actual	2050 projected
LFPR (labor force/pop 15+)	67.4	65.8	61.4
LFTP (labor force/total pop)	42.3	47.1	49

Note: The projections assume that each country's age and gender labor force
rates in 2005 remain constant and apply them to projected demographics in 2050.
Source: Beard et al. (2012).

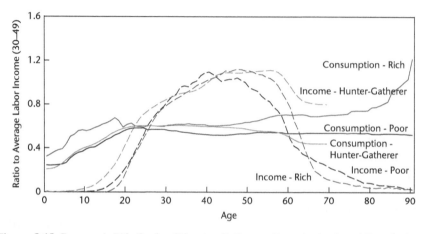

Figure 3.13 Economic Life Cycle of Hunter-Gatherers, Poor Agricultural Populations, and Rich Industrial Populations

Source: Population and Development Review, 37, Ronald D. Lee and Andrew Mason, "Generational Economics in a Changing World," p. 115–42. © 2011 The Population Council, Inc. Reprinted with permission from John Wiley and Sons.

old-age dependency rates are low, as a result of a largely accomplished fertility decline, significant gains in life expectancy, and recent declines in fertility and increases in life expectancy. At this phase in the demographic transition, there will be an increase in the fraction of the population at working ages. With associated behavioral changes and appropriate institutional frameworks, these changes in age structure may be an important contributor to economic growth.

In summary, one of the most widely cited concerns about population aging—that there will be a crushing rise in old-age dependency unless the labor force participation of the elderly drastically increases—appears not to be warranted for the world as a whole. But population aging during the next decades will exhibit considerable heterogeneity, in both the pace and the extent of aging and the social and economic challenges that stem from it. In developed countries—which already have relatively old age structures, as a result of decades of low fertility and significant increases in life expectancy during the twentieth century—additional gains in life expectancy occur primarily at older ages. Developed countries also have had low and below-replacement fertility for several decades, which is likely to persist. Together these trends imply that the size of the labor force— both in absolute numbers and as a fraction of the population—is likely to decline, if one assumes that the age range during which people are economically active remains constant—something that may not be the case.

To reduce the fiscal and economic consequences of population aging, countries can provide individuals with more choice with regard to the timing of retirement and encourage them to internalize some of the costs of early retirement and/or privatize some of the benefits of delayed retirement. This response is facilitated by improved health at "young old ages" and technological and medical progress that allows improved management of some chronic health conditions. In particular, many developed countries have social security systems that implicitly encourage relatively early retirement (at 60–65). As a consequence, despite substantial expansion of life expectancy at 65, the age at retirement in many developed countries declined or remained constant during the second half of the twentieth century. Life expectancies in 43 countries, most of which are developed, rose an average of nine years from 1965 to 2005, but the average legal retirement age rose by only about six months (Börsch-Supan 2005). Eliminating some of the incentives for early retirement by aligning the social and private costs and benefits of individuals' timing of retirement is therefore likely to result in delayed retirement.

These additional working years may be years of relatively high productivity: the evidence on decline of productivity with age is mixed, and the assumption that older people are less productive than younger people is not generally true. For example, a National Research Council (2012) report for the United States concludes that "the estimates all indicate that the age composition effect on productivity for the U.S. labor force over the next two decades is very small.... [Therefore] there is likely to be a negligible effect of the age composition of the labor force on aggregate productivity over the next two decades." Whether this optimistic assessment is accurate in the case of less developed and least developed countries, where the adult and "young old" population is often less healthy, is not clear, as detailed empirical evidence is missing.

Some countries, such as Germany and the United States, have made progress toward reducing incentives for early retirement. In other countries, raising the retirement age and making changes to the pension system that remove incentives to retire early has proven controversial and difficult. In France, for example, increases in the retirement age were reversed after social protests. Despite the difficulties of adjusting to the challenges of population aging, individually and collectively, there will almost certainly be fundamental changes in behaviors and individuals' organization of the life course.

At the same time, institutions and public policies will reflect the new meaning of aging and, along with it, the altered needs and capacities of older people. Broadly speaking, these changes will most likely entail a multifaceted response that includes raising the legal retirement age, investing in older people so that they can continue to learn and contribute to society, rethinking business practices (such as work schedules) to facilitate the participation of older workers, making sure that there are adequate social protections (such as pensions) in place, and reforming health systems to better meet the needs of older people.

In addition, recognizing that health at older ages is affected by lifelong investment in health and the cumulative effects of behaviors (including diet, smoking, and inactivity) across the life course, an important response to population aging will be to emphasize investment in both physical and mental health throughout the life course so that people remain healthy as they age. Essential elements of such policies include the promotion of healthy behaviors, the provision of education throughout the life course, regular screening for risk factors and early treatment to minimize the consequences of chronic disease, the effective management of more advanced disease through tertiary care and rehabilitation, and the creation of age-friendly environments that foster a healthy lifestyle at younger, middle, and older ages. In developed countries, substantial progress has already been made, with gains in life expectancy resulting in significant expansions of "healthy life expectancy" rather than primarily expansions in years lived with disabilities (Christensen et al. 2009; Vos et al. 2012). Significant further progress also seems possible. In contrast, in developing countries, levels of disabilities and chronic health conditions at adult and "young old" ages are frequently very high, often as a result of the cumulative effects of poor nutrition, frequent exposure to infectious disease, limited knowledge about the prevention and cure of noncommunicable diseases, and inadequate health systems. Addressing these emerging health concerns will be challenging.

Beard et al. (2012) argue that aging creates what may be the most important global public health problem of the twenty-first century: the large increase in chronic (noncommunicable) diseases. Noncommunicable diseases are currently responsible for roughly 60 percent of all deaths and nearly half of the loss of actual and effective life years to disability and death (Figures 3.14 and 3.15). The most important noncommunicable diseases are cardiovascular disease, cancer, chronic respiratory disease, diabetes, and mental health conditions, including Alzheimer's disease. Many of these diseases share four modifiable risk factors (tobacco use, physical inactivity, unhealthy diets, and the harmful use of alcohol) and one nonmodifiable risk factor (age). Reducing behavioral risk factors is critical, but doing so has often been challenging, especially where resources for the promotion of healthy behaviors are limited.

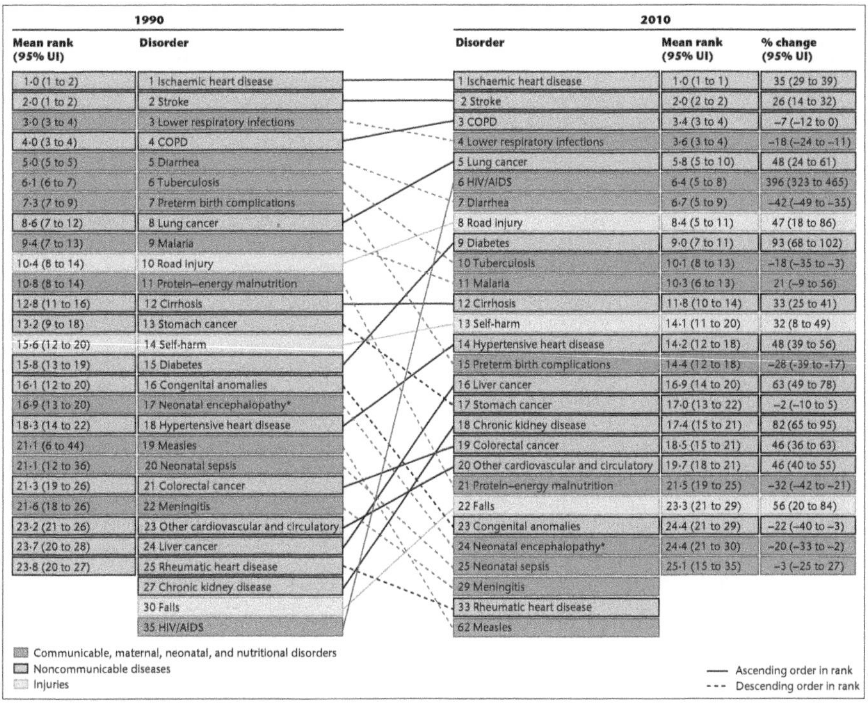

1990 Mean rank (95% UI)	1990 Disorder	2010 Disorder	2010 Mean rank (95% UI)	% change (95% UI)
1·0 (1 to 2)	1 Ischaemic heart disease	1 Ischaemic heart disease	1·0 (1 to 1)	35 (29 to 39)
2·0 (1 to 2)	2 Stroke	2 Stroke	2·0 (2 to 2)	26 (14 to 32)
3·0 (3 to 4)	3 Lower respiratory infections	3 COPD	3·4 (3 to 4)	−7 (−12 to 0)
4·0 (3 to 4)	4 COPD	4 Lower respiratory infections	3·6 (3 to 4)	−18 (−24 to −11)
5·0 (5 to 5)	5 Diarrhea	5 Lung cancer	5·8 (5 to 10)	48 (24 to 61)
6·1 (6 to 7)	6 Tuberculosis	6 HIV/AIDS	6·4 (5 to 8)	396 (323 to 465)
7·3 (7 to 9)	7 Preterm birth complications	7 Diarrhea	6·7 (5 to 9)	−42 (−49 to −35)
8·6 (7 to 12)	8 Lung cancer	8 Road injury	8·4 (5 to 11)	47 (18 to 86)
9·4 (7 to 13)	9 Malaria	9 Diabetes	9·0 (7 to 11)	93 (68 to 102)
10·4 (8 to 14)	10 Road injury	10 Tuberculosis	10·1 (8 to 13)	−18 (−35 to −3)
10·8 (8 to 14)	11 Protein–energy malnutrition	11 Malaria	10·3 (6 to 13)	21 (−9 to 56)
12·8 (11 to 16)	12 Cirrhosis	12 Cirrhosis	11·8 (10 to 14)	33 (25 to 41)
13·2 (9 to 18)	13 Stomach cancer	13 Self-harm	14·1 (11 to 20)	32 (8 to 49)
15·6 (12 to 20)	14 Self-harm	14 Hypertensive heart disease	14·2 (12 to 18)	48 (39 to 56)
15·8 (13 to 19)	15 Diabetes	15 Preterm birth complications	14·4 (12 to 18)	−28 (−39 to −17)
16·1 (12 to 20)	16 Congenital anomalies	16 Liver cancer	16·9 (14 to 20)	63 (49 to 78)
16·9 (13 to 20)	17 Neonatal encephalopathy*	17 Stomach cancer	17·0 (13 to 22)	−2 (−10 to 5)
18·3 (14 to 22)	18 Hypertensive heart disease	18 Chronic kidney disease	17·4 (15 to 21)	82 (65 to 95)
21·1 (6 to 44)	19 Measles	19 Colorectal cancer	18·5 (15 to 21)	46 (36 to 63)
21·1 (12 to 36)	20 Neonatal sepsis	20 Other cardiovascular and circulatory	19·7 (18 to 21)	46 (40 to 55)
21·3 (19 to 26)	21 Colorectal cancer	21 Protein–energy malnutrition	21·5 (19 to 25)	−32 (−42 to −21)
21·6 (18 to 26)	22 Meningitis	22 Falls	23·3 (21 to 29)	56 (20 to 84)
23·2 (21 to 26)	23 Other cardiovascular and circulatory	23 Congenital anomalies	24·4 (21 to 29)	−22 (−40 to −3)
23·7 (20 to 28)	24 Liver cancer	24 Neonatal encephalopathy*	24·4 (21 to 30)	−20 (−33 to −2)
23·8 (20 to 27)	25 Rheumatic heart disease	25 Neonatal sepsis	25·1 (15 to 35)	−3 (−25 to 27)
	27 Chronic kidney disease	29 Meningitis		
	30 Falls	33 Rheumatic heart disease		
	35 HIV/AIDS	62 Measles		

Communicable, maternal, neonatal, and nutritional disorders
Noncommunicable diseases
Injuries

— Ascending order in rank
- - - Descending order in rank

Figure 3.14 Leading Causes of Death, 1990 and 2010

Note: UI = uncertainty interval; COPD = chronic obstructive pulmonary disease. * Includes birth asphyxia/trauma.

Source: Reprinted from *The Lancet*, 380, Rafael Lozano et al. "Global and regional mortality from 235 causes of death for 20 age groups in 1990 and 2010: a systematic analysis for the Global Burden of Disease Study 2010," p. 2095–128, 2012, with permission from Elsevier.

Health systems in many developing countries are not prepared to meet the burden of chronic disease and disability that aging populations bring with them. Even in developed countries, few systems are prepared for the numbers of frail elderly who will need special living quarters, social support, and nursing homes when their needs make home care inadequate.

Many people living with chronic diseases go undiagnosed, especially in contexts with inadequate health systems, which often results in later and more costly treatment—or missed opportunities for treating them at all. The increased costs of chronic disease are difficult to bear in developed countries. The changing burden of disease and its potential costs—especially if prevention and early detection remain inadequate—risk overwhelming health systems in developing countries, threatening the allocation of public health resources and preventive measures aimed at treating infectious diseases. In most developing countries, the health care and related social systems are all ill-prepared to address the shifting population needs that

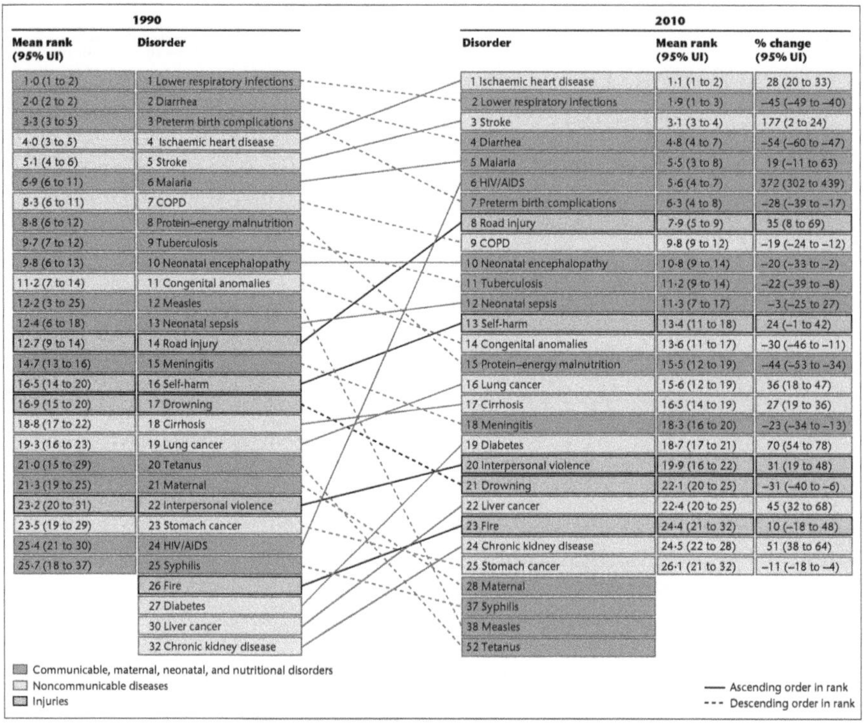

1990 Mean rank (95% UI)	1990 Disorder	2010 Disorder	2010 Mean rank (95% UI)	% change (95% UI)
1·0 (1 to 2)	1 Lower respiratory infections	1 Ischaemic heart disease	1·1 (1 to 2)	28 (20 to 33)
2·0 (2 to 2)	2 Diarrhea	2 Lower respiratory infections	1·9 (1 to 3)	−45 (−49 to −40)
3·3 (3 to 5)	3 Preterm birth complications	3 Stroke	3·1 (3 to 4)	177 (2 to 24)
4·0 (3 to 5)	4 Ischaemic heart disease	4 Diarrhea	4·8 (4 to 7)	−54 (−60 to −47)
5·1 (4 to 6)	5 Stroke	5 Malaria	5·5 (3 to 8)	19 (−11 to 63)
6·9 (6 to 11)	6 Malaria	6 HIV/AIDS	5·6 (4 to 7)	372 (302 to 439)
8·3 (6 to 11)	7 COPD	7 Preterm birth complications	6·3 (4 to 8)	−28 (−39 to −17)
8·8 (6 to 12)	8 Protein–energy malnutrition	8 Road injury	7·9 (5 to 9)	35 (8 to 69)
9·7 (7 to 12)	9 Tuberculosis	9 COPD	9·8 (9 to 12)	−19 (−24 to −12)
9·8 (6 to 13)	10 Neonatal encephalopathy	10 Neonatal encephalopathy	10·8 (9 to 14)	−20 (−33 to −2)
11·2 (7 to 14)	11 Congenital anomalies	11 Tuberculosis	11·2 (9 to 14)	−22 (−39 to −8)
12·3 (3 to 25)	12 Measles	12 Neonatal sepsis	11·3 (7 to 17)	−3 (−25 to 27)
12·4 (6 to 18)	13 Neonatal sepsis	13 Self-harm	13·4 (11 to 18)	24 (−1 to 42)
12·7 (9 to 14)	14 Road injury	14 Congenital anomalies	13·6 (11 to 17)	−30 (−46 to −11)
14·7 (13 to 16)	15 Meningitis	15 Protein–energy malnutrition	15·5 (12 to 19)	−44 (−53 to −34)
16·5 (14 to 20)	16 Self-harm	16 Lung cancer	15·6 (12 to 19)	36 (18 to 47)
16·9 (15 to 20)	17 Drowning	17 Cirrhosis	16·5 (14 to 19)	27 (19 to 36)
18·8 (17 to 22)	18 Cirrhosis	18 Meningitis	18·3 (16 to 20)	−23 (−34 to −13)
19·3 (16 to 23)	19 Lung cancer	19 Diabetes	18·7 (17 to 21)	70 (54 to 78)
21·0 (15 to 29)	20 Tetanus	20 Interpersonal violence	19·9 (16 to 22)	31 (19 to 48)
21·3 (19 to 25)	21 Maternal	21 Drowning	22·1 (20 to 25)	−31 (−40 to −6)
23·2 (20 to 31)	22 Interpersonal violence	22 Liver cancer	22·4 (20 to 25)	45 (32 to 68)
23·5 (19 to 29)	23 Stomach cancer	23 Fire	24·4 (21 to 32)	10 (−18 to 48)
25·4 (21 to 30)	24 HIV/AIDS	24 Chronic kidney disease	24·5 (22 to 28)	51 (38 to 64)
25·7 (18 to 37)	25 Syphilis	25 Stomach cancer	26·1 (21 to 32)	−11 (−18 to −4)
	26 Fire	28 Maternal		
	27 Diabetes	37 Syphilis		
	30 Liver cancer	38 Measles		
	32 Chronic kidney disease	52 Tetanus		

Communicable, maternal, neonatal, and nutritional disorders
Noncommunicable diseases
Injuries

—— Ascending order in rank
- - - Descending order in rank

Figure 3.15 Leading Causes of Global Years Lived with Disability (YLDs), 1990 and 2010
Notes: COPD = chronic obstructive pulmonary disease; BPH = benign prostatic hyperplasia. * Includes birth asphyxia/trauma.
Source: Vos and others (2012).

come with societal aging, including income support for a large population of retirees, special housing and social care needs, and new demands for adult education.

There is heterogeneity across regions within countries and across groups of countries. This heterogeneity partly reflects levels of development. For example, recent studies of settings with substantial malnutrition show that improving nutrition in early life has important outcomes decades later on such variables as adult cognitive skills, wage rates, and even intergenerational effects on the next generation (see, for example, Behrman et al. 2009; Hoddinott et al. 2008; Maluccio et al. 2009; Victora et al. 2008). Well over 150 million children under the age of five are malnourished, as reflected in stunting, primarily in South Asia but also substantially in other areas, including parts of Sub-Saharan Africa; increasing numbers of children are overweight (de Onis, Blössner, and Borghi 2010, 2011). For such children the rates of return to improving nutrition are likely to be high.

3.5 Population Mobility

The geographical distribution of population has changed substantially in recent decades, both within and across countries and regions. The basic proximate demographic factors that determine the population in a given area are fertility, mortality, and net immigration. This section first addresses the total impact of these three factors on urbanization, for which there have been and are projected to be huge movements in the future. It then considers one particular form of migration: international migration.

How do these considerations pertain to the schematic in Table 3.1? Migration, domestic or international, can cause movements within each of the cells and movements across cells if the assignment to cells is not by country but by the characteristics of subnational regions. For example, migration from poor, rural, high-fertility areas to relatively well-off low-fertility areas within some countries may be a movement along the diagonal cells in Table 3.1. Migration from poor high-fertility countries to high-income low-fertility countries also tends to be a movement along the diagonal.

3.5.1 Urbanization

As Glaeser (2011) notes, in the United States, 220 million Americans crowd together in the 3 percent of the country that is urban, while 35 million people live in the vast metropolis of Tokyo, which he characterizes as the most productive urban area in the world.[12] Increasingly, people choose to live in dense urban settlements despite the vast amounts of space available. Glaeser's research suggests that such urbanization follows from models of spatial equilibrium and agglomeration economies.

BENEFITS AND COSTS OF URBANIZATION
Heilig (2012) identifies three reasons why "the urban advantage" has important implications for development:

1. Agricultural modernization releases previously low-productive rural workers for migration to urban areas (a "push" factor for urbanization).

2. Higher-wage urban employment attracts migrants from rural areas (a "pull" factor for urbanization), particularly women, who work in urban service sectors and the garment and electronics industries.

3. Urban areas provide numerous other advantages, including better schooling and health services, more entertainment, more anonymity, greater opportunities for political participation, and freedom from traditional norms (all "pull" factors for urbanization).

---

[12] This subsection draws heavily on Heilig (2012) and UN (2012a, b, c).

Heilig claims that urbanization can moderate environmental degradation because it reduces rural population densities, decreasing population pressure on arable land and increasing possibilities of renaturalization; concentrates environmental impacts, making them easier to prevent and mitigate; and diminishes land-use impacts. He notes that the largest urban centers, with a fifth of the world's population, generate three-fifths of world output, suggesting potential productivity gains from greater urbanization (Richard et al. 2011).

There are also widely recognized costs to urbanization. Congestion and pollution are not sufficiently internalized. Heilig (2012) identifies urban policy and planning failures, including inadequate low-cost housing, basic transportation, electricity and freshwater supplies, garbage collection, sewage systems, traffic control, air pollution regulations, noise control, green spaces, and crime control. He attributes the low quality of life in many urban areas to such failures in urban policy and planning.

The gains from urbanization seem to outweigh the costs, at least privately, if expected private gains are compared with expected private costs in migration decisions (see, for example, Harris and Todaro 1970). The world has been urbanizing rapidly and is projected to continue to do so, albeit with very different patterns for less and more developed countries. Heilig (2012) notes the share of the world's population living in urban areas has risen from about 3 percent two centuries ago to about half today. Over this period, the number of cities housing more than a million people rose from one (London) to more than 450.

PROJECTIONS FOR URBANIZATION

Figure 3.16 summarizes the trend in world rural and urban populations since 1950 and projected through 2100. The changes are dramatic. In 1950, there were more than two rural residents for every urban resident. By 2010, there were slightly more urban than rural residents. By 2050, there are projected to be more than twice as many urban as rural residents, and by 2100, there will be more than five times as many. Between 1950 and 2100, the number of urban residents is projected to increase more than tenfold, while the number of rural residents is projected to peak around 2020 and decline by 2100 to below the 1950 level.

There are considerable differences in urbanization across major regions (Figure 3.17). In 1950, Europe had the most urban inhabitants, somewhat more than Asia, and Africa had a very small urban population, with only Oceania having a smaller urban population among the regions included. By 2010, the Asian urban population had expanded considerably, to almost four times the European level, and the African urban population had expanded beyond the Northern American (Canadian and U.S.) level. But the percentage of the population that was urban in 2010 was relatively low for Africa (39 percent) and Asia (44 percent) in comparison with Oceania (71 percent) and Europe (73 percent),

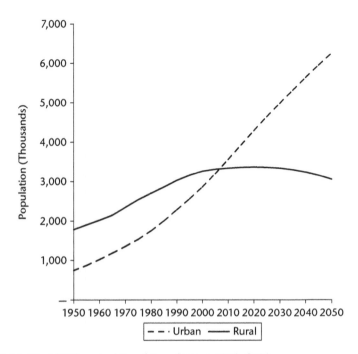

Figure 3.16 World Urban and Rural Populations 1950–2100
Source: Heilig (2012).

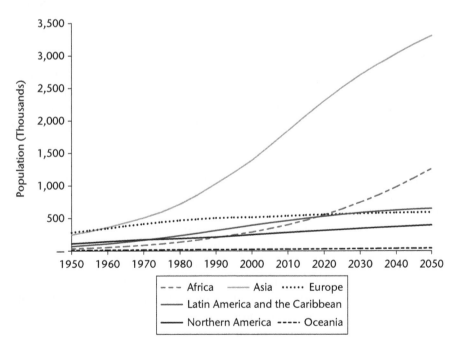

Figure 3.17 World Urban Population, by Major Region 1950–2100
Source: Heilig (2012).

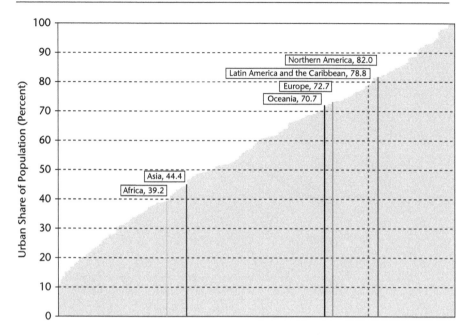

Figure 3.18 Percentage of Population Living in Urban Areas, by Region, 2010

Source: Heilig, G. K. (2012): World Urbanization Prospects. Presentation at the Center for Strategic and International Studies (CSIS) in Washington, DC, 7 June 2012 based on the United Nations World Urbanization Prospects, the 2011 Revision.

and particularly Latin America and the Caribbean (79 percent) and Northern America (82 percent) (Figure 3.18). The projections for 2010–2100 are for enormous increases in the urban populations of Asia and Africa, which are projected to account for more than 80 percent of the world's urban population by the end of the 21st century (see Figure 3.17). These projections are based on percentage changes in the urban population in these two regions between 2010 and 2100 that are more than ten times as large as in the other regions (Figure 5.19). Also of note are the reductions projected in the rural population in all regions except Africa, where the rural population is projected to increase by 59 percent. This decline is projected to be particularly large in Asia.

Megacities (cities housing more than 10 million people) have been growing very quickly. In 1970, the world had just two megacities (Tokyo and New York), with a combined population of 40 million. By 2011, the number of megacities had increased to 23 (13 in Asia, four in Latin America, and two each in Africa, Europe, and Northern America), with a total population of 359 million. By 2025, the number of megacities is projected to increase to 37, with a total population of 630 million (Figure 3.20). Most of these megacities are projected to be in Asia (22), with a few of the larger ones in the Americas (6 in Latin America, 3 in Northern America) and some of the smaller ones in Europe and Africa

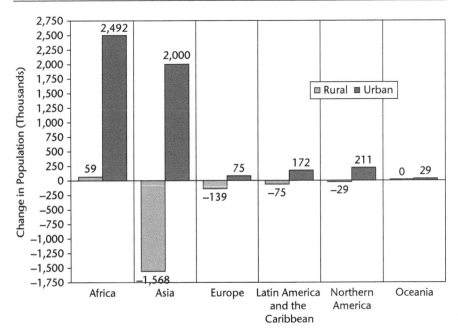

Figure 3.19 Projected Changes in Urban and Rural Population, 2010–2100

Source: Heilig, G. K. (2012): World Urbanization Prospects. Presentation at the Center for Strategic and International Studies (CSIS) in Washington, DC, 7 June 2012 based on the United Nations World Urbanization Prospects, the 2011 Revision.

(Figure 3.21). The populations of many of these megacities are projected to be in the order of magnitude of the populations of many countries.

POPULATION DENSITY

Urban population densities vary widely, with important implications for living standards and welfare, especially in relatively poor areas. For example, the global ranking of the most densely populated urban areas (areas with populations of more than 0.5 million) is led by Dhaka (Bangladesh), with a total population of about 15 million and a population density of 44,000 population/km². It is followed by Hyderabad (Pakistan), with a total population of 2.6 million and a density of 39,000 population/km². Hong Kong is ranked eighth, with a density of about 26,000 population/km². The most densely populated urban area in the United States, Los Angeles, is ranked 724th, with a density of 2,400 population/km² (Demographia 2012).

VULNERABILITY TO NATURAL DISASTERS

One concern about a number of cities pertains to the risks they face with regard to natural disasters. The United Nations Population Division (UN

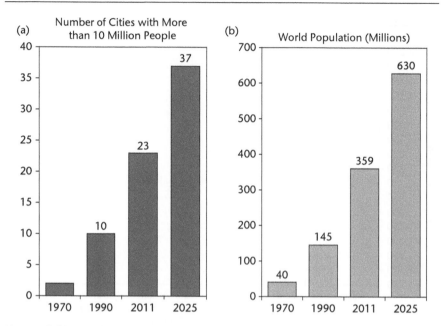

Figure 3.20 Number and Sizes of Megacities (More than 10 Million People), 1970–2025

Source: Heilig, G. K. (2012): World Urbanization Prospects. Presentation at the Center for Strategic and International Studies (CSIS) in Washington, DC, 7 June 2012 based on the United Nations World Urbanization Prospects, the 2011 Revision.

2012a, b) classifies a city as at "relatively high risk" of a particular natural disaster if it is ranked in the top three deciles of the global risk distribution in terms of scale and frequency of occurrence in recent decades. By this measure, of the more than 450 urban areas with more than 1 million inhabitants in 2011 (with 1.4 billion people), 60 percent (with about 890 million people) are in areas of high risk of exposure to at least one natural hazard. Depending on the region, between half and two-thirds of these cities face high risk of exposure to at least one natural disaster. The major cities of Europe and Africa are least exposed, with only 26 percent of European cities and 37 percent of African cities at high risk of exposure to at least one natural disaster.

In contrast, cities in Latin America and the Caribbean, Northern America, and especially Asia are often located in areas exposed to natural hazards (Figure 3.22). Flooding is the greatest and most frequent hazard for the 633 largest cities or urban agglomerations: 37 percent of these cities—13 percent of them coastal—are at risk of flooding, endangering 633 million inhabitants. The next most important natural hazards are drought (21 percent, affecting 227 million inhabitants); cyclones (11 percent, affecting 229 million inhabitants); and earthquakes (6 percent, affecting 113 million inhabitants).

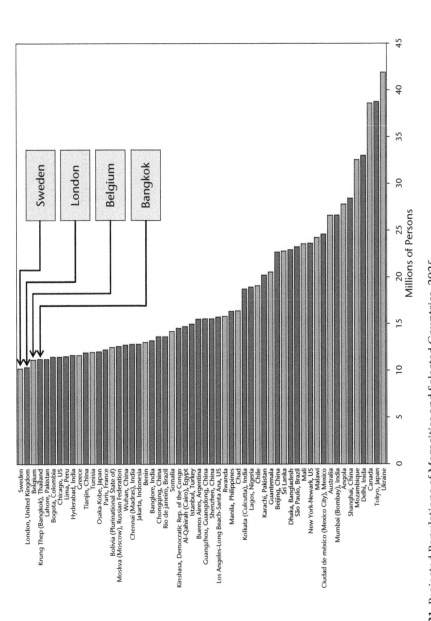

Figure 3.21 Projected Populations of Megacities and Selected Countries, 2025

Source: Heilig, G. K. (2012): World Urbanization Prospects. Presentation at the Center for Strategic and International Studies (CSIS) in Washington, DC, 7 June 2012 based on the United Nations World Urbanization Prospects, the 2011 Revision.

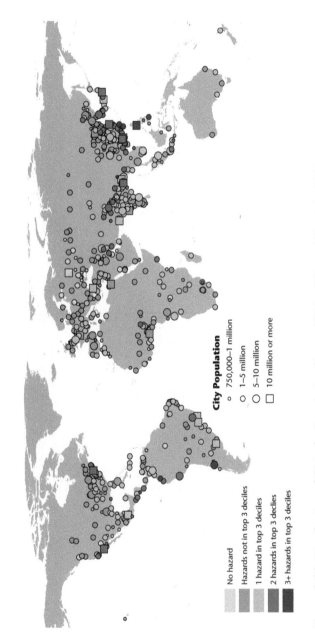

Figure 3.22 Distribution of Cities by Population Size and Risk of Natural Hazards, 2011

Source: UNPD (2012).

City Population

○ 750,000–1 million
○ 1–5 million
○ 5–10 million
☐ 10 million or more

No hazard

Hazards not in top 3 deciles

1 hazard in top 3 deciles

2 hazards in top 3 deciles

3+ hazards in top 3 deciles

Among the 63 most populated urban areas (areas with 5 million or more inhabitants in 2011), 39 are located in regions that are exposed to a high risk of at least one natural hazard; 72 percent are located on or near coasts, and 67 percent are in Asia. In 2011, the five most populated cities located in areas with exposure to at least one major natural hazard were Tokyo, Delhi, Mexico City, New York–Newark, and Shanghai. All except Tokyo face high risk of floods; Delhi faces a medium risk of drought, Mexico City a medium risk of landslides, and New York–Newark a medium risk of cyclones.

CONCERN OVER SPATIAL DISTRIBUTION OF THE POPULATION

Many governments have expressed concerns about their populations' spatial distributions. Most of these concerns relate to problems associated with urbanization, such as congestion and slums; in some cases, concerns are related to risks of natural disasters. In 2009, 83 percent of governments expressed concerns about spatial distribution (Table 3.6). Among developing countries, 58 percent expressed the desire to modify the spatial distribution of their population in major ways and 28 percent wanted minor changes. Among developed countries, 29 percent desired major changes and 43 percent minor changes. Reported dissatisfaction regarding patterns of population distribution was highest in Africa (where 75 percent of countries wished to make major changes in the spatial distribution of their population) and Asia (where 57 percent desired major changes). In Latin America and the Caribbean, Oceania, and Europe, about 40 percent of governments considered major changes in spatial distribution desirable. It is notable that such concerns are greatest in the two regions that recently experienced the highest rates of urbanization but still have a relatively small share of urban population and are projected to have the most rapid future rates of urbanization (see Figures 3.17 and 3.18). This finding suggests that governments perceive such problems, quite possibly with good justification, when changes are significant.

Table 3.6 Government Views on Internal Spatial Distribution of Population, 2009

	Major change desired	Minor change desired	Satisfactory	Total	Major change desired	Minor change desired	Satisfactory	Total
	Number of countries				Percentage			
World	99	62	34	195	51	32	17	100
More developed regions	14	21	14	49	29	43	29	100
Less developed regions	85	41	20	146	58	28	14	100

Source: World Population Policies (2009) (United Nations publication, Sales No E.09.XIII.14).

Policies aimed at modifying the spatial distribution of a population often focus on ways to reduce migrant flows to large cities. According to the United Nations Population Division (UN 2012b), in 1976, 44 percent of developing countries reported having implemented such policies; by 2011, 72 percent reported having done so (83 percent in Oceania, 77 percent in Africa, 68 percent in Latin America and the Caribbean, and 66 percent in Asia). Among developed countries, the percentage of countries with policies to reduce migrant flows to large cities declined from 55 percent in 1976 to 26 percent in 1996, before increasing to 34 percent in 2009. These policies, as well as reported concerns, thus seem related to recent and projected rapid urbanization.

3.5.2 International Migration

As a result of the differential timing of the demographic transition, population growth differs significantly across different regions and types of economies and is projected to continue to do so (see section 3.2). These differences primarily reflect differences in fertility and mortality rates, but they are also affected by international migration.

The cumulative effects of international migration flows on absolute population numbers are considerable. In 2010, the global stock of migrants (defined as people living in a country other than the one in which they were born) is estimated to have been 214 million (Figure 3.23). Although this number is large—3.4 times the population of France—it represents just 3.1 percent of the world population. Of course, migrants are not distributed equally across types of countries or regions. As would be expected from simple "push and

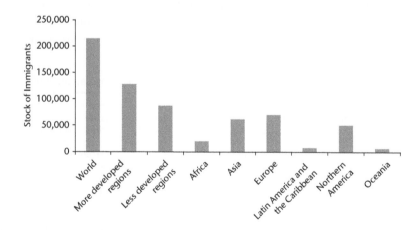

Figure 3.23 Stock of International Migrants, by Major Region, 2010
Source: Authors, based on data from UNDP (2011b).

Table 3.7 International Migrant Stock as Percentage of Total Population, by Age Range, 2010

	International migrant stock as a percentage of the total population by age		
Region	*0–19*	*20–64*	*65*
World	1.3	4.0	4.7
More developed regions	4.8	12.8	8.5
Less developed regions	0.9	1.8	2.4
Africa	1.0	2.8	2.3
Asia	0.9	1.7	2.3
Europe	4.9	11.5	8.1
Latin America and the Caribbean	0.8	1.5	2.3
Northern America	5.2	18.6	12.8
Oceania	5.9	20.8	27.5

Source: Authors.

pull" models of migration, migrants are concentrated in more developed regions, which accounted for 128 million migrants, or almost 60 percent of the total. But historically, migrant destinations have not been limited to the more developed regions of Europe, Northern America, Japan, Australia, and New Zealand. Almost 40 percent of all migrants—more than 86 million people—lived in less developed regions in 2010.

The age distribution of migrants tends to be different from that of their destination populations. Globally, people born in other countries tend to represent relatively large shares of the prime working-age population (people aged 20 to 64) and people aged 65 and over (Table 3.7). But there are striking differences between more and less developed regions, in both the share of foreign-born inhabitants and their age patterns. In more developed regions, migrants represent 12.8 percent of the 20–64-year-old segment of the population (19 percent in Northern America and 21 percent in Oceania), 4.8 percent of the population under the age of 20, and 8.5 percent of those aged 65 and older. In less developed regions, the largest percentage of migrants is in the 65 and over group (2.4 percent); migrants represent just 0.9 percent of people under the age of 20 and 1.8 percent of people aged 20 to 64. The smaller share of migrants in less developed regions is partly offset by their large absolute number of total population. As a result, the absolute number of migrants is about two-thirds as large as in more developed countries.

The stocks of migrants in 2010 are a snapshot that reflects dynamic processes of flows of net migrants over a number of years. Figures 3.24 and 3.25 summarize estimates back to 1950 and provide median projections through 2100 of the absolute numbers and proportions of international migrants (note that the number of net migrants for the less developed countries in

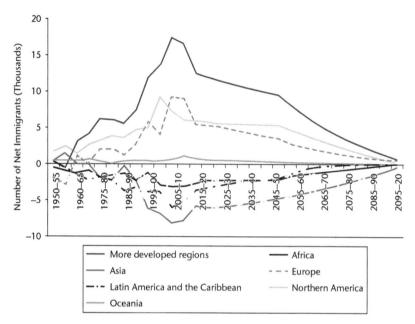

Figure 3.24 Numbers of Net International Migrants, by Major Region, 1950–2100 (Medium-Variant Projections)

Source: Authors, based on data from UNDP (2011b).

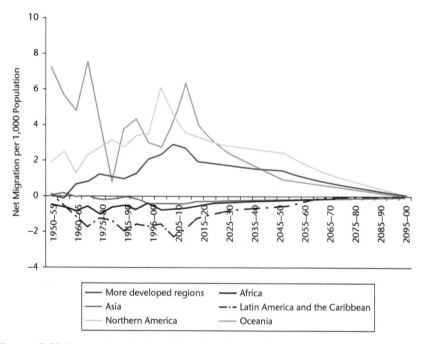

Figure 3.25 International Net Migration Rates, by Major Region, 1950–2011 (Medium-Variant Projections)

Source: Authors, based on data from UNDP (2011b).

Figure 5.9 is the mirror image with a negative sign of that for the more developed countries; also note that it is assumed for Figure 5.10 that international migration will fade out at the end of the twenty-first century).

The patterns are striking. Net international migration into more developed regions is estimated to have increased substantially to more than 17 million people in 2000–05; the figure is projected to decline over the rest of the twenty-first century at about half the rate at which it increased in the last half of the twentieth century, so that the projection for 2050–55 is less than half the estimate for 2000–05. With the exception of the first decade of the twenty-first century, Northern America has been and is projected to be the largest recipient of absolute number of net migrants, with Europe close behind. Latin America and the Caribbean was the largest source until about 1990. Since then, Asia has become the largest source. It is projected to continue to be the largest source of migrants through the twenty-first century. By the mid-twenty-first century, Africa is projected to replace Latin America and the Caribbean as the second-largest source.

If international migration rates relative to population are considered instead of absolute numbers, Oceania has tended to have the highest (positive) net rates in the past (albeit with much variation) (see Figure 3.25). Beginning around 2020, Northern America is projected to have higher (positive) net migration rates. Latin America and the Caribbean have had and are projected to continue to have the largest negative rates of international net migration over most of the period covered in the figure.

3.6 Policy Implications

There are four general considerations that are important in crafting policy recommendations for the future. These challenges for assessing probable rates of returns to alternative policies are important not only for considering policies for the quantity, quality, and mobility of the population but also for the policy areas covered in other chapters in this volume.

1. *Both distributional and efficiency policy motives are relevant for policies related to the quantity, quality, and mobility of the population.* Concern about the "average citizen" raises questions about the distributional impact of policies, presumably with more emphasis on people in the lower and middle part of the distribution than those in the upper part. But efficiency is also relevant in assessing whether policies pose tradeoffs between distributional and efficiency objectives or may instead be "win–win" in terms of both objectives. In addressing any problem, there is generally a policy hierarchy, in which alternative policies that could be used to attain a particular objective can be ranked in terms of their costs, including distortion costs,

and distributional implications. Policies that are highest in this hierarchy tend to be, but are not always, policies that most directly affect the problem being addressed and work through prices rather than quantitative restrictions and mandates.

There may also be tradeoffs between efficiency and antipoverty distributional goals for human capital investments. If, for example, such investments complement various endowments (genetics, family background), the highest rates of return accrue to investments in people with the largest endowments. But there may also be "win–win" possibilities with regard to human capital investments. If, for example, capital and insurance markets are imperfect or nonexistent for certain human capital investments and the incidence of these market imperfections falls disproportionately on the poor, a policy to correct market failures can increase both efficiency and equity.

2. *Assessing the probable rates of return to policies is challenging, because of several factors.*

- Estimation issues (unobserved heterogeneities, endogeneities) make it hard to assess both the probable impacts and the probable costs.
- Policies related to the quantity, quality, and mobility of the population require a long time horizon in many cases. But past or current data used to try to assess the impacts and costs were generated in contexts different from those that will prevail in the future, given changes of the sorts summarized here.
- Many big issues are aggregate questions that are much more difficult to assess empirically than more micro questions, because changes in the quantity, quality, and mobility of the population are likely to have market- or economy-wide effects on relative prices.

The context of the concerns of this thematic chapter are determined by the concerns of all the other chapters in this volume. These important limitations on empirical analysis circumscribe what can be said confidently about future policy options. Nevertheless, we are proceeding to venture forth, while trying to be clear about the quality of the underlying evidence.

3. *Macro heterogeneities are considerable, because countries are at differing stages of the demographic transition and economic development.* Because the quantity and quality of the population are interrelated with each other and with economic development, there are likely to be strong diagonal elements in Table 3.1, with more heterogeneity within countries and regions than across regions. The primary issues and related priorities of policies differ across table cells (though of course policies related particularly to mobility pertain to how integrated countries/regions in different cells are by human movements).

4. *Policies are more likely to be effective if they (a) create incentives for desired out-comes rather than micromanage inputs and (b) do not restrict entry or provide subsi-dies that depend on public ownership given difficult-to-observe (by policymakers and analysts) heterogeneities.* But these considerations mean that transferring "best practices" across contexts is not likely to be effective without careful atten-tion to differences in prices, resources, environments, and culture.[13] These considerations also mean that ongoing monitoring and evaluation is likely to be critical. These general considerations underlie the policies discussed below.

3.6.1 Policies on Population Quantity

- In high total fertility rate (TFR) contexts, increased investment in pro-grams providing family planning information, subsidies for contracep-tives, a broader range of reproductive health services and incentives for greater contraceptive use and better reproductive health if the social rates of return exceed the private rates of return are likely to yield high payoffs (Kohler 2013). Distributional benefits are likely to be high because the highest TFRs tend to be in relatively poor countries and regions, such as Africa. Such policies are likely to yield efficiency gains because of the public-good characteristics of information and the negative spillovers, at least under present institutions, of greater demands for subsidized schooling and health services. It is possible to reduce the efficiency costs by pricing health and educational social services to reflect their true social marginal costs. Doing so, however, would have negative effects on the poor. There is therefore a distributional argument for some form of public subsidy for the poor. As usual, lump-sum transfers would cause fewer distortions than transfers conditional on educational and health investments. However, tied transfers, such as conditional cash transfers, may provide offsetting advantages, such as reducing the stigma associ-ated with participating and increasing support for the program by non-beneficiaries, including "median voters."

---

[13] The J-PAL website (http://www.povertyactionlab.org/) provides an illustration of some of the pitfalls of efforts to identify best practice. It examines comparisons of the estimated added grades of schooling that could be obtained with $100 of additional service provider expenditures for interventions ranging from providing information about the rate of return to schooling, to deworming programs, to conditional cash transfers. Among a number of other issues—not incorporating private costs, failing to recognize that programs have multiple outcomes, focusing exclusively on increasing schooling enrollment—the comparisons presented occur in contexts with very different preprogram schooling enrollment rates, which would seem to substantially affect the possibility of increasing enrollments through the programs and make comparisons of different programs across different contexts very difficult to interpret correctly. That is, the informative comparison would seem to be of different programs in the same context, including the same preprogram enrollment rates, not different contexts including different preprogram enrollment rates.

- In low-TFR contexts, institutions and legal restrictions should be adapted to accommodate child-rearing that occurs when parents are older and more educated and often jointly active in the labor market (for example, time off from work for both fathers and mothers, more support for child care and preschool programs, neutrality regarding adult household composition for related policies). Such adaptations are not necessarily particularly pro-poor, but they may produce efficiency gains if the social gains from higher fertility exceed the private gains because of the impact on the overall age structure.

- Public pension systems should be based on expected years of remaining life given fixed characteristics (for example, gender, formal schooling, race/ethnicity, birth year) and perhaps some measure of income or wealth rather than years since birth (though there is some risk of creating negative incentives for income generation and wealth maintenance; to a lesser extent, this risk also applies to formal schooling). Basing pension eligibility on remaining life years, given fixed characteristics, rather than accumulated life years (that is, age) would reduce the bias toward the better-off (who have longer life expectancy).[14] This change might exacerbate gender differentials, however, because it would result in delays in the receipt of pensions for women relative to men, given women's longer life expectancy. Rather than using the age of pension eligibility to attempt to address lifelong gender discrepancies in economic opportunities, it would seem to be higher in the policy hierarchy to consider delinking these pension systems from formal employment histories, thereby reducing the disadvantages for people with interrupted formal employment associated with bearing and raising children.[15]

- Institutions and labor market and related policies should be adopted in low- and middle-income countries that have experienced or will soon experience large increases in the working-age share of their population in order to permit exploitation of the "demographic dividend," as a number of East Asian countries appear to have done through higher economic growth. For example, formal labor market flexibility should be increased and barriers to labor transitions reduced. Despite pro-poor rhetoric, policies that reduce labor flexibility tend not to favor the poor, but instead benefit people who are better-off and have claims to formal sector labor benefits.

[14] Kalwij, Alessie, and Knoef (2013) find that even in the Netherlands, a relatively equal society, remaining life expectancy at the statutory retirement age (65) for low-income individuals is about 2.5 years lower than for high-income individuals.

[15] The Chilean pension reform of 2008 took a step in this direction with regard to the minimum pension system.

3.6.2 Policies on Population Quality

EDUCATION

- Education should be broadly defined to include all acquisition of knowledge rather than limited to formal schooling.

- The highest social rates of return to investment in human capital are probably not to increased formal schooling, even if the social rates of return are fairly high compared with returns to investments in many assets other than human capital. In most societies, subsidies for formal schooling are much higher at higher schooling levels, the beneficiaries of which come primarily from middle- or upper-income households. From the point of view of pro-poor concerns about distribution, a shift toward a more targeted subsidy system would seem to be justified, although the transition to such a system might be difficult because of the vested interests of the middle- and upper-income classes in the current system.

- Programs to increase parental knowledge about the importance of and means of stimulating their children, particularly in the early years of life, are likely to yield high private and social rates of return, and benefit particularly children from poorer families. The limited evidence suggests that the rates of return to such preschool investments in children in a variety of developing country contexts are likely to be high (Engle et al. 2007, 2011; Victora et al. 2008). Ongoing studies on scaling up such programs in a variety of contexts, including in South Asia, are likely to be very informative for future policy development.

- Preschool programs for children aged 3–5 are likely to have high social rates of return. Moreover, expansion of such programs is likely to benefit primarily children from poorer families, given that current enrollment rates are higher for children from higher-income families. Benefit–cost estimates of reducing the gap between preschool enrollment for children from the highest income quintile and other quintiles based on data from more than 70 developing countries are well over 1 (Engle et al. 2011). Studies for the United States also indicate high rates of return to preschool children from poor families (Heckman 2006).

- More than 100 million girls, most of them in low- and middle-income countries, have never been enrolled in school. Increased incentives for enrollment of girls at all levels of schooling in contexts in which significant numbers of girls are not enrolled are likely to yield high social rates of return and benefit members of poorer families.

- Increased incentives for boys to progress through school on time are likely to yield fairly high social returns and benefit poorer families, as among students enrolled in school, boys tend to lag on average behind girls in almost all countries—particularly boys from poor families (see, for example, Grant and Behrman 2010).

- Private schooling has expanded rapidly in recent years (among poor households in rural South Asia, for example). Looking forward, it will be important to craft schooling policies that are neutral with regard to school ownership rather than favoring public ownership, successfully monitor and make available information about the nature and quality of schooling, and create appropriate incentives for improving schooling quality. Some recent studies suggest substantial promise for performance-based incentive systems, albeit with some qualifications concerning the types of behaviors that are induced to improve test scores (see, for example, Thorne-Lyman et al. 2010; Muralidharan and Sundararaman 2011; Behrman et al. 2012).

- Social returns to more general education (learning how to learn) and to education over the life cycle are likely to increase in an aging and rapidly changing world. Renewed efforts to assess formal and informal means of making education over the life cycle more effective through transparent and open institutions (rather than institutions captured by groups of employers or employees) may yield high rates of return. Such efforts are likely to be warranted on efficiency grounds, given the public-good nature of new knowledge and the social costs of hobbling potential workers through outdated knowledge. They may also be warranted on distributional grounds, although historically, investments in lifelong learning have been made by large formal sector employers and organized labor and have not served the relatively poor.

HEALTH AND NUTRITION

- Human capital is multifaceted. It is not identical to schooling or even to education more broadly defined to include all acquisition of knowledge. It is important that analysts and policies recognize that there are likely to be important human capital investments in health and nutrition.

- Nutritional investments are likely to yield high social rates of return, with beneficiaries concentrated among poorer families. Particularly important are macronutrients during pregnancy and just after birth in contexts in which women and children tend to be undernourished and micronutrients such as iron and iodine are inadequate. Such investments are particularly important in South Asia, in a number of countries in Sub-Saharan Africa, and in individual countries or regions within countries elsewhere (such as Guatemala). Recent estimates suggest high rates of return to investing in nutrition, particularly in early life (see, for example, Hoddinott et al. 2008; Victora et al. 2008, 2010; Adair et al. 2009; Behrman et al. 2009; Maluccio et al. 2009a; Martorell et al. 2010). Public support for improved nutrition in such contexts is likely to be a "win–win" scenario, as beneficiaries come primarily from poor families and efficiency improves as a result of filling gaps in knowledge and correcting market imperfections that primarily affect poor families.

- Investment in adult health and human capital may yield significant returns, especially in contexts where "healthy aging" can facilitate higher labor force participation and productivity at older ages. Currently or in the near future, the most rapidly growing age groups in some relatively poor countries, including countries in Sub-Saharan Africa, will include adults over the age of 40, many of whom who are prematurely old and limited by chronic conditions and disabilities that might be treated with current knowledge. These investments are likely to be "win–win," as beneficiaries would be primarily people from poor families, who may be marginalized within their families because of their limited productivity, and efficiency would improve as a result of filling gaps in knowledge and correcting market imperfections that primarily affect poor families.

- Prevention of common chronic diseases through behavioral changes (for example, stopping smoking); regulatory changes (for example, requiring that nutritional information be provided and restricting the use of certain ingredients, such as salt and transfats); and structural changes (such as creating walkable neighborhoods) may yield important returns by maintaining the health and human capital of aging workforces and populations in many countries. Rapidly aging populations may mean that such changes yield high social rates of return—by, for example, reducing the private and social pressures for private and public transfers to the rapidly growing older segments of the populations. Such changes in turn are likely to reduce the probability of the collapse of intergenerational transfers to support older populations who, in the absence of such transfers, would in many cases be very vulnerable, with private and social consequences.

- Health systems in low- and middle-income countries and international public and private agencies, including nongovernmental organizations and foundations, need to be reoriented to the changing realities of disease composition (the growing importance of noncommunicable diseases and accidents relative to traditional communicable diseases, on which many health systems and international agencies currently focus). Doing so is likely to result in efficiency gains given the increasing prominence of noncommunicable diseases in the developing world and various externalities associated with them. It is also likely to be somewhat pro-poor, given the relatively high incidence of diseases, including the "diseases of development," among poorer members of societies.

- Social safety nets and health and pension systems should be untied from formal labor market participation, to reduce distortions and benefit the poorer members of society, who tend to work in informal employment that is not covered by formal sector benefits.

3.6.3 Policies on Population Mobility

URBANIZATION

- Public transportation systems should be subsidized to reflect large positive externalities, and tolls should be used for private vehicles to reflect the negative externalities they generate. Both policies are likely to yield efficiency gains and positive distributional effects, particularly for poorer and middle-income citizens.[16]
- Infrastructure of new cities should be planned and built from the ground up, given scale economies and externalities. Pure market-driven approaches are likely to be inefficient, with widespread negative distributional effects.
- Megacities should be decentralized into independent districts with their own political leadership, but infrastructure planning should be centralized in order to increase efficiency. This combination would yield efficiency and distributional benefits, because it would increase the responsiveness of local leadership for many functions while recognizing the larger-scale and geographically interrelated implications of much urban infrastructure.
- Legislation on and enforcement of quality-of-life issues (air and water quality, noise reduction, sewage treatment, waste recycling, energy efficiency) should be strengthened. Doing so would increase efficiency by reducing negative externalities and improving the distribution of benefits, particularly for poorer and average citizens.
- More effective crime prevention policies should be devised, such as adoption of "smart" crime prevention ("low-tolerance" policing policy, public investments in neighborhood projects and clubs). Corruption and land grabs should be combatted by, for example, requiring greater openness, expanding/improving monitoring and evaluation, and rotating public

---

[16] This subsection draws heavily on Heilig (2012).

officials among cities. These strategies are likely to be "win–win," yielding particularly large efficiency gains for the poor.

- City zoning should include some minimum amount of green space and parks in all areas, including poor ones. Such a policy would probably yield "win–win" outcomes, given externalities and the fact that distribution of green space is otherwise likely to favor high-income citizens.

- Barriers to migration within countries should be reduced, but mechanisms should be introduced so that the incentives for migration more closely reflect social rates of return. Measures could include changes in transportation systems, quality-of-life measures, and the mandating of green spaces along the lines noted above. These strategies have the potential to yield "win–win" outcomes, particularly given the relatively high prevalence of poverty in rural areas in most countries.

INTERNATIONAL MIGRATION

- Barriers to migration within low- and middle-income countries, as well as between low- and middle-income countries and high-income countries, should be reduced.

- Receiving countries should develop migration policies that are better informed by the demographic, economic, and social needs of destination countries.

- Criteria for any restrictions on migration should be rationalized. They should be based on well-defined efficiency and distributional criteria, not family connections.

- Frameworks should be created that allow for more transitory migration between countries and improved monitoring of transitory movements across countries and regions that affect the transmission of infectious disease.

Recent studies indicate that liberalizing international migration along the lines described above could significantly increase global output. They show that millions of people could move from developing countries to developed ones without reducing wages in developed countries, particularly if the pace of movement is slow enough to allow investment to adjust.

Kennan (2012) notes that if workers are much more productive in one country than in another, restrictions on immigration lead to large efficiency losses. He quantifies these losses using a model in which efficiency differences are labor-augmenting and free trade in product markets leads to factor price equalization, so that wages measured in efficiency units of labor are equalized across countries. The estimated gains from removing immigration restrictions within a simple static model of migration costs are about as large as the gains from a growth miracle that more than doubles income levels (by $10,100 a year) in developing countries. Mukand (2012) examines the effect of movement by half of the developing world's workforce to developing countries if migration closes a quarter of the migrants' productivity gap. He estimates that migrants' average income would rise by $7,000, increasing global output by 30 percent (about $21 trillion). Pritchett (2007) estimates that even a modest easing of restrictions could produce high returns: a 3 percent increase in the labor force in developed countries through migration would yield annual benefits larger than those from eliminating remaining trade barriers. A survey of the literature on the impact of immigration on domestic wages finds that few studies report a negative impact (Blau and Kahn 2012). D'Amuri and Peri (2011) find that immigration encourages nonmigrants in Western Europe to take on more complex work. They find that such "job upgrades" are responsible for a 0.6 percent increase in nonmigrants' wages for each doubling in migrants' share of the labor force.

From a global perspective, liberalizing international migration in the developed countries would produce considerable output gains benefiting poorer people in developing countries. Thus, migration liberalization is likely to be a major "win–win" option on the global agenda. Of course, some people will lose out from competition with migrants' labor, and adjustment costs will be incurred. Despite these costs, however, liberalizing international migration would seem to have major potential.

3.7 Conclusions

Population quantity, quality, and mobility are affected by past economic development and shape current and future economic development, individual well-being, and the distribution of well-being among global citizens. In some basic sense, the quality of the population—defined to include education and health—is the essence of development, if development is defined to focus on increasing human capabilities as an end in itself, as Sen (1985) and others have suggested. This emphasis seems intrinsically related to the Global Citizens Foundation's general concern with global citizens as well as the concerns of its "Towards a Better Global Economy" project. Widely improving the quality of the human population, and reducing distributional inequalities in population qualities, is highly consonant with this project's basic aims.

Recent decades have seen enormous changes in population quantity, quality, and mobility. The world population doubled from 3.5 billion in about 1970 to more than 7 billion in 2010, a rate of increase never before experienced for a sustained period and never likely to be experienced again. Over the same period, population quality (as measured by schooling and other forms of education and by health, nutrition, and life expectancy) improved dramatically, and cross-country inequalities in some important aspects of population quality (such as schooling attainment, enrollment in preschool programs, life expectancy, and some related health measures) narrowed. Population mobility also increased, with substantial urbanization in most regions of the world as well as significant international mobility.

These changes affected the world as a whole. Because of heterogeneity across countries and regions in both their stages of economic development and the timing and duration of the demographic transition, however, they have had different effects in different places—with repercussions that will be felt throughout the twenty-first century. Differences in the stage of development and the timing and duration of the demographic transition mean that prospects and optimal policies differ across regions and countries. Much of the more developed world—including, as time goes on, middle-income countries—will experience stable or even declining populations, rapid population aging, and rising age-dependency ratios. Many middle-income and (later) low-income countries will experience declining dependency ratios and the associated challenges of accommodating "youth bulges." These countries will have opportunities to exploit the demographic dividend to enhance growth. Low-income countries with relatively high fertility rates will contribute most to world population growth during the twenty-first century (Africa's population in particular is projected to grow throughout the rest of the century, in both absolute and relative terms). In Asia and Africa, the population will become more urban, and these regions' share of the global labor market, global human capital, and the total urban population will rise.

The previous section highlights various policy implications of these changes. Four policy areas are particularly important and promising:

1. *Enhancing the freedom to move, internally and internationally.* Increasing internal and international mobility could yield enormous potential gains, particularly for poorer citizens, with possibly few offsetting losses for more affluent citizens.

2. *Strengthening the foundation for life.* The private and social gains from establishing a stronger foundation during the early years of life—through stimulation, nutrition, and health in the first five years—are substantial, particularly for children from poorer families.

3. *Supporting aging with dignity and equity.* As populations age, the potential private and social returns and equity gains from increasing the labor

force participation and productivities of aging adults—and providing social support based on expected remaining life years rather than accumulated life years (age)—appear significant.

4. *Improving incentives for social service delivery.* Improving both markets for and policies regulating the delivery of services that provide essential inputs for achieving socially desired levels of human reproduction and child-rearing; mortality; schooling, preschooling, and other forms of education; and internal and international mobility has substantial potential for enhancing productivities and well-being, with gains often largest for poorer citizens.

Improvements in these four policy areas have enormous potential to enhance future economic growth, improve the welfare of global citizens broadly, and in many cases ensure that poorer citizens share more extensively in such growth. The "win–win" characteristics of many of these policies—the fact that they both enhance economic growth and disproportionately benefit the poor—justify them both morally and economically

References

Abbasi-Shavazi, Mohammad J., Peter McDonald, and Meimanat Hossein-Chavoshi. 2009. *The Fertility Transition in Iran: Revolution and Reproduction.* Berlin: Springer.

Abbasi-Shavazi, Mohammad J., S. Phillip Morgan, M. Meimanat Hossein-Chavoshi, and Peter McDonald. 2009. "Family Change and Continuity in Iran: Birth Control Use before First Pregnancy." *Journal of Marriage and Family* 71 (5): 1309–24.

Adair, Linda S., Reynaldo Martorell, Aryeh D. Stein, Pedro C. Hallal, Harshpal S. Sachdev, Dorairaj Prabhakaran, Andrew K. Wills, Shane A. Norris, Darren L. Dahly, Nanette R. Lee, and Cesar G. Victora. 2009. "Size at Birth, Weight Gain in Infancy and Childhood, and Adult Blood Pressure in 5 Low- and Middle-Income-Country Cohorts: When Does Weight Gain Matter?" *American Journal of Clinical Nutrition* 89 (5): 1383–92.

Barro, Robert J. 1991. "Economic Growth in a Cross Section of Countries." *Quarterly Journal of Economics* 106 (May): 407–43.

Barro, Robert J. 2001. "Human Capital and Growth." *American Economic Review* 91 (2): 12–17.

Barro, Robert J., and Jong-Wha Lee. 1993. "International Comparison of Educational Attainment." *Journal of Monetary Economics* 32 (3): 363–94.

Barro, Robert J., and Jong-Wha Lee. 1996. "International Measures of Schooling Years and Schooling Quality." *American Economic Review* 86 (2): 218–23.

Beard, John, Simon Biggs, David Bloom, Linda Fried, Paul Hogan, Alexandre Kalache, and J. Olshansky. 2012. "Global Population Ageing: Peril or Promise?" PGDA Working Paper No. 89, Global Agenda Council on Ageing Society, Boston,

Becker, Gary S. 1960. "An Economic Analysis of Fertility." In *Demographic and Economic Change in Developed Countries*. Princeton, NJ: Princeton University Press for the National Bureau of Economic Research.

Becker, Gary S. 1967. "Human Capital and the Personal Distribution of Income: An Analytical Approach." Woytinsky Lecture, University of Michigan, Ann Arbor, MI. Republished in Gary S. Becker, 1975, *Human Capital*, 94–117. New York: National Bureau of Economic Research.

Becker, Gary S., and H. Gregg Lewis. 1973. "On the Interaction between the Quantity and Quality of Children." *Journal of Political Economy* 81 (2): S279–88.

Behrman, Jere R., and Nancy M. Birdsall. 1983. "The Quality of Schooling: Quantity Alone Is Misleading." *American Economic Review* 73 (5): 928–46.

Behrman, Jere R., Maria C. Calderon, Samuel H. Preston, John Hoddinott, Reynaldo Martorell, and Aryeh D. Stein. 2009. "Nutritional Supplementation in Girls Influences the Growth of Their Children: Prospective Study in Guatemala." *American Journal of Clinical Nutrition* 90 (5): 1372–9.

Behrman, Jere R., Hans-Peter Kohler, Vibeke Myrup Jensen, Dorthe Pedersen, Inge Petersen, Paul Bingley, and Kaare Christensen. 2011. "Does More Schooling Reduce Hospitalization and Delay Mortality? New Evidence Based on Danish Twins." *Demography* 48 (4): 1347–75.

Behrman, Jere R., Susan W. Parker, Petra E. Todd, and Kenneth I. Wolpin. 2012. "Aligning Learning Incentives of Students and Teachers: Results from a Social Experiment in Mexican High Schools." Working Paper Penn Institute of Economic Research (PIER) No. 13-004, University of Pennsylvania, Philadelphia, Available at SSRN: http://ssrn.com/abstract=2206883 or http://dx.doi.org/10.2139/ssrn.2206883.

Behrman, Jere R., and Mark R. Rosenzweig. 2002. "Does Increasing Women's Schooling Raise the Schooling of the Next Generation?" *American Economic Review* 92 (1): 323–34.

Behrman, Jere R., and Sergio Urzúa. 2013. "Economic Perspectives on Some Important Dimensions of Early Childhood Development in Developing Countries." In *Handbook of Early Childhood Development: Translating Research to Global Policy*, ed. P. R. Britto, P. L. Engle, and C. M. Super, 123–41. Oxford: Oxford University Press.

Black, Sandra E., Paul J. Devereux, and Kjell G. Salvanes. 2005. "Why the Apple Doesn't Fall Far: Understanding Intergenerational Transmission of Human Capital." *American Economic Review* 95 (1): 437–49.

Blau, Francine D., and Laurence M. Kahn. 2012. "Immigration and the Distribution of Incomes." NBER Working Paper 18515, National Bureau of Economic Research, Cambridge, MA.

Bloom, David E., David Canning, and Jaypee Sevilla. 2002. *The Demographic Dividend: A New Perspective on the Economic Consequences of Population Change*. Santa Monica, CA: RAND Corporation.

Börsch-Supan, Axel. 2005. "What Are NDC Pension Systems? What Do They Bring to Reform Strategies?" In *Pension Reform: Issues and Prospects for Non-Financial Defined Contribution (NDC) Schemes*, ed. Robert Holzmann and Edward Palmer. Washington, DC: World Bank.

Christensen, Kaare, Gabriele Doblhammer, Roland Rau, and James W. Vaupel. 2009. Ageing Populations: The Challenges Ahead. *Lancet* 374 (9696): 1196–208.

Cohen, Joel E. 1995a. *How Many People Can the Earth Support?* New York, NY: Norton & Co.

Cohen, Joel E. 1995b. "Population Growth and Earth's Human Carrying Capacity." *Science* 269 (5222): 341–46. doi:10.1126/science.7618100.

Demographia. 2012. *Demographia World Urban Areas (World Agglomerations),* 8th Annual ed., version 2. www.demographia.com/db-worldua.pdf.

de Onis, Mercedes, Monika Blössner, and Elaine Borghi. 2010. "Global Prevalence and Trends of Overweight and Obesity among Preschool Children." *American Journal of Clinical Nutrition* 92 (5): 1257–64.

de Onis, Mercedes, Monika Blössner, and Elaine Borghi. 2011. "Prevalence and Trends of Stunting among Pre-School Children, 1990–2020." *Public Health Nutrition* 1 (1): 1–7.

D'Amuri, Francesco, and Giovanni Peri. 2011. "Immigration, Jobs and Employment Protection: Evidence from Europe before and during the Great Recession." NBER Working Paper 17139, National Bureau of Economic Research, Cambridge, MA.

The Economist. 2009. "Go Forth and Multiply a Lot Less: Lower Fertility Is Changing the World for the Better." October 29. http://www.economist.com/node/14743589.

The Economist. 2011a. "Demography: A Tale of Three Islands. The World's Population Will Reach 7 Billion at the End of October. Don't Panic." October 22. http://www.economist.com/node/21533364.

The Economist. 2011b. "The Hopeful Continent: Africa Rising. After Decades of Slow Growth, Africa Has a Real Chance to Follow in the Footsteps of Asia." December 3. http://www.economist.com/node/21541015.

The Economist. 2011c. "World Population: Now We Are Seven Billion. Persuading Women to Have Fewer Babies Would Help in Some Places. But It Is No Answer to Scarce Resources." October 22. http://www.economist.com/node/21533409.

Engle, Patrice L., Maureen M. Black, Jere R. Behrman, Meena Cabral de Mello, Paul J. Gertler, Lydia Kapiriri, Reynaldo Martorell, and Mary Eming Young. 2007. "Strategies to Avoid the Loss of Developmental Potential in More Than 200 Million Children in the Developing World." *The Lancet* 369 (9557): 229–42.

Engle, Patrice L., Lia C. H. Fernald, Harold Alderman, Jere R. Behrman, Chloe O'Gara, Aisha Yousafzai, Meena Cabral de Mello, Melissa Hidrobo, Nurper Ulkuer, Ilgi Ertem, and Selim Iltus. 2011. "Strategies for Reducing Inequalities and Improving Developmental Outcomes for Young Children in Low and Middle Income Countries." *The Lancet* 378 (9799): 1339–53.

Ehrlich, Paul R. 1968. *The Population Bomb.* New York: Ballantine.

Ehrlich, Paul R., and Anne H. Ehrlich. 1990. *The Population Explosion.* New York: Simon & Schuster.

Ezeh, Alex C., Blessing U. Mberu, and Jacques O. Emina. 2009. "Stall in Fertility Decline in Eastern African Countries: Regional Analysis of Patterns, Determinants and Implications." *Philosophical Transactions of the Royal Society B: Biological Sciences* 364 (1532): 2985–90.

Galor, Odet 2012. "The Demographic Transition: Causes and Consequences." IZA Discussion Paper No. 6334, Institute for the Study of Labor, Bonn, Germany. http:// ssrn.com/abstract=2003667.

Glaeser, Edward. 2011. *Triumph of the City: How Our Greatest Invention Makes Us Richer, Smarter, Greener, Healthier and Happier.* New York: Macmillan.

Global Agenda Council on Population Growth. 2012. "Seven Billion and Growing: A 21st Century Perspective on Population." World Economic Forum, Geneva.

Grant, Monica J., and Jere R. Behrman. 2010. "Gender Gaps in Educational Attainment in Less Developed Countries." *Population and Development Review* 36 (1): 71–89.

Grantham-McGregor, Sally, Yin Bun Cheung, Santiago Cueto, Paul Glewwe, Linda Richter, and Barbara Strupp. 2007. "Developmental Potential in the First 5 Years for Children in Developing Countries." *The Lancet* 369 (9555): 60–70.

Harris, John R., and Michael P. Todaro. 1970. "Migration, Unemployment, and Development." *American Economic Review* 60 (March): 126–42.

Heckman, James J. 2006. "Skill Formation and the Economics of Investing in Disadvantaged Children." *Science* 312 (5782): 1900–02.

Heilig, Gerhard K. 2012. "World Urbanization Prospects: The 2011 Revision." United Nations, Department of Economic and Social Affairs (DESA), Population Division, Population Estimates and Projections Section, New York.

Hoddinott, John F., John A. Maluccio, Jere R. Behrman, Rafael Flores, and Reynaldo Martorell. 2008. "Effect of a Nutrition Intervention During Early Childhood on Economic Productivity in Guatemalan Adults." *The Lancet* 371 (9610): 411–16.

IIASA (International Institute for Applied System Analysis. n.d. CEN projections for 2000–50, World Population Program website. http://webarchive.iiasa.ac.at/ Research/POP/edu07/index.html?sb=12.

Kalwij, Adriaan S., Rob J. M. Alessie, and Marike G. Knoef. 2013. "The Association between Individual Income and Remaining Life Expectancy at the Age of 65 in the Netherlands." *Demography* 50 (1): 181–206.

KC, Samir, Bilal Barakat, Anne Goujon, Vigard Skirbekk, Warren Sanderson, and Wolfgang Lutz. 2010. "Projection of Populations by Level of Educational Attainment, Age, and Sex for 120 Countries for 2005–2050." *Demographic Research* 22 (15): 383–472.

Kennan, John. 2012. "Open Borders." NBER Working Paper 18307, National Bureau of Economic Research, Cambridge, MA.

Kohler, Hans-Peter. 2013. "Copenhagen Consensus Project 2012: Challenge Paper on 'Population Growth.'" In *Global Crises, Global Solutions*, ed. Bjørn Lomborg. Cambridge: Cambridge University Press.

Kohler, Hans-Peter, and Jose A. Ortega. 2002. "Fertility, Below-Replacement." In *Encyclopedia of Population*, ed. Paul Demeny and Geoffrey McNicoll, 405–9. New York: MacMillan Press.

Lam, David. 2011. "How the World Survived the Population Bomb: Lessons from 50 Years of Extraordinary Demographic History." *Demography* 48 (4): 1231–62.

Lee, Ronald D. 2003. "The Demographic Transition: Three Centuries of Fundamental Change." *Journal of Economic Perspectives* 17 (4): 167–90.

Lee, Ronald D. 2011. "The Outlook for Population Growth." *Science* 333 (6042): 569–573.

Lee, Ronald D., and Andrew Mason. 2011. "Generational Economics in a Changing World." *Population and Development Review* 37 (s1): 115–42.

Lee, Ronald D., and David S. Reher, eds. 2011. *Demographic Transition and Its Consequences*. New York: Wiley-Blackwell. Supplement to *Population and Development Review*.

Lutz, Wolfgang, Jesus Crespo Cuaresma, and Warren Sanderson. 2008. "The Demography of Educational Attainment and Economic Growth." *Science* 319 (5866): 1047–48.

Lutz, Wolfgang, Anne Goujon, Samir KC, and Warren Sanderson. 2007. "Reconstruction of Populations by Age, Sex and Level of Educational Attainment for 120 Countries for 1970–2000." In *Vienna Yearbook of Population Research*, 193–235. Vienna: *International Institute for Applied Systems Analysis* (IIASA).

Lutz, Wolfgang, and Samir KC. 2011. "Global Human Capital: Integrating Education and Population." *Science* 333 (6042), 587–92.

Lutz, Wolfgang, Warren C. Sanderson, and Sergei Serbov. 2004. *The End of World Population Growth in the 21st Century: New Challenges for Human Capital Formation and Sustainable Development*. London: Earthscan/James & James.

Maluccio, John A., John F. Hoddinott, J. R. Behrman, Agnes R. Quisumbing, Reynaldo Martorell, and Aryeh D. Stein. 2009. "The Impact of Nutrition During Early Childhood on Education among Guatemalan Adults." *Economics Journal* 119 (537): 734–63.

Martorell, Reynaldo, Bernardo L. Horta, Linda S. Adair, Aryeh D. Stein, Linda Richter, Caroline H. D. Fall, Santosh K. Bhargava, S. K. Dey Biswas, Lorna Perez, Fernando C. Barros, et al. 2010. "Weight Gain in the First Two Years of Life Is an Important Predictor of Schooling Outcomes in Pooled Analyses from Five Birth Cohorts from Low- and Middle-Income Countries." *Journal of Nutrition* 140 (2): 348–54.

Mukand, Sharun. 2012. "International Migration, Politics and Culture: The Case for Greater Labour Mobility." Chatham House Policy Paper, London.

Muralidharan, Karthik, and Venkatesh Sundararaman. 2011. "Teacher Opinions on Performance Pay: Evidence from India." *Economics of Education Review* 30 (3): 394–403.

National Research Council. 1986. *Population Growth and Economic Development: Policy Questions*. Washington, DC: National Academy Press.

National Research Council. 1994. *The Demography of Aging*. Washington, DC: National Academy Press.

National Research Council. 2001. *Preparing for an Aging World: The Case for Cross-National Research*. Washington, DC: National Academy Press.

National Research Council. 2012. *Aging and the Macroeconomy: Long-Term Implications of an Older Population*. Washington, DC: National Academy Press.

Oeppen, Jim, and James W. Vaupel. 2002. "Broken Limits to Life Expectancy." *Science* 296 (5570): 1029–31.

Osotimehin, Babatunde. 2011. "Population and Development." *Science* 333 (6042): 499.

Preston, Samuel H. 1986. "Are the Economic Consequences of Population Growth a Sound Basis for Population Policy?" In *World Population and U.S. Policy: The Choices Ahead*, ed. J. Menken, 67–95. New York: W. W. Norton.

Pritchett, Lant. 2001. "Where Has All the Education Gone?" *World Bank Economic Review* 15 (3): 367–91.

Pritchett, Lant. 2007. *Let Their People Come: Breaking the Deadlock in International Labor Mobility*. Center for Global Development. Washington, Washington, DC: Brookings Institution Press.

Richard, Dobbs, Smit Sven, Remes Janna, Manyika James, Roxburgh Charles, and Restrepo Alejandra. 2011. *Urban World: Mapping the Economic Power of Cities*. London: McKinsey Global Institute.

Roberts, Leslie 2011. "9 Billion?" *Science* 333 (6042): 540–3.

Rosenzweig, Mark R., and T. Paul Schultz. 1987. "Fertility and Investments in Human Capital: Estimates of the Consequences of Imperfect Fertility Control in Malaysia." *Journal of Econometrics* 36: 163–84.

Schultz, T. Paul. 1985. "Changing World Prices, Women's Wages, and the Fertility Transition: Sweden, 1860–1910." *Journal of Political Economy* 93 (6): 1126–54.

Schultz, T. Paul. 1993. "Returns to Women's Education." In *Women's Education in Developing Countries: Barriers, Benefits, and Policies*, ed. E. M. King and M. A. Hill, 51–99. Baltimore, MD: Johns Hopkins University Press for the World Bank.

Schultz, T. Paul. 2002. "Why Governments Should Invest More to Educate Girls." *World Development* 30 (2): 207–25.

Sen, Amartya K. 1985. *Commodities and Capabilities*. Amsterdam: North-Holland.

Simon, Julian 1981. *The Ultimate Resource*. Princeton, NJ: Princeton University Press.

Thorne-Lyman, Andrew L., Natalie Valpiani, Kai Sun, Richard D. Semba, Christine L. Klotz, Klaus Kraemer, Nasima Akhter, Saskia de Pee, Regina Moench-Pfanner, and Mayang Sari. 2010. "Household Dietary Diversity and Food Expenditures Are Closely Linked in Rural Bangladesh, Increasing the Risk of Malnutrition Due to the Financial Crisis." *Journal of Nutrition* 140 (1): 182S–8S.

UN (United Nations). 2009. *World Population Policies*. E.09.XIII.14. New York.

UN (United Nations). 2011. *World Population Prospects: The 2010 Revision*. CD-ROM edition. Department of Economic and Social Affairs, Population Division, New York.

UN (United Nations). 2012a. *World Urbanization Prospects: The 2011 Revision*. Department of Economic and Social Affairs, Population Division, New York.

UN (United Nations). 2012b. *World Urbanization Prospects: The 2011 Revision: Highlights*. Department of Economic and Social Affairs, Population Division, New York.

UN (United Nations). 2012c. "World Urbanization Prospects: The 2011 Revision: Press Release." Department of Economic and Social Affairs, Population Division, New York.

UN (United Nations). 2013. World Population Prospects: The 2012 Revision—*Key Findings and Advance Tables*. Department of Economic and Social Affairs, Population Division, New York.

United States Department of Agriculture (USDA) Economic Research Service (ERS), "Real Agricultural Prices have Fallen since 1900, Even as World Population

Growth Accelerated." Downloaded on 3 July 2012 from http://www.ers.usda.gov/data-products/chart-gallery/detail.aspx?chartId.

Victora, Cesar G., Linda Adair, Caroline Fall, Pedro C. Hallal, Reynaldo Martorell, Linda Richter, Harshpal Singh Sachdev, and the Maternal and Child Undernutrition Study Group. 2008. "Maternal and Child Undernutrition: Consequences for Adult Health and Human Capital." *The Lancet* 371 (9609): 340–57.

Victora, Cesar Gomes, Mercedes de Onis, Pedro Curi Hallal, Monika Blössner, and Roger Shrimpton. 2010. "Worldwide Timing of Growth Faltering: Revisiting Implications for Interventions." *Pediatrics* 125 (3): e473–e80.

Vos, T., et al. 2012. "Years Lived with Disability (YLDs) for 1160 Sequelae of 289 Diseases and Injuries 1990–2010: A Systematic Analysis for the Global Burden of Disease Study 2010." *The Lancet* 380 (9859): 2163196.

Willis, Robert J. 1973. "A New Approach to the Economic Theory of Fertility Behavior." *Journal of Political Economy* 81 (2, Part 2): S14–S64.

Wilmoth, John R., and Patrick. Ball. 1992. "The Population Debate in American Popular Magazines, 1946–90." *Population and Development Review* 18 (4): 631–68.

Wilson, Chris 2004. "Fertility Below Replacement Level." *Science* 304 (5668): 207–9.

Comments on "Population Quantity, Quality, and Mobility," by Jere R. Behrman and Hans-Peter Kohler

Ronald Lee

1. Introduction

This chapter does a terrific job of setting out many of the ways that changing demography will pose challenges for policy, income distribution, and economic development. Many important aspects of the topic are highlighted, including some that had not occurred to me. Quality gets the attention that the title of the chapter suggests it deserves. There are many fresh ideas and insights and novel ways of looking at the data. The policy recommendations are interesting and most strike me as on target.

There are some parts of the chapter where I would change the emphasis or introduce different material, and there are some policy recommendations with which I disagree. My comments draw on data from the National Transfer Accounts project (ntaccounts.org), a comparative international project that quantifies the ways in which people of different ages access economic resources in different countries.

The "demographic transition" is a useful organizing framework for this chapter, and the authors rightly emphasize that countries are distributed across different stages of the transition and that their positions in the transition fundamentally impact their economies. The transition starts with the inception of the mortality decline, which, together with continuing high fertility, leads to an increase in the number and population share of the young, the so-called "youth bulge." Members of this bulge eventually enter the labor force, where they may be productively employed, as they were in Taiwan and the Republic of Korea. Alternatively, they may experience low employment rates, as they have in Nigeria and South Africa. In either case, a decline in fertility reduces the number and population share of dependent children, raising the support ratio. This change is a benefit in the sense that per capita household incomes and per capita national income will be higher. This benefit of fertility decline, known as the "first demographic dividend," generally continues for 30–70 or more years. These aspects of the demographic transition are illustrated in Figure C3.1, which shows the support ratio for China.

This first dividend is ultimately a transitory benefit, which is reversed when lower fertility and longer life eventually lead to population aging, as support ratios fall back toward their pretransition levels or below. For the developed world and much of the developing world, this "first dividend" arising purely from rising support ratios is done or almost done. China, for example, is just about to reach its peak support ratio; other things equal, population aging will be costing it about half a percent of annual per capita income growth between now and 2050 (Lee and Mason 2012).

It is useful to consider the ways in which other things may not be equal—ways in which the transitory advantages of a high support ratio as fertility declines may be captured and made permanent in the form of increased investments in human capital and increased physical capital. These effects of the changing population age distribution are sometimes referred to as the "second demographic dividend" (Lee and Mason 2011). There is strong interest in these concepts among policymakers in parts of the developing world. For example, at the meeting of African Ministers of Finance, Economics and Planning in Abidjan in March of 2013, there were various presentations on the topic.

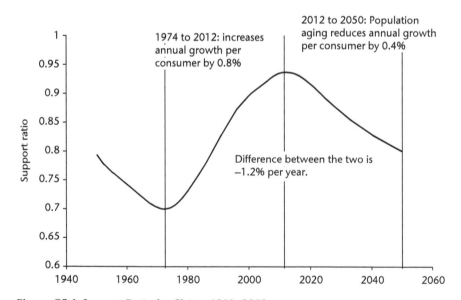

Figure C3.1 Support Ratio for China, 1950–2050

Source: Data from the United Nations Population Division and National Transfer Accounts (Li, Chen, and Jiang 2011).

While I agree with much of what the authors say about these matters, I disagree with the discussion of aging in Asia and the classification of East Asia as being "post-transition" with an "older population age structure." I also do not think the average age is the best metric for aging, since it can rise as fertility falls with no increase in the ratio of the elderly to the working-age population. Aside from Japan, the East Asian countries are not old. In fact, they are just coming to the end of their first demographic dividend phase and are now poised at their peak support ratios; they are just about to start population aging. Even in the world's oldest major country, Japan, the old-age dependency ratio will roughly double between now and 2050. In an important sense, the full force of population aging is still decades away in every country, even the richest ones, and has yet to be experienced anywhere.

One of the most striking sections of the chapter is the discussion of education. The deep and extensive use of the studies by Lutz and his coauthors presents material that has only recently been developed and has not yet been integrated in to demographers' thinking, so this section brings great value added. Another valuable contribution on education is the discussion of education other than formal schooling, including stimulation of children before they reach school age and the micronutritional quality of their diets. These points are quite new and not yet widely appreciated. They are a very welcome and valuable part of the chapter.

Within the economics of fertility, the quantity–quality tradeoff refers to the necessary choice by parents between the number of children (quantity) and the average amount they can spend (on care and investment in human capital) on each child (quality) (Becker and Lewis 1973; Willis 1973). The general idea is that as development proceeds and incomes rise, couples would like to choose both more quantity and more quality, but their desire for quality rises faster, making incremental children more costly. Consequently, the number of children declines. Development-driven increases in the rate of return to investments in quality, predominantly schooling, could also tilt parents to having fewer kids.

Figure C3.2 shows the relationship between expenditures on human capital investment per child and the level of fertility by world region. Expenditures on human capital are the sum of public and private spending. They are standardized by dividing by the average per capita labor income in each country for people aged 30–49. A strong negative relationship is evident, with an elasticity of about –0.7. While one cannot be sure about the direction of causation, it is hard to avoid the conclusion that the increase in quality is closely associated with the decline in fertility. This link is one part of the "second demographic dividend."

There is an interesting and important public–private issue here. Other data from the National Transfer Accounts reveal strong regional patterns of public

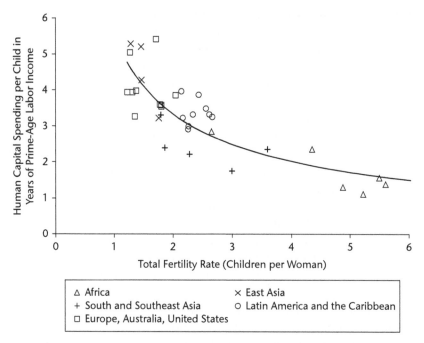

Figure C3.2 Association between Base-Period Fertility and Investments in Human Capital, by World Region

Note: Human capital investment per child is the sum of public and private per capita expenditures on health for people aged 0–17 and on education for people aged 3–26. These sums are then divided by average labor income for people aged 30–49 in each country. Fertility is measured during the five years before the base year for the National Transfer Account estimates.

Source: National Transfer Accounts data (ntaccounts.org) plus additional data not yet posted on the website.

spending on children and the elderly (Figure C3.3). Asia stands out for low public spending on both children and the elderly. In Latin America, public spending is high on the elderly and low on children. In Europe, spending is high on both.

What are the consequences of low spending on children? Taking Brazil as an informative example, high-income parents spend twice as much on private education as poor parents (ECLAC 2010). This pattern of investment in the human capital of children tends to preserve the high socioeconomic status of the children of the rich, replicating the social hierarchy in the next generation. In East Asia, there is very high private spending on education, roughly equal to public, but I do not know its class distribution. In Asia, private spending (on cram schools etc.) complements public spending; in Latin America, it generally buys alternative education (private instead of public). In the National Transfer Accounts data, most of the quantity–quality tradeoff

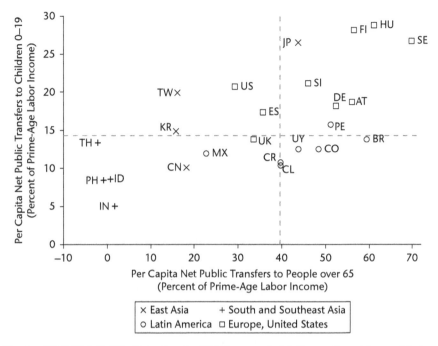

Figure C3.3 Net Public Transfers to Children and Adults, as Percentage of Labor Income of Adults 30–49

Note: Net public transfers are benefits received minus taxes. Dotted lines represent median values. Countries are identified by United Nations two-letter country codes, with plotting symbols varied by region.

Source: National Transfer Accounts (Miller 2011).

seen in Figure C3.2 is due to public spending on education rather than private spending. Countries tend to spend similar proportions of GDP on public education. As a result, the amount per child varies with fertility and the proportion of children in the population.

An increasing number of countries are in the process of population aging (all of Europe, Japan, North America, Taiwan, and Korea) or will soon be starting the process (China, much of South America). In Sub-Saharan Africa, population aging is far in the future; countries are still early in their dividend phase, and fertility is still relatively high. The chapter does a good job of taking this heterogeneity into account. It seems correct in noting that the dangers of population aging are often exaggerated.

As the population in high-income countries has aged, there has been a huge expansion of the welfare state, in the form of dramatically increased transfers to the elderly. This expansion has been driven partly by increased public provision of health care and long-term care for the elderly. It is not only the rich countries (including Japan, the United States, and Canada as well as Europe) that have followed this route; a number of Latin American countries (most strikingly Brazil) have done so as well. A consequence is that consumption by the elderly, including consumption of health care, has increased greatly relative to consumption by younger people.

Figure C3.4 shows cross-sectional age profiles of U.S. consumption in 1960, 1981, and 2009. It also shows the composition of consumption, including both public and private spending per person, on health care. The rising relative consumption by the elderly interacts with population aging to make population aging increasingly costly. Consumption expenditures have tilted dramatically toward older ages, in part due to increased public provision of health care.

I am pleased to see that problems of disability and chronic illness receive useful attention in the section on aging, with good discussion of relevant policies to improve health at older ages through interventions at earlier ages. The emphasis is on implications for health care systems and both public and familial transfer systems, presumably on the assumption that healthier elders will require less costly health care inputs, will be able to work longer, and will generally be more self-sufficient. All this is good. Let me add a couple of points.

First, a slightly different angle might be taken on old-age health, disability, and functional status (in addition to the current one). It draws on the studies on trends in disability (the Activities of Daily Living Scale, the Instrumental Activities of Daily Living Scale, and related standardized items) as measures of the quality of life of older people. I am not sure exactly what the international data show, but for the United States, disability rates were declining in the 1980s and 1990s and perhaps throughout the whole twentieth century. This is very good news, suggesting that the years of life gained through declining mortality were years of health and activity. Unfortunately, that trend appears to have ended around 2000, with some evidence of increasing disability rates by some measures and flat disability by other measures (National Research Council 2012). Furthermore, it appears that disability rates have been rising at older working ages (say, 40–64), along with obesity. These unfortunate trends, if present in other rich and also perhaps developing countries, are very bad news, both for the human welfare of the elderly and for their public and private support systems, which will already be strained by the rising proportions of elderly. There should be broader evidence on these points for other countries from the various health and retirement-type surveys now being conducted in parts of Asia and Latin America, but I don't know what they show. The chapter already covers the issue well from one angle; this would be another.

The authors present various policy recommendations. Most of them look very good, but there are some that I question or would put differently.

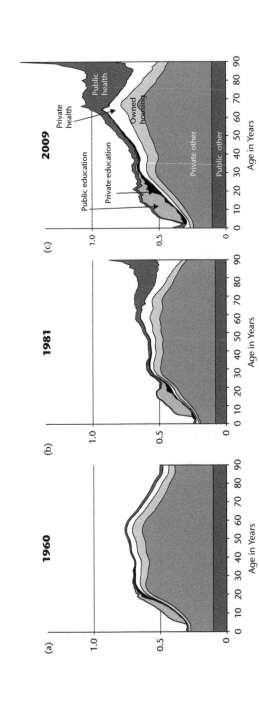

Y-axis scale: Relative to the (unweighted) profile average of labor income (YL) value for ages 30–49 for that year.

Figure C3.4 Composition of Consumption by Age in the United States, 1960, 1981, and 2009

Source: National Transfer Accounts for the United States (Lee, Donehower, and Miller 2011).

2. Capturing the Transitory Dividend by Human Capital Deepening

Some part of fertility decline is driven by the wish of parents to invest more in their children's human capital, particularly education. As I discussed earlier, spending per child on human capital is inversely related to fertility levels, reflecting both public and private spending (see Figure C3.2). Over the past few decades, fertility decline has been accompanied by greatly increased educational investment. Policy can support this natural tendency by maintaining or increasing aggregate public spending on education relative to GDP even as fertility and population shares of children fall. Human capital deepening generates positive externalities. The increase in labor productivity helps offset the decline in the number of workers relative to the elderly as populations age.

3. Capturing the Transitory Dividend through Capital Deepening

I am uncomfortable with some of the policy suggestions about pensions and agree with others. I missed any mention of funded versus Pay As You Go (PAYGO) pensions; apparently it is assumed that public pensions would be PAYGO. It was also suggested that pension benefits be delinked from earning histories and that such delinking would reduce distortions. I have two thoughts about this.

First, public old-age support is already delinked from childbearing. Some analysts suggest it should be relinked, as it was under traditional systems that provided family support for the elderly. Further delinking from earnings history would distort both labor supply decisions, including retirement age, and saving and asset accumulation decisions. It would also imperil the sustainability of public pensions as populations age. Brazil followed this policy when it extended pension benefits to the rural population. The policy reduced rural poverty, but the pension program is terribly unsustainable.

Second, in any population, older people hold far more in assets than younger people, due to a lifetime of accumulation through both inheritance and saving. As populations age, the proportion of asset-holding elders rises, leading to an increase in capital per worker (capital deepening). Whether or not capital deepens depends on how assets are invested and the openness of the economy. Longer lives and lower fertility may reinforce the pattern of asset holding by the elderly to provide for retirement consumption. In most rich countries and some middle-income countries in Latin America,

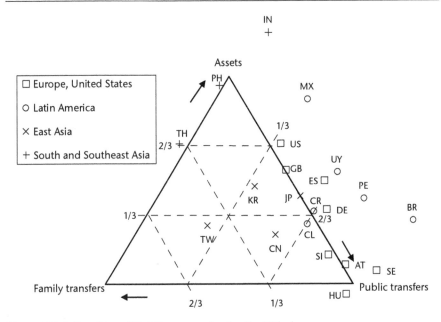

Figure C3.5 Funding of Net Consumption by the Elderly

Note: Figures shows the relative shares of public transfers, private transfers, and asset income less saving to fund net consumption (consumption minus labor income) by people aged 65 and over in selected countries. Plotting markers vary by region, identified by United Nations two-letter country codes. Points located to the right of the triangle indicate that the elderly make net private transfers to younger members of the population.

Source: National Transfer Accounts (Mason and Lee 2011).

this tendency may be undermined by excessive reliance on public PAYGO pensions. In many countries, elders rely virtually entirely on public transfers to fund their consumption, while still managing to make substantial net transfers to their children and grandchildren (Figure C3.5).

I suggest that developing countries should encourage private saving, including through mandatory saving programs for workers, starting decades before population aging is projected to begin. Prefunded public pension programs are also possible, although in practice they run a great risk of being drained by governments. A policy of growing reliable financial institutions to facilitate private retirement accounts might be preferable. Encouragement of private saving for retirement does not preclude PAYGO public pensions—it should supplement them. The idea is to harness the power of population aging to drive up the capital to labor ratio, as well as to reduce future pressure on the working-age population to fund the elderly through family transfers or public taxes and transfers. These benefits result only when actions are implemented before population aging, so that as populations age, the new elderly arrive with important asset holdings.

4. Investing in Education

It is true that pricing health and educational services for children would help bring private and social costs of children into line. However, it would also affect parents' decisions about the number of children they have and their investment in the human capital of children. The outcome might be lower human capital investments in children, with a loss of social external benefits from human capital. The recommendation does mention possible lump-sum taxes (presumably per capita at time of birth), which could be consistent with no charges for publicly provided health and education. But such policies do not seem realistic or desirable, for distributional reasons.

East Asia provides an example of what this approach might look like. It provides minimal public spending on education, which is heavily supplemented by private spending. This practice has led to (or is associated with) very low fertility and very high human capital investments. But the distributional consequences are not known. The distributional consequences of this approach are stark in Latin America: although public spending per child is similar across socioeconomic status groups (or lower for higher-status groups), the highest income group spends more than twice the public amount in Brazil and four times as much in Chile; the poorest group has almost zero private spending (ECLAC 2010). As a result, education spending on rich children in both Brazil and Chile is about three times as high as spending on poor children.

References

Becker, G., and H. G. Lewis. 1973. "On the Interaction between the Quantity and Quality of Children." *Journal of Political Economy* 84 (2, pt. 2): S279–S88.

ECLAC (Economic Commission for Latin America and the Caribbean.) 2010. *Social Panorama of Latin America 2010*. Santiago: United Nations.

Lee, R., G. Donehower, and T. Miller. 2011. "The Changing Shape of the Economic Lifecycle in the United States, 1970 to 2003." In *Aging in Asia: Findings from New and Emerging Data Initiatives*, ed. J. P. Smith and M. Majmundar, 313–26. National Research Council of the National Academies, Panel on Policy Research and Data Needs to Meet the Challenge of Aging in Asia. Washington, DC: National Academies Press.

Lee, R., and A. Mason. 2011. *Population Aging and the Generational Economy: A Global Perspective*. Cheltenham, U.K.: Edward Elgar.

Lee, R., and A. Mason. 2012. "Population Aging, Intergenerational Transfers, and Economic Growth: Asia in a Global Context." In *Aging in Asia: Findings from New and Emerging Data Initiatives*, ed. J. P. Smith and M. Majmundar, 77–95. National Research Council of the National Academies, Panel on Policy Research and

Data Needs to Meet the Challenge of Aging in Asia. Washington, DC: National Academies Press.http://www.nap.edu/openbook.php?record_id=13361&page=77.

Li, L., Q. Chen, and Y. Jiang. 2011. "The Changing Patterns of China's Public Services." In *Population Aging and the Generational Economy: A Global Perspective*, ed. R. Lee and A. Mason, 408–20. Cheltenham, U.K.: Edward Elgar.

Mason, A., and R., Lee. 2011. "Population Aging and the Generational Economy: Key Findings." In *Population Aging and the Generational Economy: A Global Perspective*, ed. R. Lee and A. Mason, 3–31. Cheltenham, U.K.: Edward Elgar.

Miller, T. 2011. "The Rise of the Intergenerational State: Aging and Development." In *Population Aging and the Generational Economy: A Global Perspective*, ed. R. Lee and A. Mason, 161–84. Cheltenham, U.K.: Edward Elgar.

National Research Council. 2012. *Aging and the Macroeconomy: Long-Term Implications of an Older Population*. Committee on Long-Run Macroeconomic Effects of Aging U.S. Population. Washington, DC: National Academies Press.

Willis, R. 1973. "A New Approach to the Economic Theory of Fertility Behavior." *Journal of Political Economy* 81 (2 pt. 2), S14–64.

4

The Hyperglobalization of Trade and Its Future

Arvind Subramanian and Martin Kessler

4.1 Introduction

The post-World War II period witnessed a rapid rise in trade between nations, reminiscent of the integration that occurred before World War 1 (see WTO 2013; Krugman 1995). This evolution was facilitated partly by reductions in policy barriers—first in the advanced economies, under the auspices of the then General Agreement on Trade and Tariffs (GATT), and later in developing countries, through unilateral liberalization actions or under programs undertaken with the International Monetary Fund (IMF) and World Bank. Trade was also facilitated by technological advances, especially in shipping and transportation costs. By the end of the 1980s and early 1990s, global trade integration had reverted to levels last seen before World War I.

The postwar period also saw a number of growth successes, beginning with Japan (and Europe), followed by the East Asian tigers and then China, and more recently India. Along the way, a few countries in Sub-Saharan Africa and Latin America also succeeded in raising their standards of living.

The authors are grateful to the project's participants, including Richard Baldwin, Nancy Birdsall, Kemal Derviş, Shahrokh Fardoust, Theo Priovolos, Dani Rodrik, and Andrew Steer, as well as to their colleagues at the Peterson Institute for International Economics and the Center for Global Development for helpful discussions. The chapter draws on work with Aaditya Mattoo and on a 2011 book by Arvind Subramanian.

Table 4.1 Convergence: Growth of Developing Countries Compared to with Growth in the United States

Indicator	1870–1960 (Maddison)	1960–2000 (Penn World Tables 7.1)	2000–07 (Penn World Tables 7.1)	2000–11 (World Development Indicators)	2008–12 (World Economic Outlook) [a]
U.S. growth rate of GDP per capita (percent)	1.7	2.47	1.28	0.65	0.02
World growth rate of GDP per capita (percent)	1.3	2.75	3.17	2.28	1.73
Number of developing countries in which growth exceeded U.S. rate	2	21	75	80	78
Percentage of developing countries in which growth exceeded U.S. rate	5.3	29.2	72.8	89.9	83.9
Average excess over U.S. growth (percentage points)[b]	0.02	1.53	3.25	2.94	3.03
Number of countries in sample	38	72	103	89	93

Note: Sample excludes oil exporters and countries with populations of less than 1 million.

a. Based on GDP in constant dollars. Other columns use GDP in PPP terms.

b. Computed as simple average growth of countries whose growth exceeds that of the United States.

Source: Authors.

In the late 1990s, however, a striking change occurred in the economic fortunes of countries: economic growth took off across the world, a phenomenon that is best described as convergence with a vengeance. Until the late 1990s, only about 30 percent of the developing world (21 of 72 countries) was catching up with the economic frontier (the United States), and the rate of catch-up was about 1.5 percent per capita per year (Table 4.1).[1] Since the late 1990s, nearly three-quarters of the developing world (75 of 103 countries) has started to catch up, at an accelerated annual pace of about 3.3 percent per capita. Although developing country growth slowed during the global financial crisis (2008–12), the rate of catch-up with advanced countries was not materially affected and remained close to 3 percent (see chapter 2).

At around the same time, perhaps just preceding this convergence phase, world trade started to surge, ushering in an era of hyperglobalization. That rising globalization (hereafter used interchangeably with *trade integration*) is

---

[1] All growth figures in this paragraph use a GDP measure in purchasing power parity (PPP) terms.

associated with stronger growth, which is a prerequisite for improving the situation of average citizens all over the world, is reason enough to seek to sustain it. This integration need not continue at the torrid pace of recent years; it should be sustained at a relatively steady rate and any serious reversal, which could set back the prospects of the average global citizen, avoided.

This chapter is divided into six sections. The next section documents some of the salient features of this era of hyperglobalization. Section 4.3 discusses three key areas where the trading system is seen as inadequate. The problems are illustrative of the proximate challenges and possible solutions but, in important ways, they cannot be solved unless the more fundamental challenges of globalization are addressed. Section 4.4 explores these deeper challenges. Section 4.5 suggests possible policy responses at the national and international levels that could help sustain globalization. Section 4.6 offers brief concluding remarks.

The chapter is not comprehensive: it focuses on the trade aspects of globalization. It does not discuss other important forms of globalization relating to the movement of finance and people; rather, it focuses on the major challenges, emphasizing aspects and arguments that have perhaps received less attention thus far.[2]

4.2 Seven Important Characteristics of the Most Recent Wave of Globalization

This section describes seven major features of the current era of hyperglobalization and of today's trading system:

- hyperglobalization (the rapid rise in trade integration);
- the dematerialization of globalization (the importance of services);
- democratic globalization (the spread of economic growth combined with the widespread embrace of openness);
- criss-crossing globalization (the similarity of North-to-South trade and investment flows with flows in the other direction);
- the rise of a mega-trader (China), the first since Imperial Britain;
- the proliferation of regional trade agreements and the imminence of mega-regional ones;
- the decline of barriers to trade in goods but the continued existence of high barriers to trade in services.

---

[2] For this reason, notable features such as the decline in transportation costs and improvements in information and communication technologies, which have been widely noted, are not studied in depth here (for discussions of these issues, see WTO 2013).

4.2.1 Hyperglobalization

Since the early 1990s, the world has entered an era of what might be called hyperglobalization (Figure 4.1). The years between 1870 and 1914 have been described as the first golden age of globalization. World exports as a share of gross domestic product (GDP) surged from 9 percent in 1870 to 15 percent on the eve of World War I. This was the era that Keynes waxed eloquently about, noting that an inhabitant of London "could order by telephone, sipping his morning tea in bed, the various products of the whole earth, in such quantity as he might see fit, and reasonably expect their early delivery upon his doorstep" (Keynes 1920, p. 11).

The period between 1914 and the end of World War II witnessed the Great Reversal of globalization, as a combustible mix of isolationism, nationalism, and militarism ignited protectionist policies. World exports plunged to a low of 6.5 percent of world GDP just before World War II began (O'Rourke and Williamson 1999; Frieden 2006; Irwin 2011).

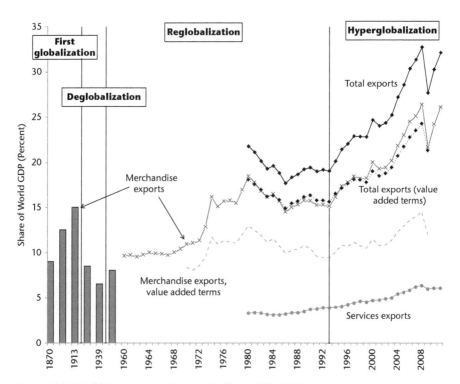

Figure 4.1 World Exports, in Current Dollars, 1870–2011

Sources: Authors, based on data from Klasing and Milionis forthcoming for historical estimates (1870–1950), World Trade Organization for 1951–2011, and Johnson and Noguera (2012) for value-added exports estimates.

A third era, starting after World War II, saw the restoration of world trade, aided by declines in transport costs and trade barriers. Only by about the mid to late 1970s did world trade revert to the peaks seen before World War I.

The world is now in a fourth era, of hyperglobalization, in which world trade has soared much more rapidly than world GDP. Over the past two decades, merchandise exports-to-GDP ratios soared from 15 percent to 26 percent, and goods and services exports rose to about 33 percent.[3] This rapid increase is somewhat surprising, because transport costs do not appear to have declined as rapidly as in earlier eras (Hummels, Ishii, and Yi 2001; Baldwin 2011a). The cost of information and communications did decline significantly, however.

Part of the increase in trade reflects the fragmentation of manufacturing across borders—the famous slicing up of the value-added chain—as individual production stages are located where the costs of production are lowest. This phenomenon, whereby technology no longer requires that successive stages of manufacturing production be physically contiguous or proximate, has been dubbed the "second unbundling" (Baldwin 2011a).[4]

This real technological impetus to trade tends to artificially inflate recorded trade. Because value is added at each stage of the production chain, it is recorded as exports at successive links in the chain. Gross exports flows therefore overstate real flows of value added (exports net of imported intermediate goods). Figure 4.1 shows that, even though value added-based exports of goods and services are about 5 percentage points lower than exports measured on a gross basis, their trajectory has been similar to that of conventionally measured exports. More recently, value added as a share of exports has not declined substantially or across all trading regions (Hanson 2012; WTO 2013).[5]

A related feature of this era of hyperglobalization is the rise of multinational corporations and the sharp surge in flows of foreign direct investment (FDI), which have both caused and been caused by cross-border and other flows of goods and services. Since the early 1990s (broadly coinciding with the era of hyperglobalization), FDI flows have surged, growing substantially faster than GDP (Figure 4.2). Global FDI as a share of world GDP, which hovered around 0.5 percent, increased sevenfold, peaking at close to 4 percent just before the onset of the recent global financial crisis. Even discounting the two surges of 1997–2000 and 2005–08, the general trend is steadily increasing. Global FDI stocks (which are less volatile than flows) jumped from less than 10 percent of GDP in the early 1990s to 30 percent

[3] Throughout this chapter, we use trade data as currently measured, on a gross basis. Wherever possible, and as a cross-check, we also present results for trade data measured on a value-added basis. The appendix explains how these values are calculated.

[4] The first unbundling reflected in the quotation from Keynes is the separation of the producer from the consumer that increased trade permits.

[5] Koopman, Wang, and Wei (2013) further refined the measurement of value-added trade by distinguishing where countries are (upstream versus downstream) in the value-added chain. The aggregate value-added measures reported here are computed as in their paper.

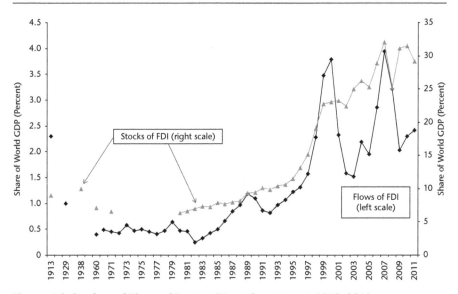

Figure 4.2 Stocks and Flows of Foreign Direct Investment, 1913–2011

Sources: Authors, based on data from Bairoch (1996) for 1913–70, Dunning (1983) for stocks, and UNCTAD various years for flows for 1970–2011.

in 2011. FDI flows, and stocks, now surpass levels achieved in the first golden era of globalization, before World War I. By 2009 there were more than 80,000 multinationals, accounting for about two-thirds of world trade (UNCTAD 2010).

4.2.2 "Dematerializing" Globalization

The rapid increase in trade has occurred in both goods and services. Based on conventional (gross) trade data, services trade represented about 17 percent of world trade in 1980 and about 20 percent in 2008. Measured in value-added terms, the corresponding numbers are 30 percent and 40 percent. The apparent paradox that we seek to explain in this section is that services trade, which represents 6 percent of world GDP in gross terms, is 40–50 percent larger when computed in value-added terms. This phenomenon arises because services are not always directly tradable but are sometimes embodied in the production of goods that are traded. In traditional trade statistics, such services are not counted as traded; in value-added terms they are considered as such, because production of the service takes place in one country and consumption in another one. Traditional measures of services trade underestimate their importance in global trade.

Two underlying factors can explain the "dematerialization" of trade. First, as Johnson and Noguera (2012) show, the ratio of value-added exports to gross exports in manufacturing goods decreased in the past 30 years (from

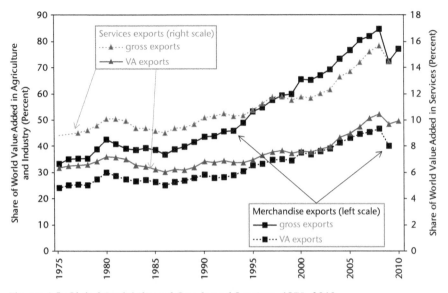

Figure 4.3 Global Tradability of Goods and Services, 1975–2010

Sources: Authors, based on data from World Bank various years and Johnson and Noguera (2012).

60 percent in 1980 to 45 percent in 2009), as a result of the rising importance of global value chains in this sector. Second, as explained in the previous paragraph, trade in services is larger and growing faster in value-added terms than traditional statistics show. Soon, trade in services could eclipse trade in goods, less because services are traded directly than because services are increasingly embodied in goods. Trade will actually be dematerializing—moving from "stuff" to intangibles—although the manifestation will be, and the data will record, the opposite effect.

Value-added-based trade data reveal how much of the total value added in a sector is traded globally. Figure 4.3 plots world exports (gross and value-added) of goods as a share of world value added in goods (defined to include agriculture and industry), as well as similar numbers for services. During the period of hyperglobalization, value-added exports of goods as a share of total value added in the sector (agriculture and industry) increased from about 33 percent to 47 percent, and services as a share of value added in the services sector increased from 11 percent to 16 percent. Thus, the pace at which services are becoming tradable mirrors that in merchandise.

The slower rise in the tradability of goods than services in the era of hyperglobalization may partly reflect the differential rise in the costs of transport versus information and communications technologies (ICT). After plummeting sharply between about 1940 and 1980, transport costs appear to have stabilized (Baldwin 2011a; Hummels 2007). In contrast, around 1990, the use of

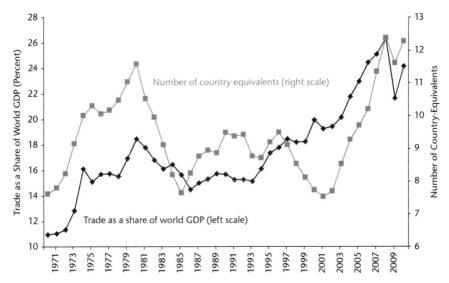

Figure 4.4 Dispersion of World Output and World Exports, 1970–2010

Note: Country-equivalents are computed as $=\dfrac{1}{\sum_i s_i^2}$, where s_i is the share of each country in world output. A higher number denotes a more equal distribution of output.

Source: Authors, based on data from UNCTAD various years.

ICT-related technologies and applications surged. A consequence could have been a differential fillip to more sophisticated goods and especially services.

4.2.3 Democratic Globalization

Part of the increase in trade also reflects convergence and the wider distribution of output and income: that is, trade has grown because output has become more widespread and "democratic." Basic gravity theory implies that smaller countries tend to trade more than larger ones.[6] A world of two equal-sized countries will experience more trade than a world in which the larger country accounts for 95 percent of world output. Over time, the world is becoming less unequal in terms of the distribution of the underlying output that generates trade.[7] For example, between 1970 and 2000 the world was constituted by about 7.0–7.5 country-equivalents (with fluctuations) (Figure 4.4).

[6] The gravity model of trade is theoretically well established and empirically validated. It shows that trade between two countries is proportional to their economic size and inversely proportional to their distance. Other things equal, a large country will trade more than a small one but will be less open (trade/GDP will be smaller).

[7] As Anderson (2011) shows, in a world without trade frictions, the share of trade in world output is given by $1-\Sigma_j b_j^2$ where b_j is the share of a country in world output. Inverting the expression gives the number of country-equivalents in the world, which increases with convergence. Baier and Bergstrand (2001) find a statistically significant effect of convergence on trade.

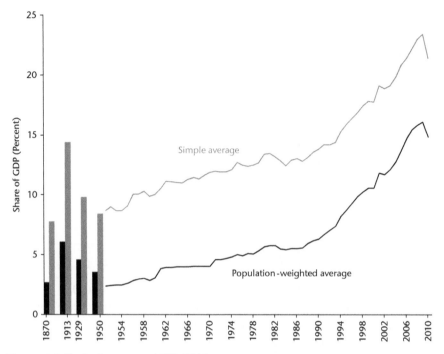

Figure 4.5 Trade Openness, 1870–2010

Note: For 1870–1950, openness is defined using Maddison's measure of current exports in dollars (deflated by the US consumer price index) and Maddison's GDP data. For 1951–2010, openness is the variable openk (Penn World Table 7.1) divided by 2. Oil exporters and small countries (populations of less than 1 million) are excluded. We chose the openk variable because it is the most comparable with the Maddison (pre–World War II) GDP data in that both are in constant purchasing power parity dollars. For the pre-War export data, there are two options for deflation: a measure of general U.S. inflation (for example, the consumer price index (CPI)) or a measure of export prices. Maddison provides a real export series based on the latter. We chose the CPI option for the simple reason that the estimates for 1950 matched better the pre–World War II estimates for the years close to 1950. If we use Maddison's real export data, the changes over time are even more dramatic than shown in Figure 4.4 (that is, export-to-GDP ratios are lower for the past when exports are deflated by an export price index than a CPI index).

Sources: Authors, based on data from Maddison (1995) and Penn World Table 7.1.

Since 2000, as more countries have started catching up with the rich, world output has become more dispersed: today, it is as if there were ten country-equivalents in the world. In the era of hyperglobalization, roughly a third of the increase in trade can be accounted for by this democratization of world output (see Figure 4.4).

Even if the rise in world trade is caused by spreading prosperity, is this rise itself broadly spread? The numbers in Figure 4.1 are in effect a GDP-weighted average of individual countries' export-to-GDP ratios. We can, instead, calculate export-to-GDP ratios that are unweighted or weighted by population to measure the reach of globalization across countries and across people, as done in Figure 4.5.

Figure 4.5 shows that in 1913, the peak of the first golden era of globalization, the unweighted average export-to-GDP ratio in the world was close to 15 percent. In 2010, it was 21.5 percent. The population-weighted export-to-GDP ratio was about 6 percent; by 2010, it was 15 percent. Hyperglobalization has thus come about not just because some rich countries are becoming more open but also because openness is being embraced more widely.[8] Keynes' paean to globalization was thus both imperialist and elitist.[9, 10]

4.2.4 Criss-Crossing Globalization

Trade has been increasing steadily. But one of the unique features of the most recent phase of hyperglobalization is the fact that similar kinds of goods (and capital) are criss-crossing global borders. In other words, it is less and less the case that a country's imports and exports are very different.

There are three manifestations of such criss-crossing globalization that can be discerned. In the immediate aftermath of World War II, the industrial countries increasingly started to export and import manufactured goods (for example, Japan, Germany, and the United States all exported and imported cars), a phenomenon at odds with the classic Ricardian model. Models of monopolistic competition (Helpman and Krugman 1985) combined with consumers' love for variety (differentiated products) provided the theoretical basis for the phenomenon of intraindustry trade that related to trade in final goods. Melitz and Trefler (2012) show that intraindustry trade's share of total trade increased by nearly 20 percentage points. But this increase occurred between 1960 and the mid-1990s rather than over the most recent period of hyperglobalization. In fact, since the 1990s, this share of intraindustry trade has stabilized (Brülhart 2009).

For the rapidly growing emerging market countries of Asia, criss-crossing globalization has taken the form of greater two-way flows of parts and components than of final goods. This phenomenon is related to the slicing up of the value-added chain and the unbundling noted above.

[8] One potential problem with Figure 4.5 is that the sample is not constant over time. The finding that trade has become more democratized holds even for the constant sample of countries (not reported here). The unweighted average is above the population-weighted average because populous countries tend to trade less.

[9] Even within the United Kingdom, the benefits of globalization were not broadly accessible. In 1912, for example, there were 0.6 million telephone subscribers in the United Kingdom, the population of which was about 46 million.

[10] Another way of describing this democratization is to note that the trade of low- and middle-income countries has grown more rapidly than their incomes and more rapidly than the trade of high-income countries and that a bulk of this growth is trade among low- and middle-income countries (Hanson 2012).

The share of parts and components in trade offers one measure of criss-crossing globalization. For the world as a whole, this share increased from about 22 percent in 1980 to 29 percent in 2000. Since then, intermediate goods trade has declined to about 26 percent of total trade, suggesting that the internationalization of production may have peaked (WTO 2013). Indeed, this form of globalization was really observed only in Asia, and even there intermediate trade has declined since 2000. Even in China, reliance on imports has declined markedly. In the computer sector (broadly defined), for example, exports were only 1.6 times imports in 1994, indicating substantial intermediate trade; by 2008, this ratio had climbed to 4.2 (Hanson 2012).

The third (and perhaps least remarked-on) dimension of criss-crossing globalization, with potentially important effects for globalization policies, relates to two-way flows of FDI. It is one of the unique aspects of this era of hyperglobalization that developing countries (especially the larger ones) are exporting FDI (which embodies sophisticated factors of production, including entrepreneurial and managerial skills and technology)—and not just to other developing countries (Mattoo and Subramanian 2010). Figure 4.6 plots a Grubel–Lloyd index of two-way flows of FDI at the global

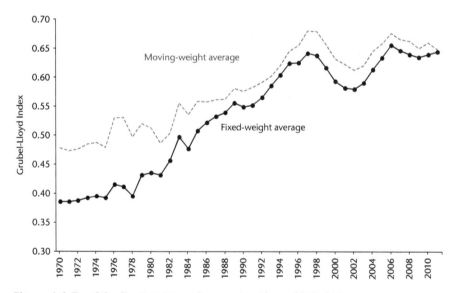

Figure 4.6 Two-Way Foreign Direct Investment Flows, 1970–2011

Note: The Grubel-Lloyd index is computed for each country with nonzero positive flows. Each country is then weighted by its share of total FDI flows, either with weights that correspond to the current year (dotted line) or with weights that are fixed at their mean over the period (solid line). The figure shows five-year moving averages (to avoid large spikes).

Source: Authors, based on data from UNCTAD various years.

Table 4.2 Merchandise Exports as Share of World Exports by Mega-Traders, 1870–2030 (percent)

Year	United Kingdom	Germany	United States	Japan	China
1870	24.3	13.4	5.0	0.1	2.8
1913	18.5	18.0	9.0	0.8	2.0
1929	15.1	16.6	14.4	2.1	3.0
1950	10.2	3.9	16.2	1.3	0.9
1973	5.1	12.9	12.2	6.4	1.0
1990	5.3	12.0	11.3	8.2	1.8
2000	4.4	8.5	12.1	7.4	3.9
2012	2.6	7.7	8.4	4.4	11.2
2020 (projected)	1.9	5.3	8.8	3.9	12.1
2030 (projected)	1.4	3.6	7.3	3.2	15.0

Sources: Authors, based on data from Maddison 1995, UNCTAD various years, Subramanian 2011 and authors' projections.

level.[11] Depending on the weighting, this index climbed from about 0.3 in 1970 to almost 0.7 by 2011.

4.2.5 The Rise of a Genuine Mega-Trader: China

When Krugman (1995) surveyed the evolution of world trade, he noted as one of the distinctive features the rise of a number of Asian super-traders, including Singapore, Hong Kong (China), and Malaysia, all of whose exports exceeded 50 percent of GDP, a feature never seen in the first era of globalization (in 1913, the United Kingdom's ratio of export to GDP was 18.5 percent). But mega-traders can be defined in two senses: globally (relative to world trade) and nationally (relative to a country's own output). Krugman clearly applied the latter criterion. Had he applied the former, one mega-trader he would have identified would have been Japan in the 1980s, which accounted for about 7.5 percent of global trade at its peak. Based on this criterion, none of the other East Asian tigers would have been noteworthy, despite their astonishing performance: the small economies of Singapore, Hong Kong (China), Taiwan (China), and Malaysia accounted for a very small share of world trade at their peaks.

Since 1990, a true mega-trader has emerged, China. It qualifies as such under both definitions of the term. Its integration into world trade accelerated

[11] The Grubel–Lloyd index, which can take values between 0 and 1, measures the degree of two-way flows for a given country or industry. An index of 0 denotes that a country's exports and imports are perfectly dissimilar—that is, a country is either fully an importer or an exporter of a good (or, in this specific case, a type of capital flow). An index of 1 denotes that a country's exports and imports are similar—that is, a country's exports and imports of a certain good are identical in magnitude.

Table 4.3 Exports and Imports as Percent of GDP in Selected Mega-Traders

Item	Actual	Percent overtrading, controlling for key gravity variables		
		Controlling for size	Controlling for size and income level	Controlling for size, income level, and oil-based economies
United Kingdom 1870 (sample includes 26 countries)				
Exports	12.2	339.3***	84.0*	n.a
United States 1975 (sample includes 121 countries)				
Exports	8.5	−9.5	−37.0***	−36.3***
Imports	7.6	−30.5***	−37.7***	−37.5***
Total trade (exports + imports)	16.1	−20.9***	−35.5***	−35.1***
Japan 1990 (sample includes 131 countries)				
Exports	10.3	−33.8***	−56.8***	−55.6***
Imports	9.4	−44.3***	−49.4***	−51.4**
Total trade (exports + imports)	19.7	−40.4***	−52.9***	−53.7***
China 2008 (sample = 136 countries)				
Exports	35.0	79.9***	68.6**	80.5***
Imports	27.3	45.7***	46.2***	38.0**
Total trade (exports + imports)	62.2	64.6***	60.8***	62.0***

Note: All coefficients were obtained by running a regression of exports, imports, trade on column heads a plus dummy for the country in question. The level of over-/under trading is exp(dummy coefficient)—1. A negative value denotes under-trading. * = significant at the 10 percent level, ** = significant at the 5 percent level, *** = significant at the 1 percent level.

Sources: Authors, based on data from Maddison 1995 for United Kingdom, IMF various years, and Penn World Table 7.1 for all other countries.

with its accession to the WTO in 2001, transforming it into the world's largest exporter and importer of manufactured goods, having surpassed the United States in 2012 (Table 4.2).

China's exports as a share of GDP are now almost 50 percent. When its size and income level are taken into account, it is a substantial over-trader, comparable to the United Kingdom in the heyday of its empire and a vastly bigger trader than the United States, Japan, or Germany at their peaks.

For example, in 1975, the United States' trade-to-GDP ratio was 13.3 percent (Table 4.3). Given the size and income level of the United States, that number represented under-trading of about 50 percent. Japan in 1990, with a trade-to-GDP ratio of 20 percent, under-traded by about 50 percent. In contrast, China's trade-to-GDP ratio in 2008 was 56.5 percent, which represented overtrading of nearly 75 percent.[12] Only Imperial Britain was a mega-trader in both senses of the term. In 1913, its exports represented 18.5 percent of world exports. Its export-to-GDP ratio was 12 percent, which represented overtrading of about 84 percent. China is thus the first mega-trader since Imperial Britain.

If trade continues to grow in line with income, China's dominance in world trade will become even greater. According to simple calculations in Subramanian (2011), by 2030 China could account for about 16–17 percent of world exports, nearly three times the share of the United States (see Table 4.2).[13] Even at the height of U.S. dominance, around 1975, it did not account for as large a share of world trade or have as great an edge over its nearest competitors (in 2000, the United States accounted for about 16 percent of world exports, compared with 8 percent for Germany and about 7 percent for Japan). Any discussion of trade and the trading system going forward must recognize this development (discussed further later in the chapter).

4.2.6 Growing Regionalization, Preferential Trade, and Impending Hyperregionalization

The era of hyperglobalization has been accompanied by a proliferation of preferential trade agreements (PTAs). Today, about half of the exports of the top 30 exporters go to preferential trade partners. Between 1990 and 2010, the number of PTAs increased from 70 to 300 (Figure 4.7). In the mid-1990s, about 75 percent of PTAs were regional; by 2003, this share had dropped to about 50 percent. All World Trade Organization (WTO) members except Mongolia have concluded at least one PTA; some, such as the European Union, Chile, and Mexico, have concluded more than 20. Some of the large traders have already concluded agreements with each other or are about to do so (examples include the European Union and Mercosul, Japan and Mercosul, the European Union and India, and India and Japan).

The fact that nearly half of world trade is covered by preferential agreements does not mean that a comparable figure enjoys preferential barrier reductions. Carpenter and Lendle (2010) estimate that only about 17 percent of world trade is eligible for preferences; the remaining 83 percent either enjoys zero nondiscriminatory tariffs (nearly 50 percent) or is excluded from preferential agreements. Moreover, where preferences can apply, margins

---

[12] This status is somewhat affected by taking into account value-added trade only. As shown in appendix table 4A.1, the "over-trading coefficient" remains high but becomes slightly lower for China in 2008; Japan's undertrading is also less acute with value added figures.

[13] The WTO (2013) projection for 2035 is exactly in line with the estimate in Subramanian (2011). The WTO's mean estimate is that China will account for 17 percent of world trade in 2035, with a range of 11–23 percent.

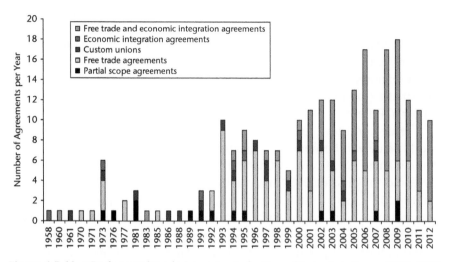

Figure 4.7 New Preferential Trade Agreements, by Year of Entry into Force, 1958–2012

Note: The year of the count is the year of entry into force of the agreement. To simplify the classification of agreements, subsumed in the "economic integration agreement" category (which corresponds to agreements covering trade in services) are all agreements that are both "economic integration agreements and customs unions" or "economic integration agreements and partial scope agreements."

Source: WTO Regional Trade Agreements Database (http://rtais.wto.org/UI/PublicMaintainRTA Home.aspx).

Table 4.4 Number and Type of Preferential Trade Agreements

Type of agreement	Pre–WTO	1995–2000	Post-2000
WTO+ issues			
Customs	13	11	56
Antidumping	12	8	53
Countervailing measures	4	5	52
Export taxes	8	8	41
State aid	10	9	34
Trade-related intellectual property rights	6	4	41
Services	7	2	39
State trading enterprises	5	3	35
Technical barriers to trade	2	2	36
Sanitary and phytosanitary standards	2	1	35
Public procurement	5	0	32
Trade-related investment measures	6	2	31
WTO plus X issues			
Competition policy	11	9	19
Movement of capital	6	5	38
Intellectual property rights	5	2	39
Investment	4	1	35

Note: WTO+ provisions concern commitments that already exist in WTO agreements but go beyond the WTO disciplines. WTOX provisions cover obligations that are outside the current WTO aegis.

Source: Baldwin 2011b.

are low. For example, less than 2 percent of world imports enjoy preferences greater than 10 percentage points.

An interesting new dimension of these PTAs is the extent to which they feature "deep integration" (Lawrence 1996)—that is, liberalize not only tariffs and quotas but other "behind-the-border" barriers, such as regulations and standards, as well. In the past ten years, for example, nearly 40 agreements have included provisions on WTO–Plus issues (competition policy, intellectual property rights, investment, and the movement of capital). This figure is four to five times greater than comparable agreements in the pre-WTO era (WTO 2011) (see Figure 4.7 and Table 4.4).

In part because of these deep integration agreements, it would be wrong on the basis of the tariff evidence to underestimate the potential discriminatory effect of preferential arrangements. In agriculture and some manufacturing sectors, such as textiles, tariffs are still high. In services, any future deepening of preferential agreements could create significant discrimination against outsiders, because most-favored-nation (MFN) levels of protection are significant and there is considerable scope for the preferential recognition of standards, licensing, and qualification requirements. Strong exclusionary effects could also arise from "deeper integration" along other dimensions: preferential agreements increasingly have provisions on investment protection, intellectual property rights, government procurement, competition policy, and technical barriers to trade. A discriminatory tariff may matter less than the selective recognition of product safety standards or selective access to government procurement markets.

On regional agreements, seismic changes are under way, with the possible negotiation of mega-regional agreements between the United States and Asia (the Trans-Pacific Partnership) and the United States and Europe (the Transatlantic Trade and Investment Partnership). Trade between these groups of countries accounts for about $2–$3 trillion a year in world trade, signifying a potentially major jump in the volume of trade covered by preferential agreements. These PTAs would represent the first between the top four major regions of the world (China, the United States, Europe, and Japan), with consequences that will be discussed below. If the Transatlantic Trade and Investment Partnership and Trans-Pacific Partnership (to the extent that it includes Japan) are concluded, more than half of global trade will be covered by those deeper regional agreements. It is not unforeseeable to think of an era in which nearly all trade becomes regional.

4.2.7 Lower Formal Barriers in Goods, High Barriers in Services

The world has become much less protectionist. Globally, MFN tariffs have declined from more than 25 percent in the mid-1980s to about 8 percent today. Border barriers (tariffs and nontariff measures) in manufacturing in the Organisation for Economic Co-operation and Development (OECD) countries are less than 4 percent.

The U.S. International Trade Commission (USITC 2011) estimates that the welfare gains in the United States from eliminating all remaining tariffs are close to zero. Border barriers in the larger emerging markets are higher, but they have declined considerably, from about 45 percent in the early 1980s to just over 10 percent in 2009 (Figure 4.8). But barriers to trade in services remain high.[14] Borchert, Gootiiz, and Mattoo (2012b) calculate restrictiveness trade indexes for services. They cover five major sectors—financial services, telecommunications, retail distribution, transport, and professional services—and the different modes of delivering these services across borders (cross-border and via investment abroad). The index ranges from 0 (completely free) to 100 (completely restricted). Barriers vary across service sectors, but the average level is high (Figure 4.9).[15] Barriers are relatively low in telecommunications and relatively high in transportation and professional services. They also vary across regions: Latin America is nearly as open as OECD countries, whereas Asia and the Middle East have high barriers. In fact, as in goods, barriers are correlated with a country's level of development (Figure 4.10). What this means is that international negotiations will increasingly focus on services and FDI.

Two points are worth noting. First, barriers to trade in goods and services have declined sharply over time; the world as a whole is thus becoming less closed. But the composition of world trade is shifting toward the poorer countries (especially toward China and India), and these countries are on average more protectionist (as Figures 4.8–4.10 illustrate). The composition of world output is also shifting toward services and away from manufacturing. Both these compositional shifts make the world as a whole less open and attenuate the liberalization trend that stems from all countries reducing barriers.

Second, the integration of goods and services markets is nowhere close to completion. One way of assessing how far from full globalization the world still is might be to compare actual trade with what is predicted by a simple gravity model without frictions. As Krugman (1995) and Anderson (2011) show, under frictionless trade, the world trade share is inversely related to the distribution of GDP across countries: the more equal the distribution,

---

[14] There are no data on barriers to trade in services going back in time that would allow a quantitative description of changes in barriers.
[15] This index cannot strictly be compared with tariffs, but the further away the number is from zero, the less open a country is.

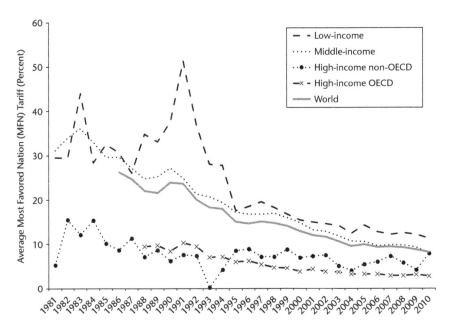

Figure 4.8 Average Most-Favored-Nation Tariffs by Income Group, 1981–2009
Note: Spikes may reflect entry and exit of countries in the sample.
Source: World Bank 2011.

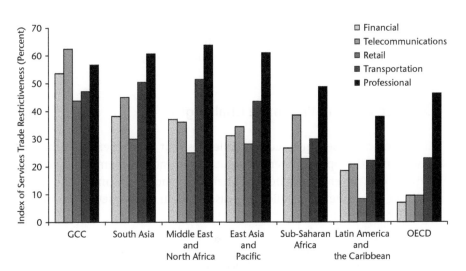

Figure 4.9 Index of Services Trade Restrictiveness, by Sector and Region, 2008–10
Source: World Bank Services Trade Restrictions Database.

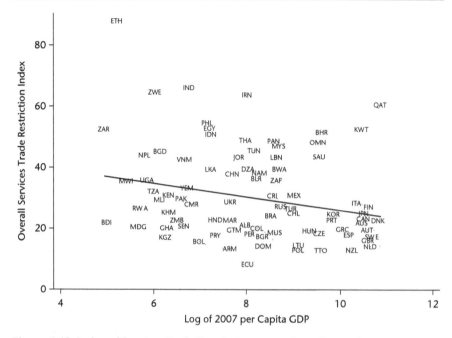

Figure 4.10 Index of Services Trade Restrictiveness and per Capita GDP

Source: Authors, based on data from World Bank Services Trade Restrictions Database and World Development Indicators.

the greater the world trade share. In 1970, actual trade was about 10 percent of the theoretical maximum predicted by the frictionless gravity model. In 2011, it was about 40 percent (perhaps less if trade is calculated on a value-added basis). Thus, although actual trade is rapidly catching up with trade in a frictionless world, there is still some way to go.[16]

4.3 Three Pressing Proximate Challenges

This section discusses three recent challenges that have emerged in the trading system and proposes potential solutions to each of them. The proposed solutions can never be reached on their own, however, unless the deeper and more fundamental challenges, discussed in subsequent sections, are addressed.[17]

---

[16] An implication of this finding on unrealized globalization is that, going forward, this potential is likely to be greater in services than in goods.

[17] The next section, on trade and currency wars, draws on Mattoo and Subramanian (2009).

4.3.1 Trade and Currency Wars

MERCANTILISM AND SELF-INSURANCE: THE DUAL ORIGINS OF
RESERVE ACCUMULATION

In the late 1990s, in the aftermath of the Asian financial crisis, a number of emerging market countries, especially in Asia, adopted an economic strategy that was dubbed Bretton Woods II (Dooley, Folkerts-Landau, and Garber 2003). This strategy had two motivations and one manifestation. Reeling from the disruption that sudden withdrawal of foreign capital had caused to their economies and chafing at the political humiliation of having to borrow from the IMF, they decided to self-insure against future crises.[18] Self-insurance took the form of building an arsenal of foreign exchange reserves (see chapter 5 of this volume; Goldstein 2009). The second motivation was mercantilism, a strategy that made trade surplus the engine of growth.

Both motivations translated into a common manifestation: countries moved from being large net importers of finance (running large current account deficits) to being less reliant on finance, or in some cases—notably China, Malaysia, and Taiwan (China)—to becoming net exporters of finance (running current account surpluses). These motivations also translated into—actually *require*—a policy of undervaluing the exchange rate in a fixed or managed peg regime, aided by intervention in foreign exchange markets. A few countries in East Asia (China and Malaysia in particular) tended to maintain restrictions on capital inflows as a way of sustaining a competitive exchange rate.

Bergsten and Gagnon (2012, p. 2) argue that more than 20 countries have been intervening in foreign exchange markets for several years "at an average rate of nearly $1 trillion annually...to keep their currencies undervalued and thus boost their international competitiveness and trade surpluses." These countries include China and a number of East Asian countries, oil exporters, and some advanced countries, including Israel and Switzerland.

This problem is not new. Similar issues of undervaluation arose relating to the Deutsche Mark in the 1960s and the yen in the 1970s and 1980s. The mercantilism or currency wars of today are related to the much deeper problem—and some would argue the greatest design flaw in the Bretton Woods system—of the asymmetric adjustment between surplus and deficit countries in the international monetary and trade system. Bergsten and Gagnon (2012, p. 10) write that "it is a huge irony that the Bretton Woods system

---

[18] The perceived humiliation was captured in the picture of the IMF Managing Director at the time, Michel Camdessus, looking over a head-bent President Suharto signing the economic adjustment program with the IMF.

was created at the end of the Second World War primarily to avoid repeating the disastrous experiences of the inter-war period with competitive devaluations, which led to currency wars and trade wars that in turn contributed importantly to the Great Depression, but that the system has failed to do so."

CONSEQUENCES OF MERCANTILISM

Why are current account surpluses combined with undervalued exchange rates a problem for the international economic system? The consequences or problems can be categorized as cyclical mercantilism, structural mercantilism, and macro-mercantilism.

Cyclical mercantilism arises when the economy is depressed relative to trend growth; such a situation is characterized by idle resources, underutilized capital, and unemployment. Mercantilism by one country threatens deflation in partner countries facing idle resources. This concern preoccupied Keynes, who argued that because of international liquidity constraints, there would always be greater pressure on debtors (countries running deficits) to adjust than on creditors. This asymmetry would impart a deflationary bias, because debtor countries would have to cut demand without surplus countries having to undertake the offsetting reflation. He therefore proposed that pressure be exerted on creditor countries by forcing them to pay instead of receiving interest on their positive balances (see Williamson 2011).

In the current context, the deflationary impact of Chinese policies on the United States, quantified by Cline (2010), has prompted some commentators to call for aggressive trade action by the United States against China and other countries practicing mercantilism (Krugman 2010; Bergsten and Gagnon 2012). Persistent surpluses by Germany and their deflationary impact, especially within Europe, have sparked similar calls for action (Wolf 2010).

Structural mercantilism arises when a country pursues policies such as undervalued exchange rates as development or growth policy for an extended period of time. Such policies can have long-run effects on partner countries. An undervalued exchange rate is both an import tax and an export subsidy; it can have adverse effects on trading partners. One way in which structural mercantilism is transmitted is by depressing the medium-run price of manufactured products, reducing opportunities for specialization in manufacturing and manufactured exports in partner countries. The concerns expressed in Sub-Saharan Africa and Latin America relate to structural mercantilism. Mattoo, Mishra, and Subramanian (2012) show, for example, that a 10 percent depreciation of China's real exchange rate reduces a developing country's exports of a typical product to third markets by about 1.5–2.0 percent. Such a decline can have long-run growth effects.

Macro-mercantilism was most evident in the recent crisis in the creation of the so-called savings glut (Bernanke 2005, 2007). Large and growing aggregate current account surpluses increase global liquidity, leading to easy credit and lending, which can easily morph into imprudence, financial excess, and asset bubbles, threatening financial stability. The savings glut hypothesis is by no means uncontested; many economists argue that monetary and regulatory policies in borrowing countries should bear the brunt of responsibility (Johnson and Kwak 2010; Haldane 2010). How much blame the bartender should bear for plying with alcohol a drinker who binges will forever be disputed. But that excess liquidity was a factor and that Chinese mercantilist policies created excess liquidity are plausible in considering deeper causes of the Lehman crisis (see Bernanke et al. 2011).

Currency wars or the resulting global imbalances are a systemic problem only if one or a few large countries pursue them. The possibility of collective action to prevent them must take account of this reality.

Exchange rates and foreign exchange intervention are centrally implicated in mercantilism. The international monetary system, under the auspices of the IMF, is therefore the best forum in which to find a solution. The prospects for any serious reform remain slim, however, because of the inherent limits to international monetary cooperation. Systemic threats arise from the policies of the largest countries, in particular when polices pursued in self-interest conflict with the collective interest. But, by definition, it is difficult for the rest of the world to change the incentives of the large country to give more weight to the collective interest. Successful cooperation is fated to falter, if not fail—and the efforts of the IMF in this matter have often resulted in failure. As Mussa (2007, p. 40) makes clear, "In *none* of these consultations has the Executive Board ever concluded that a member was out of compliance with its obligations regarding its exchange rate policies or any other matter" (emphasis in the original).[19]

Williamson (2011, p. 1) notes that "it has been 80 years since John Maynard Keynes first proposed a plan that would have disciplined persistent surplus countries. But the Keynes Plan, like the subsequent Volcker Plan in 1972–74, was defeated by the major surplus country of the day (the United States and Germany, respectively), and today China (not to mention Japan or Germany) exhibits no enthusiasm for new revisions of these ideas." The question is whether there is anything that the rest of the world could have done—by way of sticks or carrots—to have persuaded the United States in 1944, Germany in 1973, or China in 2007 to change its positions or policies for the collective good.

The IMF's ineffectiveness is a proximate manifestation of deeper structural causes related to leverage and legitimacy. Although the IMF has been

---

[19] Keynes himself recognized the asymmetry of IMF leverage between creditor and debtor countries in the discussion in the lead-up to the creation of the IMF.

able to effect changes in member country policies in the context of financial arrangements, it has not been influential without the leverage of financing. In its key surveillance function (which involves no financing), the IMF has rarely led to changes in the policies of large creditor countries, even when such policies have had significant spillover effects on countries; it has not been able to persuade large creditor countries to sacrifice domestic objectives for systemic ones. There seems to be an implicit "pact of mutual nonaggression" to use Mussa's phrase, in IMF surveillance (Mussa 2007, p. 2). Perhaps as a result, the IMF has had a history and tradition of nonadversarial dialogue between its members and has not had to develop a real dispute settlement system.[20]

Compounding this problem of limited leverage is the IMF's eroding legitimacy. Although its role and importance were rehabilitated with the recent global financial crisis, the perception of the IMF as an unreliable interlocutor in emerging market countries—Asia in particular—endures. A good example is the IMF's new conditionality-lite financing facility, which has few takers because some emerging market countries do not want to be seen even as potential borrowers from the IMF. Indeed, in 2009, a number of emerging market countries—Brazil, Singapore, and the Republic of Korea—preferred to get lines of credit from the U.S. Federal Reserve than from the IMF.

The WTO seems to be different on these two counts of legitimacy and leverage, because it works on the basis of the exchange of concessions, which ensures that all players feel they have derived a fair political "bargain." Reciprocity ensures political buy-in to cooperation. Periodic negotiations in the GATT/WTO have updated this political contract between countries, redressing some old grievances and papering over others, with the implicit understanding that there will be a future occasion on which to take up the unsolvable problems of the day.

A consequence of reciprocity and the periodic updating of the political contract to cooperate—and another reason why the WTO works—is that this process creates incentives to adhere to the dispute settlement contract. Dispute settlement by the WTO is effective largely because countries feel that they have previously (and recently) made a reasonably advantageous,

---

[20] A corollary of the observation that cooperation is least likely where the self-interest of the largest countries are at stake is that the prospects for successful cooperation are greater where these countries are less affected and when the demands on them are minimal. Building global safety nets by providing greater and more expeditious access to crisis financing is one area where the greatest progress has already been made. The IMF's lending ability tripled after the crisis, and it may increase further. For the large countries, it is both desirable and effective to push for larger safety nets. The costs are relatively small—involving larger financial contributions rather than any major change of domestic policies—and the rewards are great, because the system as a whole is strengthened while the individual clout of the large countries is increased (see Goldstein 2009).

fair, and equitable bargain, to which they must adhere. WTO governance works because negotiations to create the rules and agree on liberalization are perceived as fair and broadly equitable in outcome, rendering subsequent compliance possible.[21]

4.3.2 Trade, Climate Change, and Green Growth

Do the institutions and ideology of globalization stand in the way of tackling climate change? In one very important respect, they may.[22]

Consider two episodes from 2012. In late 2012, the United States and the European Union sanctioned the use of antidumping duties against Chinese exports of solar panels on the grounds that Chinese manufacturers were "dumping" (selling below cost) solar panels manufactured in China. In the presidential debates, President Obama was on the defensive against Mitt Romney, who tried (with some success) to tar him with the "failed industrial policy" brush in relation to government support for clean energy and Solyndra, a producer of solar panels that filed for bankruptcy two years after receiving substantial government loans and guarantees. These examples illustrate how international rules and ideology (which underlie rules) could stand in the way of efforts to tackle climate change.

Mattoo and Subramanian (2012b) argue that only radical technological change can reconcile climate change goals with the development and energy aspirations of the bulk of humanity. Technological change requires the deployment of the full range of policy instruments that would raise the price of carbon and provide incentives for research and development of non-carbon-intensive sources of energy and related green technologies. With notable exceptions, countries have shown great reluctance to raise the price of carbon directly.

International rules severely restrict the use of subsidies. Under current WTO rules, domestic subsidies for the development and production of clean energy and related energy technologies are actionable by partner countries if those countries feel that their domestic production or exports are adversely affected. Until 2000, some of these subsidies were deemed nonactionable, but the exemption has not been renewed. Moreover, all forms of export subsidy involving clean energy and/or green technologies are prohibited. These rules are in place because of the ideology that imbues globalization—the notion that subsidies and all forms of industrial policy are dubious.

---

[21] Experience suggests that the mere prospect of retaliation, as well as reluctance to be seen as a rule breaker, is sufficient to ensure compliance and that there is rarely need for action.

[22] This section is based on Mattoo and Subramanian (2013).

In relation to climate change, these rules are doubly bad. There is, of course, a logic to curtailing subsidies: even if they confer domestic benefits, those benefits are outweighed by the damage to partner countries. A multilateral rule to which there is general adherence reduces that damage, potentially leaving countries better off. But in the case of climate change, because spillovers are global, any subsidy that promotes clean energy and development confers a benefit to partner countries. On balance, therefore, rules should err on the side of promoting rather than restricting subsidies.

There is a second, arguably bigger, political economy benefit. Prospects for climate change action in the United States in the form of a carbon tax or cap-and-trade are not bright. President Obama's grand rhetoric in his 2013 State of the Union speech is unlikely to be matched by bold action because of the lack of bipartisan support in Congress. This state of affairs reflects a combination of factors—climate change denial, the strength of the carbon energy industries, and weak economic prospects. There is probably only one development that could galvanize action in the United States: the threat that China will capture green technology leadership. The United States needs a Sputnik moment of collective alarm at the loss of economic and technological ascendancy.

The problem is that China is currently constrained by WTO rules, as the actions against its firms in 2012 illustrate.[23] China and all countries that are not straitjacketed by the tyranny of the subsidies-are-bad ideology and that have the financial means to do so should be allowed to deploy industrial policy to promote clean energy and green technologies. If doing so leads to a subsidy war because partners feel threatened, that is a war that should be promoted, as it will ignite the race for the development and production of an undersupplied global public good. From this perspective, WTO rules should allow not only domestic but also export subsidies; current rules circumscribe the use of domestic and prohibit the use of export subsidies.[24]

---

[23] In fact, China stopped providing subsidies to its solar power companies in response to trade action by the United States. "The U.S. Trade Representative's Office responded by filing a complaint in December with the WTO saying China violated rules of the Geneva-based trade arbiter. China's Special Fund for Wind Power Manufacturing required recipients of aid to use Chinese- made parts and amounted to a prohibited subsidy, the U.S. said. Before the WTO acted on the complaint, China made it moot by ending that aid in June, according to the U.S" (http://www.bloomberg.com/news/2011-09-23/blame-china-chorus-grows-as-solyndra-fails-amid-cheap-imports.html).

[24] Another area in which trade restrictions should be permitted is border tariffs against imports from countries that do not tax carbon in the manner that the importing country does. Such tariffs would help overcome opposition from energy-intensive industries in countries wishing to raise the price of carbon on the grounds that they would be rendered uncompetitive relative to imports from countries that do not tax carbon. A final area in which WTO rules need to be clarified is export restrictions on natural gas, which is becoming an important fuel. The U.S. currently limits its exports to countries with which it does not have a free trade agreement. If greater global use of natural gas is desirable (because it is cleaner than substitutes such as oil and coal), then restrictions on exports may be deleterious for global energy emissions.

4.3.3 Trade and Scarcity of Food and Resources

The 2007 global food crisis was severe.[25] According to the World Bank (2009), about 100 million people are estimated to have been thrown back into the ranks of the poor because of increases in the price of food. Riots occurred in a number of countries. The Bank identified 33 countries as especially vulnerable. The poor were especially vulnerable because they spend the largest portion of their income on food. In the United States, the poor spend an estimated 18 percent of their income on food; a similar measure for households earning less than $1 a day is about 72 percent in Peru and South Africa, 66 percent in Indonesia, and 50 percent in Mexico (Banerjee and Duflo 2011).

But pressure on food supplies, and associated high food prices, could be a medium- to long-term reality, because some of the driving factors—rising prosperity in the developing world, which creates more demand; high fuel prices; stagnant agricultural productivity; and climate change-induced pressure on agricultural supplies, including through the depletion of water—could be of a durable nature. These fundamentals are being exacerbated by export restrictions on foodstuffs. According to a World Bank report, in the 2007 crisis, 18 developing countries imposed some form of export restriction (Zaman et al. 2008). Each country was trying to keep domestic supplies high, on the grounds of food security. But as more countries implemented export controls, global supply contracted, pushing prices up and exacerbating global food insecurity. The global rice market was particularly affected by trade restrictions.[26]

There are few restrictions on the use of export taxes in the WTO, and its disciplines on export restrictions are incomplete. The GATT does prohibit quantitative restrictions on exports, but temporary restrictions are permitted in order to prevent critical shortages of food or other goods.

This permissiveness on export taxes and restrictions is resulting in the worst of all possible worlds. Under "normal" agricultural conditions, costly taxpayer support reduces imports and encourages production and exports, creating huge distortions. Under abnormal conditions, such as are prevailing now, the opposite occurs: countries liberalize their imports but prevent exports. What is needed is a system in which both imports and exports remain free to flow in good times and bad. Such a system is especially important if trade is to remain a reliable avenue for food security. If in bad times importing countries are subject to the export-restricting actions of producing countries, they will consider trade an unreliable way of maintaining food

---

[25] This section draws on Mattoo and Subramanian (2012a).

[26] Food security goals are best served not by restricting trade but by deploying domestic policy instruments such as targeted safety nets. The existence of such safety nets would dilute the political economy bias in favor of trade interventions.

security and reconsider how to manage their agriculture. As a result, there will be a greater temptation to move toward more self-reliance as insurance against the bad times.[27]

The Doha Round of trade negotiations did not address these problems. It was devoted to traditional forms of agricultural protection—trade barriers in the importing countries and subsidies to food production in producing countries—which are now becoming less important as food prices have soared and import barriers declined. The trade agenda needs to be enlarged, so that trade barriers, on both imports and exports, are put on the trade agenda.

Trade policies have also exacerbated the scarcity of nonfood resources. Concerns have already arisen over China's restriction of exports of rare earth metals, for some of which (for example, scandium and yttrium) it accounts for more than 70 percent of the world's exports. It also accounts for a large share of exports of other key raw materials, including various forms of bauxite, magnesium, and zinc.[28]

4.4 Fundamental Policy Challenges

The period of hyperglobalization has been associated with the most dramatic turnaround in the economic fortunes of developing countries. Regardless of the view one takes about this association, it is safe to say that a broadly open system is good for the world, good for individual countries, and good for average citizens in these countries. Going forward, even if the pace of hyperglobalization slows, the aim of policy at the national and collective level must be to sustain steady and rising globalization and avoid sharp reversals.

The previous section illustrated some of the proximate challenges. They can be addressed only if the deeper challenges are recognized and addressed.

One way of approaching these more fundamental policy challenges is suggested in Table 4.5, which helps to identify the problems and hence to prioritize the policy response. This schematic can be applied to three broad groups of countries (high, middle, and low-income), the challenges and responses for each of which may differ.

What are the really important challenges for the open trading system, and how should they be responded to? If the next couple of decades mimic or

[27] Not surprisingly, WTO members that depend heavily on world markets for food (for example, Japan and Switzerland in 2000; the Democratic Republic of Congo, Jordan, and the Republic of Korea in 2001) have pushed for disciplines on export controls and taxes. Recognizing that importers' concerns about the reliability of supply could inhibit liberalization, some exporting countries have advocated for multilateral restrictions on the right to use export restrictions (examples include the Cairns Group and the United States in 2000 and Japan and Switzerland in 2008) (International Economic Law and Policy Blog 2008).
[28] In an earlier case, a WTO panel ruled against certain export restrictions China had maintained on a number of raw materials, including bauxite, coke, fluorspar, magnesium, and zinc.

Table 4.5 Policy Responses to the Challenges of Globalization

Level of response	Further liberalize	Maintain status quo	Retreat from globalization
National	• In low-income countries, strengthen domestic supply capacity to exploit globalization. • In China and other middle-income countries, sustain growth to enable further liberalization. • In high-income countries, revive growth and address "beleaguered middle class" and entitlements problems.	Strengthen social insurance in high-income countries.	
International/ collective	• Prevent fragmentation and conflict • Sustain multilateralism through a "China Round."	Cooperate on taxation of mobile factors to sustain domestic safety net.	Create minimum safeguards to allow some trade protection?

Source: Authors.

come close to mimicking the past two in terms of globalization, success will have been unambiguous. The challenge is thus simply to maintain the status quo and allow the forces that have shaped globalization over the last few decades to play themselves out.

Alternatively, one could argue that globalization needs to advance on a number of different dimensions—because, for example, impediments remain to the prospects of average citizens, especially in low-income countries. The need for further globalization could also stem from the perception that in some respects the current system is unsustainable, because it is differentially open and the burden of providing open markets is not equally shared, especially by China.

A third logical possibility is that the forces that will push against globalization are, or will become, so strong that a retreat from current globalization is inevitable. The challenge then will be to manage this retreat in a way that minimizes the costs to countries and citizens around the world.

The responses to each of these challenges can occur at the national level, at the international level, or through some combination of national and collective action. The responses to these challenges are discussed next.

4.4.1 The West's Challenge: Hyperglobalization Meets Economic Decline

THE BAD NEWS
Public support for free trade agreements in the United States is at its lowest point since 2006, according to the Pew Center (2010)—and the decline

occurred quickly. In 2009, the share of people who supported free trade agreements exceeded the share who opposed it by a margin of 11 percentage points. In 2010, opponents of free trade outnumbered supporters by 8 percentage points. Surprisingly, among Republican-leaning voters, the turnaround was even more dramatic: the margin in 2009 was 7 percentage points in favor of free trade agreements; the margin in 2010 was 26 percentage points against free trade agreements. This weakening collective perception of the benefits of openness is matched, mirrored, or validated by intellectual opinion.

Samuelson (2004) argues that the rise of developing countries such as China and India could compromise living standards in the United States, because as they move up the technology ladder, they provide competition for U.S. exports, reducing their price. Krugman (2008) focuses on the impact of imports from developing countries, particularly China, on the distribution of income in the United States and the wages of less-skilled workers. His conclusion is that "it is likely that the rapid growth of trade since the early 1990s has had significant distributional effects" and that "it is probably true that this increase (in manufactured imports from developing countries)…has been a force for greater inequality in the United States and other developed countries" (Krugman 2008, 134–5).

Blinder (2009) draws attention to the employment and wage consequences of the outsourcing that has been facilitated by technological change and trade in services. He estimates that 22–29 percent of all U.S. jobs will be off-shored or offshorable within the next decade or two.

Summers (2008a, 2008b) has highlighted the problems stemming from increasing capital mobility. Hypermobile U.S. capital creates a double whammy for American workers. First, as companies flee in search of cheaper labor abroad, American workers become less productive (because they have less capital to work with) and hence receive lower wages; the "exit" option for capital also reduces the incentive to invest in domestic labor. Second, capital mobility impairs the ability of domestic policy to respond to labor's problem through redistribution because of an erosion in the tax base as countries compete to attract capital by reducing their tax rates.

Spence and Hlatshwayo (2012) argue that almost all the increase in employment—27.3 million jobs—in the United States between 1990 and 2008 was in the nontradable sectors, where productivity growth was much slower than in the manufacturing and tradable sectors, explaining the long-term stagnation of wages in the last segment of the workforce.

That a constellation of intellectuals—instinctively cosmopolitan and ideologically liberal—talks like this is an important signal, not least because the objective circumstances have changed. One might call this challenge that of the irresistible force of globalization and hyperglobalization meeting the immovable object of weakening economic and fiscal fortunes in the west.

In the United States, except for a brief spell in the late 1990s, median wages have stagnated for three decades; inequality has been sharply rising, particularly because of rising incomes at the very top of the income spectrum (Piketty and Saez 2003); and mobility has declined (Haskins, Isaac, and Sawhill 2008). Worse, as in all industrial countries, indebtedness has risen (average debt in the G7 is now about 80 percent of GDP), prospects for medium-term growth in the future are not bright (according to the latest *World Economic Outlook* forecast), and aging and entitlements add to the serious fiscal pressures looming. These objective conditions are not the most propitious for sustaining globalization.

This structural malaise is captured in the following metaphor that Larry Katz, of Harvard, uses: "Think of the American economy as a large apartment block. A century ago—even 30 years ago—it was the object of envy. But in the last generation its character changed. The penthouses at the top keep getting larger and larger. The apartments in the middle are feeling more and more squeezed, and the basement has flooded. To round it off, the elevator is no longer working. That broken elevator is what gets people down the most" (quoted by Luce 2010). The policy challenge in the advanced countries is that sustaining current levels of openness will require addressing these domestic challenges at the very time when growth could be slowing and the ability to effect redistribution is being impeded by broader medium-term fiscal concerns.

In this light, the changing attitudes to globalization and free trade cited above are not surprising.

We focus here on what is now different in the west's ability to sustain globalization. A starting point is the view, described in Rodrik (1998), that sustaining openness requires a domestic social consensus in its favor, which in turn requires mechanisms of social insurance to cushion domestic actors against globalization-induced shocks. Rodrik (1998) provides evidence showing that this domestic consensus can be captured in the relationship between the size of government (a proxy for social insurance mechanisms) and openness.

More direct evidence of the importance of social insurance comes from a paper by Autor, Dorn, and Hanson (2013), who show that rising exposure to Chinese imports increases unemployment, lowers labor force participation, and reduces wages in local labor markets. They estimate that the exogenous component of this shock explains one-quarter of the contemporaneous aggregate decline in U.S. manufacturing employment. They also estimate that rising exposure to Chinese import competition explains about 16 percent of the decline in U.S. manufacturing employment between 1991 and 2000 and 27 percent of the decline between 2000 and 2007. Transfer payments for unemployment, disability, retirement, and health care also rise sharply in exposed labor markets. They estimate the increase in annual per capita transfers attributable to rising Chinese import competition at $32 in the first ten years and $51 in the last seven years of the sample, which translates into total expenditure of about $5 billion in the 1990s and almost $15 billion in the 2000s. The deadweight loss of financing these transfers is one-third to two-thirds as large as U.S. gains from trade with China.

Can the west sustain these social insurance mechanisms? According to Summers (2008a), globalization both increases the need for social insurance and undermines the government's ability to provide it, because it renders more factors, especially capital and high-skilled labor, more mobile and less easy to tax.

Has capital become less easy to tax? Figure 4.11 plots the marginal effective tax rates on capital in some important OECD countries and for the OECD as a whole. These rates have been sharply declining, and there is little pressure to reverse these trends.

For the OECD as a whole, the average marginal tax rate declined from about 55 percent to almost 40 percent, a decline of 15 percentage points. These declines were witnessed across most, if not all, countries. In the United States, rates declined from 65 percent to just over 50 percent; in Germany they fell from about 60 percent to less than 50 percent. Of course, these declines reflect pressures other than globalization and the attendant difficulty of heavily taxing mobile capital, but these pressures have been important.

A new development adds to the problems. Across the OECD, the share of the economic pie accruing to capital has been increasing, rising from about 35 percent to 40 percent in the past few years (Figure 4.12). This increasing share has prompted several commentators, including Krugman, to argue that the debate about inequality and trade and inequality in the 1990s, which related to inequality within types of labor (skilled versus unskilled), should now be viewed through a different lens, because inequality is increasingly between capital (and those who own it) and labor.

For the purposes of our argument, what is important is this: not only is the ability to finance mechanisms of social insurance being undermined by weak growth and the burden of debt (Ruggie 1998); also, slippery, mobile capital is now accounting for a larger share of the economic pie. The funding of social insurance through taxation is thus going to become more difficult.

THE GOOD NEWS: THE PROTECTIONIST DOG THAT
BARKED BUT DID NOT BITE

Several commentators have remarked on the fact that despite suffering perhaps the biggest global trade shock ever experienced in the recent global financial crisis, the world did not succumb to protectionism. This response stood in stark contrast to the experience of the 1930s. Explanations for the difference have included the facts that (a) countries could use macroeconomic policy instruments (monetary and exchange rate), which adherence to the gold standard initially prevented in the 1930s (Eichengreen and

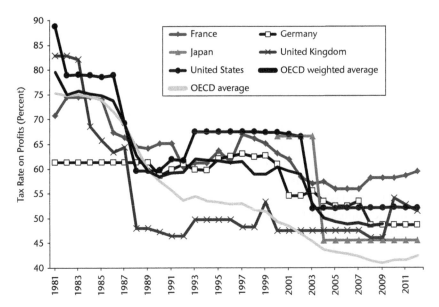

Figure 4.11 Tax Rates on Distributed Corporate Profits in Selected OECD Countries, 1981–2012

Note: Overall (corporate plus personal) tax rate on distributed profits are computed as effective statutory tax rates on distributions of domestic source income to a resident individual shareholder, taking account corporate income tax, personal income tax, and any type of integration or relief to reduce the effects of double taxation.

Source: Authors, based on data from OECD various years.

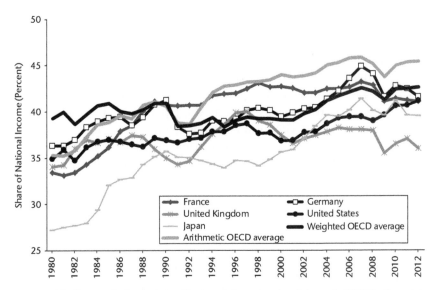

Figure 4.12 Share of Capital in National Income in Selected OECD Countries, 1980–2012

Note: The share of capital is computed from the AMECO database using the adjusted wage share at current market prices.

Sources: Authors, based on data from Annual Macroeconomic Database of the European Commission (AMECO) various years.

Irwin 2009); (b) automatic stabilizers were in place, by way of transfers and unemployment benefits (Autor, Dorn, and Hanson 2013); and (c) the deeper integration created by modern production chains rendered protectionism self-defeating (Baldwin and Evenett 2009).

The bigger puzzle is this: How did the west, and the United States in particular, adjust to arguably the biggest structural trade shock in its history—namely, rising imports from China—without any serious recourse to protectionism? Why was there less protectionist outrage in the United States against China than there was against Mexico in the 1990s or Japan in the 1980s? The domestic uproar against China did not match the backlash created in the context of the North American Free Trade Agreement (NAFTA), and actual protectionist actions did not come remotely close to the actions taken against Japan (the Reagan era witnessed the greatest upsurge in trade barriers in the postwar period; see Destler 1992).

The differences cannot be explained by the relative magnitude of the three shocks, as the Chinese shock was orders of magnitude larger than the early shocks. Figure 4.13 plots imports from Mexico, Japan, and China as a share of U.S. domestic consumption between 1962 and 2011. At their peaks, Japan accounted for 3.6 percent of U.S. consumption, whereas China accounts for about 5.2 percent.[29]

Table 4.6 quantifies the trade shocks to the United States from the three countries. The shock is computed in three ways (each scaled by the working-age population in the United States or the domestic consumption of manufacturing): (a) average imports over the relevant period (for convenience, all shocks are considered to extend over a 20-year period: Japan 1970–90, Mexico 1980–2000, and China 1990–2010); (b) the change in imports over the period;[30] and (c) both average changes and changes calibrated by per capita GDP in each country.

As Table 4.6 shows, depending on the measure used, the Chinese shock was either 4–5 or 10 times as great as the Japanese and Mexican shocks. Calibrated by per capita GDP, it was even greater. One reason to calibrate by per capita GDP is that trade with low-income countries is of the Hecksher–Ohlin variety. It therefore imposes greater domestic political costs [than, say, trade in similar goods between countries at similar levels of development], in particular because these costs are disproportionately borne by unskilled labor, which competes more directly with foreign imports.[31]

---

[29] Appendix Figure 4A.1 plots the same data but for a shorter period for which value-added trade data can be computed. Gross exports overstate value-added exports for China, but they overstate them even more for Mexico.

[30] Trefler (1993) shows that cross-industry differences in protection are associated with the change in import penetration, not its absolute value. Autor, Dorn, and Hanson (2013) use import penetration as a share of working-age population as the measure of trade shock.

[31] Krugman (1995) elaborated on the reasons for intraindustry trade posing fewer political problems compared with Hecksher–Ohlin trade.

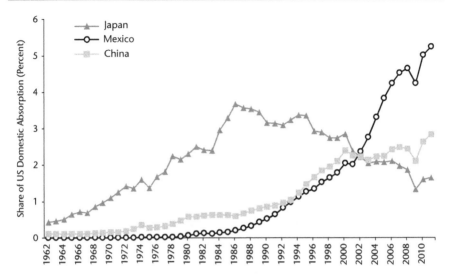

Figure 4.13 Import Shocks in the United States from Mexico, Japan, and China, 1962–2011

Note: Domestic absorption is GDP minus trade balance.

Sources: Authors, based on data from IMF various years.

Several explanations are possible for the differential response to the China shock. One could be that the measure of recorded imports exaggerates the trade shock because of the difference between gross flows and value-added flows. Chinese exports embody less value added than the exports of many other countries because of the large volume of intermediate inputs it imports and transforms into exports. Even making allowances for this distinction, however—and the problem was arguably as acute in relation to Mexican *maquiladora* exports to the United States—would hardly make a dent in the numbers presented above.[32]

A second explanation could be that in the case of Mexico, the uproar was exaggerated because there was a focal point: a trade agreement that had to be passed by the U.S. Congress. But in the case of China, there has also been an identifiable target and identifiable policies: currency manipulation. Moreover, Mexico was an ally, whereas China is a potential adversary and competitor for big-power status, which should have increased the outcry and concerns in domestic U.S. politics.

A third explanation is that by the time the China trade shock arrived, the United States had specialized so much away from unskilled labor that there

---

[32] In appendix Table 4A.1, the figures for China are recomputed based on value-added trade data (we cannot do the same for the Mexican and Japanese shocks, which would bias the comparison in favor of understating the China shock). The size of the Chinese shock declines, but it remains orders of magnitude larger than the earlier shocks from Japan and Mexico.

Table 4.6 Magnitude of Import Shocks to the United States from Japan, Mexico, and China

Country	Period	Real imports (dollars per working-age adult)		Import absorption (percent of domestic consumption)		China shock as multiple of earlier shocks (based on import absorption)			
						Average value		Change	
		Average	Change	Average	Change	Without adjusting for per capita GDP	Adjusted for per capita GDP	Without adjusting for per capita GDP	Adjusted for per capita GDP
Japan	1970–90	373.6	355.2	6.79	6.15	1.2	10.0	2.4	19.5
Mexico	1980–2000	197.3	542.2	2.93	5.46	2.9	17.2	2.9	17.2
China	1990–2010	671.8	1258.6	8.49	14.92	n.a	n.a.	n.a	n.a.

Note: Real imports are total nominal imports deflated by the unit price of imports. Import absorption is defined as (nominal) imports from each country divided by (nominal) domestic consumption (GDP less trade balance). n.a. = Not applicable.

Sources: Authors, based on data from IMF various years, U.S. Census Bureau various years, and Penn World Tables 7.1.

was less to disturb domestically. For example, the number of workers employed in the U.S. clothing sector declined from 900,000 in 1990 to 150,000 in 2013. In technical terms, the United States is no longer in the cone of diversification (Edwards and Lawrence 2013). The estimates of employment disruption by Autor, Dorn, and Hanson (2013) for the Chinese case suggest that this argument cannot be a full, or even an important, explanation, however.

A fourth argument for the relatively muted domestic response is that the size of the Chinese market and the strategy of openness to U.S. FDI essentially coopted U.S. companies and capital, which had an incentive to support rather than criticize China. The Japanese experience was different from the Chinese experience in two important respects: trade conflict with Japan reflected head-to-head competition in some specific industries (steel, cars, semiconductors) rather than conflict based on unequal endowments. It was U.S. capital rather than labor that was the victim in the Japan episode; as it had unusual influence in the political process, there was correspondingly more of a response. In addition, Japan had not created the same stake for U.S. companies in Japan as China had. Finally, it is possible that the underlying macroeconomic situation was better when the Chinese export juggernaut arrived.

One conclusion from all this is that if U.S. domestic politics could survive a shock as great as that from China, there may be an underlying resilience (helped considerably by government insurance mechanisms) that should not be underestimated. Moreover, it could be argued that structural shocks similar to China's are unlikely to repeat themselves. This fact should temper unremitting pessimism about the future of globalization.

One can generalize the Chinese experience in the United States more broadly to other advanced countries. Figures 4.14 and 4.15 and illustrate the change in OECD country imports in favor of developing countries. They plot the average income level of manufactured imports into the United States, Japan, and the European Union. The per capita GDP level of each source country, measured relative to that of the importing country, is weighted by its share in total manufactured imports of the reporting country (in Figure 4.14, the per capita GDP and import share are contemporaneous; in Figure 4.15, the per capita GDP is fixed at the 1980 level). In all cases, imports from the early 1990s are being sourced progressively from poorer countries, suggesting an increase in competition from lower-wage countries. In the European Union, for example, the average income level of imports drops from 100 percent to 75 percent. The point is that all advanced economies have experienced large trade shocks, without recourse to serious protectionism.[33]

---

[33] The value-added counterparts of Figures 4.14 and 4.15 are appendix Figures 4A.2 and 4A.3. The broad trends remain the same.

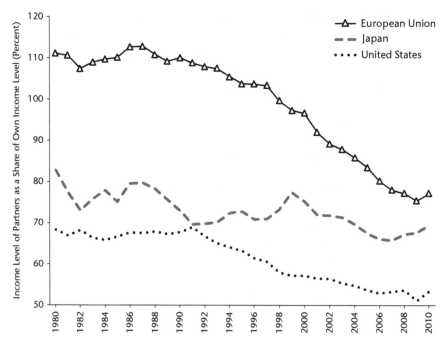

Figure 4.14 Relative Income Level of Exporters to the European Union, Japan, and the United States, 1980–2010

Note: The measure represented here is the weighted average income level of exporters to the European Union, Japan, the United States, excluding oil exporters (as defined by the IMF) and small countries (countries with populations of less than 1 million). Income level is per capita GDP (purchasing power parity) using the *rgdpch* measure in the Penn World Tables. For example, if we call this index $RI_{EU}t$ for the European Union, it is computed as

$$RI_{EU,t} = \sum_i \left(\frac{GDP_{i,t}}{GDP_{EU,t}} \right) * \left(\frac{M_{i,EU,t}}{M_{EU,t}} \right)$$

where $M_{i,EU}$ is imports by the European Union from i and $\bar{M}$ is total imports by the European Union. $RI_{JP,t}$ and $RI_{US,t}$ are identically computed for Japan and the United States.

Sources: Authors, based on data from IMF various years and Penn World Tables 7.1.

4.4.2 The China Challenge: Bretton Woods Rules or Hyperglobalization Rules?

China will play a critical role in shaping the future of globalization, just as the United States did in the immediate aftermath of World War II. Its economy is as large as the United States' (in purchasing power parity terms), and its merchandise trade is larger. Over time, unless China implodes, the differential in economic strength will widen in its favor. Under reasonable assumptions about growth, China will become the dominant economic trader, accounting for twice as much trade as the United States and four times as much as Germany in 2030.

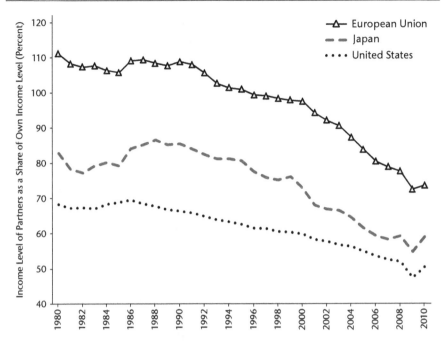

Figure 4.15 Relative Income Level of Exporters to the European Union, Japan, and the United States with Fixed Weights, 1980–2010

Note: See note to Figure 4.4. GDP weights are fixed to their initial 1980 value. The fixed-weight index $RI_{EU,t}^{FW}$ becomes:

$$RI_{EU,t}^{FW} = \sum_i \left(\frac{GDP_{i,1980}}{GDP_{EU,1980}} \right) * \left(\frac{M_{i,EU,t}}{M_{EU,t}} \right)$$

Sources: Authors, based on data from IMF various years; Penn World Tables 7.1

The China challenge will be twofold. As it becomes the world's largest economy and trader, its markets will become more important for other countries, especially low-income ones. China will thus matter to globalization not just as an exporter but also as an importer.

This tension has been best exemplified in recent years by China's mercantilist growth strategy. In this millennium, China's growth and exports have been underpinned by an undervalued exchange rate, a policy that has been successful for China from a domestic perspective. By increasing the global export supply and depressing the global price of tradables, this policy may have set back the diversification possibilities of other poorer countries, however (Mattoo, Mishra, and Subramanian 2012).[34]

---

[34] Undervalued currencies are in effect both an import tax and an export subsidy; countries that maintain them wind up reducing the profitability of industries in countries with which they trade.

The China challenge is more broadly applicable to middle-income countries. On the one hand, these countries will continue to rely on trade and foreign markets as a means of increasing their growth. On the other hand, these countries and their markets are becoming big enough (as the projection for China suggested) to offer opportunities for the average citizen in other and poorer parts of the world. If China's actions are market-opening, there will be little conflict between its domestic imperatives and the demands of an open system. If, however, it uses its policy space to implement beggar-thy-neighbor policies, conflict with other countries, including poorer ones, will ensue.

A second, possibly more important challenge from China's rise will pertain to the openness of the global system. After World War II, the United States initially bequeathed an open, rules-based trading system. Subsequently, reasonably successful cooperation between the two dominant trading powers—the United States and Europe—was achieved in the GATT/WTO through reciprocal exchange of market-opening commitments. Can this same mechanism be effective going forward with China as a dominant trader? Will it be possible to get China to reduce its policy barriers, especially in areas not covered by WTO rules, such as government procurement, investment rules, technology indigenization, and services sector policies?

There may indeed be a structural problem limiting the scope for reciprocity. When the United States and European Union dealt with each other in the postwar period, their markets were largely open; in areas where they were closed, they were broadly closed to the same extent. This symmetry facilitated reciprocity. In the future, problems could arise because the United States and European Union are, in policy terms, more open than China.

China is highly open in terms of trade outcomes, and it has made great strides in removing policy barriers as part of WTO accession. It is, however, more closed in policy terms, especially outside the traditional goods area. In services, technology, and government procurement, closed policies take the form of continuing state control over a large share of economic activity. According to Borchert et al. (2012b), China's services sector policies are about three times as restrictive as those of the United States. In the retail sector, for example, China limits foreign ownership to 49 percent if the retailer has set up 30 or more stores that sell multiple types and brands of goods. In any future bargain, the United States will, by virtue of previous liberalization, have less to offer China.

The paradox will be that China will have greater leverage in bargaining by virtue of its much larger volume of trade but will also have higher trade policy barriers. It is as if, in a duel, one party offers a smaller target and has a pistol with longer range. By 2020, China's imports will be 1.5 larger than the United States' and twice as large as Germany's, conferring the kind of power that comes with being able to determine access to its markets. Future bargaining will therefore be structurally imbalanced in China's favor, making reciprocity more difficult to achieve.

This structural imbalance will be a persistent source of tension between the United States and China. As the U.S. manufacturing sector hollows out and the United States comes to rely to an even greater degree on services, it will seek to open markets overseas, especially in China. If China's future opening is slow, over time the United States may be increasingly tempted to play the unfairness card based on the disparate levels of policy openness: "Why should our markets be more open than those of a rival and equal?"

This imbalance in bargaining could remain at the level of sparring and skirmishing without systemic consequences. But suppose failures to address its structural economic problems—stagnating median household income, rising inequality, declining economic mobility—creates a large, disaffected, and beleaguered middle class in the United States and that the intellectual consensus in favor of openness becomes increasingly frayed, as it has in the past few years. Frustrated by China's unwillingness to open the new sectors of its economy and lacking the carrots to overcome its unwillingness, spurred by a weak economic climate and shifting intellectual certitudes, and goaded by perceptions that China is not making its fair contribution to keeping markets open, the United States could be tempted to threaten to close its own market to China unless China further opens its own. In this scenario, especially if China cannot wean itself off mercantilism and state capitalism, the scope for trade conflict and tension could increase considerably, jeopardizing the openness of the global system.

Concerns about China's trade policies have not been confined to rich countries. The Chinese export juggernaut is a source of concern across the developing world. Brazil, India, Mexico, Korea, South Africa, and other emerging market countries chafe under China's mercantilist exchange rate policies. Most of the antidumping actions taken by developing countries have been against Chinese imports. And one of the dirty secrets of the Doha Round is that its collapse was caused in part by the reluctance of emerging market countries to liberalize their economies and expose themselves to Chinese competition.[35]

---

[35] In 2009, China's share of imports in the most protected sectors was substantially larger than its share of overall imports and dwarfed that of any other supplier. Its share in these sectors was more than 70 percent in Japan; more than 60 percent in Korea; about 55 percent in Brazil; and about 50 percent each in the United States, Canada, and the European Union. Even in these protected sectors, China's share increased dramatically over the course of the Doha Round. In many importing countries (for example, Brazil, the European Union, and the United States), China's share more than doubled. Also striking is how much market share China has gained even in countries such as Canada, Mexico, and Turkey, which have free trade agreements with close and large neighbors. Thus, liberalization under the Doha agenda, especially in the politically charged, high-tariff sectors, is increasingly about other countries opening their markets to Chinese exports (Mattoo and Subramanian 2012a).

So a big, first-order question for the open system is how to prompt China to adopt more open policies. The problem becomes acute if one recognizes China's economic dominance and the degree to which other countries have lost leverage to influence Chinese policies. A little over a decade ago, the west could essentially determine the terms of China's accession to the WTO; that is no longer the case today.

4.4.3 The Changing Global Governance of Trade: Mega-regionalism Meets China

For a variety of reasons, regional integration has been, along with unilateral liberalization, the preferred mode of liberalization. As a result, the governance of world trade has shifted decisively toward regionalism and away from multilateralism.

So far, preferential trade agreements (PTAs) have been North–South "deep" regional trade agreements, occasioned in part by the rise of supply chains. A Doha Round that was midwifed in an unusual bout of post-9/11 world solidarity and saddled with an agenda of issues such as agriculture and tariffs that have less relevance now than new issues (exchange rate mercantilism, services, government procurement, investment, export restrictions) also contributed to a preference for regionalism (Mattoo and Subramanian 2012a; Baldwin 2011b).

North–South PTAs have not posed a serious threat to globalization; in fact, they may have contributed to significant opening through a process of competitive liberalization. But this relatively benign outcome cannot be taken for granted in the case of the mega-regionals looming on the horizon. On the one hand, they will involve deep integration and facilitate further globalization. After all, the world trading system is already multilayered in terms of levels of integration (the European Union, the European Free Trade Agreement, customs unions, other free trade agreements, and so forth). A Trans-Pacific Partnership and Transatlantic Trade and Investment Partnership will just add another layer of integration.

On the other hand, such agreements could be exclusionary, depending on the extent to which they conform to the principles of open regionalism. Their effect will depend, above all, on how outsiders—the middle-income countries, especially China—react. If China views these agreements as economic war and containment by other means and retaliates by concluding its own regional agreements, excluding the large traders, fragmentation and conflict could lie ahead.

It is not that the WTO and multilateralism have become totally irrelevant. More and more countries, including Russia, want to join the WTO. Its dispute settlement system functions effectively; its basic rules are broadly respected.

The question is whether it retains its relevance as a key forum for facilitating further liberalization or transforms itself into an institution that serves mainly as a court of trade law and an overseer of regional trade.

4.4.4 The (Non) Challenge of Low-Income Countries

The antiglobalization and anti-WTO crusade of the 1990s (culminating in the protests in Seattle in 1998) forced policymakers into a strenuous defense of the development-friendliness of the trading system. The Doha Round, for example, was formally dubbed the Doha Development Agenda, which seems an overdone title.

The perception that the trading system is unfair to low-income countries stems from the fact that rich country trade barriers are highest in agriculture and low-skilled manufacturing (textiles, clothing, and footwear), which tend to be important exports for low-income countries. This situation changed over the past decade or so. Rich country barriers in these sectors declined in the aftermath of the Uruguay Round, with Canada, the European Union, the United States, and Japan all significantly improving preferential access to low-income countries, in terms of both country and product coverage (the European Union's Everything But Arms and the United States' Africa Growth and Opportunity Act are two notable examples). In some cases, these schemes also became less arbitrary.

As a consequence, low-income countries are at worst treated no worse than the typical country and at best treated better. Nearly all low-income countries ("least developed countries," in the jargon of the trading system) face lower trade barriers than most other countries, because they receive generous preferences (albeit with some problems, depending on which country is granting them). There are some exceptions to these preferences (Bangladesh and Cambodia in clothing; West African countries facing rich-country cotton subsidization). But even these exceptions create a situation only of parity with other countries. Increasingly, larger developing countries have also started granting preferential access to low-income countries, although the coverage and magnitude of this access are limited.

Hoekman and Nicita (2011) calculate that the average barriers facing exports of Sub-Saharan Africa are very low, and much lower than for other countries. The average level of restrictiveness (including nontariff measures) that exports from Sub-Saharan Africa face in other markets—4.4 percent in high-income countries and 6.0 percent in upper-middle-income countries, taking account of preference margins—is consistently lower than for other groups. The comparable numbers are 6.3 and 15.6 percent for high-income countries as exporters and 5.7 percent and 11.8 percent for upper-middle-income countries as exporters. (An exception is South Asia, which faces higher barriers because its exports face higher MFN tariffs and because countries such as India and Bangladesh are not included in the major preferential schemes, especially in the United States.)

Low-income countries also receive considerable space to pursue their own policies. In relation to rules on subsidies, intellectual property, and local content requirements, the least developed countries face weaker obligations. Moreover, the thresholds for taking contingent protectionist action (countervailing and antidumping) against exports of low-income countries are generally higher.

So it is not clear what more could be done for low-income countries internationally that would materially alter their growth prospects (Box 4.1). Their growth challenges are predominantly domestic, as Dani Rodrik's chapter in this volume implies. Even recognizing the important point that Baldwin (2011a) makes—that these countries need to get onto the new supply chains—it is not clear what other countries might do to galvanize this process, especially if the supply chain phenomenon is to some extent about geography.

For low-income countries, a trading system that allows them policy space to pursue appropriate growth strategies and at the same time keeps global markets open for their exports is critical. After all, such was the external environment that allowed today's middle-income countries to prosper. Despite the tightening of trade rules since the formation of the WTO, there remains enough policy space for these rules not to become a straitjacket for today's low-income countries. Apart from some specific issues (such as food security), the real concern will be whether the external environment will remain as benign as in the previous two decades, so that low-income countries can export their way to growth. The actions of high- and middle-income countries will be critical.

4.5 Policy Responses

The key challenges facing globalization are sustaining domestic support for it in the west and ensuring that China continues to open its markets. Open markets in China are an important part of China's domestic agenda for sustaining convergence. They also offer opportunities for poorer countries similar to those that China enjoyed in industrial countries over the last few decades. They are critical to keeping the trading system open and free of serious conflict. The challenge of mega-regionalism is related to the China challenge.

Box 4.1 HELPING LOW-INCOME COUNTRIES IN NEW WAYS

Discussions of trade by low-income countries increasingly focus on supply chains. Summarizing a new report, *Enabling Trade: Valuing Growth Opportunities*, Hoekman (2013, p. 13) suggests:

> reducing supply chain barriers could increase global GDP up to six times more than removing all import tariffs. Estimates suggest that an ambitious improvement in two key components of supply chain barriers—border administration and transport and communications infrastructure—with all countries raising their performance halfway to global best practice (as observed in Singapore), would lead to an increase of approximately $2.6 trillion (4.7 percent) in global GDP and $1.6 trillion (14.5 percent) in global exports. By contrast, the gains available from complete worldwide tariff elimination amount to no more than $400 billion (0.7 percent) in global GDP and $1.1 trillion (10.1 percent) in global exports.

The focus on supply chains, combined with the laudable aim of making the WTO more development-friendly and helping low-income countries, has led concerned actors to push for "trade facilitation" and "aid-for-trade." The argument for trade facilitation is that improving the procedures and institutions relating to trade and processing of trade would expand trade. Hoekman and Nicita (2011) claim that relatively limited actions to facilitate trade can boost the trade expansion effects by a factor of two, three, or more.

Leaving aside these eye-popping quantitative estimates, the real issue relates to the changes in policies and practices in low-income countries that need to be changed. One often-cited area is customs administration and procedures. The assumption underlying trade facilitation initiatives is that reforming customs is relatively easy. In fact, corruption is so rife that customs administration is fiendishly difficult to reform. A policy prescription that calls for customs reform is not very different from its behind-the-border counterpart that calls for improving institutions—something that is not easily done.

Moreover, trade facilitation assumes that governments should devote their policy effort to reforming customs administrations as opposed to reforming the judiciary or civil services more broadly. Advocates of trade facilitation never explain why trade should be prioritized.

The same assumptions pervade calls for "aid-for-trade." The question why not aid for health, or education, or other spheres is never addressed. Nor is the issue of whether aid can be effective in improving customs administration. Moreover, it turns out that reducing supply chain barriers is really about customs reform and reform of services sector policies within these countries, which are largely domestic agendas with a relatively limited role for outsiders.

As Borchert et al. (2012a) note, "Today, industrial countries provide 'aid for trade' to landlocked countries to improve their ports, airports, and telecommunications infrastructure. But they avoid the liberalisation that would let service providers compete to use these facilities. Their taxpayers and the development community need to push for services reform. Otherwise these 'trade-facilitating' investments will earn a poor return."

4.5.1 National Responses

Sustaining and furthering globalization will be determined at the national rather than the international level. For the United States and Europe, actions are needed to revive growth and address fiscal challenges, especially the challenges stemming from growing entitlements. For the United States, there is the additional challenge of addressing the problems of stagnating wages, rising inequality, and declining mobility. Success on these fronts will provide a surer guarantee that globalization will proceed apace. Several studies note that the demand for trade protection is inversely and robustly related to the state of the economy (see Rodrik 1998).

For its part, China should have a stake in preserving the open system for the simple reason that its rapid economic transformation over the past three decades was predicated crucially on openness. That transformation is still far from complete: China's standard of living is still only 20–25 percent that of industrial countries. Completing that transformation is critical for the political legitimacy of China's policymakers. In these circumstances, disrupting the open system would amount to biting the hand that has fed China and its rulers.

Indeed, going forward, the Chinese agenda for reforms, as elaborated in the government-imprimatured 2012 World Bank report *China 2030*, should be entirely consistent with an open system: China's domestic needs are broadly outsiders' wants. For example, the nontransparent practices of the state enterprises and the financial repression and closed nature of China's capital account are a big concern for foreign firms trying to access the Chinese market and for firms around the world trying to compete with an undervalued Chinese currency. The more China reforms its state enterprises and state-owned banks, the easier it will be for foreigners to do business with it.

China 2030 calls on China to move more toward an innovation-based economy, which would require stronger protection of property rights, another key demand of outsiders. China needs to reduce its pollution and move toward a more carbon-efficient economy, which would allow it to play a constructive role in global climate change efforts. In all these cases, tensions will undoubtedly arise from differing senses of urgency about specific actions. But across the board, there is no fundamental conflict between what China needs to do domestically and what it needs to do to sustain an open system.

Of course, China could falter because its domestic problems—rising inequality and corruption, increased demands for accountability and participation, environmental deterioration—cannot be easily resolved. In this case, globalization would suffer.

4.5.2 International Responses to the Challenges Facing the West

International/collective responses can help in relation to both these challenges. In relation to the first, the increasing mobility of capital and its ability to escape taxation needs to be addressed. Rodrik (1998, p. 81) argues that this phenomenon "undercuts the revenue sources needed to maintain social and political cohesion and ultimately erodes support for free trade." Two new developments have exacerbated this problem: capital has become more mobile (reflected in growing financial globalization and increased FDI flows) and the distribution of income in most OECD countries has moved substantially in favor of capital (and also in favor of high-skilled people), increasing the size of the tax base that can elude taxation.

In many emerging markets as well, especially China and India, capital is accounting for a larger share of the pie (Figure 4.16). The global tax base (not just that of the OECD) is hence becoming more slippery. If countries

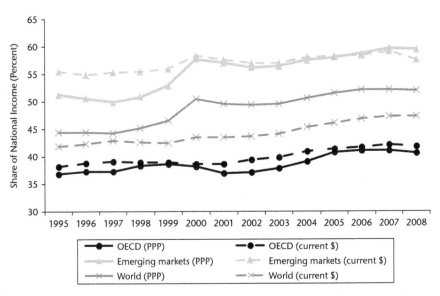

Figure 4.16 Share of Capital in National Income in Selected Country Groups, 1995–2008

Note: For emerging market countries, "compensation of employees" in the National Account Statistics was divided by GDP to compute the labor share. When series change, the last available series is used and completed by interpolation with the others using growth rates. The weighted averages (weighted by GDP in current dollars and purchasing power parity) were computed for eight emerging market countries (Argentina, Brazil, China, India, Korea, Mexico, Russia, and South Africa).

Sources: Authors, based on data from UN various years, Annual Macroeconomic Database of the European Commission (AMECO), World Bank various years, and Penn World Tables 7.1.

and companies exploit the mobility of capital, the global ability to provide social insurance will decline, creating problems for globalization. Hence, there needs to be much greater cooperation between rich and emerging market countries (and, of course, tax havens) on how to tax capital and how to share the taxes from capital (Summers 2008b). This cooperation can take the form of greater harmonization (which would be difficult and entail a degree of regulatory convergence that countries will find difficult), or it can take the form of countries doing their best to allow other countries to better enforce their own tax rules (a recent example involved Switzerland relaxing its secrecy laws to allow the United States to go after its tax evaders).

4.5.3 International Responses to the Challenge of China and Mega-Regionalism

The China challenge is a broader problem of cooperation in the face of a shift in economic power away from the United States and Europe toward a rising one. It is in this context that even the new attempt at mega-regional agreements (Trans-Pacific Partnership and Transatlantic Trade and Investment Partnership) must be seen. At one level, these agreements are about deepening integration at a time when the multilateral liberalization process has become moribund and the Doha Round remains in cold storage. At another level, the issue is how the United States and European Union deal with the rise of China.[36]

At the risk of overgeneralizing, the challenge in the trade arena can be summarized as follows: China is happy with the status quo and the United States is not. China—as well as the other larger emerging markets, such as Brazil, India, and Russia—is reasonably content to have Bretton Woods rules apply to it and hyperglobalization rules apply to its large partners. China will liberalize and open up its markets in line with domestic rather than external imperatives. Its partners, especially the United States, will increasingly refuse to acquiesce in this status quo but, given China's dominance and the weakness of the United States, the United States' ability to force or induce China to change will be limited. The mega-regionalism demarche of the United States is an attempt to exert pressure on China.

How can these differing perspectives and positions be reconciled? The larger partners of the United States and China need to deploy a strategy that

---

[36] In the case of the Trans-Pacific Partnership, containment is more political. With the Transatlantic Trade and Investment Partnership, agreement by the United States and the European Union to common regulatory standards would preempt China's imposing its standards in international markets and even force China to adhere to these common standards.

takes account of the possibility that China may occasionally be tempted into a less-than-benign economic hegemony while reinforcing its incentives to act to preserve an open economic system.

The possibility of the misuse of hegemony would not be unique to China. It was famously said of the United Kingdom that Britannia ruled the waves by waiving the rules. The United States also occasionally succumbed to this temptation. In 1955, it excluded agriculture from GATT disciplines. In the early 1970s, it unilaterally blew up the Bretton Woods system when it became a straitjacket on domestic U.S. policies. In the 1980s and 1990s, it cajoled and coerced developing countries to take on costly obligations (relating to intellectual property and capital flows, for example). In the dark Nietschzean view that "power is never held in innocence," misuse of hegemony is intrinsic to hegemony. It is inevitable given the infinite capacity for countries to succumb to the delusion that John Adams memorably warned about, that "power always thinks it has a great soul."

History suggests that the best defense against hegemony is multilateralism, which offers a modicum of protection for the weak against the dominant power. Keeping China tethered to the multilateral system, in which the United States and other major countries can exercise some countervailing influence, offers the best insurance against its unrestrained exercise of hegemony.

Multilateralism could work as a defense against China in several ways: in shaping rules, in promoting adherence to them, and more broadly in defining legitimate behavior. With China's growing size, the balance of negotiating power will be with China rather than its partners. Multilateralism ensures that China's trading partners will have enough heft to negotiate with China in a more balanced manner. For example, China might be willing to open its markets in return for the United States, European Union, India, and Brazil opening theirs. Its willingness to open up in a similar manner in negotiations with just the United States or European Union, or with some less powerful combination, is far from clear.

A similar argument carries over to enforcement and the incentives to adhere to previously agreed-upon rules. China's incentive to abide by multilateral rules will be stronger than its incentive to abide by a series of bilateral agreements, because the reputational costs of being seen as errant are much greater in the multilateral context. The opprobrium of being a deviant from multilateral norms is China's great fear, rendering multilateralism the best weapon the world can deploy against a dominant China.

These arguments for multilateralism have an important corollary for the United States and other countries. They imply less recourse to bilateral and regional dealings with China and with each other. The more countries elevate the role of bilateralism in dealings with China, the less China will be anchored in the multilateral system and the more exposed countries will be to the exercise of Chinese dominance. One operational consequence, advocated by Lieberthal and Wang (2012), is to expand the U.S.–China strategic economic dialogue to include the larger countries in the world—Europe, Japan, Brazil, and India, for a start—whose heft can be an effective counterweight to that of China.

These arguments in favor of multilateralism and against regionalism and bilateralism apply across the board in the fields of currency, finance, and trade, but they carry particularly important implications in the field of trade because of the current environment, in which the WTO appears moribund and regional initiatives are flourishing. The recent trade initiatives of the Obama administration—the Trans-Pacific and Transatlantic partnerships—are regional initiatives. As Box 4.2 suggests, they are particularly fraught in the context of a rising China.

Box 4.2 MULTILATERALISM VERSUS REGIONALISM: THE RISKS FROM THE TRANS-PACIFIC PARTNERSHIP

In the old debate between regionalists and multilateralists, the divide was not about the end-point: all parties wanted global free trade. Rather, the divide was over whether regional agreements would be, in Jagdish Bhagwati's words, a building block or a stumbling block in the way of that goal, with the regionalists falling in the former category and the multilateralists in the latter.

Regionalists would point to the evident success of regionalism in achieving deeper liberalization: in many or most cases, border barriers have been eliminated in goods and services, and in some, behind-the-border barriers have also been addressed. But both forms of regionalism involving China render this old debate less relevant.

No major country has yet embraced regional agreements with China (although the Association for Southeast Asian Nations [ASEAN] has embarked on this path). The arguments against regionalism are really the flip side of the arguments for multilateralism: negotiating with China will lead to agreements that are weighted in favor of China, because it has bargaining power. If the basic problem is the imbalance of leverage arising from China's size, regionalism will by definition be less effective than multilateralism. For the same reason, getting China to adhere to these agreements will also be difficult.

But countries are increasingly negotiating agreements around China, with the Trans-Pacific Partnership representing the best recent example. Advocates of regionalism have long relied on the competitive dynamic it creates: if two countries negotiate preferential reductions of barriers, one or several outsiders will be hurt. These outsiders will then have an incentive to negotiate preferential agreements themselves. This process would continue until the goal of global free trade is achieved—or so went the Bergsten–Zoellick theory of regionalism as promoting competitive liberalization.

But consider three ways in which the Trans-Pacific Partnership might play out. In the first, the United States embarks on a process of deep integration with a number of Asia Pacific countries without China. To avoid the dangers of hostile regionalism (that is, excluding China), Trans-Pacific Partnership countries could subscribe to the principle of open regionalism: countries get all of the agreement's benefits only if they embrace its terms.

The problem with this approach is that China would never agree to fall in line with rules it did not participate in negotiating. For example, if Trans-Pacific Partnership members negotiated rules against undervalued exchange rates, China would probably stay away. If it did, the agreement would hardly achieve the objective of disciplining problematic Chinese policies that adversely affect the open character of the trading system.

In the second scenario, the United States invites China to the Trans-Pacific Partnership negotiating table to be part of the process of creating the rules. Would its participation really be superior to negotiating with China multilaterally, where the European Union, Brazil, and India would also be at the table? If the problem of a rising China is that it will have enormous bargaining power by virtue of its economic size and dominance, then a multilateral process will add more negotiating heft on the other side of the negotiation. How can it not help to have Brazil and India and Europe as part of the group putting pressure on China to create better rules and to adhere to them? Of course, there is no guarantee that Brazil and India will always be on the side applying pressure on China. But where important interests are at stake, they are likely to do so.

In the much worse third scenario, China construes the Trans-Pacific Partnership as an act of hostile regionalism (Yao Yang's [2013] reaction is typical of this perception) and negotiates preferential agreements of its own—with, say, the European Union alone. Such a situation would create significant trade diversion for U.S. and other exporters because of high Chinese levels of protection in certain areas. The Trans-Pacific Partnership could thus provoke China into playing the regionalism game in a way that could fundamentally fragment the trading system. Down this path lies the folly of the interwar years.

In sum, the Trans-Pacific Partnership will either exclude China (and open regionalism may have little sway in persuading China to join) or be less effective in engaging China, because it would exclude other large trading countries (the European Union, Brazil, and India), whose collective heft might be crucial in balancing the bargaining power of China. The lesson is that the success of regionalism in reducing barriers and generating the competitive dynamic for further liberalization simply cannot be applied to China. The successes of regionalism typically involved a big economic power (the United States, the European Union, Japan) negotiating with smaller countries. The smaller countries did most of the incremental liberalization, because the larger countries held the balance of negotiating power and influence. With China, the power balance is reversed, rendering many of the old arguments for regionalism obsolete.

Regional and discriminatory solutions carry greater risks. The challenge of anchoring China in the multilateral trading system—as well as providing a fillip to growth in industrial countries through further liberalization—can be addressed by embarking on a new and comprehensive multilateral initiative. This initiative would anticipate the changing interests and concerns of all the big trading nations in a way that the Doha agenda did not. It would also pave the way for a reciprocal liberalization mechanism— you open your markets in return for my opening mine—that has been the basis for previous successes in the trading system.

To achieve this reciprocity, first and foremost, the world should declare that the Doha Round is dead and place a wider range of issues on the agenda. China's trading partners remain concerned by Beijing's exchange rate policies, as well as the protection and discrimination that stem from China's state capitalism. China and other countries have an interest in ensuring that their exports are not subject to antidumping and trade restrictions, uncertainty from investment regulations, and international rules on subsidies in relation to climate change.

Everyone has an interest in preventing export protectionism, liberalizing trade in goods and services, and opening government procurement markets. To achieve these goals, Mattoo and Subramanian (2012a) call for a new China Round of multilateral negotiations focused on some of these issues, with participation (initially) by a core group or critical mass of large trading countries (Low 2012).

Any new initiative will have to break from the past in one key respect. Countries in the west have been the drivers of past trade negotiations. China and the other big emerging market countries must now take the lead in negotiating further multilateral liberalization (the alternative, an orderly retreat from globalization, is explored with some skepticism in box 4.3). If they do not, there is the risk that mega-regional agreements will spread, which would be detrimental to the excluded larger emerging markets.

Box 4.3 IS AN ORDERLY RETREAT FROM GLOBALIZATION POSSIBLE?

In discussing the challenges of globalization, the possibility of a retreat from it must not be ignored. A meaningful and consequential retreat would have to be led by the major trading powers, especially the United States, Europe, and China. If it is sparked by political or security conflicts, there can by definition be no orderly retreat.

One recent historical event did represent a retreat from globalization. Although not close to the severity of protectionism seen during the 1920s and 1930s, the 1980s experience of U.S.–Japan trade relations is nevertheless instructive. In the wake of the recessions in the early 1980s and the appreciation of the dollar through 1985, the United States became more protectionist (Destler 1992). This protectionism took several forms. Some actions were consistent with the letter if not the spirit of international rules (for example, recourse to antidumping and countervailing duties). Other actions clearly violated the rules (for example, getting Japan to impose voluntary export restraints) or involved the threat of illegal trade sanctions to persuade/coerce Japan to open up its own market. This experience suggests that it will be difficult to craft rules *ex ante* that bind the very players that have the power to violate or disregard them in the very circumstances that create the greatest incentives to do so.

4.6 Concluding Thoughts on the Future of Trade Integration and Cooperation

Can and will the ongoing process of hyperglobalization of goods and services continue? Or, to use Keynes' evocative phrase, might there be "serpents to the paradise" of the ongoing process of hyperglobalization?

4.6.1 Why Optimism about Globalization?

Although trade has been rising rapidly, the process is less than half complete. On a value-added basis, the world trade-to-GDP ratio is about 25 percent, but a simple frictionless gravity model predicts that the theoretical maximum should be substantially greater.[37] At least three forces will drive globalization toward and sustain it at higher levels: economic convergence; technology; and interests, ideas, and institutions.

ECONOMIC CONVERGENCE
As more countries continue to grow and to grow more rapidly, trade will increase, as Figure 4.4 illustrates. Clearly, the pace of globalization will be affected by the pace of convergence. If Rodrik's more sober assessment prevails, the pace of globalization may slow, but it will not be reversed. If the pace described in Table 4.1 is sustained, so too will the ongoing hyperglobalization be.

TECHNOLOGY
Predicting the pace of technological progress is impossible. Revolutions in transportation, and then in information and communication technologies, have driven trade globalization. Even if the pace of new discoveries slows, there is scope for the spread of existing technologies, both directly and as embodied in FDI. Mobile telephony, Internet usage, and connectivity are still far from universal (Aker and Mbiti 2010).

INTERESTS, IDEAS, AND INSTITUTIONS
Bhagwati (1988) identifies a set of factors he calls the "three I's": interests, ideas, and institutions. The very fact of hyperglobalization deepens the enmeshing of interests across countries, people, and companies. In the current phase, the additional reinforcing factor relates to the phenomenon of criss-crossing globalization discussed earlier.

One of the widely noted features of the global financial crisis was the drop in trade that exceeded the decline in the aftermath of the Great Depression. Yet, unlike in the past, the world did not collapse into a protectionist spiral.[38] One reason why this collapse did not occur was that countries, no longer tied to the gold standard or otherwise straitjacketed, had broader macroeconomic policy options. Another reason was that the vertical integration of production

---

[37] Recall that this model suggests that the ratio of world trade to GDP should be 1 minus the sum of the squared shares of countries in world output. With convergence and a sufficiently large number of countries, the sum of squared shares should converge to 0, and the ratio of world trade to GDP should converge to 1.

[38] Global Trade Alert (2012) suggests that there was an upsurge in protectionism after the global financial crises, the quantitative impact of which remains far from clear. Hufbauer et al. (2013) document the rise of local content requirements in a number of countries.

via supply chains made it difficult and undesirable for countries to impose barriers that would undermine these chains and, hence, trading opportunities.

The supply chain phenomenon has a broader counterpart. It is not only goods that are moving back and forth—capital flows are, too. FDI flows no longer just flow downhill from rich to poor countries. Brazil, China, and India are all becoming large exporters of FDI. As capital relocates internationally, the political economy of protectionism also changes. U.S. firms in China have lobbied strongly against U.S. trade action against China. India can less afford to repel FDI if Indian companies at the same time seek to operate in and from foreign markets (Mattoo and Subramanian 2010).

The recent crises provoked an existential debate about capitalism and finance, but the ideological near-consensus that trade in goods and services, as well as FDI, should flow relatively unimpeded has not been dented.

4.6.2 Is There Reason to be Sanguine about Trade?

The cardinal sin of forecasting is to extrapolate the recent past, as Norman Angell, later a Nobel Peace Prize winner, did in 1910 when he published *The Great Illusion*. This pamphlet-turned-book acquired cult status for propagating the view that Europe had become so interlaced economically through trade, credit, and finance that war was impossible: twentieth-century wars would be so economically devastating even to the aggressor that waging one would amount to self-inflicted folly.[39]

Notwithstanding the five influences discussed above, history's lesson is that

> we cannot be 100 percent certain that the enmeshing of interests will be strong enough to sustain the status quo. Nor is there a cast-iron guarantee that the current ideological embrace of markets as the predominant basis for organizing economic relations will survive the vicissitudes of intellectual fashion and the selective and self-serving interpretations of policymakers. There is tail-side risk (that is, a small, but nontrivial probability of catastrophic outcomes) that interests, ideology, and institutions, both domestic and international, will be inadequate to the task of preserving the current system. And then there is always the unforeseeable and the irrational. World War I, after all, did happen." (Subramanian 2011, p. 170)

Section 4.5 discussed the factors that become serpents in the paradise of hyperglobalization. They include prolonged weakness in the west, a serious domestic shock in China that precipitates a retreat there, and the vacuum in international governance. The status quo power is in economic decline, and the rising power will prioritize domestic interests over international responsibilities to a greater degree than previous superpowers, because it is still

---

[39] In the words of Lord Esher, Angell's most earnest disciple, the inevitable consequences of "commercial disaster, financial ruin, and individual suffering" would be "pregnant with restraining influences."

only a middle-income country. Another unforeseeable factor is the politics and projects of militarism and imperialism (for example, a conflict between China and Japan), which could set back globalization.

Most of the actions that will allow positive influences to prevail over globalization-reversing ones will be at the national level: actions to address economic decline in the west and sustain growth in the Rest, especially China. Collective action should help strengthen the institutional underpinnings of globalization. These actions include ensuring that domestic social insurance mechanisms are not undermined by globalization and bolstering multilateral institutions to prevent conflict between the major trading partners. Greater cooperation on taxes may become necessary to preserve funding for these mechanisms. The world should declare the Doha Round dead in order to move to more meaningful multilateral negotiations to address emerging challenges, including any possible threats from new mega-regional agreements. The rising powers, especially China, will have a key role to play in resuscitating multilateralism.

The open, rules-based trading system has delivered immense benefits for all, especially today's emerging market economies. Preserving it will ensure that low-income countries can also make successful growth transitions. It is often overlooked that the international trading system has witnessed more successful cooperation, especially between the systemically important countries, than the international financial and monetary system. So, cooperation to preserve globalization, even if not in its most hyper current incarnation, is of critical importance. It may also prove less difficult.

Appendix 4A: Measuring Value-Added Trade

In national account systems trade is measured in gross terms, meaning that an export from a country is counted at its full value, whether this value was produced in the country or imported in part from another country (via foreign purchases of intermediate goods). It is thus possible to count a good that crosses frontiers at multiple stage of its production several times.

This accounting lies in contrast to the way in which GDP is computed. It is measured in terms of value added: the value of the intermediates used in production is subtracted from the value of the final good.

This distinction between gross and value-added trade has assumed significance in wake of the ongoing process of the slicing up of the value chain across national boundaries. Slicing up is not a new phenomenon, but its magnitude has accelerated sharply in recent years, increasing the importance of proper measurement. Recent attempts have been made to correct this discrepancy and measure a consistent index of "value-added trade" by linking trade data and input-output tables. The basic idea is to link sources and uses of goods and services to be able to trace to its origin the value-added embodied in an exported good.

Johnson and Noguera (2012) use estimates for 42 countries since 1970; their Table 7 is the source of the value-added trade data in Figure 4.1 in this chapter. They use the concept of value-added exports (VAX), the ratio of value added in the country and exported to total exports. Recent research has refined the under-standing of value-added trade by distinguishing various stages of production and trade (Koopman, Wang, and Wei 2013). In this chapter, for reasons of simplicity, we adopt the VAX approach. To calculate the value-added trade data presented in the tables and figures presented in this appendix, we used the publicly available World Input-Output Tables (available at http://www.wiod.org/database/iot.htm). These data span 15 years (1995–2009) and include 40 countries (including 27 EU countries and large developed and emerging market economies as well as a "rest of the world" aggregate), which represent 85–90 percent of global GDP.[40]

We faithfully follow the methodology described in Johnson and Noguera (2012) to obtain a measure of bilateral exports in terms of both domestic and foreign value added. These exports are combined in various ways to derive the numbers used in the appendix figures and tables.

The caveat is that without firm-level data, one has to make the assumption that the production function is homogeneous within a sector across exporting and non-exporting firms. This assumption is probably not accurate, as exporters generally differ in size, productivity, and technology. The value-added trade data presented, although improvements over gross trade data, should be seen as first, and necessarily imperfect, approximations to the "real" value-added data.

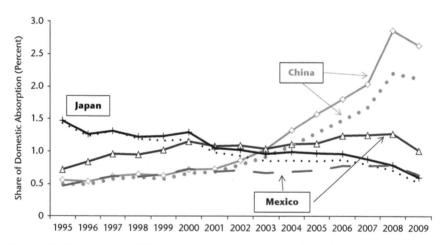

Figure 4A.1 Gross and Value-Added Imports by the United States as Share of Consumption, 1995–2009

Note: See note to Figure 4.13. Lines with (without) markers denote gross (value-added) imports.

Sources: Authors, based on data from World Input-Output Tables and IMF various years.

[40] The World Input-Output Table data are based on preliminary estimates that have since been revised, creating discrepancies for China in 2008 and 2009, and for India to a lesser extent. Data for the two years should therefore be used with caution (the problems with these years led us to use 2007 as the last year in the appendix tables).

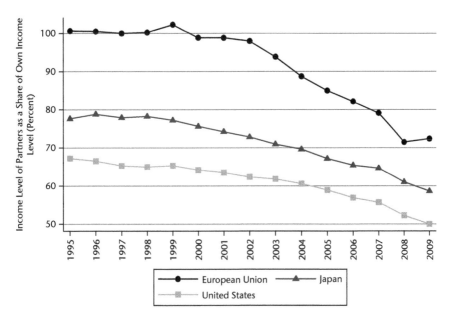

Figure 4A.2 Relative Income Level of Exporters to the European Union, Japan, and the United States, Based on Value-Added Imports, 1995–2010

Note: See note to Figure 4.14. Index here is similar but uses value-added import data.

Sources: Authors, based on data from World Input-Output Tables and Penn World Tables 7.1.

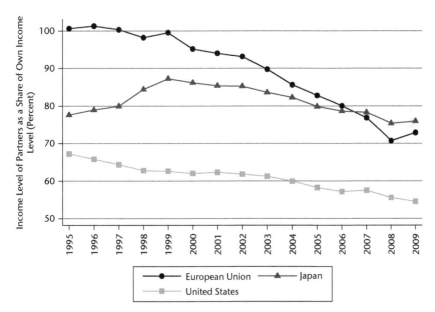

Figure 4A.3 Relative Income Level of Exporters to the European Union, Japan, and the United States, Based on Value-Added Imports at Fixed Weights, 1980–2010

Note: See note to Figure 4.15. Index here is similar but uses value-added import data.

Sources: Authors, based on data from World Input-Output Tables and Penn World Tables 7.1.

Table 4A.1 Mega-Exporters, Based on Value-Added Trade

Country/measure	Trade as a share of GDP	Overtrading, controlling for size	Overtrading, controlling for size and per capita GDP	Overtrading, controlling for size and per capita GDP and oil/small country dummies
Japan (1995) (36 countries in sample)				
Gross exports	9.2	−55.8***	−53.8***	−52.8***
Value-add exports	8.5	−46.9***	−45.5***	−44.3**
China (2007) (35 countries in sample)				
Gross exports	37.9	160.7***	155.0***	161.0***
Value-add exports	27.7	103.2***	102.1***	109.6***

Note: See note to Table 4.3; regressions are similar but use value-added exports and a restricted sample for comparability. * = significant at the 10 percent level, ** = significant at the 5 percent level, *** = significant at the 1 percent level.
Sources: Authors, based on data from World Input-Output Tables and Penn World Tables 7.1.

Table 4A.2 China Shock Based on Gross and Value-Added Imports, 1995–2007

Measure of imports	Real imports (dollars per working-age adults)		Import absorption (percent of domestic consumption)	
	Average	Change	Average	Change
Gross	562.7	957.4	6.1	10.0
Value added	485.5	766.2	5.3	7.9

Note: See note to Table 4.2.
Sources: Authors, based on data from World Input-Output Tables, Penn World Tables 7.1, and U.S. Census Bureau.

References

Aker, J., and I. Mbiti. 2010. "Mobile Phones and Economic Development in Africa." *Journal of Economic Perspectives* 24 (3): 207–32.

AMECO (Annual Macroeconomic Database). Various years. European Commission. http://ec.europa.eu/economy_finance/ameco/user/serie/SelectSerie.cfm.

Anderson, J. A. 2011. "The Gravity Model." *Annual Review of Economics* 3 (1): 133–60.

Autor, D., D. Dorn, and G. H. Hanson. 2013. "The China Syndrome: Local Labor Market Effects of Import Competition in the United States." *American Economic Review* 103 (6): 2121–68.

Baier, S. L., and J. H. Bergstrand. 2001. "The Growth of World Trade: Tariffs, Transport Costs, and Income Similarity." *Journal of International Economics* 53 (1): 1–27.

Baldwin, R. 2011a. "Trade and Industrialisation after Globalisation's 2nd Unbundling: How Building and Joining a Supply Chain Are Different and Why It Matters." Working Paper 17716, National Bureau of Economic Research, National Bureau of Economic Research, Cambridge, MA.

Baldwin, R. 2011b. "21st Century Regionalism: Filling the Gap between 21st-Century Trade and 20th-Century Trade Rules." Policy Insight No. 56, Center for Economic Policy Research Policy, Washington, DC.

Baldwin, R., and S. Evenett. 2009. *The Collapse of Global Trade, Murky Protectionism and the Crisis: Recommendations for the G20.* E-book. London: Centre for Economic Policy Research.

Banerjee, A., and E. Duflo. 2011. *Poor Economics. A Radical Rethinking of the Way to Fight Global Poverty.* New York: Public Affairs.

Bergsten, C. F., and J. E. Gagnon. 2012. "Currency Manipulation, the US Economy, and the Global Economic Order." Policy Brief 12-25, Peterson Institute for International Economics, Washington, DC.

Bernanke, B. 2005. "The Global Saving Glut and the US Current Account Deficit." Sandridge Lecture, Virginia Association of Economics, Richmond, Virginia, March 10.

Bernanke, B. 2007. "Global Imbalances: Recent Developments and Prospects." Bundesbank Lecture, Berlin, September 11.

Bernanke, B., C. Bertaut, L. DeMarco, and S. Kamin. 2011. "International Capital Flows and the Return to Safe Assets in the United States, 2003–2007." FRB International Finance Discussion Paper 1014, Federal Reserve Board, Washington, DC.

Bhagwati, J. 1988. *Protectionism.* Cambridge, MA: MIT Press.

Blinder, A. S. 2009. "How Many US Jobs Might Be Offshorable?" *World Economics* 10 (2): 41.

Borchert, I., B. Gootiiz, A. Goswami, and A. Mattoo. 2012a. "Landlocked or Policy-Locked?" Blogpost on World Bank, Africa Can End Poverty, January 23. http://blogs.worldbank.org/africacan/landlocked-or-policy-locked.

Borchert, I., B. Gootiiz, and A. Mattoo. 2012b. "Policy Barriers to International Trade in Services: Evidence from a New Database." Policy Research Working Paper 6109, World Bank, Washington, DC.

Brülhart, M. 2009. "An Account of Global Intra-industry Trade, 1962–2006." *World Economy* 32 (3): 401–59.

Carpenter, T., and A. Lendle. 2010. "How Preferential Is World Trade?" CTEI Working Paper, Centre for Trade and Economic Integration, Graduate Institute, Ecole des Hautes Etudes, Geneva.

Cline, W. R. 2010. "Renminbi Undervaluation, China's Surplus, and the US Trade Deficit." *Policy Brief 10-20,* Peterson Institute for International Economics, Washington, DC.

Destler, I. M. 1992. *American Trade Politics,* 2nd ed. New York: New York University Press.

Dooley, M. P., D. Folkerts-Landau, and P. Garber. 2003. "An Essay on the Revived Bretton Woods System." NBER Working Paper 9971, National Bureau of Economic Research, Cambridge, MA.

Dunning, J. H. 1983. "Changes in the Level and Structure of International Production: The Last One Hundred Years." In *The Growth of International Business,* ed. M. Casson, 84–134. London: Allen and Unwin.

Edwards, L., and R. Z. Lawrence. 2013. *Rising Tide: Is Growth in Emerging Economies Good for the United States?* Peterson Institute for International Economics, Washington, DC.

Eichengreen, B., and D. Irwin. 2009. "The Protectionist Temptation: Lessons from the Great Depression for Today." Vox-EU. http://www.voxeu.org/article/protectionist-temptation-lessons-great-depression-today.

Frieden, J. A. 2006. *Global Capitalism: Its Fall and Rise in the Twentieth Century.* New York: W. W. Norton.

Global Trade Report. 2012. *Débâcle: The 11th GTA Report on Protectionism.* London: Centre for Economic Policy Research.

Goldstein, M. 2009. "A Grand Bargain for the London G20 Summit: Insurance and Obeying the Rules." VoxEU. http://www.voxeu.org/article/grand-bargain-london-g20-summit.

Haldane, A. 2010. "The $100 Billion Question." Speech to Institute of Regulation and Risk, Hong Kong, March.

Hanson, G. H. 2012. "The Rise of Middle Kingdoms: Emerging Economies in Global Trade." *Journal of Economic Perspectives* 26 (2): 41–63.

Haskins, R., J. Isaacs, J., and I. Sawhill. 2008. "Getting Ahead or Losing Ground: Economic Mobility in America." Brookings Institution, Washington, DC.

Helpman, E., and P. R. Krugman. 1985. *Market Structure and Foreign Trade: Increasing Returns, Imperfect Competition, and the International Economy.* Cambridge, MA: MIT Press.

Hoekman, B. 2013. *Enabling Trade: Valuing Growth Opportunities.* World Economic Forum report, Davos, Switzerland.

Hoekman, B., and A. Nicita. 2011. "Trade Policy, Trade Costs, and Developing Country Trade." *World Development* 39 (12): 2069–79.

Hufbauer, G. C., J. J. Schott, M. Vieiro, and E. Wada. 2013. "Local Content Requirements: A Global Problem." Peterson Institute for International Economics Working Paper, Washington, DC.

Hummels, D. 2007. "Transportation Costs and International Trade in the Second Era of Globalization." *Journal of Economic Perspectives* 21 (3): 131–54.

Hummels, D. L., J. Ishii, and K. M. Yi. 2001. "The Nature and Growth of Vertical Specialization in World Trade." *Journal of International Economics* 54 (1): 75–96.

International Economic Law and Policy Blog. 2008. *Export Restrictions.* worldtradelaw.typepad.com/ielpblog.

IMF (International Monetary Fund). Various years. *Direction of Trade Statistics.* Washington, DC.

Irwin, D. A. 2011. *Trade Policy Disaster: Lessons from the 1930s.* Cambridge, MA: MIT Press.

Johnson, R. C., and G. Noguera. 2012. "Fragmentation and Trade in Value Added over Four Decades." NBER Working Paper 18186. National Bureau of Economic Research, Cambridge, MA.

Johnson, S., and J. Kwak. 2010. *13 Bankers: The Wall Street Takeover and the Next Financial Meltdown.* New York: Vintage Books.

Keynes, J. M. 1920. *The Economics Consequences of the Peace.* New York: Harcourt-Brace.

Klasing, M., and P. Milionis. Forthcoming. "Quantifying the Evolution of World Trade, 1870–1949." *Journal of International Economics.* http://dx.doi.org/10.1016/j.jinteco.2013.10.010.

Koopman R., Z. Wang, and S.-J. Wei. 2013. "Tracing Value-Added and Double Counting in Gross Exports." *American Economic Review* 104 (2): 459–94.

Krugman, P. 1995. "Growing World Trade: Causes and Consequences." *Brookings Papers on Economic Activity* 1: 327–77.

Krugman, P. 2008. "Trade and Wages, Reconsidered." *Brookings Papers on Economic Activity* 1: 103–54.

Krugman, P. 2010. "Chinese Currency Discussion." http://krugman.blogs.nytimes.com/2010/03/17/chinese-currency-discussion.

Lawrence, R. 1996. *Regionalism, Multilateralism, and Deeper Integration.* Washington, DC: Brookings Institution.

Lieberthal, K., and J. Wang. 2012. "Addressing US-China Strategic Distrust." Brookings Institution, Washington, DC.

Low, P. 2012. "The TPP in a Multilateral World." In *The Trans-Pacific Partnership. A Quest for a Twenty-First Century Trade Agreement*, ed. C. L. Lim, D. K. Elms, and P. Low, 299–31. Cambridge: Cambridge University Press.

Luce, E. 2010. "The Crisis of Middle-Class America." *Financial Times,* July 30.

Maddison, A. 1995. *The World Economy: A Millennial Perspective.* Paris: OECD Development Centre.

Mattoo, A., and A. Subramanian. 2009. "Currency Undervaluation and Sovereign Wealth Funds: A New Role for the World Trade Organization." *World Economy* 32 (8): 1135–64.

Mattoo, A., and A. Subramanian. 2010. "Criss-Crossing Globalization: Uphill Flows of Skill-Intensive Goods and Foreign Direct Investment." *Annual World Bank Conference on Development Economics 2009. Global: People, Politics, and Globalization.* Washington, DC: World Bank.

Mattoo, A., and A. Subramanian. 2012a. "China and the World Trading System." *World Economy* 35 (12): 1733–71.

Mattoo, A., and A. Subramanian. 2012b. *Greenprint: A New Approach to Cooperation on Climate Change.* Center for Global Development, Washington, DC.

Mattoo, A., and A. Subramanian. 2013. "Four Changes to Trade Rules on Climate Change." Policy Brief, Peterson Institute for International Economics, Washington, DC.

Mattoo, A., P. Mishra, and A. Subramanian. 2012. "Spillover Effects of Exchange Rates: A Study of the Renminbi." Working Paper 12-4, Peterson Institute for International Economics, Washington, DC.

Melitz, M. J., and D. Trefler. 2012. "Gains from Trade when Firms Matter." *Journal of Economic Perspectives* 26 (2): 91–118.

Mussa, M. 2007. "IMF Surveillance over China's Exchange Rate Policy." In *Debating China's Exchange Rate Policy*, ed. M. Goldstein and N. Lardy, 279–339. Washington, DC: Peterson Institute for International Economics.

OECD (Organisation for Economic Co-operation and Development). Various years. *OECD Statistics.* Paris. http://stats.oecd.org/.

O'Rourke, K. H., and J. G. Williamson. 1999. *Globalization and History: The Evolution of a Nineteenth-Century Atlantic Economy.* Cambridge, MA: MIT Press.

Penn World Tables. Penn World Table 7.1. https://pwt.sas.upenn.edu/php_site/pwt71/pwt71_form.php.

Pew Center. 2010. "Americans Are of Two Minds on Trade: More Trade, Mostly Good; Free Trade Pacts, Not So." http://www.pewresearch.org/2010/11/09/americans-are-of-two-minds-on-trade/.

Piketty, T., and E. Saez. 2003. "Income Inequality in the United States, 1913–1998." *Quarterly Journal of Economics* 118 (1): 1–41.

Rodrik, D. 1998. "Why Do More Open Economies Have Bigger Governments?" *Journal of Political Economy* 106 (5): 997–1032.

Ruggie, J. G. 1998. *Constructing the World Polity.* London: Routledge.

Samuelson, P. A. 2004. "Where Ricardo and Mill Rebut and Confirm Arguments of Mainstream Economists Supporting Globalization." *Journal of Economic Perspectives* 18 (3): 135–46.

Services Trade Restrictions Database. World Bank, Washington, DC. http://iresearch.worldbank.org/ServiceTrade/.

Spence, M., and S. Hlatshwayo. 2012. "The Evolving Structure of the American Economy and the Employment Challenge." *Comparative Economic Studies* 54 (4): 703–38.

Subramanian, A. 2011. *Eclipse: Living in the Shadow of China's Economic Dominance.* Peterson Institute for International Economics, Washington, DC.

Summers, L. 2008a. "America Needs to Make a New Case for Trade." *Financial Times,* April 27.

Summers, L. 2008b. "A Strategy to Promote Healthy Globalization." *Financial Times,* May 4.

Trefler, D. 1993. "Trade Liberalization and the Theory of Endogenous Protection: An Econometric Study of U.S. Import Policy." *Journal of Political Economy* 101 (1): 138–60.

UN (United Nations). Various years. *National Account Statistics.* New York.

UNCTAD (United Nation Conference on Trade and Development). Various years. UnctadStat. http://unctadstat.unctad.org/ReportFolders/reportFolders.aspx?sCS_referer=&sCS_ChosenLang=en.

UNCTAD. 2010. *Global Investment Trends Monitor: Global and Regional FDI Trends in 2009.* Geneva. http://www.unctad.org/en/docs/webdiaeia20101_en.pdf.

U.S. Census Bureau. Various years. www.census.gov.

USITC (United States International Trade Commission). 2011. *The Economic Effects of Significant U.S. Import Restraints: Seventh Update.* Investigation No. 332-325, USITC Publication 4253, Washington, DC.

Williamson, J. H. 2011. "Getting Surplus Countries to Adjust." Policy Brief 11-1, Peterson Institute for International Economics, Washington, DC.

WIOD (World Input-Output Database). n.d. *World Input-Output Tables and International Supply and Use Tables.* http://www.wiod.org/database/iot.htm.

Wolf, M. 2010. "China and Germany Unite to Impose Global Deflation." *Financial Times,* March 16.

World Bank. 2009. *Global Economic Prospects 2009: Commodities at the Crossroads.* Washington, DC: World Bank.

World Bank. 2011. *Data on Trade and Import Barriers.* Washington, DC. http://econ.worldbank.org/WBSITE/EXTERNAL/EXTDEC/EXTRESEARCH/0,,contentMDK:21 051044~pagePK:64214825~piPK:64214943~theSitePK:469382,00.html.

World Bank. 2012. *China 2030: Building a Modern, Harmonious, and Creative Society.* Washington, DC: World Bank.

World Development Indicators (database). World Bank, Washington, DC

WTO (World Trade Organization). 2011. *The WTO and Reciprocal Preferential Trading Agreements.* Geneva: WTO.

WTO. 2013. *The Shaping Factors of World Trade over the Next Decade.* Geneva: WTO.

Yao, Y. 2013. "America's Pivot to Asia Will Provoke China." *Financial Times*, February 12. http://blogs.ft.com/the-a-list/2013/02/12/americas-pivot-to-asia-will-provoke-china/#axzz2QTlHlbKQ.

Zaman, H., C. Delgado, D. Mitchell, and A. Revenga. 2008. *Rising Food Prices: Are There Right Policy Choices?* Washington, DC: World Bank Institute.

Comments on "The Hyperglobalization of Trade and Its Future," by Arvind Subramanian and Martin Kessler

Bernard Hoekman

A distinctive feature of the post-World War II period has been the rapid increase in international commerce, which, with the exception of a few episodes when the world went into recession (most notably in 2008), has grown more rapidly than output year in, year out. The extent to which world trade has grown since the 1950s is truly phenomenal, especially when put in historical perspective. The volume of trade increased 27-fold between 1950 and 2008, three times more than the growth in global GDP. The value of global trade in goods and services passed the $20 trillion mark in 2011 (WTO 2012), reaching 59 percent of global GDP, up from 39 percent in 1990.[1]

Subramanian and Kessler provide an interesting overview of several important dimensions of the most recent wave of globalization, which started in the early 1990s, including the increasing share of global output and trade by developing countries, especially China; the growing role of services; and the proliferation of preferential trade agreements (PTAs). They also highlight a number of important policy implications of recent trends, in particular the need for governments to address the adjustment costs of globalization and to mobilize the necessary funding for social expenditures and continued (greater) investment in education. In what follows, I provide a complementary view of some of the key challenges that confront policymakers, in particular increasing the participation in supply networks of the large number of countries that do not do so today and reducing the large current account imbalances that have emerged and are putting pressure on the trading system.

1. Trade Costs Have Been Declining, but the World Is Not Close to Being Flat

The basic driver of the developments Subramanian and Kessler describe has been the steep fall in trade costs, as a result of technological change and the adoption of outward- (export-) oriented policies. Technological changes have been both hard and

[1] Trade openness ratios were calculated from the World DataBank (the World Bank's Global Economic Prospects database).

soft. They include advances in information and communication technology (ICT), which led to a sharp drop in the costs of international telecommunications, and the adoption of containerization and other improvements in logistics, which led to a sharp fall in unit transport costs. Average tariffs were in the 20–30 percent range in 1950 (WTO 2007), complemented by a plethora of nontariff barriers (including quantitative restrictions and exchange controls) that were often more binding. Today the average uniform tariff equivalent in OECD countries for merchandise trade is only 4 percent, mostly reflecting protection of agriculture, and the average level of import protection around the world has dropped to 5–10 percent (Kee, Nicita, and Olarreaga 2009).

This increase in internationalization as a result of the fall in trade costs reflects ever greater "vertical specialization," with firms (plants) in different countries concentrating on (specializing in) different parts of the value chain for a final product. As a result, the share of manufactures in total exports of developing countries has increased from just 30 percent in 1980 to more than 70 percent today, with a substantial proportion of this increase made up of intraindustry trade—the exchange of similar, differentiated products. Since the 1990s, intraindustry trade ratios for high-growth developing countries and transition economies have risen to 50 percent or higher. Much of this trade is intraregional—for example, about half of all East Asian exports of manufactures go to other East Asian economies, often as part of a supply chain.

There is, however, substantial variation across countries and regions. The intensity of different parts of the world's participation in what the authors hyperbolically call hyperglobalization is very unequal. Sub-Saharan African countries in particular remain heavily dependent on natural resources and agricultural products. Average trade costs remain much higher for low-income countries than richer countries, and in the past 15 years trade costs have fallen much more in the former than the latter, in part because of a lack of "connectivity" reflecting weaknesses in infrastructure (Figure C4.1). Many countries in Africa as well as in South Asia, much of the Middle East, and the members of Mercosur in Latin America have not seen the shift toward intraindustry trade and participation in international supply networks that has been a driver of trade growth in East Asia, Mexico, Turkey, and Central and Eastern Europe and the emergence of what Richard Baldwin has called Factory Europe, Factory Asia, and Factory North America. As Dani Rodrik stresses in his chapter for this project, from the perspective of the "average" global citizen, much therefore depends on location. Many countries are simply not participating in the global value chains and fragmentation of manufacturing production that underlies a large share of the growth in the value of gross trade flows. Fostering greater diversification and participation by African, Latin American, and Middle Eastern economies in international supply networks is one of the great challenges confronting governments of the countries concerned, as well as the trading system.

Technological changes have had a massive impact in supporting the long boom in trade. Just-in-time, multicountry lean manufacturing would be impossible without the process innovations and ICT that permit supply chain management spanning hundreds of suppliers located in different countries. Baldwin's (2011) "second unbundling" is not affecting only the production of industrial and high-tech products (as

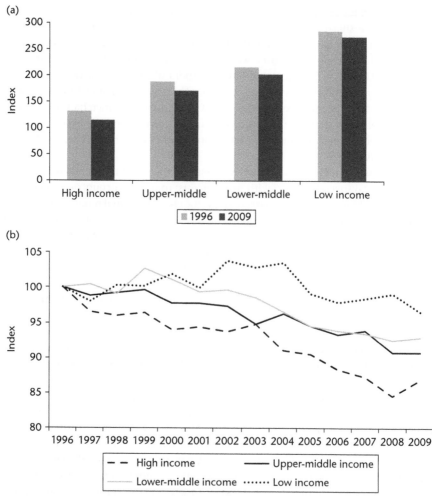

Figure C4.1 Average Trade Costs for Manufactured Exports, by Income Group, 1996–2009

Note: The unit in the first panel is average trade costs as percentage ad valorem equivalents for the ten largest importing partner countries for each country in the sample. The unit in the second panel is an index in which 1996 = 100.

Source: Arvis et al. 2013.

exemplified by the well-known examples of the Boeing airplane and the iPhone); it has also had enormous implications for firms producing basic consumer products. Walmart alone accounts for some 9 percent of U.S. imports of goods. However, as discussed below, much of the value that is embedded in U.S. imports is actually created in the United States.

Technological advances are increasingly permitting greater "dematerialization" of trade. It may be surprising therefore that the share of services in global trade has been remarkably constant since the 1980s, at about 20–25 percent. What has changed is the composition of this trade, with private business services—which includes activities such as the business process-outsourcing phenomenon—growing in importance and the share of travel and transport declining. The value of world trade in services has been expanding rapidly, but so has trade in goods. As a result, the overall ratio has not changed much. In the future, this ratio is likely to change, with potentially major implications for the tradability of white-collar jobs (Jensen 2011). Outsourcing and offshoring are increasingly going to be a feature of the organization of production and trade and a determinant of the productivity of firms. The trend toward the digitization of products to allow them to be created in one location and transmitted to another for processing or consumption could have major effects on the pattern and composition of trade. One example is the development of 3D printing, which has the potential to obviate the need to ship parts and components, which firms and consumers will "print" on demand. Such developments could have major impacts on trade flows and the pattern and composition of employment.

Although manufactures and services account for the lion's share of global trade, it is important not to lose sight of agriculture, which remains of great significance for many low-income countries. Many rich countries subsidize and otherwise support the sector, creating negative spillovers for many of the poorest economies in the world (Anderson 2009). As Subramanian and Kessler argue, a concerted push is needed to reduce the use of distorting policies, including export restrictions by producers seeking to reduce domestic consumer prices for food staples. Higher food prices resulting from climate change and the expanding size of the global middle class can be expected to generate greater supply and have been beneficial for farmers and rural communities. But such supply responses in low-income countries will depend on both domestic policies and the existence of a level playing field. More generally, beyond agriculture, a key barrier for trade expansion for many firms in low-income countries is that notwithstanding duty-free access programs, the effective market access conditions that prevail are determined in (large) part by nontariff measures, including rules of origin. A major benefit of moving toward the elimination of tariffs on a most-favored-nation basis is that doing so eliminates the need for rules of origin, thereby greatly simplifying the life of traders and reducing trade costs.

2. China and the "Rise of the Rest"

Subramanian and Kessler devote a significant part of their paper to the increasing share of world trade accounted for by China, which they define as a "mega-trader" because its trade-to-GDP ratio is much larger than what has been observed for other countries at similar stages of development in the past. It is not clear, however, that the magnitude of China's gross trade flows is a variable that is of policy interest or concern. Underlying the flow of trade from China and other developing countries that are part of global production networks are large innovative companies that are often headquartered in the North and combine labor in different locations, supply-chain management, and efficient logistics to provide their customers with a greater variety of products at lower cost. Much of this value originates at the up- and downstream ends of value chains and is created through services-related activities. Gross trade flows are therefore misleading. Of greater relevance is the extent to which China and other developing countries are generating value added. One stylized fact to note here is that in absolute terms, OECD countries have seen stagnation in the absolute amount of value added produced in manufacturing since the mid-1990s, while value added in the emerging markets has risen steadily. This is not just a China story (Timmer, Erumban, Los, Stehrer, and de Vries, 2013).

The authors stress China's mercantilist policy stance and its resulting effect of generating current account surpluses (that is, ensuring that domestic savings exceed investment through financial repression) and imply that this stance has created negative spillovers for the United States and the rest of the world. Views differ on this matter. Underemphasized are the benefits that China's growth has brought, not just in economic terms—in massively reducing poverty in one of the world's most populous countries—but also in demonstrating that using the world economy to pursue and sustain a high-growth path remains feasible for any country. The insertion of China into the world economy was inevitably going to impose adjustment pressures on the rest of the world.[2] The process was arguably effectively managed by the Chinese authorities and has certainly not been all negative for other countries. Emphasizing the negative competitiveness effects of an undervalued Chinese currency on other countries neglects the positive effects of Chinese growth for consumers (the average citizen) around the globe and natural resource exporters in Africa, Latin America, and Central Asia. As real wages in China rise, outward foreign direct investment (FDI) flows will presumably increase, including in low-income countries.

China is (still) the most populous country in the world, with 1.3 billion people, many of whom are relatively poor. It has made good use of the opportunities that exist through supply chains to put its people to work to satisfy demand in the rest of the world. The fact that China is a large trader is a reflection of initial conditions as well as its policies. What is much more relevant than China's gross trade-to-GDP ratio is the sustainability of the trade-led development strategy it has so successfully pursued over the past 30 years. The big challenge confronting both China and the rest of the world is to manage the inevitable and desirable rebalancing of the Chinese economy toward greater reliance on domestic demand and to expand domestic employment in service sectors such as retail trade, domestic logistics, and leisure, health, and financial services.

---

[2] The emergence of China as a major player following its reentry into the global economy is one element of a broader trend: the collapse of communism. The fall of the Iron Curtain also fostered the reintegration of Central and Eastern European countries with Western Europe. A good part of the increase in intraindustry, intraregional trade that occurred after 1990 involved Europe. Integration of many of the former Comecon nations helped Europe maintain its external (global) market share in manufactures until the mid-2000s (Timmer and others 2013).

3. Policy Challenges

Subramanian and Kessler identify three "pressing proximate challenges" (exchange rate undervaluation by major traders with large current account surpluses, World Trade Organization [WTO] rules that impede the use of "green" industrial policy, and the use of export restrictions for food and natural resources) as examples of the deeper, fundamental policy challenges that must be addressed in order to sustain an open global trade regime and support further globalization. Within countries a key focus, as emphasized by the authors, must be to maintain effective social insurance mechanisms and to ensure greater equality of opportunities through appropriate labor market and educational policies. Across countries the major near-term challenge is arguably to manage the adjustment of the large current account imbalances that prevail today.

China will play an important role in that adjustment process, but this matter extends to surplus countries other than China, such as Germany, the Nordic countries, and oil exporters, as well as to countries with large current account deficits, such as the United States. Policies in the rest of the world matter as much as those pursued by China. The "savings glut" during the 2000s was no doubt in part the result of policy in China, but also important was the weak regulation and absence of policies in deficit countries to manage and productively allocate the capital outflow from China and other countries where savings (greatly) exceeded investment. Focusing on what are arguably symptoms or specific dimensions of this issue, such as China's currency policy, is too narrow an approach.[3] A key question looking forward is how the further structural transformation of the Chinese economy toward services and domestic consumption will be managed by the government and how it can be supported by the rest of the world. This process will offer significant opportunities for firms in OECD countries to provide services and could lead to greater interest in China in engaging in multilateral cooperation in the WTO. Rather than assume that China needs to be forced to pursue additional policy reforms, it should be recognized that further liberalization is in China's self-interest and thus likely to be pursued autonomously in a number of areas, including in services.

Another major global policy challenge is to achieve greater participation by more developing countries in international production networks through diversification of their export structure. As noted by the authors and by Dani Rodrik in his chapter for this volume, meeting this challenge requires appropriate national policies, including, I would argue, further liberalization of trade in goods and services (such as air and road transport). But there is much that other countries can do to assist—by

---

[3] Calling for the WTO to get involved in adjudicating disputes about the level of nominal exchange rates is not the way to go. Trade policy is not an appropriate tool with which to address monetary policy-related conflicts. One reason why this is so is that it is necessary to consider the overall current account and not bilateral trade balances. One deficit country taking trade action against a surplus country may not do much to affect the balance of overall imports and exports of the two countries concerned. More fundamentally, the level of the real exchange rate reflects a mix of fiscal and monetary policies that more often than not have nothing to do with trade policy objectives (Staiger and Sykes 2010).

complementing duty-free access with simple and liberal rules of origin, by implementing regional integration agreements that provide better (lower cost) access to ports and airports, and by taking action to reduce the costs of compliance with regulatory standards, including through aid-for-trade.

The types of policy instruments that increasingly are (will be) the source of international spillovers and potential conflicts/disputes have changed. Traditional trade barriers, such as tariffs and quotas, are less and less a major factor; the policy agenda looking forward is largely one that addresses the spillover impacts of domestic "behind-the-border" regulatory policies and industrial policies (so-called nontariff measures). Examples include product regulation, certification and conformity assessment procedures, licensing requirements for service providers, data reporting and privacy standards, and border management procedures. Many of these regulatory policies often apply equally to local and foreign firms and products, but they generally increase trade costs more for foreign than for domestic suppliers, simply because regulations differ across countries or because foreign firms are subject to a multiplicity of requirements that are redundant (duplicative). Such measures cannot be "negotiated away," as presumably they fulfill a specific social or economic purpose that is not discriminatory in intent. Processes are needed that help build a common understanding of trade impacts and a search for mechanisms to reduce them without undermining the attainment of the underlying objective.

Two major challenges arise: determining how policies affect operating costs in general (that is, affect competitiveness) and determining the extent to which they distort trade. The goal should be to identify the policies that have the greatest impact on such costs and how international cooperation can reduce negative trade effects. There is no presumption that the WTO is necessarily the best forum in which to do this. PTAs or other forms of cooperation may dominate.

4. Prospects for International Cooperation

The authors lay out three possible scenarios for the future of the trade regime: liberalization (more globalization), maintenance of the status quo (preventing backsliding), and a retreat from globalization. If realized, they argue, each scenario will raise specific challenges that differ across different groups of countries. Which scenario will end up being realized is endogenous; presumably what we want to identify are the factors that may constrain the realization of the optimal scenario (which the authors argue is continued movement toward greater openness) and what could (should) be done to relax these constraints. However, much of what the authors discuss in terms of desirable (necessary) policies is not linked back to these three scenarios. In any event, it would appear that the policies that are needed to further liberalize trade and investment and to sustain an open world economy overlap to a great extent, so it is not clear how useful the three scenarios are in terms of providing insights into the likely path of the trade regime.

Facilitating a continued process of broad-based beneficial economic growth in the poorer countries of the world requires that the global trading system remain open and preferably that countries go further to liberalize trade. The global trade regime has provided an important framework for countries to agree to trade policy disciplines and commitments, as well as a mechanism through which these commitments can be enforced. The scope and coverage of multilateral policy rules has expanded steadily since the creation of the General Agreement on Trade and Tariffs (GATT) in 1947, as has membership, which now stands at 159 countries. In all, 30-plus new members—all developing countries or economies in transition—have acceded to the WTO since it was established in 1995, and another 20 are in the process of negotiating accession. The popularity of the WTO is a stylized fact of the post-1990 period that deserves greater emphasis.

Trade agreements like the WTO are self-enforcing mechanisms through which countries can cooperate to internalize negative spillovers that are large enough to matter. An important question is whether the WTO—that is, multilateral cooperation involving 159 economies—is the best mechanism to manage the (pecuniary) spillovers created by national policies. PTAs are an alternative mechanism. They have been a feature of national trade strategies of many countries for decades. What is significant is not so much the increase in the number of PTAs in recent years—many of which are not "deep," in contrast to what is sometimes claimed (including by the authors), as they often do not go much beyond the WTO in key areas such as services trade policy (see, for example, Hoekman and Mattoo 2013)—but the fact that the United States decided to join the European Union and pursue PTAs with not only (small) developing countries but also other high-income countries. The European Union has always been a serial "offender" in this area—as of the mid-2000s, European countries accounted for about half of all the PTAs notified to the WTO.[4]

It is unclear to what extent the shift to mega-regionals by the United States or a trade agreement between the European Union and the United States represents a threat to the trading system. There has been much speculation about the motivations of the United States in particular in pursuing specific PTAs, especially the Trans-Pacific Partnership (TPP). The extent to which its interest is motivated by China is arguably less important than is sometimes argued (Schott, Kotschwar, and Muir, 2013). Given the deadlock in the Doha Round, a positive implication of the many PTAs in force and under negotiation is that they are a signal that governments remain willing to make binding trade policy-related commitments in treaty-based instruments. The pursuit of mega-regionals reflects the fact that the countries involved cannot "get to yes" in the WTO, because, as the authors note, the negotiating set that is currently offered in the WTO is too small. The Doha Round has centered largely on market access issues, where there are large asymmetries in the average levels of protection that prevail in the markets of the major protagonists—the European Union/United States on the one hand and China/India on the other. At the same time, many important policy areas that create large negative spillovers are not on the table (export restrictions are an example).

---

[4] The proliferation of PTAs signed by East Asian countries starting in the late 1990s was more a reaction to than a driver of intraindustry, intraregional trade and investment flows. The evidence suggests that Asian PTAs have had virtually no impact on the pattern and growth of trade (Menon 2013).

It is not at all obvious that killing off the Doha Round and launching a new "China Round" will make a difference in this dynamic. A number of the policies for which the European Union and the United States would like to negotiate disciplines are going to be difficult to agree on (for example, the role of state ownership of companies, industrial policies, and government procurement). The fundamental constraint that is precluding the Doha Round from being concluded—namely that the United States and the European Union have little to offer—continues to apply. The same reasoning suggests that the extent to which the "mega-regionals" will put "pressure" on countries such as Brazil, China, and India to come to the negotiating table may be limited. Much will depend on the extent to which negotiations result in economically meaningful outcomes and the degree to which these outcomes imply discrimination against products coming from nonparties. Classic trade diversion costs generated by preferential liberalization are likely to be small, because average tariffs in most of the participating countries are low. There may be greater potential for de facto discrimination resulting from measures that have the effect of reducing the market-segmenting effects of differences in regulatory policies. But even here much depends on whether third-country firms will be able to benefit from access to the larger market created by the PTA if they are able to demonstrate compliance with the relevant regulatory standards. In practice, it may be difficult to exclude third-country firms from benefiting from initiatives that lower the fixed costs associated with enforcement of regulation in member countries.

The challenge for the vast majority of WTO members that are excluded from the mega-regionals is to identify actions that can be taken to reduce potential downsides and/or to benefit from these initiatives. One response is for excluded countries to pursue PTAs themselves, which has already been happening. Such agreements can help increase trade with a set of countries that is growing more rapidly than the European Union and the United States and in which traditional barriers to trade are substantially higher. If such PTAs result in meaningful preferential liberalization, the associated trade diversion could become an incentive for a renewed effort to conclude a multilateral deal, which might also become more feasible than it is today by eroding the power of the interest groups in the BRICS that currently resist market-opening on a most-favored-nation basis.

Given that classic diversion costs from the mega-regionals are likely to be limited and that their (proclaimed) goal is to be high-quality, "twenty-first-century" agreements that address the regulatory causes of market segmentation and reduce the cost-raising effects of prevailing domestic policies, one response is to focus resources on evaluating these PTAs and understand what they do. The new PTAs are a learning opportunity, not just for countries that are members but also for countries that are not. Over time, WTO members may determine that embedding some of the processes and approaches that have proven successful in a PTA context into the WTO makes sense. A precondition for such learning and "technology transfer" is information: WTO members need to invest in understanding what is being done in the PTA context. The WTO can be used for this purpose.

Another response to the proliferation of PTAs is to consider what can be done to reduce the incentive to use the PTA route for countries that want to go beyond existing WTO disciplines and to multilateralize specific features of the PTAs that are effective in reducing regulatory trade costs. The WTO allows for so-called plurilateral agreements among a subset of its members that apply only to signatories. Given that much of the "twenty-first century" trade agenda concerns regulation, there should arguably be greater flexibility and willingness by the WTO membership to allow countries to pursue cooperation on such matters inside the WTO rather than effectively forcing countries to use PTAs. Doing so would not only help reduce the fragmentation of the trading system over time, it would also increase global welfare for average citizens by providing a vehicle for all WTO members to benefit from the initiatives and experimentation that are going to be pursued in the context of PTAs.

On balance, strong forces are likely to sustain the process of international specialization and fragmentation of production that has been a driver of trade growth in recent decades. One of these forces is the fact that international production networks require low trade costs in order to operate. One reason why there was no major increase in trade barriers after the 2008 global financial crisis was that firms in countries that are most involved in supply-chain trade did not ask for them, as trade protection would not have helped them. Trade is likely to continue to be an engine of growth and global poverty reduction over the next decade or two if more low-income countries become part of the international supply chains that produce manufactures. For them to do so, they must reduce trade costs, through a mix of national action and international cooperation, and the process of current account rebalancing and adjustment must be managed well. Whatever the prospects for growth in the near term—and they are not bright in Europe, and likely to be lower than they were in previous decades for all countries—technological and environmental changes will continue to affect the pattern and composition of trade. These changes will not necessarily imply ever greater offshoring. As is already being observed, changes in technologies and the rising costs of offshoring and operating supply chains will also result in reshoring, the shortening of supply chains, and the "greening" of logistics and transport services (see, for example, World Economic Forum, 2013).

References

Anderson, K., ed. 2009. *Distortions to Agricultural Incentives: A Global Perspective, 1955–2007.* Washington, DC: Palgrave Macmillan and World Bank.

Arvis, J. F., Y. Duval, B. Shepherd, and C. Utoktham. 2013. "Trade Costs in the Developing World: 1995–2010." World Bank Policy Research Working Paper 6309, Washington, DC.

Baldwin, R. 2011. "Trade and Industrialisation after Globalisation's 2nd Unbundling: How Building and Joining a Supply Chain Are Different and Why It Matters." NBER Working Paper 17716, National Bureau of Economic Research, Cambridge, MA.

Hoekman, B., and A. Mattoo. 2013. "Liberalizing Trade in Services: Lessons from Regional and WTO Negotiations." *International Negotiation* 18: 131–51.

Jensen, J. B. 2011. *Global Trade in Services: Fear, Facts, and Offshoring.* Peterson Institute for International Economics, Washington, DC.

Kee, H. L., A. Nicita, and M. Olarreaga. 2009. "Estimating Trade Restrictiveness Indices." *Economic Journal* 119 (534): 172–99.

Menon, J. 2013. "Supporting the Growth and Spread of International Production Networks in Asia: How Can Trade Policy Help?" ADB Working Paper on Regional Economic Integration 114, Asian Development Bank, Manila.

Schott, J., B. Kotschwar, and J. Muir. 2013. *Understanding the Trans-Pacific Partnership.* Peterson Institute for International Economics, Washington, DC.

Staiger, R., and A. Sykes. 2010. "Currency Manipulation' and World Trade." *World Trade Review* 9 (4): 583–627.

Timmer, M. A. Erumban, B. Los, R. Stehrer, and G. de Vries. 2013. "Slicing Up Global Value Chains." GGDC Research Memorandum 135, Groningen Growth and Development Centre, University of Groningen, the Netherlands. http://www. ggdc.net/publications/memorandum/gd135.pdf.

WEF (World Economic Forum). 2013. *Outlook on the Logistics & Supply Chain Industry 2013.* Global Agenda Council on Logistics & Supply Chain Systems 2012–2014, Geneva: WEF.

WTO (World Trade Organization). 2007. *World Trade Report 2007: Six Decades of Multilateral Trade Cooperation.* Geneva: WTO.

WTO (World Trade Organization). 2012. *International Trade Statistics 2012.* Geneva: WTO.

5

Does Finance Accelerate or Retard Growth? Theory and Evidence

Franklin Allen, Elena Carletti, Jun "QJ" Qian, and Patricio Valenzuela

5.1 Introduction

What determines the economic welfare of global citizens? One very imperfect but important measure is gross domestic product (GDP) per capita in the country in which they live over their lifetime. This measure is determined by the level at the start of their lives and the growth rate during their lives. For poor countries, the growth rate is particularly important. As chapter 2, by Dani Rodrik, describes, policies to promote manufacturing are very important for growth. There is considerable evidence that finance is also important. However, there is a positive and a negative aspect to the effect of finance on growth. On the positive side, finance is the visible hand of resource allocation in the economy. Financial institutions and markets determine which firms in which industries receive funds to invest. There is considerable evidence, reviewed in this chapter, that finance can be beneficial for growth. On the negative side, financial crises are often very damaging for growth. The understanding of financial crises, particularly global financial crises, and

The authors are grateful to Stijn Claessens for his very helpful and constructive comments as a discussant; to Arvind Subramanian and other participants at the Geneva meeting of the Global Citizen Foundation project held December 1, 2012; and to participants at the Philadelphia meeting held March 1–3, 2013, for helpful comments and suggestions.

their effect on growth is relatively limited. The literature that addresses this issue is also considered in this chapter.

One important aspect of the growth, finance, and crises nexus is what to focus on when analyzing the interrelationship between them. A theme of this chapter is that for both the positive and negative aspects, it is the extremes of the distribution that are important for understanding how to improve the welfare of global citizens living in poor countries. Many Asian countries, particularly some in East Asia, have done extremely well in terms of growth. The "Four Tigers"—the Republic of Korea (Korea hereafter); Taiwan, China (Taiwan hereafter); the Hong Kong Special Administrative Region of China (Hong Kong hereafter); and Singapore—along with Japan showcased episodes of "economic miracles" between the 1960s and 1980s. In 1950, Taiwan's per capita GDP in purchasing power parity (PPP) was 916 international dollars—similar to the level in many African countries and 13 percent of per capita GDP in the United Kingdom and France. By 2011, its per capita GDP was higher than in the United Kingdom and France and similar to the level in Germany (Table 5.1). Assuming growth rates in per capita GDP persist, it will take less than ten years for Taiwan to catch up to the United States. Korea, which had per capita income of 845 international dollars in 1950, had a higher per capita income than Spain and Italy in 2011 (Table 5.2).

Table 5.1 Economies with Highest GDP per Capita, 2011

Rank	Economy	GDP (in international dollars)
1	United States	48,387
2	Netherlands	42,183
3	Canada	40,541
4	Australia	40,234
5	Germany	37,897
6	Belgium	37,737
7	Taiwan, China	37,720
8	United Kingdom	36,090
9	France	35,156
10	Japan	34,740
11	Republic of Korea	31,714
12	Spain	30,626
13	Italy	30,464
14	Czech Republic	27,062
15	Greece	26,294

Note: Singapore and Hong Kong are essentially city-states and are therefore excluded from the table. They have already overtaken the United States, with per capita GDPs in PPP terms of $59,710 (Singapore) and $49,417 (Hong Kong) in 2011.
Source: IMF 2012b.

Table 5.2 GDP Levels and Growth Rates of World's Largest Economies, 2011

| | GDP | | | | Growth in constant prices 1990–2011 | | | |
| | At simple exchange rates | | In PPP | | Total | | Per capita | |
Rank	Economy	Billions of U.S. dollars	Economy	Billions of international dollars	Economy	Annual growth (percent)	Economy	Annual growth (percent)
1	United States	15,094	United States	15,094	China	10.4	China	9.5
2	China	7,298	China	11,300	Vietnam	7.3	Vietnam	5.8
3	Japan	5,869	India	4,458	India	6.5	India	4.7
4	Germany	3,577	Japan	4,440	Angola	6.0	Republic of Korea	4.6
5	France	2,776	Germany	3,099	Malaysia	5.8	Taiwan	4.3
6	Brazil	2,493	Russia	2,383	Bangladesh	5.4	Sri Lanka	4.2
7	United Kingdom	2,418	Brazil	2,294	Nigeria	5.4	Sudan	4.1
8	Italy	2,199	United Kingdom	2,261	Sri Lanka	5.3	Poland	3.9
9	Russia	1,850	France	2,218	Sudan	5.3	Chile	3.9
10	Canada	1,737	Italy	1,847	Chile	5.3	Bangladesh	3.6
11	India	1,676	Mexico	1,662	Taiwan	5.0	Thailand	3.5
12	Spain	1,494	Republic of Korea	1,554	Peru	4.9	Malaysia	3.5

Notes: Economies with population less than 11 million, GDP of less than $50 billion in 2011, or less than 15 years of GDP observations are excluded from the rankings.
Source: IMF 2012b.

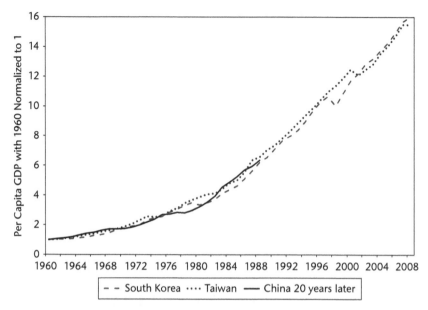

Figure 5.1 Per Capita GDP Growth in Taiwan, Korea, and China, 1960–2010

Note: Base year is 1960 for Taiwan and Korea, 1980 for China.

Source: Authors, based on data from GDP statistics from website of A. Maddison (http://www.ggdc.net/MADDISON/oriindex.htm).

Figure 5.1 shows the growth of Taiwan and Korea from 1960, together with that of China starting in 1980. It shows that China is following closely in their path. India, the third-largest economy in the world in PPP terms in 2011, has also been successful during the past two decades, as have other southern and southeastern Asian countries, such as Vietnam. Most experts would agree that Asia, and in particular China and India, will continue to be the main engines of global economic growth going forward.[1]

Other poor countries that were similar in 1950 have not fared nearly as well. For example, many African countries still have GDPs per capita not much higher than they were in 1950. Most South American countries have performed better than those in Africa, but nothing like as well as those in East Asia. Understanding the achievements of economies such as Taiwan, Korea, and China is crucial to improving the position of the global citizen.

The main theme of this chapter is that financial systems play an important role in determining variations in growth. It presents evidence that financial development has a positive impact on economic growth at adequate levels

---

[1] The size of these countries means that the strain on the environment and the earth's natural resources will be substantial. These implications of widespread growth are considered at length in chapter 6, by Andrew Steer.

of financial depth but that this effect vanishes, and even becomes negative, when finance becomes excessive. Excessive finance incubates economic booms and asset price bubbles that end in financial crises with low rates of economic growth for sustained periods. Alternative finance plays an important role in emerging economies, such as China and India. In contrast to the conventional view that strong institutions and legal systems are important for growth, we suggest that alternative systems based on trust, reputation, and other mechanisms can play a crucial role.

Section 5.2 overviews the theoretical literature on growth, finance, and crises. Section 5.3 explores the empirical relationship between finance and growth. It starts with the historical evidence from the United Kingdom, the United States, Germany, and Japan. It then examines the relationship between finance (domestic, alternative, and international) and growth. Section 5.4 investigates the main causes and consequences of financial crises and what can be done to prevent them. Section 5.5 considers the international financial architecture. Section 5.6 analyzes how finance affects several aspects of the global citizen. It covers the intersection of finance with demographics, education, labor markets, poverty, and income distribution. Section 5.7 discusses some of the ethical issues raised by the growth, finance, and crises nexus. Section 5.8 draws some lessons and policy implications.[2]

5.2 Finance and Growth: Theory

Financial systems channel funds from depositors and capital markets to people and institutions with investment opportunities. By borrowing from and lending to large groups, financial systems are able to produce relevant information and offer risk-sharing to investors through the creation of diversified portfolios. This section briefly overviews the theoretical literature exploring two channels connecting financial development and financial structure to economic growth: information acquisition and risk-sharing. It also reviews the literature that formally analyzes the relationship between bubbles, financial crises, and growth and considers the relationship between finance and inequality.

5.2.1 Producing Information and Allocating Capital

Theories assuming that capital flows toward more profitable projects usually ignore the fact that investors do not always have the capacity to collect enough

---

[2] The study draws on a number of our previous contributions, including Allen and Oura (2004); Allen and Carletti (2012); Allen, Carletti, Qian, and Valenzuela (2013); Allen, Carletti, Cull, Qian, Senbet, and Valenzuela (2012); and Allen and Carletti (2013).

information to make the most profitable investments. Acquiring information and strengthening incentives for obtaining information to improve resource allocation are key issues. A large body of theoretical literature argues that financial intermediaries improve the *ex-ante* assessment of investment opportunities, with positive ramifications for resource allocation, by reducing the costs of acquiring information acquisition (Ramakrishnan and Thakor 1984; Bhattacharya and Pfleiderer 1985; Boyd and Prescott 1986; Allen 1990).

A strand of this literature explicitly incorporates the role of information in a growth model. Greenwood and Jovanovic (1990) develop a theory in which financial intermediaries produce better information, improve resource allocation, and foster growth. Growth means that more individuals can afford to join financial intermediaries, which improves the ability of the intermediaries to produce better information. King and Levine (1993) show that financial intermediaries may boost the rate of technological innovation by identifying those entrepreneurs with the best chances of successfully initiating new goods and production processes.

Some more recent literature argues that markets potentially perform better than intermediaries where there is diversity of opinion about innovation and genuine disagreement about the optimal decision. Allen and Gale (1999) argue that with new technologies, investors' diversity of opinion reflects differences in prior beliefs rather than differences in information. The advantage of financial markets is that they allow people with similar views to join together to finance projects. In contrast, intermediated finance involves delegating the financing decision to a manager who incurs the cost necessary to form an opinion. The problem is that the manager may not have the same opinion as the investor (agency problem). The model predicts that market-based systems will lead to more innovation than bank-based systems. Hence, the role of the market may be more important in the phase of economic growth at the technological frontier.

5.2.2 Risk Sharing

A large body of research tries to understand how financial development promotes economic growth through a risk-sharing channel. One limitation of this literature is that it ignores the effect of nondiversifiable risk. The implications for financial development and financial structure on economic growth are potentially quite different when markets cannot diversify away all of the risks inherent in the economic environment.

DOMESTIC RISK-SHARING
Risk-sharing plays a key role in promoting growth when agents are risk-averse and less risky projects yield low returns. In this view, the financial system

allows agents to create diversified portfolios with higher expected returns while keeping risk reasonably low (Greenwood and Jovanovic 1990; King and Levine 1993; Devereux and Smith 1994; Obstfeld 1994).

More recent contributions emphasize that the positive effect of risk-sharing on growth depends on the level of economic development of an economy. Bose and Cothren (1996) show that the financial sector needs to reach a critical mass before advances in financial sophistication improve growth. Acemoglu and Zilibotti (1997) find that at early stages of development, the presence of indivisible projects limits the degree of diversification the economy can achieve, and that the desire to avoid highly risky investments slows capital accumulation. Gaytán and Rancière (2005) show that at early stages of economic development, risk-sharing can be achieved only at the cost of reducing investment and growth. In their model, once the economy has crossed a certain wealth threshold, the liquidity role of banks becomes unambiguously growth-enhancing.

Risk-sharing also plays a key role in promoting growth when agents face liquidity risks. Individuals are averse to both bearing risk and relinquishing control of their savings for long periods. The financial system can play a role in making projects more acceptable to the public and increasing growth prospects. Building on the Diamond and Dybvig (1983) set-up for liquidity demand, Levine (1991) models the endogenous formation of equity markets and integrates it into a growth model. As stock market transaction costs fall, more investment occurs in illiquid, high-return projects. If illiquid projects enjoy sufficiently large effects on other parts of the economy, then greater stock market liquidity induces faster steady-state growth. Bencivenga and Smith (1991) show that by eliminating liquidity risk, banks can increase investment in high-return, illiquid assets and accelerate growth. Jappelli and Pagano (1994) use an overlapping-generations model to show that liquidity constraints on households increase the savings rate and growth by limiting households' ability to smooth consumption. De Gregorio (1996) constructs a model in which financial systems can promote growth through accumulating human capital by easing liquidity constraints.

Financial intermediation in most models takes the form of a perfectly competitive banking system. Some models consider a role for stock markets, but often only as a choice between mutually exclusive banks and markets (Greenwood and Smith 1997). Analyses in which markets and intermediaries coexist are rare because including markets can eliminate the risk-sharing benefits of intermediaries.

A few studies consider the case in which banks and markets coexist. Blackburn, Bose, and Capasso (2005) develop a model in which state-dependent moral hazard conditions allow both to exist together. In this model, feedback occurs from growth in the economy to the determination of the optimal financial structure, which can be based on banking or a mixture of banks and markets. Fecht, Huang, and Martin (2008) consider a model in which financial intermediaries provide insurance to households against idiosyncratic liquidity shocks. Households can also invest in financial markets directly if they pay a cost. In equilibrium, the ability of intermediaries to share risk is constrained by the market, but it can be preserved as long as the cost to participate in markets is relatively high and the portion of individual market participants is not too large.

INTERNATIONAL RISK-SHARING

At the international level, risk-sharing allows economies to grow more by specializing according to their comparative advantages while diversifying away the risk of this specialization through the financial system. Helpman and Razin (1978) show that the risk-averse nature of consumers in an uncertain environment results in imperfect specialization that reduces the gains from trade. In such circumstances, financial development that allows the trading of contingent claims provides better risk-sharing opportunities, allowing the economy to specialize in the production of a few goods while keeping risk low. This argument is further explored by Saint-Paul (1992), who shows that stock markets that facilitate international risk-sharing enable specialization in technologies and higher growth.

International risk-sharing also involves some risks. The sudden withdrawal of capital flows increased risk in some economies, hurting growth prospects. Calvo and Mendoza (2000) and Mendoza (2001) examine the causes and consequences of sudden reversals of capital flows to emerging markets, which are typically accompanied by large declines in output and collapses in real asset prices. In these studies, risk-sharing across countries requires contract enforcement by domestic and foreign agents. The difficulty of this enforcement introduces a new source of risk. Broner and Ventura (2011) argue that the decision to enforce international contracts, which depends on the willingness of sovereigns, will depend on whether local players benefit from it. In equilibrium, this conflict can lead to the endogenous closure of some asset markets, including local ones, reducing growth and risk-sharing at both the national and international levels.

5.2.3 Financial Crises, Growth, and Bubbles

The theoretical literature that attempts to formally analyze the impact of financial crises on economic growth is at an early stage. Although some theoretical and empirical studies show that it is possible for economies to grow faster with crises than without them, there are cases in which the crises that follow bubbles in asset prices are very damaging. This section provides an overview of these issues.

On average, countries that experience occasional financial crises grow faster than countries with stable financial conditions. Endogenous growth models generate predictions that are consistent with this stylized fact. Rancière, Tornell, and Westermann (2008) present a model in which problems with contract enforceability generate borrowing constraints and impede growth. In financially liberalized economies with moderate contract enforceability, systemic risk-taking is encouraged and increases investment, leading to higher mean growth but also to greater incidence of crises. Gaytán and Rancière (2005) integrate a neoclassical growth model with Diamond–Dybvig type banks that provide insurance against idiosyncratic liquidity shocks. In their model, banks play a growth-enhancing role in reducing inefficient liquidation of long-term projects, but they may face liquidity crises associated with severe output losses. Middle-income countries may find it optimal to be exposed to liquidity crises, whereas poor and rich economies have more incentives to develop a banking system that is not exposed.

Given that bubbles are likely to exacerbate the pernicious effects of financial crises on growth, it is important to understand how they are incubated. A number of theories explain bubbles (Tirole 1982, 1985; Allen and Gorton 1993; Allen, Morris, and Postlewaite 1993; Allen and Gale 2000a; Abreu and Brunnermeier 2003; Scheinkman and Xiong 2003; Brunnermeier and Nagel 2004; Hong, Scheinkman, and Xiong 2008).

Allen and Gale (2000a) provide a theory of bubbles that is explicitly related to crises. Many investors in real estate and stock markets obtain their investment funds from external sources. If the ultimate providers of funds are unable to observe the characteristics of the investment, there is a classic asset substitution problem in which debtors want to invest in risky assets and shift risk to creditors. This problem causes investors to bid up the prices of risky assets above their fundamental values, creating a bubble. The riskier the asset, the greater the amount of risk that can be shifted to creditors and the larger the bubble. When the bubble bursts, either because returns are low or because the central bank tightens credit, a financial crisis ensues.

The survey by Allen, Babus, and Carletti (2009) provides a fuller account of the literature on bubbles and financial crises. Although there is evidence that financial crises originated by a bubble have a strong negative effect on growth, the theory is silent on the relationship between the bursting of bubbles in asset prices and growth. Better understanding of these issues is needed.

5.2.4 Finance and Inequality

Financial development affects income distribution, because it affects the economic opportunities of individuals. A large body of empirical research suggests that more developed financial systems reduce inequality, but theoretical studies are not conclusive. Demirgüç-Kunt and Levine (2009) review the literature on the finance–inequality nexus and identify three different types of effects: direct intensive margin effects, direct extensive margin effects, and indirect effects.

DIRECT EXTENSIVE MARGIN EFFECTS

Direct intensive margin effects refer to the use of financial services by individuals who had not been using those services. One set of models argues that financial development may improve income distribution because access to financial services should allow low-income individuals to improve their human and physical capital. For example, models by Becker and Tomes (1979, 1986) and Galor and Zeira (1993) highlight information and transaction costs associated with financing education. Their models predict that inequality falls when low-income families borrow to pay for the education of their children.

A second set of models argues that financial development may reduce the effects of external negative shocks that, in general, affect more strongly the unbanked, low-income segments of the population. Jacoby and Skoufias (1997) and Baland and Robinson (1998) highlight the connection between education and the smoothing of adverse income shocks. Their models predict that inequality falls when low-income families use financial services to smooth income shocks. In these models, parents with access to financial services that face a negative income shock are less likely to reduce investment in the education of their children than parents without access to those services.

A third set of models highlights the role of entrepreneurship. According to Aghion and Bolton (1997) and Bardhan (2000), low-income entrepreneurs tend to remain poor in the presence of financial markets that lend only to people with sufficient collateral rather than to people with the most profitable ideas.

DIRECT INTENSIVE MARGIN EFFECTS

Direct intensive margin effects refer to improvements in the quality and range of financial services that may primarily benefit households and firms that already have access to finance. In the Greenwood and Jovanovic (1990) model, for example, improvements in financial systems that do not lower the fixed costs of accessing financial services will not tend to broaden access to financial services; instead, they improve the quality of financial services enjoyed by people already purchasing financial services. As financial development benefits primarily the rich, it may actually exacerbate income inequality.

A direct intensive margin mechanism is consistent, for example, with recent theoretical and empirical studies that suggest that foreign banks tend to cherry-pick their customers (see, for example, Beck and Brown 2010; Detragiache, Tressel, and Gupta 2008; Gormley 2010; and Mian 2006). According to the cherry-picking hypothesis, foreign bank penetration is likely to increase the share of wealthy, urban, and professional households that already have bank accounts instead of broadening the use of financial services. Therefore, a higher level of financial development as a result of higher foreign bank penetration may increase inequality.

INDIRECT EFFECTS

A large body of theoretical research suggests that financial development may affect inequality through indirect mechanisms (Beck, Levine, and Levkov 2009; Gine and Townsend 2004; Townsend and Ueda 2006). In these models, financial development can influence both the allocation of credit and economic growth, which increases demand for both low- and high-skilled workers, with concomitant ramifications on the distribution of income. Financial development that primarily increases the demand for low-skilled workers will reduce inequality; financial development that primarily increases the demand for high-skilled workers will increase inequality (Jerzmanowski and Nabar 2007).

5.3 Finance and Growth: Empirical Evidence

5.3.1 Historical Evidence

The relationship between the growth rate of an economy and the development of its financial systems is a long-debated issue. Bagehot (1873) argued that the United Kingdom's financial system played an important role in the Industrial Revolution; Robinson (1952) suggested that the causation goes the other way. This section (based on Allen, Capie, Fohlin, Miyajima, Sylla, Wood, and Yafeh 2012) describes the historical experience of four of the most advanced economies in the world: the United Kingdom, the United States, Germany, and Japan. The fact that all four developed sophisticated financial systems and all four grew successfully despite differences in those systems suggests that a variety of financial structures can lead to high rates of economic growth.

The experience of the United Kingdom during the eighteenth and nineteenth centuries suggests that financial development is an essential precondition for growth. The Industrial Revolution of the eighteenth century that allowed the United Kingdom to experience sustained growth throughout the period was preceded by a financial revolution at the end of the previous century. This revolution involved, among other things, the foundation of the Bank of England, the adoption of sound government finances, and the development of the stock market in London. However, in terms of real and financial growth, both revolutions were limited. The growth rate was no higher than 1 percent a year, and the size of the banking multiplier remained fairly small (no more than 1.5) throughout the century.

Better support for the importance of finance is provided by the country's experience in the nineteenth century, when the intermediation provided by the banking system expanded significantly as the Bank of England started to act as lender of last resort. Moreover, higher intermediation triggered an increase of the multiplier of the banking system to about 4. These developments were followed by a jump in the growth rate in the real economy, which averaged 3 percent a year in the middle decades of the nineteenth century.

The United States was blessed from its inception with a modern, dynamic financial system. As it began its modern economic growth trajectory at the same time, the case is strong that modern financial arrangements facilitated economic growth. Alexander Hamilton, the Secretary of the Treasury from 1789 to 1795, played a significant role in the modernization of the financial system. Among other things, he created the First Bank of the United States, reformed the government's finances, and ensured the issuance of sound public debt. These actions acted as a catalyst for the emergence of a modern, articulated financial system that included sound public finances and debt management, a stable dollar currency, a central bank, a banking system, securities markets, and stock exchanges. By the mid-1790s the United States had all the elements of a modern financial system in place, allowing the economy to grow at an average real per capita growth rate of 1–2 percent per year from then until modern times.

Germany had a variety of financial institutions and markets in place well before modern growth emerged in the second half of the nineteenth century. Universal banks (banks that both make loans and underwrite securities) were part of a complex financial system that included active capital markets that worked in concert with joint-stock banks, a single monetary policy, a solid lender of last resort, and supporting financial and corporate regulations. Toward the second half of the century, the increasing financing needs of railroads and the lifting of the tight restrictions on incorporation and limited liability of the stock markets tightened the connections between finance and growth. However, despite some statistical evidence of a causative relationship between the level of joint-stock banking assets and output growth in the railroad sector during the 1850s–1870s, there is no general statistical relationship between banking assets and aggregate output.

The development of the Japanese financial system started during the Meiji Restoration, when the Bank of Japan was founded, networks of commercial banks were created, and stock exchanges were set up. The Japanese process was unique, in that its financial history began with the establishment of an entire set of institutions that typically characterize developed economies. However, throughout the period of the Meiji Restoration, business financing occurred mostly through alternative finance, retained earnings, and joint-stock for starting companies. It was not until the interwar period that bank loans, bond issuance, and equity finance began to play a more important role in funding corporations. A distinctive characteristic of the Japanese financial development was the "division of labor" between banks, which financed small family firms, and equity markets, which financed large corporate groups. Based in part on its financial modernization, Japan was a modern, growing economy by the turn of the twentieth century.

The role of different types of finance varied across the four countries. As all four were successful in terms of growth, it is difficult to conclude from this evidence that there is a unique optimal financial structure that should be widely adopted by other countries going through the development process. Different types of finance can be used to fund real economic growth. Bank loans and equity finance were important in all countries, but they operated in different ways. Although many factors were involved in economic modernization, the four cases suggest that financial development significantly facilitated the growth process.

5.3.2 Domestic Finance, Excessive Finance, and Growth

The relationship between financial development and economic development is not limited to the experiences of the four developed countries examined in the previous section. Figure 5.2 shows a positive correlation between the development of financial systems and the level of income. It also shows that financial markets have developed over time. The main task for researchers has been to provide evidence on the causality from finance to growth, as well as to confirm the robustness of the effects.

Many empirical studies find a positive causal effect from finance to growth, even after accounting for endogeneity. This literature includes cross-country growth regression analysis (King and Levine 1993; Levine and Zervos 1998; Benhabib and Spiegel 2000); instrumental variable analysis (Levine 1998, 1999; Levine, Loayza, and Beck 2000); time series analysis (Rousseau and Wachtel 1998; Rousseau and Sylla 1999); regional analysis within a country (Guiso, Sapienza, and Zingales 2004; Burgess and Pande 2005); industry-level analysis (Rajan and Zingales 1998; Beck and Levine 2002; Wurgler 2000); and firm-level analysis (Demirgüç-Kunt and Maksimovic 2002).

The global financial crises of 2007–9 and the current debt crisis in Europe highlight once again the fact that excessive finance may have undesirable effects on economic growth. A flourishing literature finds not only a

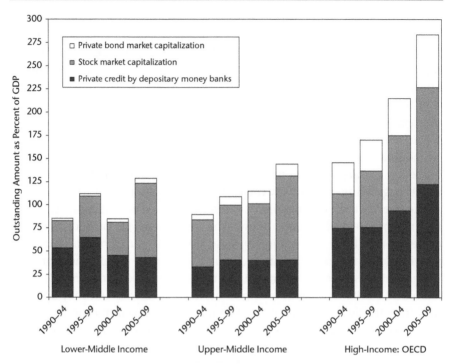

Figure 5.2 Financial Markets and Intermediaries in Lower-Middle, Upper-Middle, and High-Income Countries, 1990–2009

Source: Authors, based on data from Beck and Demirgüç-Kunt (2009).

vanishing effect in the positive impact of financial development on economic growth but also a negative effect of excessive finance on growth.

Using a dataset covering 95 countries from 1960 to 1985, De Gregorio and Guidotti (1995) find that long-run economic growth is positively correlated with bank credit to the private sector (as a percentage of GDP). In low-income economies, however, this effect is relatively small, and it is not significant in the period 1970–85. De Gregorio and Guidotti argue that this vanishing effect comes from the fact that low-income economies may be at the point at which financial development no longer affects the efficiency of investment.

Rousseau and Wachtel (2011) also find a vanishing effect in the positive relationship between financial development and long-run economic growth. They show that this relationship is positive and significant for 1960–89 but is not statistically different from zero for 1990–2004. They find evidence that this vanishing effect is associated with the incidence of financial crises. In fact, they show that the positive impact of financial development on economic growth remains intact for the whole period once crisis episodes are removed.

According to Arcand, Berkes, and Panizza (2012), the vanishing effect found in the earlier studies is driven not by a change in the fundamental relationship between finance and economic growth but by the fact that standard models do not allow for a nonmonotonic relationship between financial development and economic growth. Allowing for this relationship, they find a positive marginal effect of financial depth on economic growth in economies in which the level of credit to the private sector falls below a threshold of about 80–100 percent of GDP. Above this threshold, the relationship becomes negative (interestingly, this value is similar to the threshold at which Easterly, Islam, and Stiglitz [2000] find financial depth starts increasing output volatility). These findings are robust to controlling for macroeconomic volatility, banking crises, and institutional quality.

Overall, the findings from this new literature suggest that economies with small and medium-sized financial systems relative to their GDP tend to do better, as they put more of their resources into finance, but that this effect reverses once the financial sector becomes too large. A potential reason why excessive finance may have a negative effect on economic growth is the misallocation of resources. Beck, Levine, and Levkov (2009) show that enterprise credit is positively associated with economic growth but that there is no correlation between growth and household credit. This misallocation of resources is also likely to have a negative indirect effect on economic development through financial crises.

The global financial crisis of 2007–9 provides evidence of the relationship between excessive finance and growth. Panel a of Figure 5.3 shows the positive relationship between financial depth and economic development. It also shows that many of the economies that had levels of credit to the private sector above 80–100 percent of GDP in 2006 tended to experience costly banking crises in 2007–9. Panel b of Figure 5.3 shows that excessive finance is costly in terms of economic growth. In particular, it shows that economies that had a very high level of credit to the private sector by 2006 suffered sharper downturns in 2007–9. Moreover, the most affected countries were the ones that experienced systemic banking crises.

Loayza and Rancière (2006) reconcile the literature that finds a positive effect of financial depth on economic growth with the literature that finds a positive relationship between domestic credit and the incidence of financial crises. They find that a positive long-run relationship between financial development and economic growth coexists with a negative short-run relationship driven by financial crises. Although on average, financial depth may have a positive impact on long-run economic growth, excessive finance is pernicious for the domestic economy. Therefore, regulatory policies that reduce the size of the financial sector may have a positive effect on economic

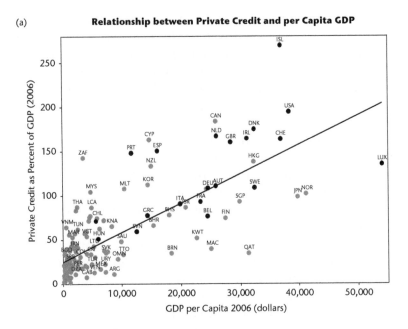

(a)

Relationship between Private Credit and per Capita GDP

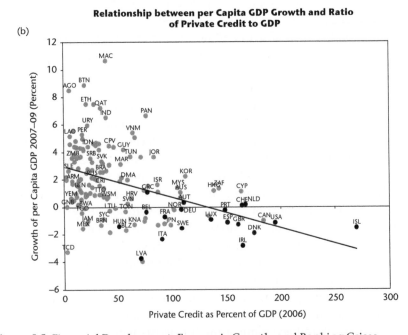

(b)

Relationship between per Capita GDP Growth and Ratio of Private Credit to GDP

Figure 5.3 Financial Development, Economic Growth, and Banking Crises

a. Relationship between Private Credit and per Capita GDP b. Relationship between per Capita GDP Growth and Ratio of Private Credit to GDP

Note: Black dots correspond to countries that experienced a banking crisis in 2007–9. The black line represents the linear least squares regression line.

Source: Authors, based on data from Beck and Demirgüç-Kunt (2009); Laeven and Valencia (2012); and World Bank (2012).

growth in countries with excessive credit, because they are likely to reduce the amplitudes of the leveraging/deleveraging cycle.

5.3.3 Financial Structure and Growth

The theme of much of the literature surveyed in the previous section is that too little finance is not good but too much finance is also not good. These findings suggest that there may be a happy medium. Financial sector development may help countries take off but be less relevant otherwise. Another possibility is that this literature focuses too much on the particular measure of depth of the financial system. Other factors—such as efficiency, stability, and access—are also important.

Some financial structures may be more efficient in driving growth than others. Lin and Xu (2012) survey a body of literature on the relationship between financial structure and growth. They identify four traditional views: the financial structure irrelevancy view, the law and finance view, the bank-based view, and the market-based view.

A number of studies provide evidence in support of the irrelevancy view (Beck, Demirgüç-Kunt, Levine, and Maksimovic 2001; Levine 2002; Stulz 2001). They contend that only financial depth, not financial structure, matters. The law and finance view holds that it is not structure that matters for growth but overall financial development, in particular the legal system and its origins; La Porta et al. (1998, 2000) provide evidence in support of this perspective. The bank-based view emphasizes the important role of banks in mobilizing resources; it is particularly associated with Gerschenkron (1962). The market-based view claims that stock markets allow investors to diversify and manage risk better, facilitate competition, and promote innovative industries (Boyd and Smith 1998; Allen and Gale 1999, 2000b).

More recent contributions focus on the idea of an optimal financial structure that depends on a country's stage of development and endowments. Xu (2011) summarizes the evidence showing that the business environment's effects on development tend to be heterogeneous and depend on the stage of development. Lin (2009) and Lin, Sun, and Jiang (2011) emphasize that financial structure must reflect the demands of the real economy and that there is an appropriate financial structure for an economy at each stage of development. Early on, for example, small banks may be better at providing finance to small firms. Carlin and Mayer (2003), Demirgüç-Kunt, Feyen, and Levine (2011), Cull and Xu (2011), and Calomiris and Haber (2013) provide a wide range of evidence that is consistent with these views.

A related issue is the role of state-owned banks in driving growth and preserving financial stability. They can potentially correct market failures and improve growth prospects for firms that would otherwise not obtain finance. They can also improve financial access by individuals and households.

Clarke, Cull, and Shirley (2005) survey the literature on bank privatization. They conclude that it usually improves bank efficiency, with gains being greater when the government fully relinquishes control and does not restrict competition. The literature on the effects of public banks suggests they are not effective in correcting market failures. However, Allen, Qian, Shan, and Zhao (2012) argue that the Chinese model of state-owned banks that combines public listing and majority government control has performed well. As a group, the five largest state-owned and listed Chinese banks significantly outperformed large non-state-owned banks from other emerging economies before and during the 2007–9 crisis.

Another important aspect of financial structure is the role of competition and its effect on the efficiency of the financial system and financial stability. Allen and Gale (2004) examine a variety of models of competition and financial stability, including general equilibrium models of financial intermediaries and markets; agency models; models of spatial competition; models of Schumpeterian competition, in which firms compete by developing new products; and models of contagion. They find a very wide range of relationships between competition and financial stability. In some situations, competition reduces stability; in others, it does not. In general equilibrium and Schumpeterian models, for example, efficiency requires both perfect competition and financial instability.

Another aspect of competition involves network-related issues. Issues such as fair access to payments and information systems and other networks are currently very important in the financial services industry. Regulation and taxation often impede competition, because they are still imposed in silos for different parts of the industry. The issue of regulation and its effect on competition and financial stability is complex and multifaceted. Sound policy requires careful consideration of all the factors at work, at both the theoretical and the empirical level.

Much of the recent debate about structure has been about whether the scope of banks' activities should be limited (the Volcker Rule and the Vickers Report). The argument for restriction is that activities such as proprietary trading may cause bankruptcy and lead to contagion and financial crisis. The argument against restriction is that permitting banks to engage in a range of activities allows diversification and improves financial stability. Very little economic analysis has been done on the trade-offs involved; there is thus no good evidence on the circumstances in which such restrictions are desirable. There has also been debate about the desirability of restricting the size of financial institutions, in order to limit the "too big to fail" problem. Little serious economic analysis has been done on the trade-offs involved.

The role of foreign financial institutions is another determinant of the structure of financial systems. Banking has increasingly become more globalized, driven by deregulation, advances in communications and technology, and economic integration. Foreign banks can have a number of advantages and disadvantages over domestic banks. Claessens and van Horen (2012) explore the relative performance of foreign banks, measured by profitability, in a large group of countries over the period 1999–2006. They find that foreign banks tend to perform better when they are from a low-income country, when regulation in the host country is relatively weak, when they are larger and have a larger market share, and when they have the same language and similar regulation as the host country. Geographical proximity does not improve performance.

5.3.4 International Finance and Financial Globalization

Over the past four decades, global financial markets have become increasingly integrated, in terms of legal restrictions on capital account transactions and in terms of outcome measures, such as the level of cross-border asset holdings (Figure 5.4). The global financial crisis of 2007–9 increased the possibility of a reversal of the previous trend toward freer capital markets, with several countries imposing new legal restrictions on capital account transactions or tightening existing restrictions. However, as shown in panel a of Figure 5.4, so far this reversal has been timid. Understanding the costs and benefits of financial globalization and its impact on long-run economic growth is crucial. (Issues of trade and other international aspects are considered in greater detail in chapter 4.)

Financial globalization has many potential benefits, but there are also potentially significant costs. The main benefit is that capital can flow from countries with a low marginal rate of return to countries with a high marginal rate, improving the funding of firms and thus spurring growth.

Financial globalization also allows improved risk-sharing across countries. This risk-sharing interacts with productive opportunities to raise growth possibilities. It allows greater specialization in the real economy based on comparative advantage, even though it reduces diversification and increases the volatility of output.

However, opening up the financial system of a country also potentially creates significant risks. There can be contagion of crises and incubation of bubbles from large capital inflows. These downsides are not inevitable; the form in which flows occur matters considerably. Foreign direct investment is more benign in that it cannot be withdrawn very easily. The possibilities for contagion are thus reduced. However, the possibility for the incubation of asset price bubbles remains. Short-term capital flows can help transmit contagion if

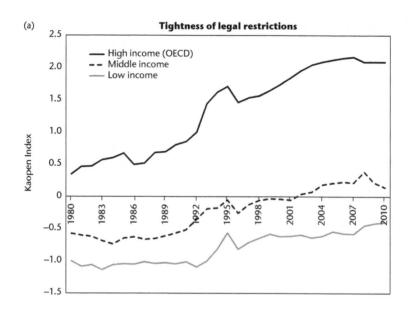

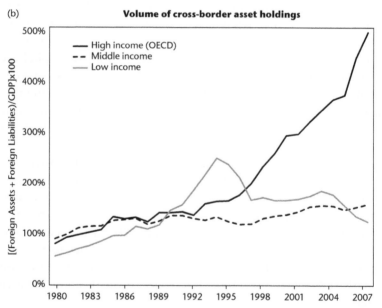

Figure 5.4 Legal Restrictions on Capital Account Transactions and Cross-Border Asset Holdings, by Country Income Level, 1980–2010

a. Degree of legal restrictions b. Volume of cross-border asset holdings

Note: The measure of legal restrictions on capital account transactions in panel a (KAOPEN) is from Chinn and Ito (2008). A higher KAOPEN value indicates fewer restrictions. Only countries for which information was available for the full period are considered. Middle-income economies include upper- and lower-middle-income economies.

Source: Authors, based on data from Chinn and Ito 2008 and Lane and Milesi-Ferretti 2007.

they result in a sudden withdrawal and can drive bubbles if the inflow is significant. These potential downsides decline with the sophistication of macroeconomic management and institutional development within a country.

The rest of this section considers the empirical evidence on these benefits and costs of financial globalization. Section 6 considers interactions between financial globalization and inequality.

The process of global financial integration has created an important source of funding for firms in both developed and developing economies. Table 5.3 reports that 36 percent of firms in developed economies and 27 percent of firms in developing economies issue debt in the international market; 5 percent of the firms in developed economies and 6 percent in developing economies issue equity in international markets. Moreover, the shares of debt and equity capital raised abroad are significant, especially for developing economies.

Table 5.3 Domestic and Foreign Sources of Financing in Developed and Developing Economies

Financing	Developed economies	Developing economies
Equity		
Total (billions of dollars at 2005 U.S. prices)	4,372	583
Percent foreign	8	28
Debt		
Total (billions of dollars at 2005 U.S. prices)	19,147	629
Percent foreign	35	47
Total		
Billions of dollars at 2005 U.S. prices	23,519	1,212
Percent foreign	30	38
Number of firms		
Equity		
Total	24	10
Percent foreign	5	6
Debt		
Total	12	3
Percent foreign	33	27
Total		
Total	36	13
Percent foreign	16	11

Note: Equity issues include initial public offerings and seasoned equity offerings. Debt issues include convertible and nonconvertible debt issues and preferred shares issues. Issues abroad are issues carried out in a public market outside of the firm's home country.

Source: Reprinted from *Journal of International Economics*, 80, Juan Carlos Gozzi et al., "Patterns of International Capital Raisings," 45–57, 2010, with permission from Elsevier.

Not all firms are able to enjoy the benefits of financial globalization. Firms raising capital abroad are larger, slower growing, more leveraged, and more profitable, and they export more than firms that raise capital only domestically (Gozzi, Levine, and Schmukler 2010). Moreover, liberalizing the capital account benefits firms with limited access to foreign currency—namely, firms producing nontradables—significantly more, as Prati, Schindler, and Valenzuela (2012) show.

Despite the large body of research on how effective capital account restrictions are and the channels through which they may affect long-run economic growth, robust conclusions remain largely elusive. Although theory predicts a number of benefits from financial openness—access to cheaper capital, portfolio diversification, consumption smoothing, emulation of foreign banks and institutions, and macro policy discipline, among others (Frankel 2010)—results from empirical studies report evidence in favor of and against capital account liberalization. Several empirical studies suggest that capital account liberalizations are often associated with higher economic growth, investment, and equity prices; lower consumption growth volatility; and reduced financial constraints (Bekaert, Harvey, and Lundblad 2005, 2006, 2011; Henry 2000a,b; Quinn and Toyoda 2008; Forbes 2007). But other empirical studies suggest that capital account restrictions make monetary policy more independent, alter the composition of capital flows toward longer maturities, reduce real exchange pressures, and reduce leverage and dependence on short-term debt (De Gregorio, Edwards, and Valdes 2000; Gallego and Hernandez 2003; Reinhart and Smith 1998).

In view of the multiple dimensions of financial globalization, Prasad et al. (2003) argue that it is difficult to establish a robust causal relationship between the degree of financial integration and output growth. Rodrik and Subramanian (2009) argue that the benefits of financial globalization, even leaving financial crises aside, are hard to find. In fact, Figure 5.5 shows a slightly negative unconditional correlation between capital account liberalization and growth in both periods of global financial stability and periods of global financial distress, although dispersion is very high.

One of the main problems with financial globalization is that strong capital inflows have the potential to incubate bubbles that can burst as a result of unpredictable external contagion or liquidity shocks, triggering major credit disruption. Reinhart and Rogoff (2008) show the close relationship between capital mobility and the incidence of banking crises. Although the cost of occasional crises can be relatively small compared with the growth-enhancing effect of financial liberalization (Tornell, Westermann, and Martinez 2004), crises following bubbles in investment and asset prices seem to unleash extremely costly recessions. These observations suggest that a cost–benefit analysis of financial liberalization is needed. Occasional costly

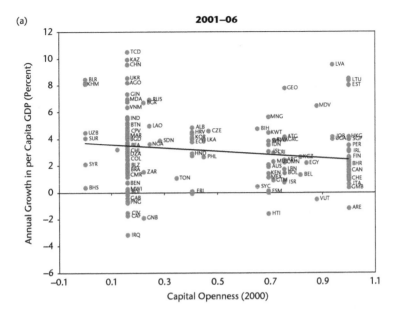

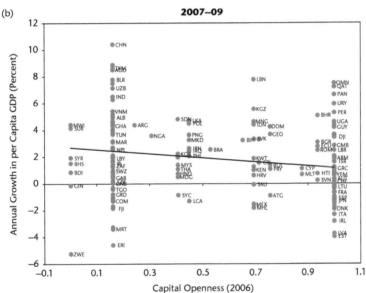

Figure 5.5 Relationship between Economic Growth and Financial Openness during Periods of Stability and Crisis

a. 2001–6 b. 2007–9

Note: Capital openness corresponds to the KAOPEN index from Chinn and Ito (2008), a *de jure* index of capital account openness. The index is normalized between 0 and 1. Higher values of the index indicate that a country is more open to cross-border capital transactions.

Source: Authors, based on data from Chinn and Ito 2008 and World Bank 2012.

crises seem to be likely in a deregulated environment. At the same time, however, deregulation and globalization allow more risk-taking, higher expected returns, and better allocation of capital.

Among the many possible reasons for the lack of consistent empirical results, three factors are probably important. First, it is likely that financial globalization is effective only under certain conditions. Second, aggregate data may hide important heterogeneities in the extent to which subsets of an economy are affected, concealing significant underlying effects (Prati, Schindler, and Valenzuela 2012). Third, different types of capital account restrictions aim to achieve different goals. Capital account restrictions on inflows are a crisis prevention tool; capital account restrictions on outflows seek to contain crises. Most studies do not distinguish capital account restrictions by the direction of flows, making it difficult to evaluate their consequences.

Understanding the effects of financial openness requires better knowledge of the specific conditions under which financial globalization is effective. Obstfeld and Taylor (2004) emphasize the role of good institutions in increasing productivity in an economy and hence increasing the benefit from financial opening. Chile is an interesting case study, for two reasons. First, the best-known example of a tax on capital inflows aimed at discouraging shorter-term borrowing is the *encaje* adopted by Chile from 1991 to 1998. IMF officials suggested that other emerging markets could benefit from adopting similar capital controls in certain circumstances (Forbes 2007). Stanley Fischer, the former First Deputy Managing Director of the IMF wrote, "The IMF has cautiously supported the use of market-based capital inflow controls, Chilean style" (Fischer 2002). Second, Chile has managed to prevent real exchange appreciation for a sustained period of time, thanks in part to reliance on capital controls. Figure 5.6 shows that Chile experienced an intense process of capital account liberalization during the past decade. Despite being a small, open economy, Chile has been more resilient to the current episode of global financial distress than most of the rest of the world. Moreover, it has been less vulnerable to this crisis than previous ones. A potential reason for Chile's resilience is that it invested in improving the quality of its institutions before liberalizing its capital account.

Our take on the relationship between financial globalization and growth is that the benefit of financial opening may be much smaller in an economy facing agency problems and other market failures compared with first-best outcomes. In a second-best world with agency problems, excessive risk-taking may result in bubbles in investment and asset prices that tend to form, at the time of increased uncertainty, from deregulation and structural change. These effects eventually increase the costs of subsequent financial crises. This view shares some elements with the Obstfeld–Taylor view, which

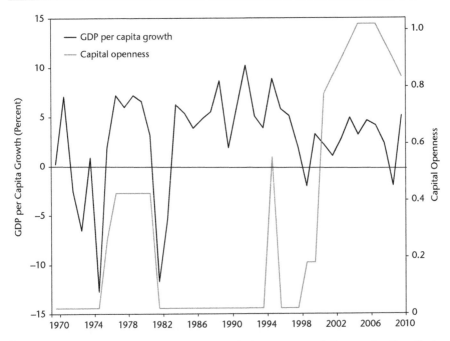

Figure 5.6 Relationship between Financial Openness and Economic Growth in Chile, 1970–2010

Note: Capital openness corresponds to the KAOPEN index from Chinn and Ito (2008), a de jure index of capital account openness. The index is normalized between 0 and 1. Higher values of the index indicate that a country is more open to cross-border capital transactions.

Source: Authors, based on data from Chinn and Ito 2008 and World Bank 2012.

emphasizes the role of better institutions and higher effective productivity in increasing benefits from financial opening. The agency problems we emphasize are based on underlying distortions, which give importance to institutional aspects, such as contract enforceability, shareholder rights protection, and rule of law.

5.3.5 Alternative Financing Channels

Financial markets and the intermediation sector are generally viewed as the main sources of funds for firms. However, in many emerging economies, the banking sector is limited and vulnerable to banking crises, and equity and bond markets are accessible only to large firms in a small number of industries. For firms without access to traditional financial markets, two financing channels become more relevant: internal finance (for example, retained earnings) and alternative (external) financing channels, defined as all nonmarket, nonbank external sources. The institutional structure that supports

Table 5.4 Access to Bank Credit by Firm Size and Country Income Level (percent)

Type of firm/country income level	Small firms (5–19 employees)	Medium-size firms (20–99 employees)	Large firms (more than 10 employees)
Firms with line of credit or loan from a financial institution			
High	45	60	66
Upper-middle	38	54	65
Lower-middle	25	39	51
Low-income	17	33	46
Firms identifying access to finance as a "major" or "very severe" obstacle			
High	22	18	18
Upper-middle	29	25	20
Lower-middle	31	28	23
Low	44	39	30

Source: Allen, Carletti, Qian, and Valenzuela 2013, based on data from World Bank Enterprise surveys (http://www.enterprisesurveys.org) for 2002–10.

much of this alternative financing is not based on standard legal mechanisms but rather on a range of mechanisms such as reputation, relationship, and trust.

Allen, Carletti, Qian, and Valenzuela (2013) show that in most countries, small and medium-sized firms, especially firms that are unlisted, rely more on alternative finance. This finding is consistent with the fact that a large proportion of firms—particularly small firms and firms in developing economies—lack access to credit from any financial institution (Table 5.4). In low-income countries, only 17 percent of small firms, compared with 66 percent of large firms, have bank credit. In low-income economies, 44 percent of small firms identify lack of access to credit as a "major" or "very severe" obstacle to the development of their businesses. Among large firms in high-income economies, the figure is 18 percent.

Although many economists view financial markets as the ideal and most important source of funds for firms, this view of the world is not entirely supported in the data (Table 5.5). Internally generated funds are the most important source of capital in all countries; these funds are far more important than external finance raised through markets, banks, and alternative channels. Internal financing is more important for firms in low-income economies than in high-income economies. Financial markets (equity and debt markets) provide the least important source of external capital; alternative finance is, on average, as important as bank finance.

There are different views regarding whether alternative finance is as conducive as bank and market finance to supporting growth. The predominant

Table 5.5 Internal and External Sources of Financing, by Country Income Level (percent)

Country income level	Number of countries	Internal sources	External sources		
			Market finance	Bank finance	Alternative finance
High	15	60	6	16	17
Upper-middle	27	64	2	18	16
Lower-middle	31	61	4	18	17
Low	24	72	3	14	11

Source: Allen, Carletti, Qian, and Valenzuela 2013, based on data from World Bank Enterprise surveys (http://www.enterprisesurveys.org) for 2002–10.

view—as illustrated in cross-country studies (for example, Beck et al. 2005, 2008) and within-country studies (for example, Ayyagari, Demirgüç-Kunt, and Maksimovic 2010)—states that firms with access to bank and market finance are of superior quality and grow faster than firms that rely only on internal and alternative finance. This evidence is more likely to support this view in developed economies with advanced markets, banks, and formal institutions. Alternative finance seems to have a strong relationship with economic growth in emerging market economies.

The very high rates of economic growth achieved by China and India, two of the largest and fastest-growing economies in the world, are difficult to explain in terms of finance provided by banks and organized equity and bond markets. Allen, Carletti, Qian, and Valenzuela (2013) argue that, in both countries, alternative finance played a major role in funding fast-growing small and medium-sized enterprises. According to the World Bank's Enterprise Surveys, alternative finance accounts for 52 percent of funding in China; the rest comes from bank finance (15 percent), retained earnings (15 percent), market finance (12 percent), and other sources. In contrast to the conventional view that strong institutions and legal systems are important for growth, we suggest that alternative systems based on trust, reputation, and other mechanisms play a crucial role.

Allen, Chakrabarti, De, Qian, and Qian (2012) explore the impact of alternative finance on growth in India. Specifically, they test the null hypothesis that access to bank and market finance is associated with higher firm growth rates in India. Their main finding is that the positive relation between bank finance and firm growth does not hold for Indian firms, after controlling for firm characteristics including location and regional development and correcting for possible survivorship biases as a result of higher death rates among smaller firms. The results are robust to controlling for potential endogeneity associated with the fact that firms chose the type of financing.

An important issue is the extent to which alternative finance poses a systemic risk that could result in a crisis. This risk depends on the nature of the financing. Financing from family and friends does not pose a systemic risk. To the extent that chains of trade credit run through many firms to banks, trade credit may pose some systemic risk.

In China, there has recently been discussion of the risks posed by the shadow banking system. These risks depend on the nature of the transactions undertaken. One widespread form of transaction is loans brokered by financial institutions. This type of transaction creates little systemic risk, as the bank arranges a loan from the creditor to the borrower in exchange for a fee, without taking on any credit risk itself; the risk of default is borne by the lender. Another type of transaction is loans made by banks to entities set up by local authorities. These entities often have no revenue source. The total amount of these loans is substantial. The problem here is that local governments do not have proper funding sources, such as the ability to tax: if they did, there would be no systemic risk. Ultimately, these debts are likely to be the responsibility of the central government. Given its strong fiscal position, they should not pose a systemic threat.

5.3.6 Formal versus Alternative Institutions

Economists have long argued that efficient institutions that facilitate business transactions are a key driver of long-run economic growth (see, for example, Coase 1960; North and Thomas 1973; Williamson 1979). Much of institutional economics developed over the past two decades has emphasized the role of two types of formal institutions: a legal system and a financial system. The law and finance literature, pioneered by La Porta et al. (1997, 1998), posits that a strong legal system that enforces contracts and resolves disputes is important for finance and growth. Similarly, a developed financial system, in particular financial markets and a banking sector, are vital sources of external financing to fund firm growth.

Allen, Qian, and Qian (2005) argue that China provides a significant counterexample to the literature. During China's high growth period (1980–2005), neither its legal nor its financial systems were well developed, and the government was regarded as autocratic and corrupt. Yet its economy grew at the fastest pace in the world.

Other research shows that the legal system plays a very limited role in finance and commerce in other successful Asian economies, including Taiwan, Korea, Vietnam, and Japan. Despite India's English common law origin and British-style judicial system, formal legal and financial institutions are of limited use there (Allen, Chakrabarti, De, Qian, and Qian 2012). Even in developed countries such as the United Kingdom and Germany, where financial markets and formal legal and financial institutions were first developed, the importance of the role of the law and legal system during their early stages of economic development is debatable.

The conventional wisdom would characterize the economic performance in China as successful despite the lack of western-style institutions. By contrast, Allen, Qian, and Zhang (2011) argue that China has done well *because of* this lack of western-style institutions: conducting business outside the legal system in fast-growing economies, such as the current economies of China and India and the economies of Taiwan and Korea in the 1960s–80s, can be superior to using the law as the basis for finance and commerce. In China and India, state-owned enterprises and publicly listed firms have much easier access to legal institutions and banks and financial markets than nonstate, nonlisted firms. Even these nonstate, nonlisted firms conduct business outside the legal system and do not rely on financial markets or banks for most of their financing needs. Instead, they use methods based on reputation, relationships, and trust to settle disputes and induce good behaviors and rely on alternative financing channels such as trade credits and funds from family and friends to finance their growth, as discussed in the previous section. In both countries, especially in China, it is the nonstate, nonlisted firms that provide most of the economic growth and employ most of the labor force. To a large degree, similar alternative institutions are also behind the success of other Asian economies, and they have played an important part in developed countries, such as the United Kingdom and Germany, at least during early stages of their growth.

Allen, Qian, and Zhang (2011) argue that alternative finance backed by nonlegal mechanisms can actually be superior to bank and market finance backed by the legal system. Research on political economy factors (for example, Rajan and Zingales 2003a, 2003b; Acemoglu and Johnson 2005) suggests that rent-seeking behavior by interest groups can turn the legal system, a monopolist institution, into a barrier to change. These problems are expected to be much more severe in developing countries. The "alternative" view thus argues that by not using the legal system, alternative finance can minimize the costs associated with legal institutions. These papers also point out that in a dynamic environment, characterized by frequent fundamental changes in the economy, alternative institutions can adapt and change much more quickly than formal institutions.

Alternative finance has important implications. The first is that in rapidly growing economies and during the early stages of economic growth, the disadvantages of using the legal system can overshadow its advantages. Thus, conducting business without using the law and legal system and relying on alternative finance as the main source of external funds for corporate sectors can be a superior model. A second important implication is that alternative finance is likely to become a more important source of financing during periods of financial distress, when access to credit and financial markets becomes more difficult. Nilsen (2002) shows that small firms are more likely to rely on trade credit during episodes of financial distress.

5.4 Financial Crises

High growth may well require that firms and entrepreneurs take significant nondiversifiable risks in order to obtain high returns. This risk-taking may lead to high growth but also to financial crises. The main problem is that in some cases, the negative effects of boom–bust cycles are so extreme that the variation in growth is harmful, as the current crisis illustrates. Moreover, as Bordo et al. (2001) emphasize, in recent decades financial crises have occurred twice as often as during the Bretton Woods period (1945–71) or the Gold Standard era (1880–1993); only during the Great Depression were they as frequent. Since 1970, the world has experienced 147 banking crises, 218 currency crises, 67 sovereign debt crises, and multiple double and triple crises (Table 5.6).

The empirical research on crises and growth is sparse. One of the few studies is by Loayza and Rancière (2006), who note that the growth literature finds a positive relationship between financial development measures, such as private domestic credit and liquid liabilities, and economic growth, whereas the currency and banking crises literature (Kaminsky and Reinhart 1999) often finds such variables useful in predicting crises. Loayza and Rancière find that a positive long-run relationship between financial development and output growth coexists with a mostly negative short-run relationship. Rancière, Tornell, and Westermann (2008) document that on average, countries that have experienced occasional crises have grown faster than countries with smooth credit conditions.

The following subsections explore some of the most important causes and consequences of financial crises, as well as policies to try to prevent them.

5.4.1 Systemic Risk, Financial Crises, and Macroprudential Regulation

Asset price bubbles are by no means the only form of systemic risk that can trigger crises. This subsection examines four categories of systemic risk:

- panics (banking crises as a result of multiple equilibria);
- banking crises as a result of asset price falls;
- contagion;
- foreign exchange mismatches in the banking system.

Table 5.6 Annual Number of Financial Crises, by Type, 1970–2012

Year	Banking crisis	Currency crisis	Sovereign debt crisis	Double crisis	Triple crisis
1970	0	0	0	0	0
1971	0	1	0	0	0
1972	0	5	0	0	0
1973	0	1	0	0	0
1974	0	0	0	0	0
1975	0	5	0	0	0
1976	2	4	1	0	0
1977	2	1	1	0	0
1978	0	5	3	0	0
1979	0	3	2	0	0
1980	3	4	3	3	0
1981	3	10	6	1	0
1982	5	5	9	1	1
1983	7	12	9	2	1
1984	1	10	4	0	0
1985	2	10	3	0	0
1986	1	4	3	0	0
1987	6	6	0	1	0
1988	7	5	1	0	0
1989	4	8	3	1	1
1990	7	10	2	0	0
1991	10	6	0	1	0
1992	8	9	1	1	0
1993	7	8	0	1	0
1994	11	25	0	2	0
1995	13	4	0	2	0
1996	4	6	0	1	0
1997	7	6	0	4	0
1998	7	10	2	3	3
1999	0	8	2	0	0
2000	2	4	0	0	0
2001	1	3	2	1	1
2002	1	5	4	0	0
2003	1	4	1	1	1
2004	0	1	1	0	0
2005	0	1	0	0	0
2006	0	0	0	0	0
2007	2	0	0	0	0
2008	22	3	2	2	0
2009	1	5	0	0	0
2010	0	1	1	0	0
2011	0	0	0	0	0
2012	0	0	1	0	0
Total	147	218	67	28	8

Note: A twin crisis indicates a banking crisis in year t and a currency crisis during $[t-1, t+1]$. A triple crisis indicates a banking crisis in year t, a currency crisis during $[t-1, t+1]$, and debt crisis during $[t-1, t+1]$.

Source: Laeven and Valencia, 2012.

This subsection also examines macroprudential regulatory measures and policies that could be put in place to counter these risks. What is important is that the new macroprudential regulation deals with systemic risk, that the focus of regulation not be solely on the risk of failure of single financial institutions. The current crisis has clearly shown that the microprudential approach to financial regulation does not suffice to prevent financial crises. Systemic risk is a complex phenomenon that needs to be combated with a wide range of policies.

PANICS (BANKING CRISES AS A RESULT OF MULTIPLE EQUILIBRIA)
The importance of panics in the current crisis is unclear. However, historically there is evidence that panics have been an important source of systemic risk. In the seminal work by Bryant (1980) and Diamond and Dybvig (1983), panics are self-fulfilling events. Agents have uncertain needs for consumption, and long-term investments are costly to liquidate. They deposit their endowment in a bank in exchange for a demand deposit contract that provides insurance for their liquidity needs. If all depositors believe that other depositors withdraw their funds only according to their consumption needs, then good equilibrium is reached in which the bank can satisfy all depositors' demands without liquidating any of the long-term assets. If, however, depositors believe that other depositors will withdraw prematurely, then all agents find it rational to redeem their claims and a panic occurs.

In their classic book, Friedman and Schwartz (1963) argue that the systemic risk and financial instability in the United States in the late nineteenth and early twentieth centuries were panic-based, as evidenced by the absence of downturns in the relevant macroeconomic time series before the crises.

Introducing deposit insurance for retail depositors is one policy measure that can prevent panics. However, it covers only small depositors. As shown in the recent crisis, large deposits and wholesale funding constitute the majority of funding for many financial institutions. As a result, deposit insurance alone is no longer adequate to solve the problem of panics.

Deposit insurance could be extended and all forms of short-term debt guaranteed. Although doing so could prevent panics, it would generate moral hazard (if banks have access to low-cost funds guaranteed by the government, they have an incentive to take significant risks). A better solution may be to remove deposit insurance and deal with the problem of panic runs through lender-of-last-resort policies. If depositors know that the central bank will provide the needed liquidity if they attempt to withdraw early, they will not do so.

The other significant problem with deposit insurance and short-term guarantees is that they can be extremely costly to implement if there are other types of systemic risk. In Ireland, for example, the blanket bank debt guarantees of September 2008 effectively bankrupted the country and forced the government to seek funds from the European Financial Stability Fund.

BANKING CRISES AS A RESULT OF ASSET PRICE FALLS
The prices of assets held by banks can fall for many reasons. Some of the most relevant for causing financial crises include the following.

- fluctuations in the business cycle;
- bursting of real estate bubbles;
- mispricing as a result of inefficient liquidity provision and limits to arbitrage;
- sovereign default;
- increases in interest rates.

Fluctuations in the business cycle. A longstanding alternative to the panic view of banking crises was that such crises were not random events but a natural outgrowth of the business cycle (see the survey by Allen, Babus, and Carletti 2009). The idea is that an economic downturn will reduce the value of bank assets, raising the possibility that banks are unable to meet their commitments. As Gorton (1988) explains, if depositors receive information about the impending downturn in the cycle, they will anticipate financial difficulties in the banking sector and try to withdraw their funds prematurely, precipitating the crisis. In contrast to the Friedman and Schwarz (1963) view of crises as panics, Gorton (1988), Calomiris and Gorton (1991), and Calomiris and Mason (2003) provide evidence that many of the crises that occurred in the United States were based on fundamentals.

One of the goals of macroprudential policy is to prevent fundamental crises. Standard macroeconomic measures designed to mitigate the depth of the recession may be helpful. Deposit insurance and other forms of guarantee may also help prevent a fundamental crisis but may have large fiscal consequences, as in the case of Ireland just discussed. The nature of this trade-off is not yet well understood.

Bursting of real estate bubbles. Herring and Wachter (1999), Reinhart and Rogoff (2009), Glick and Lansing (2010), and Crowe et al. (2011) provide persuasive evidence that collapses in real estate prices (residential, commercial, or both) are one of the major causes of financial crises. In many cases, these collapses occur following bubbles created by loose monetary policy and the excessive availability of credit.

Allen and Carletti (2010) argue that the main initial cause of the current crisis was the bubble in real estate in the United States and a number of other countries, such as Ireland and Spain. When the bubble burst in the United States, many financial institutions experienced severe problems because of the collapse in the securitized mortgage market. Problems then spread to the real economy.

It can be argued that the real estate bubble in these countries was the result of loose monetary policy and a build-up of foreign exchange reserves that led to excessive credit availability. Central banks, in particular the Federal Reserve, set very low interest rates during 2003–04, to avoid a recession after the bursting of the tech bubble in 2000 and the terrorist attacks of September 11, 2001. As Taylor (2007, 2008) argue, interest rates were much lower than in previous U.S. recessions relative to standard economic indicators as captured by the Taylor Rule, which describes the historic relationship between interest rates and various macroeconomic variables.

Figure 5.7, taken from Taylor (2007), reports the effective federal funds rate and its counterfactual according to the Taylor Rule. The rate was cut to the very low level of 1 percent in 2003 and stayed there until 2004. For almost four years, it fell well below what historical experience would suggest it should have been. This deviation of monetary policy from the Taylor Rule was unusually large; no greater or more persistent deviation from actual Fed policy has been observed since the 1970s.

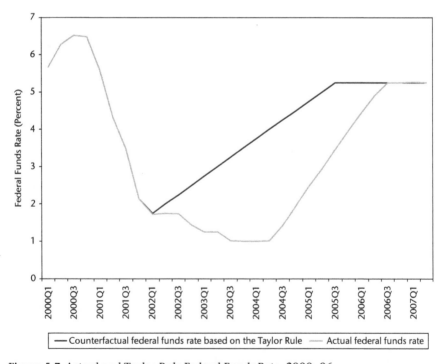

Figure 5.7 Actual and Taylor Rule Federal Funds Rate, 2000–06

Source: John Taylor, "Housing and Monetary Policy," in *Housing, Housing Finance, and Monetary Policy*, Federal Reserve Bank of Kansas City, September 2007, pp. 463–76.

This loose monetary policy was adopted during a period in which housing prices were still growing at significantly more than the inflation rate of about 3 percent. During 1997–2005, the Case–Shiller 10 City Composite Index, one of the most frequently used house price indexes, rose annually by 5–15 percent. Given the positive serial correlation in housing prices documented by Glaeser and Gyourko (2007) and others, this low level of interest rates created an incentive for people to buy houses, as they could borrow at 1 percent and buy assets whose value was growing much faster.

Like the United States, several European countries exhibited deviations from the Taylor Rule. These deviations explain an important fraction of the cross-country variation in housing booms in Europe, measured by the change in housing investment as a percentage of GDP (Ahrend, Cournède, and Price 2008).

Growth in credit also plays an important role in asset price bubbles (Allen and Gale 2000a, 2007). During the recent crisis, credit expanded rapidly in countries with loose monetary policy as a result of the investment of large foreign exchange reserves accumulated primarily by Asian countries since the late 1990s and oil producers since the mid-2000s. Allen and Hong (2011) suggest that the Asian countries affected by the crisis of 1997 started accumulating reserves in response to the tough conditions the IMF imposed on them in exchange for financial assistance. The motivations for the reserve accumulation of China, the largest single holder, are probably more complex. In addition to the precautionary reason, China started accumulating reserves to prevent its currency from strengthening, in order to protect its exports. Perhaps most important, reserves increased China's political influence significantly.[3] Most of the accumulated reserves were invested in U.S. dollars and euros. The large supply of credit in the United States helped drive down lending standards in order to ensure that there was enough demand for debt from homebuyers and other borrowers. Funds did not flow only to the United States; Spain and Ireland also ran large current account deficits, which helped fuel their property bubbles.

When real estate bubbles burst, the financial sector and the real economy are adversely affected. Mian and Sufi (2009) show that zip codes in the United States that experienced the largest increases in household leverage tended to experience the sharpest jumps in loan defaults and the most severe recessions.

Asset price bubbles typically go through three phases. The first starts with financial liberalization, a conscious decision by the central bank to increase

---

[3] For example, before the 2008 Beijing Olympics, many European leaders met with the Dalai Lama to protest China's human rights policies in Tibet. Since the start of the euro zone crisis in 2010, European leaders have been much more interested in borrowing from China and have refrained from drawing attention to its human rights policies.

lending, or some other similar event. The resulting expansion in credit is accompanied by an increase in the prices of assets such as real estate. This rise in prices continues for some time, possibly several years, as the bubble inflates. During the second phase, the bubble bursts and asset prices collapse, often in a short period of time, such as a few days or months, but sometimes over a longer period. The third phase is characterized by the default of agents that borrowed to buy assets at inflated prices. Banking and/or foreign exchange crises may follow this wave of defaults. The difficulties associated with the defaults and banking and foreign exchange crises often cause problems in the real sector of the economy that can last for years. There is significant interaction between the financial system and growth.

Consistent with the first phase, Glick and Lansing (2010) shows that countries that experienced significant increases of household debt in 1997–2007 experienced significant increases in housing prices (Figure 5.8). This relationship suggests that the link between easy household credit and rising property prices held globally. Consistent with the second phase, Figure 5.9 shows that countries that experienced excessive increases in housing prices exhibited a significant drop in those prices once the bubble burst. Consistent with the third phase, Figure 5.10 shows that GDP per capita in the United States significantly dropped after the bust of the real estate sector.

In order to avoid crises, it is very important for macroprudential policymakers to be able to predict bubbles and prevent their emergence. Borio and Lowe (2002) argue that although it is difficult to predict asset price bubbles, particularly real estate bubbles, it is not impossible. They provide evidence that rapid credit growth combined with large increases in real estate prices can lead to financial instability. They suggest that in low-inflation environments, inflationary pressures can first appear in asset prices rather than in the prices of goods and services. In such cases, it may be appropriate to use monetary policy to prick bubbles and preserve financial and monetary stability.

Bubbles, in particular real estate bubbles, seem to be associated with loose monetary policy and excessive credit supply. One way to prevent them is, then, through interest rate policy. In particular, interest rates should not be kept very low when property prices are surging.

Once bubbles begin to form, it may be possible and desirable to raise interest rates in economies with a high degree of homogeneity, such as small countries like Sweden or possibly the United Kingdom. However, doing so may be difficult for political reasons. In particular, when such policies are first introduced, it may be difficult to explain why it is worth causing a recession to burst a property'bubble.

The problem is more complicated in heterogeneous economies like the United States, China, and the euro zone, where economic fundamentals and the rate of property price increases differ across regions. Using interest rates to prick

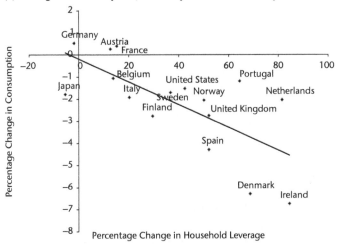

Figure 5.8 Housing Prices and Household Leverage, 1997–2007

a. Changes in housing prices 1997–2007 b. Changes in consumption, second quarter 2008-first quarter 2009

Source: Glick and Lansing 2010.

bubbles would adversely affect areas that do not have them. Recent events in the euro zone constitute a clear example. The interest rate policy followed by the European Central Bank was correct for countries such as Germany, where there was no bubble, but inappropriate for Spain, where it helped inflate the bubble. A tighter policy might have been effective in preventing the bubble in Spain— but at the cost of a recession or at least slower growth in some other countries.

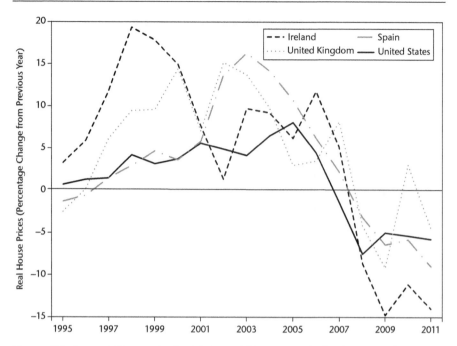

Figure 5.9 Annual Change in Real Prices of Housing in Ireland, Spain, the United States, and the United Kingdom, 1995–2011

Source: Authors, based on data from OECD (2012).

When interest rates cannot be used, it may be better to use other forms of macroprudential regulation to prevent bubbles. One example is limits on loan-to-value ratios, which could be lowered as property prices increase at a faster pace. Using this tool can be effective for residential property but it may be difficult to enforce for commercial property, because firms may be able to use pyramids of companies that increase leverage. Another option is to impose property transfer taxes that rise with the rate of property price increases. A more direct measure is to restrict real estate lending in certain regions.

These measures have been tried in several Asian economies, including Hong Kong, Korea, and Singapore. Crowe et al. (2011) show that they appear to have been effective in the short term but less so in the medium and long term.

Saying that monetary policy should not be used to prick bubbles in larger economies or in monetary unions where countries have different economic conditions does not imply that monetary policy should not be constrained. Loose monetary policy is arguably one of the main causes for the emergence of bubbles, as the recent crisis has shown. One of the most important macroprudential measures should be constraining monetary policy so that it does

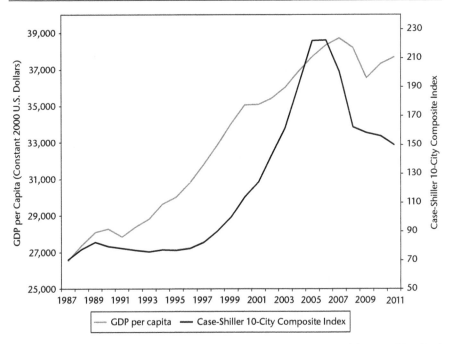

Figure 5.10 Real GDP and Index of Real Housing Prices in the United States, 1987–2011

Note: The Case–Shiller 10-City Composite Index is a widely used indicator of changes in house prices.

Source: Authors, based on data from Standard and Poor's (2012) and World Bank (2012).

not trigger bubbles. Interest rates should not be kept excessively low, particularly when real estate prices are rising.

During the recent crisis, excessive credit emerged because of large global imbalances in foreign exchange reserves. To prevent bubbles in the future, it is important to solve this problem. Although it is individually advantageous for countries to self-insure by accumulating reserves, this mechanism is inefficient from a global perspective. What is needed to solve this problem is a reform of the international financial system, as will be discussed in section 5.

Mispricing as a result of inefficient liquidity provision and limits to arbitrage. Asset pricing theory relies on the assumption of fully rational agents and perfect and complete markets. Under these assumptions, assets are always correctly priced at their fundamental values. The recent crisis illustrated the flaws in this theory in practice.

Theories explaining the role of liquidity in creating systemic risk combine the functioning of financial institutions and markets in a model of liquidity (see, for example, Allen and Gale 2007; Allen, Carletti, and Gale 2009). Financial intermediaries provide liquidity insurance to consumers against their individual liquidity shocks. Markets allow financial intermediaries (and hence their depositors) to share aggregate risks. If financial markets are complete, the financial system provides liquidity efficiently, by ensuring that banks' liquidity shocks are hedged. By contrast, where markets are incomplete, banks cannot hedge completely against shocks, and the financial system stops providing an efficient level of liquidity. This inability to hedge can cause assets to be mispriced, with the prices of even safe assets falling below their fundamental values.

An illustration of this phenomenon in the current crisis is the fact that many securitized products appear to have been mispriced. The challenge for macroprudential policy is to design interventions that allow this problem to be corrected, as the Troubled Asset Relief Program (TARP) program in the United States sought to do. The idea was that by buying large volumes of toxic assets, the Treasury could restore the functioning of the market. In practice, the Treasury was unable to implement the program effectively. This type of direct intervention seems problematic. Political economy issues are clearly important. It is also not clear that such a scheme can restore the market to proper functioning. No convincing proposals have yet been suggested for this critical area of macroprudential policy.

Given the lack of an immediate solution to this problem, what should governments do? A major problem is that recent reforms have ensured that financial institutions mark their assets to market. In normal times, this system is undoubtedly the best. Financial institutions have traditionally used historic cost accounting for many of their assets. This system has the disadvantage that it allows institutions to conceal declines in asset values for significant periods of time. A good example is the savings and loans crisis in the United States in the 1980s. This kind of episode encouraged the move to mark-to-market accounting by the International Accounting Standards Board and U.S. Financial Accounting Standards Board (FASB) (see, for example, Allen and Carletti 2008a; Plantin, Sapra, and Shin 2008). The divergence between asset prices, particularly prices of securitized products, and apparent fundamentals in the current crisis meant that mark-to-market accounting came under severe criticism by financial institutions and was relaxed by the FASB under political pressure from Congress.

How should the advantages and disadvantages of mark-to-market accounting be balanced? As long as markets are efficient, mark-to-market accounting dominates. When, during times of crisis, they cease to be efficient, market prices do not provide a good guide for regulators and investors. The key issue becomes how to identify whether financial markets are working properly. Allen and Carletti (2008b) suggest that when market and model-based prices diverge significantly (by more than, say, 5 percent), financial institutions should publish both. If regulators and investors see many financial institutions independently publishing different valuations, they can deduce that financial markets may no longer be efficient and can act accordingly.

Sovereign default. The introduction of the euro led to significant integration of the European bond market. The spread on the sovereign debt of different euro countries decreased significantly over the past decade, reflecting the idea that the monetary union together with the fiscal rules of the Maastricht Treaty and the Growth and Stability Pact would suffice to increase fiscal harmonization across Europe and thus the solvency of all euro countries.

Since May 2010, it has become clear that the architecture embedded in the Maastricht Treaty, and in particular the Growth and Stability Pact, is not sufficient to achieve its goals. The Greek default in 2012 showed that there is credit risk in sovereign debt—a serious problem in its own right, but also a critical problem because of its effect on the stability of the banking system. The relation works both ways: the euro zone crisis puts pressure on the financial system, and the financial crisis in Europe puts pressure on the euro zone.

The Growth and Stability Pact contained rules on the amount of current public deficits and overall debt allowed. The possibility that a country would go into default was not even contemplated in the architecture of the euro zone. When the Greek crisis emerged, there were no guidelines or regulations that could be used. In the end, the European Union and the euro zone dealt with the problem by setting up a bailout fund. This response creates moral hazard, by changing the incentives of governments to deal with fiscal excesses. In addition, there is the question of how sustainable the bailout mechanism is politically. If Greece and any other countries default, Germany will pay a large share of the cost. How much German voters—and voters in other countries that make large contributions to bailout funds—will be willing to subsidize defaulting countries remains to be seen.

Interest rate risk. Perhaps the most immediate systemic risk going forward is that of a sharp rise in interest rates. In many countries, both short- and long-term interest rates are at all-time historical lows. When they start to rise, as a result of either policy moves by central banks to restrain inflation or market moves in anticipation of inflation, the price of all securities, including government debt, will fall. In many countries, this decline in security prices has the potential to cause significant solvency problems for banks.

If central banks raise rates, they should do so over an extended period, so that the effects on financial stability are limited. One of the risks of pursuing low interest rate policies is that a crisis could lead to a rise in long-term interest rates that would be very difficult for central banks to prevent. For example, foreign holders of U.S. Treasuries could decide to sell at the same time, creating a financial crisis. In designing plans for an exit from low interest rate and quantitative easing policies, it is very important to take into account financial stability.

CONTAGION

One source of systemic risk that appears to have been important during the recent financial crisis is contagion: the possibility that the distress of one financial institution propagates to others in the financial system, ultimately leading to a systemic crisis. Central banks often use the risk of contagion to justify intervention, especially when the financial institution in distress is big or occupies a key position in particular markets. Fear of contagion is the origin of the term "too big to fail."

The recent crisis abounds with examples of fears of contagion. Federal Reserve chairman Ben Bernanke (2008) argues that the takeover of Bear Stearns by J.P. Morgan arranged by the Federal Reserve in March 2008 was justified by the likelihood that its failure would lead to a chain reaction that would have caused many other financial institutions to have gone bankrupt. Contagion could have spread bankruptcy throughout the network of derivative contracts that Bear Stearns was part of.

When Lehman Brothers failed, in September 2008, the Federal Reserve presumably expected that its failure would not generate contagion. In fact, there was contagion, but the form it took was complex. The problem spread first to money market funds. The government had to intervene rapidly by guaranteeing all money market mutual funds. The failure of Lehman also led to a loss of confidence in many financial firms, as investors feared that other financial institutions might also be allowed to fail. Volumes in many important financial markets fell significantly, and there was a large spillover into the real economy. World trade collapsed. In trade-based economies such as Germany and Japan, GDP fell significantly in the fourth quarter of 2008 and the first quarter of 2009. This dramatic decline in GDP in many countries underlines the importance of contagion.

The effects of contagion are not well understood. The literature has provided a few explanations of the mechanisms at play, but much work is still needed. Research on contagion takes a number of approaches (see the survey by Allen, Babus, and Carletti 2009). In looking for contagious effects through direct linkages, early research by Allen and Gale (2000c) studied how the banking system responds to contagion when banks are connected by different network structures. They show that incomplete networks are more prone to contagion than complete structures. Following research focused on network externalities created from individual bank risk, they applied network techniques to the study of contagion in financial systems. The main result in this theoretical literature is that greater connectivity reduces the likelihood of widespread default. However, shocks may have a significantly larger impact on the financial system when they occur.

Wagner (2010), Ibragimov, Jaffee, and Walden (2011), and Allen, Babus, and Carletti (2012) consider a second type of contagion, in which systemic risk arises from common asset exposures. Diversification is privately beneficial but increases the likelihood of systemic risk as portfolios become more similar. The use of short-term debt can lead to a further significant increase in systemic risk.

Several macroprudential policies and regulations may be needed to address the different channels and types of contagion. Capital regulation has been the main tool for regulating banks in recent years, coordinated internationally through the Basel agreements. It is the main tool for ensuring stability in the international financial system. The traditional justification for capital regulation has been that it is needed to offset moral hazard from deposit insurance (for an example of an exception, see Hellmann, Murdock, and Stiglitz 2000). Because banks have access to low-cost funds guaranteed by the government, they have an incentive to take significant risks. If the risks pay off, banks profit; if the risks do not pay off, the government bears the losses. Capital regulation is needed to offset the incentives for banks to take risks, as it ensures that shareholders will lose significantly. Moreover, capital acts as a buffer to absorb losses, thus making banks more resilient to shocks and losses and, perhaps most important, reducing the risk of contagion.

There is a longstanding debate over how much capital banks should hold (for a recent contribution, see Admati et al. 2010). The recent crisis and the discussions of the proposal for a new regulatory framework have highlighted the difficulties embodied in these proposals. The starting point of the discussion is usually that capital is a more costly form of funding than debt, so that, left unregulated, banks minimize the use of capital; regulation is needed to force banks to hold minimum capital levels. The same argument is typically assumed in the academic literature (see, for example, Gorton and Winton 2003).

Modeling the cost of equity finance for financial institutions is one of the major problems in designing capital regulation. The first issue is whether equity is in fact more costly than debt. If it is, the second issue is whether equity is more costly only in the financial industry or in all industries. Financial institutions hold much less equity (about 10 percent) than industrial companies (30–40 percent). Understanding the reasons for this large difference in capital structures is of crucial importance in designing capital regulation.

One simple answer as to why equity is more costly than debt is that in many countries interest on corporate debt is tax deductible but dividends are not. It is not clear why this is the case or whether it should be the case. There does not seem to be any good public policy rationale for the deductibility of interest on corporate debt, which seems to have arisen as a historical accident. When the corporate income tax was introduced, interest was regarded as a cost of doing business, in the same way that paying wages to workers was a cost. However, from a modern corporate finance perspective, equity and debt are just alternative ways of financing the firm. If tax deductibility is the reason why firms prefer to use debt rather than equity, then the simple solution is to remove it. If without deductibility, financial institutions are willing or can be induced through regulation to use more equity, then financial stability could potentially be considerably enhanced.

Other possible rationales for the high cost of equity are agency problems within the firm. According to this rationale, equity does not provide the correct incentives to shareholders or managers to provide the right monitoring. High leverage is needed to ensure such monitoring. There is little empirical evidence that this problem is severe in the banking sector. In private equity and venture capital firms, where the agency problem seems much greater, leverage is typically lower than in banks.

A final point concerns the reason why financial institutions hold so little capital relative to other industries. Debt in the financial industry is implicitly subsidized through government guarantees and bailouts. If this implicit subsidy explains why financial institutions rely so heavily on debt, then it is necessary to limit guarantees and create credible enforcement mechanisms such as proper resolution procedures.

In the current debates on capital regulation, two main proposals have been put forth. The first concerns countercyclical capital regulation. The second concerns the use of hybrid instruments in the form of contingent convertible debt (CoCos).

The idea behind countercyclical capital regulation is that during normal times, banks and other financial institutions can accumulate capital reserves and buffers that will allow them to survive serious shocks to the financial system. These measures are related to countercyclical loan reserves that have been implemented by the Bank of Spain for some time. The accumulation of loan reserves in the period before the crisis helped Spanish banks weather the crisis, suggesting that countercyclical capital ratios may be helpful. However, the accumulation of loan reserves did not prevent the credit boom in Spain or the bubble in property prices, so not too much reliance should be placed on them.

It has been widely suggested that banks should issue convertible debt that could be converted into equity in the event of a crisis. The Royal Bank of Scotland and Lloyds in the United Kingdom and Unicredit in Italy have issued this kind of security. CoCos have two main advantages: they obviate the need for banks to raise capital in difficult times, and they allow losses to be shared with debt holders. This possibility of conversion would also have a disciplinary role, inducing bank managers to behave more prudently.

Another way to stabilize markets and prevent contagion is through a combination of public and private financial institutions. Chile's Banco Estado is a publicly owned commercial bank that competes with private sector banks. In times of crisis, it can expand and help stabilize the market, as all market participants know that it is backed by the state and will not fail.

Many central banks have been playing this role by buying large quantities of commercial paper. These central banks have become like large commercial banks—but the officials in charge of central banks do not usually have much expertise in running a commercial bank or know much about credit risk. It would be better to have expertise in the public sector that allows the state to perform commercial banking functions during times of crisis. These state institutions would act as firebreaks, limiting the damage that can be done by contagion.

CURRENCY MISMATCHES IN THE BANKING SYSTEM

One of the major problems in the 1997 Asian crisis was currency mismatch. Banks and firms in Korea, Thailand, and other countries had borrowed in foreign currencies, particularly dollars. When the crisis hit, they were unable to borrow. Central banks did not have enough foreign exchange reserves and were unable to borrow in the markets. As a result, a number of countries had to turn to the IMF.

During the current crisis, the major central banks agreed on foreign exchange swaps. These swaps eased the international aspects of the crisis, compared with 1997. Allen and Moessner (2010) describe the problems raised by banks lending at low interest rates in foreign currencies. The foreign currencies that were typically used to make loans were the U.S. dollar, the Japanese yen, and the Swiss franc. These loans were funded in two ways. The first was through the international wholesale deposit market; the second was by taking deposits in domestic currency and then using the foreign exchange swap market to convert them into the required foreign currency. The largest currency-specific liquidity shortages were $400 billion in the euro zone, $90 billion worth of yen in the United Kingdom, $70 billion worth of euros in the United States, and $30 billion worth of Swiss francs in the euro zone. The central bank foreign exchange swaps ended the problems these mismatches posed.

Allen and Moessner (2010) document how the swap system worked. There were four overlapping networks:

- the Federal Reserve's network to supply U.S. dollars;

- the European Central Bank's network to supply euros;
- the Swiss franc network;
- the Latin American and Asian networks.

These swap networks involved considerable overlap (see Allen and Moessner 2010). As they were organized between central banks, the credit risk borne was sovereign rather than commercial. The receiving central bank then passed on the foreign currency to firms and financial institutions, which bore the commercial credit risk. Some of the swaps between central banks were collateralized with the currency of the counterparty central bank. These swaps considerably eased foreign exchange problems during the crisis and are widely regarded as having been successful.

5.4.2 Domestic Financial Deregulation

As suggested by Moss (2010), the experience of the United States exhibits a significant correlation between financial deregulation and financial crises (Figure 5.11). Until 1933, a period characterized by very little financial regulation, bank failures were frequent in the United States. After financial regulation was dramatically strengthened, bank failures practically vanished for nearly 50 years. When financial deregulation began in the 1980s, bank failures reappeared.

The international evidence is not much different from the experience of the United States. The negative experience of the Great Depression was so severe that extensive financial regulation and other measures were put in place around the globe to prevent another Great Depression. These measures, particularly the measures implemented in much of Europe and Asia, restricted risk-taking to a great degree and prevented banking crises. From 1945 until 1971, there was only one banking crisis in the world, which occurred in Brazil in 1962 together with a currency crisis.

One way to stop crises is thus to prevent financial institutions from taking risks. However, the prevention of crises during this period was achieved at a high cost. The measures were so severe that they effectively prevented the financial system from allocating resources.

As shown in Table 5.6, starting in the 1970s and accelerating in the 1980s, financial systems were deregulated and banking crises returned. Kaminsky and Reinhart (1999) document the importance of financial liberalization and deregulation in causing crises in a wide range of circumstances. Their results suggest that great care needs to be taken in deregulating financial systems and ensuring that it does not lead to credit booms and other excesses that result in financial crises.

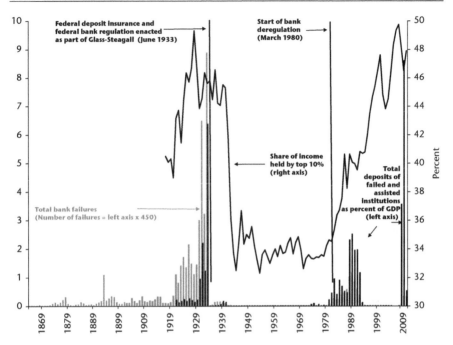

Figure 5.11 Banking Crises, Financial Regulation, and Income Inequality in the United States, 1864–2009

Note: The left y-axis measures two variables. The first is total deposits of failed and assisted institutions. It is measured as a percent of GDP. The second variable is total bank failures. The number 1 represents 450 failures, 2 represents 900 failures, and so on. The right axis measures the share of income held by the top 10 percent.

Source: Moss (2010).

5.4.3 Income Inequality

According to Moss (2010), income inequality in the United States has also followed a similar pattern to the frequency of banking crises and financial deregulation. This correlation is mainly observed in the two peaks in inequality that occurred in 1928 and 2007—immediately before the Great Depression and the Great Recession (see Figure 5.11). As a consequence of these stylized facts, a series of theories argue that income inequality may create incentives that put the financial system at risk.

Rajan (2010) and Kumhof and Rancière (2011) investigate how high leverage and financial crises can arise as a result of changes in income distribution. Rajan (2010) argues that the subprime crisis was a manifestation of an underlying and longer-term dynamic driven by income inequality. The main argument is that increased income inequality created political pressure to encourage easy credit in order to keep demand and job creation robust despite stagnating incomes. Kumhof and Rancière (2011) argue that in periods of high inequality, the rich lend a large part of their increased income to the low-income segments of the population. In this way, investors allow workers to smooth the drop in their consumption following their loss of income, at the cost of a large and highly persistent increase in workers' debt. These high levels of debt create financial fragility, which eventually makes an economy more vulnerable to financial crises. Their findings suggest that a reduction in income inequality, through an increase in the bargaining power of the lower income group or other redistributional policies, can lead to a sustained reduction in crisis risk.

In contrast to U.S. economic history, the international empirical evidence on the relationship between income inequality and crises is not conclusive, suggesting that the experience of the United States may be an outlier by historical standards. For example, the experiences of some Scandinavian countries that underwent financial crises without much inequality suggest that other factors may play a more important role. Using a panel of 14 advanced economies for the period 1920–2008, Bordo and Meissner (2012) find that after controlling for a number of variables, income inequality plays no significant role in explaining credit growth. The two key determinants of credit booms are economic expansion and low interest rates.

A main lesson from these studies is that income inequality or high levels of debt (caused by income inequality) can lead to financial crises. However, as Bordo and Meissner (2012) emphasize, an increase in the supply of credit that incubates a financial crisis requires different policy responses from the responses that might be prescribed for an increase in the demand for credit. In the former case, financial regulations and reforms to limit excessive credit seem to be more appropriate actions to achieve financial stability.

5.4.4 Financial Globalization

Financial globalization can trigger financial crises. Episodes of strong capital inflows could incubate bubbles, which could burst as a result of unpredictable external contagion or liquidity shocks, triggering major credit disruption. Reinhart and Rogoff (2008) shows a strong correlation between capital mobility and the incidence of banking crises. The cost of occasional crises can be small compared with the growth-enhancing effect of financial liberalization (Tornell, Westermann, and Martinez 2004). But crises that follow the bursting of bubbles in investment and asset prices seem to be followed by extremely costly recessions. The costs and benefits of financial liberalization thus need to be considered. Occasional, costly crises seem to be inevitable in a deregulated environment. At the same time, deregulation and globalization allow more risk-taking, higher expected returns, and better allocation of capital.

Table 5.7 Outcomes of Banking Crises in Advanced, Emerging, and Developing Economies, 1970–2011 (percent)

Countries by income level	Output loss	Increase in debt	Fiscal costs	Duration in years
All	23.0	12.1	6.8	2
Advanced	32.9	21.4	3.8	3
Emerging	26.0	9.1	10.0	2
Developing	1.6	10.9	10.0	1

Source: Laeven and Valencia 2012.

5.4.5 Consequences of Crises

Financial crises have pernicious consequences. According to Reinhart and Rogoff (2009), on average, financial crises result in the following:

- 35 percent real drop in housing prices over six years;
- 55 percent drop in equity prices over three and a half years;
- 9 percent decline in output over two years;
- 7 percent increase in the unemployment rate over four years;
- 86 percent increase in central government debt over its precrisis level.

Laeven and Valencia (2012) also find significant costs associated with financial crises. Output losses (measured as deviations from trend GDP) of systemic banking crises can be large, averaging about 20 percent of GDP during the first four years (Table 5.7). Output losses and increases in public debt tend to be larger in advanced economies, consistent with the fact that with deeper financial systems, a banking crisis is more disruptive. In contrast, fiscal costs are larger in developing and emerging economies, whether measured as a percentage of GDP or as a percentage of financial system assets (to account for differences in the relative size of financial systems).

The greater reliance on macroeconomic tools may also explain why crises tend to last longer in advanced economies. If macroeconomic policies are used to avoid a sharp contraction in economic activity, they may discourage more active bank restructuring that would allow banks to recover more quickly and renew lending to the real economy, with the risk of prolonging the crisis and depressing growth for a prolonged period of time.

5.5 Reforming the International Financial System

As the discussion of financial globalization in the previous sections makes clear, the international financial system has an important effect on the average global citizen. The most important institution in the international financial system since the end of World War II has been the IMF.[4] With regard to growth, finance, and crises, it can be argued that the IMF needs to be reformed to reduce the need for large foreign exchange reserves that many countries, particularly in Asia, apparently feel.

As Allen and Hong (2011) argue, the accumulation of reserves by the Asian countries was at least partly a response to the policies the IMF imposed on a number of countries during the late 1990s. For example, although Korea was one of the most successful economies in the world in the preceding decades, the IMF forced it to raise interest rates to maintain its exchange rate and to cut government expenditure. This prescription was the exact opposite of what the United States and many European countries did when faced with similar circumstance in the current crisis. Given that Korean firms used significant amounts of trade credit, the rise in interest rates was very damaging, driving many thousands of firms into bankruptcy. Unemployment rose from about 3 percent to 9 percent, and there was a long recession. It was this experience that impressed upon the Koreans that they must accumulate sufficient reserves going forward in order to avoid being forced to go to the IMF.

Since its foundation at the end of World War II, the IMF has been dominated by the United States and European countries. Its head has always been a European, and the deputy head has always been an American. Nobody from Asia or any other part of the world has held either of these posts. In addition, the voting shares of European countries exceed their share of world GDP, particularly when measured in purchasing power parity terms, whereas the shares of China and many other Asian countries are significantly below their GDP weight. During the 1997 Asian crisis, Asians were not well represented among the senior staff of the IMF. Their underrepresentation contributed to the problems arising from the policies pursued, as there was effectively no appeal mechanism.

Going forward, it is therefore important to reform the governance structure of the IMF and the other international economic organizations so that Asian countries are properly represented. Doing so would help ensure that they receive equal treatment when they need financial help. It would also reduce the need of these countries to accumulate reserves as a self-insurance mechanism. This self-insurance is very wasteful from an economic point of view. It involves some of the economies with the best investment opportunities in the world, such as Taiwan, Korea, and China, investing substantial amounts in low-yielding U.S. Treasuries and euro zone government securities. These funds would be much better employed by domestic firms.

---

[4] In her chapter in this volume (chapter 7), Birdsall considers the role of the IMF and its governance at some length.

Although such reforms are desirable, they seem unlikely to be implemented in the short or even medium term. To reduce the large accumulation of reserves, particularly by China, other measures are necessary. For example, senior Chinese officials have proposed replacing the dollar with a global currency as a reserve currency. Reserves could be created initially without large transfers of resources and the attendant risk of a crisis. All countries could be allocated enough reserves in the event of a crisis to survive shocks. The problem with this proposal is that an international institution like the IMF would need to implement the currency. There would then again be the issue of whether all countries, in particular the Asian ones, are properly represented in the governance process.

A more likely medium-term scenario is that the yuan becomes fully convertible and joins the U.S. dollar and the euro as the third major reserve currency. With three reserve currencies, there would be more scope for diversification of risks, and China itself would have little need of reserves. This idea is perhaps one of the most practical solutions to the global foreign exchange reserve-imbalance problem. The Chinese have already taken some steps in this direction. They have started to allow the settlement of trade in yuan and the issuance of yuan-denominated bonds by western companies such as McDonald's in Hong Kong. Of course, the most important aspect of being a reserve currency is full convertibility. Capital controls thus need to be removed and unrestricted capital movements allowed. The Chinese government has made moves in this direction by increasing the amounts Chinese citizens can invest overseas and citizens and foreigners can invest in China.

Convertibility of the yuan and establishment of it as a reserve currency are arguably the most important reforms of the international financial system. These reforms would allow countries to manage their foreign exchange reserves much better, because there would be one currency for each of the three major economies in the world. Countries, particularly China, could reduce their foreign exchange reserves, as countries with a reserve currency do not need significant foreign exchange reserves. These reductions in holdings would considerably increase the financial stability of the global financial system.

5.6 Finance and the Global Citizen

This section analyzes how finance affects the global citizen in a variety of dimensions. It explores how financial inclusion is related to demographics and examines the impact of financial inclusion on education, labor, poverty, and income inequality. It also describes how financial crises are likely to have heterogeneous effects in the population, with the underprivileged segments of the population suffering the longest-lasting effects. It closes by examining how the process of financial globalization has affected income inequality.

5.6.1 Financial Inclusion and Demographics

Access to financial services plays an important role in economic development and poverty reduction. Financial inclusion permits vulnerable segments of the population to save and to borrow. Through these financial services, individuals can build their assets, invest in human capital, and improve their standard of living.[5] Inclusive financial systems allow poor people to smooth their consumption and insure themselves against negative shocks such as illness, unemployment, and natural disasters. Burgess and Pande (2005) find that financial development has a significant impact on economic development in rural areas. Given the potential impact of access to finance on the lives of the poor, the role of financial inclusion cannot be ignored.

With low levels of development, there is evidence that some financial services matter more for people's welfare than others. In their research on the financial lives of poor households, for example, Collins et al. (2009) find a pattern of intensive use of savings instruments. Payment services may also allow people to avoid problems of theft associated with the use of cash. In contrast, the granting of credit is more problematic, particularly among people with low incomes, suggesting that savings and payment services may be more important than credit for poor people and low-income countries. The path for development may involve opening up the savings markets before the credit and other financial markets.

Karaivanov and Townsend (2012) develop a range of dynamic models of constrained credit and insurance that allow for moral hazard and limited commitment. They compare these solutions with full insurance and exogenously incomplete regimes. Using data from Thai households, they find that savings-only and borrowing regimes provide the best fit to data for rural households; data from urban households suggest they are considerably less constrained.

Financial inclusion varies significantly across regions and countries. Although finance is likely to benefit the underprivileged segments of the population (for example, women, young people, and people in rural communities) more, these segments of the population face more difficulties in accessing financial services. Table 5.8 reports four measures of access to financial services by country income levels and individual characteristics. At least three stylized facts emerge from the table. First, the use of formal financial

---

[5] Behrman and Kohler examine these demographic and human capital issues in chapter 3.

Table 5.8 Financial Inclusion, by Country Income Level and Individual Characteristics, 2011 (percent)

Measure/ country income level	Gender			Income		Location		Education	
	Men	Women	Total	Top 60 percent	Bottom 40 percent	Urban	Rural	Secondary or more	Primary only
Has account at formal financial institution									
High	92.3	88.9	90.5	93.3	87.4	90.8	88.0	93.5	75.7
Middle	48.0	38.5	43.3	53.2	30.9	50.5	39.9	53.8	36.8
Low	27.0	20.4	23.7	29.3	16	34.8	21.9	36.4	15.1
Has loans from family or friends									
High	11.9	11.9	11.9	10.3	13.7	12.5	9.6	13.3	11.1
Middle	26.0	23.3	24.7	23.2	26.2	24.9	24.5	23.8	24.9
Low	32.1	28.5	30	31.2	29.1	28.4	30.6	28.8	30.5
Has account used to receive government payments									
High	45.2	41.9	43.5	42.4	44.7	40.7	41.2	44.6	38.3
Middle	7.2	5.8	6.5	7.4	5.3	8.5	5.6	8.5	5.3
Low	3.4	1.6	2.5	3.4	1.2	3.6	2.3	4.5	1.0
Has account used to receive remittances									
High	14.8	12.2	13.5	14	12.9	14.9	6.2	15.6	9.8
Middle	6.1	5.9	6	7.5	3.9	8.5	4.4	6.8	5.5
Low	5.4	4.1	4.7	7.0	1.7	8.2	1.9	8.5	4.1

Note: Figures are for people 15 years old and older.

Source: Global Financial Inclusion Dataset from the World Bank (http://datatopics.worldbank.org/financialinclusion).

services is more common in higher-income economies. Second, women, the poor, rural residents, and people with less education have less access to both formal and alternative financial services. Third, the use of alternative finance mechanisms, such as loans from family and friends, is more common in lower-income economies.

Despite the low penetration of formal financial services in some low-income areas, latent demand for financial services is strong. In Kenya, for example, even rural poor respondents mention a "commercial bank" would be their preferred saving mechanism if they had access to all the alternatives (Dupas et al. 2012). Two innovations in Kenya have expanded access to finance to isolated areas and minority groups. Equity Bank is a pioneering commercial bank that devised a banking service strategy targeting low-income clients and traditionally underserved territories. Its branch expansion targeted clients speaking minority languages and a key part of its strategy involved the use of low-cost services that were possible because of the use of computers (Allen, Carletti, Cull, Qian, Senbet, and Valenzuela 2012). M-Pesa is a mobile phone-based service that greatly facilitates money transfers and remittances by the poor. It has been used primarily to transfer money from individual to individual rather than as a vehicle for saving. Mbiti and Weil (2011) find that the use of M-Pesa also increased the probability of people having bank accounts.

The examples of Equity Bank and M-Pesa illustrate the possibilities for using new technologies to leapfrog. These examples suggest ways around the current financial markets and institutional structure that can also help deal with vested interests. Mobile phones and the development of low-cost banking through the use of computers seem a good way for many banks to pursue strategies that increase financial inclusion. Both of these strategies were profitable and thus can be left to the private sector. There is no need for public subsidies. However, it is necessary that regulators permit the use of such strategies.

Financial markets can also hurt the poor, through financial crises. Paxson and Schady (2005) explore some of the consequences of the crisis of 1988–92 in Peru. They find that spending on health contracted sharply during the crisis, resulting in a significant rise in infant mortality. Ferreira and Schady (2008) find that in poorer economies, child health is procyclical: infant mortality rises and nutrition falls during recessions.

5.6.2 Finance, Education, and Labor Markets

Empirical evidence suggests that access to financial services such as saving and credit accounts promotes investment by parents in the education of their children, especially when negative shocks reduce household income. Jacoby and Skoufias (1997) show that households from Indian villages without access to credit markets tend to reduce their children's schooling when they receive transitory shocks. Using cross-country data, Flug, Spilimbergo, and Wachtenheim (1998) find that lack of access to financial markets reduces average secondary school enrollment rates.

Excessive finance is likely to have a negative effect on education, through the effects of financial crises. Financial crises generally have heterogeneous effects, across and within countries. Ferreira and Schady (2008) show that in low-income countries, schooling rates tend to drop during a macroeconomic or agro-climatic crisis. In contrast, in middle- and high-income countries, schooling tends to increase.

The impact of financial crises on children and young people is of great concern. Pulling children from poor families out of school in response to negative income shocks has a lasting impact on poverty, because dropouts tend to earn less as adults. Therefore, providing schooling and training support to the underprivileged segments of the population should be a policy response in times of financial crisis.

Labor markets are also directly affected by financial crises. As suggested by Calvo, Coricelli and Ottonello (2012), the persistence of unemployment following recessions has concerned economists and policymakers since at least the Great Depression. The high and persistent unemployment during the recent global financial crisis of 2007–9 has brought the discussion of the jobless recovery to the debate once again. Although by September 2013, output had reached its precrisis level in the United States, the unemployment rate was still significantly above its precrisis level (Figure 5.12). Calvo, Coricelli, and Ottonello (2012) explore the hypothesis that the joblessness nature of the recovery from a recession is related to the financial nature of the episode. They find that financial crises tend to be followed by jobless recoveries in the presence of low inflation and by "wageless" recoveries in the presence of high inflation.

The European debt crises had a significant effect on the unemployment rate between 2007 and 2010, with several countries increasing their unemployment rates by more than 5 percentage points (panel a of Figure 5.13). During financial crises, young people are particularly vulnerable. They are often the first to exit and the last to enter the labor market, because they have to compete with job seekers who have more experience in a market with fewer job opportunities.

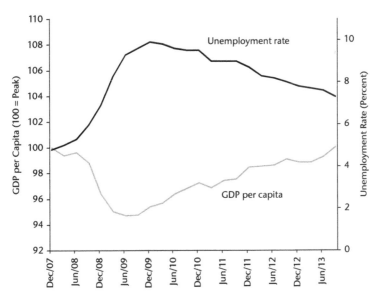

Figure 5.12 Jobless Recovery following the Great Recession, 2007–11
Note: Figures are seasonally adjusted.
Source: Calvo, Coricelli, and Ottonello 2012.

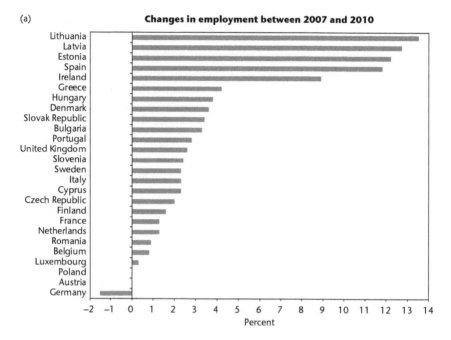

(a)

Changes in employment between 2007 and 2010

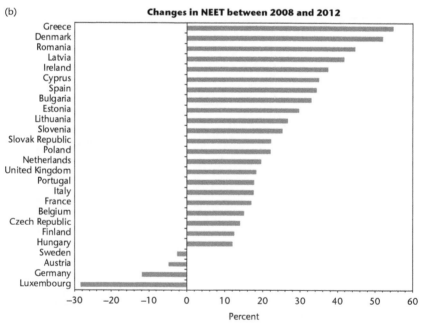

(b)

Changes in NEET between 2008 and 2012

Figure 5.13 Changes in Unemployment and Share of Population Not in Employment, Education or Training (NEET) in Europe, by Country

a. Changes in employment between 2007 and 2010 b. Changes in NEET between 2008 and 2012

Source: Authors, based on data from World Bank (2012) and Eurofound (2011).

As a consequence of the debt crisis, a group of people has emerged in Europe that is at high risk of social exclusion, namely young people not in employment, education, or training (the so-called NEET group). This group typically includes people between the ages of 16 and 24 who have disengaged from both education and work. Panel b of Figure 6.2 shows that most European countries have experienced a significant increase in this group. Among the worst-affected countries are Greece, Denmark, Ireland, and Spain. According to Eurofound (2011), people with a higher probability of being NEET include people with disabilities, immigrant backgrounds, low education levels, low household income, and parents who experienced unemployment, and people who live in remote areas.

5.6.3 Finance, Income Distribution, and Poverty

Access to finance affects income distribution, because it affects individuals' economic opportunities. Access to credit is an important determinant for paying for education or starting a business, for example.

The direction of the impact of access to finance on income distribution is not obvious. On the one hand, access to finance may improve income distribution, because access to saving and credit instruments should allow underprivileged individuals to increase their human and physical capital. Access to finance may also reduce the pernicious effects of external negative shocks (such as natural disasters), which in general affect low-income segments of the population more than other segments. On the other hand, because the poor do not have the same access to financial services as higher-income segments of the population (for example, as a result of lack of collateral), financial markets may actually exacerbate income inequality. Similar to the finance–growth nexus, excessive finance is likely to increase the incidence of financial crises, worsening the distribution of income.

According to Baldacci, de Mello, and Inchauste (2002), financial crises adversely affect the distribution of income for at least three reasons. First, they typically cause significant currency depreciations, which may increase the cost of imported food, which mainly hurts poor people. Second, a financial crisis can cause workers' earnings to fall as jobs are lost in the formal sector, demand for services provided by the informal sector declines, and working hours and real wages are cut. When formal sector workers who have lost their jobs enter the informal sector, they put additional pressure on informal labor markets. Third, governments often respond to crises by spending on social programs, transfers to households, and salaries. However, Ravallion (2002) finds that the nonpoor benefited significantly from countries' main antipoverty programs; such changes may thus actually exacerbate income inequality. Something similar is apparently happening in the current European debt crisis, in which budget cuts are directly affecting the most underprivileged sectors of the population.

5.6.4 Financial Globalization and Income Distribution

Although financial globalization is likely to affect income inequality, the net effect is not clear. Some economists argue that greater financial globalization may increase access to resources for the poor; others suggest that by increasing the incidence of financial crises, greater financial globalization may hurt the poor. Greater inequality can lead to more financial opening, however, so the direction of causation is unclear. Possible perverse effects on inequality have to control for that possibility. Open markets have also been shown to help overcome vested interest.

International evidence suggests that both globalization and income inequality increased significantly in most countries and regions over the past two decades. Jaumotte, Lall, and Papageorgiou (2011) find that increasing trade and financial globalization have had separately identifiable and opposite effects on income distribution. Trade liberalization is associated with lower income inequality; increased financial globalization is associated with higher inequality. However, their combined contribution to rising inequality has been much lower than that of technological change at the global level, especially in developing countries. The impact of financial openness (felt mainly through foreign direct investment) and technological progress on income inequality appears to be working through similar channels by increasing the premium on higher skills rather than limiting opportunities for economic development. This observation is consistent with evidence in the United States and the United Kingdom.

A large body of research suggests that the quality of institutions plays a significant role. Financial globalization may allow better consumption smoothing and reduce volatility for the poor in countries with good institutions. In countries with weak institutions, however, financial access is biased in favor of the better off; the increase in finance from tapping global and not just domestic savings may exacerbate inequality.

5.7 Ethical Issues

The interaction of growth, finance, and crises raises a number of important ethical issues. One is the intergenerational distribution of the fiscal burden. In the long run, growth raises living standards. In general, fiscal burdens should therefore be borne more by future generations than current ones; the old should be protected relative to the young. However, in the short run, financial crises can place heavy fiscal burdens on governments. How should such burdens be split between younger and older generations? Currently, the young appear to be bearing a considerable part of the cost. They will have to pay down large amounts of government debt, directly or through inflation. Youth unemployment rates are also much higher than overall unemployment rates. High unemployment will make it difficult for today's younger generation to deal with the government debt burden it will have to bear. For these reasons, young people today may not be better off than the generation that preceded them, suggesting that older people should bear a large proportion of the burden than they are currently bearing. Cuts in pension benefits and health care would ensure that they did so.

Another important ethical issue is the extent to which the poor versus the rich should bear the burden. Typically, it is the rich who benefit from the boom phase of the cycle. Although they may suffer in the bust phase, many of them will often still be better off than they were at the start of the boom. The poor suffer through increased unemployment and, to the extent they are homeowners, by the decline in the price of their homes. In most countries, the rich have not borne a greater burden than the poor. For example, very few countries have suggested a one-off wealth tax to solve the fiscal problem.

A third ethical issue is the extent to which people in the financial services industry should be singled out for special treatment after financial crises. The recent restrictions imposed by the European Union on bankers' bonuses are one example of negative special treatment. The paucity of criminal prosecutions of financial executives after the crisis in response to apparent fraudulent behavior such as the LIBOR scandal may be an example of positive special treatment. Whether such special treatment is appropriate is a very important issue going forward.

5.8 Lessons, Policy Implications, and Conclusions

The main conclusion in the literature surveyed is that there is an optimal depth in financial structure. Too little finance is not desirable—but too much is not desirable either. The policy implications of this literature can be summarized as follows:

- The global financial crises of 2007–9 and the current debt crisis in Europe highlight the fact that excessive finance may have undesirable effects on economic growth. A growing literature finds not only a vanishing effect on the positive impact of financial development on economic growth but also a negative effect of excessive finance on growth.

- Long-run economic growth is positively correlated with bank credit to the private sector as a percentage of GDP. In low-income economies, however, this effect is relatively small, and it vanishes in some periods, possibly because these economies may have reached the point at which financial development no longer affects the efficiency of investment.

- Economies with small and medium-size financial systems relative to their GDP tend to do better as they put more of their resources into finance, but this effect reverses once the financial sector becomes too large.

- Although the literature traditionally focuses on financial depth, financial structure is also important. Recent contributions focus on the optimal financial structure, which depends on a country's stage of development and endowments. Early on, for example, small banks may be appropriate for providing finance to small firms.

- Although theory predicts a number of benefits from financial openness—access to cheaper capital, portfolio diversification, consumption smoothing, emulation of foreign banks and institutions, and macro policy discipline among others—results from empirical studies report evidence in favor of and against capital account liberalization.

The literature from which these conclusions are drawn is based on the experiences of a wide range of countries. From the perspective of the average global citizen, it might be better to base policy advice on success stories. The experiences of Taiwan, Korea, and China suggest that countries can grow quickly for many years. Within 50–60 years, per capita income can rise from African levels to Western European and possibly U.S. levels. Hong Kong and Singapore, both of which achieved this kind of improvement, are small city-states, but Taiwan and Korea have substantial populations. The problem from the global citizen's perspective is to understand how these countries achieved these spectacular growth paths and to implement their policies in other countries.

In China, alternative finance and institutions rather than traditional strong institutions and rule of law have allowed this growth. One of the most important policy conclusions is that alternative finance and the enforcement mechanisms associated with it should be encouraged rather than hindered. Conventional wisdom characterizes the economic performance in China as successful despite the lack of western-style institutions. We argue that China has done well because of this lack of western-style institutions: conducting business outside the legal system in fast-growing economies can be superior to using the law as the basis for finance and commerce. Research on political economy factors suggests that rent-seeking behavior by interest groups can turn the legal system, a monopolist institution, into a barrier to change.

The "alternative" view argues that by not using the legal system, alternative finance can minimize the costs associated with legal institutions. In a dynamic environment, characterized by frequent fundamental changes in the economy, alternative institutions can adapt and change much more quickly than formal institutions.

There is also a dark side to finance, excessive levels of which can lead to asset price bubbles and financial crises. Other systemic risks that can lead to financial crises include panics (banking crises as a result of multiple equilibria), banking crises as a result of asset price falls, contagion, and foreign exchange mismatches in the banking system. Macroprudential policies are designed to counter these systemic risks. The most important of these policies include the following:

- Deposit insurance and government debt guarantees can prevent banking panics. However, they create moral hazard and can be extremely costly if in fact the systemic risk is not from a panic but is from the collapse of an asset price bubble or some other source.

- On some occasions it may be possible to use interest rates to burst real estate bubbles. However, in large diverse economies such as China, the euro zone or the United States, doing so will not usually be possible, because bubbles tend to be regional and higher interest rates may cause slowdowns in regions without bubbles. When interest rates cannot be used, policymakers can limit loan-to-value ratios, which could be lowered as property prices increase at a faster pace; impose property transfer taxes that rise with the rate of property price increases; or restrict real estate lending in certain regions.

- If limits to arbitrage and other market failures lead to a serious malfunctioning of markets, it may be necessary to suspend mark-to-market accounting for financial institutions.

- One of the most significant systemic risks is the raising of interest rates by central banks and markets as normalcy returns. These increases will cause asset values to fall and pose a significant risk to the stability banking system. The return to normalcy needs to be carefully planned and carried out over time to minimize systemic risk.

- Contagion is one of the most serious and least understood forms of systemic risk. Several macroprudential policies and regulations may be needed to address the different channels and types of contagion. Perhaps the most important is capital regulation.

- Implementing permanent swap facilities for foreign exchange between central banks is an important policy to prevent currency mismatches in the banking system and reduce the need for large foreign exchange reserves.

The global imbalance in foreign exchange reserves was a significant contributor to the financial crisis, because these funds helped fuel the real estate bubbles that triggered the crisis. Going forward, it is important to reform the governance structure of the IMF and the other international economic organizations so that Asian countries are properly represented. This reform would help ensure that they receive equal treatment when they need financial help. It would also reduce their need to accumulate reserves as a self-insurance mechanism. Self-insurance is very wasteful from an economic point of view.

A more likely medium-term scenario is that the yuan becomes fully convertible and joins the U.S. dollar and the euro as the third major reserve currency. With three reserve currencies, there would be more scope for diversification of risks by central banks holding reserves and China itself would have little need of reserves.

With regard to financial inclusion, two innovations in Kenya have expanded access to finance to isolated areas and minority groups. Equity Bank is a pioneering commercial bank that devised a banking service strategy targeting low-income clients and traditionally underserved territories. Its branch expansion targeted clients speaking minority languages. A key part of its strategy involved the use of low-cost services that were possible because of the use of computers. M-Pesa is a mobile phone-based service that greatly facilitates money transfers and remittances by the poor. It has been used primarily to transfer money between individuals rather than as a vehicle for saving. Equity Bank and M-Pesa illustrate the possibilities for using new technologies to leapfrog. Both strategies were profitable and thus can be left to the private sector. There is no need for public subsidies. However, it is necessary that regulators permit the use of such strategies.

References

Abreu, D., and M. Brunnermeier. 2003. "Bubbles and Crashes." *Econometrica* 71: 173–204.

Acemoglu, D., and S. Johnson. 2005. "Unbundling Institutions." *Journal of Political Economy* 113: 949–95.

Acemoglu, D., and F. Zilibotti. 1997. "Was Prometheus Unbound by Chance? Risk, Diversification, and Growth." *Journal of Political Economy* 105: 709–51.

Admati, A., P. DeMarzo, M. Hellwig, and P. Pfleiderer. 2010. "Fallacies, Irrelevant Facts and Myths in the Discussion of Capital Regulation." Stanford Graduate School of Business Research Paper No.2065, Stanford, CA.

Aghion, P., and P. Bolton. 1997. "A Theory of Trickle-Down Growth and Development." *Review of Economic Studies* 64: 151–72.

Ahrend, R., B. Cournède, and R. Price. 2008. "Monetary Policy, Market Excesses and Financial Turmoil." OECD Economics Department Working Paper 597, Organisation for Economic Co-operation and Development, Paris.

Allen, F. 1990. "The Market for Information and the Origin of Financial Intermediaries." *Journal of Financial Intermediation* 1: 3–30.

Allen, F., A. Babus, and E. Carletti. 2009. "Financial Crises: Theory and Evidence." *Annual Review of Financial Economics* 1: 97–116.

Allen, F., A. Babus, and E. Carletti. 2012. "Asset Commonality, Debt Maturity and Systemic Risk." *Journal of Financial Economics* 104: 519–34.

Allen, F., F. Capie, C. Fohlin, H. Miyajima, R. Sylla, G. Wood, and Y. Yafeh. 2012. "How Important Historically Were Financial Systems for Growth in the U.K., U.S., Germany, and Japan?" Wharton Financial Institutions Center Working Paper 10–27, University of Pennsylvania, Philadelphia.

Allen, F., and E. Carletti. 2008a. "Mark-to-Market Accounting and Liquidity Pricing." *Journal of Accounting and Economics* 45: 358–78.

Allen, F., and E. Carletti. 2008b. "Should Financial Institutions Mark to Market?" *Bank of France Financial Stability Review* 12: 1–6.

Allen, F., and E. Carletti. 2010. "An Overview of the Crisis: Causes, Consequences and Solutions." *International Review of Finance* 10: 1–27.

Allen, F., and E. Carletti. 2012. "Systemic Risk and Macroprudential Regulation." In *The Global Macro Economy and Finance*, ed. F. Allen, M. Aoki, J. Fitoussi, N. Kiyotaki, R. Gordon, and J. Stiglitz, 191–210. International Economics Association Conference Volume 150–III. New York: Palgrave Macmillan.

Allen, F., and E. Carletti. 2013. "What Is Systemic Risk?" *Journal of Money, Credit and Banking* 45 (s1): 121–7.

Allen, F., E. Carletti, and D. Gale. 2009. "Interbank Market Liquidity and Central Bank Intervention." *Journal of Monetary Economics* 56: 639–52.

Allen, F., E. Carletti, R. Cull, J. Qian, L. Senbet, and P. Valenzuela. 2012. "Improving Access to Banking: Evidence from Kenya." Working Paper 12-11, Wharton Financial Institutions Center, University of Pennsylvania, Philadelphia.

Allen, F., E. Carletti, J. Qian, and P. Valenzuela. 2013. "Financial Intermediation, Markets, and Alternative Financial Sectors." In *The Handbook of the Economics of Finance*, ed. G. Constantinides, M. Harris, and R. Stulz, 759–98. Amsterdam: Elsevier.

Allen, F., R. Chakrabarti, S. De, J. Qian, and M. Qian. 2012. "Financing Firms in India." *Journal of Financial Intermediation* 21: 409–45.

Allen, F., and D. Gale. 1999. "Diversity of Opinion and Financing of New Technologies." *Journal of Financial Intermediation* 8: 68–89.

Allen, F., and D. Gale. 2000a. "Bubbles and Crises." *Economic Journal* 110: 236–55.

Allen, F., and D. Gale. 2000b. *Comparing Financial Systems*. Cambridge, MA: MIT Press.

Allen, F., and D. Gale. 2000c. "Financial Contagion." *Journal of Political Economy* 108: 1–33.

Allen, F., and D. Gale. 2004. "Competition and Financial Stability." *Journal of Money, Credit and Banking* 36: 433–80.

Allen, F., and D. Gale. 2007. *Understanding Financial Crises*. Clarendon Lecture Series in Finance. Oxford: Oxford University Press.

Allen, F., and G. Gorton. 1993. "Churning Bubbles." *Review of Economic Studies* 60: 813–36.

Allen, F., and J. Y. Hong. 2011. "Why Are There Large Foreign Exchange Reserves? The Case of South Korea." *Korean Social Science Journal* 38: 1–33.

Allen, F., S. Morris, and A. Postlewaite. 1993. "Finite Bubbles with Short Sale Constraints and Asymmetric Information." *Journal of Economic Theory* 61: 206–29.

Allen, F., and H. Oura. 2004. "Sustained Economic Growth and the Financial Systems." *Monetary and Economic Studies* 22: 95–119.

Allen, F., J. Qian, and M. Qian. 2005. "Law, Finance, and Economic Growth in China." *Journal of Financial Economics* 77: 57–116.

Allen, F., J. Qian, S. Shan, and M. Zhao. 2012. "The IPO of Industrial and Commercial Bank of China and the 'Chinese Model' of Privatizing Large Financial Institutions." *European Journal of Finance*, 1–26.

Allen, F., J. Qian, and C. Zhang. 2011. "An Alternative View on Law, Institutions, Finance and Growth." Wharton Financial Institutions Center, Working Paper 11-64, University of Pennsylvania, Philadelphia.

Allen, W., and R. Moessner. 2010. "Central Bank Co-operation and International Liquidity in the Financial Crisis of 2008–9." Bank for International Settlements Working Paper 310, Basel.

Arcand, J.-L., E. Berkes, and U. Panizza. 2012. "Too Much Finance?" IMF Working Paper 12/161, International Monetary Fund, Washington, DC.

Ayyagari, M., A. Demirgüç-Kunt, and V. Maksimovic. 2010. "Formal versus Informal Finance: Evidence from China." *Review of Financial Studies* 23: 3048–97.

Bagehot, W. 1873 (1962). *Lombard Street*. Homewood, IL: Irwin.

Baland, J.-M., and J. A. Robinson. 1998. "A Model of Child Labor." Working Paper 9803, Department of Economics, University of Southern California, Los Angeles.

Baldacci, E., L. de Mello, and G. Inchauste. 2002. "Financial Crises, Poverty, and Income Distribution." IMF Working Paper 02/4, International Monetary Fund, Washington, DC.

Bardhan P. 2000. "The Nature of Institutional Impediments to Economic Development." In *A Not-So-Dismal Science: A Broader View of Economies and Societies*, ed. M. Olson and S. Kähkönen, 245–68. New York: Oxford University Press.

Beck, T., and M. Brown. 2010. "Which Households Use Banks? Evidence from the Transition Economies." ECB Working Paper 1295, European Central Bank, Frankfurt.

Beck, T., and A. Demirgüç-Kunt. 2009. "Financial Institutions and Markets across Countries and Over Time: Data and Analysis." World Bank Policy Research Working Paper 4943, Washington, DC.

Beck, T., A. Demirgüç-Kunt, and R. Levine. 2005. "Bank Concentration and Fragility: Impact and Mechanics." NBER Working Paper 11500, National Bureau of Economic Research, Cambridge, MA.

Beck, T., A. Demirgüç-Kunt, R. Levine, and V. Maksimovic. 2001. "Financial Structure and Economic Development: Firms, Industry, and Country Evidence." In *Financial Structure and Economic Growth: A Cross-Country Comparison of Banks, Markets, and Development*, ed. A. Demirgüç-Kunt and R. Levine, 189–242. Cambridge, MA: MIT Press.

Beck, T., A. Demirgüç-Kunt, and V. Maksimovic. 2008. "Financing Patterns around the World: Are Small Firms Different?" *Journal of Financial Economics* 89: 467–87.

Beck, T., and R. Levine. 2002. "Industry Growth and Capital Allocation: Does Having a Market- or Bank-Based System Matter?" *Journal of Financial Economics* 64: 147–80.

Beck T., R. Levine, and A. Levkov. 2009. "Big Bad Banks? The Impact of U.S. Branch Deregulation on Income Distribution." NBER Working Paper 13299, National Bureau of Economic Research, Cambridge, MA.

Becker, G. S., and N. Tomes. 1979. "An Equilibrium Theory of the Distribution of Income and Intergenerational Mobility." *Journal of Political Economics* 87: 1153–89.

Becker, G. S., and N. Tomes. 1986. "Human Capital and the Rise and Fall of Families." *Journal of Labor Economics* 4: 1–39.

Bekaert, G., C. Harvey, and C. Lundblad. 2005. "Does Financial Liberalization Spur Growth?" *Journal of Financial Economics* 77: 3–55.

Bekaert, G., C. Harvey, and C. Lundblad. 2006. "Growth Volatility and Financial Liberalization." *Journal of International Money and Finance* 25: 370–403.

Bekaert, G., C. Harvey, and C. Lundblad. 2011. "Financial Openness and Productivity." *World Development* 39: 1–19.

Bencivenga, V., and B. Smith. 1991. "Financial Intermediation and Endogenous Growth." *Review of Economic Studies* 58: 195–209.

Benhabib, J., and M. Spiegel. 2000. "Cross Country Growth Regressions: Are Primitives All That Matter?" *Journal of Economic Growth* 5: 341–60.

Bernanke, B. 2008. "Opening Remarks." *Maintaining Stability in a Changing Financial System*, 1–12. Jackson Hole Symposium, Federal Reserve Bank of Kansas City.

Bhattacharya, S., and P. Pfleiderer. 1985. "Delegated Portfolio Management." *Journal of Economic Theory* 36: 1–25.

Blackburn, K., N. Bose, and S. Capasso. 2005. "Financial Development, Financing Choice and Economic Growth." *Review of Development Economics* 9: 135–49.

Bordo, M., B. Eichengreen, D. Klingebiel, and M. S. Martinez-Peria. 2001. "Is the Crisis Problem Growing More Severe?" *Economic Policy* 16: 51–82.

Bordo, M., and C. Meissner. 2012. "Does Inequality Lead to a Financial Crisis?" NBER Working Paper 17896, National Bureau of Economic Research, Cambridge, MA.

Borio, C., and P. Lowe. 2002. "Asset Prices, Financial and Monetary Stability: Exploring the Nexus." Bank for International Settlements Working Paper 114, Basel.

Bose, N., and R. Cothren. 1996. "Equilibrium Loan Contracts and Endogenous Growth in the Presence of Asymmetric Information." *Journal of Monetary Economics* 38: 363–76.

Boyd, J., and E. Prescott. 1986. "Financial Intermediary-Coalitions." *Journal of Economic Theory* 38: 211–32.

Boyd, J., and B. Smith. 1998. "The Evolution of Debt and Equity Markets in Economic Development." *Economic Theory* 12: 519–60.

Broner, F., and J. Ventura. 2011. "Globalization and Risk Sharing." *Review of Economic Studies* 78: 49–82.

Brunnermeier, M., and S. Nagel. 2004. "Hedge Funds and the Technology Bubble." *Journal of Finance* 59: 2013–40.

Bryant, J. 1980. "A Model of Reserves, Bank Runs, and Deposit Insurance." *Journal of Banking and Finance* 4: 335–44.

Burgess, R., and R. Pande. 2005. "Do Rural Banks Matter? Evidence from the Indian Social Banking Experiment." *American Economic Review* 95: 780–95.

Calomiris, C., and G. Gorton. 1991. "The Origins of Banking Panics, Models, Facts, and Bank Regulation." In *Financial Markets and Financial Crises*, ed. R. G. Hubbard, 109–73. Chicago: University of Chicago Press.

Calomiris, C., and S. Haber. 2013. *Fragile Banks, Durable Bargains: Why Banking Is All about Politics and Always Has Been*. Princeton, NJ: Princeton University Press.

Calomiris, C., and J. Mason. 2003. "Fundamentals, Panics, and Bank Distress during the Depression." *American Economic Review* 93: 1615–47.

Calvo, G., F. Coricelli, and P. Ottonello. 2012. "The Labor Market Consequences of Financial Crises with or without Inflation: Jobless and Wageless Recoveries." NBER Working Paper 18480, National Bureau of Economic Research, Cambridge, MA.

Calvo, G., and E. Mendoza. 2000. "Rational Contagion and the Globalization of Securities Markets." *Journal of International Economics* 51: 79–113.

Carlin, W., and C. Mayer. 2003. "Finance, Investment, and Growth." *Journal of Financial Economics* 69: 191–226.

Chinn, M., and H. Ito. 2008. "A New Measure of Financial Openness." *Journal of Comparative Policy Analysis* 10: 309–22.

Claessens, S., and N. van Horen. 2012. "Being a Foreigner among Domestic Banks: Asset or Liability?" *Journal of Banking and Finance* 36: 1276–90.

Clarke, G., R. Cull, and M. Shirley. 2005. "Bank Privatization in Developing Countries: A Summary of Lessons and Findings." *Journal of Banking and Finance* 29: 1905–30.

Coase, R. 1960. "The Problem of Social Cost." *Journal of Law and Economics* 3: 1–44.

Collins, D., J. Morduch, S. Rutherford, and O. Ruthven. 2009. *Portfolios of the Poor: How the World's Poor Live on $2 a Day*. Princeton, NJ: Princeton University Press.

Crowe, C., G. Dell'Ariccia, D. Igan, and P. Rabanal. 2011. "How to Deal with Real Estate Booms: Lessons from Country Experiences." IMF Working Paper 11/91, International Monetary Fund, Washington, DC.

Cull, R., and L. Xu. 2011. "Firm Growth and Finance: Are Some Financial Institutions Better Suited to Early Stages of Development than Others?" Working Paper, World Bank, Washington, DC.

De Gregorio, J. 1996. "Borrowing Constraints, Human Capital Accumulation, and Growth." *Journal of Monetary Economics* 37: 49–71.

De Gregorio, J., S. Edwards, and R. Valdes. 2000. "Controls on Capital Inflows: Do They Work?" *Journal of Development Economics* 63: 59–83.

De Gregorio, J., and P. Guidotti. 1995. "Financial Development and Economic Growth." *World Development* 23: 433–48.

Demirgüç-Kunt, A., E. Feyen, and R. Levine. 2011. "Optimal Financial Structures and Development: The Evolving Importance of Banks and Markets." Working Paper, World Bank, Washington, DC.

Demirgüç-Kunt, A., and R. Levine. 2009. "Finance and Inequality: Theory and Evidence." NBER Working Paper 15275, National Bureau of Economic Research, Cambridge, MA.

Demirgüç-Kunt, A., and V. Maksimovic. 2002. "Funding Growth in Bank-Based and Market-Based Financial Systems: Evidence from Firm-Level Data." *Journal of Financial Economics* 65: 337–63.

Detragiache, E., T. Tressel, and P. Gupta. 2008. "Foreign Banks in Poor Countries: Theory and Evidence." *Journal of Finance* 63: 2123–60.

Devereux, M., and G. Smith. 1994. "International Risk Sharing and Economic Growth." *International Economic Review* 35: 535–50.

Diamond, D., and P. Dybvig. 1983. "Bank Runs, Deposit Insurance and Liquidity." *Journal of Political Economy* 91: 401–19.

Dupas, P., S. Green, A. Keats, and J. Robinson. 2012. "Challenges in Banking the Rural Poor: Evidence from Kenya's Western Province." NBER Working Paper 17851, National Bureau of Economic Research, Cambridge, MA.

Easterly, W., R. Islam, and J. Stiglitz. 2000. "Shaken and Stirred, Explaining Growth Volatility." *Annual Bank Conference on Development Economics*, 191–211. Washington, DC: World Bank.

Eurofound. 2011. "Young People and NEETs in Europe: First Findings." December, European Foundation for the Improvement of Living and Working Conditions, Dublin.

Fecht, F., K. X. D. Huang, and A. Martin. 2008. "Financial Intermediaries, Markets, and Growth." *Journal of Money, Credit and Banking* 40: 701–20.

Ferreira, F., and N. Schady. 2008. "Aggregate Economic Shocks, Child Schooling and Child Health." Policy Research Working Paper Series 4701, World Bank, Washington, DC.

Fischer, S., 2002. "Financial Crises and Reform of the International Financial System." NBER Working Paper 9267, National Bureau of Economic Research, Cambridge, MA.

Flug, K., A. Spilimbergo, and E. Wachtenheim. 1998. "Investment in Education: Do Economic Volatility and Credit Constraints Matter?" *Journal of Development Economics* 55: 465–81.

Forbes, K. 2007. "One Cost of the Chilean Capital Controls: Increased Financial Constraints for Small Traded Firms." *Journal of International Economics* 71: 294–323.

Frankel, J. 2010. "Monetary Policy in Emerging Markets: A Survey." NBER Working Paper 16125, National Bureau of Economic Research, Cambridge, MA.

Friedman, M., and A. Schwartz. 1963. *A Monetary History of the United States, 1867–1960*. Princeton, NJ: Princeton University Press.

Gallego, F., and L. Hernandez. 2003. "Microeconomic Effects of Capital Controls: The Chilean Experience during the 1990s." *International Journal of Finance and Economics* 8: 225–53.

Galor, O., and J. Zeira. 1993. "Income Distribution and Macroeconomics." *Review of Economic Studies* 60: 35–52.

Gaytán, A., and R. Rancière. 2005. "Banks, Liquidity Crises and Economic Growth." Banco de Mexico Working Paper 2005–03, Mexico City.

Gerschenkron, A. 1962. *Economic Backwardness in Historical Perspective: A Book of Essays.* Cambridge, MA: Harvard University Press.

Gine, X., and R. Townsend. 2004. "Evaluation of Financial Liberalization: A General Equilibrium Model with Constrained Occupation Choice." *Journal of Development Economics* 74: 269–307.

Glaeser, E., and J. Gyourko. 2007. "Housing Dynamics." Working Paper, Wharton School, University of Pennsylvania, Philadelphia.

Glick, R., and K. Lansing. 2010. "Global Household Leverage, House Prices, and Consumption," *FRBSF Economic Letters*, January, Federal Reserve Bank of San Francisco.

Gormley, T. 2010. "Banking Competition in Developing Countries: Does Foreign Bank Entry Improve Credit Access?" *Journal of Financial Intermediation* 19: 26–51.

Gorton, G. 1988. "Banking Panics and Business Cycles." *Oxford Economic Papers* 40: 751–81.

Gorton, G., and A. Winton. 2003. "Financial Intermediation." In *Handbook of Economics and Finance*, ed. G. Constantinides, M. Harris, and R. Stulz, 431–552. Amsterdam: North Holland.

Gozzi, J. C., R. Levine, and S. Schmukler. 2010. "Patterns of International Capital Raisings." *Journal of International Economics* 80: 45–57.

Greenwood, J., and B. Jovanovic. 1990. "Financial Development, Growth, and the Distribution of Income." *Journal of Political Economy* 98: 1076–107.

Greenwood, J., and B. Smith. 1997. "Financial Markets in Development, and the Development of Financial Markets." *Journal of Economic Dynamics and Control* 21: 145–81.

Guiso, L., P. Sapienza, and L. Zingales. 2004. "Does Local Financial Development Matter?" *Quarterly Journal of Economics* 119: 929–69.

Hellmann, T., K. Murdock, and J. Stiglitz. 2000. "Liberalization, Moral Hazard in Banking, and Prudential Regulation: Are Capital Requirements Enough?" *American Economic Review* 90: 147–65.

Helpman, E., and A. Razin. 1978. *A Theory of International Trade under Uncertainty.* New York: Academic Press.

Henry, P. B. 2000a. "Do Stock Market Liberalizations Cause Investment Booms?" *Journal of Financial Economics* 58: 301–34.

Henry, P. B. 2000b. "Stock Market Liberalization, Economic Reform, and Emerging Market Equity Prices." *Journal of Finance* 55: 529–64.

Herring, R., and S. Wachter. 1999. "Real Estate Booms and Banking Busts: An International Perspective." Wharton Financial Institutions Center Working Paper 99–27, University of Pennsylvania, Philadelphia.

Hong, H., J. Scheinkman, and W. Xiong. 2008. "Advisors and Asset Prices: A Model of the Origins of Bubbles." *Journal of Financial Economics* 89: 268–87.

Ibragimov, R., D. Jaffee, and J. Walden. 2011. "Diversification Disasters." *Journal of Financial Economics* 99: 333–48.

IMF (International Monetary Fund). 2012a. *World Economic Outlook.* January, Washington, DC.

IMF. 2012b. *World Economic Outlook Database.* April, Washington, DC.

Jacoby, H., and E. Skoufias. 1997. "Risk, Financial Markets, and Human Capital in a Developing Country." *Review of Economics Studies* 64: 311–35.

Jappelli, T., and M. Pagano. 1994. "Saving, Growth, and Liquidity Constraints." *Quarterly Journal of Economics* 109: 83–109.

Jaumotte, F., S. Lall, and C. Papageorgiou. 2011. "Rising Income Inequality: Technology, or Trade and Financial Globalization?" IMF Working Paper 08/185, Washington, DC.

Jerzmanowski, M., and M. Nabar. 2007. "Financial Development and Wage Inequality: Theory and Evidence." MPRA Working Paper 9841, *Munich Personal RePEc Archive.*

Kaminsky, G., and C. Reinhart. 1999. "The Twin Crises: The Causes of Banking and Balance-of-Payments Problems." *American Economic Review* 89: 473–500.

Karaivanov, A., and R. Townsend. 2012. "Dynamic Financial Constraints: Distinguishing Mechanism Design from Exogenously Incomplete Regimes." Working Paper, Economics Department, Massachusetts Institute of Technology, Cambridge, MA.

King, R., and R. Levine. 1993. "Finance, Entrepreneurship and Economic Development." *Journal of Monetary Economics* 32: 513–42.

Kumhof, M., and R. Rancière. 2011. "Inequality, Leverage and Crises." IMF Working Paper 10/268, International Monetary Fund, Washington, DC.

La Porta, R., F. Lopez-De-Silanes, A. Shleifer, and R. Vishny. 1997. "Legal Determinants of External Finance." *Journal of Finance* 52: 1131–59.

La Porta, R., F. Lopez-De-Silanes, A. Shleifer, and R. Vishny. 1998. "Law and Finance." *Journal of Political Economy* 106: 1113–55.

La Porta, R., F. Lopez-De-Silanes, A. Shleifer, and R. Vishny. 2000. "Investor Protection and Corporate Governance." *Journal of Financial Economics* 58: 3–27.

Laeven, L., and F. Valencia. 2012. "Systemic Banking Crises Database: An Update." IMF Working Paper 12/163, International Monetary Fund, Washington, DC.

Lane, P., and G. Milesi-Ferretti. 2007. "The External Wealth of Nations Mark II: Revised and Extended Estimates of Foreign Assets and Liabilities, 1970–2004." *Journal of International Economics* 73: 223–50.

Levine, R. 1991. "Stock Markets, Growth and Tax Policy." *Journal of Finance* 46: 1445–65.

Levine, R. 1998. "The Legal Environment, Banks, and Long–run Economic Growth." *Journal of Money, Credit and Banking* 30: 596–613.

Levine, R. 1999. "Law, Finance, and Economic Growth." *Journal of Financial Intermediation* 8: 36–67.

Levine, R. 2002. "Bank-Based or Market-Based Financial Systems: Which Is Better?" *Journal of Financial Intermediation* 11: 398–428.

Levine, R., N. Loayza, and T. Beck. 2000. "Financial Intermediation and Growth: Causality and Causes." *Journal of Monetary Economics* 46: 31–77.

Levine, R., and S. Zervos. 1998. "Stock Markets, Banks, and Economic Growth." *American Economic Review* 88: 537–58.

Lin, J. 2009. *Economic Development and Transition: Thought, Strategy, and Viability.* New York: Cambridge University Press.

Lin, J., and C. Xu. 2012. "Some Recent Progresses on Financial Structure and Development." In *The Global Macro Economy and Finance*, ed. F. Allen, M. Aoki, J. Fitoussi, N. Kiyotaki, R. Gordon, and J. Stiglitz, 224–44. International Economics Association Conference Volume 150–III. New York: Palgrave Macmillan.

Lin, J., X. Sun, and Y. Jiang. 2011. "Toward a Theory of Optimal Financial Structure." Working Paper, World Bank, Washington, DC.

Loayza, N., and R. Rancière. 2006. "Financial Development, Financial Fragility, and Growth." *Journal of Money, Credit and Banking* 38: 1051–76.

Mbiti, I., and D. Weil. 2011. "Mobile Banking: The Impact of M-Pesa in Kenya." NBER Working Paper 17129, National Bureau of Economic Research, Cambridge, MA.

Mendoza, E. 2001. "Credit, Prices, and Crashes: Business Cycles with a Sudden Stop." NBER Working Paper 8338, National Bureau of Economic Research, Cambridge, MA.

Mian, A. 2006. "Distance Constraints: The Limits of Foreign Lending in Poor Economies." *Journal of Finance* 61: 1465–505.

Mian, A., and A. Sufi. 2009. "The Consequences of Mortgage Credit Expansion: Evidence from the U.S. Mortgage Default Crisis." *Quarterly Journal of Economics* 124: 1449–96.

Moss, D. 2010. "Bank Failures, Regulation, and Inequality in the United States." Harvard Business School, Cambridge, MA. http://rof.oxfordjournals.org/content/early/2013/10/03/rof.rft039.full

Nilsen, J. 2002. "Trade Credit and the Bank Lending Channel." *Journal of Money, Credit and Banking* 34: 226–53.

North, D., and R. Thomas. 1973. *The Rise of the Western World: A New Economic History.* Cambridge: Cambridge University Press.

Obstfeld, M. 1994. "Risk-Taking, Global Diversification, and Growth." *American Economic Review* 84: 1310–29.

Obstfeld, M., and A. Taylor. 2004. *Global Capital Markets: Integration, Crisis, and Growth.* Japan–U.S. Center Sanwa Monographs on International Financial Markets. Cambridge: Cambridge University Press.

OECD (Organisation for Economic Co-operation and Development). 2012. "House Prices." *Economics: Key Tables from OECD* No. 17, Paris.

Paxson, C., and N. Schady. 2005. "Cognitive Development among Young Children in Ecuador: The Roles of Wealth, Health and Parenting." *Journal of Human Resources* 42 (1): 49–84.

Plantin, G., H. Sapra, and H. Shin. 2008. "Marking-to-Market: Panacea or Pandora's Box?" *Journal of Accounting Research* 46: 435–60.

Prasad, E., K. Rogoff, S.-J. Wei, and A. Kose. 2003. "Effects of Financial Globalization on Developing Countries: Some Empirical Evidence." IMF Occasional Paper 220, International Monetary Fund, Washington, DC.

Prati, A., M. Schindler, and P. Valenzuela. 2012. "Who Benefits from Capital Account Liberalization? Evidence from Firm-Level Credit Ratings Data." *Journal of International Money and Finance* 31: 1649–73.

Quinn, D., and A. M. Toyoda. 2008. "Does Capital Account Liberalization Lead to Growth?" *Review of Financial Studies* 21: 1403–49.

Rajan, R. 2010. *Fault Lines: How Hidden Fractures Still Threaten the World Economy*, Princeton, NJ: Princeton University Press.

Rajan, R., and L. Zingales. 1998. "Financial Development and Growth." *American Economic Review* 88: 559–86.

Rajan, R., and L. Zingales. 2003a. "The Great Reversals: The Politics of Financial Development in the Twentieth Century." *Journal of Financial Economics* 69: 5–50.

Rajan, R., and L. Zingales. 2003b. *Saving Capitalism from Capitalists: Unleashing the Power of Financial Markets to Create Wealth and Spread Opportunity.* New York: Random House.

Ramakrishnan, R. T. S., and A. Thakor. 1984. "Information Reliability and a Theory of Financial Intermediation." *Review of Economic Studies* 51: 415–32.

Rancière, R., A. Tornell, and F. Westermann. 2008. "Systemic Crises and Growth." *Quarterly Journal of Economics* 123: 359–406.

Ravallion, M. 2002. "Are the Poor Protected from Budget Cuts? Evidence for Argentina." *Journal of Applied Economics* 5 (1): 95–121.

Reinhart, C. and K. Rogoff. 2008. "This Time Is Different: A Panoramic View of Eight Centuries of Financial Crises." NBER Working Paper 13882, National Bureau of Economic Research, Cambridge, MA.

Reinhart, C., and K. Rogoff. 2009. *This Time Is Different: Eight Centuries of Financial Folly.* Princeton, NJ: Princeton University Press.

Reinhart, C., and T. Smith. 1998, "Too Much of a Good Thing: The Macroeconomic Effects of Taxing Capital Inflows." In *Managing Capital Flows and Exchange Rates: Perspectives from the Pacific Basin,* ed. R. Glick, 436–64. Cambridge: Cambridge University Press.

Robinson, J. 1952. "The Generalization of the General Theory." In *The Rate of Interest and Other Essays*, ed. J. Robinson, 67–142. London: Macmillan.

Rodrik, D., and A. Subramanian. 2009. "Why Did Financial Globalization Disappoint?" *IMF Staff Papers* 56: 112–38.

Rousseau, P., and R. Sylla. 1999. "Emerging Financial Markets and Early U.S. Growth." NBER Working Paper 7448, National Bureau of Economic Research, Cambridge, MA.

Rousseau, P., and P. Wachtel. 1998. "Financial Intermediation and Economic Performance: Historical Evidence from Five Industrial Countries." *Journal of Money Credit and Banking* 30: 657–78.

Rousseau, P., and P. Wachtel. 2011. "What Is Happening to the Impact of Financial Deepening on Economic Growth?" *Economic Inquiry* 49: 276–88.

Saint-Paul, G. 1992. "Technological Choice, Financial Markets and Economic Development." *European Economic Review* 36: 763–81.

Scheinkman, J., and W. Xiong. 2003. "Overconfidence and Speculative Bubbles." *Journal of Political Economy* 111: 1183–219.

Standard and Poor's. 2012. "S&P/Case-Shiller Home Price Indices."http://us.spindices.com.

Stulz, R. 2001. "Does Financial Structure Matter for Economic Growth? A Corporate Finance Perspective." In *Financial Structure and Economic Growth: A Cross–Country Comparison of Banks, Markets, and Development*, ed. A. Demirgüç-Kunt and R. Levine, 143–88. Cambridge, MA: MIT Press.

Taylor, J. 2007. "Housing and Monetary Policy." In *Housing, Housing Finance, and Monetary Policy*, 463–76. Kansas City: Federal Reserve Bank of Kansas City.

Taylor, J. 2008. "The Financial Crisis and the Policy Responses: An Empirical Analysis of What Went Wrong." NBER Working Paper 14631, National Bureau of Economic Research, Cambridge, MA.

Tirole, J. 1982. "On the Possibility of Speculation under Rational Expectations." *Econometrica* 50: 1163–81.

Tirole, J. 1985. "Asset Bubbles and Overlapping Generations." *Econometrica* 53: 1499–528.

Tornell, A., F. Westermann, and L. Martinez. 2004. "The Positive Link between Financial Liberalization, Growth and Crises." NBER Working Paper 10293, National Bureau of Economic Research, Cambridge, MA.

Townsend, R. M., and K. Ueda. 2006. "Financial Deepening, Inequality and Growth: a Model–based Quantitative Evaluation." *Review of Economic Studies* 73: 251–93.

Wagner, W. 2010. "Diversification at Financial Institutions and Systemic Crises." *Journal of Financial Intermediation* 19: 333–54.

Williamson, O. 1979. "Transaction Cost Economics: The Governance of Contractual Relations." *Journal of Law and Economics* 22: 233–61.

World Bank. 2012. *World Development Indicators*. Washington, DC.

Wurgler, J. 2000. "Financial Markets and the Allocation of Capital." *Journal of Financial Economics* 58: 187–214.

Xu, L. 2011. "The Effects of Business Environments on Development: A Survey of New Firm-Level Evidence." *World Bank Research Observer* 26: 310–40.

Comments on "Does Finance Accelerate or Retard Growth? Theory and Evidence," by Franklin Allen, Elena Carletti, Jun "QJ" Qian, and Patricio Valenzuela

Stijn Claessens

I want to start with much praise for the chapter. It is a very comprehensive review of the roles of finance in economic development and citizens' welfare. It covers all relevant aspects—the drivers of financial sector development; the impact of finance on growth; the relationship between finance and crises; the determinants and impact of access to financial services, especially for small firms and low-income households; and the relationship between finance and inequality—and offers many suggestions for policy improvements and paths of financial reforms. It provides extensive theoretical perspectives and is rich on historical and recent evidence, presenting many facts and relationships. It also reviews many countries' experiences, covering advanced countries, emerging markets, and low-income countries. In addition to the many specific suggestions and concrete policy advice, it highlights areas of unknowns. Importantly, it focuses on the issues of key interest to the Global Citizen Foundation (GCF): globalization, inequality, financial inclusion, poverty, and income distribution.

Given the quality of the chapter, reflecting the erudition of the authors and their extensive research in this area, it is hard to be critical. It is even harder to add much to the chapter, particularly as I had a chance to do so at the interim workshop. As a modest attempt to add value at this stage, I have put together a set of ruminations on possible policy implications—in part inspired by the chapter but largely my own thoughts—as well as possible implications for the GCF project.

I begin with some policy issues. I then continue with some broader lessons, as I see them, and a possible agenda for going forward. My broader lessons focus on governance and oversight in the financial sector, both national and international. I argue that a financial sector to service all citizens in better ways requires better governance and engagement with a broader group of stakeholders in designing financial reforms. I conclude with a possible agenda for how to conduct better reform processes and build relationships among stakeholders.

1. Policy Issues

I focus on four themes: financial sector development, risk prevention, crisis management, and making finance work for more.

1.1 Financial Sector Development

It has become clearer with the recent financial crisis that the market-driven approach, while still the starting point for designing financial reforms, needs to acknowledge more explicitly two aspects: the many market failures that can arise in the financial sector and the large (implicit) role of the state in the financial sector, which, although necessary in many ways, has not always been productive. The chapter devotes much attention to these policies and problems. It highlights the recent call for macroprudential policies that can possibly correct some of the many externalities that arise in financial services provision. And it is very cognizant of the fact that, although a large role of the state is needed (for regulation and supervision, for example), this comes with drawbacks. Distortions can arise, for example, as a result of moral hazard (associated with "too big to fail" institutions, for example) or the deductibility of interest payments, leading to increased systemic risks.

Although these issues have been acknowledged, the often poor provision of financial services provision and the repeated occurrence of financial crises shows that the profession is still not able to design regulatory frameworks or implement them consistently in a way that creates financial systems that are efficient, serve the needs of all, and are reasonably "fail- and fool-proof." Although many deeper issues are at fault here—notably political economy factors, which I address later—more needs to and can be done, in academia as well in practice, regarding the "optimal" design and sequencing of financial reforms.

Specifically, in my view, too little attention has been given to how to coordinate and phase various types of financial reforms. There is a need—and I am borrowing here from the thoughts of Joseph Stiglitz—to conduct more "dynamic portfolio analyses" of financial reforms. Doing so would attempt to explicitly model the actions of financial agents given the various incentives for profit and growth opportunities and the risks they face at a given point in time. These opportunities and risks would depend in turn, at least in part, on prevailing and expected regulatory and market structures. The analysis would then aim to achieve some "optimal" degree and paths of financial liberalization (or conversely a certain degree of "repression") in market segments or activities, given the effects that the associated degree of competition, rents, and franchise values have on agents' incentives, including regarding the efficient provision of financial services, in terms of quantity and quality, and the degree of (systemic) risk-taking.

It would be very challenging to model these dynamic aspects, which would therefore be very imprecise. The idea would be to proxy how financial reforms affect the behavior of financial markets' participants. Doing so could address aspects such as the fact that over time basic services (such as deposit and payments services) become more contestable, and new financial markets develop that allow for more scalable transactions. This increased competition in basic services may lead banks to undertake more market-based transactions (for example, trading of derivatives). Such transactions, which are easier than other services to scale up, could be a way for banks to use their franchise value in traditional banking in the face of competition. Yet this practice could be risky from a system point of view. Limiting this behavior (for some time) could therefore be beneficial, at least until other supporting institutions are in place.

A dynamic portfolio approach could be beneficial not just from a financial stability perspective but also from an access to financial services point of view. For example, providing information-intensive banking services may require some "rents" for banks to be willing to invest in information acquisition. This approach could call for a specific or slower path of financial liberalization. Given a level of development in a country, some financial services may also matter more for "welfare." For example, payment services may be more important than credit for low-income people and low-income countries. These differences may have implications for reform paths—for example, opening up the savings markets first, before credit and other financial markets, may be best. Or the approach may help determine when it is feasible, useful, and prudent to develop "new" financial services. Many countries have struggled, for example, to develop well-functioning capital markets, notably stock markets. One reason why may be that the incentives for financial agents to actively support such markets are not yet sufficiently present, as the development of a stock market would undermine their existing franchise values.

Approaching financial reforms dynamically from financial stability and access perspectives can have important implications for reform processes. Such an analysis could lead to policy implications similar to those used at some point for industrial policy in East Asia (as reviewed in chapter 2, by Dani Rodrik): give some rents to some segments or forms of financial services that have the highest social value at that point in time, and then take those rents away as the economy changes and systems develop. Such an analysis could also help identify thresholds for specific liberalization and reforms (for example, only when the institutional environment—regulation and supervision, market discipline, institutional infrastructure, and so forth—is adequate to allow for some new types of financial services).

1.2 Risk Prevention

As the chapter shows, financial crises can have very adverse impacts on not only economic growth but also on inequality and poverty. Preventing financial crises should thus be an important objective. At a minimum, the goal should be to prevent countries from experiencing "old"-type financial crises. For example, one would hope that enough has been learned that "frontier markets" do not have to suffer the types of financial crises which emerging markets (in, for example, East Asia or Latin America) experienced more than a decade ago, or that advanced countries experienced recently (and many still endure).

Reducing systemic risks is closely related to the need for better implementation of basic regulations, such as higher capital adequacy requirements, good supervision, clear resolution frameworks for weak financial institutions, better cross-border coordination, and, more generally, incentive structures that are less prone to incentivize excessive risk-taking. Some *ex ante* measures could limit the risk of financial institutions that become too big to fail and that are subject to the moral hazard of a bailout. Some institutional infrastructures, such as central counterparties, could help reduce the risks of and problems of contagion.

As the chapter amply notes, however, lessons have also been learned on what types of reforms, financial system structures, and types of capital flows can be considered more susceptible to crises. For example, a fairly robust finding suggests that rapid financial liberalization, including capital account liberalization, can increase the risks of crises. Some types of capital flows (for example, bank flows) seem to raise countries' vulnerability to a balance of payments crisis, whereas others (for example, foreign direct investment) are less closely associated with crises. Also, it appears that a model in which foreign banks obtain funding locally leads to fewer vulnerabilities than one in which foreign and domestic banks in a country rely heavily on cross-border lending.

Findings thus suggest that, in addition to basic reforms, certain types of financial systems or configurations of financial exposures or flows can make countries less prone to crises. A general lesson from recent crises is that there is a greater need for policies aimed specifically at reducing market failures and externalities. As such, there has been a renewed interest in capital account openness in recent years. This interest questions the fully liberalized model and supports the notion that capital account management tools can be used to prevent or deal with the build-up of financial sector vulnerabilities and systemic macroeconomic risks. And while it is still early to draw conclusions, macroprudential policies seem to offer promising new tools to reduce the build-up of systemic risks, notably in real estate booms, reducing the chances of a bust.

Many questions remain about both capital flow management and macroprudential policies. Among others, these include evidence on their effectiveness and optimal calibration to reflect country conditions and circumstances; the interactions of these policies with other policies, notably macroprudential policies and monetary policy; the institutional design (who is in charge of these policies); and general political economy considerations (for example, how to ensure that they will be implemented properly when needed). Further thought and research (on, for example, how to design optimal externality "taxes") would be useful, so that these policies can help reduce the frequency of crises and mitigate their impact if they do occur.

1.3 Crisis Management

Unfortunately, as noted in the chapter, although more needs to be done to reduce risks *ex ante*, many policies have had limited success. Crises have recurred partly because knowledge of their causes remains imperfect. The "this time is different" syndrome highlighted by Reinhart and Rogoff in *This Time is Different: Eight Centuries of Financial Folly*—that is, the fact that in the face of the build-up of vulnerabilities, the collective view remains that systemic risks are limited "because conditions and institutional environment have changed"—is often likely to prevail.

With crises likely to continue to occur, the question of how to best manage their aftermath remains very relevant. Unfortunately, the record here, although better than for crisis prevention, is also poor. Interventions are often too late, too timid, and insufficiently coordinated across policy areas, let alone countries. The latest crisis—which has been drawn out and included large cross-country spillovers within the euro zone—is a case in point.

Poor management leads to higher economic costs (in the form of lost output) and increases the final fiscal bill (incurred directly when governments resolve failed financial institutions and indirectly when they support the economy in the aftermath of a crisis). It can also have both direct and indirect adverse impacts on inequality, income distribution, and poverty. The weight of paying for the fiscal costs incurred, for example, may fall disproportionally on lower-income households. And, following a financial crisis and its resolution, small and medium-size enterprises (SMEs) may have less access to finance than large firms. Small savers may be worse off, while richer households may escape the high inflation or financial repression that often follows a crisis. There is thus a critical need to manage crises better from an inequality perspective.

Relatively well-known lessons at both the national and international levels could be applied better. The main one is the need to absorb any losses resulting from the crisis—in the financial, corporate, or household sectors or at the level of the sovereign debt restructuring—as quickly as possible. In practice, doing so means recapitalizing banks quickly when needed; having strong, efficient, less creditor-biased financial resolution and restructuring mechanisms to resolve overindebted corporations and households; and restructuring sovereign debt, if necessary, quickly, including through the use of coordination mechanisms (such as collective action clauses and the like). Disseminating and applying these best practices more widely would be very useful.

1.4 Making Finance Work for More

I think this area, as the analysis of the chapter shows, is one of the most complex and raises many fundamental questions. Financial systems typically serve a relatively small set of the population and the corporate sector; low-income people and SMEs, especially in developing countries, have little access to financial services at reasonable costs. Although "demand" factors, such as creditworthiness, obviously play a large role in hindering access, "supply" factors matter as well. Such supply incentives can relate to the financial system structure; the return to banks and other financial institutions to cater to these segments is often too low relative to other opportunities. Although technology has reduced costs in many areas, for many services they remain high, in part because service provision often still involves human input. Consideration of financial sector structures can be important here.

Relative lack of access also arises because finance has become more rules-oriented, with a multitude of new rules following the global financial crisis. Obviously rules can have benefits, but they also have compliance and other indirect costs. They can hinder access, as when money laundering rules are applied to very small financial transactions or the opening of a bank account. Especially when they need to be harmonized internationally, rules can also suffer from the lowest common denominator problem. New rules are not always subject to proper cost–benefit analyses. More generally, many rules and regulatory approaches have limited analytical foundations, as the academic discussion on the level of capital adequacy requirements, noted in the chapter, shows.

Some weaknesses in the design of rules can be overcome by better processes, an issue I take up later. More generally, though, it may be good to move away from the very detailed Basel III and other Financial Stability

Board "standards" approaches and allow more room for different models of financial services provision, particularly given the scope for countries to leapfrog. Innovations can increase access to financial services and improve equality, especially in emerging markets and developing countries. Some case study evidence cited in the chapter, including on the extensive use of mobile payments in Kenya, suggests that there are ways around the current financial market and institutional structures and related constraints. Some of these new approaches can also help overcome vested interests (for example, provision of mobile phone-based financial services may not be subject to the same capture as traditional banking services). More analyses on which of these models are best for enhancing access would be useful.

In addition to less emphasis on standards and more on innovative approaches, more work could be done on legal and institutional reforms. Judicial systems, information systems, and competition policies are often barriers to the efficient provision of financial services in many (low-income) countries. Countries need such systems for their overall development, particularly as they are important for overall private sector development. Because they are less driven by financial sector-specific needs, these reforms may be less subject to capture than other reforms (there are no guarantees, of course: as the chapter notes, when legal reforms hurt insiders, they may be blocked as well). Property rights protections—including both vertical property rights (which protect citizens against expropriation by the state) and horizontal property rights (which foster private sector transactions)—are key. Both affect financial sector development, with vertical property rights being more important for general financial development and horizontal property rights more important for capital market development.

2. Broad Themes

Let me now move from these specific policy issues to broader themes. I think the big question here is the governance of finance, a theme that is common to some of the other chapters in this volume (for example chapter 7, by Nancy Birdsall). This question has both national and international dimensions, including those relating to processes and stakeholders. I discuss each in turn, ending with some ideas on how governance of finance can become a forward-looking agenda for the project.

2.1 National Governance

Capture is a big problem in the financial sector, with adverse effects on access to financial services and financial stability. Capture occurs in many ways. Some are subtle: insiders—both people within the financial services industries and important users of financial services—set the rules, standards, and institutional designs, mostly to benefit themselves. As rents arise, the costs of financial services increase and access declines for some groups. In some cases, capture occurs in very blatant ways, such as corruption, which includes not only "stealing" (as when state-owned banks lend to cronies who subsequently default) but also the misallocation of resources. Capture often occurs *ex post*—through, for example, bailouts induced by the moral hazard of too-big-to-fail financial institutions or more relaxed monetary policy and fiscal policies to help avoid the risks of a systemic financial crisis. Regulators, supervisors, and many other officials often fail in their public policy roles, with little ex post costs (in terms of loss of jobs or reputations, for example).

The question of how to improve national governance is a complex matter. Despite the costs of capture, the general public is little involved in financial sector matters, *ex ante* or *ex post*, both because it is poorly informed about the causes of crises—financial systems and regulations are complex—and because it is not easily mobilized. Other "whistleblowers" (including auditors, accountants, rating agencies, investors, and financial markets more generally) have a poor track record in disciplining financial agents, markets, and countries, partly because groupthink is often prevalent. One would want to retain the bias toward private sector-led, open financial systems and not assume that controls can easily correct for these deficiencies. Yet the high cost shows clearly that more balance to counter capture is needed.

For one, more attention to the governance of regulators and supervisors would be useful. In many countries, regulators lack sufficient legal, financial, and operational independence from legislative bodies and political economy pressures more generally. There is also often too little formal public oversight of regulators and supervisors. Through objective assessments and regular checks, weaknesses in their independence, accountability, integrity, and transparency of operations could be brought out and corrected. It would also help if the standards assessors (the IMF, the World Bank, the Financial Stability Board, and the like) moved away from assessing formal compliance of countries with international "standards" to assessing the "governance" of regulators and the transparency of "processes" (and outcomes).

Better governance should also involve more transparency and greater participation of the public in the design of rules. There needs to be more transparency in rules-setting, with more views allowed to be expressed. Better and perhaps new institutions are likely needed, in part as the public is hard to mobilize. The establishment of the Consumer Financial Protection Bureau in the United States can be seen as an attempt to create a counterforce to insiders designing and applying the rules. Although few other such bureaus exist so far, and the one in the United States remains incipient, it could be a sensible model, as it replicates what often exists for other products (for example, consumer product safety bureaus).

There could also be additional formal oversight, both *ex ante* and *ex post*. For example, some academics have proposed a "sentinel"—an informed, expertly staffed, and independent institution evaluating financial regulations and regulators' actions from the public's point of view. Although a sentinel seems hard to design, as the problem of groupthink often arises, it is worth considering. Perhaps requiring formal, *ex ante* Food and Drug Administration-style approval of new financial instruments could be useful to ensure that they are not only "safe" for the general public but also socially valuable. Or—and maybe more realistically, as each new financial service would be hard to approve *ex ante*—a National Transportation Safety Board-like agency for finance could be set up. Such an agency could systemically investigate and report on failures. It would be better than maintaining financial crises commissions, which are too ad hoc and often have too little standing.

2.2 International Governance

Issues are even more complex internationally than nationally. International regulators and supervisors often fail in their (macroeconomic and financial stability) surveillance roles. More attention has been placed on international governance and legitimacy in recent years, and some progress is being made to broaden the set of stakeholders (as reflected in the greater role of the G20). Still, international governance has proven hard to change (witness, for example, the ongoing governance and quota debate for the IMF, as noted in the chapter). Also, although transparency at the international level has improved, more is still needed, in terms of both specific issues and countries (for example, on country surveillance and program decisions) and data availability (for example, on cross-border exposures).

Overall, one should be skeptical of the scope for rapid progress in international formal governance arrangements, if only because of the multitude of actors involved. Perhaps there is scope for improving some of the processes for decision-making internationally. One step could be further opening up the standards-setting processes, including by soliciting public input more explicitly (although many users will need support given the technical nature of the discussions). At the margin, there may also be some scope for involving existing institutions. Although expertise may be an issue, there could perhaps be a greater role for broader agencies such as the World Trade Organization in both debates about rules and in various processes, including dispute resolution.

In the end, changing the financial sector paradigm and the way in which the benefits and risks are allocated has to be about changing governance.

Doing so will be complex and require changing both the set of stakeholders involved as well as the processes that set the rules of the game, in both static and dynamic ways. Although many stakeholders are involved in financial services, not all are well represented. In most countries, providers of financial services are well represented; users—notably households, but also many institutional investors—are much less well represented. As much of financial sector regulation is determined through standards set by groups such as the Basle Committee on Banking Supervision, the international dimension is crucial as well. Internationally, advanced countries dominate, emerging markets are much less represented than their current economic size warrants, and low-income countries are hardly represented at all. With the shifts in income and financial assets toward emerging markets and developing countries, these discrepancies are likely to increase.

Improving governance thus requires greater representation of some groups. Representation is largely an (international) political economy question, on which economists have less to say. How can relevant parties, including the general public, be better mobilized to demand a bigger say in discussions? How can one better harness the power of nongovernmental organizations, 99 percent-type movements, and other groups? Of course, it is also relevant to better understand existing stakeholders' objectives and views. How uniform or diverse are they? The lack of an effective voice of emerging markets, for example, in part reflects their diversity, with groups like the BRICs not necessarily unified in their views. How can they be made to coalesce better?

2.3 Moving Forward

With these "answers," one can try to assess what a better model might be. Here, as in many other areas of international governance, the path is not obvious. Should one, for example, work through existing mechanisms? Should "new" stakeholders try to play a greater role in formulating rules and standards, assessing public bodies and countries, and the like? It may be that using existing mechanisms is not the most efficient means of reforming financial systems, because it risks entering a (losing) game of being coopted. I have no insights on this; perhaps political economy experts and others could help design better ways to influence financial sector reforms around the world. Such an agenda could benefit all global citizens.

Comments on "Does Finance Accelerate or Retard Growth? Theory and Evidence" by Franklin Allen, Elena Carletti, Jun "QJ" Qian, and Patricio Valenzuela

Thorsten Beck

The chapter is a very complete literature survey as well as a forward-looking think piece. Rather than commenting on it, I would like to drill deeper into three specific topics. First, I discuss different explanations for the nonlinearity of the finance and growth literature. Second, I make a suggestion on how to conceptualize the bright and dark sides of finance under one framework. Third, I discuss two channels through which financial deepening can influence societal outcomes, especially by contributing to poverty reduction.

1. Finance and Growth: Reasons for Nonlinearities

Recent research has pointed to important nonlinearities in the relationship between finance and growth. There is evidence that the effect of financial development is strongest among middle-income countries; other work finds a declining effect of finance and growth as countries grow richer (Rioja and Valev 2004a, 2004b; Aghion, Howitt, and Mayer-Foulkes 2005). More recently, Arcand, Berkes, and Panizza (2011) find that the finance-and-growth relationship turns negative for high-income countries. They identify a value of 110 percent private credit to GDP as the approximate turning point, with the negative relationship between finance and growth turning significant at about 150 percent private credit to GDP, levels reached by some high-income countries in the 2000s.

There are several, not exclusive, explanations for such nonlinearities, as put forward by the recent literature and partly informed by the recent crisis. I briefly mention four of these explanations before discussing two more in some detail.

First, the measures of financial depth and intermediation that the literature has been using might simply be too crude to capture quality improvements at high levels of financial development. In addition, the financial sector has gradually extended its scope beyond the traditional activity of intermediation toward so-called "nonintermediation" financial activities (Demirgüc-Kunt and Huizinga 2010). As a result, the usual measures of intermediation services have become less and less congruent with the reality of modern financial systems. Second, some argue that the reason for the nonlinearity of the finance–growth relationship might be that financial development helps countries catch up to the productivity frontier but has limited or no growth effect for countries that are close to or at the frontier (Aghion, Howitt, and Mayer-Foulkes 2005). Third, the financial system might actually grow too large relative to the real economy if it extracts excessively high informational rents and in this way attracts too much young talent to the financial industry (Bolton, Santos, and Scheinkman 2011; Philippon 2010). Fourth, and related, the financial system can grow too large because of the safety net subsidy that results in overly aggressive risk-taking and overextension of the financial system. Fifth, a critical question is: who is the beneficiary of financial deepening—a question I discuss in more detail below. Although the theoretical and most of the empirical finance and growth literature has focused mostly on enterprise credit, financial systems in high-income countries provide a large share of their services, including credit, to households rather than enterprises. As countries grow richer and financial systems develop, a larger share of bank credit is given to households rather than enterprises. Even within high-income countries, this trend has been increasing over time, as documented by Beck, Buyukkarabacak, Rioja, and Valev (2012). Household credit constitutes more than 80 percent of overall bank credit (mostly mortgage credit) in several countries, including Canada, Denmark, and the Netherlands.

Although the theoretical and empirical literature has clearly shown the positive impact of enterprise credit for firm and aggregate growth, theory has made ambiguous predictions on the role of household credit. On the one hand, Jappelli and Pagano (1994) argue that alleviating credit constraints on households reduces the savings rate, with negative repercussions for economic growth. On the other hand, Galor and Zeira (1993) and De Gregorio (1996) argue that household credit can foster economic development if it increases human capital accumulation.

Tentative cross-country evidence shows that the positive effect of financial deepening comes mostly through enterprise credit; there is no significant relationship between the importance of household credit and economic growth (Beck, Buyukkarabacak, Rioja, and Valev, 2012). These results hold controlling for an array of other country characteristics and for endogeneity. The relationship between enterprise credit and GDP per capita growth is more accurately estimated and significant for a larger number of countries than the relationship between overall bank lending and GDP per capita growth. This finding, together with the observation of an increasing share of household credit in total bank lending in many developed economies over the past decades, mostly for mortgages, can go some way toward explaining the diminishing growth benefits from financial deepening in high-income countries.

A final explanation for the nonlinear relationship between finance and growth that I would like to briefly discuss concerns the role of the financial system vis-à-vis the rest of the economy. Whereas academics have focused mostly on the facilitating role of the financial sector, which consists of mobilizing funds for investment and contributing to an efficient allocation of capital in general, policymakers, especially before the crisis and in some European countries, have often focused on financial services as a growth sector in itself. This view sees the financial sector more or less as an export sector, one that seeks to build an (often) nationally centered financial center stronghold by building on comparative advantages, such as skill base, favorable regulatory policies, subsidies, and so forth.

The differences between these two approaches toward the financial sector can be illustrated with measures that are being used to capture the importance of the financial system. Academic economists typically focus on private credit to GDP—defined as the outstanding claims of financial institutions on the domestic nonfinancial private sector relative to economic activity—as a crude and imperfect measure of the development and efficiency of the financial system, as it captures the intermediation function of financial institutions. In contrast, the financial center view focuses on the financial sector's contribution to GDP or the share of the labor force employed in the financial sector.

There is strong evidence for the facilitating role of finance. There is less evidence for the growth benefits from building a financial center. Recent cross-country comparisons show that, controlling for the effects of financial intermediation, a larger financial sector may bring short-term growth benefits in high-income countries, but certainly brings higher growth volatility (Beck, Degryse, and Kneer 2014). Based on a sample of 77 countries for the period 1980 and 2007, they find that intermediation activities increase growth and reduce volatility in the long run, but that expansion of the financial sectors along other dimensions has no long-run effect on real sector outcomes. Over shorter time horizons, a large financial sector stimulates growth at the cost of higher volatility in high-income countries. Intermediation activities stabilize the economy in the medium run, especially in low-income countries.

These results were obtained for the period before 2007, but recent experiences confirm them. The 2008 collapse of the Icelandic banking system and the turmoil in the Cypriot banking system shed significant doubt on the premise that more is better when it comes to finance. The recent crisis has certainly exposed the risks of such a financial center approach, which brings with it high contingent taxpayer liabilities which, in a crisis, turn into real taxpayer costs and turn a banking crisis more easily into a deep recession, and potentially into a sovereign debt crisis. Refocusing attention on the facilitating and intermediation role of finance might therefore be useful.

2. The Bright and Dark Sides of Finance: A Conceptual Framework

I would like to discuss how we can reconcile the bright and dark sides of financial deepening in one analytical framework, which can serve as a basis for policy discussion. In order to understand the policies and institutions needed for a sound and effective financial system and reconcile the bright and dark sides of financial deepening into one analytical framework, I would like to briefly discuss the concept of the financial possibility frontier. This concept not only allows us to better understand the relative performance of financial systems relative to other countries and over time; it also identifies the necessary policies to achieve the optimal level of financial deepening.

To develop the frontier, I start from basic concepts. Financial systems are constrained by two major market frictions, transaction costs and risks, which can constrain the deepening and broadening of financial systems in developing countries.[1] As I discuss in what follows, financial intermediaries and markets arise exactly because these market frictions prevent direct intermediation between savers and borrowers. However, their efficient operation is limited by the same market frictions.

Fixed transaction costs in financial service provision result in decreasing unit costs as the number or size of transactions increases.[2] The resulting economies of scale at all levels explain why financial intermediation costs are typically higher in smaller financial systems and why smaller economies can typically sustain only small financial systems (even in relation to economic activity). They also explain the limited capacity of small financial

---

[1] For the following, see a similar discussion in Beck and de la Torre (2007) and Barajas and others (2013).

[2] These fixed costs exist at the level of the transaction, client, institution, and even the financial system as a whole. Processing an individual payment or savings transaction entails costs that are, at least in part, independent of the value of the transaction. Similarly, maintaining an account for an individual client implies costs that are largely independent of the number and size of the transactions the client makes. At the level of a financial institution, fixed costs span a wide range—from the brick-and-mortar branch network to computer systems, legal and accounting services, and security arrangements—and are independent of the number of clients

systems to broaden their financial systems toward clients with needs for smaller transactions.[3] In summary, fixed transactions costs can explain the high level of formal financial exclusion in many developing countries. Fixed costs can also explain the lack of capital markets in many small developing economies.

In addition to costs, the depth and outreach of financial systems, especially in credit and insurance services, is constrained by risks, particularly default risk. These risks can be either contract-specific or systemic in nature. Although idiosyncratic risks are specific to individual borrowers, projects, or policy holders, their management is influenced by the systemic risk environment. High macroeconomic uncertainty and deficient contract enforcement institutions exacerbate agency problems, and the lack of diversification possibilities can hinder the ability of financial institutions to diversify nonagency risks. As systemic risk increases, it enlarges the set of borrowers and projects that are effectively priced out of credit and capital markets. Similarly, it makes insurance policies unaffordable for larger segments of the population. At the same time, the easing of agency frictions in the absence of adequate oversight can create incentives for excessive risk-taking by market participants (who fail to internalize externalities), fueling financial instability.

The efficiency with which financial institutions and markets can overcome market frictions is critically influenced by a number of state variables—factors that are invariant in the short term (often lying outside the purview of policymakers)—that affect provision of financial services on the supply side and can constrain participation on the demand side. State variables thus impose an upper limit of financial deepening in an economy at a given time. These variables are either directly related to the financial sector (for example, macroeconomic fundamentals, available technology, contractual and information frameworks underpinning the financial system, prudential oversight) or related to the broader socio-political and structural environment in which the financial system operates. Among the state variables is also the size of the market. Problems in many developing countries are related to the oft-found triple problem of smallness—small transactions, small financial institutions, and small market size—which reduces the possibilities to diversify and hedge risks while at the same time increasing concentration risks. However, there

served. Fixed costs also arise at the level of the financial system (for example, regulatory costs and the costs of payment, clearing, and settlement infrastructure) which are, up to a point, independent of the number of institutions regulated or participating in the payment system.

[3] The effect of fixed costs on financial service provision can be reinforced by network externalities, where the marginal benefit to an additional customer is determined by the number of customers already using the service (Claessens et al. 2003). This effect is especially relevant in the case of payments systems and capital market development, where benefits, and thus participation and liquidity, increase as the pool of users expands.

are also important demand factors—such as the demographic composition of the population, which determines the aggregate savings rates, or cultural and religious preferences, or aversion with respect to formal financial services and the concept of interest rates.

Using the concept of state variables allows us to define the financial possibility frontier as a rationed equilibrium of realized supply and demand. This frontier shows the maximum sustainable depth (for example, credit or deposit volumes); outreach (for example, share of population reached); or breadth (for example, diversity of domestic sources of long-term finance) of a financial system that can be realistically achieved at a given point in time. The financial possibility frontier can move over time, as income levels change, the international environment adjusts, new technologies arise, and—most important—the overall socio-political environment in which financial institutions work changes. Policy levers, including the macroeconomic environment and contractual and information frameworks, can be used to push out the frontier, although such benefits are rarely to be reaped in the short term.

The financial possibility frontier also allows us to distinguish several challenges to deepening and broadening financial systems in developing countries and the corresponding policies. Depending on where a financial system stands relative to the frontier and where the frontier stands in comparison with other countries with similar characteristics, different policy priorities and thus different functions for government apply. In what follows, I discuss situations in which a financial system is below the frontier, above the frontier, and at too low a frontier.

The financial possibility frontier may be low relative to countries at similar levels of economic development due to deficiencies in state variables. Here we can distinguish between the role played by structural and other state variables. Among structural variables, low population density and small market size increase the costs and risks for financial institutions, excluding large segments of the population from formal financial services. In addition, economic informality of large parts of the population reduces both the demand for and the supply of financial services. Among nonstructural variables, the absence of an adequate legal, contractual, and institutional environment or persistent macroeconomic instability can explain a low frontier. For instance, limited capacity to enforce contracts and poor protection of property rights can discourage long-term investments and arms-length financial contracting. Persistent macroeconomic instability can prevent deepening of markets for long-term financing.

A financial system can also lie below the frontier—that is, below the constrained maximum defined by state variables—as a result of demand-side constraints, supply-side constraints, or both. Demand-side constraints can arise if, for instance, the number of loan applicants is too low because of self-exclusion (because of lack of financial literacy, for example) or a lack of viable investment projects in the economy (as a result of short-term macro-economic uncertainty, for example). Supply constraints affecting idiosyncratic risks or artificially pushing up costs of financial service provision might hold the financial system below the frontier.[4] For instance, lack of competition or regulatory restrictions might prevent financial institutions and market players from reaching out to new clientele or introducing new products and services. Regulatory barriers can prevent deepening of certain market segments, as can weak systems of credit information sharing or opacity of financial information about firms.

The financial system can move beyond the frontier, indicating an unsustainable expansion of the financial system beyond its fundamentals. For instance, boom–bust cycles in economies can occur in the wake of excessive investment and risk-taking (often facilitated by loose monetary policy) by market participants. Experience from past banking crises suggests that credit booms and subsequent busts typically occur in environments characterized by poorly defined regulatory and supervisory frameworks. As underscored by the global financial crisis, financial innovation and regulatory ease can foster rapid deepening, but they also pose challenges for financial stability.[5] Fragility in many developing countries is often linked to governance problems: overshooting of the financial possibility frontier may be related to limited supervisory and market discipline.

In summary, the concept of the financial possibility frontier clearly illustrates that there can be too much of a good thing—finance—and that more finance is not always better, especially if it implies moving beyond the sustainable frontier.

3. Finance and Poverty: The Channels

Financial deepening affects societal outcomes, especially poverty alleviation, through various mechanisms: recent evidence shows that financial deepening is not only pro-growth but also pro-poor. Beck, Demirgüç-Kunt, and Levine (2007) show that countries with higher levels of financial development experience faster reductions in income inequality and poverty levels. Clarke, Xu,

---

[4] Lack of private sector participation could also result from other frictions in the economy. Barriers to doing business, tax distortions that discourage firm growth, and direct subsidies to industries and sectors are examples of distortions complementary to credit market frictions that constrain participation.

[5] See Beck, Chen, Lin, and Song (2012) for evidence on the bright and dark sides of financial innovation.

and Zou (2006) show a negative relationship between financial sector development and the level of poverty. At the country level, Beck, Levine, and Levkov (2010) show that branch deregulation across U.S. states in the 1970s and 1980s helped reduce income inequality. Giné and Townsend (2004) show that financial liberalization can explain the reduction in poverty in Thailand. Ayyagari, Beck, and Hoseini (2013) show that financial deepening following the 1991 liberalization explains reductions in rural poverty across India. Given that changes in poverty can be decomposed into changes caused by growth and changes caused by movements in income inequality, this evidence suggests that financial sector development is not only pro-growth but also pro-poor. Unlike other policy areas, which might have opposing effects on growth and equity, financial sector development does not present such concerns. But how does finance help reduce poverty? Much attention has focused on increasing access to financial services. However, theory and empirical work also point to important indirect effects through labor markets.

Theory provides possible channels for both a direct and an indirect impact of financial deepening on poverty reduction. On the one hand, providing access to credit to the poor may help them overcome financing constraints and allow them to invest in microenterprises and human capital accumulation (see Galor and Zeira 1993; Galor and Moav 2004). On the other hand, there may be indirect effects through enterprise credit. By expanding credit to existing and new enterprises and allocating society's savings more efficiently, financial systems can expand the formal economy and pull larger segments of the population into the formal labor market.

Initial empirical explorations of the channels through which finance affects income inequality and poverty levels point to an important role of such indirect effects. Specifically, evidence from the United States, India, and Thailand suggests that an important effect of financial sector deepening on income inequality and poverty is indirect. By changing the structure of the economy and allowing more entry into the labor market of previously un- or underemployed segments of the population, finance helps reduce income inequality and poverty, but not by giving access to credit to everyone (see Beck, Levine, and Levkov 2010; Giné and Townsend 2004; Ayyagari, Beck, and Hoseini 2013). This finding is also consistent with cross-country evidence that financial deepening is positively associated with employment growth in developing countries (Pagano and Pica 2012).

These findings are in contrast to more ambiguous results on the effect of expanding access to credit to households and microenterprises. As surveyed by Karlan and Morduch (2009), some studies find a positive effect whereas others find insignificant effects, with some studies showing different results depending on the econometric method being used. More recent evidence points to important differential effects across borrowers of different characteristics

(Banerjee and others 2010), with households that are inclined to become entrepreneurs more likely to do so with improved access to credit or savings services and households that are not so inclined more likely to increase consumption.

4. Conclusions

The recent literature and the recent and (at least in Europe) still ongoing crisis has taught us important lessons about the impact of the financial sector on the real sector. Going forward, it is important to move away from the idea that finance is good or bad, instead trying to harness the positive forces of the financial sector while mitigating its risks. A conceptual framework that combines the bright and dark sides of finance can be useful in this discussion. In the context of the discussion of the societal impact of financial deepening, it is important to look beyond direct effects to indirect effects of financial deepening on labor and goods markets, and the structural transformation that financial deepening can cause.

References

Arcand, Jean-Louis, Enrico Berkes, and Ugo Panizza. 2011. "Too Much Finance?" IMF Working Paper, International Monetary Fund, Washington, DC.

Aghion, Philippe, Peter Howitt, and David Mayer-Foulkes. 2005. "The Effect of Financial Development on Convergence: Theory and Evidence." *Quarterly Journal of Economics* 120: 173–222.

Ayyagari, Meghana, Thorsten Beck, and Mohamad Hoseini. 2013. "Finance and Poverty: Evidence from India." CEPR Discussion Paper, Center for Economic Policy Research, Washington, DC.

Banerjee, Abhijit, Esther Duflo, Rachel Glennerster, and Cynthia Kinan. 2010. "The Miracle of Microfinance? Evidence from a Randomized Experiment." MIT Working Paper, Department of Economics, Cambridge, MA.

Barajas, Adolfo, Thorsten Beck, Era Dabla-Norris, and Reza Yousefi. 2013. "Too Cold? Too Hot? Or Just Right? Assessing Financial Sector Development across the Globe." IMF Working Paper 13/81, International Monetary Fund, Washington, DC.

Beck, Thorsten, Berrak Buyukkarabacak, Felix Rioja, and Neven Valev. 2012. "Who Gets the Credit? And Does It Matter? Household vs. Firm Lending Across Countries." *B.E. Journal of Macroeconomics* 12 (1): 1–46.

Beck, Thorsten, Tao Chen, Chen Lin, and Frank Song. 2012. "Financial Innovation: The Bright and the Dark Sides." Working Paper, Tilburg University, the Netherlands.

Beck, Thorsten, and Augusto de la Torre. 2007. "The Basic Analytics of Access to Financial Service." *Financial Markets, Institution and Instruments* 17: 79–117.

Beck, Thorsten, Hans Degryse, and Christiane Kneer. 2014. "Is More Finance Better? Disentangling Intermediation and Size Effects of Financial Systems." *Journal of Financial Stability* 10: 50–64.

Beck, Thorsten, Asli Demirgüç-Kunt, and Ross Levine. 2007. "Finance, Inequality and the Poor." *Journal of Economic Growth* 12: 27–49.

Beck, Thorsten, Ross Levine, and Alexey Levkov. 2010. "Big Bad Banks? The Winners and Losers from Bank Deregulation in the United States." *Journal of Finance* 65 (5): 1637–67.

Bolton, Patrick, Tano Santos, and Jose Scheinkman. 2011. "Cream Skimming in Financial Markets." NBER Working Paper 16804, National Bureau of Economic Research, Cambridge, MA.

Claessens, S., G. Dobos, D. Klingebiel, and L. Laeven. 2003. "The Growing Importance of Networks in Finance and Its Effects of Competition." In *Innovations in Financial and Economic Networks*, ed. A. Nagurney, 110–35. Northampton, MA: Edward Elgar Publishers.

Clarke, George R. G., Lixin Colin Xu, and Heng-fu Zou. 2006. "Finance and Income Inequality: What Do the Data Tell Us?" *Southern Economic Journal* 72 (3): 578–96.

De Gregorio, José. 1996. "Borrowing Constraints, Human Capital Accumulation, and Growth." *Journal of Monetary Economics* 37: 49–71.

Demirgüç-Kunt, Asli, and Harry Huizinga. 2010. "Bank Activity and Funding Strategies: The Impact on Risk and Return." *Journal of Financial Economics* 98: 626–50.

Galor, Oded, and Omer Moav. 2004. "From Physical to Human Capital Accumulation: Inequality and the Process of Development." *Review of Economic Studies* 71 (October): 1001–26.

Galor, Oded, and Joseph Zeira. 1993 "Income Distribution and Macroeconomics." *Review of Economic Studies* 60: 35–52.

Giné, Xavier, and Robert M. Townsend. 2004. "Evaluation of Financial Liberalization: A General Equilibrium Model with Constrained Occupation Choice." *Journal of Development Economics* 74: 269–307.

Jappelli, Tullio, and Marco Pagano. 1994. "Saving, Growth, and Liquidity Constraints." *Quarterly Journal of Economics* 109: 83–109.

Karlan, Dean, and Jonathan Morduch. 2010. "Access to Finance." In *Handbook of Development Economics*, vol. 5, ed. Dani Rodrik and Mark Rosenzweig, 4703–84. Amsterdam: Elsevier.

Pagano, Marco, and Giovanni Pica. 2012. "Finance and Employment." *Economic Policy* 27: 5–55.

Phillipon, Thomas, 2010 "Financiers vs. Engineers: Should the Financial Sector be Taxed or Subsidized?" *American Economic Journal: Macroeconomics* 2 (3): 158–82.

Rioja, Felix, and Neven Valev. 2004a. "Does One Size Fit All? A Reexamination of the Finance and Growth Relationship." *Journal of Development Economics* 74: 429–47.

Rioja, Felix, and Neven Valev. 2004b. "Finance and the Sources of Growth at Various Stages of Economic Development." *Economic Inquiry* 42 (1): 127–40.

6

Resource Depletion, Climate Change, and Economic Growth

Andrew Steer

Natural resources are an essential input in the production process. This is true for marketed resources (such as metals, minerals, and land) and nonmarketed resources (such as clean air, weather, and myriad ecosystem services). Over the past century, as the global population quadrupled and economic production increased about 20-fold, demand for natural resources rose greatly. The extraction of construction materials grew by a factor of 34, ores and minerals by a factor of 27 (UNEP 2011a). The human footprint on the natural world is now vastly greater than ever before. In a real sense, we have moved from a relatively empty world to a full one. For the first time, the scale of the human footprint has grown to the extent that human economic activity has the power to influence major planetary systems, prompting some scientists to note that we may be moving into a new epoch, from Holocene to "Anthropocene."

It is now four decades since the Club of Rome's famous report *Limits to Growth*. The economics profession was generally critical at the time, noting the report's massive underestimation of the power of price effects, substitution, and new technology. Although economists appeared vindicated, at least then, a growing number in the profession are now questioning whether there are indeed limits to growth.

In assessing the two-way relationship between economic growth and the natural world, it is important to distinguish market resources, for which price

The author is grateful to Nicholas Bianco and Aaron Holdway, research associates at the World Resources Institute, for research support; to Sara Nawaz, a research assistant at the World Resources Institute, for assistance in the publication process; and to Franklin Allen, Jere Behrman, Nancy Birdsall, Shahrokh Fardoust, Jennifer Morgan, Jeremy Oppenheim, Theophilos Priovolos, Janet Ranganathan, Dani Rodrik, and Arvind Subramanian for valuable comments.

signals prompt substitution, from nonmarketed resources. Many resources—forests, soils, and water quality, for example—have elements that lie within the market system and elements that lie outside it. Forests, for example, provide marketed resources, such as timber, as well as an array of nonmarketed services, such as climate regulation, soil creation, and erosion control. It is also necessary to distinguish externalities that are primarily local or national from those that are global. Currently, it is global problems that pose the greatest threat. But fresh questions are also being raised about whether the pace of growth in the demand for marketed natural resources is now so rapid that technologies for substitution will not emerge quickly enough, causing rising commodity prices and supply interruptions to limit further economic growth, jeopardizing development aspirations.

In this chapter, the term *resource depletion* is used to refer to all natural resources: marketed, nonmarketed, and those in between. The place of climate change in resource depletion may not be intuitive to some, as the upper atmosphere may not appear as a natural resource of relevance to the production system. In fact, the atmosphere, and the climate it influences, is among the most valuable of all natural resources. Because climate change is the greatest and most complex problem to solve, it is the primary focus of this chapter. Further, if climate change can be successfully addressed, other resource problems will be easier to solve, providing another reason for this focus.

This chapter seeks to shed light on the following questions:

1. Are current patterns of growth sustainable throughout the twenty-first century?
2. With current and expected technology, are alternative paths available that will allow healthy rates of growth into the indefinite future? Will the economy automatically tend towards greener paths as problems become ever more evident?
3. Does new understanding of "green growth" offer new opportunities for spurring economic growth as well as improving the quality of life?
4. What are the implications of the above for policy at the national and international levels, particularly for climate change?

6.1 Are Current Patterns of Growth Sustainable?

Evidence suggests that current patterns of energy and resource use, agricultural practices, and urbanization will lead to increased costs and decreased productivity that will reduce growth, as conventionally measured, with sharp, unpredictable threshold effects likely. The impact will be felt differentially across countries. Environmental damage already imposes a deadweight loss to the economy approaching 10 percent of gross domestic product (GDP) in many emerging economies—even before adding likely impacts from climate change (World Bank 2012a). Moreover, the costs of resource depletion will not be borne equally. The bottom half of the income distribution—both across and within countries—will suffer most from the direct effects, which will include higher prices of food, fuel, and fiber, and lower rates of growth and job creation.

6.1.1 Impacts of Resource Depletion Today

The pace and scale of environmental damage has been well documented. More than one quarter of the world's land surface has been degraded as a result of soil erosion, salinization, nutrient depletion, and desertification (Bai et al. 2008). Water withdrawals tripled in the past 50 years, leading to water scarcity and groundwater depletion. In developing countries, withdrawals are projected to increase by another 50 percent by 2030, by which time more than 5 billion people—two-thirds of the world's population—could be living in areas facing moderate to severe water stress (WRI forthcoming).

Growth has also strained ecosystems. Roughly 60 percent of the world's ecosystem services are now of lower quality than they were 50 years ago (Millennium Ecosystem Assessment 2005), the current rate of species extinction is 100–1,000 times higher than in prehuman days (IUCN 2004), and all of the planet's 13 hottest years on record have occurred since 1997 (WMO 2013).[1]

The economic cost of such damage is significant. In China, for example, air pollution alone is estimated to cost the equivalent of 3.8 percent of GDP per year (Cropper 2010). Figure 6.1 summarizes the estimated costs of environmental damage across a range of countries. The bulk of these costs come from pollution and the associated health and productivity costs. Such estimates generally do not place monetary values on more complex issues, such as the loss of biodiversity or the degradation of ecosystem services. They are also generally based only on current costs, ignoring future and less certain costs, such as the costs of climate change.

Evidence is growing that the human cost of environmental damage is very high. Some estimates suggest that carbon-intensive growth is already responsible for about 5 million deaths a year—400,000 as a result of hunger and

---

[1] The year 2012 broke yet more records. It was the 36th consecutive year in which global temperatures were above the average for the previous century and the hottest year in U.S. history (DeConcini and Thompson 2013).

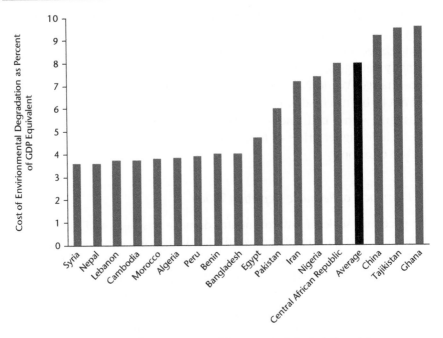

Figure 6.1 Annual Cost of Environmental Damage in Selected Countries
Source: Data from World Bank 2012a.

communicable diseases exacerbated by climate change and 4.5 million as a result of associated air pollution (DARA and the Climate Forum 2012).

The costs of environmental damage can have major impacts on economic production. They include, for example, the impacts on agriculture from the rise in temperature and the increase in the frequency and severity of extreme weather events (not necessarily caused by climate change but made much more likely by it). The drought in the United States that began in 2012 is expected to cost 1 percent of GDP; it may be the most costly natural disaster in U.S. history. The combination of adverse climate and rapidly growing demand has led to sharply higher food prices over the past few years. The spike in food prices in the second half of 2010 alone was estimated to have driven more than 40 million people into poverty.[2]

The rise in food prices mirrors a more general trend in commodity prices. The past century saw a broad decline in overall commodity prices (except for energy)—an astonishing fact given that real incomes and consumption rose by a factor of 20. But such gains were fully reversed during the first decade of the current century (Figure 6.2). It is too early to say whether this change

---

[2] Some recent analysis suggests greater resilience on the part of the poor, with a smaller overall impact (IFPRI 2013).

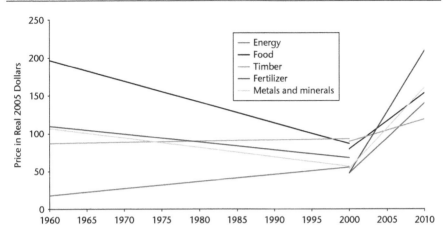

Figure 6.2 World Prices of Selected Commodities, 1960–2010: From Abundance to Scarcity?

Source: World Resources Institute analysis, based on 2012 World Bank data.

represents a permanent upward shift, but a growing number of analysts are concluding that it does. Prices are not only higher; they are also more variable and more highly correlated with one another than at any time over the past century (McKinsey 2011).

6.1.2 Measuring Sustainability

Whether current patterns of economic activity are "sustainable" depends on the extent to which depletion of natural forms of capital can be (and is) compensated by the accumulation of other forms of capital, especially human and fabricated capital.[3] Efforts have been made to assess such sustainability, albeit with a limited array of natural assets. Arrow et al. (2010) analyze this question for the United States and China. They find that in both countries, the accumulation of (especially human) capital has more than compensated for high levels of resource depletion. Given the massive scale of resource depletion and environmental damage in China, this finding may seem surprising. But given its rate of investment and the limited range of environmental assets included in the analysis (basically extractive resources, forests, and soils), the results are to be expected. The authors recognize the limitations of such analysis. Estimates address a limited range of natural assets,

---

[3] The "Hartwick Rule" (Hartwick 1977; Solow 1986) provides a rule of thumb for resource-dependent economies. It shows that if the rents from nonrenewable resources are invested rather than consumed, consumption over time can be sustained. For an overview of the sustainability of growth, see Heal (2010).

Table 6.1 Distribution of per Capita Wealth by Type of Capital and Country Income Level, 2005

Country income level	Total per capita wealth ($)	Produced capital	Intangible capital[a]	Natural capital
Low	6,138	13	57	30
Lower-middle	16,903	24	51	25
Upper-middle	81,903	16	69	15
High-income	588,315	17	81	2
Total	120,475	18	77	5

a. Intangible capital comprises human and institutional capital.
Source: World Bank 2011a.

assume a high (and probably unrealistic) degree of substitutability among different forms of capital, and do not include, in any real depth, uncertainty or the risk of threshold effects or catastrophic, irreversible change.[4]

Led by the World Bank, researchers have tried to measure national capital stocks, including manmade, human, and natural stocks, in order to assess the extent to which the inclusion of natural capital affects the direction and pace of change of the overall productive capacity of the economy, and hence its prospects for sustained rising consumption and welfare levels. The importance of natural capital—narrowly defined to include metals, minerals, soils, and forests—is much greater in lower-income countries than in richer countries, accounting for an estimated 30 percent of total wealth in low-income countries but only 2 percent in high-income countries (Table 6.1).

This difference helps explain why poorer countries are more vulnerable to resource depletion than richer countries, and why the sustainability stakes may be even higher for developing countries than more-developed countries.[5] Compensation for the depletion of natural capital by increases in other forms of capital is likely to be easier where the share of natural capital is smaller. Particularly striking from Table 6.1 is the importance of "intangible" capital (encompassing human and institutional capital), which accounts for more than 80 percent of total wealth in rich countries. The importance of intangible capital suggests how important it is that developing countries reinvest income from natural resources into these assets. It also perhaps warns against assumptions of high substitutability between natural and intangible assets.[6]

---

[4] See, for example, Hamilton (2010), who provides a theoretical framework for sustainability using the concept of "genuine savings." He points out that estimates of sustainability are based on assumptions about the future that may turn out to be too optimistic.

[5] These estimates are narrow; taking the impacts of climate change into account, for example, would change this weighting. Indeed, including the monetized value of a stable climate as a productive asset would change these percentages substantially.

[6] The "Hartwick Rule" (Hartwick 1977; Solow 1986) provides a simple rule of thumb for sustainable development in countries that depend on nonrenewable natural resources. It holds that consumption can be maintained—the definition of sustainable development—if the rents from

One approach to assessing the sustainability of countries' development paths is to measure the rate of "genuine savings" by adjusting the rate of savings to take account of resource depletion (and the accumulation of human capital). For low-income countries, especially those dependent on natural resource exploitation, the picture is not encouraging. Calculations show that genuine savings in Sub-Saharan Africa became negative in 2004 and remained highly negative throughout the decade, implying that consumption levels were not sustainable (World Bank 2011a).

About 30 countries have now institutionalized such "natural wealth" accounting, although most of them focus almost exclusively on the depletion of mineral and energy assets rather than on a more complete set of resources, including forests, clean water and air, and ecosystem services. In 2013, at the Rio + 20 UN Summit, more than 50 countries and 85 major institutions signed up to a Natural Capital Declaration, committing to revising their accounts to incorporate nature. This commitment builds on a growing call for revisions in the way nations and corporations report their assets and income (Stiglitz, Sen, and Fitoussi 2009).[7]

6.1.3 Impacts of Natural Resource Depletion in the Future

A number of drivers suggest that the impacts of natural resource depletion will accelerate in the future, especially for resources outside or only partially within the marketplace, such as water, soil, ecosystem services, and climate. An increase in the world population of more than 2 billion people between 2010 and 2050 will place additional pressures on natural resources. The impacts will be magnified because the increased population will be located primarily in cities, often in low-lying areas vulnerable to storm surges, and in vulnerable agricultural areas (see chapter 3, by Behrman and Kohler).

Although environmental stresses brought about by population growth are significant, rising incomes will be of even greater impact. During the two decades since 1990, the size of the global middle class rose from 1 billion to 2 billion (as defined by the OECD as having purchasing power parity per capita income of $3,000–$15,000). In the coming two decades, it is probable that another 3 billion will join the middle class (OECD 2011; McKinsey 2011).[8] This transition—in which the majority of the world will be able to afford

nonrenewable resources are continuously invested rather than used for consumption. Many resource-rich developing countries do not reinvest the rents.

[7] Efforts to incorporate environmental assets and liabilities in financial statements of companies are gaining momentum. In 2011, Puma became the first company to seek to fully value its environmental impacts in its financial statements. Other major companies are following.

[8] Nearly 90 percent of this increase is projected in the Asia Pacific region. The OECD projects that global per capita average incomes will rise 4.7 percent a year during the period. See Kharas (2010) for a review of the emerging middle class in the developing world.

a private motor vehicle,[9] modern appliances, and a diet that includes meat daily—represents an important threshold in human pressure on the natural world.

6.2 The Unique Challenge of Climate Change

Climate change is among the greatest and most difficult challenges facing the world today. A number of characteristics—its global nature, its intergenerational impact, the uncertainty and massive downside risks associated with it—combine to make it an unparalleled challenge of global collective action.

Climate change is also highly significant in that successfully addressing it will go a very long way toward addressing other environmental problems. Efforts to deal with air pollution, water risks, soil degradation, and the loss of forests, natural habitats, and biodiversity will benefit greatly from actions to address climate change. These spillover effects provide another reason for focusing attention on climate.

The atmospheric concentration of carbon dioxide (CO_2) has risen from about 285 parts per million (ppm) in the preindustrial era to 400 ppm today.[10] To have a 50 percent chance of limiting average temperature rise to 2°C above preindustrial levels (the target maximum increase negotiated under the United Nations Framework Convention on Climate Change), atmospheric CO_2 concentrations need to remain below 450 ppm. Achieving this goal is a receding possibility; meeting it would require global greenhouse gas emissions to peak by 2020 and then fall to 50 percent of today's levels by 2050 (including an 80–90 percent reduction from current levels in industrial countries). Current trends suggest that concentrations could reach 700 ppm by the end of this century, implying a mean temperature increase of about 5°C. Such temperatures have not occurred for 30 million years.

The impact of climate change on economic activity has been studied for the past two decades (Tol 2009). Estimates of impact vary greatly, depending on the assumptions made about the scale of warming, the pathways through which the impact takes place, and the costs of adaptation.

---

[9] Most projections suggest a motor vehicle fleet of almost 2 billion by 2030, up from 800 million in 2010 (Dargay, Gately, and Sommer 2007).

[10] Concentrations of greenhouse gas emissions controlled under the Kyoto Protocol were measured at 444 ppm CO_2e in 2010. If all greenhouse gas emissions are measured, including aerosols, which have a cooling property, the figure is about 400 ppm CO_2e (European Environment Agency 2013).

Climate change can affect economic activity through four principal paths:

- increases in temperature and the associated impacts on agriculture, energy demand, disease, and so forth;

- rises in sea level and the associated threat to infrastructure and production capacity, especially in urban areas;

- increased intensity of extreme weather events and the associated destruction of infrastructure and agriculture;

- shifts in the hydrological cycle and the associated impacts on agriculture, power and industrial systems, and drinking water.

The most complete models seek to account for all of these channels. Few modeling efforts claim to do a thorough job on all four, however, and fewer still address the kinds of multiplicative interactions described later in this chapter.

The Stern Review (Stern 2006, pp. vi–vii), which remains the iconic statement on the costs of climate change, reached the following conclusion:

> Using the results from formal economic models, the Review estimates that if we don't act, the overall costs and risks of climate change will be equivalent to losing at least 5 percent of global GDP each year, now and forever. If a wider range of risks and impacts is taken into account, the estimates of damage could rise to 20 percent of GDP or more. In contrast, the costs of action—reducing greenhouse gas emissions to avoid the worst impacts of climate change—can be limited to about 1 percent of global GDP each year.

All researchers estimating the impacts of climate change would acknowledge that uncertainties exist from many sources, including the impact of atmospheric carbon intensity on climate (including the possibility of discontinuities), the impacts of climate change on production processes, and the technological ability of production processes to adapt to such impacts. Although there is great variance around the mean, most researchers would probably agree with the following statements:

- It will be difficult to limit the average increase in global temperature to 2°C above preindustrial levels, as the countries of the world agreed to do at Cancun in 2010. Global greenhouse gas emissions would need to peak by about 2020 to have a good chance of achieving this goal. Given that no global agreement will be in effect this decade, this is unlikely. Instead, an average temperature increase of 2°C–5°C should be assumed to be the most likely estimate during this century.

- The first-round economic impact of climate change, estimated in terms of costs as a share of GDP, varies greatly, from 1 percent to 10 percent for a 3°C increase in warming and up to 20 percent for a 5°C increase. The estimates are substantial in absolute terms but relatively modest compared with the projected growth of the global economy. They are also large compared with the cost of addressing the impacts of climate change.

- Costs vary greatly by geography, with benefits in some high-latitude countries and much higher costs closer to the Equator. Tropical countries, which tend to have higher rates of poverty, will generally be more affected than cold climate countries. For a 2°C warming scenario, it is estimated that about 75–80 percent of the impact would fall on developing countries.[11]

- The probabilities of estimates being wrong are highly asymmetrical, especially when larger temperature increases are assumed. Discontinuities triggered by ice melt, tropical forest dieback, ocean acidification, and other events would all multiply the impacts substantially.

There is a growing sense that current modeling techniques do not do justice to the seriousness of the problem, for two reasons. First, they fail to take into account the interaction of risks, which can multiply the drag on growth and the quality of life. Second, as temperature increases rise above 2°C, the smooth-line assumptions of most models are no longer tenable.

6.2.1 Risk Interaction and Multiplication

Interaction among the various stressors makes the future highly uncertain and highly risky. Consider, for example, water and its links to food production and energy supply. Water shortages pose serious threats to food and energy security in the decades ahead:

- Global water models suggest a sharp increase in water-related risks over the coming decades, as demand for water doubles. Water will become scarcer in some areas (with scarcity likely to increase where there is already a shortfall), and floods and droughts will become both more extreme and less predictable. A recent corporate survey found that more than 50 percent of Global 500 respondents report that water risks are already adversely affecting their profitability. Figure 6.3, mapped with the World Resource Institute's Aqueduct model, a major tool for mapping water risk, presents the best current scientific estimates of water stress in 2040.

[11] Some researchers have sought to identify direct relationships between temperature and income levels. Dell, Jones, and Olken (2009) estimate that a 1°C increase in a given year reduced economic growth that year by about 1.1 percentage points in poor countries while having no discernible effect on growth in rich countries.

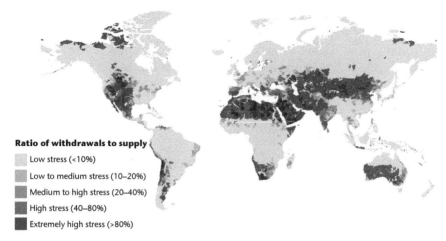

Figure 6.3 Predicted Water Stress in 2040
Source: World Resources Institute 2014.

- Food production will need to increase by nearly 70 percent by 2050, implying broadly the same rate of production growth as in the past 40 years, when Green Revolution technologies and the massive expansion of irrigated and rain-fed crop land fueled growth. Agriculture already accounts for 70 percent of all freshwater withdrawals from rivers, lakes, and aquifers; achieving the required additional growth will demand vast amounts of additional water. This increased demand is likely to coincide with a shrinkage in availability, even for existing irrigated areas in Asia, and much more variable rainfall in much of Africa, all at a time when rising temperatures will reduce yields in the tropics and subtropics. A rough rule of thumb suggests that absent adaptive strategies, every 1°C in temperature rise will reduce productivity by 10 percent. According to the current best understanding of the impacts of climate change on agricultural yields of a 3°C average increase in global temperature (now rapidly becoming a central estimate), impacts will be intense. To add to the challenge, agriculture currently accounts for about 24 percent of global greenhouse gas emissions (from methane emissions from livestock and rice paddies and nitrous oxide emissions from fertilizers, soil erosion, and agriculture-induced changes in land use). These emissions will need to be reduced dramatically if climate change is to be addressed.

- Primary energy demand will rise by an estimated one-third over the next 20 years, with growth especially high in Asia and Africa. Energy security is increasingly dependent on plentiful and reliable water supplies. Hydropower is already vulnerable in many parts of the world. The development of shale gas and coal-powered generation is highly dependent on water supplies. For a country like China, which will account for 40 percent of all new planned generation from coal in the coming years (Figure 6.4) and which faces increasingly severe water shortages, such dependence poses a serious threat to economic security. Current models fail to capture the scale of such risks.

6.2.2 Threshold Effects

There is growing recognition that both physical and economic models have seriously underestimated the risks of climate change. Inability to model critical tipping points, such as major ice melting (leading to sharp increases in sea level) or permafrost melting (leading to massive leakage of methane and a sharp acceleration of climate change), has meant that these impacts have implicitly been zero when translated into economic models. This failure was less important when it appeared that increases in temperatures might be kept to a maximum of 2°C. Now that realistic expectations are for a 3°C–5°C increase, such omissions may prove fatal in encouraging complacency in policymaking.

To illustrate this point, when global average temperatures were last 3°C warmer than today (3–5 million years ago), sea levels were 20 meters higher than they are today (Miller et al. 2012). Such an increase would take several centuries to occur, but once started it would be irreversible. Such potential impacts are almost totally lacking from current models. Even absent any ice melting, current best estimates suggest an increase in sea level of 1–2 meters during the current century. When combined with increased storm surges, this increase may require relocating hundreds of millions of people, with the biggest impact on the poor (Nichols et al. 2011).

Such tipping points may apply not only to sea level rise but also to shifts in the hydrological cycle. Whether through shifts in the monsoon pattern in Asia or self-reinforcing forest dieback in the Amazon, impacts on food production and other ecosystem services are largely missing from current models. The growing awareness of such threats is leading to a call for a new generation of models (Stern 2013), in which a range of probabilities are assigned to these very high-cost outcomes.

6.3 The Prospects for Greener Growth

With current and expected technology, are alternative paths available that will allow healthy rates of growth into the indefinite future?

Evidence suggests that it is possible to decouple environmental damage from growth, decarbonize production, use resources more efficiently, farm

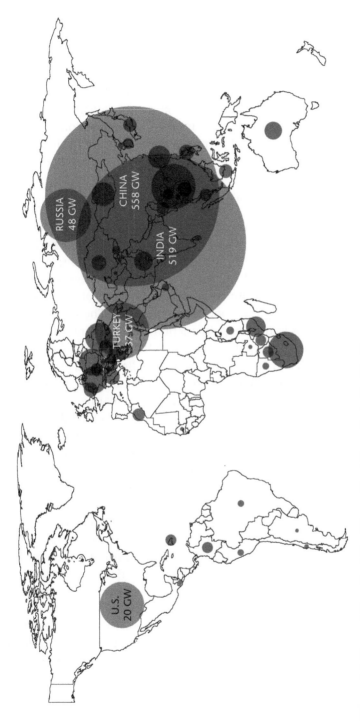

Figure 6.4 Planned New Coal-Fired Power Plant Capacity in the World

Note: Figure incorporates 1,200 new plants currently proposed.

Source: World Resources Institute 2012.

differently, and design smarter urban infrastructure at a reasonable cost (1–3 percent of GDP per year). Traditional models suggest that such action would result in a modest reduction in the rate of overall economic growth, at least in the short run. More recent analysis, in which technological change is endogenous, suggests that the impact on growth could even be positive.

Moving from current to "greener" paths will require two interrelated transitions. The first is the decoupling of environmental damage and growth (a special case relates to climate change and the decarbonization of the economy). The second transition will involve a major increase in the efficiency with which resources are used and reused in the production process.

6.3.1 Decoupling Economic Growth from Environmental Damage

Since the early 1990s, there has been a lively empirical and theoretical debate over the existence of environmental Kuznets curves (that is, whether environmental damage first rises with income levels and then falls; World Bank 1992; Grossman and Krueger 1993). For some forms of damage—local pollutants with well-understood health costs and modest costs of abatement—the evidence appears to strongly support the hypothesis. The mechanism can involve citizens' voices leading to public action, or it can simply be the result of compositional shifts in output and advances in technology (Andreoni and Levinson 2001; Brock and Taylor 2005; Smulders, Bretschger, and Egli 2011). History is full of examples of environmental crises leading to tipping points in public and official opinion and rapid action, in a manner that would not have occurred at lower income levels. The "Great Stink" of London in 1858—in which the extreme odor, new knowledge about cholera, and new sanitary technology led to major legislation being passed through Parliament in just 18 days for the construction of a sewerage system—was among the most dramatic but by no means the first or last case in modern history.

Global and longer-term challenges show a much weaker tendency, as a result of the absence of paths for citizen voices to be heard, weaker knowledge, and the need to allocate costs among competing nations. Consider the case of East Asia, which has been growing faster than any other region. Simple air pollution (PM_{10}) has been decreasing there since 1990, even as real output has risen more than fourfold. In many places, levels are still well above those recommended by the World Health Organization but are declining (Figure 6.5).[12] Indeed, it can legitimately be argued that growth has enabled and created the demand for progress. Figure 6.6 shows a counterintuitive acceleration of progress on reducing particulates during periods of high growth. One has

[12] Other forms of pollution, such as $PM_{2.5}$, remain at record levels in some cities, and as the air pollution crisis in China indicates, one should not count on any automatic tendency for a solution to pollution.

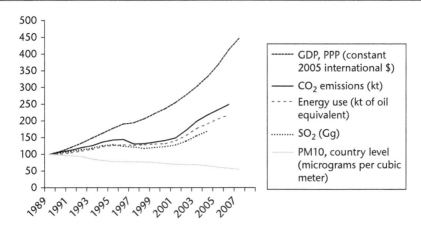

Figure 6.5 Air Pollution, Energy Use, and GDP in the East Asia and Pacific Region, 1990–2008

Source: Author's own calculation, based on World Bank data.

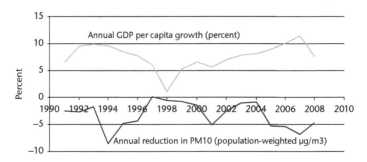

Figure 6.6 Faster Growth, Lower Pollution? Particulates and Economic Growth in the East Asia and Pacific Region, 1990–2007

Source: Author's own calculation, based on World bank data.

to be careful not to read too much into these data, but there is strong evidence that higher growth makes resources available to invest in pollution control.

As might be expected, this pattern is less evident for pollutants that cost more to address and for which the health impact is less severe. Figure 6.5 shows that reductions in sulfur dioxide emissions, for example, have been much less pronounced in East Asia, although they may be approaching an inflexion point. Chinese sulfur dioxide emissions, which account for a quarter of the global total, increased at an annual growth rate of 7 percent between 2000 and 2006, as a result of the massive expansion in coal-fired power plants. Since 2006, sulfur dioxide emissions have begun to decrease, because of flue-gas desulfurization and the closing of small inefficient units (Lu et al. 2010). This trend has been induced mainly by government policies aimed at reaching the targets set in China's 11th (2006–10) and 12th

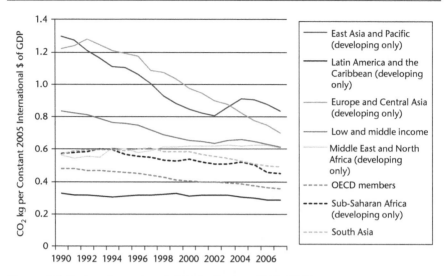

Figure 6.7 Carbon Intensity of GDP, by Region, 1990–2007
Source: Author's own calculations, based on World Bank data.

(2010–15) Five-Year Plans. This inflection point in China illustrates an important interaction between income, policy, and technology. Increased resources and the declining costs of technology made a major shift in the way power is generated attractive, but the change was facilitated only as a result of strong government policy (World Bank 2010).

The same principles underlie the use of energy. In 1990, East Asia used more energy to generate a unit of GDP than any other region in the world. In the past two decades, it made more progress than any other region, cutting energy intensity in half.

Parallel to the gains in energy efficiency has been the overall reduction in carbon intensity of East Asian economies—although these economies continue to exhibit the highest carbon dioxide emissions-to-GDP ratio of all regions (Figure 6.7). Driving a wedge between GDP and carbon dioxide emissions is a societal choice, as shown in Figure 6.8, which compares the recent trajectories of Denmark and China.

6.3.2 Decoupling Growth from Greenhouse Gas Emissions: Limitations of Cost–Benefit Analysis

The global nature of the externality, coupled with the perceived high cost of action and the long-term and uncertain nature of the impacts, may explain why greenhouse gases have shown no evidence of fitting within the environmental Kuznets curve framework. Estimates of the costs of addressing climate change depend not only on the depth and speed of cuts but also on

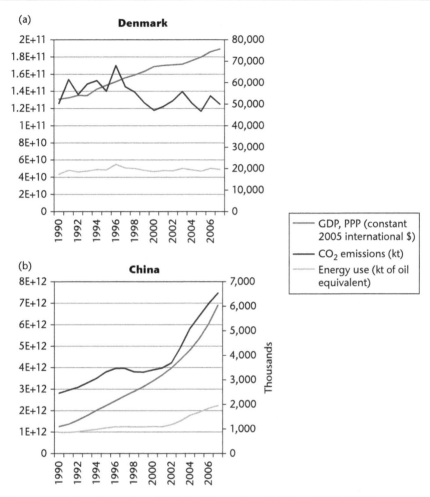

Figure 6.8 Carbon Intensity of GDP in Denmark and China, 1990–2005
Source: Author's own calculations, based on World Bank data.

numerous assumptions regarding technology and cost trends, substitution elasticities, and the like. The Stern Review estimated the costs of stabilizing greenhouse gas concentrations at 500–550 ppm CO_2e—which, according to the IPCC's Fourth Assessment (2007), would lead to an average temperature rise of about 3°C—to be in the order of 1 percent of GDP a year through 2050. It estimates the cost of stabilizing emissions at 450 ppm CO_2e (which would provide about a 50 percent probability of limiting average temperature rise to 2°C) at about three times greater.

Given the stock nature of the problem—that is, the fact that the problem slowly builds as the stock of greenhouse gas emissions rises—the time trajectory of emissions matters: each year of delayed action can raise costs. To limit atmospheric concentrations to 450 ppm, the allowable "emissions budget" from fossil fuels and land use change in the first half of the current century is about 1,440 gigatons (Meinshausen et al. 2009). Between 2000 and 2011, 420 gigatons were emitted, and another 136 gigatons from nonenergy sources is expected to be emitted through 2050, leaving an allowable budget of about 884 gigatons for 2012–50, or an average of about 23 gigatons per year. Current annual emissions are estimated at about 32 gigatons (IEA 2012a) and are still rising. Delaying action means that more will need to be done in the remaining years, with cost increases compounded as emissions are increasingly "locked in" as a result of ongoing infrastructure investments.

The Stern Review calculated the annual deadweight loss to the economy without estimating the impact on the growth rate. Other estimates, such as the *Environmental Outlook to 2050* (OECD 2012), explore the impacts on growth. Under an aggressive program to accelerate the energy and agricultural transformation and stabilize emissions at 450 ppm CO_2e, the OECD projects that the average annual world growth rate would decline from 3.5 percent in the baseline scenario to 3.3 percent, yielding a world GDP that is 5.5 percent lower in 2050 than under the baseline scenario. Stabilization at 550 ppm would cost as little as 1 percent of real income. Moreover, these numbers fail to take into account positive feedback impacts on growth from such policies. They thus likely overestimate the costs. The OECD report finds that the costs of inaction would reduce global consumption by 13 percent. It thus concludes that the proposed actions are warranted.

Conventional cost–benefit analysis yields results based on three sets of calculations: the future streams of benefits and costs of action and the discount rate that enables them to be compared. On all three sets of calculations, there may be a bias encouraging inadequate action on climate change. First, on the costs of climate change (the benefits of action), most calculations fail to account for the risk of catastrophic impacts. Weitzman (2009) suggests that this failure—and the difficulty of addressing such unknowable risks with existing tools—may render conventional analysis of little value. Second, an emerging literature suggests that although the costs of inaction may be seriously underestimated, the costs of action may be overestimated (as discussed later in the context of green growth). Third, ethicists and most economists differ regarding discount rates.

DISCOUNT RATES MATTER

The economic case for urgent action on climate change depends in most studies on low discount rates. The reason is clear: the worst impacts of climate change will occur decades from now, whereas the costs of action must begin in earnest today. The power of discounting is huge in affecting the weight given to future events. A discount rate of 6 percent makes a benefit of $100 a century from now worth only 25 cents today.

In the tradition of Frank Ramsey, the discount rate, r, is the sum of two components:

$$r = \delta + ng$$

where δ is the rate of pure time preference, g is the growth rate of per capita consumption, and η is the elasticity of marginal utility of consumption, measuring how much utility drops as consumption increases.

There have been disagreements on both components of the discount rate. One senses that the economics profession, aided by ethicists and philosophers, is moving toward acceptance of a lower (zero or near zero) pure rate of time preference, on the simple grounds that all generations should be treated equally. This intuitively ethical notion follows a long tradition of economic thought, including contributions by Frank Ramsey, Arthur Pigou, Roy Harrod, Robert Solow, James Mirrlees, and Amartya Sen (Stern 2008). Nonetheless, it represents a shift from mainstream economic theory (Nordhaus 2007; Weitzman 2007), which argues that such an assumption is inconsistent with observed savings behavior of individuals and that assuming a low rate will hurt future generations because it will result in less growth and less prosperity being available to them. The Stern Review argued that morality and common sense call for a pure rate of time preference very close to zero and assumed a rate of 0.1 percent (different from zero as a result of the small but not inconceivable possibility that future generations will not exist).

The second term in the discount rate identity reflects the fact that if future generations will be richer than the current one, there is less need to invest today for their benefit. Here, too, there are grounds for disagreement. The future path of income and consumption is often assumed to be independent of decisions made on climate change. But in the absence of action against climate change, it would be foolish to assume that future generations will be better off than the current one. In such circumstances, the second term in the Ramsey equation may need to be negative, giving greater weight to the future than the present, thereby making an irresistible case for strong, immediate action on climate change.

Another concern relates to distributional issues. Even if the average citizen in 2050 will be better off than today's average citizen, the impacts of climate change will be highly unequal, with the poor bearing the brunt. Compensation schemes from the richer to the poorer may be possible, but they will almost certainly not occur.

The Stern Review assumed per capita consumption growth of 1.3 percent and a unitary elasticity of utility with respect to consumption. Adding the two components yields a discount rate of 1.4 percent. This discount rate is much lower than the rates in traditional economic models, which can be as high as 6 percent, with huge implications for the overall result. Benefits of $100 a century from now, discounted to the present using a 1.4 percent rate, will be worth 100 times as much ($25) as when discounted by 6 percent (25 cents).

THREE REASONS TO RETHINK CONVENTIONAL WISDOM

Does new understanding of "green growth" offer new opportunities for economic growth as well as the quality of life? Are the costs of action on climate change, as conventionally measured, overestimated?

In the past few years, the concept of "green growth" has been popularized, in part replacing the concept of "sustainable development." At root, its distinctive insight is that environmental problems can be turned to good advantage. Smart environmental and growth policies combined can actually promote efficiency gains and technological advances, increase investment, and generate competitive advantage, the argument goes.

Belief in green growth may help explain why more than 50 developing countries are now imposing costs on themselves (through feed-in tariffs, renewable energy standards, and so forth) that at first sight seem not to be in their country's narrow interest. China, for example, introduced cap-and-trade policies for CO_2 emissions on a pilot basis in 2013, with a nationwide program planned for 2015. A large research agenda lies ahead in this field, with the issue of "green jobs" acting as a strong political impetus in many countries.

New empirical and theoretical insights suggest that economists need to rethink their models of how an economy adjusts to tighter environmental policies, for three main reasons:

1. Numerous win–win gains that would benefit both efficiency and the environment are being left unexploited, as a result of a range of barriers, rigidities, and market imperfections. New understanding from psychology and behavioral economics helps explain why these opportunities remain unexploited and how rising concerns about resource depletion can help unlock these constraints.

2. Smart, market-based environmental policies, coupled with public–private partnerships in technology research, can trigger innovation and investment that can create new markets, jobs, and economic growth.

3. Risks about the future impact of climate change, compounded by growing belief by the business community that policy action to address climate change will occur in the future, is leading to concerns about "stranded assets," a reduction in the appetite for investment, and a plea for a consistent long-term policy framework.

The three reasons are discussed in the next three sections. All argue for early action on climate change.

The first two mechanisms are illustrated by the marginal abatement cost curve shown in Figure 6.9. Beneath the horizontal axis are a range of

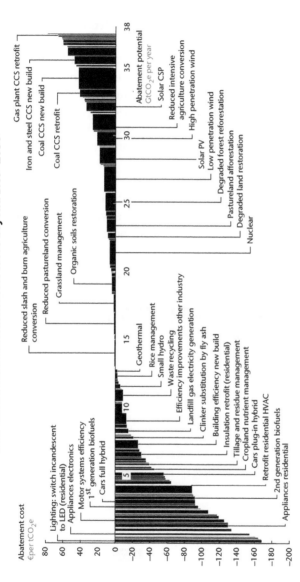

Figure 6.9 Estimated Costs of Abating Global Greenhouse Gas Emissions

Source: Exhibit from "Impact of the Financial Crisis on Carbon Economics: Version 2.1 of the Global Greenhouse Abatement Cost Curve," 2010, McKinsey & Company, www.mckinsey.com/insights. Reprinted by permission.

investments, much larger than earlier thought, that have positive returns independent of their benefits for the environment. These investments often remain largely unexploited. Investments in energy efficiency, which have been shown to have extremely high rates of return, are the iconic example of such opportunities. One-hundred-dollar bills are systematically left on the sidewalk as a result of a range of barriers associated with principal–agent issues, information gaps, operational policies of financial institutions, and so forth (Jaffe and Stavins 1994). These opportunities are not free; they require investment, but the investments pay for themselves in a commercial sense in the short run. When local environmental co-benefits, in the form of pollution reduction, are included, these investments become even more attractive (Figure 6.10). The urgency of acting on climate and environmental issues can help unlock some of the barriers preventing action.

RESOURCE EFFICIENCY
For many years it has been understood that efforts to improve resource efficiency will also benefit climate change and the environment (World Bank 1992; Steer 1992). But how much are these agendas overlapping, and how

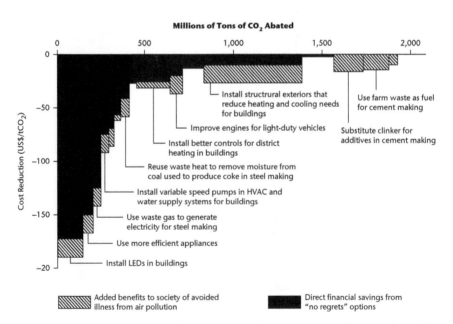

Figure 6.10 No-Regrets Options for Reducing CO_2 Emissions in China, Adjusted for Local Environmental Benefits

Source: World Bank 2013, China 2030: building a modern, harmonious, and creative society, © World Bank. http://documents.worldbank.org/curated/en/2013/03/17494829/china-2030-building-modern-harmonious-creative-society. Licence: Creative Commons 3.0 Unported license (CC BY 3.0).

much of the reduced emissions required to address climate change can be obtained from investments that are justified on efficiency grounds alone? The answer appears to be about half in the period up to 2030.

The most complete effort to date to analyze these win–win options is provided by McKinsey's *Resource Revolution: Meeting the World's Energy, Materials, Food, and Water Needs* (2011). Between 2010 and 2030, global resource demand is likely to grow by 27 percent for food, 33 percent for energy, 41 percent for water, and 80 percent for steel. Meeting such demand can be done by increasing supply or using existing resources more efficiently. The study estimates costs and benefits of both options. It finds that increasing efficiency requires more upfront capital but yields a much higher rate of return than investments required to increase the supply of food, energy, water, and steel, which would require annual investments of $3 trillion through 2030—roughly $1 trillion per year more than was invested in the recent past. Such investments would come at a time in which global risk capital is likely to be expensive and geopolitical and environmental risks high.

Resource-efficiency gains will be insufficient to address growing demand for resources, but an extra $900 billion per year of investment in efficiency would reduce the needed investment in supply by $700 billion. More important, by 2030, it would yield annual savings to society of $2.9 trillion. Of the 150 resource productivity measures examined, the top 15 account for 75 percent of the benefits.[13]

Such "no regret" investments deliver nearly half the required adjustment in greenhouse gas emissions, a number broadly consistent with a range of other climate studies. In order to stabilize greenhouse gas concentrations at 450 ppm, global emissions would need to be reduced from a projected 61 gigatons in 2030 under a "business as usual" case to 35 gigatons. A full set of resource productivity investments would reduce the figure to about 48 gigatons.

DIRECTED TECHNICAL CHANGE

Although such win–win options can thus solve about half of the problem, they are not enough. Measures beyond "no regrets" are required. Whether it is possible to implement these measures in a way that does not impose a drag on output and growth remains an open question. Above the horizontal axis in Figure 6.8 are opportunities that in a static context do not pay for themselves; these investments will not be adopted in the absence of regulation or government incentives. Conventional economic thinking held that such policies would impose costs on the economy. More recent analysis, beginning

---

[13] The top five measures are building energy efficiency, increasing yields on large-scale farms, reducing food waste, reducing municipal water leakage, and making urban areas denser (leading to major transport efficiency gains).

with Porter and van der Linde (1995), suggests that policy promotes innovation that reduces the cost of regulation (the weak Porter hypothesis) and can lead to increased competitiveness and profitability (the strong Porter hypothesis). The weak hypothesis has been widely supported by empirical studies. Evidence for the strong hypothesis has been mixed, with more recent studies tending to be more supportive (Ambec et al. 2011).

Acemoglu et al. (2011) provide the theoretical underpinning for this hypothesis and for an activist role for government. Many traditional computable general equilibrium models assume exogenous technology, with no learning; in these models, the costs to growth of action on environmental problems can be substantial. Such approaches tend to come out in favor of gradual environmental policy changes. But the evidence is clear that technology responds quickly to price and policy shifts. Patent data have been used in a number of studies to illustrate this point. Figure 6.11 shows how patent applications have responded to environmental regulations and awareness. Acemoglu and others demonstrate that a combination of a carbon tax and directed public expenditures on research can result in no decline in growth and an optimization of intertemporal welfare.

A small number of empirical modeling exercises work on similar lines. On behalf of the German government, Jaeger et al. (2011) explore the impacts on European economies of more ambitious climate targets. Their model allows for learning by doing and recognizes that clearer policy signals from the

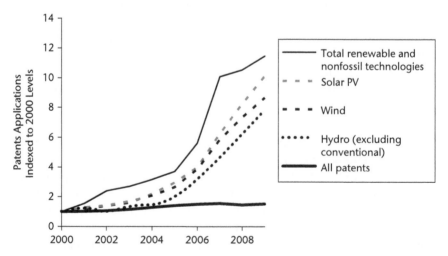

Figure 6.11 Index of Innovation in Climate Change Mitigation Technologies, 1975–2007

Note: Figure shows total worldwide applications in the EPO PASTAT database by priority date. It includes only "claimed priorities" (patents for which an application was filed at an office other than the original "priority" office).

Source: World Bank 2012b, citing OECD 2010.

government on the needed move toward a greener economy could shift investor expectations and build confidence. It indicates that a unilateral commitment by the European Union to increase its ambition in abating climate change from its existing commitment of a 20 percent reduction in greenhouse gas emissions by 2020 to 30 percent over a 1990 baseline would lead to higher investment, growth, and competitiveness. This result contrasts sharply with most existing models, which conclude that greater ambition would reduce growth.

NEW UNDERSTANDINGS OF INVESTMENT: CLIMATE CHANGE DELAYS INVESTMENT

A third reason to believe that tighter environmental policy and near-term economic growth may be positively rather than negatively linked relates to new understanding of investment behavior. The past two decades have yielded new insights into how common characteristics of investment decisions—in particular their irreversibility, their context of uncertainty, and the ability to choose their timing—suggest that options theory rather than maximization of net present value has better predictive value in explaining how decisions are made (Dixit and Pindyk 1994). These insights help explain why, for example, investment is surprisingly unresponsive to interest rate changes, yet highly responsive to changes in outlook.

They also shed light on common concerns expressed by the investor community, which faces a double uncertainty related to climate change. First, investors are increasingly concerned about the possible impact of climate change on returns. Second, a growing number of investors are concerned about the expectation that, at some stage in the future, price signals will shift sharply as new climate policies are implemented with great urgency. Both risks are growing and may be reaching the stage at which major investment decisions are delayed and overall investment is lower than it would otherwise be. Concerns are rising rapidly about the possibility of "stranded assets"—capital stock that appeared a good investment at the time but whose value is sharply diminished by a changing policy context or a changing climate. These concerns explain why a growing number of major corporations are calling for a price on carbon to be introduced now, to provide greater predictability of investment returns. It is the voices of these people that provide perhaps the greatest hope for early action.

GREEN GROWTH AND JOBS

For the three reasons above, tighter environmental policy, carefully chosen and phased, can lead to increased investment and higher growth. An important test for the green growth hypothesis has been to look at shifts in the demand for skilled labor following the tightening of environmental policy. A review of 21 country studies (ILO 2011) shows a shift in labor demand: across industries, away from polluting and toward more modern sectors; within industries, toward greener activities, driven by profitability; and toward totally new occupations, induced by environmental policies. There is also evidence of labor market shortages in skills required for a low-carbon and resource-efficient economy, which undermines the effectiveness of environmental policies and prospects of dynamic gains in competitiveness.

The impact of environmental policies on jobs is of great political importance and forms a link to trade policy. Critics of environmental legislation commonly criticize its "job-killing" characteristics. There has also been a view that tighter environmental controls in one country will lead to outmigration of dirtier industries to countries with looser controls. There is almost no evidence to support the notion that tight environmental policies and open trade and capital movements lead to job migration. Firms move—but pollution abatement costs represent too small a share of total costs to make the difference (Copeland 2012).

Low-carbon development is generally relatively labor-intensive; it therefore probably has a net positive impact on employment, but knowledge gaps remain (Bowen 2012; Fankhauser, Sehlleier, and Stern 2008). Renewable energy and energy-efficient investments employ much larger numbers of workers than fossil fuel production and transmission; recycling and retrofitting are also labor-intensive. The renewable energy sector employed more than 2.3 million people in 2006. The sector has grown very rapidly since then, with China accounting for the largest share. Some 10 million people are believed to be employed in recycling in China (UNEP 2008). The Chinese government estimates that energy efficiency and environmental protection will generate more than 10 million jobs over the next 5–10 years; exports of green goods could create 4–8 million jobs. In the United States, an estimated 1.3 million jobs were created in recycling in 2006 alone (Bezdek 2007).

A recent study of South Africa (World Bank 2011b) finds that although developing green industries could have a cost-effective benefit on new jobs, it will do so only if labor market and regulatory obstacles are also addressed. Investment in research and development (R&D) in green industries will do little if educational and financial systems produce few skilled workers and little risk capital. The key conclusion: green growth requires not only good green policies but also good growth policies.

6.4 Policies and Politics of Low-Carbon Growth

Three considerations are important when thinking through a low-carbon growth policy framework to move from current to more sustainable paths:

- Although the tools needed to internalize externalities have been well known for decades, they are generally not adopted, for a range of well-known (and lesser-known) reasons. The political economy and psychology of policy prescriptions needs to be of central concern.

- The level of uncertainty and potentially irreversible threshold effects implies that the value of conventional cost–benefit analysis may be severely limited and that precautionary principles should drive action.

- The global nature and intergenerational implications of today's resource-depletion problems present challenges of collective action that appear to be well beyond the means of current governance mechanisms to address. Meeting these challenges will demand new approaches.[14]

- Although climate change is easily understood as the result of a fundamental market failure (the lack of property rights and thus a market value of climate services), it actually reflects several market failures (Stern 2013), each requiring different instruments.

In the light of these considerations, actions to address climate change—and many other environmental externalities—require a great deal of creativity and a combination of policies.

The scale and nature of the challenge is captured in Figure 6.12 (IEA 2012b), which shows possible trajectories for energy-related emissions (which account for two-thirds of total greenhouse gases). Under current policies and practices, emissions will continue to rise into the indefinite future. Fortunately, more than 90 countries have made statements of intent to address greenhouse gas emissions. The New Policies scenario captures these goals, which, while laudable, are inadequate to the task. The Efficient World scenario assumes that all countries exploit the win–win opportunities (options that can be justified purely on efficiency rather than environmental grounds). Although this scenario slightly reduces greenhouse gas emissions, further policies and investments are required from the section of the marginal abatement cost curve above the horizontal axis in Figure 6.8.

Figure 6.12 highlights two important features of the challenge. First, global emissions will need to peak by 2020 if concentrations are to be limited to 450 ppm; delays beyond this point would increase the costs sharply, probably making the task politically and economically prohibitive. Second, about 70 percent of the reduction from a business-as-usual path needs to be achieved outside the OECD, illustrating the urgent need for international cooperation.

6.4.1 Removing Subsidies on Fossil Fuels

Subsidies on fossil fuel production and consumption are pointing economic agents in the wrong direction and wasting large sums of money that could be

---

[14] See Matoo and Subramanian (2013) for a lively exploration of this theme.

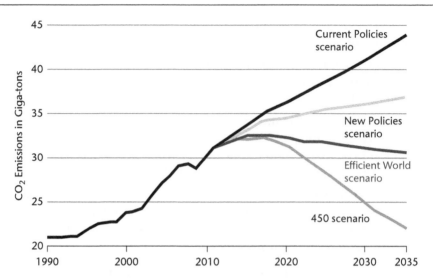

Figure 6.12 Alternative Scenarios for Global Energy-Related CO_2 Emissions, 1990–2035: Growing Gap between Current Policies and What Is Needed

Note: The Efficient World scenario assumes that the long-term economic potential of energy efficiency is realized by 2035. The 450 (ppm) scenario is consistent with limiting global warming to 2°C above preindustrial levels. Almost two-thirds of emissions come from non–OECD countries in the New Policies scenario; emissions avoidance in these countries makes up the majority of abatement in the 450 scenario.

Source: IEA 2012b. World Energy Outlook 2012. Paris: International Energy Agency © OECD/IEA, 2012

used to help set economies on more sustainable paths. Such subsidies cost about $400 billion per year in emerging and developing counties, mainly in the form of consumption incentives, and about $50–$80 billion in advanced countries (OECD 2012), more often in the form of production incentives. If the subsidy is measured not with regard to the free market price of the energy source but with regard to what the price should be (after adjusting for the rate of optimal taxation and negative externalities), the global subsidy is much higher, amounting to $1.9 trillion in 2011, about 2.5 percent of global GDP or 8 percent of total public revenue (IMF 2013). Eliminating such subsidies would reduce global CO_2 emissions by 13 percent—and, if well spent, help economic growth. By contrast, total global public research on renewable energy is less than $100 billion a year.

Subsidies encouraging the overuse of other natural resources account for another $500–$800 billion per year (McKinsey 2011; World Bank 2012a).[15] Water subsidies for groundwater extraction and irrigation systems account for $200–$300 billion per year. Public subsidies for fishing amount to $10–$30 billion per

[15] These estimates come from a variety of studies by multilateral institutions and academic researchers. Because the data are sometimes unreliable and definitions complex, estimates vary widely. These estimates appear to be roughly in the mid-range.

year, mainly in the form of direct cash payments, concessional credit, and insurance subsidies (UNEP 2011b). Agricultural subsidies account for another $370 billion (OECD 2011), although not all are environmentally harmful.

The benefits of removing such subsidies have been discussed for decades, but these subsidies remain as high as ever, as a result of the political difficulties of removing them. A few governments (for example, Indonesia and Iran) have demonstrated that using savings from subsidy reduction to provide cash transfers to the lower third of the income distribution can enable such price adjustments without increases in poverty and with manageable political fallout. Modern information technologies that enable the targeting of compensation programs open up new opportunities for doing things better.

Removing subsidies has more than just first-round effects; cost savings make other initiatives possible. In East Asia, for example, the estimated additional net financing required (above the gains from investments in energy efficiency) for a sustainable energy path is $80 billion per year. If implemented in conjunction with removing the $70 billion per year the region currently spends on fossil fuel subsidies, the new path becomes economically and politically attractive (Wang et al. 2010; IEA 2008).

6.4.2 Pricing Carbon

Beyond subsidy removal, a price on carbon is required. Market-based mechanisms can be significantly more cost-effective than regulatory regimes. The adoption of permit trading for sulfur dioxide in the United States in the 1990s yielded annual compliance costs savings of more than $300 million over standards-based regulation, as a result of the flexibility to find solutions that it gives polluters (Anthoff and Hahn 2010).

A number of studies have sought to calculate the appropriate price of carbon. Economists argue that it should be set by calculating the point at which two curves intersect. The marginal abatement cost curve captures the rising cost of reducing each ton of greenhouse gases as the level of ambition increases. The marginal benefit curve captures the falling marginal benefit from each ton not emitted as the level of ambition rises. The social cost of carbon is estimated by calculating where these curves intersect—that is, where the marginal benefits and costs are equated. This calculation requires the use of cost–benefit analysis and is thus subject to the weaknesses discussed earlier in this chapter. Estimates tend to range widely, based on the assumptions made about discount rates and the likely impacts and costs; they tend to be lower than many scientists would support, given the inability of existing tools to capture the possibility of extreme events.

Tol (2004) combines 103 estimates to produce a probability-density function of the social cost of carbon. He finds a median of $14 per ton and a mean of $93. The IPCC Fourth Assessment notes that peer-reviewed estimates of the social cost of carbon averaged about $12 per ton of CO_2, with a range of –$3 to +$95. The U.S. government–convened Interagency Work Group came up with a "central value" estimate of the social cost of carbon of $21 per ton of CO_2 (U.S. EPA 2010; see Hausker 2011 for a critical assessment).

Carbon can be priced by imposing either a carbon tax, which would provide certainty on the price but no guarantee on the impact on emissions, or a quantity cap, which would guarantee quantity impact but create uncertainty over the price. In a world of perfect information, the two would be fully equivalent. The choice in the real world depends on whether it is more important to have certainty on the limits on carbon emitted (the view of many scientists and environmentalists) or confidence on the prices faced by investors and consumers and the revenues raised (the view of many ministries of finance, on the grounds that price and revenue volatility is inefficient). The fact that confidence on both emissions and prices is desirable has led to the design of hybrid approaches that combine quantity and price targets.

The countries of the European Union have led the way in placing a price on carbon, choosing a cap-and-trade system. The EU Emissions Trading Scheme, which accounts for more than 90 percent of all global trades, and the Clean Development Mechanism (CDM), the global offset system introduced under the Kyoto Protocol, illustrate both the strengths and the weaknesses of a cap-and-trade system. They have significantly reduced the cost of mitigation within Europe. In addition, by purchasing credits through the CDM, Europeans and other participants have provided finance for more than 6,500 projects in the developing world with a combined investment of more than $350 billion in low-carbon development (Purvis et al. 2013).

However, the price of carbon in international markets has been driven by the ambition of EU targets rather than any rational calculation of the social price of carbon. When the EU goals of reducing greenhouse gas emissions by 20 percent by 2020 were set, it was assumed that the recovery from the economic crisis would be relatively prompt, promoting demand for more energy. The economic stagnation in Europe since 2008 has made the greenhouse gas targets for 2020 relatively easy to achieve, driving down the carbon price within Europe and globally (Figure 6.13). This trend has not only created economic uncertainty but has undermined confidence in carbon markets, as much of the infrastructure—brokerage firms, developers, and so forth—exited the markets or sharply cut back operations. Price signals facing investors are now discouraging action on climate change, not because the problem has lessened (it has seriously worsened) but because the depth of the recession was underestimated. In this situation, a carbon price would have been preferable to a cap-and-trade system.

The long-term prospects for carbon markets, however, remain strong, as a result of the sheer need to act soon to prevent a catastrophe. A number of countries

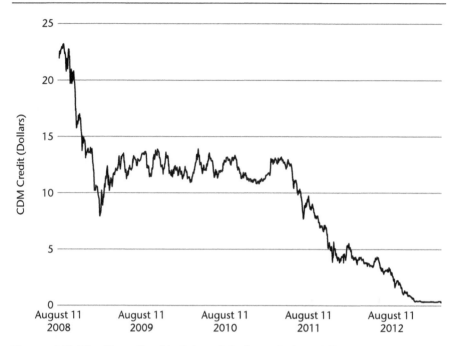

Figure 6.13 The Unpredictable Price of Carbon: Carbon Offset Prices Transacted through the Clean Development Mechanism, 2008–12

Source: Purvis, Grausz, and Light (2013), citing Thomson Reuters Point Carbon 2013.
This material was originally created by the Center for American Progress (www.americanprogress.org)

and regions are introducing trading schemes in that anticipation. In 2012–13, Australia, China, California, Kazakhstan, the Republic of Korea, and Quebec are all designing, launching, or deepening their trading systems. Australia's program covers 60 percent of emissions and combines a price and trading element. In 2013, China began trading in seven cities and provinces accounting for more than 25 percent of national GDP; these pilots were planned to inform the design of a nationwide program by 2015. India has chosen an innovative variant by introducing a trading scheme for Renewable Energy Certificates (RECs), whereby obligations to increase the share of renewable production can be met through market transactions. Korea has passed legislation to introduce emissions trading by 2015 as a key element of its "green growth" proposals.

6.4.3 Climbing the Marginal Abatement Curve: Addressing Other Market Failures

Although placing a price on carbon is perhaps the single most important measure required, it is not enough. The unpriced global externality caused by greenhouse gas emissions is not the only market failure (Stern 2013). Information asymmetry, coordination failures (the need for networks), imperfections in capital markets and R&D, and the existence of substantial co-benefits in the form of other environmental benefits are all discouraging action on climate change. They must be addressed through a portfolio of policies.[16]

Emissions standards, applied carefully and phased in over time, have been found to have high rates of economic return, even when they require significant investment for compliance. The benefit–cost ratio of the U.S. Clean Air Act, for example, is estimated to be 25:1 by 2015 (U.S. EPA 2011). Compliance costs have been consistently found to be lower than predicted by industry associations and to promote technology responses that are greater than anticipated. A notable example is vehicle standards (An et al. 2007). In some instances, such regulations are a second-best alternative to pricing measures, but in other cases they are effective complements—and, in the presence of information asymmetries, principal–agent problems, and other market failures, superior alternatives—to pricing measures.[17] If the goal is to change household energy use, imposing (mandatory) energy efficiency standards and (voluntary) appliance labeling is much more cost-effective than, for example, placing taxes on electricity use.

New insights from behavioral psychology help explain why individuals and even firms do not always respond to price signals. They are encouraging a new emphasis on "nudge" policies (Thaler and Sunstein 2009). Labeling, certification schemes, and power use monitors are examples that are proving effective. Relatedly, there is evidence that consumers and voters are biased toward the status quo: they tend to view new environmental policies as a burden while discounting the costs of existing or future environmental damage (World Bank 2012a). This phenomenon helps explain why it is very difficult to create political coalitions for strong action on climate change and suggests that progress could be greater if low-carbon choices were presented as the default option, with the high-carbon path an active choice (Picherta and Katsikopoulos 2008).

The role of government in the development of technology requires careful attention. Although price and nonprice policies can spur innovation, there is also a role for the use of public funds (Acemoglu et al. 2012). To date, worldwide public spending on renewable energy and energy efficiency has been dwarfed by public support for fossil-based energy (Bloomberg New Energy

---

[16] For an overview of environmental policy choice, see Sterner (2003), and Goulder and Parry (2008).

[17] Achieving the U.S. commitment to reduce greenhouse emissions by 17 percent between 2005 and 2020 will require a mix of regulatory standards and measures. Analysis at the World Resources Institute by Bianco and others (2013) shows how new power plant standards, methane leakage standards, the phase-out of hydrofluorocarbons, and new energy efficiency can, if firmly implemented, enable the goals to be reached at low cost and significant technological gain—even in the absence of political support for pricing measures, although these measures would be more effective in the presence of complementary pricing measures.

Finance 2010). Emerging economies like China and Morocco are adopting aggressive public spending programs to support renewables, however, and more than 40 countries now have feed-in tariff arrangements to support investment in renewables. The past two decades have witnessed a birth of a new form of industrial policy in which externalities and spillovers are identified by public–private collaboration, and incentives and public spending have focused on addressing them (Rodrick 2004). Green technologies have been an important component of this trend.

Denmark became a global leader in wind technology through a focused program of support between the mid-1980s and late 1990s, combining market creation through feed-in tariffs and research support. China is an important current example in photovoltaic technology (De La Tour, Glachant, and Ménière 2011).

6.4.4 International Cooperation

As the greatest of all global market failures—and one in which the countries that caused the problem will not be those that will suffer most from it—climate change poses huge problems of international collective action, especially in an environment in which the costs of action have dominated the discourse and, too often, a zero-sum game mentality has pervaded negotiations. The United Nations Framework Convention on Climate Change (UNFCCC), which came into force in 1994 and has been ratified by 195 countries, has achieved some notable achievements, including the Kyoto Protocol, the introduction of global carbon trading through the Clean Development Mechanism, and a broad range of technical agreements on how to measure and account for greenhouse gas emissions. The failure of the Copenhagen Conference of the Parties (COP) in 2009 to deliver a global agreement was partly compensated for by the agreement to create a registry of voluntary (and nonbinding) commitments to reduce greenhouse gas emissions up to 2020. More than 90 countries have now registered such aspirations.[18] They represent by far the greatest commitment to act against climate change ever. But adding up all the aspirations still falls far short of what is necessary (UNEP 2012), as the New Policies scenario in Figure 6.12 shows.

---

[18] For many developing countries, these aspirations are contingent on financing from developed countries. Sometimes two figures offered are offered—one independent of additional finance and a more ambitious one if adequate finance is forthcoming. Indonesia, for example, has committed to a reduction of 26 percent (from business-as-usual trends) to be achieved by its own efforts and 41 percent if additional subsidized funding is forthcoming. Some countries have expressed greenhouse gas goals as a percentage of GDP. China, for example, has committed to reduce the carbon content of real GDP by 40 percent between 2000 and 2020.

Following the breakdown of negotiations in Copenhagen, subsequent annual COPs—in Cancun, Durban, and Doha—sought to raise the level of ambition. Agreement was reached to finalize a global deal, with legal force, in 2015, to become effective in 2020. The goal would be to limit average temperature increases to a maximum of 2°C. Although this achievement is important, two serious problems remain. First, views differ vastly on the legal form of such a deal, with some insisting on a global treaty strictly limiting greenhouse gas emissions, with international penalties for violations, while others advocate a much looser, bottom-up "pledge and review" approach. The problem is complicated by the fact that UNFCCC rules specify that any decisions be made by consensus, which has been understood to mean that every country has veto power.[19] As a result, few observers are optimistic that the degree of ambition, and subsequent impact, will be sufficient. Second, as noted earlier, although it is action in the current decade that will be essential if global emissions are to peak by 2020, in this critical decade there will be no global arrangements whatsoever.[20]

Although a globally inclusive intergovernmental agreement remains as essential as ever, it is clear that a process that allows any country, however small, to defeat any decision cannot be relied upon to solve a problem of such great global importance. Many observers regard today's UNFCCC processes as indicative of the inadequacies of global governance mechanisms to address the key international problems of the current century (see chapter 7, by Birdsall). Calls for new approaches are growing.

The idea of smaller groupings of committed players helping to create momentum for change is a growing theme in international dialogue and practice. Existing regional blocs, such as the European Union, are demonstrating that greater ambition is possible when fewer players are engaged. New (voluntary) "clubs" are being designed to show that success is possible. Examples include the creation in the past three years of coalitions to address short-term air pollutants, new clubs of countries committed to renewable energy and energy efficiency, and governments committed to the adoption of green growth paths. Their purpose is to share information and technology, demonstrate that success can be achieved at reasonable (or negative) economic and political costs, and in some cases provide financial assistance to developing country members. Morgan and Weischer (2013) explore 17

---

[19] At the conclusion of the Cancun COP, in 2010, the chair pronounced consensus, even though one country (Bolivia) was opposed. This decision was met with opposition among some parties as undermining the integrity of the UNFCCC process, but it provided new hope for more rational decision-making.

[20] A second commitment period under the Kyoto Protocol was agreed to at the Durban COP, in 2011, which will be effective during the current decade, but it includes only 37 countries, which together account for only 13 percent of global emissions. Its significance is political rather than substantive.

such clubs, identifying the conditions under which they can help move the needle, increasing the likelihood of achieving a strong global deal.

Many of the most innovative coalitions include private corporations, subnational governments, and civil society, as well as ambitious national governments. For example, the Sustainable Energy for All Initiative, led by the United Nations and the World Bank, consists of 77 countries; dozens of major corporations, financial institutions, and civil society organizations; and tens of billions of dollars of committed finance devoted to specific targets on renewable energy, energy efficiency, and universal access to electricity by 2030. The C40 grouping of the world's major cities has made significant and specific commitments to reduce greenhouse gas emissions and to help one another do so through technical assistance, toolkits, and political support. None of these efforts can substitute for the need for a global deal, but they can help change the political and economic calculus, making such a deal more likely. An increase in such arrangements should be expected and encouraged, not only on climate change but also to address much broader issues of resource risks in the coming decades (see Lee et al. 2012).

6.4.5 Facilitating Citizen Voice through the Marketplace

Governments rarely initiate efforts that lead to environmental progress. In most instances, it is citizens who demand change. The combined leadership of consumers and business leaders who recognize that continuation of present behavior is unsustainable now offers the greatest hope for change. Certification schemes and associated roundtables for a range of commodities, such as timber and palm oil, are playing a major role in preventing deforestation and reducing carbon footprints. More than 80 percent of Global 500 firms now report their carbon dioxide emissions—not because governments require that they do so but because institutional investors, led by citizen shareholders, demand it. New technologies (remote sensing, crowd sourcing, GPS tracking, and protocols for measuring emissions) are enabling green companies and products to distinguish themselves. Environmental auditing and voluntary disclosure schemes are springing up in support, slowly transforming supply chains among leading companies. Policy options exist that can make these efforts more effective.

6.5 Concluding Thought

These initiatives will play an important role in transforming economic processes toward a more sustainable footing. Sadly, they will not be sufficient unless they succeed in demonstrating that the benefits of climate action are greater than have been widely understood and the language of burden-sharing and costs is replaced with that of opportunity and greater well-being for citizens everywhere. This area will be a big battlefield in the coming years. The stakes are high, and time is running out.

References

Acemoglu, D., P. Aghion, L. Bursztyn, and D. Hemous. 2012. "The Environment and Directed Technical Change." *American Economic Review* 102 (1): 131–66.

Ambec, S., M. A. Cohen, S. Elgie, and P. Lanoie. 2011. "The Porter Hypothesis at 20: Can Environmental Regulation Enhance Innovation and Competitiveness?" Discussion Paper 11-01, Resources for the Future, Washington, DC.

An, F., D. Gordon, H. He, D. Kodjak, and D. Rutherford. 2007. *Passenger Vehicle Greenhouse Gas and Fuel Economy, Standards: A Global Update.* Washington, DC: International Council on Clean Transportation.

Andreoni, J., and A. Levinson. 2001. "The Simple Analytics of the Environmental Kuznets Curve." *Journal of Public Economics* 80 (2): 269–86.

Anthoff, A., and R. Hahn. 2010. "Government Failure and Market Failure: On the Inefficiency of Environmental and Energy Policy." *Oxford Review of Economic Policy* 26 (2): 197–224.

Arrow, K. J., P. Dasgupta, L. H. Goulder, K. Mumford, and K. Oleson. 2010. "China, the US, and Sustainability: Perspectives Based on Comprehensive Wealth." In *Is Economic Growth Sustainable?* ed. Geoffrey Heal, 92–145. London: Palgrave MacMillan.

Bai, Z. G., D. L. Dent, L. Olsson, and M. E. Schaepman. 2008. *Global Assessment of Land Degradation and Improvement. 1. Identification by Remote Sensing.* ISRIC (World Soil Information) Report 2008/01, Wageningen, Netherlands.

Bezdek, R. 2007. *Renewable Energy and Energy Efficiency: Economic Drivers for the 21st Century.* Boulder, CO: American Solar Energy Society.

Bianco, N, F. Litz, K. Meek, and R. Gaspar, 2013. *Can the U.S. Get There from Here? Using Existing Federal Laws and State Action to Reduce Greenhouse Gas Emissions.* Washington, DC: World Resources Institute.

Bloomberg New Energy Finance. 2010. "Subsidies for Renewables, Biofuels Dwarfed by Supports for Fossil Fuels." Press release, July 29.

Bolinger, M., R. Wiser, and W. Golove. 2002. "Quantifying the Value that Wind Power Provides as a Hedge against Volatile Natural Gas Prices." *Proceedings of Windpower 2002.* American Wind Energy Association, Washington, DC.

Bowen, A. 2012. "Green Growth, Green Jobs, and Labor Markets." Policy Research Working Paper 5990, World Bank, Washington, DC.

Brock, W. A. and M. S. Taylor. 2005. "Economic Growth and the Environment: A Review of Theory and Empirics." In *Handbook of Economic Growth*, ed. P. Aghion and S. Durlauf, 1749–821. Amsterdam: Elsevier.

CDP (Carbon Disclosure Project). 2012. *CDP Global Water Report 2012.* London: CDP.

Copeland, B. R. 2012. "International Trade and Green Growth." Paper presented at the Green Growth Knowledge Platform Inaugural Conference, Mexico City, January 12–13.

Cropper, M. 2010. "What Are the Health Effects of Air Pollution in China?" In *Is Economic Growth Sustainable?* ed. G. Heal, 10–47. London Palgrave Macmillan.

DARA, and the Climate Vulnerable Forum. 2012. *Climate Vulnerability Monitor 2nd Edition: A Guide to the Cold Calculus of a Hot Planet.* Madrid: DARA.

Dargay, J., D. Gately, and M. Sommer. 2007. "Vehicle Ownership and Income Growth, Worldwide: 1960–2030." *Energy Journal* 28 (4): 143–70.

De la Tour, A., M. Glachant, and Y. Ménière. 2011. "Innovation and International Technology Transfer: The Case of the Chinese Photovoltaic Industry." *Energy Policy* 39 (2): 761–70.

DeConcini, C., and F. Thompson. 2013. *2012: A Year of Record-Breaking Extreme Weather and Climate.* Washington, DC: World Resources Institute.

Dell, M., B. F. Jones, and B. A. Olken. 2009. "Temperature and Income: Reconciling New Cross-Sectional and Panel Estimates." *American Economic Review* 99 (2): 198–204.

Dixit, A., and R. Pindyk. 1994. *Investment under Uncertainty.* Princeton, NJ: Princeton University Press.

European Environment Agency. 2013. *Atmospheric Greenhouse Gas Concentrations.* Copenhagen: European Environment Agency.

Fankhauser, S., F. Sehlleier, and N. Stern. 2008. "Climate Change, Innovation and Jobs." *Climate Policy* 8: 421–9.

Goulder, L. H., and I. W. H. Parry, 2008. "Instrument Choice in Environmental Policy." *Review of Environmental Economics and Policy* 2: 152–74.

Grossman, G. M., and A. B. Krueger. 1993. "Environmental Impacts of a North American Free Trade Agreement." In *The US Mexico Free Trade Agreement*, ed. P. Garber, 165–77. Cambridge, MA: MIT Press.

Hamilton, Kirk. 2010. "Wealth, Saving and Sustainability." In *Is Economic Growth Sustainable?* ed. Geoffrey Heath, 76–92. London: Palgrave Macmillan.

Hartwick, J. M. 1977. "Intergenerational Equity and the Investing of Rents from Exhaustible Resources." *American Economic Review* 66: 972–4.

Hausker, K. 2011. "The Social Cost of Carbon and Competing Decision Frameworks for Climate Policy." Paper presented at the fall meeting of the American Bar Association, section on the environment, energy, and resources, Indianapolis, October 12–15.

Heal, G., ed. 2010. *Is Economic Growth Sustainable?* London: Palgrave Macmillan.

IEA (International Energy Agency). 2012a. "Global Carbon-Dioxide Emissions Increase by 1.0 Gt in 2011 to Record High." Paris. http://www.iea.org/newsroomandevents/news/2012/may/name,27216,en.html.

IEA (International Energy Agency). 2012b. *World Energy Outlook 2012.* Paris: International Energy Agency.

IFPRI (International Food Policy Research Institute). 2013. *2012 Global Food Policy Report.* Washington, DC: International Food Policy Research Institute.

ILO (International Labor Organization). 2011. *Skills for Green Jobs. A Global View: Synthesis Report Based on 21 Country Studies.* Geneva: ILO.

IMF (International Monetary Fund). 2013. *Energy Subsidy Reform: Lessons and Implications.* Washington, DC: IMF.

IPCC (Intergovernmental Panel on Climate Change). 2007. Climate Change 2007: Synthesis Report. Contribution of Working Groups I, II and III to the Fourth Assessment of the Intergovernmental Panel on Climate Change.

IUCN (International Union for Conservation of Nature). 2004. *A Global Species Assessment.* Gland, Switzerland, and Cambridge, United Kingdom.

Jaeger, C. C., L. Paroussos, D. Mangalagiu, D., R. Kupers, A. Mandel, and J. D. Tàbara. 2011. *A New Growth Path for Europe: Generating Prosperity and Jobs in the Low-Carbon Economy. Synthesis Report.* European Climate Forum, Potsdam, Germany.

Jaffe, A., and R. Stavins. 1994. "The Energy-Efficiency Gap: What Does It Mean?" *Energy Policy* 22 (10): 804–10.

Kharas, H. 2010. "The Emerging Middle Class in Developing Countries." Working Paper 285, OECD Development Centre, Organisation for Economic Co-operation and Development, Paris.

Lee, B., F. Preston, J. Kooroshy, R. Bailey, and G. Lahn. 2012. *Resources Futures.* London: Chatham House.

Mattoo, Aaditya, and Arvind Subramanian. 2013. *Greenprint: A New Approach to Cooperation on Climate Change.* Washington, DC: Center for Global Development.

McKinsey & Company. 2010. *Impact of the Financial Crisis on Carbon Economics: Version 2.1 of the Global Greenhouse Gas Abatement Cost Curve.*

McKinsey & Company. 2011. *Resource Revolution: Meeting the World's Energy, Materials, Food, and Water Needs.* http://www.mckinsey.com/insights/ energy_resources_materials/resource_revolution.

Meinshausen, M., N. Meinshausen, W. Hare1, S. C. B. Raper, K. Frieler, R. Knutti, D. J. Frame, and M. R. Allen. 2009. "Greenhouse-Gas Emission Targets for Limiting Global Warming to 2°C." *Nature* 458: 1158–62.

Millennium Ecosystem Assessment. 2005. *Ecosystems and Human Well-Being: General Synthesis.* Washington, DC: Island Press.

Miller, Kenneth G., James D. Wright, James V. Browning, Andrew Kulpecz, Michelle Kominz, Tim R. Naish, Benjamin S. Cramer, Yair Rosenthal, W. Richard Peltier, and Sindia Sosdian. 2012. "High Tide of the Warm Pliocene: Implications of Global Sea Level for Antarctic Deglaciation." *Geology* 40: 407–10.

Morgan, J., and L. Weischer. 2013. "Two Degrees Clubs: How Small Groups of Countries Can Make a Big Difference." *WRI Insights*, World Resources Institute, Washington, DC.

Nicholls, R. J., N. Marinova, J. A. Lowe, S. Brown, P. Vellinga, D. de Gusmão, J. Hinkel, and R. S. J. Tol. 2011. "Sea-Level Rise and Its Possible Impacts Given a 'Beyond 4°C World' in the Twenty-First Century." *Philosophical Transactions of the Royal Society A* 369: 161–81.

Nordhaus, W. D. 1974. "Resources as a Constraint on Growth." *American Economic Review* 64 (May): 22–26.

Nordhaus, W. D. 2007. "A Review of the Stern Review on the Economics of Climate Change." *Journal of Economic Literature* 45 (3): 686–702.

OECD (Organisation for Economic Co-operation and Development). 2010. *Climate Policy and Technological Innovation and Transfer: An Overview of Trends and Recent Empirical Results.* Paris: OECD.

OECD (Organisation for Economic Co-operation and Development). 2011. *Towards Green Growth.* Paris: OECD.

OECD (Organisation for Economic Co-operation and Development). 2012. *Environmental Outlook to 2050.* Paris: OECD.

Picherta, D., and K. Katsikopoulos, 2008. "Green Defaults: Information Presentation and Pro-Environmental Behaviour" *Journal of Environmental Psychology* 28: 62–73.

Porter, M., and C. van der Linde. 1995. "Toward a New Conception of the Environment-Competitiveness Relationship." *Journal of Economic Perspective* 9 (4): 97–118.

Purvis, N., S. Grausz, and A. Light. 2013. *Carbon Market Crossroads: New Ideas for Harnessing Global Markets to Confront Climate Change.* Washington, DC: Center for American Progress.

Smulders, S., L. Bretschger, and H. Egli. 2011. "Economic Growth and the Diffusion of Clean Technologies: Explaining Environmental Kuznets Curves." *Environmental & Resource Economics* 49 (1): 79–99.

Solow, R. 1986. "On the Intergenerational Allocation of Natural Resources." *Scandinavian Journal of Economics* 88 (1): 141–9.

Steer, A. 1992. "The Environment for Development." *Finance & Development*, June.

Steer, A., and S. Csordis. 2011. "Green Growth in Emerging East Asia?" Paper presented at conference on East Asian Development, Singapore, March 21–22.

Stern, N. 2006. *The Stern Review on the Economics of Climate Change.* Cambridge: Cambridge University Press.

Stern, N. 2008. "The Economics of Climate Change." *American Economic Review* 98 (2): 1–37.

Stern, N. 2013. "Economic Growth, Poverty Reduction and Managing Climate Change." Paper presented at the International Monetary Fund, Washington, DC, April 2. http://www.wri.org/event/2013/04/fostering-growth-and-poverty-reduction-world-immense-risk.

Sterner, T. 2003. *Policy Instruments for Environmental and Natural Resource Management.* Washington, DC: Resources for the Future Press.

Stiglitz, J, A. Sen, and J.-P. Fitoussi. 2009. *Report of the Commission on the Measurement of Economic Performance and Social Progress.* Paris.

Thaler, R. H., and C. R. Sunstein. 2009. *Nudge: Improving Decisions about Health, Wealth and Happiness.* New York: Penguin.

Tol, R. 2004. "The Marginal Damage Costs of Greenhouse Gas Emissions: An Assessment of the Uncertainties." *Energy Policy* 33: 2064–74.

Tol, R. 2009. "The Economic Effects of Climate Change." *Journal of Economic Perspectives* 23 (2): 29–51.

UNEP (United Nations Environment Programme). 2008. *Green Jobs: Towards Decent Work in a Sustainable, Low-Carbon World.* Washington, DC: Worldwatch Institute, for the United Nations Environment Programme.

UNEP (United Nations Environment Programme). 2011a. *Decoupling Natural Resource Use and Environmental Impacts from Economic Growth*. A Report of the Working Group on Decoupling to the International Resource Panel.

UNEP (United Nations Environment Programme). 2011b. *Towards a Green Economy: Pathways to Sustainable Development and Poverty Eradication. A Synthesis for Policy Makers*. Geneva. http://www.unep.org/greeneconomy.

UNEP (United Nations Environment Programme). 2012. *The Emissions Gap Report, 2012*. UNEP Synthesis Report, United Nations Environment Programme.

UN Water, and FAO (Food and Agriculture Organization). 2007. *Coping with Water Scarcity: Challenge of the Twenty-First Century*. http://www.fao.org/nr/water/docs/escarcity.pdf.

U.S. EPA (Environmental Protection Agency). 2010. *Social Cost of Carbon for Regulatory Impact Analysis under Executive Order 12866*. February, Interagency Working Group on Social Cost of Carbon, Washington, DC. www.epa.gov/OTAQ/climate/regulations/scc-tsd.pdf.

U.S. EPA (Environmental Protection Agency). 2011. "The Benefits and Costs of the Clean Air Act from 1990 to 2020." U.S. EPA: Washington, DC.

Weitzman, M. L. 2007. "A Review of the Stern Review on the Economics of Climate Change." *Journal of Economic Literature* 45 (3): 703–24.

Weitzman, M. L. 2009. "On Modeling and Interpreting the Economics of Catastrophic Climate Change." *Review of Economics and Statistics* 91 (1): 1–19.

World Bank. 1992. *World Development Report 1992: Development and the Environment*. Washington, DC: World Bank.

World Bank. 2008. *Framework Document for a Global Food Crisis Response Program*. Washington, DC: World Bank.

World Bank. 2010. *Winds of Change: East Asia's Sustainable Energy Future*. Washington, DC: World Bank.

World Bank. 2011a. *The Changing Wealth of Nations: Measuring Sustainable Development in the New Millennium*. Washington, DC: World Bank.

World Bank. 2011b. *South Africa: Economic Update; Focus on Green Growth*. Washington, DC: World Bank.

World Bank. 2012a. *Inclusive Green Growth: The Pathway to Sustainable Development*. Washington, DC: World Bank.

World Bank. 2012b. "Seizing the Opportunity of Green Development in China." In *China 2030*. Washington, DC: World Bank.

WMO (World Meteorological Organization. 2013. *Powering Our Future with Weather, Climate and Water*. Geneva: WMO.

WRI (World Resources Institute). 2012. *Global Coal Risk Assessment: Data Analysis and Market Research*. Washington, DC. http://www.wri.org/publication/global-coal-risk-assessment.

WRI (World Resources Institute). Forthcoming. *Food Futures: The 2013–14 World Resources Report*. Washington, DC: World Resources Institute.

Comments on "Resource Depletion, Climate Change, and Economic Growth," by Andrew Steer

Jeremy Oppenheim

This chapter lays out the core case for incorporating a set of variables in models of economic growth that are insufficiently accounted for in more conventional models. These variables include the following:

- climate risk, which affects the steady-state growth pathway as a potentially negative exogenous shock and as a source of uncertainty, on both direct and policy-related dimensions, which results in lower investment rates and hence lower aggregate growth;

- the potential for endogenous technological progress in key sectors (energy, transport, building materials, agriculture) to accelerate as a result of low-carbon policies, contributing to faster overall economic growth;[1]

- the potential to drive resource efficiency (in water, energy, land-use, carbon) by correcting for a set of market failures and imperfections.

The chapter makes the point that the low-carbon economy model is not a priori likely to deliver more or less growth than the high-carbon model. Under certain circumstances (including a high climate change scenario or high induced rates of technological progress), the low-carbon model may actually deliver a higher rate of growth (the chapter does not push the "strong" version of the argument). The chapter argues that the thesis applies as much, if not more, to low-income countries as it does to high-income countries, given that low-income countries are disproportionately exposed to natural resource and environmental risk. At the heart of the narrative is also the proposition that the right combination of technology, markets, and policy can accelerate the transition to a low-carbon economy with no or little impact on aggregate

---

[1] Investing to accelerate progress on "clean technologies" would presumably be at the expense of other R&D investments, which might have higher economic returns, unless the argument is that the world would simply increase its rate of R&D spending.

growth. This proposition requires considerable institutional sophistication to work in practice, given the risk of gaming, asymmetric information, and poorly designed policies (captured by specific interests).

The chapter is probably the most comprehensive and compelling synthesis of the case for "green growth" currently available. It pulls on many different threads of the literature and integrates a highly diverse field, from natural resource economics to behavioral economics (with respect to investor conduct) and endogenous growth theory.

The mystery of why it is so hard to land the argument with policymakers and investors in a decisive fashion remains. Currently, key decision-makers (both public and private) continue to invest in options that appear small relative to both the risks of climate change and the benefits of a more resource-efficient, clean technology-intensive model. China provides a particularly challenging case in point. The direction of change—in the sense of the Kuznets environmental curve—is toward a more resource-efficient, lower-carbon economy. However, China's hugely successful transition from low-income to middle-income status was based largely on a resource-intensive, carbon-intensive economic model, fuelled largely by cheap coal. Other countries—from Vietnam to Turkey—have followed or are following a similar paradigm. For their part, the developed economies have not shifted their economic models in any significant way, other than offshoring a large share of their historic emissions (to China), as Denmark has done. The theory of green growth appears to be significantly ahead of the reality—and the gap does not appear to be closing particularly quickly, if at all.

Given my broad agreement with the overall contents of the chapter and its framing of the theoretical case for a shift to a low-carbon economy, let me simply point to four potential areas where further research would be helpful:

- the challenge presented by cheap hydrocarbons, especially gas;
- the technology/industrial policy challenge;
- the distributional impact of the shift to a low-carbon model;
- the case for a greater focus on local environmental goods.

1. Cheap Hydrocarbons

The expanded supply of hydrocarbons is a serious problem for the transition to a low-carbon economy. Shale gas (and oil shale) represents the most profound energy revolution currently playing out, affecting investment decisions across the world economy, from China to Brazil. Until three to five years ago, a central element of the low-carbon narrative was that it would simultaneously solve two problems—climate and energy security—not just one. Now, this story is much harder to tell, for three reasons. First, accessible hydrocarbon supplies appear to be increasing, given technological shifts. Second, the expansion of gas complicates the picture, because it crowds out coal but also crowds out renewable energy (and reduces energy costs). Third, the biggest owners of hydrocarbon assets—especially oil, still the most valuable form of energy per unit—have no or little incentive to leave their resources in the ground. The design of any kind of incentive or payment system for countries or companies not to exploit their hydrocarbon resources is a critical technical (and political) challenge. Given relative values, the challenge will be an order of magnitude more difficult than designing the (highly complex) features of the market to incentivize reduced deforestation (through reducing emissions from deforestation and forest degradation [REDD] credits). Under what set of conditions would it ever be incentive-compatible for countries/companies not to exploit their hydrocarbon assets—or to do so in a way that sequesters the majority of the associated carbon emissions?

2. The Technology/Policy Challenge

The chapter touches lightly on the question of technology. At the macro level, accelerated progress on clean technologies—across a number of sectors—is a necessary condition for the transition to a low-carbon economy. At the micro level, accelerated, large-scale deployment of low-carbon technologies is likely to be a major challenge in almost every sector. For most low-carbon technologies in the energy sector, outside niche applications, competitive deployment at scale remains challenging at carbon prices less than \$30–\$50 a tonne. (This price point would of course be significantly lower if the air-pollution externalities of coal-fired power were properly priced). For precommercial low-carbon technologies, such as carbon capture and sequestration, electric vehicles, and offshore wind, the carbon price necessary to make the low-carbon technologies competitive is still well over \$100 for early vintages.[2]

The main problems of accelerated progress relate to two key features of the relevant technology set. First, many of these technologies play into a commodity market. In practice, it is hard to distinguish green electrons from brown electrons, at least in terms of their functionality. As a result, it is hard to generate a differentiated market proposition that can, absent policy support, tap into an autocatalytic segment of early adopters. Second,

---

[2] Some technologies yield a pure resource efficiency gain. These technologies are economically attractive as long as institutional and behavioral barriers can be overcome.

many green technologies are relatively capital-intensive, and their cost performance improves primarily through additional deployment (rather than primarily through exogenous technological change, driven by more R&D). These features make the coupling of policy support and technological progress particularly tight—and analytically different from, for example, traditional approaches justifying government investment in basic R&D as a public good. These two features compound each other in critical technology bets, such as carbon capture and storage, which take on more of the characteristics of defense procurement programs than of conventional public R&D. They also generate extra challenges for the deployment of low-carbon technology in many developing countries which are still relatively capital-constrained.

In general, given the current rate of stock accumulation of carbon dioxide equivalent (CO_2e) in the atmosphere, a number of big technology bets will be essential if concentrations are to stay within the 450–550 parts range or the world is to adapt to the consequences of higher CO_2e levels. The selection, design, and institutional arrangements/economics for these big bets (including their cross-country dimensions) deserve significant further attention, as a matter both of theory and of practice.

3. Distributional Implications

The distributional implications of a low-carbon economic model are hard to predict. The most obvious losers appear to be carbon-intensive players, although the incidence depends as ever on policy design (and lobbying power).[3] But there are significant concerns about the potential impact of a low-carbon, resource-efficient economic model on poorer segments of the world's population. This seems paradoxical, as the poor are highly dependent on a stable natural environment and hence much more exposed to weather, energy, and food volatility. However, many mainstream economists argue that policies that increase energy or food prices (by shifting to renewable energy or pricing water) may have a disproportionately negative impact on poor households. They also argue that low-carbon technologies are typically more capital-intensive than high-carbon technologies and hence, absent suitable capital market interventions, disproportionately penalize the poor.

---

[3] In the European Trading System (ETS) for CO_2, precisely the opposite result played out, with the most carbon-intensive players receiving the most permits and hence capturing the lion's share of economic value from the new currency. Polluting pays, it seems!

Reality is, as ever, much more complex. Many poor households pay very high effective prices for their energy, food, and water, when one takes account of quality factors, associated costs (for example to health), and labor input requirements (water is never free). Systematically analyzing the impact of low-carbon versus high-carbon models at the "bottom of the pyramid" is a key unresolved area, on which further research is needed.

4. Local Environmental Goods

The chapter focuses on the global public good of climate change. There is a good case for doing so. Addressing climate change makes many of the local environmental challenges much easier. At the same time, it is worth recognizing that all politics—and most policies—are local. It is hard to imagine most politicians—or citizens, for that matter—putting global environmental risks above local pollution and damage to the local environment. The catalyst for China's transition to a lower-carbon economy is much more likely to be air pollution and water pollution—local effects—than anything global. Strengthening and accelerating the case for local environmental goods is critical, especially for rapidly industrializing nations, which are most likely to experience major lock-in effects as they develop their infrastructure and urban footprints.

There is a useful discussion of the Kuznets environmental curve at the start of the chapter. It would be good to see that set of issues addressed more systematically in future research. Arguably, the biggest challenge to the environment—both local and global—is the rapid process of industrialization and urbanization, both in China and in the next wave of countries. So far, there is little evidence that the critical phase of middle-income growth (which lifts the next 1–2 billion people out of poverty) can be achieved through a low-carbon model. More profoundly, there is little evidence that it can be achieved through a model that requires changing preferred tradeoffs between faster economic growth and environmental costs (whether local or global). Defining an environmentally efficient, politically attractive model of middle-income growth—for Indonesia, India, Pakistan, Nigeria, and the wave of countries that follows them—may be the most acute practical challenge to the agenda presented in this excellent chapter.

This chapter represents a major step forward in synthesizing many of the key aspects of the "green growth" case. There are, as ever, unanswered questions, some of which are highlighted above. There are also the perennial debates, not specific to this chapter, about the effectiveness and efficiency of government intervention. Although market failures and imperfections associated with resources/environmental capital are rampant, so are government failures and public–private rent-seeking partnerships. I have not sought to address these issues, although they have some acute features in the natural resource sector. However, it is precisely these problems that may be the Achilles' heel of the transition to a cleaner, greener model of economic growth.

7

Global Markets, Global Citizens, and Global Governance in the Twenty-first Century

Nancy Birdsall, with Christian Meyer and Alexis Sowa

7.1 Introduction

Consider two tales of global governance. A Ghanaian woman testifies before the U.S. Congress, hoping members of Congress will tell U.S. Treasury staff to push the World Bank to reverse its support for imposition of user charges for health services in Africa. In this case, an international institution creates an opening she may not have at home to influence her own and other African countries' policies and practices by influencing views in the United States (Figure 7.1).

Or: international nongovernmental organizations (NGOs) fight intellectual property rules adopted at the World Trade Organization (WTO) at the behest of the United States and other rich countries that are keeping anti-AIDS drugs prices high in developing countries, winning changes that

[1]Dr. Birdsall is grateful to Pratap Mehta and the other core and project management members of the Global Citizen Foundation Towards a Better Global Economy project team for their comments on earlier versions of this chapter, as well as to Owen Barder, Kemal Derviş, Alan Gelb, Devesh Kapur, Inge Kaul, David Lindauer, Paul O'Brien, William Savedoff, participants in a seminar at the Center for Global Development, and participants in the Global Citizens Foundation Geneva conference.

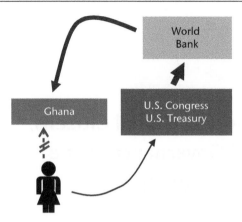

Figure 7.1 A Tale of Global Governance
Source: Authors.

eventually permit dramatic gains in access to those drugs in poor countries. In this case, the international institution provides the setting for an unofficial, nonstate global movement to embarrass democratic states into accepting a change in the global rules.

These are but two examples of how multilateral institutions can advance the interests of people in the bottom half of the global income distribution. Too often, however, global rules and institutions fail the world's poorer people. Decision-making—whether by the G20 group of the world's largest economies, the International Monetary Fund (IMF), the WTO, or the multilateral development banks—does not instill confidence, either in the global market's stability or, more importantly, in its fundamental fairness. In this sense, economic globalization has far outstripped politically democratic globalization.

To be sure, market-based growth and globalization have brought many benefits. Millions of people in the developing world have escaped poverty and, for the first time in 100 years, the yawning gap between the rich countries and the developing world has narrowed, as China, Brazil, India, and other developing countries grow faster than the United States and Europe.

But the global market has also resulted in ever greater concentrations of wealth within countries, destabilizing capital flows that hurt the average working person, new risks of job loss for middle-class people in advanced economies, and food and fuel price hikes that have had devastating effects on poor households in low-income countries. Problems of the global commons that will not be addressed by the global market itself, most prominently climate change, continue unattended.

What can be done to make the global politics of managing the global economy more effective and more legitimate?

This chapter is about the norms and politics behind the resulting loop of influence, including the role: of citizens, often supported by nongovernmental institutions (NGOs); of dominant compared with other sovereign states; and of global institutions. It is about the shortfall of adequate management of the global economy, or of adequate "global governance." The term *global governance* as I use it here refers to political decision-making processes and outcomes, within and among countries, on issues that create spillovers across borders and thus affect people outside any one country. "Adequate" global governance refers to the idea that the processes and outcomes that result should adequately represent the interests of ordinary citizens, including and especially the world's more than 3 billion people in the bottom half of the global distribution of income who live in developing countries. Adequate global governance would do more to bend the path of future growth in the direction of better shared or equal opportunity or "fair" growth and more environmentally sustainable, climate-friendly "far-sighted" growth.[1]

I argue that the politics, rules, and institutions of cooperation among nations are not keeping up with the pace of economic globalization; the reality of increasing interdependence among nations and peoples; and changing norms, evidenced by increasing demands from globally aware citizens for growth in their own and other countries that is better shared and more sustainable. On the positive side, the Internet revolution is giving citizens greater opportunities to make demands on powerful authorities, including beyond their borders; evidence from worldwide surveys of individuals suggests that those demands are shaped by increasing awareness of interdependence and changing norms about civic responsibilities that extend beyond any one nation's borders. On the negative side, growth and global markets are increasing the risks associated with other governments' regulatory and other failures on ordinary people's lives and well-being—from the spread of resistance to antimicrobial drugs, to the costs of climate change, to the problems of financial markets—and the supply of good governance at the global level seems increasingly inadequate to meet the resulting challenges.

Global governance is a huge topic that extends from security, to health, to human rights, international criminal courts, and more. The focus here is on global economic and financial governance, in particular the shortfall of global cooperation among nation-states that matters not just for economic growth itself but for the future path of economic growth—how shared and sustainable it will be. Global inequality and climate are issues on which there

---

[1] The 1996 *Human Development Report* expressed concern about growth that was, among other problems, "ruthless. . . where the fruits of economic growth mostly benefit the rich" and "future-less. . .where the present generation squanders resources needed by future generations" (UNDP 1996, 2–4).

are solutions that are win–win for most countries and their citizens. But they require that domestic policies in the richest and largest countries be better aligned with the demands of an interdependent world—often at short-run costs to key interest and ideological groups in those countries.[2] Domestic policy failings put a premium on the possibility that changing awareness and norms on these issues within countries, particularly within countries like the United States and China, could affect their internal politics. Moreover, changing norms could provide a vehicle for the political leadership within those countries, in their own enlightened self-interest, to bind themselves to rules and policies that would otherwise be politically difficult to manage at home.

To a very large extent, a country's growth and the extent of its inequality depend primarily on its own policies and politics and "governance," not on global rules and institutions or "global governance." Rapid growth and increases in inequality in China and India following their firm embrace of market principles in the last several decades are evidence of that. Similarly, weak growth since the financial crisis, and several decades of wage stagnation in the United States, are as much or more a product of the United States' own fiscal, monetary, and financial sector policies as of increasing competitiveness elsewhere and resulting global imbalances over which it has had less control.

But it is also true that no country can insulate itself from the risks to its growth posed by other countries' economic and financial policy mistakes and by the trend of increasing emissions of greenhouse gases. The enormous differences in income between the richest and poorest countries—and within countries between the elite and the marginalized—constitute a moral challenge in an interconnected world. That challenge commands global collaboration to help bind all countries to trade, migration, aid, tax, and anticorruption and other policies and programs that would ensure that growth benefits the bottom half of the world's population. Greater cooperation and collaboration can make more likely and more effective individual countries' own efforts to bend the path of future growth toward greater equality and sustainability.

In section 7.2, I define global governance and set out the nature of the challenge, arguing that the current system is flawed in two ways. First, it is too weak to adequately and consistently represent the interests of ordinary citizens in an interdependent global economy. The problem is less an intrusive "world government" than a weak and often ineffective global polity; there is no analogue at the global level to the role of the state in forging and managing a domestic social contract that corrects for initial inequalities at birth and deals with such market externalities as pollution. Second, where the system

---

[2] I am grateful to Pratap Mehta for helping clarify the different underlying problems—ideological differences, distributive conflicts, technological superiority of some countries—with which global governance needs to contend.

does act (or fails to act), it often reinforces and better reflects the interests of the rich and powerful in the world—countries, corporations, and people—than those of the ordinary citizen. Sometimes global rules and institutions give more voice to people than they have in their own countries, as in the opening stories. But much of the time they do not.

In section 7.3, I summarize evidence that despite tremendous progress in the past several decades in developing countries, the bottom half of the world's population that lives in those countries is and will be relatively poor and deeply insecure in income terms for another two decades at least, with little political voice in their own countries, let alone in the global community. Within developing countries, even equally shared growth will result in growing distance between the income and political clout of the relatively rich and that of the relatively poor. In the advanced economies, the middle class (as well as labor versus capital) has gained little or nothing in income terms, undermining confidence in the market model itself and in the benefits of global markets.

In section 7.4, I discuss evidence from worldwide surveys showing high levels of global consciousness, or what might be called "global citizenship"; younger and better-educated respondents are more likely to think of themselves as global citizens and have higher apparent demand for more globally fair and far-sighted policies in their own countries. Attitudes and norms seem to be ahead of the institutions and rules that make up official global governance.

In section 7.5, I turn to the "stuck" supply side of global governance, focusing on the economic institutions and clubs that operate across countries, including the G20, the IMF, the multilateral banks, and the recently established Green Climate Fund. Although wholly dependent on their sovereign members, particularly on their larger and more powerful members, they have delegated autonomy to act in the broad interests of all people and for that reason constitute a global public good in themselves. For the most part, the world, especially the world's bottom half, is better off with than without them. But they are less legitimate and effective than they need to be. A key problem is that collective action among sovereigns is difficult in the first place, particularly so with the relative decline of the United States and the reality of today's G-0 (zero) world.

In section 7.6, I suggest some implications. How can the moral force of changing norms for fairer and more farsighted growth be better reflected in the institutions and the rules that matter at the political level? How can the activism of "global citizens" in demanding better rules and policies on global issues be more effectively harnessed? What are the implications for policies at global institutions, including a focus on transparency, crowd-sourcing, even mechanisms equivalent to global "voting"? In the most advanced democracies, they include development at the political level of a better narrative in support of multilateralism and cooperation in general on economic issues.

7.2 The Nature of the Challenge: Interdependent Global Markets without Global Governance

In an increasingly interdependent global system, there is an inherent logic to the idea of what is commonly called global governance. Though economic globalization, or the globalization of markets, has been a key contributor to better lives around the world, bigger and deeper markets, unfettered and unmanaged, will never be sufficient to improve lives for the people in the bottom half of the world's distribution. The theory is straightforward. Within and across countries, markets are inherently asymmetric, favoring the already rich and connected, and they do not deal with critical intergenerational and other externalities, such as climate change.[3] Within countries, it is the function of the nation-state to provide the basic public good of security of citizens and to use taxes, subsidies, and regulatory powers to offset initial inequalities (by, for example, financing equal access to schooling and forcing polluters to internalize the costs they would otherwise impose on others). Across countries, there is an analogous function for global governance, in addition to protecting citizens from violence, to compensate for initial and ongoing inequalities across nations and peoples and to deal with climate, financial, and other market failures at the global level.

What exactly is global governance? In this chapter, it is defined in terms of national and international political decision-making processes, rules, and institutions that affect outcomes that matter beyond any one nation's borders. It is more than what the familiar transnational institutions and clubs (the United Nations, the WTO, the G20) are and do. As an outcome, it cannot be thought of as independent of decisions (or lack of decisions) at the level of sovereign states that bear on citizens in other sovereign states—including but not restricted to decisions of sovereign states, particularly states that are large and powerful, in the context of transnational and intergovernmental institutions. It can be thought of as the more formal portion of the "global polity"—a broader concept including less formal arrangements sometimes seen as the political counterpart of the global market.[4]

---

[3] There is less agreement on the role of government in dealing with "asymmetric markets" and resulting inequality (Birdsall 2002) than with the market failures that result in environmental problems.

[4] The "global polity" includes both "institutions with a street address" (Risse 2006, 181) such as the WTO and the IMF and international regimes that Krasner defines as "sets of implicit or

Global civil society operates alongside global governance. Global civil society includes nongovernmental service and advocacy clubs and organizations (NGOs such as Médecins Sans Frontières, charitable and advocacy organizations such as Oxfam, and philanthropic individuals and foundations such at the Bill & Melinda Gates Foundation), as well as the many transnational professional associations and business organizations (such as the Business Coalition for Sustainable Development) that operate at the global level.

The argument in this chapter simplifies the distinction between global civil society and global governance using a simple demand-and-supply framework.[5] As shown in Figure 7.2, global civil society and active global citizens make up the demand for better rules and policies that matter at the global level, including both local and national policies with global spillovers and internationally agreed rules and policies. They work to influence the supply of those decisions, rules, and policies of national or sovereign states with global implications or spillovers, as well as the decisions and policies of the transnational and global clubs and institutions that operate at the behest of various sovereign states. The challenge is to make the supply side—the

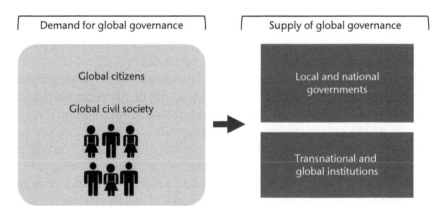

Figure 7.2 Demand for and Supply of Global Governance
Source: Authors.

explicit principles, norms, rules, and decision-making procedures around which actors' expectations converge in a given area of international relations" (1983, 2; see also Ruggie 1975. It is beyond the scope of this chapter to summarize the extensive literature in sociology, political science, and international relations on the concepts of the global polity and global governance. The approach here is most closely related to Held (2003), Held and McGrew (2003), and Norris (2003). Essays in Held and Koenig-Archibugi (2005) provide a comprehensive summary of the debate on global governance, sovereignty, and public accountability. For a more general treatment of globalization and global governance, see also Keohane and Nye (1974) and Keohane (2001).

[5] Anheier, Glasius, and Kaldor (2001a) and other essays in Anheier, Glasius, and Kaldor (2001b) and Kaldor, Moore, and Selchow (2012) provide a conceptual and empirical introduction to the idea of global civil society.

more and less powerful sovereign states themselves and the institutions, regimes, and clubs in which sovereign states cooperate—more effective and more responsive to the needs and demands of citizens on the demand side.

The focus on global governance does not imply that decision-making at the global level can or should always or often substitute for decision-making at the national or lower levels of government. The subsidiarity principle calls for political decision-making to be as decentralized as possible, in order to maximize the influence of the people whose welfare will be most affected by particular decisions. Moreover, it is sovereign states that are the locus of most decisions and policies that have implications beyond any country's borders (financial services, trade, taxes, immigration, fishing, forests and other climate-relevant policies), and it is states that have the tax, regulatory, and enforcement powers needed to back up coordinated policies and cooperation in and through international institutions.

However, as global markets become bigger, deeper, and more integrated, the resulting greater interdependence increases the global space within which citizens of any one country are more likely to be affected by decisions made in other countries over which they have no political control.[6] On the one hand, citizens are better able than ever to make demands on powerful authorities beyond the borders of their own countries; on the other hand, they are more vulnerable than ever to the harm authorities and governments other than their own can do to their own well-being.

Governments as well as countries are vulnerable to others' decisions. This century is likely to see a continuing unbundling of the tight relationship between geographic territory and sovereign control. Sovereignty will continue to be the dominant order. But changes in communication, the consolidation of formerly nation-based corporations into global entities, the increase in the reach and influence of international nongovernmental and other civil society groups, changes in production (as a result of robotic and other technologies), and the increasing mobility of money and people across borders all make it harder for sovereign states to collect taxes, enforce laws, and generally impose political order inside their borders.[7] The optimal size or reach of governance arrangements seems to have increased, for good and for ill, as markets and people have become more connected. Governance has moved from families, to parishes, to towns, to states, to nations, to federal

---

[6] Held (2003, 471) invokes a principle of "inclusiveness and subsidiarity." In drawing "proper boundaries around units of collective decision-making. . .those significantly. . .affected by public decisions. . . should, ceteris paribus, have an equal opportunity, directly or indirectly through elected representatives, to influence and shape them [and] to have a say in their making."

[7] In what is an exaggeration with a grain of truth, globalization has been called "the twilight of sovereignty" (Wriston 1992, cited in Fukuyama 2011).

states, as trade and mobility of people have increased and transportation and communications costs fallen.

In this sense, the problem is that the current global polity is weak in managing the global economy in the common interest, compared with the traditional powers of the typical state in managing the domestic economy. One reason why this is so is that cooperation and coordination among states is hard; it is difficult for sovereign states to cede the equivalent of tax and other powers to regional and global institutions, even when it is in their long-run interests to cooperate. The result is that the global polity is too weak to represent ordinary citizens on many issues where global coordination and cooperation are necessary, or where global coordination and cooperation would make everyone better off. It is too weak to keep the peace and prevent genocide. On economic issues, it is too weak to eliminate tax havens and restrain "race-to-the-bottom" tax competition among countries desperate to attract capital; to extend and enforce agreed safety standards to protect industrial workers at the bottom of complex multinational supply chains; to rationalize rich-country immigration policies that deprive citizens in developing countries of the right to move even as they impede growth in already rich countries; to generate agreement to price emissions of heat-trapping gasses and otherwise deal with the high and rising costs of climate change in tropical Africa, India, China, or elsewhere in the developing world.

A related problem is that the current system of global governance lacks the legitimacy of the democratic state, often representing the global elite better than the ordinary citizen, through economic and political power that reinforces rather than tempers the excesses of the global market. As is often the case at the local and national levels, powerful interests sometimes block rules and decisions that would yield benefits for most people (as in the case of regulatory failures in financial markets or immigration or climate) and sometimes impose rules and decisions that violate the larger interests of the majority affected (as in the case of the initial WTO Agreement on the Trade Related Aspects of Intellectual Property Rights [TRIPS] regime).

The opening stories illustrate, however, that the system of global governance can be a vehicle for enhancing the interests of ordinary people, by providing a voice to people advocating for better rules and policies in countries other than their own. It is in this sense that the ordinary citizen can be better off with than without a system of global governance—and that a stronger and more representative system is desirable.

7.3 The Bottom Half: Is the World on the Right Path?

Growth in the past two decades, and especially the past decade, has been high in many developing countries. Because China and India together account for so much of the world's population, and had high rates of poverty two decades ago, their growth has reduced global poverty dramatically. As a result, the typical person in the developing world is immensely better off today than her counterpart of the past. New technologies, better organization, and delivery of services within countries, and programs financed by private and public aid, have contributed to gains in education, health, and other social indicators that have been faster and more dramatic than gains in income in the decades since the end of World War II (Kenny 2012).

Life has been getting better in other domains as well. In his treatise on the decline of violence over the thousands of years of human history, Steven Pinker (2011b) credits the spread of democracy, trade, and international organizations associated with the end of proxy wars in the developing world; the rights revolution; and the expansion of international peacekeeping. In short, what has made the world a better place has been the combination of the state, with its monopoly on legitimate force and its ability to use tax revenue for basic services; the global market and the trading system; and the beneficent effects of globally organized cooperation on not only peacekeeping but also smallpox eradication, tariff reduction, and more.[8]

However, for the world's typical citizen in the developing world, at the median of the distribution of developing world income, life is still harsh. Though her income has risen from perhaps $1 a day 50 years ago, it is still less than $3 a day today—well below the estimate of daily income, closer to $10 a day, associated with a permanent escape from poverty and entry into the secure middle class in developing countries.[9] This typical citizen is likely to live in a country—Bolivia, China, India, Nicaragua, Nigeria, Tanzania—where, though not poor by the international standard of living on less than $1.25 a day, her ability to hold the state accountable to her as a citizen with rights is limited. Consider the case of Mohamed Bouazizi, the Tunisian man who immolated himself when the local police destroyed his vegetable cart, triggering the Arab Spring. He was not poor, but he was not materially secure either, and for him the state was more predator than protector.

In this sense, there is a long way to go in reducing global income inequality. Though China, India, Brazil, many countries in Africa, and other countries in the developing world are now growing faster than countries in the rich world, bringing unconditional convergence in income for the first time in several hundred years, the absolute differences in income between the advanced economies and developing countries—and between the richest and

---

[8] Pinker refers to "the expansion of people's parochial little worlds through literacy, mobility, education, science, history, journalism and mass media" (Pinker 2011a).

[9] The estimate of median daily income is based on Milanovic (2012). On the $10 line, see Lopez-Calva and Ortiz-Juarez (2011), based on panel data from three countries of Latin America, and Birdsall (2010).

the poorest people, wherever they live—are still enormous. Current median household income per capita in the United States is about $50 a day,[10] more than ten times that in the developing world. Relative poverty and indignity are still the reality for at least half the world's population.

Assuming that growth is shared equally within each country, so that country distributions of income do not change, projections of country-specific growth for the next 25 years imply a near doubling of the income of the median-income citizen, to more than $5.[11] But even with this increase, most people's income will still be well below the level associated with material security. For example, households in Bangladesh at per person consumption of about $5 a day allocate more than 60 percent of their total spending to food, leaving little for other basics. And many will still have only limited political agency in their own countries. If democracy works in countries like India, where people with income of $5 a day are above the median, their interests and aspirations will be represented reasonably well in the political system. But the reality is that the poor are poorly represented in even the most mature democracies of the advanced economies. In much of the developing world, democracy, where it exists, is fragile, and systems of accountability do not work well.

For the "typical" citizens who follow Bouazizi, much depends on the long-run politics of distribution within their own countries. The politics of distribution, in turn, may well depend on the extent to which the rising middle classes see their interests aligned with those of the still larger majority of citizens in the vulnerable or struggler group (larger in virtually all developing countries through 2030), rather than with the richer elite in their own countries. For the former condition to hold requires that the new middle classes support the kind of institution and state-building in their own countries (see Rodrik 2013) that will sustain the growth of the recent past; whether they will is not clear and certainly depends on specific countries' political and other circumstances.

Our projections of income growth imply an increase in the size of the ($10–$50) middle class in the developing world from about 15 percent to about 30 percent of the population (that is, from about 800 million in 2010 to

[10] Pritchett and Spivack (2013). The median income household in the United States spends about 10 percent of its income on food (based on median household total money income divided by the mean household size (U.S. Census Bureau 2012)).

[11] These estimates are explained in Birdsall, Lustig, and Meyer (2013). They use a simple model to project growth and to rescale the global income and consumption distribution data for 2005 from the World Bank's World Income Distribution (WYD) database. Growth projections rely on a three-factor production model from the Centre d'Études Prospectives et d'Informations Internationales (Fouré, Bénassy-Quéré, and Fontagne 2012). They then assume that household income and consumption increase by 70 percent of the real GDP per capita (at purchasing power parity) growth rate. This methodology follows Ahluwalia, Carter, and Chenery (1979) and Dadush and Shaw (2011).

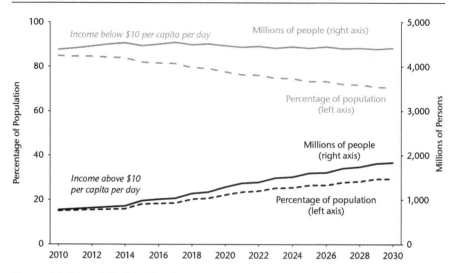

Figure 7.3 Rise of the Middle Class in Low- and Middle-Income Countries, 2010–30

Note: Income distributions for 2005 are rescaled using real GDP per capita growth forecasts, assuming no changes in the distributions.

Source: Birdsall, Lustig, and Meyer 2014.

more than 1.9 billion in 2030; Birdsall, Lustig, and Meyer 2014).[12] Figure 7.3 plots the projected increase in the share of people in the developing world with income of more than $10 per day (that is, the middle class and the rich) with respect to the poor and the vulnerable (see Birdsall 2012 for an explanation of the income groups).

Projections are not predictions; they almost surely overstate the extent to which recent trends will persist, both in the level of growth and the distribution of its benefits. The sustained growth in East Asia for more than 40 years relied heavily on increasing manufactured exports—a strategy, as Rodrik points out, that may not be available to current low-income countries. The equally shared growth built into the projections may also be optimistic; the trend since the 1990s of increasing inequality in many (though not all) countries makes the politics of sustaining the free market

[12] These numbers refer to the middle class in low- and middle-income countries. Globally, we estimate the middle class to grow from about 1.5 billion in 2010 to 2.6 billion in 2030. This definition of the middle class is based on evidence from Latin America that on average it is at an income or consumption level of $10 a day that people are relatively secure from falling back into poverty, defined as $4 or less per day. The relevant minimum might well be somewhat lower in poorer regions. In a similar exercise, Ravallion (2012) finds that between 2008 and 2015, the number of poor people could decline from more than 1.2 billion people (22.4 percent of the developing world's population) to a little more than 1.0 billion (16.3 percent of the total population). He assumes distributional changes, whereas Birdsall, Lustig, and Meyer (2013) assume constant 2005 income distributions. Both apply country-level growth projections to baseline poverty data, assuming a pass-through of national accounts growth to survey means.

and globalization itself difficult, especially in the advanced economies, where the middle class has had little if any increase in its real income over the past two decades.

Most problematic of all is the fact that even equally shared growth across all parts of the income distribution increases the absolute difference in income between the income-secure middle class and the rich (more than $10) and the poor and vulnerable (under $10), as shown for Brazil and India in Figure 7.4. Within countries, absolute differences can generate increases in the prices of positional goods and in the social tensions associated with high inequality (Frank 1985, 2005). They also imply growing distance between the political clout of the relatively rich and that of the relatively poor. It is impossible to predict how these changes will affect the politics of distribution within countries and the interests and values of the middle class with respect to their poorer citizens, or how they will interact with evolving views of the new middle class on global issues.

Finally, the rise of the middle class in the developing world is leading to huge increases in the consumption of energy. In the absence of higher pricing of carbon and the early elimination of the link between energy consumption and carbon emissions, this increase is exacerbating climate problems and could reduce growth itself (see chapter 6, by Andrew Steer).

In short, even healthy rates of growth in the developing world, even equally shared, do not move the bottom half of the world's future population into the secure middle class. They imply continuing high levels of poverty in the

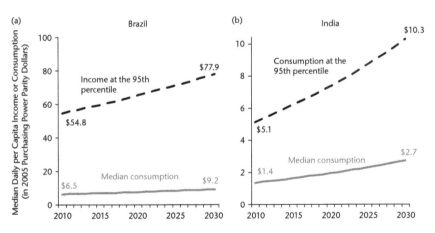

Figure 7.4 Divergence between Top and Middle (Median) of Income Distribution in Brazil and India, 2010–30

Note: Income and consumption distributions for 2005 are rescaled using real GDP per capita growth forecasts, assuming no changes in their distributions.

Source: Birdsall, Lustig, and Meyer 2014.

relative sense and inequality of outcomes overall, while adding to the risks of climate change.

For the next several decades, the average citizen—a person with global median income—will continue to be mostly a victim or beneficiary of others' actions and decisions, in her own country but also abroad. She may enjoy the benefits of living in a more democratic and accountable state—or not. She may or may live in a fragile or frontline state, where poverty, inequality, and local injustices may lead to civil conflict—or not. Her situation and that of the rest of the bottom half of the world's population might in itself create risks for other countries around the world—or not.

What does her situation have to do with global governance? The moral challenge for the global "system" is to minimize the risks from abroad that she faces—SARS or other pandemics, a new financial crisis, damage to her natural environment and livelihood caused by climate change—and to maximize, to the limited extent possible from outside, her opportunities for a better life. Projections of growth rely in part on the assumption that the current institutional arrangements for managing the global economy will continue to play this role, at least to the extent they have up to now. The next section suggests demand that they do so is growing.

7.4 Norms Not Politics: Global Citizens and the Demand for Better Global Governance

Consider a simple model of citizens' demand for "global governance" in the form of a better or better-managed globalization. Individual demand takes the form of interest in and advocacy of policies that maximize positive global spillovers and minimize negative ones, both within individuals' own countries and in supranational institutions.

Demand for better managed globalization is difficult to observe directly. However, it is possible to observe aspects of "globality" or global consciousness at the individual level, in at least three forms: awareness of the global forces that affect one's life, at home or abroad; an attitude accepting or internalizing some rights and responsibilities in the face of those forces as a global citizen and the logic of nations cooperating through international institutions; and activism or lobbying at some level for changes in policies and practices at home or abroad to alter those global forces—including in one's own interests, given greater awareness of interdependence. Over time, an increase in these three As (awareness, attitude, activism) on the part of individuals could be viewed as the natural outcome of cheaper and faster communications across borders and cheaper and more reliable transportation, which provide new opportunities to work, live, study, and vacation outside one's own country. They also bring increased exposure and vulnerability to global forces: global financial crises, wage competition, climate change, cyber-warfare, terrorism, drug trafficking, and so on. Across individuals, at any one time, education, exposure to media, income, childhood travel, living outside one's country of birth, and sector of work are likely to be associated with one or more of the three As.

The identification of greater global consciousness of individuals in terms of awareness and attitude is different from the concept of "cosmopolitanism" or "cosmopolitan citizens" proposed by Pippa Norris and Ronald Inglehart, for example (Norris and Inglehart 2009). Norris defines cosmopolitans in terms of personal identity and contrasts them with "nationalists" (Norris 2003). Cosmopolitans are understood as identifying more broadly with their continent or with the world as a whole than with their country, and in particular as having greater faith in regional and global institutions of global governance than do nationalists, who identify primarily with their own country.

I take the view that the AAA of individual globality need not substitute for—indeed, can enhance—national identity.[13] And I prefer to treat institutions of global governance not as an indicator of individuals' global consciousness but as an outcome of demand for policies and practices relevant to managing globalization (as in Figure 2.1), both because global AAA need not reduce an individual's primary identity with her country (or local community) and because demand, as proxied by AAA citizens, may well be for changes in national policies in their own countries and in their own interests that affect global forces, fully independent of confidence or lack thereof in another regional or global institution.[14]

7.4.1 Awareness and Attitudes

The most comprehensive country coverage in a single set of surveys of global awareness and attitudes comes from the World Values Survey, which covers up to 70 countries in a series including 1981–84 and four additional waves

[13] Mayda and Rodrik (2005) cite Smith and Jarkko (1998, 1) as noting that "national pride is not incompatible with cosmopolitanism (literally being a 'world citizen')." I allow for the possibility that identifying primarily with one's own country is not incompatible with a high degree of global consciousness in terms of awareness, attitude, or activism.

[14] In the long run, confidence in global institutions could be a determinant of globally oriented activism at some level (for example, as a result of the effect of global institutions on welfare at the national level). That effect is likely to be greater in weak and poor countries, where welfare is more likely to be affected by global institutions' practices, as suggested by the opening story of the Ghanaian testifying at a U.S. Congressional hearing. However, even in these countries, the role of global institutions in affecting real long-term welfare is limited compared with the role of national policies and conditions, as most studies of the impact of outside aid, trade, anticorruption and other policies conclude. A possible exception is UN peacekeeping in countries like Somalia and Liberia.

that are publicly available.[15] Survey questions regarding supranational identity and world citizenship provide some insight into the extent and possible future trend of individuals' awareness of global interdependence. Table 7.1 summarizes the results of simple tabulations of the responses to these two questions. Supranational identity (most recently asked about only in the survey wave conducted in 1999–2004) is defined as the percentage of respondents answering "world" as their primary identity, given the choices locality, region, country, continent, or world. About 11 percent (up to 16 percent if "world" as a second choice is counted) did so; there is some association with being younger and better educated and a possible association with higher relative income within one's own country. The responses for the United States were particularly high, second only to Moldova among the more than 50 countries for which these data are available, at 20 percent for world as first choice and 33 percent as second choice.

Almost 30 percent of all respondents asked the question "Do you see yourself as a world citizen?" (2005–07) "strongly agreed" that they did. (In this case, respondents did not need to rank seeing themselves as a world citizen against seeing themselves as citizens of their own country.) On a question about the degree of confidence in the United Nations (not shown), 58 percent in the 1994–99 wave and 50 percent in the 2005–06 wave were positive, suggesting not only awareness but acceptance of the idea of an international institution (Birdsall and Meyer forthcoming). These results are consistent with largely favorable ratings of the United Nations, the IMF, and the World Bank in other surveys conducted over the last decade. In France, Germany, and the United States, for example, more than half of respondents had favorable views because "many global problems can't be solved by a single country" (Pew Global Attitudes Project 2009, 2011 and German Marshall Fund 2005, cited in Council on Foreign Relations 2011).

Statistical analysis indicates that identifying oneself as a world citizen is strongly associated with education, especially higher education (Figure 7.5), and to some extent with higher income and younger age in all countries (see appendix table 7A.1).

The question about supranational identity was asked in four successive survey waves between 1981 and 2004; there is no upward trend in the responses, as might be expected. However, the relationship of education, age, and income to the responses on both questions implies that awareness is likely to increase over time, especially with continuing gains in education in developing countries. In principle, the age effect could be a life-cycle

---

[15] Nancy Birdsall is particularly grateful to Christian Meyer for his contribution to this section.

Table 7.1 Awareness of Global Citizenship, by Socioeconomic Characteristic

Characteristic	Supranational identity[a]	World citizen[b]
Total	10.6	28.6
Age		
15–29	13.5	31.6
30–49	11.0	28.7
50 and over	7.4	25.4
Gender		
Male	11.4	29.4
Female	9.9	27.8
Size of town		
Small (< 50,000)	8.7	26.9
Large (≥ 50,000)	13.6	29.7
Highest education level attained		
Incomplete elementary	6.3	31.5
Complete elementary	8.3	27.1
Incomplete lower-secondary	8.8	27.9
Complete lower-secondary	10.3	26.6
Incomplete upper-secondary	11.1	27.6
Complete upper-secondary	11.5	27.8
Incomplete tertiary	15.1	29.6
Complete tertiary	15.5	30.7
Income decile		
1	11.3	32.1
2	9.9	27.6
3	9.4	26.1
4	10.2	26.6
5	9.9	28.2
6	10.5	29.5
7	10.3	29.2
8	12.6	30.0
9	11.7	28.9
10	14.6	32.2

a. Percentage of respondents reporting "world" as first choice in question in wave 4: "To which of these geographical groups would you say you belong first of all? Locality, Region, Country, Continent, World."

b. Percentage of respondents responding "strongly agree" in question in wave 5: "People have different views about themselves and how they relate to the world. Using this card, would you tell me how strongly you agree or disagree with each of the following statements about how you see yourself? 'I see myself as a world citizen.'"

Note: Figures show results for full sample of all countries in each wave. Observations are weighted using integrated *N*-preserving weights.

Source: Author's calculations, based on data from wave 4 (1999–2004) and wave 5 (2005–07) of the European and World Values Surveys.

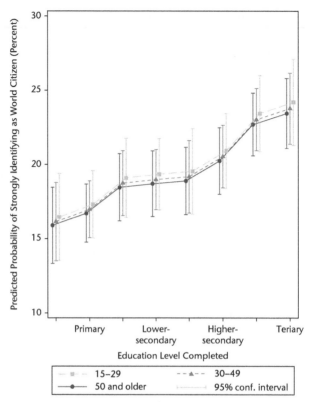

Note: Standard errors are clustered at the country level.

Figure 7.5 Predicted Probabilities of Strongly Identifying as World Citizen, by Education and Age

Note: Figure shows adjusted predictions, holding all independent variables at their means. Calculations are based on an ordered logit regression (appendix Table A.1, second column). Robust standard errors are clustered at the country level. Ranges show 95 percent confidence interval.

Source: Birdsall and Meyer (forthcoming), based on data from wave 5 (2005–07) of the European and World Values Surveys.

rather than a generational one.[16] But cohort and trend analysis of age effects in election surveys in nine western societies over several decades indicates that age effects were indeed intergenerational, reflecting a marked shift to what Inglehart calls "postmaterialist" values among people who grew up after World War II (Inglehart 1971, 1997, 2008; Inglehart and Baker 2000).[17]

---

[16] Similarly, within countries, the effect of education could be related to relative rather than to absolute levels of schooling. However, in contrast to age, statistical analysis suggests similarity across countries in the effect by level.

[17] The measure of postmaterialist values is based on respondents' choice of goals among a set designed to tap economic and physical security on the one hand and self-expression and the nonmaterial quality of life on the other. The result is similar to that first reported by Easterlin

To go beyond awareness to an indication of attitudes relevant to global interdependence, consider questions on immigration (2005–07), economic aid to poorer countries (1999–2004), and the global environment (2005–07).[18] Table 7.2 provides simple tabulations of these results; appendix table 7A.2 provides the results of an ordered logit regression.

Asked about immigration policy, a relatively high 13 percent of respondents would "let anyone come" from another country; 41 percent would let immigrants come "as long as jobs are available" (not shown). Strong support for immigration is, not surprisingly, higher in low-income than high-income countries (Figure 7.6); in high-income countries, it increases with education, especially higher education.[19]

Attitudes toward aid are even more positive. A majority of respondents in all countries surveyed favored providing more economic aid to poorer countries, and 16 percent favored providing "a lot more" aid. Support was even greater in a subsample of rich countries, where about 60 percent of all respondents and almost 70 percent of respondents aged 15–29 favored providing more aid to poorer countries. In other surveys, overall support for economic aid was similar or greater. In 17 of 20 developed countries, more than 80 percent of respondents said they had "a moral responsibility to work to reduce hunger and severe poverty in poor countries"; in only three developing countries were the percentages lower than 80 percent: 72 percent in India, still high, and 54 percent in Russia (World Public Opinion 2008, as cited in Council on Foreign Relations 2011). The majority of people polled in eight advanced economies were willing to finance the cost of achieving Millennium Development Goal 1 (eradicating extreme poverty and hunger), as long as other countries pulled their weight.

Support for aid at these levels is surprising, given that aid budgets are seen as vulnerable in many of the traditional donor countries. In the United States, for example, with the possible exception of aid for humanitarian and health needs, aid is not considered a big vote-winner, unless tied to particular commercial interests or security concerns. It may be too easy to "favor" aid in surveys; attitude questions do not capture well the priority respondents would put on sending aid abroad compared with spending at home. The

(1995) and more recently reported in surveys of well-being, namely of diminishing (though not to zero) returns to increases in personal income. See Kahneman and Deaton (2010), Graham (2012), and Stevenson and Wolfers (2008).

[18] Questions regarding attitudes provide only an indication of possible demand, as respondents are not given any budget constraint or indication of the potential opportunity cost associated with their choices.

[19] These findings mirror earlier findings by Mayda (2006), who shows that education is positively correlated with pro-immigration attitudes in richer countries but negatively correlated with pro-immigration attitudes in poorer countries. For attitudes on trade, see Mayda and Rodrik (2005), who find that a pro-trade attitude is positively associated with pride in a country's democracy and negatively associated with pride in a country's political influence in the world.

high level of positive responses does, however, signal widespread awareness of the substantial needs in other countries and some sense of responsibility for attending to them in an interconnected global system.

Asked about global warming, 60 percent of respondents in all 25 advanced and developing countries surveyed judged it a "serious" problem (majorities in 15 of 25 found it to be a "very serious" problem), as shown in Table 7.2. In a similar global survey, majorities in 23 of 25 countries agreed that "dealing with the problem of climate change should be given priority, even if it causes slower economic growth and some loss of jobs" (Pew Research Global Attitudes Project 2009, as cited in Council on Foreign Relations 2011). And in one of the few statistically robust results associated with gender, women in high-income countries are more likely than men to be concerned about global warming, perhaps because they are more likely than men to take into account the risks to their children and grandchildren.[20]

As in the case of questions about identity as a world citizen, there is no clear trend over time on the questions on immigration and economic aid; the framing of the questions, changes in economic and other circumstances, and the changing sets of countries included in various waves could obscure any trend.[21]

What is the bottom line? Though no trend emerges between the late 1980s and the mid-2000s, the likelihood of growing future awareness about global issues and changing attitudes—more positive about immigration and aid, more concerned about climate change—is built into the education and possibly the age results in the cross-sections. The growing proportion of young people in developing countries (at least for the next decade); the continuing emphasis on increasing access to education; projected increases in the size of the middle class (reaching 30 percent in many middle-income countries by 2030); the high levels of financial, commercial, and social interdependence among countries (supply chains, food and toy standards, weather and disease monitoring); and the "exponential

---

[20] Overall, concern about climate change also appears to be positively associated with country GDP per capita, although the relationship is not statistically significant. In country cross-sections, demand for local environmental services such as antipollution controls and increased habitat protection does not seem to kick in until GDP per capita reaches at least $10,000; concern about global warming could be independent of income altogether and might not have any income relationship with willingness to accept the costs of dealing with it. There is a large body of literature on the environmental Kuznets curve; see Stern (2004) for a good overview of the debate. Using the World Values Survey data, Dunlap and York (2008) find no clear relationship between country income and environmental concern. Torgler and Garcia-Valiñas (2005) offer a comprehensive analysis of individual-level determinants of environmental concerns using World Values Survey data for Spain.

[21] Efforts were made to identify trends using both a constructed constant sample of countries across waves and a changing sample. In both approaches, time dummies were statistically significant but not in any order suggesting a consistent trend.

Table 7.2 Attitudes toward Immigration, Global Warming, and Economic Aid, by Socioeconomic Characteristic

Characteristic	Immigration [a]		Global warming [b]		Economic aid [c]	
	Full sample	High income	Full sample	High income	Full sample	High income
Total	13.3	6.8	60.0	60.5	52.9	60.1
Age						
15–29	16.1	9.4	59.6	61.3	56.2	68.8
30–49	13.0	7.3	61.0	61.7	51.9	57.9
50 and older	10.9	5.2	59.2	59.0	50.4	56.0
Gender						
Male	13.6	7.1	59.4	58.1	52.0	59.1
Female	13.0	6.6	60.6	62.7	53.8	61.0
Size of town						
Small (< 50,000)	13.7	6.0	58.9	60.7	55.9	66.2
Large (≥ 50,000)	15.3	10.9	60.1	61.6	51.8	59.6
Highest education attained						
Incomplete primary	21.7	6.1	55.6	52.1	56.9	70.6
Complete primary	12.8	5.9	55.5	58.2	51.7	61.3
Incomplete lower-secondary	17.4	6.1	59.6	62.1	50.7	50.5
Complete lower-secondary	11.6	4.5	58.2	57.1	49.5	54.0
Incomplete upper-secondary	10.0	5.9	61.6	59.6	49.9	52.8
Complete upper-secondary	10.1	6.9	60.9	62.4	52.8	58.9
Incomplete tertiary	11.2	8.5	66.5	63.9	54.0	60.6
Complete tertiary	11.7	10.0	66.3	63.6	58.1	69.1
Income decile						
1	15.1	7.7	60.7	61.5	56.1	63.4
2	14.8	5.9	60.0	61.3	55.0	62.4
3	12.5	5.6	60.3	60.7	53.1	56.5
4	12.2	5.5	60.4	58.9	49.7	61.3
5	13.5	6.8	60.2	60.1	51.0	62.4
6	13.7	6.7	57.3	57.8	53.9	54.0
7	13.5	8.6	56.4	59.9	52.6	57.8
8	13.3	7.5	58.7	60.9	49.8	54.0
9	12.5	8.4	61.1	63.2	48.0	56.1
10	13.1	9.3	62.9	62.7	50.9	62.2

a. Responses to wave 5 question: "How about people from other countries coming here to work. Which one of the following do you think the government should do?" Percentage refers to respondents answering "let anyone come."

b. Responses to wave 5 question: "Now let's consider environmental problems in the world as a whole. Please, tell me how serious you consider each of the following to be for the world as a whole. Is it very serious, somewhat serious, not very serious or not serious at all? Global warming or the greenhouse effect." Percentage refers to respondents answering "very serious."

c. Responses to wave 5 question: "Some people favor, and others are against, having this country provide economic aid to poorer countries. Do you think that this country should provide more or less economic aid to poorer countries? Would you say we should give. . .?" Percentage refers to respondents answering "a lot more than we do now" or "more than we do now."

Note: "Full sample" refers to full sample in each World Value Survey wave. "High income" is a subsample based on the World Bank country classification. Observations are weighted using integrated *N*-preserving weights.

Source: Author's calculations, based on data from wave 4 (1999–2004) and wave 5 (2005–07) of the European and World Values Surveys.

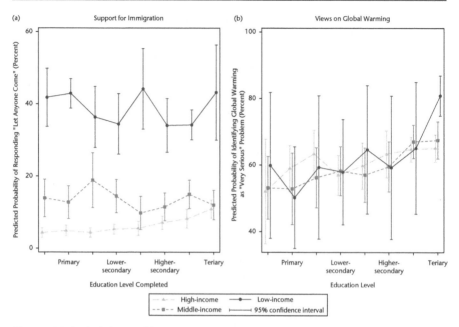

Figure 7.6 Probabilities of Strong Support for Immigration and Believing that Global Warming Is a Very Serious Threat, by Income and Education

Note: Figures show adjusted predictions, holding all independent variables at their means, based on three separate ordered logit models of subsamples for low-, middle- and high-income countries. Income groups follow World Bank classifications. Results include a respondent-level dummy for gender. Standard errors are clustered at the country level. Ranges show 95 percent confidence interval.

Source: Birdsall and Meyer (forthcoming), based on data from wave 5 (2005–07) of the European and World Values Surveys.

technology" (Diamandis and Kotler 2012) of Facebook and other social media associated with the Arab Spring, which clearly reached more people with less education and income faster than would have been possible 20 years earlier, all suggest that the surprise would be a lack of increase in awareness of global issues. What the survey results show is that more educated and younger people are not only more aware but also more supportive of policies in their own countries that would be more friendly to people elsewhere. The surprise would be to observe a decline in the implicit demand for better management, or governance, of globally relevant challenges over the next several decades.[22]

---

[22] The surveys do not give respondents anything that could be said to represent a budget constraint, so I use the word *demand* here in the colloquial rather than the economic sense.

At the same time, the results indicate that awareness of interdependence (and its tradeoffs in terms of individual interests) and support for policies to deal better with interdependence are largely a product of at least some post-secondary education. This finding is consistent with the observation that it is often university students who first take to the streets (and even then often primarily to protect their own narrow interests). Support for fairer and more far-sighted domestic and foreign policies is likely to increase, but from a low base, in the developing world, where over the next several decades, most people in the rising middle class will have at most secondary education. In 2009/10, for example, only about 14 percent of households in middle-income Latin America included an adult who had completed tertiary education; the numbers are even lower in South Asia and much of Africa. The median number of years of schooling of people in Latin America living on $5 a day today—the projected daily per capita income for the median-income person in the world in 2030—was only about six a few years ago (Birdsall 2012). It will thus be many decades before a substantial majority of adults has any postsecondary education.[23]

In short, worldwide surveys indicate that citizens everywhere are aware of the implications of a global market and global interdependence. In the advanced economies, that awareness is reflected in strong concern about climate change and broad support for immigration and foreign aid—what might be viewed as their responsibilities as global citizens—especially among the young and people with university education. In the developing world, awareness of global interdependence is high. But the "demand" for more globally friendly policies at home and in other countries will remain limited for the next two or three decades, even in rapidly growing middle-income countries with rising numbers of people in the new middle class.

7.4.2 Activism

At the individual level, awareness and attitudes as measured crudely above can be thought of as prefatory to activism. At the same time, activist movements may be central to increasing awareness and changing attitudes, by mobilizing individuals who otherwise would not have become engaged.

The decline in the costs of communication and information in just the past ten years as a result of the mobile phone has surely increased awareness of global interdependence everywhere, perhaps even among people in the

---

[23] This figure is the unweighted average of Brazil, Chile, Costa Rica, the Dominican Republic, Honduras, and Mexico in 2008/9, all of which used a harmonized definition. The quality of these estimates varies widely. Own estimates, based on data from the Socio-Economic Database for Latin America and the Caribbean (CEDLAS and World Bank 2012).

bottom half of the world's income distribution. However, the "typical" person in the bottom half of the world's income distribution is much less likely to have the time or tools to participate or the sense of political agency that invites activism. For these people, the costs relative to the benefits of activism are far higher. Such people may have supported the protests at Tahrir Square in Egypt in 2011—but the survey analysis suggests they did not participate in them.

Citizen activism is fueled by the educated and relatively secure middle class, as it was in nineteenth-century Europe. In the early nineteenth century, antislavery advocates organized into societies and associations, initially within their own borders but eventually crossing geographical boundaries as the movement assumed a transnational form. A variety of other movements emerged during this time, from peace groups lobbying at international conferences, to civil society associations focused on trade issues, to the International Committee of the Red Cross, which advocated for the protection of lives and the dignity of victims of armed conflict (see Florini 2000). A 1963 study of international cooperation in Europe in the nineteenth century identified 450 private and nongovernmental international organizations and nearly 3,000 international gatherings (Savedoff 2012, who cites Berridge, Loughlin, and Herring 2009, who in turn refer to a study by Frances Stewart Lyons).

International movements sometimes gained nation-states as allies—Great Britain, for example, used its naval power to discourage the slave trade—resulting in what Savedoff (2012) calls "mixed coalitions" of private and public advocacy. In the twentieth century, philanthropic organizations became advocates for social and political change: the Rockefeller Foundation—the Bill & Melinda Gates Foundation of its day—provided up to half of the budget of the League of Nations Health Office between the wars (Weindling 1995, as cited by Savedoff 2012).

After World War II, the number of civil society and mixed coalition movements operating at the international level increased again, from an estimated 200 in 1909 to more than 35,000 in 2013, with a marked acceleration in the early 1970s and after 2005 (Figure 7.7). The increase in the number of official intergovernmental organizations (such as the IMF and WTO) to about 3,000 today pales in comparison. The number of well-organized and well-funded NGOs that have made the effort to obtain "consultative status" from the United Nations (enabling them to send representatives to UN consultations and conferences) has grown from a handful 50 years ago to about 3,500 today, with a marked acceleration in the late 1990s (Figure 7.8).[24] This growth

[24] These figures are from the Global Policy Forum, based on data from the United Nations Department of Economic and Social Affairs. Categories are determined by the UN Economic

Figure 7.7 Number of Active Intergovernmental and International Nongovernmental Organizations, 1909–2013

Note: Figures include organizations classified by the UIO as types A–G; for 2013, the breakdown of IGO/NGOs is estimated from the total number of active organizations.

Source: Union of International Associations 2012.

was not confined to high-income countries: between 1995 and 2011, their numbers increased nearly fivefold in Asia and eightfold in Africa.

The information and communications revolution is generating new platforms for citizen engagement and advocacy, dramatically reducing the cost of participation and raising the potential for participation to make a difference on the ground and through policy change. This potential is no longer confined primarily to people in high-income countries. Of the 1 billion monthly active users of Facebook (as of December 2012), 82 percent were outside the United States and Canada; Jakarta is one of the top three cities in terms of Twitter (Semiocast 2012). These platforms provide the basis for hundreds of new virtual organizations. Users of Change.org, a petition platform launched in 2007, grew from 1 million in 2010 to 25 million in 2012. Facebook Causes has had 1 billion "actions taken" by 153 million people. Avaaz, a global web movement that seeks to "bring people-powered politics to decision-making

and Social Council (ECOSOC). "General consultative status" is reserved for larger international NGOs that cover most of the issues on the agenda for ECOSOC and its subsidiary bodies; these NGOs tend to have broad geographical reach. "Special consultative status" is for NGOs that cover only a few of the fields of activity of the ECOSOC; these NGOS tend to be smaller and more recently established. "Roster status" is for organizations with a narrow or technical focus that do not cleanly fit into the other categories.

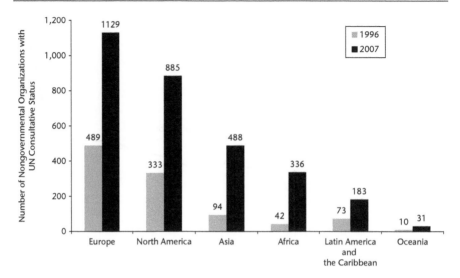

Figure 7.8 Number of Nongovernmental Organizations with UN Consultative Status, by Region, 1996 and 2007

Source: Global Policy Forum, based on data from UN Department of Economic and Social Affairs.

everywhere" has had 50 million "actions" and raised $15 million since its online launch in 2007.[25]

Citizen activism (the NGOs and the mixed coalitions that are part of global society in Figure 7.2) has been successful in pushing the global polity on policies and programs to deal with global inequality; the people active in these groups can reasonably be presumed to be motivated by altruism in improving lives, primarily in developing countries. The Jubilee 2000 movement was an international coalition with members in more than 40 countries that, beginning in the 1990s, lobbied the G8, the IMF, and the multilateral development banks for full cancellation of low-income country debt. Initially a largely Christian movement, Jubilee was famously supported by Bono and Bob Geldof of Live Aid fame, by the establishment and evangelical churches, and by the Jewish leadership in the United States. The movement played a role in triggering considerable economic analysis of the debt issue for poor countries;[26] by the early 2000s, it had succeeded in securing commitments by

[25] A more recent online movement is Globalsolutions.org, with nearly 60,000 members who "want the United States to take a responsible and cooperative role in the world." Since its creation in 2012, the movement has run campaigns to protect the rights of the disabled, include a climate change debate in the presidential debates, and strengthen the arms trade treaty, among others. Members can contribute to the "Global Citizen" blog prominently positioned on the organization's homepage.

[26] This analysis included the book I co-authored with John Williamson (Birdsall and Williamson 2002). The co-founder and initial patron of the Center for Global Development was inspired in part by a film financed by the Ford Foundation and shown on television in which

the G7 and other high-income country creditors to write off virtually all the debt owed to them and to finance equivalent write-offs by the multilateral institutions—at a cost (depending on how their debt is valued) of $130 billion (Jubilee Debt Campaign 2012).

The Jubilee movement operated outside of official government and intergovernmental institutions to change those institutions' policies. But there are other models. The Global Alliance for Vaccines and Immunizations, founded in 2000, and the Global Fund to Fight AIDS, Tuberculosis and Malaria, founded in 2002, were created through nongovernmental initiatives, including the Bill & Melinda Gates Foundation, which used its own funds to leverage substantial additional public financing from willing governments.[27] Since the launch of the Extractive Industries Transparency Initiative (EITI) at the 2002 World Summit for Sustainable Development, 37 countries have signed up to implement a transparency standard jointly agreed to by a coalition of governments, companies, civil society groups, investors, and international organizations. Countries have embodied the EITI principles in national legislation. The 2010 financial sector regulatory reform legislation in the United States includes the Cardin-Lugar provision, which mandates that mining firms raising capital in U.S. markets report their payments to foreign governments; hundreds of policy and advocacy groups seeking to reduce the corruption and waste in extractive industries that ultimately hurt the poor in developing countries lobbied long and hard for the provision.[28] Other movements and organizations—the Robin Hood movement; the Tax Justice Network; the IF Campaign, founded in January 2013—focus on reducing tax evasion and other illicit financial flows and pushing for a financial transactions tax or some other form of international tax that could be used to increase transfers to poor countries and poor people.[29]

These efforts are drawn from hundreds of examples of citizen activism on global issues. Perhaps the most illustrative is the example given in Figure 7.9.

A citizen-based movement harnessed international public opinion that embarrassed the U.S. pharmaceutical industry and the U.S. government into modifying their insistence on strict adherence by developing countries to an internationally agreed upon intellectual property regime. In the run-up to the completion of the multilateral Uruguay Round of trade negotiations, U.S. business interests pressed hard for and won the inclusion of trade-related

the high debt of poor countries in Central America was cited as one culprit in those countries' difficulties in dealing with their social problems.

[27] Savedoff (2012) notes that these and other health initiatives eclipsed the activities of the World Health Organization, the intergovernmental body.

[28] On the work of lobby groups, see the website of Publish What You Pay, a global network of more than 650 organizations (www.publishwhatyoupay.org).

[29] See http://www.robinhoodtax.org/, http://www.taxjustice.net/, and http://enoughfoodif.org/.

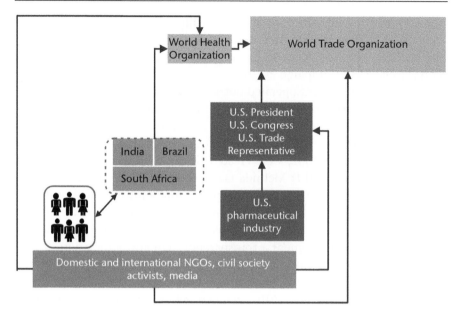

Figure 7.9 A Second Tale of Global Governance
Source: Authors.

intellectual property rules in a multilateral trade agreement—the first time such regulations had been included. In principle, these rules achieved a balance between private incentives for innovation and invention and the public interest in access to new products, including new medicines to save lives. Under pressure from the influential and powerful pharmaceutical lobby in the United States (at the time among the top five in spending on lobbying in Washington, DC; it is now the leading spender), U.S. negotiators won agreement to a system that required that all developing countries adopt a tough minimum standard of protection of intellectual property by 2000 (with additional time for the least developed countries), including patent protection for new medicines and drugs of 20 years, comparable to the period of such protection in the United States. Developing countries as a group, including India and other countries that manufacture generic drugs, agreed only reluctantly; they might not have agreed at all except in the context of the broader benefits of the trade agreement (Devereaux, Lawrence, and Watkins 2006 provide a full discussion). Though aware of the potential benefits of encouraging invention and production in their own industries in the long run, they also feared the costs and the disincentives at home associated with the first-mover advantages of high-income country producers enjoying patent protection.

The deal was done. In the official global governance system, U.S. commercial interests, backed by the powerful U.S. government, got what they sought.

In the several years that followed, with the spread of AIDS in Africa and other developing countries, activists in the health field began calling attention to the high costs of patent-protected AIDS medications sold by the major pharmaceutical firms. These medications cost as much as $10,000 a year, obviously unaffordable in countries where annual per capita public health spending was as low as $10. Civil society mobilized under the leadership of Health Action International, a nonprofit network of 70 organizations; eventually, Médecins Sans Frontières (Doctors without Borders), the Consumer Project on Technology (a Ralph Nader group led by Jamie Love), Oxfam, and other organizations joined in what became an international campaign to change the public understanding and official approach to TRIPS to take into account public health. In 1998, they took the issue of access to medicines to the World Health Organization (WHO), calling on all of its members to acknowledge the primacy of public health over commercial interests. The resulting resolution was approved by the Executive Board of the WHO and followed by a highly contentious discussion between U.S. and developing country officials at the ensuing World Health Assembly. Though never formally agreed to, even at the WHO, the controversy got press attention and contributed to growing concern in the larger public about the effect of high-priced AIDS drugs on loss of lives in poor countries.

However, at the same time, the Clinton Administration and the U.S. Trade Representative (USTR), under the influence of the pharmaceutical industry and members of Congress, continued to pressure Thailand, South Africa, and then Brazil to retract domestic legislation, particularly the 1997 South African legislation allowing parallel importation of medicines, compulsory licensing of patented drugs, and generic drug substitution. The USTR threatened sanctions on South Africa, invoking TRIPS; U.S. officials allegedly also quietly threatened reprisals in other areas of trade and security. President Clinton sent Vice-President Al Gore to South Africa in search of a compromise in late 1999, and hearings were scheduled in Congress about the U.S. policy in South Africa. By September 1999 U.S. trade negotiators had eased their demands, agreeing to accept a pledge from South Africa that the law would not violate TRIPS.

Under growing public pressure, by late 1999, the pharmaceutical firms announced deep discounts for AIDS treatment drugs benefiting the poorest countries. Eventually, they also donated drugs outright—partly in response to the pricing by CIPLA, an Indian generic producer, of $600 per patient per year. In April 2001, the 39 western pharmaceutical firms that had sued the South African government in 1997 dropped their suit.

By late 2001, the activists and developing countries had won an initial victory. A Declaration on the TRIPS Agreement and Public Health was agreed on at a WTO ministerial meeting, stating that the TRIPS Agreement "does not and should not present Members from taking measures to protect public health." WTO negotiations dragged on for another two years; the poorest countries without manufacturing capacity could not take advantage of compulsory licensing, and activists wanted it made clear that they could import low-cost generics.

By 2003, the victory was complete. With the Bush Administration sponsoring a huge new program to fight AIDS in Africa, the Clinton Foundation fully engaged, and the pharmaceutical firms fearing further bad publicity, language opening the door for generic imports was agreed to. The major international pharmaceutical firms agreed to compulsory licensing of their patented AIDS medications and to sales of South African manufactured generic drugs in 47 African countries.

The situation illustrated in Figure 7.9 was unusual in two ways. First, by linking TRIPS to AIDS, citizen activists invoked the moral imperative to save lives, harnessing public opinion to their cause in the rich world. It is not as easy to build the kind of coalition they built, between health activists and the governments of developing countries, when the enemy is not a corporate lobby backed by a powerful government of an advanced democracy but instead, for example, the millions of consumers of coal-fired electricity all over the world. Second, their position on TRIPS was nicely aligned with the obvious interests of some of the poorest people in the poor world.

Of course, asymmetry of power operates in the nongovernmental system as well; activists in the richer countries are richer, and their objectives and values do not always necessarily align with those of the bottom half in poorer countries. Energy access is an example; it is not the consumers of energy in the poor world, at rates far below consumers in the rich world, who are the "enemy" in the case of reducing carbon emissions.[30] Yet power asymmetries operate not only at the official level in the global economy, but at the unofficial, citizen-based level as well. Western NGOs have disproportionate voice and ability to affect the fate of the poor and the weak through the very efforts, such as preventing climate change or protecting global biodiversity, that they might view as globally progressive. Journalist Sebastian Mallaby refers to this phenomenon as the "cacophony of our advanced democracies." He elaborates on the case of the Bujagali dam in Uganda, a World Bank project that was famously brought to a halt by a campaign organized by the International Rivers Network, based in Berkeley, California. Given the World Bank's troubled history with dams, western journalists tended to believe the NGOs' charges about the Bank's bad behavior without validating their

---

[30] As Todd Moss, of the Center for Global Development, recently wrote, "While climate change is a very real concern, Africans are understandably more focused on the problem that seven in ten people living in the continent have no electricity at all." On the question of what is fair and equitable in the case of climate change policies, see Mattoo and Subramanian (2012, chapter 2).

claims. Upon closer inspection on a 2003 trip to Uganda, Mallaby reported that the local villagers would have gladly accepted the financial compensation that was being offered for relocation; in fact, the only people who objected to the dam were people living just outside its perimeter, who would not benefit from the dam's construction because they were not going to be relocated. [31]

Still, the lesson is clear: activism powered in part by altruism and the norm that global rules should not do visible harm to people without a voice in the system can be effective. Norm-driven activism has changed international rules, from the land mines treaty, to the international criminal court, to the 2013 treaty to regulate the arms trade. The Millennium Development Goals did not change any formal rules, but they seem to have influenced behavior by setting a new international norm that developing country leaders and G7 ministers acknowledged: that every person, independent of where she is born, deserves the opportunity to lead a healthy, productive life.

The demands of globally aware citizens—citizens with more education and political voice in their own societies—for a better world seem likely to increase, barring a complete disruption of the global economy and the global interdependence that, for good and ill, affects citizens wherever they live. As interdependence and instant communications expand the global space in which citizens can operate, more people are eager and able to do so— whether as workers, consumers, or political or social networkers, whether using Google map maker to track election fraud in Kenya or Kiva to borrow directly from people-creditors around the world. That is the implication of continuing declines in the transaction costs of organizing, communicating with, and mobilizing citizens and the projected increases in education and income set out above.

Citizen demand is rooted in the growing concern and activism over global inequality and climate change, as well as concern over microbial resistance to medicines, global financial crises, drug trafficking, terrorism, and many other global problems (Goldin 2013). It is also rooted in the growing awareness of unexploited opportunities to increase equality of opportunity and the sustainability of higher living standards across borders—in many ways, including trade, more open borders, and the leveraging of private investments in basic infrastructure. Many people living at a comfortable standard are increasingly aware of the potential harm done by failures of policy in their own countries—guns, drugs, immigration, climate—that create

---

[31] Mallaby (2004, 8) concluded that the story was a "tragedy for Uganda, since millions of Ugandans are being deprived of electricity—deprived by Californians whose idea of an electricity 'crisis' is a handful of summer blackouts. . . and a tragedy for the antipoverty fight worldwide, since projects in dozens of countries are being held up for fear of activist resistance."

burdens for fellow global citizens elsewhere. Despite these concerns, what there is of a "global social contract" (Birdsall 2008) is much thinner than the domestic social contract in high-income countries. Despite the high levels of income inequality across countries, cross-border spending by the richer for the poorer in the form of official aid is less than 0.2 percent of global GDP (based on OECD 2013; compared with 10–20 percent, depending on how the social contract is measured, within countries).[32]

If the effects of citizen activism for a less unequal world are measured in terms of charitable transfers to developing countries, they are small—an estimated \$56 billion in 2010, compared with about \$130 billion of official aid and about \$190 billion of remittances from countries in the Organisation for Economic Co-operation and Development (OECD; Adelman, Marano, and Spantchak 2012). Combined official aid and charitable transfers amounted to less than 0.3 percent of the global economy in 2010.[33] But, as the TRIPS story shows, a large proportion of the activity of "global society" does not have to do with raising money but with lobbying for different policies and practices on the part of the "global polity"—in effect, trying to translate the moral imperative of individual global citizens, or the norm that there ought to be a less unequal world, into change at the political level in the rules of the global game: norms into politics.

7.5 Politics, Not Norms: The Troubled Supply Side

The supply side of the global polity (see Figure 7.2) deals directly or indirectly with the global economy. It is made up of two parts: sovereign states whose actions and policies have implications beyond their borders and various intergovernmental clubs and institutions at the regional and global level in which sovereign states are members.

Like government at the domestic level, "government" at the global level is far from perfect; we should celebrate the extent to which there is global cooperation at all among sovereign states. The "trouble" in this section's title refers to the weakness of the global polity today relative to the challenges of global inequality and climate (among many others), and the difficulty of imagining that official global governance arrangements will get markedly better.

---

[32] Germany, for example, spent about 8.6 percent of GDP on public health and another 4.5 percent on public education in 2008 (OECD 2012a, 2012b).

[33] One estimate, based on weighted per person averages for 14 developed economies, is that national governments spend 30,000 times as much helping each poor person at home as each foreigner abroad. (see www.ghemawat.com).

7.5.1 Weak Global Governance Today

On the problem of inequality across countries, many high-income states act on their own to encourage growth and higher living standards in poorer countries—for example, through aid and trade relations and preferences. But they also cooperate through clubs and the more formal institutions, on the grounds that through cooperation and collaboration they can be more effective at lower cost. On the problem of climate change, cooperation among sovereigns would not only be cheaper; it is also necessary because of the public good nature of the challenge at the global level. In the absence of enforcement of agreed steps by at least the major emitters, free-riding would be too tempting.

The intergovernmental clubs and institutions are state-based political entities; they constitute the global "polity" that is the counterpart to global society and the global economy. They provide some of the global public goods, or aspects of a global social contract, that global citizens are demanding. This is not to suggest that they are the principal suppliers of global public goods or good global policy. Nation-states supply a large portion of global public goods voluntarily, because it is in their own interests to do so. Optimal policies at the domestic level will often be perfectly aligned with the global good, in principle eliminating the need for international cooperation were all nations able politically to act in their own interests (Rodrik 2009; see also Rodrik 1999). Alignment of domestic interests with global benefits also explains many international programs sponsored by countries. The United States has provided the security umbrella for the western world for decades; with its highly competitive industries and financial services, it was very much in its interests to ensure that the international trading system functioned well.

Examples of intergovernmental clubs and institutions dealing with the global economy are the G7 and the G20, the IMF, the World Bank and other multilateral development banks, the WTO, the Financial Stability Forum, the United Nations and some of its agencies, and the recently created Green Climate Fund. These institutions were created by sovereign governments to shape and manage implementation of agreed-upon programs and, in the case of the more formal institutions, to enforce agreed-upon rules. With a few exceptions (the International Labour Organization has union representatives; the Global Environment Fund has civil society on its board), they were generally set up by and for sovereign nations, under formal rules of leadership selection and voting arrangements that are in varying degrees representative and "democratic."

These global entities make up only a limited portion of what some would see as the global polity. Many other official and informal organizations and movements exist in which states participate, including the landmine initiative and the EITI; the Global Fund to Fight AIDS, Tuberculosis and Malaria; and the International Business Coalition for Sustainable Development. There are also dozens of international standard-setting associations and organizations, such as the Bank for International Settlements and the International Auditing and Assurance Standards Board. Their shortcomings are emblematic of the weakness of the global polity overall in the face of growing challenges.

The G20 and the major international financial institutions can be thought of as sitting at the top of the heap in political terms. They have the most visible and well-embedded political standing and are made up entirely of their sovereign members. The G20 matters because it operates at the level of heads of state, who in principle can make commitments with political backing; because they dominate the governance of the institutions, they can turn to those institutions to monitor and sometimes implement agreed-upon decisions and actions. The institutions have financial and rule-making power—the equivalent of tax and enforcement powers at the level of nation-states. And, except in the case of the Green Climate Fund, they have embedded legal, financial, and technical assets and rules that provide them with a measure of independence. On the one hand, they are not immune to the interests of their most powerful members; on the other, they provide their members with a setting in which they are able to cooperate at lower cost and at a step removed from the immediate demands of each member's domestic politics.

Still, weakness of these institutions is inherent in the difficulty of sovereign states cooperating, even in their long-term interests, because in doing so they give up a measure of their own control. On long-term distributional and environmental issues, it is especially hard to be effective—that is, to agree to act and in some cases contribute financially (perhaps compared with acting cooperatively on immediate security threats). When sovereign states do cooperate, they do so because the benefits of locking themselves and others into rules and policies—as, for example, in the open trading system—are visible and would be difficult to sustain domestically, or can be implemented at lower cost or greater effectiveness collectively (examples are the World Bank for reducing lending costs, the IMF for maintaining global financial stability, and the WHO for preventing global pandemics). But cooperation is the exception, not the rule.

The problem of the global system of governance is not only weakness; it is also that decision-making among sovereign states is inherently undemocratic and unrepresentative. Where this quality undermines legitimacy, it can contribute to weakness or lack of effectiveness. Governance arrangements of international institutions cannot help but reflect inequalities within and among states, and they will not generally adequately represent the interests of even the typical citizen of the larger and more powerful states, let alone the interests of the world's poor.[34] Almost all of the people in the bottom half of the global income distribution suffer a double democratic deficit. They are unlikely to be well represented by their own governments, because many live in states that lack mature democratic institutions, and their countries have limited control and influence in the global institutions. The institutions are in this sense far more imperfect democracies than many national governments. The solution is not necessarily governance structures within intergovernmental institutions that are more "democratic" in representing smaller and poorer states. The UN General Assembly is highly representative of all states but is widely viewed as ineffective; the new Green Climate Fund, in which small developing countries are well represented, appears to suffer from the same problem. In contrast, the G20 and the World Bank, which combine and reflect the economic power of relatively rich members, are viewed as reasonably effective but unrepresentative and lacking legitimacy.

The apparent tradeoff between effectiveness and legitimacy is not necessary; many observers believe that the limited representation of developing countries in the governance and management of the IMF and the World Bank has at times limited those institutions' effectiveness—for example, when country programs supported by the institutions lose popular support because they are seen as imposed by outsiders. Of course, "outsiders" may be misguided technically, as well as ineffective, because they lack political legitimacy (as some would argue was the case for IMF programs during the East Asian crisis or in Greece and Ireland in the past several years). But the misguided technical stance is itself likely to reflect the ideological and political dominance of the traditional powers and the lack of sufficient input from countries that are poorly represented. In other situations, the institutions' lack of legitimacy undermines their ability to effectively support sound pro-poor reforms because of civil society or populist suspicions within countries.[35]

In the introduction to this chapter, I emphasized the apparent inability of today's global governance arrangements to reduce the inequities of the global economy. Weakness also reduces global growth and the stability and efficiency of the global market, often with disproportionately high costs to the welfare of the bottom half of the world's people. The global financial crisis and its aftermath provide a telling illustration. On the one hand, the

---

[34] Saying that governance arrangements at the global level "cannot help" but reflect inequalities may be too strong. Owen Barder raised an interesting question in his review of this chapter. Why, he asked, is the realpolitik view of politics as "a-ethical" taken for granted for international decision-making, whereas for national decision-making the possibility of an ethical sense of responsibility as a citizen is acknowledged? In a sense, the point of this chapter is that the idea of global citizenry with ethical responsibilities is rising.

[35] Derviş (2005) reports that the World Bank's lack of legitimacy in Turkey complicated its ability to support a program intended to help the poor there in the early 2000s.

existence of the IMF and the resources of the multilateral banks provided critical liquidity in the aftermath of the 2008 Lehman Brothers collapse, complementing the coordinated stimulus of the largest economies in 2009 under the umbrella of the G20. On the other hand, the global imbalances that contributed to the crisis persist despite the multilateral surveillance work of the IMF, and they may be worsening, as slow-growing countries resort to monetary easing to stimulate their economies (in a twenty-first-century currency version of trade wars) and the advanced economies fail to implement regulatory and other reforms, unable to resist pressure from their own financial services industries concerned with competitiveness.

Global governance also fails in nonfinancial markets. As the cushion between the demand and supply of staple foods declined in 2008 and food prices rose, food surplus countries restricted food exports, panic ensued, and food prices spiked. The WTO has no code of conduct on export restrictions, and there are no standards or rules on the management of emergency food stocks.

In the energy sector, many of the same problems exist. The International Energy Agency is effective, but it is fundamentally an OECD agency, without the full engagement of major consuming nations like China. It is impotent in the face of shortages, price volatility, poor access to energy in the low-income countries, and the looming climate disaster.

Even so, cooperation among states through clubs and institutions can make a difference.[36] It can help lock in optimal domestic policy—the argument for the G20 agreement during the global financial crisis to avoid trade protectionism. The mechanisms of cooperation themselves constitute a global public good; cooperation complements the process of securing and locking in the better policy at home, particularly when domestic political decisions are at risk of capture by short-term and powerful vested interests.

The stories at the beginning of this chapter (see Figure 7.1) illustrate three points about the characteristics and roles of the intergovernmental institutions. The three points illustrate their weaknesses and their strengths. They capture the tensions between sovereign independence and the readiness to cooperate, and between the interests of powerful states and the problem of representation in the institutions in which all states are members.

First, the intergovernmental institutions are creatures of their sovereign members and fundamentally beholden to the most powerful among them. They are not immune to the prevailing ideologies and interests of those members (on such issues as the respective roles of the state and the market, the benefits of liberalized capital markets, and so on). At the same time, they can

---

[36] Consider nonproliferation, the landmine treaty, the elimination of smallpox, the Montreal Protocol for the near abolition of chlorofluorocarbons.

benefit from the institutional strengths of those members. The Ghanaian witness was testifying before the Congress of the United States, at the turn of the century the most powerful nation in the world. The support for her testimony came indirectly from U.S. and international NGOs, which correctly viewed the U.S. government as influential inside the World Bank.

The TRIPS story is equally illustrative. In this case, activists fought for a change in the U.S. position because it was the U.S. position that mattered for the nature of the WTO intellectual property regime. Ultimately, the U.S. government—pushed by a coalition of developing country members, activists, and the broader health community, including at the WHO, and embarrassed by critical press coverage—yielded to compromise.

Second, the World Bank (and to varying degrees other international institutions) is more open or porous to views of "stakeholders" on its programs and policies than many of the developing countries in which it operates.[37] These institutions sometimes represent and reflect in a democratic sense the views of global citizens who have limited voice and representation in their own country. The Ghanaian expert and supporters of her view adeptly exploited this fact. She was urging the World Bank to promote changes in the approach to financing health in Africa—something she may not have been able to influence directly in Ghana. Some might see the issue as one of the World Bank imposing its views on Ghana, and there would be some truth in that. But the volume and vigor of criticisms of the World Bank by civil society groups, NGOs, and think tanks reflects their view that they can ultimately influence the Bank. Though their policies will often reflect the ideological views and narrow interests of their most influential members (most famously in the case of the so-called Washington Consensus[38]), institutions like the World Bank are not impervious to change. As Keohane, Macedo, and Moravcsik (2009) argue, when international institutions are more open and responsive to outside parties than some of their member governments, they can be democracy-enhancing (though Ghana is one of the more open and democratic countries in its region).

The TRIPS story looks different in its details but in the end illustrates the same point. The less powerful developing countries and most vulnerable of their people are better off with a multilateral institution in which even the most powerful countries subject themselves to agreed rules (Arvind

---

[37] In a zen-like coincidence, these two tweets popped up on my browser as I was revising this paragraph: "44% of @WorldBank projects #engagevoices with citizen feedback systems" and "All of @WorldBank's #OpenData work is at Data.worldbank.org—now with @IMF data too!" Both tweets are from @DGateway, a World Bank-sponsored program, on April 18, 2014 at 11:29 and 11:32 a.m. Eastern daylight time.

[38] On this issue, Birdsall, de la Torre, and Caicedo (2011) provide a useful summary and analysis of the critique of the "damaged brand."

Subramanian and Martin Kessler make the same point in chapter 4). In this case, the United States ended up compromising its apparent domestic interests because citizens used convening, the Internet, and the influence of the press in an age in which those matter.

Third, though creatures of their members, the international institutions have considerable independence. Their staffs have a mandate to use their technical judgment in line with strong professional standards; as bureaucracies, they are one step removed politically from their sovereign members. Indeed, that is the point. Sovereigns create institutions to precommit in their own long-term interests to rules or arrangements that may be politically difficult to manage at any particular moment domestically. That is most obviously the case for members of the WTO, who trade a measure of sovereignty for the benefits of mutual gain.

7.5.2 Will These Institutions Get Stronger and More Effective?

Overall, the system has strengths and weaknesses. These institutions' ability to make the global system less unequal and less environmentally destructive varies depending on the issue and the institution. Specific examples suggest that the direction is not particularly positive, however. The limited role of the major institutions and the problems of legitimacy of the intergovernmental institutions are emblematic of the broader point of a weak global polity and the resulting shortfall of global governance in management of the global economy.

G20

The G20 group of finance ministers was created at the time of the Asian financial crisis in the late 1990s, at the initiative of the U.S. Treasury. The G20 at the head of state level was created at the end of 2008, with the initiative coming from the White House in the closing days of President George W. Bush's term. Though it has not fully replaced the G7 group of advanced economies, its creation bespeaks the arrival of China and other emerging markets onto the global economic stage. Its focus on economic and financial issues has meant that it has become for practical purposes a kind of steering committee for the IMF, and to a lesser extent the World Bank. In both cases, the leading western power had the convening power to initiate a process bent on collaboration, a point I return to later in the chapter. The G20 was the setting that enabled the increase in the financial resources the IMF had available to help deal with immediate liquidity problems in 2009. It has since provided the framework for the ongoing "multilateral assessment program" under which in principle the major economic powers use peer review of one another's policies to help minimize the imbalances and distortions that can arise from uncoordinated macroeconomic policies. Many observers also credit the resolve of the G20 leaders to avoid a trade war for the avoidance of protection in the aftermath of the crisis.

The G20 is a self-appointed club, not an institution. It fails any reasonable tests of representation; many of the world's most populous countries have no seat at the table.[39] Still, it represents an advance over the G7, and the world is probably better off with it than without. Many observers question its ability to retain relevance and leadership even as a club, invoking, for example, the failure at the international level to resolve the issue of global imbalances that contributed to the crisis in the first place.

INTERNATIONAL MONETARY FUND
The Fund was rescued from decline by the global financial crisis. Some healthy reform steps in the two years preceding the crisis may have been important in the G20's essentially turning to the Fund as a major channel for financing the agreed global stimulus. However, the Fund was unable to impose discipline on China and other surplus countries or on the United States in dealing with the tremendous imbalances that contributed to the global financial crisis. In the past few years, its role has been compromised in Europe, where it has participated in lending packages as a minor player (sometimes to the chagrin of its non-European members concerned about the financing risks) without the ability to impose any form of conditionality on Germany or the European Union institutions; the European Central Bank is in the troika instead of being on the other side of the table.[40]

There is no real consensus in the G20 on whether the Fund should be bigger, with more financial heft in a more vulnerable and independent global financial system. Even if there were, there is no source of a major increase in financing, given the fiscal situation in the United States and Europe and China's reluctance to take a financing lead in an institution in which it still has limited votes or influence. A negotiated agreement that would double the quotas and shift at least some greater voting power to China and other emerging market economies consistent with their size and impact on the global economy cannot advance without the United States, whose agreement is needed because a quota increase requires 85 percent of the weighted votes and the United States holds 17 percent. Figure 7.10 illustrates the post-2010 reform governance structure of the IMF by dividing the total voting share

[39] Rueda-Sabater, Ramachandran, and Kraft (2009) make a sensible and feasible proposal for membership that would combine effectiveness and representativeness. But it seems unlikely that a self-appointed club of sovereigns could easily toss out any of its founding members.

[40] Economist Ted Truman made this obvious (once you've heard it) point at a conference in the fall of 2012. See also Mandeng (2013), who wrote, "To save itself, the IMF needs to leave the troika."

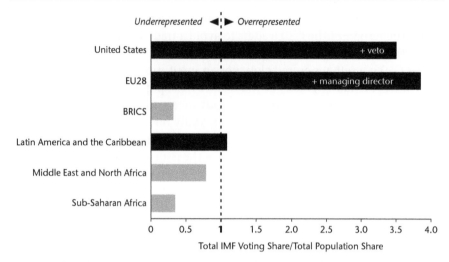

Figure 7.10 National and Regional Under- and Overrepresentation within the International Monetary Fund, 2010

Note: BRICS are Brazil, Russia, India, China, and South Africa. Regional groupings follow World Bank classification (June 2013). Voting shares reflect quota increases agreed to at the conclusion of the 14th General Review of Quotas in November 2010. As of July 31, 2013, the quota and governance reform was not yet in effect.

Source: Author's calculations, based on Penn World Tables 8.0 and IMF.

of members by their total population share. The U.S. Treasury supports the increase but waited a very long time to find a propitious moment to ask Congress for the necessary authorization (Birdsall 2013).

The Fund has struggled with adjustments to its governance that would recognize the increase in the relative size of major emerging markets. The Europeans hold 8 of 24 Board seats and have been unable to agree among themselves on how and when to change their constituencies and give up two seats. Like the United States, the European countries have continued to hang on to the privilege of naming the IMF managing director. The fact that a European heads the IMF (in line with the historic privilege established more than 60 years ago, at the institution's founding) has not helped strengthen the technical credibility of IMF-supported programs in the euro zone periphery.

The IMF plays a critical role in supporting global financial stability through its periodic surveillance at the country and global level, though in the global case without any mechanisms to effect change. But other potential roles the IMF might play—promoting the sharing of tax information by countries, monitoring illegitimate capital flows, accepting even a modest global tax function through a centrally controlled currency transaction tax (Task Force on International Financial Transactions and Development 2010)—are not on the table.

WORLD BANK

The World Bank's role as a provider of financial transfers was on a declining trend in middle-income countries before the financial crisis. Its value-added as a lender in middle-income countries over and above that of the generally leaner regional development banks is not obvious; its strength is in its technical and fiduciary expertise and its global experience.

The recent recapitalization of the Bank was allegedly smaller than it might have been because of the reluctance of the United States to agree to the additional capital that would have been necessary to avoid further diminishment of U.S. shares, votes, and influence. Its former major borrowers are considering establishing their own new BRICS bank, hoping to gain access to more capital for borrowing at a lower cost than they can obtain individually and to avoid the onerous procedures that delay and complicate many World Bank projects, especially infrastructure projects. The United States is pushing for ever-tighter and risk-free environmental and other "safeguards" meant to protect against environmental damage, corruption, and violation of indigenous peoples' rights. Borrowers argue that these safeguards impose unreasonable costs and delays in preparing Bank-funded operations and fail to reflect the tradeoffs in poorer countries between, for example, the role of greater energy supply in improving livelihoods and raising growth compared with protecting natural resources.

Among the 70 low-income states eligible for the Bank's concessional window (the International Development Association [IDA]), as few as 20 will be eligible in 2025 (Severino and Moss 2012), with India, Pakistan, and possibly Bangladesh having "graduated" (assuming the current income cut-off is not increased). The remaining countries will be largely fragile and "flailing" states, in which the Bank's strengths in infrastructure will be difficult to exploit and its weaknesses in public sector reform and state-building (IEG 2006) make it hard to envision it being effective. The IDA window is in a sense one more aid agency in a crowded and fragmented aid system; it is, however, more efficient and effective than most bilateral agencies and provides some of the glue that holds a fragmented system together on overall strategy and vision. It faces increasing difficulty playing a strategic role in that system, however, as more than 22 percent of its operational budget is now covered by member countries and other entities through contributions for specific purposes to Bank-managed trust funds.[41]

---

[41] According to World Bank data (IEG 2011), trust fund spending represents 22 percent of the Bank's administrative budget; it represents an even larger percentage of country operations (knowledge products and lending), as the administrative budget covers the Bank's revenue or treasury operations, human resources, building maintenance, and so on.

Meanwhile, the potential contribution of the Bank in using its financial and technical strengths to contribute to the creation and diffusion of global public goods, including new ideas and products, cannot be realized in the absence of a mandate from its members to move beyond its historical role as a lender to countries. A key problem is the reliance of the Bank for more than 60 years on a single instrument: the sovereign-guaranteed loan (Birdsall and Subramanian 2007; Birdsall 2014).

The discussion of governance reform of the Bank continues, to little real effect. Modest increases in the voting power of the developing countries are more symbolic than real. In 2012, the United States once more pushed through the selection of an American as president of the institution. Many civil society organizations, particularly in the developing world, see the Bank as the arrogant proponent of what they view as misguided Washington Consensus policies and do not consider the Bank a legitimate institution. In the United States, this perception does not help shore up declining support for multilateral institutions in general.

GREEN CLIMATE FUND

The Green Climate Fund (GCF) is the product of hundreds of hours of contentious negotiations, primarily among foreign affairs and environmental officials in the context of the UN-managed conferences in search of a global climate agreement over the last few years. It came into existence in 2012, with a mission to raise and deploy financing of climate mitigation and adaptation programs in developing countries.

The negotiations created a governance arrangement in which developing countries have more influence and veto power than in the traditional financial institutions of the IMF and World Bank. One apparent result has been a reluctance on the part of the traditional transatlantic donors to put any resources they are currently dedicating to climate in developing countries through traditional aid programs into the GCF. This stance is likely to change only when some formal or informal adjustments are agreed that build confidence among potential donors that the GCF's operations will be effectively managed.

7.5.3 The Future of International Cooperation: From Benign Bully to the G-Zero

Behind the governance shortcomings of each of these institution is the ongoing gradual disruption of the twentieth-century postwar geopolitical order. In that order, the United States provided the leadership, generally but not always benign, in managing the liberalization of international trade and finance, with Western Europe for the most part a reliable follower. Equally important, the United States provided a kind of canonical example of the economic and political direction all countries should take: an open market and a liberal democracy, in which individual freedoms and protection of minority rights in the political sphere and property rights and contract enforcement in the economic sphere buttress each other to minimize elite capture and guarantee sustained and widely shared prosperity.

Economic historians are likely to mark the global financial crisis of 2008–09 and its aftermath as the end of the twentieth-century postwar era of the United States' near hegemony as a (largely) benign bully.[42] The rapid growth of China and other emerging market economies and the resilience of the developing world's economies following the crisis are changing perceptions as well as reality—and in geopolitics, perceptions matter. The United States is still the indispensable superpower: without its leadership, global cooperation flounders. But it no longer has the will or the means—or, some would say, a credible economic model—for its leadership to automatically command followers. It can now manage but not bully.

In his book *Eclipse*, Subramanian uses an index of economic dominance as the basis for predicting that China will dominate the United States economically by 2020 (Subramanian 2011). Based on this index (which comprises GDP in purchasing power parity, exchange rate terms, trade data, and external financial strength), Figure 7.11 illustrates the difference between a dominant country and the second most dominant, the second and third most dominant, and the second through fifth most dominant countries since 1870. In 2008, the United States is still the dominant power but, using Subramanian's index, China (the second most dominant) is close behind.

For the next several decades, in contrast to the second half of the twentieth century, the world will not enjoy the benefits—mixed as they might have been—of a single dominant economic power: one that is more productive and competitive than all the others and able to provide its large middle class with jobs and other benefits of growth. In a unipolar system, one country has the incentives to preserve order and competition and, indeed, to build more democratic states in its own interests. It has an interest in locking in allies and rivals to rules and institutional arrangements that reduce the costs of cooperation and lock in their benefits.[43]

The decline of the United States is only relative, but it is a decline beyond that measured by economic indicators. The United States is no longer in command of the moral and political high ground; its politics are increasingly

---

[42] The more conventional term is *global steward*.

[43] Naim (2013) argues that the issue is less the relative decline of the United States as hegemon than the general loss of power of sovereign states in the face of other forces. Malloch-Brown (2011, 239) is more hopeful about the "momentum toward a fairer and more inclusive world."

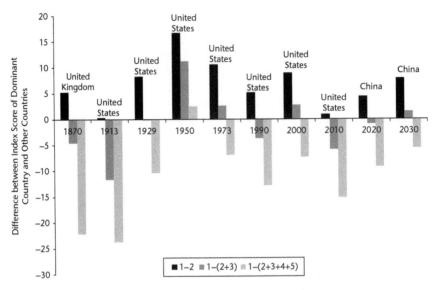

Figure 7.11 Extent of Dominant Country's Economic Dominance, 1870–2030

Note: Figure shows difference between the Subramanian Economic Dominance Index scores of the most dominant country and the second most dominant country, the sum of the scores of the second and third most dominant countries, and the sum of scores of the second through fifth most dominant countries. Scores are the scores in the convergence scenario using IMF weights as opposed to reserve currency weights (see discussion in Subramanian 2011).

Source: Author's calculations, based on index scores from Subramanian 2011.

dysfunctional; it has among the lowest rates of social mobility in the OECD; its leading public intellectuals failed to warn of the risks of the policy and regulatory failures that triggered the crisis in the United States that became global.

A benign bully is difficult to deal with and makes mistakes, even at times violating its own interests in its actions around the world, as the United States has done. A beleaguered bully raises the deeper problem that the impetus for cooperation is less compelling for everyone.

The new power, China, is not willing or interested in taking leadership on common global challenges (Kapur and Suri 2012). China is a big economy and a big market, but it is still poor in per capita terms, and its domestic interests are not yet obviously aligned with the shared interests of other nations in the global economic system. Figure 7.12 adds GDP per capita to the Subramanian index, as a crude proxy for domestic institutional capability and the readiness and ability to take leadership on the global stage. The figure illustrates a G-Zero world, a geopolitical and economic system closer to that in Europe when the then large powers stumbled into World War I. In this century, the immediate risk is not war but the health of

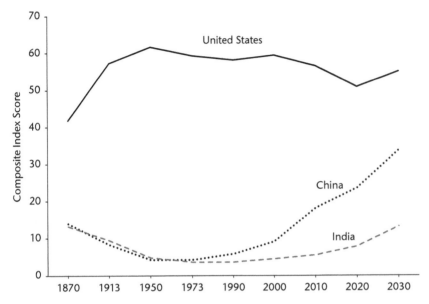

Figure 7.12 Composite Index of Economic Dominance and GDP per Capita, 1870–2030

Note: Figure plots a weighted average of the Subramanian Economic Index score (50 percent) and past or projected GDP per capita (50 percent) in each year shown. Projections start in 2010.

Source: Author's calculations, based on data from Maddison (2009) and Subramanian (2011).

the model of market-led democracy that has, for all its failures—including in dealing with climate change—helped bring millions of people out of poverty.

7.6 Conclusions and Implications

Few people would argue that the global economy is in great shape. Europe is stumbling, and the U.S. economy is not yet out of the woods. The advanced economies as a group face medium-term problems as their populations age and perhaps as the latest wave of robotic and nanotechnologies further loosens the connection between productivity growth and the creation of "good" jobs that provided a reasonably secure middle-class living stand-ard. Emerging market economies are doing better, but their future growth depends in part on uncertain demand for their products from the advanced economies and on healthy sustained growth in China to drive demand for natural resource-based commodities on which many developing countries still rely for export income. Among low-income economies, the prospects for getting on what Rodrik (in chapter 2) calls the escalator of manufactured exports, which powered the East Asian Tigers in the twentieth century to middle-income status, seem poor.

So healthy growth is not a given. And though growth is necessary for a better world, it is not sufficient. Overall, the current path of market-led growth is at best neutral in reducing global and within-country inequality; at worst it could reinforce such trends. Even equally shared future growth in India, China, and Brazil can leave behind a large and frustrated income-insecure group compared with the rising middle class in those countries. And in the absence of a dramatic technological breakthrough in the production and distribution of carbon-free energy, market-led growth is also potentially destructive because of its effect on climate change (see chapter 6).

The global market built on the capitalist system and on democratic and accountable government as the political guardian of that system will probably survive the next several decades, but it is not entirely secure.[44] The official governance of the global market is inadequate in representing and protecting the bottom half of the world's population, which lives on just $3 per person per day in the developing world. It is currently inadequate to manage collective action to deal with climate change. There is also a global political problem: in the advanced economies, where the middle class is no longer benefiting from growth, there is growing suspicion of the costs of "globalization" and lack of confidence that the global "system" overall is fair.

That is the problem. But there is also an opportunity.

Worldwide surveys show that citizens everywhere are becoming more aware and more active in seeking changes in the global norms and rules that could make the global system and the global economy fairer—in processes if not outcomes—and less environmentally harmful. Across the world more people, especially the more educated, see themselves as "global citizens," aware that what happens inside their own country matters for others outside and that what happens outside matters for them and for their children and grandchildren. Global citizenship is seen not in opposition but alongside national citizenship. This sense is highest among the young and better educated, suggesting that over time it will increase.

Views on the two global challenges on which I have focused—inequality and climate—are emblematic. The young and educated in the rich countries favor increased foreign aid and more immigration; in all countries surveyed, poor and rich, large majorities are deeply concerned about climate change. Along with increasing global awareness there is an apparent upsurge in levels

---

[44] Democracy and accountability are the hallmark of what Acemoglu and Robinson (2012) call inclusive politics. They help sustain inclusive economics and, they argue, the nation-state itself.

of organized citizen-based activism at the international level, especially in the past 5–10 years, perhaps fueled by the zero-marginal-cost magic of Internet-based communications.

Of course, activist movements can be misguided and are not always benign. Activism will not always lead to policy changes that represent gains for the world's bottom half. Even within the mature democracies, the poor normally have little time or resources to participate in politics or citizen movements. It is students and the relatively rich who are activists, especially on global as opposed to local issues—and their organizations sometimes end up reinforcing asymmetries of power in the corporate and political worlds, as the Bujagali dam story above suggests. Still, the direction of history has been for the better angels of human nature—altruism, not selfish and parochial interests—to prevail (Pinker 2011a). As often as not, citizen-based movements represent and help the world's bottom half, sometimes working with willing states in mixed coalitions (the EITI, the Global Fund) and sometimes fighting to change or enforce policies or rules at the official level in the interests of the poor, as in the TRIPS story.

At the same time, citizen movements and mixed coalitions have their limits. They cannot substitute for a weak and unrepresentative system of global governance. In the absence of a global tax, for example, redistributive transfers from the world's rich to the world's poor are minuscule; in the $70-trillion-dollar global economy of 2010, perhaps $200 billion—less than 0.3 percent—was transferred from advanced to poor economies through voluntary (foreign aid) public channels and private charitable and philanthropic programs. In this sense, the global social contract is a mere shadow of the domestic social contract in advanced economies.

Though transfers are not the key to reducing global inequality, they do illustrate the limits of citizen-based movements to make a real difference without a stronger and more representative global political order, if not a world government. What matter more than transfers for reducing inequality are open markets in the rich world, including for agriculture, and development-friendly immigration policy, enforcement of anticorruption laws, prevention of tax evasion, and domestic policies to reduce carbon emissions. These domestic policies of the advanced economies would do more to create opportunities for the world's poor and vulnerable than aid would (Birdsall, Rodrik, and Subramanian 2005). On these policies, however, activists in the rich world cannot make changes on their own; they can effect change only through the political process—in their own countries and governments and in the intergovernmental institutions their governments still largely control.

Citizen movements and mixed coalitions are also unable to address effectively an issue like climate change, which requires a formal or informal agreement on minimum mutual monitoring and enforcement of agreed actions among the major emitting states. Climate change involves irreversible damage;[45] the tax power of government and publicly financed basic research are key to minimizing long-term damage.[46]

What, then, is the opportunity? It is to close the gap between the demands of global citizens for a better world and the supply of better global governance. It is to exploit mechanisms that amplify the voices of global citizens, strengthen the ties among them, and link their good intentions to effective national and international policies, giving global society better channels by which to influence the global polity. The results of the surveys and polls reported above are a contribution in themselves; they demonstrate the will of the "aggregated consciousness of the people" (Kull 2010, 28). They can be more influential the more they induce the people surveyed to "vote" for or against policies, to make choices among different priorities, and to do so in frameworks that provide clear if imagined limits on public resources.

Individual and official supporters of reducing global inequality and managing climate change can support not only polls and informal voting but also civil society groups and think tanks, including in the developing world, that generate information, monitor performance of governments and intergovernmental organizations against their commitments, inform the media, and in general contribute to deliberative discourse. They can insist on transparency of their own governments and of intergovernmental institutions as a critical input to citizen monitoring and activism.

The highly empowered global citizens in the world's largest economies—the United States, China, Europe, Japan—have a particular responsibility. It is their governments' actions and lack of actions on financial, trade, immigration, investment, anticorruption, tax, and climate policies that matter most for people everywhere. It is these countries' domestic policies that often impose negative spillovers on others. For these citizens, a priority should be to lobby that their own houses be put in order—whether it is for a carbon tax in the United States or fiscal expansion in Germany. The same can be said for the small but powerful corporate and political elite within developing countries—which could back forest conservation in Indonesia, protection of indigenous people in Brazil, and reform of patronage-based school systems in India.

The first-best solution to many global problems would be a stronger and more "activist" system of global governance—if not a world government then

---

[45] Savedoff (2012) emphasizes irreversibility as the defining characteristic of problems requiring collective action among sovereigns.

[46] The failure of governments to provide countercyclical stimulus on the fiscal side in the advanced economies also involves irreversible damage to young people who lose out on early entry to the job market.

something more legitimate, more democratic, and more effective than the current set of intergovernmental rules, processes, and institutions. But the world is made up of sovereign nations, and it is within them that democratic and representative systems of government are rooted. It is within sovereign nations that citizens of the world have the possibility and the responsibility to make their governments accountable for policies and practices that have impacts beyond their borders.

The world's rich and the secure middle class, wherever they live, have a second responsibility: to support the idea of multilateral cooperation and to contribute to a narrative in their own countries in support of the multilateral institutions. These institutions, for all their shortcomings, allow powerful sovereigns to precommit to rules and practices that are in the broad common interest and protect the interests of the world's poorer countries. Where multilateral institutions are weak and ineffective—as is the new Green Climate Fund—the common interest is shortchanged and the world's poor in particular lose out.

In the United States in particular, the most influential citizens would do well to recognize their personal interest in a more effective and legitimate set of international institutions and the risk to them and to the world if the longstanding bipartisan support for the IMF, the World Bank, and the United Nations continues to waver—with Congress indifferent to IMF reform and reluctant to fund increases for the World Bank rather than fund with American bilateral aid programs.[47] Global citizens in the United States and Europe should endorse the governance reforms at the IMF and the World Bank that would give China and the big emerging markets a larger stake; they should recognize that without these reforms, increasingly powerful countries will disengage, further weakening the institutions and undoing the potential benefits of global cooperation. The big risk of a more fractured global political order is greater in an interdependent global economy than the small risk of less control over policies and patronage at the institutions. The long-run risk is that in a G-Zero, multipolar world, the values and norms embedded in the rules and practices of the institutions, for all that they are not perfectly honored, will be eroded if they lose the legitimacy on which their effectiveness in the long run ultimately depends.

Multilateral institutions and global governance do not provide immunization against capture by ideology and narrow interests; they are weakened by the lack of clear legitimacy. But their problems reflect the larger challenge of collective action among sovereign states, especially in the absence of a

---

[47] The United States channels 13 percent of its aid through multilateral institutions, compared with 50 percent in the United Kingdom. This figure is lower than any other OECD donor (Birdsall and Kharas 2012).

single dominant power. The creation of the IMF, the World Bank, and the seeds of what later became the WTO at Bretton Woods in 1945–46 was a singular event, triggered by the political and security catastrophe of World War II and helped along by the commercial and security interests of the United States in a prosperous and stable global economy. Some would view the agreement among 13 fully sovereign and independent states in North America to join together in "these united states" at the time of the creation of the U.S. Constitution as an even more singular event, as would be further economic and political consolidation in Europe. The point is that if today's global economic and financial institutions did not exist, they would be hard to reconstitute. If they become more marginal or less legitimate, or fail to get off the ground in the first place (as in the case of the Green Climate Fund), the world as a whole will be worse off, the world's bottom half especially so.

The politics, rules, and institutions of cooperation among nations have not kept up with the demands from global citizens for fairer and more farsighted global political order. The question is whether the moral force of that rising demand can generate an increased supply of good global governance. The jury is still out.

Appendix 7A

Table 7A.1 Ordered Logit Regressions Results on Awareness of Global Citizens

Variable	Supranational identity[a]	World citizenship[b]
Gender		
Female	−0.171***	−0.0239
	(0.0191)	(0.0255)
Highest education level attained		
Complete primary	0.137*	0.0604
	(0.0552)	(0.0621)
Incomplete lower-secondary	0.267***	0.181**
	(0.0696)	(0.0683)
Complete lower-secondary	0.340***	0.197**
	(0.0618)	(0.0678)
Incomplete upper-secondary	0.427***	0.209*
	(0.0833)	(0.0887)
Complete upper-secondary	0.555***	0.295***
	(0.0726)	(0.0719)
Incomplete tertiary	0.682***	0.441***
	(0.0723)	(0.0701)
Complete tertiary	0.832***	0.483***
	(0.0889)	(0.0726)

(Continued)

Table 7A.1 (Continued)

Variable	Supranational identity[a]	World citizenship[b]
Age		
30–49	−0.0900**	−0.0232
	(0.0287)	(0.0338)
50 and older	−0.308***	−0.0417
	(0.0464)	(0.0482)
Decile of income distribution		
2	−0.119*	−0.0718
	(0.0542)	(0.0532)
3	−0.118*	−0.0995
	(0.0580)	(0.0622)
4	−0.0713	−0.0573
	(0.0562)	(0.0658)
5	−0.0367	0.0350
	(0.0637)	(0.0605)
6	−0.0268	0.0320
	(0.0654)	(0.0718)
7	−0.0272	0.0251
	(0.0698)	(0.0764)
8	0.0440	0.0136
	(0.0666)	(0.0833)
9	0.0718	−0.0105
	(0.0649)	(0.0955)
10	0.218**	0.138
	(0.0793)	(0.0967)
Sample size	80,552	58,764

Note: Table shows ordered logit results with country dummies and country fixed effects. Lowest level of each dummy omitted. Robust standard errors, clustered at the country level, in parentheses.

a. Based on responses to question in wave 4: "To which of these geographical groups would you say you belong first of all? Locality, Region, Country, Continent, World."

b. Based on responses to question in wave 5: "People have different views about themselves and how they relate to the world. Using this card, would you tell me how strongly you agree or disagree with each of the following statements about how you see yourself? 'I see myself as a world citizen.'"

* $p < 0.05$; ** $p < 0.01$; *** $p < 0.001$.

Source: Birdsall and Meyer (forthcoming), based on data from wave 4 (1999–2004) and wave 5 (2005–07) of the European and World Values Surveys.

Table 7A.2 Ordered Logit Regressions Results on Attitudes of Global Citizens

Variable	Immigration[a]	Global warming [b]	Economic aid [c]
Gender			
Female	−0.0175	0.0788*	0.0504
	(0.0202)	(0.0342)	(0.0360)
Highest education level attained			
Complete primary	−0.0561	0.157*	−0.0778
	(0.0467)	(0.0632)	(0.0939)
Incomplete lower-secondary	−0.124	0.308***	−0.0759
	(0.0762)	(0.0651)	(0.109)
Complete lower-secondary	−0.0818	0.408***	−0.173
	(0.0586)	(0.0539)	(0.0904)
Incomplete upper-secondary	−0.0459	0.448***	−0.154
	(0.0603)	(0.0618)	(0.0981)
Complete upper-secondary	0.117*	0.497***	−0.0942
	(0.0554)	(0.0648)	(0.0848)
Incomplete tertiary	0.180*	0.750***	−0.129
	(0.0828)	(0.0855)	(0.112)
Complete tertiary	0.293***	0.765***	0.0432
	(0.0806)	(0.0795)	(0.117)
Age			
30–49	−0.0639*	0.102***	−0.155***
	(0.0274)	(0.0279)	(0.0431)
50 and older	−0.137***	0.105**	−0.242***
	(0.0406)	(0.0378)	(0.0511)
Decile of income distribution			
2	0.0146	−0.0354	−0.123
	(0.0565)	(0.0769)	(0.0737)
3	−0.0437	−0.0183	−0.186**
	(0.0498)	(0.0890)	(0.0674)
4	0.000514	−0.0186	−0.284***
	(0.0479)	(0.0888)	(0.0805)
5	0.0278	0.0229	−0.322***
	(0.0465)	(0.0855)	(0.0740)
6	0.0859	−0.0837	−0.205*
	(0.0492)	(0.0998)	(0.0870)
7	0.158*	−0.0946	−0.201
	(0.0618)	(0.0948)	(0.104)
8	0.108	−0.0415	−0.263**
	(0.0727)	(0.0969)	(0.0933)
9	0.251***	−0.0899	−0.180
	(0.0662)	(0.0979)	(0.0944)
10	0.369***	−0.129	−0.152
	(0.0735)	(0.130)	(0.101)
Sample size	61,476	56,630	28,667

(Continued)

Table 7A.2 (Continued)

Variable	Immigration[a]	Global warming [b]	Economic aid [c]

Note: Table shows ordered logit results with country dummies and country fixed effects. Lowest level of each dummy is omitted. Robust standard errors, clustered at the country level, are in parentheses.

a. Based on responses to wave 5 question: "How about people from other countries coming here to work. Which one of the following do you think the government should do?"

b. Based on responses to wave 5 question: "Now let's consider environmental problems in the world as a whole. Please, tell me how serious you consider each of the following to be for the world as a whole. Is it very serious, somewhat serious, not very serious or not serious at all? Global warming or the greenhouse effect."

c. Based on responses to wave 4 question: "Some people favor, and others are against, having this country provide economic aid to poorer countries. Do you think that this country should provide more or less economic aid to poorer countries? Would you say we should give. . ."

* $p < 0.05$; ** $p < 0.01$; *** $p < 0.001$.

Source: Birdsall and Meyer (forthcoming), based on data from wave 4 (1999–2004) and wave 5 (2005–07) of the European and World Values Surveys.

References

Acemoglu, Daron. 2012. *Why Nations Fail: The Origins of Power, Prosperity and Poverty.* New York: Crown Publishers.

Adelman, Carol, Kacie Marano, and Yulya Spantchak. 2012. "The Index of Global Philanthrophy and Remittances 2012." Center for Global Prosperity, Hudson Institute, Washington, DC.

Ahluwalia, Montek S., Nicholas G. Carter, and Hollis B. Chenery. 1979. "Growth and Poverty in Developing Countries." *Journal of Development Economics* 6 (3): 299–341.

Anheier, Helmut, Marlies Glasius, and Mary Kaldor. 2001a. *Global Civil Society 2001.* Global Civil Society Yearbook 1. Oxford: Oxford University Press.

Anheier, Helmut, Marlies Glasius, and Mary Kaldor. 2001b. "Introducing Global Civil Society." In *Global Civil Society 2001*, ed. Helmut Anheier, Marlies Glasius, and Mary Kaldor, 3–32. Global Civil Society Yearbook 1. Oxford: Oxford University Press.

Benavot, Aaron, and Phyllis Riddle. 1988. "The Expansion of Primary Education, 1870–1940: Trends and Issues." *Sociology of Education* 61 (3): 191–210.

Birdsall, Nancy. 2002. "Asymmetric Globalization: Global Markets Require Good Global Politics." Working Paper 12, Center for Global Development, Washington, DC.

Birdsall, Nancy. 2008. "The Development Agenda as a Global Social Contract; or, We Are All in This Development Boat Together." Lecture presented at the Dutch Scientific Council (WRR), The Hague, December 8.

Birdsall, Nancy. 2010. "The (Indispensable) Middle Class: Or, Why It's the Rich and the Rest, Not the Poor and the Rest." Working Paper 207, Center for Global Development, Washington, DC.

Birdsall, Nancy. 2012. "The World Bank and Climate Change: Forever a Big Fish in a Small Pond?" CGD Policy Paper 007, Center for Global Development, Washington, DC.

Birdsall, Nancy. 2013. "A Missed Opportunity for Sensible US Action on IMF—and Why It Matters." *Views from the Center Blog*. http://www.cgdev.org/blog/missed-opportunity-sensible-us-action-imf%E2%80%94and-why-it-matters.

Birdsall, Nancy. 2014. "A Note on the Middle Class in Latin America." In *Inequality in Asia and the Pacific: Trends, Drivers, and Policy Implications*, ed. Ravi Kanbur, Changyong Rhee, and Juzhong Zhuang, 257–87. London: Routledge and the Asian Development Bank.

Birdsall, Nancy, Augusto de la Torre, and Felipe Valencia Caicedo. 2011. "The Washington Consensus: Assessing a 'Damaged Brand.'" In *The Oxford Handbook of Latin American Economics*, ed. José Antonio Ocampo and Jaime Ros, 79–107. Oxford: Oxford University Press.

Birdsall, Nancy, and Homi Kharas. 2012. *Quality of Official Development Assistance Assessment (QuODA)*. Washington, DC: Brookings Institution and Center for Global Development.

Birdsall, Nancy, Nora Lustig, and Christian J. Meyer. 2014. "The Strugglers: The New Poor in Latin America?" *World Development* 60 (1): 132–46.

Birdsall, Nancy, Dani Rodrik, and Arvind Subramanian. 2005. "How to Help Poor Countries." *Foreign Affairs* 84 (4): 136–52.

Birdsall, Nancy, and Alexis Sowa. 2013. "The United States: From Multilateral Champion to Handicapped Donor . . . and Back Again." Prism V.4, N.3, Center for Complex Operations, National Defense University, Washington, DC. Also available as Working Paper 029, Center for Global Development, Washington, DC.

Birdsall, Nancy, and Arvind Subramanian. 2007. "From World Bank to World Development Cooperative." CGD Essay, October, Center for Global Development, Washington, DC.

Birdsall, Nancy, and John Williamson. 2002. "Delivering on Debt Relief: From IMF Gold to a New Aid Architecture." Center for Global Development and Peterson Institute for International Economics, Washington, DC.

CEDLAS (Center for Distributive, Labor and Social Studies), and World Bank. 2012. "Socio-Economic Database for Latin America and the Caribbean." http://sedlac.econo.unlp.edu.ar/eng/.

Commission on Growth and Development. 2008. *The Growth Report: Strategies for Sustained Growth and Inclusive Development*. Washington, DC: World Bank.

Council on Foreign Relations. 2011. "Public Opinion on Global Issues." New York. www.cfr.org/public_opinion.

Dadush, Uri, and William Shaw. 2011. *Juggernaut: How Emerging Powers Are Reshaping Globalization*. Washington, DC: Carnegie Endowment for International Peace.

Derviş, Kemal. 2005. *A Better Globalization: Legitimacy, Governance, and Reform*. Washington, DC: Center for Global Development.

Devereaux, Charan, Robert Z. Lawrence, and Michael D. Watkins. 2006. "Trade-Related Aspects of Intellectual Property Rights." In *Case Studies in US Trade Negotiation*, vol. 1, *Making the Rules*, 37–133. Washington, DC: Peterson Institute for International Economics.

Diamandis, Peter H., and Steven Kotler. 2012. *Abundance: The Future Is Better Than You Think*. New York: Free Press.

Dunlap, Riley E., and Richard York. 2008. "The Globalization of Environmental Concern and the Limits of the Postmaterialist Values Explanation: Evidence from Four Multinational Surveys." *Sociological Quarterly* 49 (3): 529–63.

Easterlin, Richard A. 1995. "Will Raising the Incomes of All Increase the Happiness of All?" *Journal of Economic Behavior & Organization* 27 (1): 35–47.

Florini, Ann, ed. 2000. *The Third Force: The Rise of Transnational Civil Society*. Tokyo and Washington, DC: Japan Center for International Exchange and Carnegie Endowment for International Peace.

Fouré, Jean, Agnès Bénassy-Quéré, and Lionel Fontagne. 2012. "The Great Shift: Macroeconomic Projections for the World Economy at the 2050 Horizon." CEPII Working Paper 2012-3, Centre d'Etudes Prospectives et d'Informations Internationales, Paris.

Frank, Robert H. 1985. "The Demand for Unobservable and Other Nonpositional Goods." *American Economic Review* 75 (1): 101–16.

Frank, Robert H. 2005. "Positional Externalities Cause Large and Preventable Welfare Losses." *American Economic Review* 95 (2): 137–41.

Fukuyama, Francis. 2011. *The Origins of Political Order: From Prehuman Times to the French Revolution*. New York: Farrar, Straus and Giroux.

German Marshall Fund. 2005. *Transatlantic Trends 2005*. Washington, DC.

Global Policy Forum. 2012. "NGOs with Consultative Status with ECOSOC by Category." http://www.globalpolicy.org/component/content/article/176-general/3 2119-ngos-in-consultative-status-with-ecosoc-by-category.html.

Goldin, Ian. 2013. *Divided Nations: Why Global Governance Is Failing, and What We Can Do about It*. Oxford: Oxford University Press.

Graham, Carol. 2012. *Happiness around the World: The Paradox of Happy Peasants and Miserable Millionaires*. New York: Oxford University Press.

Held, David. 2003. "Cosmopolitanism: Globalisation Tamed?" *Review of International Studies* 29 (04): 465–80.

Held, David, and Mathias Koenig-Archibugi, eds. 2005. *Global Governance and Public Accountability*. Oxford: Blackwell.

Held, David, and Anthony G. McGrew. 2003. *Global Transformations: Politics, Economics and Culture*. New York: John Wiley & Sons.

IEG (Independent Evaluation Group). 2006. *Engaging with Fragile States: An IEG Review of World Bank Support to Low-Income Countries under Stress*. Washington, DC: World Bank Group.

IEG (Independent Evaluation Group). 2011. *Trust Fund Support for Development: An Evaluation of the World Bank's Trust Fund Portfolio*. World Bank Group, Washington, DC.

ILO (International Labour Organization). 2012. *Global Employment Trends for Women 2012*. Geneva: International Labour Organization.

Inglehart, Ronald. 1971. "The Silent Revolution in Europe: Intergenerational Change in Post-Industrial Societies." *American Political Science Review* 65 (04): 991–1017.

Inglehart, Ronald. 1997. *Modernization and Postmodernization: Cultural, Economic, and Political Change in 43 Societies*. Princeton, NJ: Princeton University Press.

Inglehart, Ronald. 2008. "Changing Values among Western Publics from 1970 to 2006." *West European Politics* 31 (1–2): 130–46.

Inglehart, Ronald, and Wayne E. Baker. 2000. "Modernization, Cultural Change, and the Persistence of Traditional Values." *American Sociological Review* 65 (1): 19–51.

Jubilee Debt Campaign. 2012. *Review 2012: History Repeating.* London: Jubilee Debt Campaign.

Kahneman, Daniel, and Angus Deaton. 2010. "High Income Improves Evaluation of Life but Not Emotional Well-Being." *Proceedings of the National Academy of Sciences* 107 (38): 16489–93.

Kaldor, Mary, Henrietta L. Moore, and Sabine Selchow, eds. 2012. *Global Civil Society 2012: Ten Years of Critical Reflection.* Global Civil Society Yearbook 10. Basingstoke: Palgrave Macmillan.

Kapur, Devesh, and Manik Suri. 2012. "Geoeconomics vs. Geopolitics: Implications for Asia and the US–Australia." In *Emerging Asia and the Future of the US-Australia Alliance.* Canberra: Australian National University. http://www.alliance21.org.au/themes/emerging-asia.

Kenny, Charles. 2012. *Getting Better: Why Global Development Is Succeeding—and How We Can Improve the World Even More.* New York: Basic Books.

Keohane, Robert O. 2001. "Governance in a Partially Globalized World." *American Political Science Review* 95 (01): 1–13.

Keohane, Robert O., Stephen Macedo, and Andrew Moravcsik. 2009. "Democracy-Enhancing Multilateralism." *International Organization* 63 (01): 1–31.

Keohane, Robert O., and Joseph S. Nye. 1974. "Transgovernmental Relations and International Organizations." *World Politics* 27 (01): 39–62.

Krasner, Stephen D. 1983. *International Regimes.* Ithaca, NY: Cornell University Press.

Lopez-Calva, Luis F., and Eduardo Ortiz-Juarez. 2011. "A Vulnerability Approach to the Definition of the Middle Class." Policy Research Working Paper 5902, World Bank, Washington, DC.

Mallaby, Sebastian. 2004. *The World's Banker: A Story of Failed States, Financial Crises, and the Wealth and Poverty of Nations.* New York: Penguin Press.

Malloch-Brown, Mark. 2011. *The Unfinished Global Revolution: The Road to International Cooperation.* New York: Penguin Books.

Mandeng, Ousmène. 2013. "The IMF Must Pull Out of the Troika If It Wants to Survive." *Financial Times,* April 18.

Mattoo, Aaditya, and Arvind Subramanian. 2012. *Greenprint: A New Approach to Cooperation on Climate Change.* Washington, DC: Centre for Global Development.

Mayda, Anna Maria. 2006. "Who Is Against Immigration? A Cross-Country Investigation of Individual Attitudes toward Immigrants." *Review of Economics and Statistics* 88 (3): 510–30.

Mayda, Anna Maria, and Dani Rodrik. 2005. "Why Are Some People (and Countries) More Protectionist than Others?" *European Economic Review* 49 (6): 1393–430.

Meyer, Christian J., and Nancy Birdsall. 2012. "New Estimates of India's Middle Class." CGD Note, Center for Global Development, Washington, DC.

Milanovic, Branko. 2012. "Global Income Inequality by the Numbers: In History and Now—An Overview." Policy Research Working Paper 6259, World Bank, Washington, DC.

Morrisson, Christian, and Fabrice Murtin. 2007. "Education Inequalities and the Kuznets Curves: a Global Perspective since 1870." Working Paper 2007, Paris School of Economics.

Naim, Moises. 2013. *The End of Power: From Boardrooms to Battlefields and Churches to States, Why Being in Charge Isn't What It Used to Be.* New York: Basic Books.

Ncube, Mthuli, Charles Leyeka Lufumpa, and Steve Kayizzi-Mugerwa. 2011. "The Middle of the Pyramid: Dynamics of the Middle Class in Africa." Market Brief, April 20, Chief Economist Complex, African Development Bank, Abidjan.

Norris, Pippa. 2003. "Global Governance and the Cosmopolitan Citizens." In *Global Transformations Reader: An Introduction to the Globalization Debate*, 2nd ed., ed. David Held and Anthony G. McGrew, 287–99. Cambridge: Polity Press.

Norris, Pippa, and Ronald Inglehart. 2009. *Cosmopolitan Communications: Cultural Diversity in a Globalized World.* Cambridge: Cambridge University Press.

OECD (Organisation for Economic Co-operation and Development). 2008. *Latin American Economic Outlook 2009.* Paris: OECD Development Centre.

OECD (Organisation for Economic Co-operation and Development). 2012a. "OECD Family Database 2012." Paris. http://www.oecd.org/social/soc/oecdfamilydatabase.htm.

OECD (Organisation for Economic Co-operation and Development). 2012b. "OECD Health Data 2012." Paris. http://www.oecd.org/health/healthdata.

OECD (Organisation for Economic Co-operation and Development). 2013. "Development Co-operation Directorate, International Development Statistics Online Database." Paris. www.oecd.org/dac/stats/idsonline.

Pew Research. 2009. "Global Attitudes Project." Spring 2009 Survey Dataset, Washington, DC.

Pew Research. 2011. "Global Attitudes Project." Spring 2011 Survey Dataset, Washington, DC.

Pinker, Steven. 2011a. *The Better Angels of Our Nature: Why Violence Has Declined.* New York: Viking Penguin.

Pinker, Steven. 2011b. "Violence Vanquished." *Wall Street Journal*, September 24.

Pritchett, Lant and Marla Spivack. 2013. "Estimating Income/Expenditure Differences across Populations: New Fun with Old Engel's Law." Working Paper 339, Center for Global development, Washington, DC.

Ravallion, Martin. 2012. "Benchmarking Global Poverty Reduction." Policy Research Working Paper 6205, World Bank, Washington, DC.

Risse, Thomas. 2006. "Transnational Governance and Legitimacy." In *Governance and Democracy: Comparing National, European, and International Experiences*, ed. Arthur Benz and Yannis Papadopoulos, 179–99. Routledge/ECPR Studies in European Political Science 44. New York: Routledge.

Rodrik, Dani. 1999. "Governing the Global Economy: Does One Architectural Style Fit All?" In *Brookings Trade Forum 1999: Governing in a Global Economy*, ed. Susan M.

Collins and Robert Z. Lawrence, 105–93. Washington, DC: Brookings Institution Press.

Rodrik, Dani. 2009. "Economics Focus: A Plan B for Global Finance." *The Economist* March 12.

Rodrik, Dani. 2013. "The Past, Present and Future of Economic Growth," Working Paper 1, Global Citizen Foundation.

Rueda-Sabater, Enrique, Vijaya Ramachandran, and Robin Kraft. 2009. "A Fresh Look at Global Governance: Exploring Objective Criteria for Representation." Working Paper 160, Center for Global Development, Washington, DC.

Ruggie, John Gerard. 1975. "International Responses to Technology: Concepts and Trends." *International Organization* 29 (03): 557–83.

Savedoff, William D. 2012. "Global Government, Mixed Coalitions, and the Future of International Cooperation." CGD Essay, July, Center for Global Development, Washington, DC.

Semiocast. 2012. "Twitter Reaches Half a Billion Accounts, More than 140 Millions in the U.S." *Geolocation Analysis of Twitter Accounts and Tweets by Semiocast.* http://semiocast.com/publications/2012_07_30_Twitter_reaches_half_a_billion_accounts_140m_in_the_US.

Severino, Jean-Michel, and Todd Moss. 2012. *Soft Lending without Poor Countries: Recommendations for a New IDA.* Final Report of the Future of IDA (International Development Association) Working Group, Center for Global Development, Washington, DC.

Smith, Tom W., and Lars Jarkko. 1998. *National Pride: A Cross-National Analysis.* National Opinion Research Center (NORC), General Social Survey Project, University of Chicago, Chicago.

Stern, David I. 2004. "The Rise and Fall of the Environmental Kuznets Curve." *World Development* 32 (8): 1419–39.

Stevenson, Betsey, and Justin Wolfers. 2008. "Economic Growth and Subjective Well-Being: Reassessing the Easterlin Paradox." *Brookings Papers on Economic Activity* 39 (1): 1–102.

Subramanian, Arvind. 2011. *Eclipse: Living in the Shadow of China's Economic Dominance.* Washington, DC: Peterson Institute for International Economics.

Task Force on International Financial Transactions and Development. 2010. *Globalizing Solidarity: The Case for Financial Levies.* Report of the Committee of Experts to the Taskforce on International Financial Transactions and Development, French Ministry of Foreign and European Affairs, Permanent Leading Group Secretariat, Paris.

Torgler, Benno, and Maria A. Garcia-Valiñas. 2005. "The Determinants of Individuals' Attitudes towards Preventing Environmental Damage." *Ecological Economics* 63 (2): 536–52.

UNDP (United Nations Development Programme). 1996. *Human Development Report 1996: Economic Growth and Human Development.* New York: Oxford University Press.

Union of International Associations. 2012. *Yearbook of International Organizations 2012–2013: Statistics, Visualizations, and Patterns*, 11th ed., vol. 5. Leiden, Netherlands: Brill.

United Nations. 2012. *World Urbanization Prospects, the 2011 Revision*. Final Report with Annex Tables, Department of Economic and Social Affairs, Population Division, New York.

Weindling, Paul. 1995. "Social Medicine at the League of Nations Health Organization and the International Labour Office Compared." In *International Health Organizations and Movements, 1918–1939*, ed. Paul Weindlig, 134–53. Cambridge: Cambridge University Press.

World Bank. 2013. *World Development Indicators*. Washington, DC: World Bank. http://data.worldbank.org/data-catalog/world-development-indicators.

World Public Opinion. 2008. "Publics in Developed Countries Ready to Contribute Funds Necessary to Cut Hunger in Half By 2015." http://www.worldpublicopinion.org/pipa/articles/btdevelopmentaidra/554.php?lb=btda.

Wriston, Walter B. 1992. *The Twilight of Sovereignty: How the Information Revolution Is Transforming Our World*. New York: Charles Scribner's Sons.

Comments on "Global Markets, Global Citizens, and Global Governance in the Twenty-first Century," by Nancy Birdsall, with Christian Meyer and Alexis Sowa

Pratap Bhanu Mehta

There is widespread agreement that there is a "global governance" deficit. The architecture of global governance does not serve the interests of the poor. This architecture is increasingly producing a series of deadlocks on the major global challenges, such as climate change, trade, inequality, and cyber security. And this architecture does not adequately recognize our deep interdependence: the political processes at the global level do not adequately take into account issues that create spillovers and affect citizens in other countries.

The chapter by Birdsall, Meyer, and Sowa provides a moderately hopeful assessment of the prospects for global governance. Their optimism comes from one sociological claim: that there is a greater global consciousness among newly emerging middle classes, who increasingly think of their identity in global terms. Truly global communication is now possible. It comes from one organizational claim: that civil society movements are now so organized as to be able to have their voice heard at the global level. It comes from one geopolitical claim: that the balance of power is such that no single country or small group of countries can dominate the global system without challenge. These changes may give more incentives to countries to cooperate and create a consensus on important issues, since powerful countries can no longer assume that they can simply command and others will follow. Finally, there is an implicit normative claim that we recognize the desirability of cooperation.

These large-scale changes might provide a propitious backdrop for the reform of global governance. Even if we do not have a global demos, the prospect of transnational solidarity is enticing. Even if global institutions are not fully representative, they can act as deliberative forums that take diverse civil society voices into account. Even national governments can and do engage

486

with civil society groups from other parts of the world. A shift in the global balance of power will produce pressures to make global institutions such as the IMF more representative. New organizational forms such as the G20 are emerging to challenge older, more exclusive clubs. And finally, we are beginning to recognize that our destinies are intertwined.

Most of what the chapter says is correct and characteristically well argued, and I don't disagree with the claims advanced. Many of the institutional proposals, particularly on the reform of the IMF, World Bank, and G20, are eminently practical. But just to push the boundaries of the discussion and to offer a provocation, let me ask the old question: "So what?" If these trends are propitious, what is the problem? Why is it that, as the chapter puts it, "the politics, rules, and institutions of cooperation among nations have not kept up with the demands from global citizens for fairer and more farsighted global political order?" Is it because of an undersupply of global governance? Or does the problem lie in the ways in which domestic politics functions in countries? And can these seemingly propitious trends overcome those constraints?

We all agree that better global governance is a desirable outcome. But will global governance be achieved if we make it into a project, something we self-consciously aim at and design? Or, rather than assume that better global governance is the solution to global problems, should we not focus on how domestic governance generates these problems in the first place? The global order does not represent the poor, the chapter argues. But by the same token, neither do domestic political orders. Why do we think a solution at the global level will solve that particular problem?

1. The Poison in the Cure

The chapter hints at but does not fully explore an alternative but more dispiriting story. The very trends the authors see as providing momentum for better global governance might also work in the opposite direction: there may be a tinge of poison in the cure, as it were. A newly emerging middle class might display greater global consciousness, but it might also lend momentum to another old sociological adage: no middle class, no nationalism. The rise of a global consciousness, we have known since the time of the French Revolution, is quite compatible with and sometimes gives a boost to nationalism. The rise in global consciousness can take the form of emulation and comparison, but it ultimately creates competition. It is not an accident that politicians in most countries seem to think there are very stringent limits on what they can sell to their middle-class constituents in terms of the necessity for international cooperation. The problem is not an undersupply of global governance; the problem is that global governance has relatively little traction in domestic politics. The urgent need of the hour is not making global institutions more representative: it is giving those institutions a voice, a narrative, and a constituency in domestic politics. Even worse: the jury is still out on whether the structures of interdependence will ultimately trump the rise of nationalism. From China to the United States, from Japan to Turkey, middle-class nationalism creates pressures to ensure that countries commit to doing only what is minimally necessary. The problem is that minimally necessary is not good enough for the nature of the problems we face.

The second trend—the rise of a global civil society—is similarly ambiguous. A vibrant, active, and admirable world of NGOs has done much to raise global issues and transform global consciousness. These networks are now a vital part of the global governance landscape. But I think the authors underestimate the degree to which such movements are also seen as undermining representative institutions. Most states are very suspicious of transnational civil society movements and are increasingly regulating them. There is also a sense that civil society movements, which deepen the deliberative process, also undermine representative ones. The unkind quip that those who can join politics, while those who cannot join civil society is very much the common sense construction of NGOs in most countries. Their ability to work outside of representative politics and find a presence in global institutions makes them objects of suspicion rather than tools of global governance. Indeed, one could argue that the more international institutions are seen to be privileging some NGOs and civil society movements against the positions of national governments, the less likely it is that national governments will sign up for global cooperation. It is not an accident that the United Nations' greater openness to NGOs has coincided with its greater irrelevance for most governments. The world order still sees empowering NGOs by the backdoor as undermining democratic processes. NGOs are most effective not when they are key pivots in global governance but when they transform the structure of domestic politics by changing norms.

The third trend—the shift in the balance of power—contains both possibilities and pitfalls. It creates pressures for new structures of global cooperation, but it also makes collective action more difficult. It is important to be very precise about the kinds of power shifts we are talking about and the implications they have for global governance. In some areas—such as cyber security and drone warfare, for example—countries that have an immense technological lead have little incentive to cooperate and will risk world peace by unilateral action. For a while, it looked as if necessity would force governments to cooperate globally on energy governance. But recent developments in the United States, including the discovery of shale gas, have dimmed the prospects of such global governance of energy markets emerging. There might still be a propitious outcome for global energy, not because of more global governance but because incentives for individual countries have changed. In other areas, such as climate change, it is precisely this shift in the balance of power that is making a solution difficult.

At one level, one could argue that global governance has worked too well: in areas such as climate change, there is a global negotiating process that is as wide-ranging and representative as it can be. There is a balance of power such that no country can impose an unjust solution on any other. There is even a scientific consensus. And there is the full flow of NGOs and civil society groups. Yet we still end up with what philosopher Stephen Gardiner has evocatively called the "perfect moral storm." The challenge is not the undersupply of global governance; it is the structure of countries' domestic politics. Progress on climate change will not be achieved primarily through global governance reform; it will be achieved through changing the nature of politics in the United States and other large countries.

The same could be argued for trade. The deadlock in trade negotiations is a success for global governance, yet at the same time shows how domestic politics rule the roost. Countries cannot now easily be pushed into doing what they do not want to do: hence the deadlock. Receptivity to breaking the deadlock will depend less on reform of the WTO and more on tackling the political economy in the major countries.

It is in this context that it is important to draw the right lesson from the Agreement on Trade Related Aspects of Intellectual Property Rights (TRIPS) story mentioned in the chapter. At one level, the limitations placed on intellectual property rights in the agreement are trotted out as a prime example of what global governance can do for the poor. A coalition of developing country NGOs forced the United States to yield on intellectual property rights in ways that protected the interests of the poor. Was this a triumph of global governance? In a way, yes. But what made it possible were the following conditions. First, there was pressure in the domestic politics of the major countries not to give in to the United States on the issue of access to pharmaceuticals by the poor. Second, because of the protectionist choices some of these countries had made, there was a powerful industry lobby for producing generics. In short, a good global outcome was achieved not because of more global governance but because domestic politics moved in a certain direction. It is not an accident that when India's domestic drug industry became more diversified and had a lobby to move for more stringent intellectual property rights protection, the Indian government began to move away from its traditional concern with cheap drugs. Only a decision by the Indian Supreme Court allowed the local generic industry to subvert the United States' views on patent protection. In short, the nature of global governance was an outcome of other processes, not the solution.

489

2. The Cure in the Poison

Under what conditions does global governance arise? To simplify matters somewhat, one could argue that institutions arise when they serve the interests of power. Institutions of global governance were designed for two objectives. The first objective was to prevent armed conflict that could assume the proportions of a world war. In some ways, these institutions managed to do so, although they could not prevent the costs of competition between great powers being imposed on a range of regions such as the Middle East or Pakistan. It could also be argued that what created the "stability" of the world order was not global governance but exogenous developments like the development of nuclear weapons.

The second objective was to create conditions that would guarantee the stability of global capitalism. You don't have to be a Marxist to recognize this. Creating the conditions for this stability often required appropriating resistance to the global order, providing space for it, and thereby neutralizing its radicalism. Stability also required creating conditions for its legitimacy. It is not an accident that mechanisms of global order have been rather swiftly improvised when the fundamental stability of the global financial and economic order is at stake. The G20 was born in such a crisis, first during the East Asian Crisis and then at a higher level during the recent financial crisis. Under these conditions, it did its job of being a global steering committee rather well. But there is a lesson here. Global governance reform, like domestic reform, is invariably the product of a crisis. It is seldom a product of calls for "reform." Areas of global attention that are not experienced as crises will not receive attention.

The nature of global governance will be shaped not by the middle class, not by shifts in balance of power or NGOs, but by the nature of global capitalism. The real issue is not going to be global governance, but how different states conceptualize the relationship between state and market.

The global economic order, crafted under American leadership, proved fairly resilient because countries such as China and India decided it was in their interests to join that order. And it could be argued that for all its antipoor bias, that order provided the opportunity for lifting millions out of poverty. The authors point out that even with modest improvements, much of the "global" citizenry will remain very poor.

Part of the reason why there is a sense that there is a global governance deficit is not so much that there is an undersupply of global governance; it is that our confident assumptions about what regulatory measures and norms would conduce to the stability of global capitalism have been shaken in two different ways. First, globalization increases the divergence between "elites" and the rest of the population within a country. I do not use the term "inequality" for this divergence, though certainly inequality could be one facet of it. Divergence is a broader political idea that can include the idea that some sections of society have more options, can potentially "secede," and so forth. It can also point to the fact that global governance has largely been about the mobility of capital, not labor. But making the mobility of labor a priority again takes us back not to an undersupply of global governance but to ways in which the identities of political communities are constituted. Giving global voices an opportunity in domestic political debates may help. It may also be necessary, as the chapter argues. But the objective is not global governance; it is transforming the structures of local politics.

Second, there is now a real contest over the rules of capitalism. This contest will be played out over diverse terrains, such as the permissibility of "industrial" policy to exchange rates. Most "developed country" states are covering up, as it were, for domestic inequality or stagnant wages by taking actions that kick problems down the road. In short, the issue is not so much what global governance will look like. The issue is what the nature of global capitalism will be. Can we no longer assume that productivity growth, income growth, and job generation will go together? If we can no longer do so, will we now get a very different kind of competition in the international system?

Part of the crisis of global governance is the lack of confidence that the private sector can measure and price risk correctly. But at the same time, states have incentives that lead to great regulatory failures. More than a rising middle class, the central issue for global governance will arise from confidence in states and markets. This confidence will have to be domestically generated. It seems unlikely that the causality will run from global governance to restoring faith in states and markets at the national level. It seems to me that both the problem of and appetite for global governance will depend on the call one makes on these fundamental propositions. But here is the tricky question: are these debates going to be better served by focusing on reform of global governance institutions such as the World Bank and the IMF, whose declining relative importance is generally a good thing? More options have been generated for the developing world not by global governance reform but by the cumulative outcome of domestic reform. Will better outcomes be achieved by focusing on the formal design of global institutions, or is a "bottom-up" approach, which focuses on domestic politics in these countries without burdening that debate with arcane issues of global governance reform, preferable?

The problem is not where there is an undersupply of global governance; the real question for global governance is what norms will underpin it. How are global norms generated? How do norms get institutionalized? It may be that the cause of institutionalizing the right norms is not always best served by focusing on global governance. Think of two different ways in which this might happen. First, there is great skepticism about global governance because, as the last financial crisis showed, it did not provide immunity against ideological capture; indeed, it may have encouraged it. Although power and cronyism played roles in the financial crisis, there was also a great deal of intellectual failure. It was not the undersupply of governance that produced the crisis but a seeming oversupply, where dubious norms became institutionalized rather too quickly.

Second, think of climate change. The climate action plans of most developing countries are far more progressive than their stance in international negotiations. Indeed, this is one reason why many observers think that a European-style top-down architecture will not work. The best chance for an agreement is based on the idea of a bottom-up architecture, which evolves out of existing shifts in norms. Converting the debate about climate change to a debate about global governance architecture, rather than about the dissemination of norms, diminishes rather than increases the chances of a solution. This proposition is debatable, but it does suggest the possibility that we need to think of dissemination of norms rather than creation of institutions.

If what I am suggesting is correct, there is a silver lining. What looks like a weakness (the undersupply of global governance) may mask the strength of this moment. The poison (the lack of collective action) may contain the cure, as it allows for the possibility that new norms will emerge in a way in which focusing on global governance does not.

If the issue is the dissemination of norms, then the problem is not an undersupply of global governance but the fact that "global issues" have very little "representation" in national politics. The chapter's great strength is that it recognizes this. Ironically, the issue is not that ordinary citizens do not have access to the IMF or the United Nations Framework Convention on Climate Change (UNFCC); it is that the kinds of issues that the IMF or the UNFCC have to wrestle with do not find a place in national debates in the right kind of way. The relevant measure of "global citizenship" may not be identification with the globe but the degree to which global issues get reflected in national politics. These are two slightly different things. We need more research on this.

3. By Way of Conclusion

We need to be a bit wary of use of the term "governance." The term was a conceptual innovation that signaled the idea that governance is about more than governments, but it has also become a strategy of depoliticization. We all look for "governance solutions" as a way of avoiding the rough-and-tumble of power politics, organization, socialization, leadership, and contestation of norms. Take a quick typology of global issues:

- Issues that involve dealing with massive asymmetries of power. I suspect cyber security and drones and possibly weaponization of space are good examples of this. These are areas where the technological superiority of the United States or possibly China will be such that they will have no incentive to even begin a serious conversation on norms. Here the global governance problem is mobilizing in the face of massive technological superiority.

- Issues where there needs to be coordination among national economies. There are win–win solutions, but much depends on the contingency of political cycles. Global rebalancing might be one of these issues (assuming no exogenous changes). This is the problem of aligning domestic politics with the demands of an interdependent economic world. It is a coordination more than a governance problem.

- Issues where there is genuine distributive conflict over who bears the burden of change. Climate change may be such an issue. But there are fundamental distributive conflicts. Here the question is what kinds of coalitions will emerge.

- Issues where there is a contest over norms or a contest of world views. Regulatory contests can often disguise distributive conflicts, but often they can also be genuinely good-faith disagreements.

- Issues over which norms should take priority. It may be the case that two norms, environmental protection and open trade, may both have traction but different weights are assigned to them. For example, environmental concerns might suggest that countries should be given leeway in developing their own technology base in renewables such as solar panels. Yet existing WTO rules potentially block the dissemination and creation of new solar related technologies.

- Issues where we simply need to generate new norms (global arms trade regulation, for example).

The great lesson of the twentieth century was that great reallocations in global power are often precipitated by small groups or small renegade countries. The problem is not matching power for power but taming the paradoxical power of weak states to disrupt the system. I must confess I find these indexes of great power domination practically useless when it comes to dealing with tricky problems. The blunt truth about globalization is that small entities can also make the world fragile: China cannot tame North Korea any more than the United States can tame Pakistan on nuclear proliferation.

These instances pose different types of challenges and need different types of political responses. More than institutions, they require a distinct kind of politics. My fear is that talk of "governance" has become a substitute for talking about politics: governance or the emphasis on institutional solutions can also represent a kind of depoliticization. I like the fact that the chapter is somewhat open-ended in its conclusions. I take that to mean that it does not offer the false illusion of institutional design. Instead, it reminds us that we need to do the political hard work at every level. There is no solution outside the conditions of politics. Politics is, as Max Weber said, the slow boring of hard boards. It requires less sincerity about designing institutions and a lot more strategic and Machiavellian thinking about how to use contingent conjunctures to humanity's advantage.

Index